First published by Inside Corner Books Ltd 2005

Inside Corner Books
19 The Hollins
Holloway
Derbyshire DE4 5BA
E-mail: insidecorner@btinternet.com
Webpage: www.insidecornerbooks.com

ISBN 0-9549672-0-8

Printed by Butler and Tanner, England

INSIDE CORNER BOOKS

ROADS TO REDEMPTION

A Guide to Major League Baseball

Craig W Thomas

Graphic design and typesetting: Sarah Keeling

Thanks.........

My major buddy Stateside, Josh Alexander, to whom I owe a huge debt for a ton of things, most notably the fact that this book has actually come into existence and for his many supporting comments, such as *"They want $10,000? Fuck 'em, that's extortion!"* To Nigel Coulson for the lend of his house; to Sarah Keeling, my absolute rock in the design area; to Tim Wiles, Bill Burdick, Brad Horn at the Hall of Fame; to Geedon Bruce, the Inside Cornerstone; to the *Bo5* gang for lighting the flame: Erik Janssen, Jonny Gould, David Lengel and Josh Chetwynd; to Penny Clifton for her crucial PR support; to Andy Turner for lending me some books and to Rachel Samuels at Getty for being efficient and friendly where a certain photo person at another company was rude and unprofessional. Big up to my children Nastassja, Lyall and Jordan for not distracting me with too many self-destructive tendencies. And who knows what the hell I'd be doing without Louise, the boss? Probably not this.

Musical provision was unknowingly laid on by Rufus Wainwright (thanks to Nigel Coulson). To heaven with all his works.

All black and white photography and the colour photos of Eckersley and Clemente were licensed by the Baseball Hall of Fame Archive. The photo of Tony Bastista of the Expos was licensed by the Montreal Gazette/Marcus Townsend. All other colour photography was licensed by Getty Images.

Couple of Notes:

The Dictionary is the original work of the author, as is everything else between the front and back cover except for the photos. Mind, I did choose them and where they went. However, the term "original work" is a slight misnomer: this project would have been a complete non-starter in the relatively short time it took to research, write and put together without the magnificent websites out there in the electronic ether.

Had I seen the Dickson dictionary before I began work in October 2003 or in the book's early stages I doubt I would have had the nerve to do one of my own. However, I didn't know of its existence until I was nearly finished (if a thing like that is ever *nearly* finished, never mind finished). I would like to thank Mr Dickson particularly for about twenty entries where it was really helpful for checking the accuracy of what I already had.

If you come across any errors in the book, I hope you'll feel much more smug than disappointed.

CT February 2005

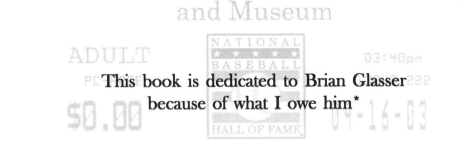

This book is dedicated to Brian Glasser
because of what I owe him*

---

*about £2600 for all the times I've slept at his house.

FOREWORD

by Jonny Gould, presenter of *Baseball On 5*

"I've always wanted to write a book. Seeing your name in print - it all sounds so very glamorous. Of course the reality is anything but glamorous. Long nights, writers block and a computer screen for a bed partner. Luckily for me, as presenter of Five TV's Major League Baseball show, I can do the next best thing - write a forward to someone elses book.

Craig is a big fan of the show and passionate about everything he does - which is why I'm so overjoyed to be part of his epic journey through this great and crazy sport that we call baseball. And you do have to be a bit crazy to be a UK baseball fan. Starved of coverage in the pre-Five TV days, most hardcore fans had to rely on US Services Radio or MLB.com for their daily fix. Add into the mix the fact that "live" baseball only occurs in the UK in the middle of the night, and that most Brits still unenlightedly refer to this great sport as "glorified rounders", and you can appreciate big shoulders and a hardy nature are a must for any potential fan.

In fact Five TV once did some research into who watched the show. Apparently most of our viewers are students (no surprise there!), train drivers (hmmm!), night-shift workers, insomniacs and breast-feeding mothers!! You can imagine the latter made a piece-to-camera a little tough to focus on.

But you don't have to have lactating nipples to be a confirmed "baseball-nut". It appeals to all sorts from Premiership footballers (Charlton FC's Chris Perry apparently has been known to go to training on 3 hours sleep), to rugby World Cup winners (England skipper Martin Johnson), to showbiz types (TV comedian Phil Jupitus), and even allegedly members of the Royal family (diplomacy prevents me from saying who!)

We do around 60 shows a year and since going to air on 5 in 1997, three viewers have asked me to pop the question for them; one viewer wondered if I could help him out and ask his wife for a divorce. We've ruined the academic careers of a host of late-watching students, and in 1998 famed film director Francis Ford Coppola e-mailed us his thanks for our live coverage of the World Series. My favourite story though involved the shows original pundit Todd "the Mooseman" Macklin. Rated by many as the best sport analyst in recent years, one viewer was such a big fan that he built a website dedicated to "the Toddster". It only had one page - a photo of Todd with the words:

"TODD IS GOD!"

Is Craig crazy to write this book? Probably. But what I love about it, is that there's something for everyone inside these covers. Historical content (ideal for TV presenters who still have a long way to go before they can claim expert status), and an insiders view of the people and programme that have become family for all baseball-nuts!

I hope you enjoy it as much as I have and look forward to spending many more sleepless nights with you all, as we play ball!

Jonny Gould

INTRODUCTION

In the August of 2004, nine months down the road, I had to break off from writing *Redemption* to go on a family holiday. For the best part of a year I had thought about, read about and written about baseball for a sizeable portion of every single day, Monday to Sunday. In retrospect I think the work must have begun to send me a little crazy because I kept thinking to myself, 'Let's see if there really is a place I can go where there is no baseball and where it doesn't matter to anybody.' You'd have thought that would be easy in this country, but with Britain being saturated with American culture, I couldn't seem to go a day without watching a TV drama or film and finding references to baseball: if it wasn't a *Seinfeld* episode built around Kramer spotting Joe DiMaggio dunking a donut in a New York coffee shop it was a casual lines like "stepping up to the plate," "swinging for the fences" or "being thrown a curve" in *CSI*, *24* or the director's commentary on a DVD of *Donnie Darko*. It's like that thing where you've never seen an Audi TT until a Steely Dan lyric is built around it and suddenly you see one every day. It was like that for me with baseball and television 'n the movies. I also wanted to clear myself of it, just for a while you understand, because my wife has a way of looking at me sometimes when I'm talking about sport of even thinking about it (she can read my mind) as if to say, "do you have to spend *all* your life obsessing yourself with the meaningless and trivial?"

So off we all flew to Bavaria in the south-east corner of Germany, doing that sightseeing thing. No problem; I like Germany and I like sightseeing. I say, 'getting myself clear': I took some Roger Kahn with me to read, and some Roger Angell too, just to tide me over.

The pleasant days passed by. Very pleasant. The beautiful towns, the wonderful and varied history, the splendid cafés, restaurants and ice cream parlours. And the Germans will put in an immaculate glass of beer for you if that is your need. About a week in, staying near Berchtesgaden, we spent a long day in the wake of the Hitler nightmare. We went to a museum at the foot of a mountain on which stood a holiday home, the Eagle's Nest specially built for the Dictator by Martin Bormann in honour of his 50th birthday, before boarding a bus that would take us up to the house itself. The private road along which the Fuhrer and just about no one else was ever driven, pulls up at a short tunnel that leads to a lift that rises 150 ft through a shaft cut through solid rock. Tourists ride this gold plated elevator in the very same confined space that the Dictator fretted in (he hated the house because he hated heights), to be deposited right into the heart of the house itself.

The views from this eyrie in the Obersaltzburg are stupendous, but more amazing to me is to be able to sit, eat, drink and look around you in the private sitting room Adolf Hitler himself once sat, ate, drank and looked around in, contemplating the invasion of eastern Europe and the eradication of over 90% of European's population of Jews. A long way from the majors I was then.

Afterwards, we went for a stroll on the mountain top in the drizzly afternoon weather. It isn't a place for quiet contemplation of the weight of movement of time and tragedy, however. Negotiating my way along the rocky path, a man's voice pulled me out of my historical reverie with stunning suddenness.

"Go Sox!" he said in a plain, strong, friendly American accent.

I looked to my left to see a guy I'd actually already noticed a while before, accompanied by a loud, gregarious wife and a couple of young children. He was grinning at me with an unmistakeable air of confidence.

"Oh, the cap," I said, referring to my headwear of choice, a plain blue fitted Boston Red Sox cap with the traditional red 'B' posted on the front. "Are you a fan?" I said instinctively, trying to make polite conversation, like you do.

"Yeah. I know a few of the players."

"Huh?"

"I used to play with Jason Varitek and Doug Mirabelli."

"The catchers," I replied, wearing my "Brit trying to prove to an American he knows something about the man's national sport" insecurity right there on my sleeve. An obvious thought dropped into the slot as I looked hard at the guy. He looked right to be a pro-sportsman: in his thirties, but tall, lean and handsome.

"So, did you...erm, make it to the majors?"

"Yeah, I did," he said, not smiling.

"Um," I said, trying to make sure he didn't think I was being rude, "who did you play for?"

"The Rangers and the Giants."

We walked along for a little. I wanted to smash him on the head with a rock, just to the point of temporary unconsciousness, so I could drag him off to a lonely place for six or seven hours and ply him with about six hundred questions. I knew I couldn't actually do this, of course, but I did ask him his name. 'You better not be lying to me, you bastard, I thought.'

"Dan Pell-tee-air," he told me.

"Dan Pell-tee-air," I repeated quietly so as not to forget it. 'Dan Pell-tee-air, Dan Pell-tee-air, Dan Pell-tee-air,' I went in my head.

"How are you spelling that?"

"Dan P-e-l-t-i-e-r."

It looked like I'd bagged my first major leaguer, right there on Hitler's mountain. I spent most of the next two hours shaking my head and laughing.

Back home in England, shortly after dropping the bags on the floor, I logged on to Baseball Reference dot com to see if Dan Peltier genuinely existed. Sure enough, there he was. Three seasons in the Big Show, 1992, 1993 and 1996, then gone. He wasn't quite there for merely three end of season cups of coffee though. He played 65 games in 1993 for the Rangers, batting .269. Not so bad. I looked for his home runs: did he hit one in the majors? I scanned across: there in the 'HR' column stood a figure '1.' So you hit a homer in the big time, Dan. Good on you. I bet that was a great moment. Was he thinking about that on the mountain? I imagined him in a Texas Rangers uniform stood alone in the green outfield spaces, wondering whether he would actually really make it and become an everyday player. For whatever reason, he never did. But I also thought, 'wow,' so you really were a Giant - John McGraw, Christy Mathewson, Carl Hubbell, Willie Mays, Barry Bonds - even if you only played 31 times. 31 is a lot better than 3.

The question that really bugged me, right there talking to Dan P-e-l-t-i-e-r on a mountain top in Germany was this one: 'what on earth is a committed British football fan doing writing a book about American baseball?' This has haunted me on every leg of my journey from original idea to this fruition. What am I doing? This isn't my game, this isn't my country.

I have one single answer.

America is full of descendent Europeans. Their forefathers and mothers went there – no, escaped there from religiously intolerant monarchs in the seventeenth century, firstly from my country, then from France and Holland and Germany and Scandinavia. The Spanish also colonised it for their King, and later the Irish were driven there in droves by starvation and cruelty. Here is me, English and European, but always I have been fascinated by this outsized giant of a place, this land of mystery, magic, terror and tragedy. It hit me many months ago that just like Paul Simon I was looking for America. I realised that you don't have to live there to feel the compulsion to go searching for it. Though thousands of miles removed, it is my fate still to go looking for America and this book about baseball is a part of my journey.

Craig Thomas, December 10th 2004.

Author Biography:

Craig Thomas was born in Tottenham in 1957. Whilst teaching he wrote for the Chesterfield football fanzine *The Crooked Spireite* from 1988, then was its editor for five years until 1997. The need to quit an addiction to CFC as an academic and obsessional subject led to the publication of *Losing My Religion* in 2002. *Roads To Redemption* is his second book. A novel, an adult school story, *Fairest Of All Yarrow* will be published by Inside Corner in the autumn of 2005.

1

A ROUGH, INCOMPLETE SHORT HISTORY OF BASEBALL

Once Upon A Time West Of Here

"Whoever wants to know the hearts and minds of Americans had better know baseball."
Jacques Berzun

"I did nothing of the sort, dammit! I played the next day and got three base hits."
Ty Cobb, asked by biographer Al Stump, if he went in search of a doctor
after being slashed with a knife in a street attack in August 1912.

Though the game has changed over time, America's educated classes have tried consistently over the past forty years or so to preserve it. Hand in hand with this has gone the need to explain the deep hold the game has always had over the fan. In carrying through this process, they have tried to explain to *themselves*, as much as to us, what it is that makes them love the game so deeply (this is the thing about being educated: you have to *explain* everything). One of the recurring themes of this dialogue between writers and their audience of fellow baseball lovers is the timelessness of the game. 'Yes of course,' they say, time has re-shaped and re-moulded the game in all sorts of subtle and unsubtle ways, but it is still essentially the same game as it was when the northern Yankees took it south in the Civil War of the 1860s, and if this is a little hopeful, then it is without doubt the same game, give or take gloves the size of buckets and one or two other things, that the first major leaguers played in 1886. From this notion emanates much of the mystique of baseball: its thick, treacle richness and depth. We can watch Derek Jeter make hit a double and tear around the bases and know that what Nap Lajoie and Rogers Hornsby did on the diamond all that vast expanse of lost time ago was pretty much exactly the same.

This is the American's desperate grab at personal-historical identity, won through the historical continuity of baseball. We in Britain, perhaps unfortunately, grow up with so much history, you want to shake it off your clothes and leave it as far behind as you can. At least, this is true if you were born in the sixties or earlier. Those of us who were alive to witness *Please Please Me* jetting to the top of the charts for The Beatles' first number one (in 1963) were made to believe that winning two World Wars had made us the greatest country in the world. We were told this from potty training onwards. We were pulled through our childhood to the sound of *God Save The Queen* (the national anthem, that is) and tales of Churchill, Nelson and Monty, while our radios and televisions programmed us to believe that God, after several noble experiments, made the British, discovered He'd reached perfection and stopped making any more nations.

In Britain today, no sport has the same status as baseball has in America, the same value. Probably our society is too fractured, in terms of social class and in terms of geography. The English upper class for the last one hundred years have been able to look to a variety of sports and leisure activities expressing their world view and reflecting their status: rugby union, rowing, horse racing and show jumping, tennis even. Here, sport performs the function of ritual, display and leisure. The English working class had football, whippet and pigeon racing and some actually followed cricket. Scotland embraced rugby union, but only among the rural middle classes in the south. For working class Scots, there has been football and it has shaped national identity, but only to a point: the sport became nationally important to Scotland only when they were defeating the English.

The Welsh looked to rugby union in the twentieth century for national identity, but again, there were limitations to the ability of the sport to express the feelings and attitudes of a nation downtrodden for centuries by English power: only in the south was it important, and as in Scotland in terms of football, only among the working classes. As for Ireland, well, the English lost control of most of it. But here has played a political role: the games of Gaelic football and hurling belong to the Irish and confirm Gaelic identity. In late nineteenth century America, one game came to dominate its leisure life, not just from a spectating point of view. It was easy to play and it was simple: you needed only a ball, a stick and some open space and fun was there for the taking. The game was simple too: you throw, you hit, you run, you catch and throw some more. That's it.

For the American, the matter is more complex and difficult. America, the "can and must-do" country is in many senses still young. Its obsession with freedom is partly about freedom from the reins and the restrictive shadows and shackles of the past. Actually, I should have said that America is still *youthful*, not young; it is being wearied and aged by its struggles with foreign enemies and by internal problems. That, I'm afraid, is an inevitable part of the organic ageing of nations. This process means that its people naturally demand more history to make reference to as they think more often about their past (they have progressively more past to think about). A nation's past needs to be filled with values and beliefs, just as does its present. For many mature Americans, baseball is a fundamental strand in its historical structure. Further, It seems to be a truism that a national history has to contain heroes. Well, then. If Americans looks at baseball they see almost nothing but heroes: mythical men peering easily at us now in the magnificent pages of monochromatic photography, rugged, strong and full of the life force. These are men who look as though they knew how to live and knew how to have fun. We know they suffered various privations too as they travelled in hard conditions across a seething summer continent, playing practically every day and providing America with a tobacco juicy slab of its national entertainment. As the now thoroughly organised and established baseball rolled into the twentieth century, the hard-living boys of summer were the likes of Speaker, Cobb, Mathewson, Ruth and Wagner. And Grover Cleveland Alexander: how did he come to be called just 'Pete'? The sport's history is flooded with names that capture our imagination now, as they must have done the vast crowds then. You want romance in sport? Well, you got it down baseball's still glimmering ancient decades: Napoleon Lajoie (pronounced "Laj" – as in leisure – "oo-way"); Rube Marquard; Rogers Hornsby; Cornelius McGillicuddy (mystifyingly, or is it "mystically?" planed down to 'Connie Mack'); Burleigh Grimes; Smokey Joe Wood and the seductively romantic Shoeless Joe Jackson. How that name conjures up a storehouse of mystery: a poor waif child swinging a mean, back street bat on his way along a true rags to riches glory trail, bootless and desperate. Small wonder the man was canonised on late-twentieth century film. And if that isn't enough, how about his fall back to rags again?

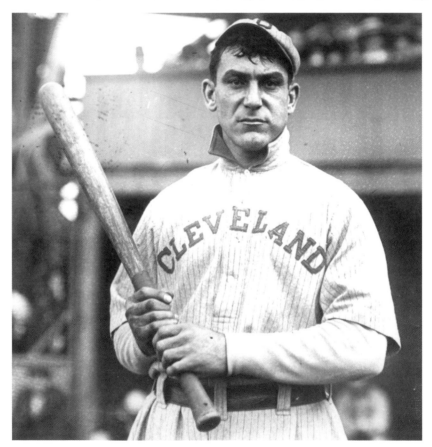

Napoleon Lajoie   1874-1959
b Woonsocket, Rhode Island. (Cleveland Blues, Second Baseman, known as "Nap" or "Larry") Could this rough looking ballplayer, plug of tobacco wedged in the side of his gob, be just anyone? This is one of the most brilliant hitters of all time, so great that he actually rivalled the greatest, Ty Cobb. When he was offered the skipper's job of his club and took it, the whole organisation was named after him; they became the Cleveland Naps in 1905 and remained so until 1914 whence they became the Indians.

It doesn't matter that Joe was only Shoeless because he went out to field in his socks because his new game shoes hurt his feet. The man was a batting genius and that was enough to make a baseball legend. The game is more than littered with historical figures ripe for historical reverence. Baseball is rubbish dump high with men of daring-do and mighty deeds. A country with a huge population, most of them immigrants from ball-playing Europe (it matters not which ball game develops hand-eye co-ordination), with the right cultural conditions – hungry poor looking for an escape route, reared at a time with a tiny number of leisure pursuit distractions, a massive, baying audience, progressively wealthy, lusting for an American sport to follow – was bound to produce dozens of prodigiously talented flingers and swingers. Further, it was certain to produce men of boundless energy and potential, aching for achievement and record-breaking as well as money. But there's more. The game was also chased hungrily by more affluent, educated Americans who loved playing the game in their backwoods towns and hamlets, and who refused to take their place in more humdrum professions. The idea of playing ball in the sun for money all summer long was too glorious to refuse, and imbued with the spirit of America, they went to the big leagues too, Ty Cobb among them.

Cobb lost a father's love over his choice of baseball over college. Other fathers were affected, perhaps infected, with the culture of immigrant America, and let their similarly infected sons go, however reluctantly. For the boys, "Why shouldn't I?" is the American question where "I suppose I can't then" is the mirror statement for the British. Some ballplayers dared to run away from home to play pro-ball. The huge distances required to reach professional clubs didn't deter many. For a young kid, the notion of actually being paid money to play a game must have been deliriously attractive. America as an idea must have pushed them to make the journey or take the risk too. The vast continent of success awaited those who need only prove they had the guts to try and make it. There were no class boundaries in baseball itself, while the inhibiting class factor pulling back the ambitious youth was only skin light compared to the dead weight of class culture in the old country.

A mention too should be made of the climate. America's summers were and are hot, fine and long (away from the east coast); it's an outdoors country. The availability of practise time was only limited by farm chores, homework and tired muscles. But for some, even these limits can be overcome. More than one future pitching star was aided by farmer fathers building faux-mounds in the barn, complete with home-patented floodlights flickering according to caprices of the Depression generator.

America in the late nineteenth century was a perfect environment then for professional sport. As well as having young men in abundance with the desire to play, there was a massive market for the game amongst the population. Back then there was no competition from basketball, (American) football or soccer. Cricket had not taken root. Humans will always make entertainment for themselves on whatever continent they live. It only needed a business culture to fill the gaping need for sporting entertainment and the financial wherewithal for the public to pay a fraction of their earnings to turn out near their homes to watch it. This existed in the form of America's famed entrepreneurial spirit, and this staggering energy produced a vast number of professional baseball clubs all over the burgeoning states – there were only 39 (11 to go) when the big leagues began in 1876 – which provided almost immeasurable opportunities for talented young American athletes to develop their playing skills. "Build it and they will come," we might say at this juncture. The men of business built the ballparks, and come they did, both spectators and ballplayers. Not only did individual players make their way from the deepest backwoods to win local, metropolitan or national renown, but also groups of hungry Negroes came barnstorming across the mid-west from the cities of the east even in the face of terrible racism, often playing against white Nines. You can hardly require better evidence for the gargantuan reservoir of capacity for the development of pro-baseball than this.

The drawing of a widely dispersed population of talented ballplayers to semi-pro and pro-ball clubs in the opening fifty years or so of organised baseball must be unique in the history of world sport. Small wonder we have the phrase "land of opportunity" for this New World. Furthermore, tens of millions of Americans needed a diversion from work at that point in time just as hundreds of millions devour televised international soccer across the planet in this new century. In short, by 1875, held in place in the United States of America were the most perfect ingredients for the development of a professional sport. There is still one not mentioned yet here: the game itself. Was it interesting enough to do the job of engrossing the people?

The subsequent history of baseball renders the question somewhat ridiculous, but to a Briton, it isn't so daft. To those of us reared on football and cricket, the game takes on a strange appearance upon encountering it. There is also the echo of "glorified rounders" in one's mind, a beloved phrase of Brits who know nothing of the game save that it's a game of bat and ball played by those awful, brash Americans ("overpaid, oversexed and over here," etc) and therefore assume that the American pastime is nothing more than a feeble, not even watered-down form of cricket. For this writer, the alien aspect of the sport emanates from the shape of the stadiums. It has taken me four years for my mind to become accommodated to the fact that one end of the park is left open and unenclosed, unlike a football ground. "How can this be a proper stadium?" I would hear myself thinking, especially when seeing

Ty Cobb – 1886-1961
b. Narrows, Georgia. (Detroit Tigers, Center-fielder) "The Georgia Peach", fearsome, terrifying, ruthless, racist, selfish, friendless, rich and almost beyond dispute, the best batter who ever lived.

pictures of ballparks in books. "They've got the double-decker stands and the floodlights, why hasn't it been finished off properly?"

As for the game itself, there are no nets to lovingly cradle a football or sets of stumps to be broken in one dramatic and unexpected moment, but baseball lacks for nothing. The literature of baseball tells the foreigner over and over again how complete and satisfying the shape of the game is. Perhaps talk of "*mysteries of nines and threes*" (in Richard Behm's poem, "*The Origin And Purpose Of Baseball*") is trying to stretch the properties of the game to a sacred snapping point, but a vital impression is left by such men (and a few women) who have tried to capture in words the depth of their feeling for it: that the sheer shape of the game has almost magical properties: the shape the "square propped up on one of its four points," also inaccurately known as the "diamond," makes; the smooth expanse of outfield green; the seductive flow of movement from the pitcher; the graceful stroke of the master batter; contact or no contact; the swooping of gloved athletes moving gracefully upon the ball hit along the ground; the effortless flick of the infielder's wrist that sends the ball like a missile to the waiting glove of the first baseman. To the baseball writer and thinker, there is a visual poetry to the playing of the game: something of classic and classical import, irrespective of and separate from the mere totting up of scores and games won and lost. To me, this is not a desperate attempt of a new country's intellectual elite, lacking in self-esteem, trying to match something possessed by the English with their cricket (as described by Cardus, Arlott and Swanton). Not a lame and jealous stab at finding a hopeful strand of pure classicism flowing from the playing of a sport that really, is only attainable in the Old World. The admiration and appreciation for baseball as an aesthetic endeavour is genuine; the sense of wonder in their prose is all too real. It communicates itself to you, whatever your nationality. You find yourself wanting to make the journey across the Atlantic Ocean to watch a big league game there all the more strongly. Then you find yourself on a train from Boston to New York passing a minor league stadium and discover your mind now thinking how much of a picture the shape of the outfield and the low stands makes. You buy a book on baseball stadiums and notice that the more you look at the inside cover photograph of the sun going down on a packed Midway Stadium in St Paul, Minnesota (capacity 6, 329), the more beautiful you think it looks. Till you reach the point where you say to yourself, "shit, I've got to go there;" and sit in those stands myself, on a hot summer night, eating a hot dog, watching the pitcher fold up his leg and hurling his sliders in dreams of his own manifest destiny. Then, if you're not stupid, you may think, "well if I'm British and baseball is possessing me like this, how great must this game be to an American?"

If it's hard to separate the distilled art of playing baseball from the surrounding culture of the sport, some writers have tried. It is a false perspective, because it is a romantic one. No hitter ever swung a meaningful bat that wasn't watched by thousands of spectators who may actively have caused the magnificent home run through the game atmosphere they have created. It's also impossible to seriously imagine a game of baseball, especially one from the past, where the split second of action bears no relation to the relationship between pitcher and manager, batter and front office. And how is baseball "baseball" without vicious arguments between players and umpires, insults (and objects) thrown at visiting ballplayers, tobacco juice and sputum gobbed onto the ground, scorecards and programmes, eating and drinking? More than any sport I have encountered, baseball is less about some microbe-free pure sporting aesthetic in the hallowed arena of the noble sportsman. Frankly, it doesn't need to be placed in the abstract any more than it can be. Ted Williams' stroke may well be famously beautiful (even I've watched it on tape), but how much meaning does it have without our knowledge of the man taking batting practice every day of his working life saying out loud, "I'm fucking Ted Williams and I'm the best fucking hitter the game's ever seen" all the while? Or his relentless pursuit of technical perfection? Baseball is wonderful for many reasons; one of them is that it is gives us an insight into what it is to be human as much if not more than any other sport. Actually that's a mistake. Baseball probably gives us a better insight into what it was to be an American than any sport does in telling us of a people's national characteristics. As the man said, if you want to know America, you better know baseball. Probably for the that reason, writers with the sensibilities of a Roger Angell can type dreamily of spring training or college games of ball drifting to their nine innings conclusion as if God him or herself carved out the rules of a perfect game and handed them and it down to a chosen people. Perhaps it isn't that the game is utterly fantastic – it can be, but it can also be very dull indeed – but that the game is so perfectly and fully American. Even though it is played fanatically in Japan, Cuba, the Dominican Republic, Puerto Rico and Venezuela, baseball belongs to one nation more than any one sport belongs to anyone. Perhaps it is this that satisfies so many baseball lovers so profoundly.

*Footnote. It's a tempting proposition, the one that goes, "America was too democratic for cricket. A sport where a man could bat for hours, meaning the rights of others are naturally restricted wouldn't wash in a society where everyone was expected to be allowed an equal share in the available entertainment. It doesn't help explain why the Australians didn't reject it, though.

Honus Wagner - 1874-1955
(Pittsburgh Pirates, Shortstop) Johannes Peter Wagner - the noble Dutchman was one of a rare breed in any sport: a
true giant of his time in terms of stature as both a man and as a player. He won 8 batting titles. Here we see his magnificent
features in his scruffy club blazer. At 60 while coaching his old club, he put on the glove and took infield practice at short.
Every player stopped to watch him, awed just to see the old man in action once again (see Ritter, page)

So when we read of a game of baseball's eternal rhythms, perhaps the writer's mind is tricked; what is seen and felt is probably the slow *tick*, then *tock*, or ebb, then flow, of America's rhythms, or one of them.

At this point, as a Brit one ought to leave any further discussion on what baseball means to America, to Americans and stick to what it means to one of us. If you love sport and you love history, and you're fascinated by America, baseball lies in wait for you whether you were born in Nice, Munich or Grimsby. I think wherever you're from baseball lends itself to flights out of the everyday (and into the world of bullshit, I can hear my wife saying) because its history, thankfully preserved in astounding depth by its writers, is full of fantastic stories. Our football and cricket just cannot compete. Here's just an obvious sample: Germany Schaeffer's dramatic performance upon hitting a home run in 1906, the death of Ed Delahanty, Ty Cobb's demonstration of the what he detested, hitting home runs near the end of his career in 1927, Ty Cobb's beating a man to death, Babe Ruth's called shot in 1932, Babe Ruth's generosity, Buck Weaver's long, heartbreaking protestation of innocence in the thirty-six years between his expulsion from the game in 1920, the year after the Black Sox Scandal, and his death in 1956, the enduring myth of Shoeless Joe , the sheer cussedness of the Cubs' infielders retrieving the ball to seal Merkle's Boner, all the Rube Waddell stories, any of the large number of baseball suicides.

Given this outpouring of excitement, horror, pain and exultation, it isn't any wonder that baseball's tentacles reach out over the water to grab you. It's only a wonder that baseball didn't find us sooner.

Compared to British sport, the stage on which baseball history is played out appears as something of huge imagining. Envisioned as a painting, think Picasso's *Guernica*. Examples: the impact made by Babe Ruth on America is not matched by the dent made on our culture by any single man or woman in British twentieth century history. The nearest thing to the Ruth phenomenon in Britain is The Beatles. Neither has there ever been in our sport an "issue" as big as that caused by Branch Rickey, owner of the Brooklyn Dodgers, deciding to sign the first black man to a major league organisation – Jackie Robinson in 1945 – then to bring him up to the big leagues in 1947. The scandal of Basil D'Oliveira not being selected by the MCC for the 1968-9 tour of South Africa and the subsequent torpedoing of the 1970 South African tour to England by the anti-apartheid movement was large, but plays Ben Nevis to Rickey breaking the colour bar's Mount Washington (or Matterhorn). The D'Oliveira Storm was a subject of vital moment to Britain's intelligentsia, but frankly, the masses couldn't have given a tuppenny shit about it. But when Robinson stepped out onto Ebbett's Field in a Dodgers uniform on April 15th 1947 the whole of America as whites knew it, seemed to be rocking on its foundations. (One wonders too how deep was the impact of the other huge English cricket controversy of the century, the Bodyline Series of 1932-3. The upper echelons of British society choked on their dinner rolls and sharp words were sent in letter form to The Times, but I doubt that the English – cricket has never been a British game - working man was distracted by Jardine taking on the Aussies in such a confrontational and physical way. At least the English can boast of big events in one of its sports: I think we might explain this in terms of Britain here in its expanded imperial form. These days are long gone, of course.)

If British sports seem to be taking a pounding for their smallness of stature compared to baseball, we should be unsurprised. After all, America itself is a vast continent which sucked in over a hundred million Europeans and Africans stolen from their homeland by the British in a very short space of time, as if part of some semi-global experiment by Gods as imagined by the Greeks. If the unloading of these millions upon a literally awesome landscape represents the playing out of a game of human chemistry of monstrous proportions, then we should have expected a country somewhat larger than life, something approaching mega-human. Consequently, this new and unique by-product of mass human migration was fated to paint itself large in terms of culture. America has delivered enormous and ecstatic pleasures and advances for the human race: the motion picture industry and the movie-star; colour television; the development of penicillin; modern youth culture; luxury cars; jazz, soul and R n'B (which led inexorably to The Beatles in a gargantuan example of muso-geographical cross-fertilisation and which caused an over-sized kick forward in human musical development); the nightclub; air travel; Coca-Cola and the saving of European civilisation (in 1945). It has also delivered disasters and follies of epic proportions: the genocide of the indigenous peoples, Prohibition, the use of the first nuclear bomb, the guzzling of fossil fuel allegedly causing climate change and unwanted military and corporate interference across the continents least able to defend themselves. It is hardly surprising then that its national sport mirrored all this with events and trends on a grand scale: every ballplayer held in serfdom by the Reserve Clause until 1975; the raising up of national icons such as Ruth and DiMaggio, play by electric light (from 1936); the establishing of monstrous salaries for its superstars, the Black Sox Scandal when gamblers fixed the World Series in 1919, the exclusion of non-whites from professional baseball until 1947, the sanitisation of the game in the television age, a player strike wiping out post-season play completely in 1994. This is sports history writ large: another reason, I think, why when foreigners collide with it, they are often drawn to it irresistibly.

Christy Mathewson – 1878-1925

b. Factoryville, Pennsylvania (New York Giants, right-hand pitcher) "Big Six" was not far behind Johnson as a golden age of great pitching at the elite level. He won 373 games in a one-club career spanning 16 whole seasons and was one of the original Hall of Fame inductees with Cobb, Ruth, Johnson and Wagner in 1936. He died of TB as a result of gas inhaled during a training exercise during The Great War in France. What was that oxymoron, now: military intelligence?

For a people in search of heroes, then, baseball provided them. But there must also be something crucial about the game itself, however, which made and makes baseball so precious, so deeply felt by Americans, and therefore that caused them to raise and nurture its history so carefully and so successfully.

The game of baseball in the days of Cobb, Wagner and Johnson was undoubtedly the baseball that is known and loved today. Significantly though, to enable America to practically dissolve into ecstasies of sentimental reverence, it needed to be different and was.

The crucial thing then, is that the game changed shape over time, in sync with changes in American society as a whole. Baseball could be America's game because it was as close to everyday American life as our heart is close to our minds. This could be so because of the class system, or more to the point, the lack of one. Games would begin at four o'clock in the afternoon, when most ordinary working men had done their shift. The ballparks belonged to the people. Midweek crowds could be low: but three of the weekly games were played at the weekend, with the double-header taking centre-stage. In the fifty years that spanned the watershed of 1900, the fans more than watched the game: they got involved. Constant ribald shouting wasn't even the half of it. Junk would rain down on outfielders and intense verbal blastings would be sent from the first and third baseline home rooters. All would regularly be aroused to fury and excitement by fights among players, or fights between players and umpires. These typically might include an almost ritual spitting of tobacco juice at the umpire (or pushing, shoving or decking him with a punch), concluding in the inevitable throwing of the player from the game. Why umpires put up with it, in the days when they were on their own out there, is a question I find hard to answer.

Just as daily life was lived in the raw in the cities of America at this time, so was baseball. The two were entwined in a national embrace of stunning intensity. This is perfectly illustrated by the habit of fans being allowed to mass on the playing field, right up to and around the dug outs (which at first were only benches), before the games. Pitchers warmed up in front of grandstands and when the occasion was a massive pennant chasing game or the World Series, space might be drastically limited by the closeness of the masses, clamouring for a magnifying glass view of men who were local and national heroes.

The game itself was played by the same rules of today by 1920, but the culture was tantalisingly different. Games more often than not were duels between gladiator pitchers who became low paid megastars. Seen now through the romantic haze of the black and white still (and occasionally some scratchy, fast-flickering film), Johnson and Matheson et al cause an intake of awed breath. So they really exist, we think. Their tough, lined faces, in uniforms of almost impossibly classic design, reveal all. These are hard-looking men of a by-gone age who are like us, but recognisably more battle-hardened by their life experiences.

There are two other histories of baseball, however: the one of the statistic and the other of the game shaping event or development. The former of iceberg significance was what became known as the Black Sox Scandal. To have a World Series thrown by players (of the Chicago Cubs against the underdog Cincinnati Reds) devastated a baseball media and public when it was revealed a year later. Fortunately, the damaged was fully repaired. Firstly, the owners handed power to a very un-American institution, a Tsar fully loaded with autocratic power. Not only did he attempt to flush out corruption with life bans for the Guilty Nine, but he saw in the adoption of a new type of ball that dramatically altered play. His name was Kennesaw Mountain Landis and he played the role of fearsome dictator of the game for the next twenty years.

Cy Young – 1867-1955

b. Gilmore, Ohio. (Boston Red Sox, Right-handed pitcher) To win "a Cy Young" remains the accolade all pitchers seek and here is the man himself, in uniform. Winner of 511 games of baseball, he is the Daddy, though he is probably not the greatest pitcher of all time. Interestingly, his record includes his 1890s career whilst with the Cleveland Spiders of the National League. Young actually has 225 wins if you begin counting from the start of the modern majors in 1901 (which American statisticians don't).

Sam Crawford 1880-1968

b. Wahoo, Nebraska (Detroit Tigers, Left-fielder)
The biggest triples hitter who ever lived: 312. He was the Tigers' number one star until Cobb came along in 1905. He had almost 3000 hits and is very memorably described in Ritter's foreword. The mystifyingly failure with the bat of both Wahoo Sam and Ty Cobb cost the Tigers possibly three World Series, 1907-09.

Rogers Hornsby – 1896-1963
(St Louis Cardinals, Second Baseman) One of the greatest hitters of all-time, he hit .309 as a young man in the Dead Ball era, before exploding his numbers into the .400s after 1920. Has the second highest average ever behind Cobb, of .358. He didn't smoke, didn't drink, didn't drink coffee and refused to read or watch movies, lest they damage his fantastic eye for striking a baseball.

George Sisler – 1893-1973
b. Manchester, Ohio. (St Louis Browns, First Baseman, left-hand bat) "Gorgeous George", smiling here in fielding pose,
this is the man Ichiro deposed last season, as everyone knows, from the Most Hits In A Season pedestal. Two years after
his 257-hit season, in 1922, he could "easily" have taken his mark higher still: he had 246 safeties in 142 games. If he'd played
a full 154-game season – he did in '20 – a mark of around 265-270 could have been established.

HISTORY 1920-50

"Son, when you pitch a strike Mr. Hornsby will let you know."
Bill Klem, Hall of Fame umpire, to complaining rookie pitcher that his pitches
to Rogers Hornsby were being called balls.

From the 1920 season a new harder ball was to be used which flew much further. It was also accepted that the balls
had to be replaced regularly during play. Before this, one ball could last a whole game (the crowd threw it back
when it dropped in their midst) and would quickly become worn and darkened. This created two problems for the
batter: one, he wouldn't be able to pick it out of the crowd or advertising hoardings behind the pitcher and two, a
roughened shell caused it to dart and dive unpredictably through the air from pitching arm to batter's box. Worse,
it was legal for the pitcher to assist the above-described process. Mud or dirt was applied to the ball to alter its flight
and make it all but impossible to see, or spit or Vaseline to make it dart like a swallow. Yet in the chaos, Ty Cobb
managed to leave the game with the highest lifetime batting average of all time: .368. What a player he must have
been. He is frequently touted as being the greatest of all time (we're coming to Ruth in a moment). History needs
some thinking out, though. If the ball was as hard to see and hit as is said, how was Cobb able to hit .400? Was he
superhuman? Were others like Wagner, Sam Crawford and Tris Speaker too?

We're told too that this period yielded the greatest pitcher of all time, one Walter Johnson. He was said also to
throw at lightning speed. Something isn't right. Hitting a dark projectile coming at you at 90 mph from a crowd
background on a dark afternoon ought to have been totally impossible. True, scores were very low then: all 1-0s and
2-1s and pitchers going not just through the nine inning and pitching on what today would be short-rest, but pitching
through fifteen, sixteen innings and more when required. But to square the situation, the best batters today would

have to be hitting .600 if they were alive today. The problem can only be resolved by one of two explanations: the spitball, the mudball and the dark backgrounds and balls are nothing more than made up stories or the pitchers weren't that fast. Or to offer a third, the gap between a narrow stratum of quality hitters and the rest was huge, with pitchers only needing to get the ball across the plate to strike most of the men, the dross, out. There were no speed guns in those days. Naturally the fastest pitchers then threw bullet-hard, but exactly how fast was a matter of perception. Doubtless had the fastest pitcher's fastest pitch been thrown at a mere 80 mph it would have whistled past the batter like a rocket to the eye and mind of the 1910 batter. This explains the reminiscences of the players. Furthermore, in the days of thinner catcher's mitts, pitchers of modern speed would have smashed their hands to pieces.

If it seems sacrilege to suggest that Mathewson, Johnson and Alexander didn't throw that hard, it shouldn't be. Doubtless had they all been born fifty years later, they would be throwing as hard as anyone today. Talent doesn't change across time, but diet does and so does the amount of body conditioning and so does expectation. They threw as hard as they needed to. Before 1920 then, pitchers had it easy and threw men out as if they were children. Runs were scarce. And yet, baseball was still phenomenally popular. It was about to become more so.

The strangeness of great pitchers, great hitters, no runs, is also explained by the lack of depth in pitching. A few men stood out from the crowd, have become immortal names in the Hall of Fame and all the books. Doubtless they were good enough for even Lajoie and Cobb to struggle to hit consistently. On days when the best weren't pitching, the presence of pie throwers on the mounds of the sixteen major league franchises (eight in each league) would have caused eyes to light up of the best hitters, who even in miserably unpromising circumstances could now get bat on ball and cash in.

In a bid to make the game more exciting, and obviously fairer, the new "lively" ball, as it was called, had come in. It was now changed frequently during the game and hitters filled their boots. Heilmann hit .394 in the first season of the new age and Rogers Hornsby hit .397. The previous year, the total base leaders in the leagues hit for 284 and 227 bases. Now the leaders hit 399 and 329. Balls began flying out of ballparks almost everywhere, helped by shrinking outfields, and pitchers had to suffer the consequences to their win-loss records and earned run averages. Pitchers were now in trouble. Walter Johnson's ERA, 1.27 and 1.49 in '18 and '19, fell to 3.13 in 1920 and 3.51 the following year. In nine of the previous ten seasons he'd pitched over 300 innings; after the Dead Ball Era came to an enforced stop, he never threw 300 innings again or even got close. No longer leaning on legalised cheating, and without modern pitches like the slider and the splitter, hurlers had to throw harder and so wore out more quickly. It was no longer easy to go nine and they needed more rest between games. More pitchers were needed on the roster, which reduced quality. Batting averages swelled on the flood tide of constant slap hitting and relentless power hitting. Home run "champions" in what now became known as the Dead Ball Era had sometimes only needed around ten to do it, sometimes less. Now the leaders were hitting twenties, then forties within a couple of years. It was a long time before the standard of pitching improved to match the new, revolutionary situation. One can only imagine the numbers if Landis had illogically allowed a group of spitball pitchers to continue using their flight-bending toss.

Ruth

"I get back to the dugout and they ask me what it was I hit and I tell them
I don't know except it looked good."

George Herman Ruth 1894-1948

Just as it is impossible to imagine or understand the history of Europe without Adolf Hitler, it is impossible to imagine and understand the history of baseball without Babe Ruth. The game would probably have had its hitting revolution without him, certainly in terms of rising averages, but America would have been deprived of a titanic hero. America is not just about excess and indulgence, but if it was and a group of futuristic bionic engineers had created a quintessential humanoid to lead not just the national pastime but America itself into the decade of impossible roaring boom, they might easily fallen short of George Herman Ruth. A gargantuan eater, drinker and fucker (by all accounts), he was perhaps the most extraordinary sportsmen in human history. No one changed a sport, to my knowledge, as Ruth changed baseball. True he exploited the new ball and gradually shrinking parks, but this guy was already hitting 29 home runs in 1919 (the National League leader, Gavvy Cravath, hit 12). It takes more than size to hit a baseball a long way – though Ruth was always tall with a muscular build – it takes hand to eye co-ordination of exceptional ability. Anyone can swing lustily: it takes an athlete with the eye of an eagle to time the 80-90 miles per hour projectile with a narrow stick of wood sufficiently well to send it shooting through the sky to new distances far beyond those being reached before and with fresh consistency. This rough orphan boy from Baltimore, this pitcher, mark you, *pitching* star of the Boston Red Sox domination of the 1912-18 period, not only blasted balls

George Herman Ruth 1895-1948
b. Baltimore, Maryland. (Boston Red Sox, 1913-19, New York Yankees 1920-33, Boston Braves 1934,
right-fielder, right-handed pitcher). "The Babe."

into orbit almost as a matter of daily course, he did it with considerable style and grace. His probable equivalent in cricket, Don Bradman - a contemporary from 1927 onwards - smashed records and achieved a level of consistent success of super-human proportion, but he was no stylist. There is little surviving film of "Jidge," but that you will see shows baseball hitting to be a thing of beauty. He struck out a lot, for sure, but he wasn't the Neanderthal slugger one might have imagined if we hadn't all read and seen differently.

Ruth, in the first year of the new era, hit 54 home runs, way out beyond his own record from 1919, and batted in a record-breaking 137 runs. He crossed home plate 177 times, a ludicrous figure given that Ty Cobb's 1916 record of 144 was itself huge. Cobb had inflated his record with base running of unknown relentlessness and bravery, but Ruth did it all by simply demolishing pitchers to shattered, shambling flesh and bone. The figure of 177 has never been broken. No one has even come close. He is known for home runs, and here he changed how the game would be played ever after. Once crowds had witnessed the ball in glorious, heaven-bound flight, there was no going back to small ball bunt, sacrifice and steal. And what hitter, given sufficient skill, would want to deprive themselves of launching a crowd into instant ecstasy and themselves to instant headlines? Ruth hit 59 in 1921, then 60 in 1927. What happened in between? The good life isn't that good for a ballplayer. If the Babe had lived a healthy life, he may have hit 80 home runs. If baseball had a rule disallowing the deliberate walk, he'd have hit 80 anyway, possibly more. Jidge's biggest problem on the field, when not being able to resist fighting umpires - the result of residual alcohol in his system from the night before likely as not - was finding pitchers brave enough to pitch to him. His career record in walks is only now being approached by the greatest hitter of modern times cursed by the same problem, Barry Bonds.

Two things amaze me about George Herman Ruth: in his last season, with the Boston Braves, in 1935, old before his time at 40, fat and all but washed up, he went to Pittsburgh and Forbes Field. It was the last game but five of his whole career. He hit three home runs that afternoon, but that isn't it. His third, according to his best biographer (by all accounts), Robert Creamer, a sober writer, was "unbelievably long." "It's probably still going," said the pitcher, Guy Bush. No one had ever hit a ball out of Forbes Field before, but Ruth did, when he was as good as finished and could hardly play.

The second thing that always gets me is that Ruth was a very fine left-handed pitcher before he was a slugger. In 1916 and 1917 he won more than 20 games, making him statistically one of the game's best. For 42 years he held a World Series record for the most innings pitched without conceding a run, 29, set in 1918, stolen from Christy Matthewson. His club, the Boston Red Sox, won the Series that year. At the time of writing the first draft of this, they had never won it since. Thus emerged over time "The Curse Of The Bambino," something many people in Beantown have been foolish enough to believe in. It's bad enough that it's even thought about. The BoSox haven't won it since then because either the front office, the players, or the manager, simply haven't been good enough.

The 20s and 30s have gone down as two decades of power hitting and huge numbers. The pitching superstars of the Dead Ball Era were not replaced, casting further doubts on how good the old masters truly, purely were. Only four pitching names stand out from this period: Dizzy Dean of the Cardinals and the Cubs; Lefty Grove of the Philadelphia A's and the Red Sox; Carl Hubbell of the Giants and Bob Feller of the Cleveland Indians. All made it to the Hall, but none achieved the stature in the game of Cy Young, Grover Cleveland Alexander, Christy Mathewson and Walter Johnson. To say that a decade 'belongs' to this player or that player is facile, but in potted histories is virtually unavoidable. After Ruth left New York in 1934, the 30s seems to be most remembered for the ascendancy of the great hitter Lou Gehrig who hit behind Ruth for almost his entire career there. A brilliant hitter, he played 2,130 consecutive games before the onset of a rare terminal illness, amyotrophic lateral sclerosis broke his streak. He retired on July 4th 1939 after a famous farewell day at Yankee Stadium where he made his "luckiest man alive speech," not knowing that his disease was life threatening. He died in 1942. Gehrig is acknowledged in all the rating systems as one of the best ten or twelve position players (non-pitchers) ever to play the game.

The decade also saw the arrival of two giants of baseball history, both hitters. One was of such fame and magnitude that he didn't actually need to marry Marilyn Monroe to become an icon. Not to half of New York at least. He was Giuseppe Paulo DiMaggio, son of a Sicilian fisherman immigrant (and his Sicilian immigrant wife). The other didn't have music in his name and so didn't make it into song. He was Ted Williams. Joe DiMaggio, the Yankee Clipper, batted in 125 runs in his rookie year in 1936 and went on from there to vast fame as probably the best all round player - batter and fielder - of all time. The Splendid Splinter (Ted was so tall and thin he resembled a toothpick as a cocky young man) came into the game three years later and lasted eight years longer (he retired in 1960). To him has fallen the common assessment as the best hitter of all time. He is the last man to hit .400, a feat most believe will never be done again.

As the world loomed towards war, America in December 1941, baseball still exercised an enormous hold over huge swathes of the American people. Of American football and basketball, there is no history as far as this country is concerned. The game of hitting continued: there is no return to gladiator conflicts between master pitchers, just an ongoing struggle of hurlers with the curve ball and the fastball and no spit to contain the sluggers. The larger struggle for the game was to come after the A-bombing in Japan in the spring of 1945: the absorption of the black people of America into the major leagues.

By the beginning of the 40s, there were actually two major league baseballs: black and white. The 20s and 30s saw the growth of an organised system of two leagues, 140 game schedules, a World Series and an All-Star game. The Crowds were often huge, accommodated by the lending of the white major league stadiums to the black clubs. Teams such as the Kansas City Monarchs, the Homestead Grays and the Crawford Coloured Giants were the best of the period and on them were players who were as good if not better than anyone from the white game. Names now immortalised in the Hall of Fame as well as oral history, Satchel Paige, Cool Papa Bell, Oscar Charleston, Josh Gibson and Judy Johnson echo down from the past with the same stardust attached to Williams, DiMag, Greenberg, Hubbell and Grove for true scholars and liberal writers. Deservedly so. When barnstorming (travelling) white teams in the off-season met black teams doing the same, the whites often got taken. In 1934 Dizzy Dean played in a barnstorming game against Satchel Paige and pronounced him the best pitcher he had ever seen. The statistics don't lie there eternally on the page and Paige never got to pitch to Babe Ruth on the bona fide stage of organised baseball, but no one in America who is taken seriously would seriously contend that the black stars would not have blazed a trail through the game had they been given the chance.

Ludwig "Lou" Gehrig – 1903-41
b. (New York Yankees, First Baseman) The man who played in the shadow of Babe Ruth but who was deeply loved by the Bronx crowds and acknowledged as a very great hitter indeed. Played games consecutively for 2 130 games, a record overtaken by Cal Ripken Jr who took the record on to 2 632. Hence his nickname, "The Iron Horse".

That they were not is due simply to the 100% proof racism of white owners, league presidents and baseball commissioners. They wanted a white game. They held out until enough black blood was shed on the battlefields of Europe and the Far East to force them to give way and until a small proportion of their number broke ranks. The Pittsburgh Pirates tried to sign stellar hitter-catcher Josh Gibson; Landis blocked it. When Bill Veeck tried to buy the ailing Philadelphia Phillies and rejuvenate them with a raft of Negro players, Landis blocked him. Then Landis died. Branch Rickey, owner of the Brooklyn Dodgers, signed a black man in 1945 to the Dodgers' farm team in Montreal. He was an infielder and hitter and he was Jackie Robinson. He played brilliantly, ate, slept and changed separately, endured tidal waves of racist abuse from fans and players. The Montreal Royals won their championship and the Little World Series. Jackie was headed for the big leagues.

Jimmy Foxx – 1907-67

(Philadelphia Athletics, Boston Red Sox, First Baseman). We can't see his arms here, but apparently they were thickly muscled, which explains his status as one of the game's best ever sluggers. A Triple Crown winner in 1933, his statistics make a sea of RBIs, home runs and massive hits across all the old ballparks of the American League. He hit 58 homers in 1932 and would probably have broken Ruth's record had he not carried an injury for part of that season. He choked to death on a piece of meat.

Harold Henr "Pee Wee" Reese 1918-99

b. Ekron, Kentucky. (Brooklyn Dodgers, Shortstop) This little guy comes from an age where the Shortstop was supposed to be quick and supple, sprites almost. He was the infield anchor of the great Dodgers line up of the 50s.

Reading the story of the 28 years-old Jackie Robinson's first season in white major league baseball for the first time was intensely fascinating. It is a mixture of heroism and miserable shame for the white race of people, not just American whites: all of us. After all, what are white Americans if not ex-Europeans? Never, surely, has a professional sportsman ever had to perform under such stress. He endured constant verbal abuse from players, fans and umpires, every day for a season. Before this all started, he faced death threats too, naturally. This venomous bile continued to be directed at him everywhere he went. Crowds were huge everywhere too, to see this phenomenon, not just of baseball, but of American history. Daily he faced pitchers, the best in the game, snarling as they flung a ball at around 90 miles per hour not just near his body but frequently at it. At St Louis, Enos Slaughter, later a Hall of Famer, leapt feet in the air as he "slid" into second base, Robinson's station, to deliberately carve a gash in his thigh.

On and on it went, through the spring and summer months of 1947. But Jackie hit well and played an incredible running game on the bases, stealing them and beating tags and throws. His enthusiasm and explosive play gradually won over bigots and casual racists in number. The Sporting News, the media arm of organised ball, who had opposed integration in April, inaugurated their new rookie of the season award by giving it to Jackie Robinson. He averaged .297, stole 29 bases and hit 12 homers. His teammates, some of who threatened to boycott the team at the beginning, were within months ready each game to avenge anyone who attacked their guy on the field. Racism was and is learned from others.

(Above) Brooklyn Dodgers 1949 team picture. The year baseball was blown apart by Branch Rickey, owner of the Dodgers, and Robinson himself who refused to be other than brilliant at second base. Did white on shirts ever appear so white?
(Below) Jackie is seen here being tagged out at the plate on another hot day.

Jackie Robinson 1919-72

b. Cairo, Georgia. (Brooklyn Dodgers, Second Baseman) The man could hit too. He hit .297 in '47, making him the very first Rookie of the Year. The award is now named after him. He hit the majors at the age of 28, so his career numbers do not reveal his true worth. And anyway, statistics clearly are not what is important with this man. He was an incredible force of nature, whose psychological strength and moral courage make him perhaps the greatest man ever to step on to a sports field.

It can only exist where whites and blacks do not work and live side by side. When they do, the Robinson story proves, racial prejudice comes crashing down destroyed, as it deserved to be. Jackie Robinson's first season in major league baseball is one of the most sensational, awful but ultimately beautiful stories in human history. How he found the strength to be so good under what appeared to be unendurably difficult conditions is impossible to fathom. He did, and baseball was never the same again. In fair honour of this man who died prematurely in 1972 aged 53, his uniform number has been retired throughout all of baseball.

I have it on good authority here in 2004 that race is still the third rail of American life. Blacks are not equal, but in baseball they are perhaps more equal than anywhere else. After Robinson and Rickey stormed the citadel, others steadily trickled into the game. By the mid-50s, we have to talk of superstars again, but now we read about and stare at photographs of black men: Willie Mays of the Giants, one of the best five players of all time, a home run champion four times; Larry Doby of the Cleveland Indians, the first Negro to play in the American League; Henry Aaron, eventually the breaker of Ruth's lifetime record of 714 home runs; Ernie Banks of the Cubs, an eventual 500 home run hitter.

History 1950-70

"An outfield of Cobb, Speaker and Ruth, even with Ruth, lacks the combined power of DiMaggio, Musial and Williams."
Connie Mack, manager of the Philadelphia Athletics from 1901-50.

Studying baseball in the 50s means colliding inevitably with a different baseball phenomenon, the rise of the team behemoth of baseball history, the New York Yankees. The Bronx Bombers were a nothing team called the New York Highlanders until Babe Ruth arrived in 1920. Although Gehrig was a true great also, it is likely that Ruth would have catapulted at least half the teams in either league to pennants and Series with some decent support on the mound. With Ruth, the Yankees won 7 American League championships and 4 World Series. Under the fantastic hitting of DiMaggio, they won 5 more Series between 1936 and 1941. They were now threatening to become a dynasty, a Holy (or unholy, depending on your point of view) Roman Empire of the sport. They won again in 1943 and 1947. Then from 1949 they won five consecutive World Series, cementing the monolith in place: it seems to dwarf the game when we study their success from this distance. It's easier to list the years they *didn't* win the American League after 1936: 1940; 1944; 1945; 1946 (two of the three without DiMaggio); 1948; 1954; 1959 and 1965. Twenty-two pennants in thirty seasons.

The 1950s was the decade of a third Yankee outfielder and slugger of great importance: Mickey Mantle. Here in another in most everyone's top ten of all time, and the Yankees had him. They also had Whitey Ford, a great pitcher, but above all, by now there was a spirit of the New York Yankees, an attitude to and a standard of playing the game that made for an extra player or two. "We are the Yankees," it went, " and we win." Success, given sufficient talent and intelligent management, can be learned behaviour. At team level it also requires a preparedness of great players to prepare not to be separate: to give themselves to the team. If Ruth didn't have it, and he didn't, fundamentally nice and kind man though he was, his greatness aligned to Gehrig was enough to slay the field. DiMaggio was a team man, a Yankee. His spirit lives on in the team more than Ruth's, although it took the acquisition of the greatest scorer and maker of runs of all time and all time to come, to plant the Yankee flag on America's moon.

Somehow, you feel, they must have cheated, or that God was on their side. But they didn't and He wasn't. There was enough money in the rest of America for other teams to buy great stars, and there is only room for nine players on the field at any one time. They had Ruth, DiMaggio and Mantle, spanning 1920 and 1965. When the outfield superstar supply gave out, so did the dynasty and for a time, so did the spirit. For eleven years, they won nothing.

The Sixties is a decade which in baseball terms I've yet to come to terms with.

For me, baseball is a game either played in the first decade of this century, or the first fifty of the last. Baseball now is a process of historical continuation. When I watch it on tape today I feel somehow that I'm watching a historical programme. The Sixties to me is The Beatles and flower power and Hendrix and Woodstock, drugs and Bob Dylan. If I link that to America in my head, the only other event that flashes up is the Vietnam War. What has this to do with baseball? I think. Base hits and the Vietcong? The slider and Napalm? I find it hard to reconcile Americans worrying about Al Kaline's run production with that naked child running away from a burning village.

Who the fuck cares about baseball while Kennedy, Johnson and Nixon engaged their country in a war that had nothing to do with national security, killing and maiming men, women and children on both sides pointlessly. The same, you may be thinking, can be said now about the Iraq War, only anti-American terrorism is not a figment of a political organisation's paranoid imagination. And the Vietnam War removed no one from tyranny whereas the Iraq War did, unquestionably. There's a question of scale here too.

Much as I love *Ball Four* by Jim Bouton, his account of the 1969 baseball season makes very few references to the war, when you feel it should, that his knuckleball is comically irrelevant to American history at that point. It's another trick of perception on the writer's part, however. Young Americans had their minds shot or blown and their balls blown off in Vietnam while by all accounts, huge numbers of Americans took baseball as seriously as they ever had. If Jim Bouton is anything to go by, and I have no doubt that his diary is as authentic as any historical document you can produce, baseball was still fascinating. Gone were the days of scruffy, poor players fighting half the time: we're now in the modern age of jet planes and synthetic, brightly coloured uniforms. Hair is long to go with the times and there are groupies for third basemen and pitchers just as there were for guitarists and drummers. Whether the batboy picked up the crumbs the roadies used to, I don't know.

Strands of miserable continuity remained, however. The ballplayer was still owned by the ball clubs and salaries, though better than the days of yore, were still artificially held down. Critical uncertainty for the marginal player remained. Bouton, with exquisitely painful accuracy, reveals to us the precipitous life of the major leaguer who isn't a star. He's a man who one day can be on the St Louis roster on a Thursday afternoon, but be on the way to Portland, Oregon on a Friday morning as a minor leaguer, which will for the rest of the season at least, be his home city. The drop from the majors to the minors is like dropping off a flat earth. Constantly travelling, practising (if you're a hitter at least) and playing, the pro in The Show in 1969 is oblivious to Vietnam but desperate to look up a chick's skirt at the game, stare through a hotel window at her undressing away from it and screw one if she comes within orbit. He's macho to the point of imbecility and a freak if he reads anything but the box scores and the funny papers. Not only does he screw, great as long as his wife or girlfriend doesn't find out, but he drinks and takes drugs. He does amphetamines as a matter of course and if possible, times the ingestion to coincide perfectly with an at bat. He is not a perfect role model for a middle class American family out of *The Lucy Show*.

When *Ball Four* hit the shops, the establishment freaked out completely. Bouton put baseball where it belonged: in the crack between old and new America. When the media covered baseball fully in the early 60s, with television as well as baseball, it tried to do what the newspapers had done: sanitise it and package it as wholesome entertainment, something it never was. What the wonderful memoirs of the past do is put baseball back where it belongs: in its place reflecting the warp and weft, the good and evil, of American society. Everyone who wants real baseball and who has written about it has much to thank Jim Bouton and his publisher for, surely.

Perhaps more prosaically, baseball in the Sixties was about the rise of the pitcher over the batter once again. This he or they, did, by discovering a new pitch, the slider and pitching from higher and higher mounds, which now brought the ball to the batter at a trajectory that was much harder for him to hit hard. In 1968 amid falling attendances and with Carl Yastrzemsky of the Red Sox becoming batting champion with a mere .301 average, time was called on the Incredible Rising Hill. It was shaved to its present height of ten inches. Numbers rose immediately and batters began the process of learning to cope with the slider, this devil of a trick pitch which veered away from the batter sideways just as it was about to be launched at the fences by slugger.

The Los Angeles Dodgers owned the best pitcher of the 60s, one Sandy Koufax, so good he slipped into the scripts of films and comedies of the time, along with Mickey Mantle, so even we knew roughly who he was. St Louis had the first black pitching great of the post-Robinson era: Bob Gibson. Fast to pitch, fast through the air and one who hated batters. The Dodgers won the Series in 1963 and 1965, the Cardinals in 1964 and 1967. The deflating Yankees left room for others to find World Championship glory. In 1969, the shock of all, another team from the five boroughs hit the heights: the New York Metropolitans, or as they were soon known, The Miracle Mets.

Giuseppe DiMaggio 1914-1999
b. Martinez, California. (New York Yankees, Center-fielder) The "Dago" or "Daig" – can you believe that despite his brilliance he was regularly called this on account of his Italian origins? This is the swing that crashed against the self-belief of a hundred pitchers time after time.

Ted Williams – 1918-2002
b. San Diego, California. (Boston Red Sox, Left fielder) This man is quite widely believed to be the most brilliant striker of a baseball that ever lived. He couldn't field much and wasn't a quick baserunner. But he is down in history for the time being as the last man to hit .400, .406 to be precise. Going into the last day of the season he would dip below the mountainous stat if he had a bad day: his manager suggested he miss the game to preserve it, but Williams knew that if he did, his reputation would be forever tarnished. He got three hits.

Willie Mays – 1931-
b. Westfield, Alabama. (New York Giants, Center-fielder) Don't let anyone get away with the claim that great baseball players wouldn't have made great cricketers. This photo proves to me that had the slave ship dropped off Willie's ancestor in the Caribbean instead of one of the southern states, he may well have been as great as George Headley or Vivian Richards. Just look at that balance and that natural poise. The game he's playing here is stickball.

History 1971-Present

"One day, he will put up numbers no one can believe."
Pittsburgh Pirate contemporary of Barry Bonds. Robert James Reynolds.

Baseball has gone through convulsions in recent times too. The strike in 1981 threatened to destroy that season: the 1994 strike did so. The fall out from that was a four-year decline in the public's interest while national interest in football ("American football" to us) grew steadily. But essentially, given the amazing change that took place in the last part of the 20th century in technology, thought and lifestyle, baseball has more than survived. Audiences actually in the stadium are arguably pretty huge - even 20 000 people watch Brewers games at a rate of 81 per season – are well looked after and watch with enormous enthusiasm. Money is not only bursting out of the players' pockets: new ballparks are being built at a steady rate with shed loads of private and public cash. This investment in baseball capital, above all, is a statement of big institutional America having great faith in baseball future. It will go on and on, and will be watched and played in a style that resembles the Beverly Hillbillies more than The Jetsons or Futurama.

This was not the case as the Play Off Era began in 1969. The next decade saw changes to the look and texture of baseball that alarmed anyone who wanted the pastime to remain fairly static in shape and form, there being little wrong with it. There were four big difficulties (at least): one, the stadiums had become soulless, concrete monstrosities. Two, the game was increasingly played on green carpet, not grass. Three, the players played in garb that resembled the acid-fuelled dreams of Jimi Hendrix. Four, the players' rising salaries were making them lazy, spoiled players the fans could no longer relate to. Five, as a result of their free agency which was soon to arrive, they were merely hired guns with zero loyalty to a team. Six, as *Ball Four* told us, the pill bottle had replaced the plug of tobacco, a habit that would ruin the sport.

For younger readers (cf. you students), you ought to know that in the Sixties and Seventies it was pretty much assumed that by 2000 we'd all be riding around in the sky on scooters eating food out of toothpaste tubes and the world would be made of plastic. Sex would be abolished for something less messy while governments, themselves controlled by either dictators or corporations, would control our minds. In short, the future would change the human species beyond recognition. Pretty much everything would get worse and anything you regarded as traditional would be swept away by the insatiable thirst for the new. So baseball during this time was changed by owners to fit this expectation, daft as it sounds. Players wore uniforms in almost luminous colours in ghastly synthetic material that made them look like actors in a space-aged drama rather than highly tuned sportsmen. To accompany this development, the game "that used to be played on grass" (see Honig and Venables, as in Terry) was played on plastic stained green. So a ball chopped down hard would fly over the head of the pitcher and the infield and be heading for Mars in no time. *Boing!* When you see footage of Baseball In The Synthetic Age, it looks completely wrong (thankfully football, as in soccer, managed to escape most of this). This is because – and I don't want to sound like one of those ludicrous fuddy-duddies like Richard Ingrams here, but... - it *was* completely wrong. Grass was to baseball what butter is to a cake. Uniform shirts of cotton (we'll accept that earlier heavier materials weren't such a great thing) were to the game what canvas is to a painting. Interesting logos and a small number of colour embellishments on uniforms are salt and vinegar to the bag of chips. And perfect conformity is to stadium design what an office suit is to a day at the beach. The incredible thing to this observer is that the corporations of America who move and shake baseball have turned the course of history around 180 degrees. Retro irregularity and grass are now not considered fashionable but essential to steer baseball forward in time correctly. Uniforms have returned to a style we can fairly regard as classic: simple, clean but pleasingly colourful.

Modernists or post-modernists may regard this development as a futile and unnatural attempt to stop time. But is life on the planet supposed to consist of endless progression? One of the beauties of baseball is the fact that it is a sport that doesn't need much changing. Its essentials, like those of our football, cricket and rugby, work just fine. Like its counterparts, baseball has evolved over time. The preparedness to evolve is essential; what may seem to have been working well enough in 1904, the spitball for example, may not be appropriate to a later time. But if we look at baseball in 2005, it's a game that still works and still satisfies the players and the public. Of course, reform is demanded by some: some regard games to be too high-scoring and want the strike zone increased; some want to restrict the number of pick off throws a pitcher can make; many regret the Designated Hitter rule in the American League and would happily go back to hitting pitchers; a chunk of folk resent the play off system, especially the Wild Card rule. This is all good, actually. A game that isn't worth arguing about is one that is too static and can't be worth playing. To be annoyed is as human as wanting things to change. But the baseball the North Americans have is beautifully balanced: it entertains, it engrosses, it angers, it worries people and it has problems. Frantically worrried conservatives can calm down because baseball has always had them. Do players take steroids? Players used to drink too much. Do they care any more about playing seriously (they don't need to, to make money)? Old timers used to take bribes. And they weren't that fit. They were knackered from all that travelling on uncomfortable trains. Isn't the game is being taken over by players from the Hispanic countries? Until 1947 the game was exclusively preserved for whites and when a black was allowed to join the club he was treated worse than a scabby dog. Magnificent black players were deprived of the right to enthral the public with their magical skills and the average standard of play was artificially and immorally depressed.

Roberto Clemente 1934-72
b. Carolina, Puerto Rico (Pittsburgh Pirates, Right-fielder) A great hitter, a wonderful fielder and a man of great substance and honour. Died helping his countrymen and women.

Dennis Eckersley – 1954-
b. Oakland, California. (Boston Red Sox, Oakland Athletics, right-handed pitcher) Vitally important in developing the role of the closer, we see this brilliant pitcher wrapped in what today appears as extremely dodgy garb, typical of the 90s period. The material is too synthetic, too bright and too tight. But to pitching. Eckersley became closer at the A's in 1986 almost by accident and became the first ninth inning closer in the game – and was brilliant at it. He has 390 saves (4th AT) and pitched in the 2nd highest number of games ever, 1071, behind Jesse Orosco, in what became a 23-year long career.

Actually, as English soccer writer David Lacey found when twenty years ago he got his hands on the 1953 Cup Final, a game which in his memory represented perfection in the sport, and saw twenty-two men playing at practically walking pace and showing quite considerable ineptitude, if we could go back and watch the game as played in the 20s we'd no doubt be horrified about its slowness and scrappiness. The memory of ballplayers recalls great fielding, lightning pitching and spectacular hitting but in the absence of film and speed guns, there is absolutely no proof whatsoever that Walter Johnson was as fast as Randy Johnson. Or that pitching generally was as good as it is today. For example, what about them all getting hammered in the age of Ruth and the banned spitball? No one bats .400 any more. Don't tell us that's because fitter, stronger batters aren't as good. Not when pitchers are fitter, stronger, armed with more technical and tactical information that a heart transplant surgeon. Yet people say too many runs are scored. Could it be that hitters 6,7 and 8 are far more talented than their counterparts in the 1940s? So is the case that the standard of baseball today is actually better than it used to be. It has to be. But the key question is this: is baseball better than it was? And the answer is 'no.' A game of baseball, a game of anything, is as good as the feeling it gives you inside. The home runs, stolen bases, strikeouts and double plays of yore clearly inspired young men (and women), drove tens of thousands to frenzied excitement, engrossed serious growing children and caused endless hot stove talk when it was all over for another year. You only have to see photographs of the vast throngs of American humanity who choked city main squares just to see World Series play-by-play scores posted on signboards, of teams they didn't root for, to know that baseball was desperately important and deeply loved by Americans in the past. It is likely - certainly it is possible - that baseball meant more to the American in the first sixty years of the 20th century than it does today. And that might be the most meaningful thing of all.

If baseball cannot quite mean quite as much to America now in the age of the endless option, that doesn't mean it isn't one of the best times for the fan to be alive. To present to you a fairly obvious example: the crowds returned to baseball in large numbers in 1998 when the public imagination, dragged down by accusations of player greed (encouraged by supposedly rapacious, parasitic agents) amid the '94 strike, was re-fired by the home run race of 1998. Two super-sluggers of the modern age, Mark McGwire of the St Louis Cardinals and Sammy Sosa of the Chicago Cubs fought titanically to beat the 1961 home run record that both immortalised and destroyed the career of Roger Maris. McGwire, at 32, hit 52 for the Athletics in '96, and 58 for the Athletics and the Cardinals the following year. The Dominican Sosa, 29 years old in '98, had a season peak of 40 going into the season, notched in '96. When in '97 he fell back to 36 homers, it was only the third time he'd hit 30 in his career. Then in 1998 he exploded. He ended the season with what would have been a Maris-breaking 66, but McGwire hit 70. The race of that year brought the playing of the game back to the centre stage instead of what ideally should always be peripheral matters. The hint that summer of a new golden age was cemented three years later when Barry Bonds, tore through McGwire's new mark with 73. Poor Sosa had gone on from 1998 to hit 63, 50 and 64 long balls, sensational hitting, but was reduced to so much film on the cutting room floor by the San Francisco Giant who previous to '91 hadn't shown any signs that he was about to become an immortal. His record to that point put him among the near-greats, he'd hit the 40 HR mark four times and hit 49 the year before, but 49 is a long, long way from 70 and no one saw this coming.

Roger Maris –1934-85
b. Hibbing, Minnesota (like Bob Dylan) (New York Yankees, Right-fielder) "Maybe I wasn't the chosen one, but I was the one who got the record." This picture doesn't appear to lie: he was a distressed young man even while chasing successfully, Babe Ruth's 1927 home run record in 1961. His hair later fell out as he came apart as a result of the stress of chasing the record, of beating it, and living down the fact that he'd done it in more games than Ruth, thus causing a huge debate in the game over whether the record was truly his.

Bonds in 2004 went past his godfather Willie Mays' career total of 660 a couple of weeks in, then in August hit his 700th, only the third man in history so to do. In 2005 he will glide past Ruth, barring a personal disaster; in 2006, at the age of 43, he will most probably become the man with the most home runs in the history of the American Pastime. It's not easy to say ¡°this is a new golden age of baseball,¡± but it's not that difficult. Wonderful things are happening. The Red Sox winning the Series for the first time since 1918 isn't just wonderful for BoSox fans: it's so for all baseball fans. Even with the game debased as a currency by its availability seven days a week through television, the event provides us with what we need to live in the bliss of present golden age possibility: the pleasure of the new. For the Sox, it's like the World Series has been won for the first time. Perhaps Bonds will take the career home run total into new territory. It's not a good age, much less a golden one, when events are happening over and over again. The Yankees can never make another golden age. Higher, faster, farther, better. There is a terrible relentlessness implied by the thought that these phenomena are required for baseball to be truly great, but it seems – at least it did last October to be so: is Bonds not the *best* player at his age in history? Is Clemens not possibly the *best* pitcher aged over 40 of all time? Isn't the standard of fielding *higher* than it's ever been? Is not pitching more refined than it has ever been, more thoughtful, more expert? Is the general standard not *better* than *ever*?

The disease-ridden answer is that because of steroid use, the extent of which is anyone's guess, we have absolutely no idea. The cosy romantic historical view of the game has now been trashed for the foreseeable future as well as our ability to pronounce judgement on the present crop of superstars and all who toil in their wake. Doubts no longer just surround Bonds and Sheffield, they appear to make a charade of the 1998 Sosa-McGwire revival story and call into complete question the home run/hitting bulge that began in the 90s. It's a sad thing to watch players throw their talent to the birds through a taste for coke and alcohol, but a disaster of meltdown proportions for them to be allowed to cheat their way to glory. The game of baseball now has its road of redemption to travel, to treat steroid users as it treated the 1919 Black Sox, to root out this monstrous deceit and stamp it into history like it did the spitball and spiking. Let us hope that the guardians of the game – the Commissioner and the owners – understand what baseball has meant to America for over one hundred years and believe in its myths and legends so as to protect its reality. As Rufus Wainwright almost put it, "'wouldn't it be a lovely headline: 'Baseball Is Beautiful Again' in the New York Times.'"

Historical Addendum: Pitching

"Clean living and the spitball."
Preacher Roe, when asked to what he attributed his long career.

Studying and discovering baseball for the first time, the most surprising thing to me was how complex pitching is. The literature of the game takes this further. The pitcher of tradition plies a profound and mystical trade; he is somewhere between snake charmer and back street bully, or technocrat and philosopher. Historically too each pitcher is the team's gladiator, carrying the team's hope on his back as he takes on opposing killer lions with a mixture of brute strength and the wisdom of the ages.

This might all be fanciful bullshit. However, the fact that the old pitchers of yesteryear, truly legendary names - Walter Johnson; Grover Cleveland "Pete" Alexander; Christy Mathewson; Dizzy Dean and Bob Feller, to name a bunch of the most commonly found in the annals – are presented in this way is fascinating and important in itself. And the fact is, in the first part of the twentieth century, a period where few runs were scored in baseball games, ball parks were often stuffed full with thousands of ordinary sports loving Americans desperate to see these men do battle with each other.

The oral history of this period reveals an integral element in the frantic and pleasurably complex social history of the country that is gritty and real, but not without natural elements of romance. The story woven by their tales consists of a rough everyday reality of uncertainty and poor wages. The legends were men who could throw a baseball with great speed and accuracy, whose deeds and proficiency are now preserved for as many years as baseball is taken seriously. But the ranks of professional major league pitchers consisted of a small elite whose livelihood was constantly under threat from serious injury. The precious arm could wear down with the years of wear and tear or suddenly blow. The famed boy of summer could soon be looking forward to a future career of manual labour. He would have been underpaid by mean and greedy owners who owned his ass for all time, but now he could be back among the farm and factory workers scratching for a living if he didn't come, as some did, even before the Depression, from an educated background. After October 1930, the ruined hurler was in the same mess as just about everyone else and levelled back to obscurity unless they could find a sinecure in the game as some sort of coach. The Depression itself (the years 1930 to 1938) should make us wary of romanticising baseball. Crowds fell cutting franchise revenues, which led directly and rapidly to lower baseball wages. Great as it clearly was for the everyday player to be much better off financially and otherwise compared to his fellow American, this was no golden age. The black and white photographs might mesmerise, stories of the Gashouse Gang tantalize and the tale of the Called Shot make us fantasize about being there in person to have seen a precious moment in time, but we should be aware of how easy it is for our non-presence in this imagined reality to chronically distort how it really was for those who really did live it. A mental note of the frequency of baseball suicides would be a good starting point to get a handle on the truth about the daily fabric of the game.

That said, over and over in the Ritter book and its successor by Honig, the old player "loved every minute" of life in the major leagues. Sure. Being paid to play a sport because your skills are a world above the ordinary and so avoiding the mine, the workshop, the farm and the office must have been very nice work indeed if you could get it and still is, I guess. But to pitching.

The more I have read about it, the more I have had to appreciate the importance of pitching and the pitcher. Since major league play began in the 1880s until, say, 1980, each game was mostly seen as a battle between two individuals throwing a baseball not one between two hitting line-ups. That the MLB websites for each club display the daily notice of the night's game underpinned by "Wood 6-5 (4.32 ERA) v Schmidt 9-4 (2.98 ERA)" tells us how hard it is for baseball to lose this notion of baseball as a gladiatorial contest. The old pre-eminence of the pitcher dates back to a now different game. Time was when batters were dominated by the hard-throwing guy on the mound who never had to worry about the excruciating personal crucifixion of the given up home run because no one tried to hit them. In case you're wondering, this was because ballparks before 1920 were so huge that the long ball wasn't possible. Until Ruth, anyway. A sharp pull could get it out down at the end of the foul lines, but mostly place hitting was the order of the decades. And besides, the power hit to send the outfielders sprinting away into the distance was considered vulgar and not quite right. This is the closest baseball ever got to cricket.

Pitchers were called hurlers because that's what they did: they threw their little projectile as hard as they could past the batter. If he hit you hard you came back next time and threw at his body. Or his head. This was a game for the provably courageous. No speed guns existed to tell us how hard Walter Johnson threw, but it would likely as not have been up around the late eighties or early nineties. The hard throw was called the "fastball" and it has stuck fast through to this day. The pitcher had just two clear alternatives to the throw of pure speed. In the 1860s, way before overhand (overarm) pitching was allowed in 1884, one Candy Cummins discovered and used the curveball. This was thrown with top or over spin through a "snap" of the wrist and caused the ball to rise then drop; it has been defeating batters with effortless regularity ever since. The other was the "change up" which came out of the hand with much less speed than the fastball. The big deal is that the speed of the arm delivery was the same as that for the fastball; this causes the batter to swing early and miss or put the ball up in the air for an easy out. This pitch also prospers today as much as it ever did and is a staple of the hurler's arsenal just as the curve and the fastball are.

The third alternative was (and still is) became illegal in 1920: the spitball. Most often wetted with saliva, but also scuffed and cut, this pitch caused the ball to drop alarmingly as it reached the plate. Between them, these pitches were enough, before 1921, to make major league baseball a game based firmly upon batting failure. A player coming to the plate and making three and a half hits in ten was a genius. To us now, the odds stacked up against the batter towered so ridiculously against him that we might wonder that anyone wanted to watch men playing a game of Swing and Miss. Mean games of one-nothing ball were common (and in fact, in terms of the full length of history have only very recently died out). If the dark, wet, soft (or 'dead') ball thrown to him in the dusk against a dark background didn't make things next to impossible, to grind his nose into the dirt, umpires essentially allowed intimidatory pitching. It isn't surprising then that this period has left us few "immortal" batters. Only three come bursting out of the books: Cap Anson, Napoleon Lajoie, Honus Wagner and perhaps the greatest hitter of all time: Ty Cobb.

To reduce a long story to take away size, the end of the wet and dirty ball in the immediate aftermath of the 1919-20 Black Sox Scandal saw an explosion of hitting and batters' numbers that lasted for two decades. Babe Ruth started to hit a prodigious number of home runs with the new 'lively' ball. The electrified fans who flooded stadiums wherever Ruth played, urgent to witness his soaring hits encouraged owners to cut the size of their ballparks to produce their own home run hitters and so make more money at the gate. The Hall of Fame is flooded with the men who exacted revenge upon the throwers in the new conditions. Ruth, Gehrig, Greenberg, Collins, Sisler, Hornsby, Gehringer, Ott, Foxx, Traynor, Heilman and Appling, to name the most obvious. At the end of the period came DiMaggio and Williams. The 1940 to 1970 period saw a gradual re-establishment of balance to the batter-pitcher power struggle. It was caused by the slow evolution of better, smarter pitching to cope with the humiliation of being constantly hit and the invention and spread of a new and devastating pitch, the slider.

A Detroit Tigers pitcher, George Uhle claimed to have invented it. Whereas the curve ball worked its now old magic through overspin, this new pitch operated through sidespin. It moved sideways on the batter and could drop also. It was thrown faster than a curve too, causing more damage (it was known as a 'sailing fastball' by Uhle and his colleagues). Thrown by a right-hander to a right-hander, the movement was away. As most all hitters liked to pull the ball, it presented an extremely serious difficulty to the slugger. How do you pull an accurate, well thrown slider out of the park? How, even, do you make contact with it without giving up an easy out through a mis-cue? The last hitter to average .400 for an entire season was Ted Williams in 1941. One frequently asked question in the game is, "will anyone ever again hit four hundred?" The answer is almost always "no." The slider is one of the explanations. A poor quality ball was used in the war years, the Balata Ball, but the return of the harder ball with peace didn't revive batting numbers to the heights of the 30s. Stan Musial hit .376 in 1948, but not until 1980 was four hundred again a possibility (George Brett of the Kansas City Royals inexplicably hit .390 that year.)

The pitcher fight back was rocked by Roger Maris's defeat of the Ruth home run record of 60 in 1961, but by 1964 they were aided by the introduction of a bigger strike zone. A new trend developed too in this decade to stymie the slugger. In a rash of conservatism, pitching mounds were allowed to grow higher and higher, cutting successful hitting back to the point where legislation was introduced to restrict the height of the hill to 10 inches (where it has remained). The mid to late-sixties was a period of Gibson-Koufax-led domination and austerity. In 1969 the AL batting champion, Carl Yastrzemsky of the Boston Red Sox could only muster .301. RBI leaders Harrelson and McCovey brought home only 109 and 105 respectively. If you think about the implications of the seminal *Ball Four*, it could have been the case that drug-taking batters couldn't do the job their predecessors had done of old – there's a surprise – and had to be helped. Were they not balanced by bleary-eyed, pill-popping, coke-snorting hurlers though? Probably not: hitting is sexy and immediate. Pitching has always been considered to be a craft, an art even. The fragility of the job caused fewer to risk it all for the cheap psychotropic thrills of the Woodstock age, I would suspect (though I wouldn't know for sure).

The Seventies saw batting numbers safely recover, and so a period of stability was achieved. It gave us great pitchers: Steve Carlton; Don Sutton; Nolan Ryan; Tom Seaver; Fergie Jenkins; Phil Niekro; Gaylord Perry; Catfish Hunter and Dennis Eckersley. But great or highly effective hitters come more readily to mind and went to the Hall in bigger numbers (almost all of them): Roberto Clemente; Joe Morgan; Pete Rose; Wade Boggs; George Brett; Rod Carew; Mike Schmidt; Orlando Cepeda; Willie Stargell; Reggie Jackson; Robin Yount; Don Mattingly; Dave Winfield.

A shrinking strike zone again, caused the beginning, in 1990, of the period we're in now, one of high numbers of hits, homers and batting average. Now we expect the top fifty batters to hit .300 and the best hitters to be hitting 40 homers and more. Crowds are huge because they are well looked after and they see hits and runs. Just as no one wants to go to their local football ground to see a 0-0 draw or a drab, ground out one-nil, fans, purists apart, don't want pitching duels. No one hits .400 but more than three times out of ten, a lot of players will connect well and get to first base. A fair proportion of those times, the ball screams through the air like a shell, line driven for a single or double. Occasionally, sometimes more than occasionally, it is a launched missile that leaves the playing area in a drama only those who have experienced themselves can tell you how arresting and deep. Those poor saps who paid their quarters in the Dead Ball Era and died before it ended, thankfully never knew what they missed.

Pitching is the same now as it has always been: a highly technical craft or as near to an art as you get in sports. It is still the case that the gift of great (or even successful) pitching is considered delicate and mysterious – ironically practised by the physically robust throwing a potentially life-threatening missile – and one where success is known to be often fleeting, temporary, transitory. Some operators – and I'm talking present day ones now – seem to have attained the Holy Grail of marvellous consistency: Roger Clemens; Pedro Martinez; Mariano Rivera. But even these come to the mound some days and get shelled. They "can't find their location;" they "didn't have it" on that day. They do walk a precipice and have done since Ruth pulled down the home run from heaven and gave it to us. Three bad pitches could cost you five runs and an early, ignominious ejection. And they can't, unless they're a reliever, go to sleep knowing that 'hell, tomorrow's another day,' because tomorrow he won't pitch. Nor the next day nor the next. Roped on Sunday afternoon, the guy won't be able to put things right until Saturday. For we now live in the period of the five-man starting rotation and no bullpen activity unless it's the late play offs or the World Series and no play on Mondays (normally). And what if he comes to the pitching mound and doesn't have it then? The fastball isn't jumping, the sinker isn't sinking and the confidence isn't there to throw that normally devastating change up? He goes for seven runs this time. Another five day wait to pitch again. How slowly must the time pass and with what mental uncertainties and agonies? How much comfort the vast salary? (Derek Weaver was paid $4 million in 2003 by the New York Yankees). What if in his desperation to get back to his normal five-hit, three run game he overthrows and injures his shoulder or a crucial arm muscle. That ain't going to happen to a hitter (and you've thought a hundred times too how the 0 for 5 hitter on a Tuesday can come out on Wednesday and hit a nice double second time up and it all starts flowing again). He can be out for months. The rest of the season. If he's Pedro, or Pettite, well fine, everyone's running round worrying about that arm and desperate, fans too, for him to come back as soon as you can. After all, you're one of the best in the league. But what if you're the fifth starter, just promoted from three seasons in Triple A ball? You have no track record in the majors; you haven't proved to anyone that you can cut it up here in the Big Show. There are plenty more out there just like you: young guns

Walter Johnson – 1887-1946

b. Humboldt, Kansas (Washington Senators, right-hand pitcher) You are looking at the man who is widely regarded as the greatest pitcher in the history of baseball. For ten straight seasons – 1910-19 - he won over 20 games for a weak team. In his first 13 seasons, his ERA reached 2 runs given up per 9 innings once. His 417 career wins is second only to Cy Young. Baseball Library describes him having "a wholly admirable character" in a "rowdy game". A gentle, old-fashioned human being was The Big Train, and he threw a lethal, mighty fastball.

. *"This boy throws so fast you can't see 'em and he knows where he is throwing, because if he didn't there would be dead bodies all over Idaho."*
Joe Cantillion, on Walter Johnson before joining the Washington Senators

overflowing with energy and ambition to show there's a place in this heaven for them and you, you busted your arm so get out the fuckin' way and let someone else show them how to slow a slider on a full count with two on and none out. And each year the June College/High School draft reminds you that each year the next Woods, Santanas and Schmidts lurk there waiting to take your place away.

This is the worse case scenario, however. The pressures on the modern pitcher are enough to explain many a mental crack up, but all the modern day major league ball clubs have deep networks of support and most important all, they don't want you to fail. If you make it all the way to the starting rotation you have already proved yourself to be great, superb at what you do to earn yourself what is, let's face it, an incredibly good material living. When you struggle there are pitching coaches to nurse you back to form aided and abetted by a web of technical back up devices such as video and so on. The days of *Ball Four* and a hopeless coaching squad of mean spirited buffoons whose system amounts to no more than doing what he did when he was in the majors are now past. The emotional support is professional and the physical conditioning is second to none. In the case of physical breakdown, referral to surgical treatment will bring you procedures which are production line smooth or in the case of more drastic damage being delivered to cutting edge specialists pushing the frontiers of surgery back just so they can save you. It is true that careers can be ruined by injury, but in the first decade of the twenty-first century you have every chance of making it back from anything short of losing your whole arm in an off-season argument with farm machinery.

On the mound the hitters might be as brilliant as they've ever been: fitter, stronger and more patient than at any time in the history of the game, also with more support and a technical approach to hitting that would have made Ted Williams drool. Batters and *their* coaches are studying the art of hitting, as they have never done before; their science is advancing continually: all those home runs are no longer smashed by guess-hitters. In Oakland and now Boston the technocrats are devising more and more ways to force you to expose your weaknesses.

So what do you have to beat them? Eight out of ten will have, first and foremost, their fastball. The fastest can throw consistently at 94 or 95 miles per hour. If you work hard enough at it, it can move in the air too. The two-seam fastball can be used to produce sideways movement, at high speed, remember, or can be made to sink. Get this right and it will fall "right off the table" making the batter look like he's grovelling on the floor for dimes. Right alongside your fastball will be the slider. Everyone throws it now. Late movement again and potentially a fantastic strikeout pitch. Third you have the change up to master and deploy. When the ninety miles-per-hour fastball arrives at seventy-five the batter is so far out in front of the ball he's half way out to the mound to embrace you. And if these fantastic weapons aren't enough you have your brain to help administer the coup de grace. First pitch you threw a fastball that A Rod didn't even swing at. Having succeeded once, he's thinking you're going to throw another for strike two so you slip him a change up instead which he missed by so much that his wondrous, classically elegant swing had him looking like a fuckin' ballet dancer when he'd got to the end of that fancy-Dan follow through. Okay, then, the 0-2 pitch. He doesn't know what's coming. So. Tell you what. As you've got a reputation for using the blazing fastball as a strikeout pitch, and knowing that he's got to swing now at whatever you throw next, if he knows what's good for him, you'll throw him another change up. Look in at A Rod fuckin' sweatin' there in the batter's box, reach back and *grmmmph*. "*Streeeough!*" See ya A Rod, you're gone.

Normally, you're not going to have to meet Jeter, Sheffield and Alex Rodriquez, so you'll have an easier time of it. And look it: you beat A Rod with just your fastball and change up. You didn't need the curve, you didn't need your slider and you didn't even need two fastballs, putting all that strain on your arm. Really, it isn't fair on the batter: there's too much stuff I can use on them to get them out that the rules ought to be changed.

Alternatively things can pan out like this:

Oh shit, here comes A Rod. Lofton forced me to throw him four balls. My catcher kept picking pitches for me I didn't want to throw. I wanted to throw Jeter my change up first pitch but my battery mate signalled fastball, which Derek lined over short like a scud for a single and Lofton slid in at third. First inning, no one out and already they've men on the corners. And did I not tell you? I don't decide what to throw, my catcher does that. I'd like to shake him off more often, but with a record so far of 0-3 and an ERA of 5.65, I'm not in a position to argue. My first pitch to Sheffield, a slider, was wide, then he smacked a fastball high to my centre fielder who made the out but Lofton tagged up to score (Jeter to third); and now Rodriguez. Okay now, keep it together. I look in at Pudge and he's signalling slider. Good choice. I throw it. Shit, wide again. Pudge is now running out toward me to give me some advice.

"Okay, man, what do you want to throw this guy next?"

"Let me throw him a change up."

"What, are you crazy? He spots it coming someone's going to get their windshield smashed to fuckin' pieces. And it'll be four-nothing with one out."

Clarence "Dazzy" Vance – 1891-1961

b. Homosassa Springs, Florida. (Brooklyn Robins, Right-hand pitcher) I love this picture very much. This is the face of
the wily old hurler, a man who ruined his arm as a fireballer in his 20s only to emerge as an expert curveball specialist in his 30s.
He was a 31 year-old rookie (!) who went on to win 197 games. He (very) famously tore his white shirt to ribbons so that
on washday in Brooklyn, he was practically un-hittable at Ebbetts Field. He was in his mid-40s when he finished his career.

"Hrrmph." Pitcher scuffs pitching mound with toe of right foot.
"Look, we need a groundball for the double play. How are you feeling about your sinker?"
"Not so good."
"Okay, throw him a couple of sliders, down and in. We'll take it from there."
"Okay."
Okay, off we go again. One slider in the right place and we're out of here....

Our pitching friend here throws the slider. Down and in it's a wonderful pitch. Located right, A Rod watches it curl in on the corner for a strike. Better than nothing. If he does swing, located right he's going to hit the ball straight to short or third and he gets the double play or at the very least one. But pitching is a confidence thing. To throw a breaking pitch with such precision under such pressure takes tremendous pitching know-how and some luck. Throw a round projectile at 88 mph with your adrenaline surging like high tide at Big Sur; you can't expect it to be inch perfect. You can only hope....

"Grrmmmph......fuck no, not on the outside........."

Alex Rodriquez watches the first slider nearly take him in the knee for ball two, and then fancies taking a pop at the next one, another slider. The location is wrong, it's away. It's low though, so it's actually a pretty good pitch. But A Rod is a great hitter and gets a piece of it. It tears through the hole between shortstop and second base, only three feet away from our pitcher, and finds the power alley in left. He got enough of the barrel on the pitch to send it to the wall in left-centre field and helps himself to a double. Jeter scores, Sheffield scores and it's 3-0 Yankees with still only one out. A Rod is in scoring position and next is Posada, an excellent hitting catcher.

At this time in baseball history, pitchers do have a lot going for them. They're not always facing this quality of hitter by any means. There are a number of teams in each league whose number seven, eight and nine hitters are never going to make the All-Star team. Form and confidence is almost everything. Without it, a pitcher with the same skill, power, brains and variety of pitches can be easy prey for major league hitting. Carrying self-belief and an ERA of 2.82 he seems unhittable and to all but the best in the league, probably, for now, is.

The decisive factor for the pitcher in terms of outcome is location. Throw that slider to the edge of the strike zone and Larry Walker looks at a strike going by. Leave it up another four inches and in another three and not sliding very much, Larry hits in 420 feet and you're wearing a donkey's head. Just watching two games a week on the TV you see this time and time again. A pitcher can be going very well indeed, throwing fast, mixing his pitches and locating all of them with exceptional skill. But these days, with the pool of hitters starting from a population of 250 million people in the United States, extends now to Mexico, Venezuela, Puerto Rico, the Dominican Republic, Cuba and Japan, never have the major leagues had such quality to deploy against their rivals, surely. *Never!* Thus it is that you see a top quality pitcher leave one pitch in the middle of the strike zone, make one mistake, and get taken clean out of the yard. The solo shot is no disaster, but you can't expect not to make that mistake when you've walked one guy while another has got on base with a blooper or something. You're facing quality guys all the time: they're all, however humble in hitting skill, capable of getting something on the pitch and poking it through the infield for a base hit. And that walk: does that look bad? Another problem for that pitcher is the margin for error. Hitters are getting so smart and so patient that throwing balls is easy. The target, home plate, is only 17 inches wide: one foot and five inches. And these days around three feet high. You have to throw fast or clever now to defeat all these quality guys coming in from the south so you are bound to miss what is, in effect, a tiny target a fair amount. And remember, the pitcher is not throwing at a target 17 by 36 in size: he's trying desperately to miss the chunk in the middle. Sometimes - and I've seen this in both the last two televised games – hitters will hit something out of the bottom of the strike zone and outside for a home run. So given the choice, only my immense reserve of cowardice would cause me to choose pitching over hitting if I could live in a perfect world. That aside, who'd be a pitcher given a choice? Not me. Me, I'd be Manny Ramirez, but then again, none of us is perfect.

Carl Hubbell – 1903-88
(New York Giants 1928-43, Left-handed pitcher) Known as "The Meal Ticket" for his brilliance and reliability, he was the best pitcher of the 30s, leading in wins in '37 and ERA from '34 to '37. He won the MVP honour in '33 and '36. His staple pitch, remarkably, was the screwball that could ruin the arm. Yet with it he pitched with great accuracy and longevity. Across the end of '36 and the end of '37 he racked up an unbroken record of 24 consecutive wins.

Sandy Koufax 1935-
b. Brooklyn, New York (Brooklyn and Los Angeles Dodgers, Left-hand pitcher) "The Jewish Kid is probably the best of them," said Casey Stengel after his Yankees has been destroyed by Sanford Koufax ("Ko-fax") in the 1963 World Series. He hit the majors in '55 but it wasn't until '61 that he discovered truly how to pitch. When he did he was virtually untouchable. He retired at 30 through a damaged arm in '66. Here he is holding up four souvenir balls from his four no-hit games.

2
Belief In The Unseen
The 2004 Post-Season

"There is only one road to redemption and it lies right down the middle of Yankee Stadium."
Josh Alexander, October 2004, Boston, Massachusetts.

ALCS Game 5. Damon has just come home on a muscled Ortiz single to beat the Yankees 5-4 in the bottom of the 14th inning, ending the longest game in post-season history

I'm badly positioned to do this because I am a Boston Red Sox fan. I was born with a double dose of the tribal football supporter gene, so when I first went to America in 2001, to Boston, and saw the floodlights (as I called them then) rising above the roofs beside what remains of the fens, I was on my way down. So it's great, yes, that "my team" won the Big Cahuna three and a half years later, but that tribal feeling usually is a matter of cost, of debit not benefit. Even now a big part of me wants to be a Pirate or a Tiger because the emotional memories of football for me are not being a small boy and watching Manchester United – my team via my father – winning the European Cup in 1968, but listening to them lose an FA Cup semi-final third replay two years later at the hands of Leeds, and of walking down a Chesterfield side street moping about another home defeat with promotion as far out of reach as the moon. Pain and disappointment are the norm for almost all football supporters and I'm most comfortable there. But alas, Hope and Expectation, the eternal parents of this pain, made it so that by 2003 I'd been sucked into a manic Red Sox ride towards destroying The Curse as easily as a New Year reveller accepting another drink. Before the cold of April was gone, a new supporters' ritual was born in this house. Each morning I'd be the first in the family to wake up, go downstairs, open the fridge, take out the cat food, the coffee and the water jug, then feed the cats, switch on the kettle, spoon the coffee in the pot and slice the bagel in two for the toaster and complete twenty other manoeuvres (in a stupor I counted them one morning). In the crack between any one of those rituals, I'd switch on the computer. After going back in the kitchen to take down two mugs, pour some milk in them and open up the honey jar, I'd go back to the office to click the mouse so that Internet pony could start to ride, before going back to the kitchen to preside over the breakfast developments and wait for the default page to fill up with the Red Sox result from the night before.

By mid-summer this had become important. By the beginning of August I'd get a nervous stomach from about the second I hit "Connect." I'd pad back into the kitchen and perform the meaningful/meaningless groundhog tasks, waiting like a panicking Wall Street broker from October 1929 for the ticker tape to spit out the final prices. Awaiting the news of the rubber game in Baltimore isn't a matter of life and death but it sure feels something like it. One of the great things about baseball is that you ride a hurtling roller coaster whereas football fanatics ride a slow train. When I heard, or thought I heard that the season consisted of one-hundred-and-sixty-two games, I knew I'd made a mistake. *162? Come off it!* It turned out in due course that I was wrong, but it took about two weeks for this fact to just float on the surface of my conscious mind. The great thing I quickly found about the season that never ends was that you didn't have long to dwell on a defeat, unless you followed the Tigers, because a win was often less than a day away.

The American League Championship Series of 2003 feels like ancient history already, but the two mornings I came down to see if the Sox had managed to stave off elimination after going 2-3 behind in Boston are still flesh pink fresh in the memory. The 3-3 morning was a glorious jolt to the senses but the next was unforgettable: a numb plod to the office from a coffee ritual after making the click that would seal my fate for the immediate future. The suspense as I waited for all the clicking and whirring to rush off and fetch me an electronic triumph or disaster was painful-beautiful. What would life be without such dramas? (bloody great, I imagine).

The screen, from the hallway, (the door to the office is always left open) is eight feet away from me. That morning I could see a big patch of white in the middle, with two big, black words above; best to blast towards it to get it over with quickly, I thought. Almost simultaneously I saw a cruel photograph of the drained figure of David Ortiz in a Yankee Stadium locker room and "*Sox Lose*" above. It was just awful, I don't care if living this fan life is a male deferral of reality; this is something I was born to do, I've accepted it. But the thing here was that I was suffering as real a sport-related pain as any I could remember but I wasn't even an American, never mind from Boston! As if the Aaron Boone walk off home run in the 11th inning wasn't punishment enough, I didn't feel as though I had the right to own that excruciating pain. This was actually beyond awful: it was *fucking* awful.

Also forgotten now, as fresh baseball pulls fresh tissue over the scars like tide over sandcastles that went completely wrong, is Grady Little's boner. Some of you will be so new to baseball I suspect that you won't know what I'm talking about. This is probably a very good thing and I'm not going to re-hash the whole history of G's B right here and now. Maybe I will next time, because it is a great sporting story. Suffice it to say that the manager of the Red Sox, on the verge of victory (bottom of the eighth, Boston 5-2), thought, "wait a minute: let's make this more interesting." Or had a brain haemorrhage or something. And you missed a hell of a fight during Game 4 between a short, tubby old man over seventy and one of the greatest pitchers of modern times (the old man hit the canvas in short order and never really recovered). So humour me and come forward in time with me one year.

The 2004 Red Sox story is something you probably all know. It started well, then collapsed and by mid-season was heading absolutely nowhere. The starting pitching stank, apart from big, new star from the Diamondbacks and their brilliant 2001 World Series victory, or half of it anyway (the other half is still in Arizona, Randy Johnson), and the hitters weren't hitting well enough to cover them. For a month leading up to the All-Star Break they could hardly play .500 ball, so how they were going to get past the Yankees this time was nobody's guess. Unless they had a mysterious hot line to the future, Red Sox fans knew that 2004 was nothing but somebody's idea of a mistake. Yet another.

Pedro, Manny and Millar. In the modern day game, the superstar cannot move more than a couple of public steps without the media on their tale. Having just downed the Yankees to win the first Boston American League pennant since 1995, two playing lynchpins and one clubhouse leader (of two: the other is catcher Jason Varitek) come out to face all the dumb questions with looks of pleasure for a change. Note too, Johnny Damon and Curt Schilling in the background doing their media chores too. (Pedro Martinez, b. 1971, Managuyabo, Toronto Blue Jays, BRS, Dominican Republic; Manny Ramirez and Kevin Millar, b. 1971, Los Angeles, California, Florida Marlins, BRS)

Then – again, 'as everyone who followed this knows' - the young tyro General Manager who looks about twelve, Theo Epstein, got rid of superstar shortstop Nomar Garciaparra and brought in some decent infielders before the end of the July trading deadline. I remember looking up the batting averages of Dave Roberts (Los Angeles Dodgers), Doug Mientzkevich (Minnesota Twins) and Orlando Cabrera (Montreal Expos) and wincing with disgust. "How are mediocrities like this going to get us out of the mire?" If it's true that only Cabrera made the regular starting nine, the other two still played an important role in blowing out the gremlins that were gumming up the machine. Cabrera after a slow start batted nearly .300 for the Sox through to the end of September and was a clubhouse livewire where Nomah was allegedly Mr Sulk. Mientkiewicz, that permanent spelling mistake, woke up the sleeping bat of Kevin Millar (who significantly had begun to shed weight), while Roberts, if his bat was a little chilly, would come in as a lightning pinch runner to steal a base or turn third into a run. Crucially, the changed chemistry changed the results. By the end of August the team had won 30 of 33 and the pitching was fast becoming reliable, both starters and bullpen.

A similar thing had happened to the Astros over in Texas, only a change of manager rather than player personnel untied the knot. Jimy Williams was given the pink slip while a loose Phil Garner came in and got the vast talent on the roster – a true embarrassment of future Hall of Famers – to spring into gear. There was one new playing arrival too: Carlos Beltran, acquired from Kansas City. He came in batting .278 but completed the season as a .258 Astro. Not to worry, the team snuck into the play offs via the Wild one, just like Boston. That Beltran could hit a pretty home run though: 23 in 90 games.

The Houston revival was also pretty. On the Sunday night of June 11, the start of the All-Star break, they were 44-44 on the season and had just lost for the sixth time in eight games. They were 6 and 10 for the last sixteen. Garner didn't wave a magic wand and make everything alright: they lost four of the next five. Then they won four of the next five, to get back to .500, then won five of the next eight. Then for whatever reason, they lost eight of the next ten to stand at 56-60. It was August 14th. Why the same bunch of players can produce such differing results in the space of a few weeks is utterly mystifying. .200 ball over ten games is pretty disgusting. Good job it represents only one sixteenth of a whole season. By the 26th of the month another eleven games had passed and the Houston Astros had won eight of them. Then they won the next twelve straight. I make that 20-3 since the 14th of the 8th. To end the dream though, they went down in four of the next seven before crushing the Cards 8-3 and sweeping the Phillies. They were now sixteen games over .500 and Clemens was 18-3 on his season at 41 years-old. Then, they dropped three of the next five to stand on September 25th at 85-70. To make the Wild Card spot they had to win their last eight games and hope that the second placed threat, the Cubs had a monumental crisis of self-belief and form. With four games left, the Astros had caught them Cubs, both teams standing 88-70. Then Chicago lost the next three and it was over for them.

But the remarkable thing about Houston's triumphant regular season, and it seems ridiculous that they didn't win a big pennant for it, is that they had another adversary to deal with too: the San Francisco Giants. They also stood at 88-70 with four to go, and both they and the Astros were 90-70 with two to go. The only thing preventing the thing having an inevitable play-off game look to it was the fact that if Houston won their last two games, and they 'only' had to knock over Colorado with their incandescent form, the Giants had to take two from the Dodgers. With three to go, LA had to win just one of the last three to beat out the Giants for the Division. First game the Giants won 4-2. Two more defeats like that and the Dodgers would be left with a Wild Card tie after 162 with the Astros if Houston could win *their* last two (I hope all you students are following this). What Garner et al needed was for LA to win the next day, the Cubs to lose and themselves to beat Colorado. Both events transpired. The Dodgers took the pennant in the West, and now, if they won on the last day, even a Giants last day win would them one game back. They did, narrowly, 5-3. Nerves got the better of the batters after they went 5-0 ahead in the third, but the Rockies couldn't rally hard enough.

But here's the thing about these end of season events: if Houston wins the Series in 2005, and if they still have Beltran (unlikely) when you read this, back here is where they got the belief and the form to do it. And a second point: if the Astros hadn't squeaked through to the 2004 post-season, where would Carlos be right now in terms of a career? Not a good-looking young man on the lip of superstardom. So it goes.

Meanwhile, over in the American League, the Yankees were being the Yankees. After a hundred games they were already 26 games over .500. After another ten they were 71-39. It all looked easy, with Boston faltering in mid-summer. On August 14th they were 75-41. Then they went Coney Island. Losing seven of the next ten and going 5-4 over the next nine. Then they were the Yankees again, winning four straight then going 6-3. They were clearly going to win the pennant for the millionth time, but it was odd that such a good team could lose two September series to Toronto, could lose 7 of the last 13 of the season, but in the midst of this rolled over the AL Central champions Minnesota in three very tight games. They ended up winning 101 games and it looked as though when they needed to, they could still turn on winning baseball like a tap. But two things are worth pointing out and were noticed by wise acres at the time: one, they had to keep coming from behind to win games. The problem was very suspect pitching. Those huge bats: Sheffield, ARod, Matsui, Williams, Jeter and Posada, would have to keep bailing them out, and once in the lead, in would come arguably the most soul destroying closer of all time (Eric wait in line, there patiently), Mariano Rivera, to nail the win. The second problem was that by the end of the season, the Red Sox had scored a significant crack in one of the Yankees' most frightening weapons. On the night of 18th August, the Sox had their best comeback win of the season when Cabrera ruined Mariano Rivera's easy stroll towards 50 saves for the season by hitting a go-ahead RBI single in the ninth. After a fantastic sequence of wins – they had won 25 of their previous 30 games on this night - the Sox were now only 2 ½ games out of the Bombers. It was the closest they got, however. The last two games of the rubber were blowouts for the Pinstripes who went on to do enough to win the division yet again, but by only three games. It wasn't significant to anybody at the time but to get that go-ahead run, Dave Roberts had stolen a base from Rivera. It may not have escaped everyone's notice that almost four week's previously, Bill Mueller had carpeted a Rivera pitch for a two-run walk off homer at Fenway. For the first time in a long time, the Red Sox finished the season of fights with their bitter rivals with a winning record, 11-8. They took the last series too, 2-1, but in the process laying down another marker, notching two large wins, 12-5 and 11-4. When the two teams met for another Championship Series, some pundits actually had the BoSox down as favourites.

The big threat to the other three was the St Louis Cardinals. The starters looked strong, the bullpen, led by KRod, stronger. And what a line up of batters: Pujols, Rolen and Edmonds was a bad enough trio for opposing pitchers to deal with, but in midsummer in came the sweet power of Larry Walker from the Rockies to turn a powerful line up look impregnable. Once they'd disposed of the Dodgers 3-1 in their Division series, and the Astros had felled the Braves, who had done brilliantly just to win their division with a mediocre crop of talent (for the Braves, that is) 3-2. This series was not as close as it looked. In the decider, the Astros crushed the opposition 12-3. The Cards and Houston's finest did mighty, mighty battle for the right to compete in the World Series. It was a howitzer NLCS. The struggle went to seven games and produced a record LCS number of home runs, 24. Houston's mid-season acquisition, Carlos Beltran, stole the opera (Wagnerian) with white-hot form: 20 post-season runs scored, 8 post-season home runs (a joint record) and 47 post-season bases (also a tied record) told the story of a player still young (27, April 28) who was suddenly playing like a lost natural found. Yet he didn't make the World Series. Behind the great Roger Clemens, the Astros failed to hold this new Murderers Row, as many were now calling them, losing 2-5 in Busch Stadium. The key plays were two: firstly, a remarkable

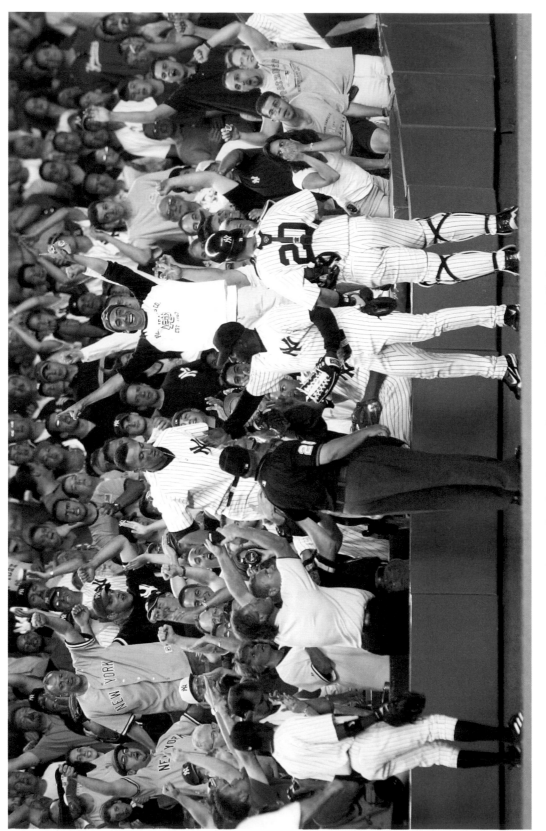

Derek Jeter. (b. 1974, Pequannock, New Jersey, New York Yankees)

If there is one player I would like to have beside me if I'm stuck in a nightmare playing a game of baseball to save me from the suffocating red-hot jaws of hell it is this bloke. Here he's returning to the playing field having jumped headlong over the wall to make a catch in a regular season game against the Boston Red Sox at Yankee Stadium, August 2004. He is on the way to the Hall of Fame with more justification than is enough for 4 players. His .292 2004 season will probably be forgotten, but it took true greatness, I think, to turn the disaster of his early season batting form into a 188 hit one. He also ended up batting in the 3rd highest number of runs in his 10-year career.

catch in the outfield by Jim Edmonds to hold back a Houston rally in the second, making the third out at 1-0 Astros with two on base. Catcher Brad Ausmus was the batter and a double and two runs were a certainty had Edmonds not made the diving grab.

Yankee Stadium – No general book on baseball can be complete without a shot of the place home fans just call "The Stadium." Here she in the first inning of Game 6 on October 19 against the Red Sox, Jon Lieber throwing a pitch in the first.

Secondly, a two-run homer from Scott Rolen off Clemens in the sixth to prise open a 2-2 game that threatened to become a cliffhanger. Remarkably the home team was victorious in each of the seven games. Would the Astros had won then if they'd had pennant winner advantage? Dunno. Having slugged their way to that 'ol National League mountain, the 2004 St Louis Cardinals looked across to the American League peak to see the survivor of the latest Sox-Yankees war of attrition.

The thing about the New York Yankees from the Boston point of view, is that when you face them to get to the big prize, you are not just taking on the 25-man roster and coaching staff of a ballclub: you are taking on the dead, dense weight of the absolutely impossible. You are trying to defeat a historical object the size of Alaska that contains the oppressive burden of 26 World Series wins for the Bombers and none for us. Consequently you are taking on a fight against an entire institution that forms one of probably the most successful sports club in the world. Men in pinstriped uniforms, talented enough to start with, seem to play with that gale of historical forces at their backs the whole time. Now they have an outstanding leader in Mr Torre, they win the American League East division as a matter of natural justice if not Mother Nature. The Yankees Win. They win because they win, because they win. For the Boston Red Sox they are insurmountable as well as unbeatable. Or to correct myself, they were after the Boston Red Sox made a light meal of the Anaheim Angels in the AL Division Series, winning all three games unanswered. To beat them you have to get a superhero to do something strange with the primal forces of the universe, to allow the team to tap into them.

If the Sox-Yankees 2003 ALCS clash in this seemingly ancient war had been tense and dramatic, the events of October 2004 completely re-wrote history. If you are coming this new to baseball, you have to buy the DVD to believe me. If you're writing a sports novel, you don't put the mighty Yankees 3-0 ahead and then decide that the underdogs are going to scale Everest breaking all-time records as they went, to actually win 4-3. Novels these days have to be believable. In real life, when a team has never, *never*, in baseball history, come back from 0-3 to win a post-season series, you let the Yankees win it and make the drama out of the Red Sox deciding on a mass self-poisoning or blowing up Yankee Stadium on the final out with 57 000 in the Bronx Zoo screaming their heads off. Yet this is what the 2004 Boston Red Sox did.

Said Tyler Kepner in the New York Times on October 17th, "If there are any believers left, the Yankees are stomping on their faith." They had just iced the Sox 17-8. He went on to say this in the next paragraph: "No team in baseball history has recovered from a 3-0 deficit to win a post-season series and the Red Sox seem ill-equipped to try."

17-8. The manner of the third victory seemed to be more than one more post-season game chalked off in the history of America's pastime. It was a pronouncement. You Will Never Beat The Yankees.

Carlos Beltran – (b. 24 April 1977, Manati, Puerto Rico, Kansas City Royals, Houston Astros)
Beltran makes the traditional hi-5 of this Astro team after yet another 2004 post-season home run. This one came in the bottom of the ninth of Game 3 of the NLCS against the Cardinals in Minute Maid Park, Houston on October 16. His season was heading for Nowheresville, somewhere east of Mediocre, until he was traded in the All-Star break from Kansas City to Houston, and ended with the richest franchises in the majors hot on his trail.

Meanwhile, clubhouse mover and shaker Kevin Millar was saying this to his adversaries to a vast spread of microphones hemming him in: "Don't let us win one game, that's all I'm saying," In truth, he and his team were staring down the barrel of a gun that could wipe out Illinois. Kepner finished his article thus:

"The faithful need a miracle, which is never a Red Sox specialty. The devoted must believe in the unseen."

The thing is, Kevin Millar knew what he was talking about, and unlike the rest of us, thank God, he is not a fan. To him, Derek Jeter is only flesh and blood. It's as well he doesn't know the truth. Millar knew his team of Idiots, as they were calling themselves, disarmingly. Down the stretch they had won a hell of a lot of games, more than the Bombers.

Scott Rolen - (b. 1975, Evansville, Indiana, Philadelphia Phillies, St Louis Cardinals)
If the St Louis Cardinals had won the World Series, this would have been the cover of this book. A great shot, I think, of Rolen saluting the crowd after his 2-run homer off Clemens in the bottom of the 6th in Game 7. Despite an abysmal World Series, he hit .300 in the regular season for the first time (.314) and had best seasons for home runs (34), RBIs (124) and strikeouts (92). He is also a superlative Gold Glove winning Third Baseman.

After three games they'd screwed up, blown it, let everybody down, choked, you name it. But he knew that they could play the game, and crucially, above everything, *everything* else, he seemed to truly believe that in the most grim of clutch situations, they could hold their nerve. If you didn't know what was about to happen you'd say, "what an idiot."

Oh, how they were tested. Game 4, late over here, very late, I quit and went to bed after Jeter hit a three run triple to put the Yanks 4-2 ahead in the sixth. I "watched" the game on Gameday (see end of book if you haven't a clue what I'm saying) but couldn't face the outs leaking away. This, surely, was the end. So long to the Series for another five years or however long it took for the organisation to rebuild a roster that had a bunch of coming up free agents. Nomar gone, Manny would leave, so would Pedro, Lowe definitely (no loss) and maybe Jason Varitek, the team's heart and soul. The sheer weight of 86 years without a World Series flag to fly over Fenway was said to have done in Garciappara; for the rest, there had to be an easier way to earn a fat living. 0-3 down, 2-4 down. Francona, Sox manager, later paid huge tribute to Dave Roberts, the lead-off guy being kept out of the line-up by Johnny Damon, who came in to pinch run for Millar, who here in the ninth inning represented the tieing run at first base. Roberts stole second then came home with practically Olympic speed on a Bill Mueller single up the middle to make it 4-4, Fenway Park going crazy. But the story gets more bizarre. The Sox won, 6-4, on a 2-run Ortiz home run in the bottom of the 12th inning straight out of the book of Drama-Baseball Impossible . But wind back a bit. When Mueller ripped that single, it was off the great Rivera and one of his 93 mph trademark cutters. Thus ended the longest game in Championship Series history. An epic game, an epic performance by Boston, against the odds, holding on, holding on, holding on, after being out-hit and out-pitched in the first three games.

But after a night of practically unbearable drama, it was only 1-3. The next night, a Monday, saw a desperately tight game just go right into the ridiculous and beyond. Again the Red Sox had to come from behind, and levelled once more through Roberts pinch running and speeding home to make it 4-4 in the eighth following an Ortiz solo home run. This time the game went over the abyss into five extra innings. In the 14th, to end the longest game in post-season history, at 6 hours 49 minutes, David Ortiz, at 1.25 am, managed a mis-timed muscled single for the second walk off win in two nights. This stuff was beyond drama into something new and unheard of. Nerve endings had all but been shredded in extra innings the previous night. By the fifth extra inning of a second night, everyone played or watched, almost numb, the players producing what they had on a wing and a prayer, or from memory; "on fumes" as Francona put it.

But although one can say that Boston's starting and relief pitching had somehow held it together, by luck or brilliance, where were the New York Yankee hitters when they were needed just to finish off a bleeding opponent? With players weak with adrenalin surges, it took mental strength and perhaps something as simple and as complex as team spirit, for Boston to win these two games. The famed "We Are The Yankees" intangible somewhere along the line packed up and went home. Their relievers were brilliant too, one should say that, or, maybe the occasion got to Boston bats almost as badly as it undid that awesome collection of sluggers in pinstripes who had got their pitchers out of the mire with clutch hits all season long.

At 2-3, the psychology of this now monstrous series had completely, and as it turned out, irrevocably switched. The Red Sox could go to Yankee Stadium and play with more freedom that the home team. The team had collectively peered over the edge into oblivion, into nothingness; what now did they have to lose? In a sense they had already lost, or at least been given up for dead, which almost amounted to the same. It must have been incredible to be a player on that team after the two comeback games. To have produced not just winning ball but ultimate survivor ball, against the biggest team in baseball, in the thin air of extra innings, must have given those men a surging inner strength few sportsmen can ever have felt. Me, the distant fan, went nowhere near the game and thank God for that. I've watched Dave Waller score an 87th minute goal at 0-0 in a must-win game to stave off relegation for Chesterfield and the same team lose at Wembley in a play-off final against Cambridge United and lose; just the thought of being in anyway involved in following six hours of shit or bust baseball makes me physically ill. I woke up the next day, went through the normal morning rituals and just saw Boston 5 New York Yankees 4. That was excitement enough.

They inevitably drew level on the Tuesday, and new stars were appearing. Mark Bellhorn, a strikeout and walk King but nothing else throughout the regular season, bashed the Sox ahead with a three-run homer in the 6th. That old hero, Schilling was piling another layer of myth onto the saga by pitching thanks only to untried patch-up surgery. He'd lost his team Game 2 through the pain in his right ankle, but with a dislocated tendon sutured in place, but with the wound coming apart on the mound, he stayed strong and pitched a beaut to stave off the Big Yankee Bat in Game 6. He went seven innings and handed on a 4-1 lead to the bullpen. This was stuff sheer Greek legend. The warrior in pain. Well it actually was like that. I'm sure I'd have wussed out after G2 if it'd been me: there's always next year after all. But then that sort of attitude would have kept me far from the majors even if I'd had Schilling's prodigious talent. Fact is, anyway, he was a model of sporting desire and determination gone to the nuthouse. If anyone deserved a Cy Young award for all this – he was to do it once again in Game 2 of the World Series - it was this man, only baseball culture says the award can only be merited by regular season play only, so there. Pity.

Curt Schilling throws the two-and-two pitch to Marlon Anderson with two out in the third, Game 2 of the World Series at Fenway Park, Boston 2-0 ahead. October 24th 2004.

Curtis Montague Schilling (b. 1966, Anchorage, Alaska; Philadelphia Phillies, Arizona Diamondbacks, Boston Red Sox). Here is the face of the guy with more guts than an abbatoir working at full capacity, celebrating the end of his second victorious World Series with milling press types or Red Sox back room staff. There's no sign of pain from that dislocated ankle tendon now it's all been done. The injury may have cost the Red Sox Game 1 of the ALCS, but his outstanding, utter determination to return compete and win, was a core reason for this improbable team victory. In short: no Schilling? no Rings.

There are more men to mention yet. Keith Foulke, for example, Boston's closer, throwing a tired arm to stop runs and close out games, another one blazing and a-burning with a desire that produces winners. But there are questions coming from this too: what causes men to go through pain barriers, to produce their best form, when it really and truly matters, when there is no tomorrow if you don't do it almost perfectly *now*? Is it team spirit molecules that bounce from player to player all day and night rubbing off over and over and over again? Is it individual inner strength? What is it? (Don't know).

After six games, the New York Yankees were beaten. All the keepers at the Bronx Zoo must have realised that. The "Not In My House" banner I saw on the TV looked pathetically hopeful rather than the show of brute strength it was supposed to project. On this night Johnny Damon, a dead-loss throughout the post-season thus far came out and hit not one but two homers in Game 7, one a grand slam that put his team up 6-0 in the second. Starter Kevin Brown had already departed and Vasquez on his way out. Earlier in 2004 Brown was still a great pitcher; now he'd been emphatically broken on the Red Sox wheel.

That suspect pitching problem that seemed to have been gaffer-taped over at 3-0 at Fenway had suddenly unravelled under the white bright play-off glare. The Boston hitters were feasting on the carcass now and if you didn't want the losers since 1918 to win, it was embarrassing. Before the Yankees could come out and pressurize the aggressive, now relentless Red Sox, Damon announced himself, rose to the occasion, produced the goods – use whatever expression you like. Bellhorn again hit a homer, later on, when the game was already beyond the Yankees, at 1-8 in the fourth. This wasn't drama like his shot off Pesky's Pole, it was just a laughing insurance run. Ortiz had hit a solo shot in the 4th but things were so good for the Red Sox, so bad for the Yankees, that it wasn't even news. The astonishing thing here is that from being effectively beaten, in three nights this team had smashed their tormentors to pieces. The reversal was so complete that Game 7 was almost anti-climactic.

That morning it had "forgone conclusion" written all over it. I emailed my Boston man, Alexander: "You know the Sox are going to win tonight, don't you." He knew. Ten minutes or something shy of 5am British time the phone woke me. "Ring me if we win," I'd told him an hour before I went to bed. No repeat of 2003, thank you. I was tossing and turning before the contraption blurbed into life beside me. I was half awake, thinking, 'the phone hasn't rung, we've lost.' Not really conscious, I could feel the hollowness beginning to expand like a slow-motion air bag. I must have drifted away again before an awful synthetic bleeping began cracking off to my left. I picked up: "We did it. 10-3," said a lively, smug but relieved voice 3,200 miles away (how did I work out his tone? I thought about it later). This was no time to sleep, not with a video having taped every minute of it from the Baseball On 5 show. I pulled on dirty clothes and went down to the set to see all kinds of Red Sox making merry in The Stadium, tramping the dirt down. Champions. Epstein, interviewed in the immediate aftermath in the locker room, said, "Now we want to win this thing."

Game 4. Boston Red Sox 3 St Louis Cardinals 0

There are times in sport where a team develops beyond the expectations of everyone, comes together as a unit and triumphs spectacularly, gloriously. The Arizona Diamondbacks, the Anaheim Angels and the Florida Marlins all did it, and in consecutive years. Now it was Boston's turn in the beautiful light. Of course, it is nobody's "turn." There never was a Curse, though Grady Little's bizarre faith in Pedro Martinez against all baseball percentages may suggest otherwise. But remember here: to Grady, he was doing what he thought was logical. Players have to make victory happen. The luck involved occurs in the right players making a team chemistry that perhaps not even a genius of a General Manager can ever see. Luck occurs in events unexpected, like Dr Morgan fixing up Curt Schilling's ankle after practising a hitherto untried procedure on a corpse. Was it also lucky that the Yankees failed so dramatically in all those extra innings in Boston, the place where to all intents and purposes the series was lost and won? Maybe, but probably not. Shit happens. Sometimes good shit happens. It happened to Boston in 2004. Were they lucky they played the Yankees in the ALCS? Had they played the Twins, would they have been strong enough for the New Murderers?

What we can say is that the whole team had been well tested by the time they took on the great St Louis Cardinals in their first World Series since 1986. They weren't so much battle hardened as ruggedly bullet proof. The Cards had come through a tense and tough seven- game series but Houston are not, or were not, even with Biggio, Beltran, Bagwell, Berkman and Clemens, the New York Yankees. The Pinstripes were at one time were 6-1 in games in this here post-season. If the pundits expected the Cardinals to win the Series, and many did, they didn't understand team sport very well. In the space between the CS's and Game 1, it is not the time to look at the relative talents of the two line ups, at regular season stats. What they failed to understand is that the Red Sox hadn't won through to the World Series, they had swallowed a gigantic monster. It turned out that the Redbirds were a bunch of poisonous spiders: dangerous and possibly fatal if you don't know what you're doing, but no behemoth with the huge, slavering jaws of six mouths. The collective determination of the Boston Idiots was like a protective force-field around them and more. Additionally, it produced crucial work at do or die moments. The G4 Damon homer is a case in point, as was the G3's Ramirez blast, as was Mark Bellhorn's 2-run shot at 9-9 in G1. The thing about baseball though is that there is always another way of reading things: these guys could arguably do these deeds because the St Louis pitching wasn't good enough and because their best starter Chris Carpenter was missing injured. Conversely, these pitchers had been good enough to deal with the Astros's stellar offense. Just. There is always another way of looking at things.

The Red Sox even made four fielding errors in Game 1 and managed to come through in a scrappy game, 11-9. Was that luck? In reviewing the last two series, perhaps in every baseball triumph, they could point to individuals producing in the moment: Ramirez had hit no home runs in the New York series though his average was more than .320, but he came through in Game 1 quickly and dumped a Williams pitch over the Green Monster. He did it early on in G3 too over in Busch, to announce to the Cardinals and the watching baseball fraternity that he didn't give a shit that St Louis hadn't lost a post-season game in 2004 at home. That must do something to and for the team. Character, we talk about character, but "character" has to come from people actually doing something. In 2004, Boston had the doers. We might talk right here about another of these, Tim Wakefield. He pitched his knuckleball indifferently in his Game 2 start against the Cards, but when the walls were being blown out of the house in the third game against the Yankees he volunteered to get beat up out of the bullpen to save everyone else's arm for the fourth game. If he'd been as selfish as modern sportsmen are supposed to be, game four would have been Goodnight Kansas. Better, in the game of fourteen innings, it was Wakefield who pitched three innings of shutout ball, shutout *knuckleball* mark you, in extras. Did it take character or did it add character to his team mates who watched him carve out defiant victory from a fingertip hold on the alpine precipice? Both. There were many World Series winning moments, where different players displayed exceptional skills (I was going to say 'at key times' but the wonderful thing about baseball is that every at bat is a key time) before, as well as during it. Wakefield's sacrifice meant his giving up his allotted start the following night. This brought in Derek Lowe from the cold, the pitcher who had been dropped from the play off rotation. Lowe was so good in G4 he pitched again three nights later and was superb. He turned in a great performance in Game 4 in Busch. The result of Wakefield's actions revived Lowe's career. Lucky Boston, or was Lowe inspired? We come back to questions of team spirit and character, which we should now turn into answers.

And so to Manny. David Lengel was perfect in 2003 when he said, "Manny doesn't care about nothin'! Manny is Manny" Manny Ramirez, one part clown, the rest of him genius, is acutally a very serious player indeed, won the MVP for his consistent hitting, just one of the components that helped to push over the Cardinals. This Series was decided by

Johnny Damon (b. 1973, Fort Riley, Kansas; Kansas City Royals, Oakland Athletics, Boston Red Sox) The Boston Red Sox
lead off man and huge crowd favourite. After his best regular season, hitting .304 and with great on base percentage, his
post-season was poor until Game 7 against the Yankees. Here he's just struck his second home run of the game, a grand slam,
to put the Sox 6-0 ahead in the fourth inning. The Bombers never recovered from this. His swing is, to me, incredible; not a full
swing, but a flip, which thanks to strong wrists and profoundly good timing, has here propelled the ball into the upper deck
in right field. He was to go on to open the last game of the World Series with a lead off home run to signal the
beginning of the end for the huge St Louis Cardinals challenge of 2004.

these kind of signals of strength, of resolution and defiance just as the last two games in New York had been. Crucially,
crucially, Francona's pitchers got stronger and stronger with each game. If you look at the stats for their starting pitchers
on the MLB website for the Series, you'll see a vertical line of 0.00's in the ERA column for three of them: Schilling,
Martinez and Lowe. They went 21 innings and gave up not a single run. The Cardinal pitchers looked tired or couldn't
hack the pressure. Lowe was a post-season revelation. He pitched great ball not once but twice in the series against the
Yankees over 13 innings and again, in Game 4, the last game of baseball in the 2004 season, he went seven again and was
too good for a bunch of hitters who by now were low in confidence, self-esteem and it seemed, energy.

I don't know enough about Terry Francona to know how good he was, so I'd better say little. Obviously, most of what
a skipper does, you don't see. He put Roberts in at perfect times, so we'll give him that. He let Wakefield in to relieve and
he brought Lowe back, so he has much going for him there too. What he was doing giving Pedro the ball in G7 in Yankee
Stadium though is anyone's guess. But he stuck by Bellhorn when everyone said 'bench him' so he earns big points there,

Derek Lowe (b. 1973, Dearborn, Michigan; Seattle Mariners, Boston Red Sox). Happy is the sportsman who comes back from the dead to prove his greatness. An over-compliment? There is an uncomfortable disjunction in baseball between standard player performance measurement: regular season only and don't argue! And the fact that it takes a great player to play superbly when the chips are really on the table in the post-season. Lowe pitched three great games against the Yankees and the Cards in shit-or-bust situations. Who in 20 years will remember outside of Boston? ('04 PS Record: 3-0, Pitched 19.33 innings, for 11 hits and 4 ER)

I guess. But you have to be much closer to the Boston players than me to be able to assess just how much credit he should take for his players taking out all the ghosts, ghouls and nasties that have lurked around Fenway Park since whenever people started to talk about 1918 out of all the closets and made them all disappear.

In the last analysis, one can't help feeling very strongly that the Serious wasn't even close because the New York Yankees had sharpened the Red Sox mentally beyond anything normally experienced by sports teams. They also had this abnormal disregard for every independent observer's expectation of how they should view their situation. A World Series is supposed to exert an almost intolerable pressure on a player individually and collectively. Incapacitating tension is thought to be the norm, a horribly difficult enemy to subdue. The 2004 Red Sox made these notions look like very tired nostrums. Manny's ribbing of Pedro Martinez, hitter, as he came back to towards the dugout having just struck out hopelessly sticks in the memory. Indelibly imprinted there is a TV shot of Manny (again) and Kevin Millar going through an elaborate hand slapping routing in the dugout before G7 in Yankee Stadium. I saw it and I assumed it was videotape being replayed from an earlier hour or after the previous night's victory. I was completely wrong-footed. It was live, five minutes before first pitch. This made no sense in terms of sports science, which is supposed to be the God to worship these days. Just relax, be yourself and go out and do it. This wasn't the BoSox; these guys weren't idiots either. These were simply The Incredibles. They should consider renaming the whole ballclub in their honour. How they worked out that they could be this way is a guess I for one am not capable of making.

The 2004 Boston Red Sox took on the favourites and ruined them. It may have been boring for the neutral, but for the aficionado it had to be fascinating to see this unfold. The supposed Curse of the Bambino, in truth the long, woeful inadequacy of the Red Sox organisation, had dragged on and on like a tedious opera. It was time to lay it all aside, to bury it in some landfill of history. Pundits said, 'what are the fans going to do without all that misery? They won't know what to do, they'll be, erm, miserable.' I doubt it. I'm no *true* Red Sox fan: too new and too foreign. But in my long experience of sporting tribalism, I can't believe that the relief of it won't feel sensationally good. There is nothing in sport, in life perhaps, like winning. And I think Red Sox Nation will love, will glory in their team being World Champions. That failure of the years was something I could feel, just reading the hacks that camp follow it all, the rotten weariness of all those barren years. They wanted the monkey off their backs like cancer sufferers want to undo the facts of their personal pathology. I think, 2004 will go down as the year the Nation could feel truly free for the first time.

"It is done. In my lifetime."

Josh Alexander, October 27 2004

Stats Selection

Game Scores

Game 1 At Fenway Park:	St Louis Cardinals 9 Boston Red Sox 11
Game 2 At Fenway Park:	St Louis Cardinals 2 Boston Red Sox 4
Game 3 At Busch Stadium:	Boston Red Sox 4 St Louis Cardinals 1
Game 4 At Busch Stadium:	Boston Red Sox 3 St Louis Cardinals 0

World Series

St Louis Cardinals Hitting

"Murderers Row"	Hit Ratio	%	HR	RBI
Jim Edmonds	1/15	.067	0	0
Scott Rolen	0/15	.000	0	0
Albert Pujols	5/15	.333	0	0
Larry Walker	5/14	.357	2	3

Championship Series

St Louis Cardinals Hitting

"Murderers Row"	Hit Ratio	%	HR	RBI
Jim Edmonds	7/24	.292	2	7
Scott Rolen	9/29	.310	3	6
Albert Pujols	14/28	.500	4	9
Larry Walker	7/29	.241	2	5

World Series

Boston Red Sox Hitting

"The Idiots" Offense	Hit Ratio	%	HR	RBI	BB
Jonny Damon	6/21	.286	1	2	0
David Ortiz	4/13	.308	1	4	4
Manny Ramirez	7/17	.412	1	4	3
Mark Belhorn	3/10	.300	1	4	5
Jason Varitek	2/13	.154	0	2	1
Kevin Millar	1/8	.125	0	0	2
Bill Mueller	6/14	.429	0	2	4
Trot Nixon	5/14	.357	0	3	1

Championship Series

Boston Red Sox Hitting

"The Idiots" Offense	Hit Ratio	%	HR	RBI	BB
Jonny Damon	6/35	.171	2	7	2
David Ortiz	12/31	.387	3	11	4
Manny Ramirez	9/30	.300	0	0	5
Mark Belhorn	5/26	.192	2	4	5
Jason Varitek	9/28	.321	2	7	2
Kevin Millar	6/24	.250	0	2	5
Bill Mueller	8/30	.267	0	1	2
Trot Nixon	6/29	.207	1	3	0

Addendum

Carlos Beltran – ALDS Hitting Stats

Player	Hit Ratio	%	HR	RBI	TB	BB
Carlos Beltran	10/22	.455	4	9	24	1

Carlos Beltran – ALCS Hitting Stats

Player	Hit Ratio	%	HR	RBI	TB	BB
Carlos Beltran	10/24	.417	4	5	23	8

2004: Also The Year of Suzuki San

By Josh Alexander

SEATTLE | Friday, October 1, 2004

Entering another team's baseball park for the first time is always a grand affair for me – an unveiling of another house of baseball, a chance to watch a game without being invested in its outcome, and to just soak up the unique history of ups and downs that surrounds each Park – it's an experience that always varies by geography and circumstance. As a Boston Red Sox fan, I'm used to the grit and grime of history in Fenway Park and the sometimes pitched battles of rivalries that make up the AL East. But, then again, Fenway Park is somewhat unique.

As fate would have it, I found myself in Seattle on a weekend business trip, with the last-place Mariners in town playing the Texas Rangers in a game that should have been a coda on the season for both teams. Both the Mariners and the Rangers had already been eliminated from the playoffs - the Mariners were 22 games out of the AL West – and this was their last series of the regular season. But I felt lucky to have a ticket in my hand as I walked through the wide boulevards along Puget Sound to Safeco Field on a beautiful warm autumn Friday evening. Seattle is a jewel of a city, quite accessible by foot, with a coffee barista on every corner, wi-fi access for every laptop, a chicken in every pot. Thoroughly Western and metropolitan, it enjoys the good fortune of sitting on some excellent real estate on the edge of the Pacific Rim, and serves as a gateway for the tourist and fishing industries of Canada and Alaska. On that sun-drenched evening, it felt great to be in Seattle, and even greater to be holding a ticket to Safeco Field.

As I strolled along and got closer to the Park, it was obvious from the industry of scalpers and parking attendants that rimmed the outer reaches of Safeco's gravitational pull that much of the rest of Seattle was desperate for a ticket. Tickets were flying, people were biting, serious money was changing hands – it was clearly an event.

The idea of even trying to see the Mariners in Seattle had first entered my mind earlier in the week. Though I was watching the Boston Red Sox and NY Yankees Division standings and the AL wild card race with the typical obsession that takes over in September, the Mariners were at the bottom of the AL West, and of no concern to any Red Sox fan. But on Monday, I noticed in the morning paper that the Mariners' Ichiro Suzuki, a free agent from the Japanese League who signed with the Mariners in 2000, was closing in on George Sisler's 84-year-old record of 257 hits in a season. This wasn't an entire surprise. Ichiro – as he's known to wider baseball world, having been elevated to single-name status after just four seasons in the Majors – had over 200 hits in each of his first three seasons with the Mariners, a feat last accomplished by Johnny Pesky in the 1940s, who was never elevated to single-name status, although he does have the Fenway Park right field foul pole, Pesky Pole, as his legacy.

It was an amazing story: A diminutive 5'9" right fielder in his fourth year of the Majors, and a great example of a latter-day Major League Specialist. Ichiro hits singles, and then he tries to steal bases. He doesn't have much power, or at least he chooses not to use it. In 2003, he had 212 hits, and 161 of them were singles. His talent and consistency rely on crisply hitting sharp zingers past the infielders, and then to steal bases. That's what he does.

On Tuesday, Ichiro got 2 hits against the Oakland As, and stood at 254. I called a friend in Seattle Tuesday night, told him my flight was arriving Friday at noon and basically begged him to somehow snare me a ticket for Friday night's game. He's a reliable friend, and my ticket was waiting at my hotel where I arrived. As he told me later, "it's a good thing you called Tuesday night, because tickets were scarce on Wednesday, and impossible to find on Thursday. And by the way, you owe me $20."

Meanwhile, Ichiro clicked off hit 255 on Wednesday and 256 on Thursday. The stars were aligning, and George Sisler was looking down at his durable 84-year record as it was about to become an asterisk in Major League history. Friday night's game was Ichiro's first chance to tie or beat Sisler's single season hit record, and everyone in Seattle knew it. Despite their abysmal season and the meaningless outcome of the game, this game with the Texas Rangers was going to be one for the record books. Maybe. Probably, given that Ichiro gets a hit almost every game.

I wore my Red Sox jersey, something I always proudly do when I travel to other cities and get a chance to go to a game – the Red Sox Nation Diaspora takes quite seriously what it sees as its mission to demonstrate that Red Sox fans can appear anywhere, anytime – and slipped into the park about 20 minutes before game time. Safeco was filling to its 45,000-seat capacity. At first, I was a little lost as I tried to line up my seat coordinates printed on my ticket with the array of overhead signs to point me in the right direction. Finally, I found an attendant, an older guy, and I said, "look, I'm from

Ichiro Suzuki – (b. 22 October 1973, Kasugai, Japan, Seattle Mariners)
Ichiro batting champion of the National League with .372 and was second in Bill James list for Runs Creators for 2004. Here he
makes the record hit overtaking the Sisler record. He was Rookie of the Year in his first year after leaving Japan in 2001.
He made 242 hits that year, so we should have seen last season coming. His career average in MLB in his four seasons is .339.
He has made 200 hits each year.

Boston, and Fenway is a lot smaller than Safeco. How do I get to Section 315?" He chuckled, and pointed me down the gently curving corridor to the right. "Down deep in right field, in the upper section," he said.

Off I went, found the entrance to my section, and then emerged – as you always do, no matter what stadium – into the light, the 45,000 capacity crowd packing into their seats with armloads of food and beer, and most of all, the brilliant green carpet laid out before me. This was not anything remotely like Fenway Park, which stands low over the Fens in Back Bay like a leviathan iron crustacean studded with all manner of added-on seating rimmed along the top of the walls to wring the last dollar out of the place, a hulking piece of 19th century history with its cavernous facilities, obstructed views, and childlike seats. Safeco Park is a beautiful, expansive and sloping stadium, with a retractable roof, and wide seats designed to accommodate the generous suburban backsides that would pay to sit in them and have a wonderful afternoon. It was all breathtaking, except I found myself suddenly 500 feet up from the playing field, a feeling that I'm not used to, or frankly fond of. You could stack 4 or 5 Fenway Parks, one on top of the other, and you might not reach the scale of Safeco Field. I was feeling a touch of vertigo, looking down across all that distance.

As I made my way up from there (yes, up! It began to dawn on me why my ticket cost only $20), I began to get a smattering of encouragement for my Red Sox Jersey from the crowd. "Go Sox!!" "We hate the Yankees, too!!" "Reverse the Curse!" This too was different. At Fenway, fans sporting other teams' shirts are often treated with outright derision and hostility (I'm thinking Yankees here) or at best a quiet dismissive sniff. Where were the cheap seats fans I have learned to grow fond of at Fenway, the bleacher creatures, who might erupt in a fight in front of you, or perhaps throw watered down beers at each other behind you? There was none of that at Safeco. The crowd was friendly and pleasant enough, and it had a family-oriented, carnival-like quality about it – it was collegiate, it was polite, it was comfortable and civil. After all, no one there really cared about the outcome of the game, which was beside the point. So the legions of rabid fans, hungry for a win at any cost, were not part of the atmosphere. To add to the festivities, sharing the bill with Ichiro and George Sisler's 84-year old record, was Edgar Martinez, the career Mariner DH and a Seattle institution since 1982, who was retiring at the end of the season. It was a game, but it was a giant party, too.

As I settled into my seat, it was suddenly game time. In the bottom of the first inning, Ichiro, top of the order, immediately went to work, with tens of thousands of digital cameras flashing all at once trying to capture history for their owners, and the crowd chanting "EE-CHEE-ROW! EE-CHEE-ROW!!" Just four pitches into his first at bat he tied Sisler's record, smacking a looping chopper over third baseman Hank Blalock's outstretched glove. Then, a half hour later, Ichiro came to bat again in the third inning (and all of Safeco once again began popping with flashbulbs), and hit a stinging grounder by second base, past the Rangers shortstop Michael Young, where it dribbled into center field for the record-breaker. Ichiro scampered to first. It was, in a couple of heartbeats, finished.

It was lacking in the high athleticism of, say, a Hank Aaron hitting his record-breaking home run over the left field wall at Braves Stadium, or a Barry Bonds lifting another long arcing HR over the high walls of SBC Park and into the water outside, where kayakers lay in wait like alligators to grab the next valuable ball that hopefully plops down beside them. It was just a sharp single and about 3 seconds while Ichiro ran quickly to first base. It happens all the time; this one just happened to matter more.

The historical baseball was taken out of play – no doubt to be exhibited under glass somewhere, someday – fireworks above the left-field bleachers exploded in fanfare, and Ichiro was congratulated by his teammates, who swarmed onto the field. Then he stopped and turned sharply with an almost military precision to the crowd by the first base line, and bowed deeply, slowly and reverentially to a gathering of George Sisler's relatives who were placed right in front of the bag so as to witness the passing of what had been a remarkably durable record of achievement. After the Sisler family came out on to the field, officials and executives suddenly appeared. A presentation was made. Achievement on a decades-old scale was recognized with pomp and short speeches, and then they folded up tent and it was all over. The smoke from the fireworks hung over the Park.

And then, of course, the game went on. A new record set, it was time to get on with it and play some more baseball. Ichiro got his next hit, extending the record again, to 259 (he finally achieved his new watermark of 262 hits two nights later on the last game of the year), and the Mariners won, 8-3, but the record had been broken, the score was largely immaterial, and the Safeco crowd partied on until the last out. Ichiro was the story of the evening, and quite literally one for the books.

BARRY BONDS

"He's not going to hit 70 homers but he thinks he can. That's frightening."

Shawn Dunston, 2000

The word on Barry Bonds that came through to us in Britain before the first week of December 2004 was that this player was probably one of the three or four best batters of all time. In a sport where play is measured microscopically by the Court of Baseball History, that is one heavyweight piece of reckoning. His 2004 season was yet another spectacular one to toss on a steadily mounting pile. He broke the Walks In A Season record because no one would pitch to him. Why? Because if you didn't pitch brilliantly to him, he was liable to put the game beyond you right there and then. In only 373 at bats he had 137 hits, 21 doubles and 45 home runs. His slugging percentage was a towering .812. Put simply, teams refused to pitch to this guy because he was so good it was almost like throwing a baseball at a God.

There have been players like him before. Ty Cobb, Ted Williams and of course, Babe Ruth come most obviously to mind. For long periods, otherwise great pitchers were pretty dismal about their chances when hurling the ball in Joe DiMaggio's direction. And here was Bonds, just about ready to join this elite group of the elite. He began in April on 658 homers, two behind his Godfather Willie Mays, and quickly reached 660 in his home park. Before the whiff of firework sulphur had left the air, he'd advanced to 661 and run on to make the season become a procession of walks and demonstrations of the man's magnificent eye, great judgement and brutal power. The 700-barrier came right up close in September, was breached and, by the conclusion of his nineteenth campaign in the majors, had begun already to recede. Barry Bonds' home run total stood at seven-hundred and three, eleven behind Ruth and fifty-two behind Hank Aaron's gigantic all-time record of 755.

Batting Average last 3 years:	.357	
Batting Average last 5 years:	.341	
Batting Average last 10 years:	.316	
Home Run Average last 6 years per at bat:	2004: 8.29	2001: 6.52
	2003: 8.67	2000: 9.79
	2002: 8.76	1999: 10.44
Home Runs 1986-1990	117	
Home Runs 1991-1995	175	
Home Runs 1996-2000	202	
Home Runs 2001-2004	209	

For the UK fan, starved of the constant daily drone of baseball news minutae through the corporate news prism, Bonds appeared clearly to be the number one superstar of the game. But there seemed to be a lack of appropriate awe and scale in the coverage, given the importance of baseball in the United States and the enormity of the numbers. This deficiency is explicable in one word: steroids. Through to the end of the 2004 season, only one player had been out-ed as a user/abuser of performance enhancing substances – steroids – and he, Ken Caminiti, was seemingly only raised into public sight by dying. He was 43. Tony Gwynn, one of the great late-20th century hitters and a team mate of Caminiti's, wrote after his death in May that he thought around 20% of the game's players were – are – users of steroids to bulk up muscle and improve stamina. "Although I still love the guy," he said, "knowing that he took steroids taints what he accomplished as well as baseball's integrity." For many observers, Barry Bonds' improvement with age (see table) – at 40 years of age he is supposed to have gone into decline several years ago – defied belief. He was either arguably the most remarkable man ever to have wielded a stick, or a cheat. His magnificently honed physique explained a power that made baseball lovers of the home run drool, but the nagging question for the dubious observer was that of whether this was an ill-gotten gain. And if certain substances out there could improve a player's stamina through the long and gruelling sixth month, six days a week season, might Bonds be defying the inevitable limitations age must impose upon even a world class athlete by imbibing?

On December 3rd 2004, a leaked report from a Grand Jury investigation into the Bay area company BALCO back in the previous January, hit the news. It emerged that Barry had admitted taking substances administered by his trainer Greg Anderson, a guy who worked for BALCO: a liquid ("the clear"), a salve ("the cream") and some tablets ("red beans"). He claimed he had no idea that the substances he'd taken to help his arthritic knees and his general conditioning were illegal; in short, were steroids (the word, you'll notice, has the same sort of power in sport as the word "cancer" has in everyday life). Ignorance was and remains his defence. Very quickly however, the press began sending out their own verdict. Post columnist Michael Wilbon, like Bonds an Afro-American, commented, "It looks like they've used up their benefit of the doubt, if they ever had any," speaking of BB and Jason Giambi, the New York Yankees slugger, who had in fact come

Barry Lamar Bonds – (b. 24 July 1964, Riverside, California, Pittsburgh Pirates, San Francisco Giants).
A rare shot of Barry smiling and a rare shot of Barry striking out. In 2004 despite ending the season with a record tally of walks, 232, he made 135 hits, batted in 101runs, hit 27 doubles and 45 home runs from only 373 at bats. His 41 strikeouts was the lowest total of his career. He batted .362, second in the Major Leagues only to Ichiro. I don't think we'll be seeing him smile much in 2005.

Bonds Records
Most Intentional Walks in one season - 120 (2004)
Most Intentional Walks in a career – 604
Most Walks in a Career: 2302
Most Times Winner of a league MVP: 7 (1990, 1992, 1993, 2001-2004)
Most Times Winner of a league MVP in consecutive years: 4 (previous record, 2)

clean about his steroid use when facing the same Grand Jury probe. Giambi's career and reputation was immediately in tatters, but Bonds' response was predictably stout. But if the esteemed Washington Post of December 4 was anything to go by, he'd already lost his credibility as a champion. Columnist Thomas Boswell laid into it with a large mallet: "Bonds' reputation has lived by his statistics. Now let it die by them. Forever."

To the end of 2004, the steroids issue began to unravel at speed. Giambi's club were desperately looking for ways to dump his $120 million contract. Deep suspicions now clouded the great home run race of 1998 when Sammy Sosa and Mark McGwire jumped all over the Maris '61 home run record, the latter ending with 70, the former with 66. Sosa had a mediocre '04: 34 homers, his lowest for ten years and a batting average of .253, a drop of 26 points on his '03. This cemented a decline in his reliability as a hitter which began in 2001. Pertinently, his impressively muscular build has fallen away during the season (Giambi's was described as having 'shrivelled up like a prune' since the off-season of 2003-4), causing some to wonder whether Sammy had ceased abusing his body, perhaps knowing that investigations into substance abuse were in the wind (it could of course be the case that he was unwell or had just ceased to be interested in going to the gym).

The players' one union, the Players Association and Commissioner Selig were now put under great pressure to respond. Supremo Selig faced loud criticism in terms of baseball's chronic failure to address a problem that his office had seemed prepared to turn a blind eye to for far too long. Drug testing had increased in frequency in 2004 and had revealed abuse, but no players were named nor, obviously, suspended or fined. Selig ended the calendar year promising to get tough. The PA, however, was standing rock solid behind a wilfully stubborn refusal to accept responsibility for what was now clearly a deadly serious problem rather than a rumour of one. They seemed chronically and curiously blind to the consequences of steroid abuse not being brought to a complete and immediate halt. The general and binding agreement they'd thrashed out with MLB and the owners was due to run out in 2006 - it included drug testing - and they were not going to budge from it. Nor were they doing anything but supporting Giambi completely as his people fought to stop the Yankees dumping every outstanding penny on his bloated contract. Their stance was deemed ugly and crass by just about everybody.

The year 2005 is going to be a hugely significant for the sport, to understate the case almost irresponsibly. To what extent are fans going to come out and see pumped up steroid users launching home runs? Perhaps even more worrying is the issue of baseball statistics, one of the key props that hold up baseball's existence as an authentic historical American institution. If the argument that some of the highest profile stats in the game – the home run piles of the 90s and 00s sluggers for example – are essentially false is sustained, then are they going to be wiped from the record and who is going to do the wiping? Even more significantly, what does that mean for baseball? Does that not send a wrecking ball crashing into the castle walls of modern baseball history?

Oh, yes,' is surely the answer to that one. However, a more optimistic take on these matters may convince us all that the record books will absolutely need correcting if baseball is to be restored to equilibrium. Otherwise, in the case of the super-sluggers being found to have built their numbers with illegal performance enhancing substances, what will be the point of comparing McGwire with Ruth or Sosa with Mantle? How, even, will be compare Sosa with Bonds?: decide who was taking the best shit? The most? Perhaps only the setting up of a Congressional Committee of Baseball Statistic Restitution will be capable of delivering sufficiently sagacious judgment that will allow the discussion of baseball numbers to continue with minimal controversy in the future.

Of huge further interest in the wake of these accusations, different light is already being shed on the deeds of the pre-modern era: how good a player does Roger Maris now look to everybody? Would it not be a great thing for baseball if the Veterans Committee of the Hall of Fame were to vote him into the grouping of the supposed immortals in 2005? Is it not the only appropriate thing for them to do?

When I began this article in the autumn of 2004, I wrote:

"The Barry Bonds question, apart from whether he will pass Hank Aaron to become baseball history's biggest hitter of home runs (he will), is whether he is the greatest of all time. Such a thing was ridiculous to people in the game as recently as three or even two years ago, but his form has been so magnificent and so sustained in the past two seasons that you can palpably feel baseball people shuffling their feet or looking at each other quizzically wondering whether the best hitter of all-time is right here, right now, in their midst."

Most of us thought his fantastic body was attributable only to dedication and the gym, the rest of the explanation for his genius-like performance down to the non-miracle of modern diet, modern healthcare and a refreshing self-discipline. In a puff of wind, a reputation is ruined and a writer looks like a fool. Amid the impending predictions of earthquake and doom, there is still the tingle of electricity as huge shifts in the historical ground take place beneath our feet. Is it genuinely a shame that the wrong kind of history is being made? Or do we not secretly love this type of disaster?

Maybe it's only me.

3
GOOD TIMES AND HARD TIMES
Major League Franchise Performance 1901-2004

I love the poetry, the mystery and the romance of baseball, but the geek in me is always ready to rise to the occasion and challenge the unmeasurable in the game and beat it up with statistics. The Geek Boy that sits in a corner of my brain called across to the nerd that twitches not far away and posed him a question: "which, 1 to 30, are the best and by definition, the worst franchises in the history of baseball?" I love a good, simple number crunch and so, over a number of mornings, afternoons and evenings over the past year, I've done some light wrestling with the problem.

I think these are fair questions to ask. Everyone knows that the New York Yankees is the most successful baseball organisation in US history and we all think we know that the St Louis Cardinals come second, but after that, what? Or rather who, is next in the pecking order?

The problem naturally, as you try to take a step in the shoeprints of the SABRmeisters of this world, is how to balance several historical factors: only sixteen franchises existed as major league entities from 1901 to 1960. How do we compare the Angels, Astros and Mets with the established teams when their history is so much shorter? To highlight the main difficulty, how do we deal with the fact that they have had so much less time to pick up World Series ranking points? And as time flows forward toward 2005, we pick up more expansion franchises with the same problem increasing in scale. How do we meaningfully make a league table of the franchises now thirty in number? To which the plausible answer is, "with difficulty," but we can do it, revealing some interesting things in the process. And if we enjoy doing it and looking at the results, what the hell!

If we take the pre-expansion period alone and compare the teams' regular season and World Series performance combined, The Sixteen spread out reasonably well. In the table below, the regular season success figure is calculated using a simple points method where first place in an 8th placed team in the league table merits 8 points, second place 7 and so on down. The total for 68 seasons is then divided by 68 to produce a points-per-season figure, which you see here. The World Series figures are arrived at by another simple points award system, averaged out over the same time period. Some obvious analytical thoughts quickly emerge, such as "****!" (choose your own personal favourite expletive) the Phillies were absolute shite! Swiftly followed by, "****** my auntie, I knew the Browns and the Senators were supposed to have been God-awful; but no one told me about the Phillies. Surely this is a mistake?" No, it isn't. The Phillies remember, have won only one World Series in their history, in 1980, and won the National League twice (1915 & 1950), whilst finishing last no less than twenty-one times. They also had twelve seventh places in this period too.

I think looking at failure here is actually more interesting that noticing success. If you read a lot of old baseball books you pretty quickly pick up the idea that the Giants, the Cards, the Red Sox and the Dodgers were huge and that the Tigers were a big deal in the game for many years along with the Pirates, the A's, the Cubs and the Reds. But hang on a minute: look at the statistics which I think don't lie here, and you find yourself being brought up pretty short. The Cubs have a World Series figure of less than 1? and the Indians almost nothing? Even doubling the numbers to bring them more into line with the regular season averages the Indians still don't make 1, and neither do the White Sox nor the Phillies. Which means that essentially, over this period of time we have to assign to these clubs the three 'F's: Failure; Failure and Failure.

Original 16 Franchises, Pre- and Post-Moves, 1901-68

	Team	RS Pts	Ave.	WS Ave. x 2		Total
1	New York Yankees	422	6.13	3.61	7.22	13.35
2	New York Giants/SF	413	6.07	1.08	2.16	8.23
3	St Louis Cardinals	349	5.13	1.33	2.66	7.79
4	Brooklyn Dodgers/LA	348	5.11	1.19	2.38	7.49
5	Detroit Tigers	358	5.26	0.78	1.56	6.92
6	Pittsburgh Pirates	342	5.02	0.67	1.34	6.36
7=	Boston Red Sox	310	4.55	0.81	1.62	6.17
7=	Philadelphia /Oak/KC/A's	249	3.66	1.24	2.48	6.17
9	Cleveland Indians	354	5.15	0.36	0.72	5.87
10	Chicago Cubs	324	4.76	0.51	1.02	5.78
11	Cincinnati Reds	285	4.19	0.74	1.48	5.67
12	Chicago White Sox	328	4.82	0.32	0.64	5.46
13	Boston/Milwaukee/Atlanta Braves	267	3.92	0.60	1.20	5.12
14	Washington Senators/Minn. Twins	273	4.01	0.49	0.96	4.97
15	St Louis Browns/Baltimore Orioles	254	3.73	0.53	1.06	4.79
16	Philadelphia Phillies	233	3.42	0.24	0.48	3.90

Note: World Series points award system: 20 pts for a Series win and 3 pts for each game won. The total per season for each team has been doubled to balance regular and World Series performance – the doubled figures are arguably still too low.

If we jump forward and examine the 1969-Present seasons, we see a new order having emerged. We may ask first of the stats, how have the Mobile and Expansion franchises fared? Answer, extremely well. In the ranking table below which puts together points-awards for Play-Offs and the World Series, we can see how the move west has really suited the A's, while the switch east for the St Louis Browns has transformed their fortunes. The Braves have now emerged as a potent force, having exited both Boston and Milwaukee. The Dodgers have maintained stability, but look for the Giants in the Top 10 and you'll be there for eternity. They're not even Top 15. In fact, the last 36 seasons for them has witnessed a fiasco in terms of playing performance. True they're ninth in games-won, but they haven't won a lot of divisions (6) and when they've made it to the play offs they have imploded or fizzled out a wet firework. They have won not a single World Series since 1969 while 18 organisations of the 30 have. That has to be perhaps the most startling statistic from this period of 'modern' play off baseball.

Expansion teams have fared much less well than the mobiles. Only three franchises have managed to burst through into the Top 16. However, the Mets have a pretty splendid record, having made four Series, winning two, while the extraordinary Marlins have amassed 122 points in only 12 seasons. Even more extraordinary is the fact that they have won two World Series without ever winning their division. Many would cry "foul and get out of here!" at this point because of the lack of traditionalism in the modern play off system which allows the best second placed team to advance in order, to turn an unwieldy six into a smooth eight (teams). However there is a strong counter argument to this – and four times now has the Wild Card team gone on to win the Series since inception on 1994 – that a second placed team can actually have a better regular season percentage than some of the division winners, which was the case last year with the Red Sox in their 98 game-winning season.

Regular & Post-Season Performance of the 30 Franchises Since 1969 Table 1

	Franchise	Seas	1st Places	WS Wins	WS Pts Tot	PO Pts Tot	Tot Pts
1	New York Yankees	36	13.5	6	213	276	490
2	Oakland Athletics	36	12.5	4	131	133	267
3	Cincinnati Reds	36	9	3	108	97	205
4	Baltimore Orioles	36	8	2	85	114	199
5	Los Angeles Dodgers	36	9.5	2	79	101	180
6	Atlanta Braves	36	15	1	41	138	179
7	St Louis Cardinals	36	8	1	50	128	178
8	New York Mets	36	4	2	76	100	176
9	Boston Red Sox	36	6	1	50	85	135
10	Florida Marlins	12	0	2	64	58	122
11	Pittsburgh Pirates	36	9	2	64	54	118
12	Minnesota Twins	36	7	2	64	53	117
13	Toronto Blue Jays	36	5	2	64	46	110
14	Philadelphia Phillies	36	6.5	1	41	58	99
15	Cleveland Indians	36	6	0	15	83	98
16	Kansas City Royals	36	5.5	1	38	44	82
17	Anaheim Angels	36	3	1	32	41	73
18	San Francisco Giants	36	6	0	9	59	68
19	Arizona Diamondbacks	6	3	1	32	29	61
20	Detroit Tigers	36	3	1	32	22	54
21	San Diego Padres	36	3	0	3	45	48
22	Seattle Mariners	28	3	0	0	45	45
23	Milwaukee Brewers	36	1.5	0	9	20	29
24	Houston Astros	36	6.5	0	0	19	19
25	Chicago Cubs	36	3	0	0	18	18
26	Montreal Expos	36	1.5	0	0	11	11
27	Chicago White Sox	36	4	0	0	6	6
28=	Colorado Rockies	12	0	0	0	2	2
28=	Texas Rangers	36	4	0	0	2	2
30	Tampa Bay Devil Rays	6	0	0	0	0	0

Another point about the table above you is that the placings depend upon the values the author places on the different stages of progress to the World Series. In this system, twice the number of points, 20, are awarded for a Series win than are netted by a Championship Series win (10). If this underestimates the achievement of actually cresting all other twenty-nine teams and we award 30 points for each Series win, then I should tell you only one pair of teams flip-flop: the Diamondbacks climb up over the Giants into 18th place. If however we award 40 points for a win and keep the CS award at 10 then things begin to move: the Mets leap two to become the 6th best team since 1969, the Red Sox drop three to 12th, the Giants now drop below the Tigers into 20th and the Royals climb over the Indians. I then wondered whether increasing the points per World Series game win from 3 to 5, exaggerating the achievement of the ultimate winners still further, would make further changes to the pecking order; there was only one change: the Red Sox dropped again, one place below the rising Toronto Blue Jays (who won 2 Series in '92 and '93) to 13th. How a player of this statistical game divvies out the relative points between Division, Championship and World series is entirely moot: there really is no correct way of doing it.

The thing that staggers me each time I look at this table is to see how appalling the records of the two Chicago Clubs are over the period. To me, 25th and 27th for the Cubs and White Sox respectively is staggering. Being around for a long time gives you more time to fail – it'll be interesting to see in ten years time where spectacular arrivistes the Marlins and Diamondbacks sit in this context – but 104 years indisputably gives a franchise a lot more time to pull disastrous failings apart and put things back together intelligently and again to increase competitiveness. I mean to say: 18 organisations have won a Series in the past 36 seasons. Another 4 (the Giants, Indians, Padres and Brewers) have made it to the Series and lost. Of the remaining 8, 6 are Expansion clubs, two of which have only been around for only a short while. The two complete duds with no excuse are from Chicago. In terms of wins-per-season, the consistency mark, the Cubs have done better, averaging 73.9 wins per season, which puts them 22nd. But the same measure has the White Sox at 11th. Cubs have 5 seconds and 3 first places. The Sox however, have 10 seconds and 4 wins. In the past 8 seasons they have been runners up in the AL Central 6 times. They're good, but they're not good enough quite to win. Without their 2003-04 improvement, the Cubs would be so bad, writers would be lost for whole winters trying to find words to describe how big a failure the whole enterprise has been. To remind you: this club won 4 of the first 10 National League pennants, won 2 of the next 20, 3 of the next 8, then 1 of the next 30, which takes us to the beginning of divisions. They have won 3 of 36 division races, competing against only 4 other teams. Just compare that with a middle-ranking team, the Kansas City Royals. Though having a very thin time of it lately, no division pennants since 1985, since 1969 when they began their existence, they have won 6 races and come second 9 times also.

The success of some teams surprised me: the Oakland Athletics are the second most successful team on this rating system since 1969. The Baltimore Orioles are in the top five. Somehow, one imagines that the Dodgers, the Giants, the Red Sox, the Cardinals, the Cubs, the Braves and the Yankees are the MLB equivalent of Arsenal, Chelsea, Everton, Spurs, Aston Villa (I know, I'm not sure either), Newcastle and Manchester United. But these are simply the ballclubs who grab most of the headlines, the "big market teams". The Braves of course are chronic underachievers. Fact is, it is the image created in the minds of the image-makers by their history and great players that creates the impression of their aristocracy. In playing terms, the Athletics, the Orioles, the Reds and the Mets should be in any top group of baseball organisations for you can easily argue that what you did in 1920 counts for nothing: what you've done in the past 30 years counts for a hell of a lot more (I should have probably placed the Cincinnati Reds in the media aristocracy, but, speaking as I only can as a new and British fan of American baseball, they don't seem to be pushed forward into this group).

After completing a post-season order of merit it was time to introduce some reward for consistent regular season play. After all, with teams separated only by a few wins each year, it's patently unfair to load up the system so that only the one team who squeezes through the division net each year (plus the Wild Carder) grab all the points. So in addition to the post-season points won, I added the average number of games per season won by each. This hurts teams like the Marlins who, despite stellar seasons of lunatic proportions, have actually had a number of struggling seasons since starting out in 1993. I then added some more balance by rewarding the teams who could win a division race but who haven't been able to get themselves started in the play offs.

You can't quote me on that . . .

"The only thing my father & I have in common is that our similarities are different."
Dale Berra, Pittsburgh shortstop and son of Yogi, King of the Malapropists.

Regular & Post-Season Performance of the 30 Franchises Since 1969 Table 2

	Franchise	No. Of Seas	Ave. Games won	1st Place	WS Pts	PO Pts	Tot Pts	+ 1st Places	+Ave Games per s
1	New York Yankees	36	85	13.5	213	276	490	625	710
2	Oakland Athletics	36	80.4	12.5	131	133	267	392	472
3	Atlanta Braves	36	78.9	15	41	138	179	329	408
4	Cincinnati Reds	36	81.3	9	108	97	205	295	376
5	Baltimore Orioles	36	73.3	8	103	114	217	297	370
6	Los Angeles Dodgers	36	82.3	9.5	79	101	180	275	357
7	St Louis Cardinals	36	78.9	8	50	128	178	255	334
8	New York Mets	36	76.8	4	76	100	176	216	293
9	Pittsburgh Pirates	36	77.4	9	64	54	118	208	285
10	Boston Red Sox	36	82.6	6	50	85	135	195	278
11	Minnesota Twins	36	75	7	64	53	117	187	262
12	Philadelphia Phillies	36	75.2	6.5	41	58	99	164	239
13	Toronto Blue Jays	36	75.4	5	64	46	110	160	235
14	Cleveland Indians	36	73.8	6	15	83	98	158	232
15	Kansas City Royals	36	76.6	5.5	38	44	82	137	214
16	San Francisco Giants	36	78.6	6	9	59	68	128	207
17	Florida Marlins	12	66.4	0	64	58	122	122	188
18	Anaheim Angels	36	75.2	3	32	41	73	103	178
19	Chicago White Sox	36	76	4	0	6	6	100	176
20	ArizonaDiamondbacks	6	75	3	32	29	61	91	166
21	Houston Astros	36	79	6.5	0	19	19	79	163
22	Detroit Tigers	36	74	3	32	22	54	84	158
23	San Diego Padres	36	70	3	3	45	48	78	148
24	Seattle Mariners	28	72	3	0	45	45	75	147
25	Chicago Cubs	36	73.9	3	0	18	18	48	122
26	Texas Rangers	36	76	4	0	2	2	42	118
27	Milwaukee Brewers	36	72.5	1.5	9	20	29	44	117
28	Montreal Expos	36	74.7	1.5	0	11	11	26	101
29	Colorado Rockies	12	67.8	0	0	2	2	2	70
30	Tampa Bay Devil Rays	6	54.4	0	0	0	0	0	54

Methodology. World Series Points System: 20 points for each Series won and 3 points for each game won, win or lose. Play Offs Points System: 5 points for Division Series won and 2 points for each game won, 10 points for each Championship Series won and 3 points for each game won.

".5" – the strange looking .5 first places refers to the 1981 season where because of strike action the season was split into two halves with a first place awarded at the end of each. The two winners in each league played off against each other in a division series in each league.

The results? Up come the Braves! Sixth place originally looks pretty good, but this is the team that can claim more success than any other franchise since the play off-big expansion era: more division wins than any other ballclub including the New York Yankees. And of course, crash go the Marlins. The White Sox rise towards mediocrity (some might say they've now achieved it). But although almost everyone is shuffled around, the changes are almost entirely small ones.

The relative performance of mobile, expansion and original franchises is interesting still, I think. Of the Top 10, only 5 clubs have neither moved base nor come into major league baseball "late." One, or "only one" club makes it. Of the next ten, five are expansioners and two more have moved. It's impossible to prove conclusively that the Dodgers, the Giants, the Browns, the Athletics, the Braves and the Senators would have won fewer games and glories had they remained in their old ballpark locations, but I should imagine that serious baseball thinkers who believe that movement hasn't been of fundamental importance to the progress of the last four of the above are very thin on the ground.

For the traditionalists who hate the whole notion of expansion and would have baseball back as it was in 1959 or maybe a Bigs of say, twenty franchises, they have this going for them: 8 of the bottom 10 performers were born of post-1960 expansion. Back at them, 55 division races since expansion have been won by Expansioners, spread among 11 of the later 14. And notice how 28 of the 30 clubs have made it to post-season play at least once. That's quite remarkable, I think. It also occurs to me that only a real hard-bitten hardliner with an angry fist permanently being shaken at the world could deny that expansion and, though it grieves me a little to say it, movement, has added tremendous energy to the progress of baseball history. That isn't to say that the apparent chronic neglect of baseball in Montreal is totally unforgiveable. It goes against the grain of history, actually: Montreal is only the second expansion club to move, after a panic flight of the Pilots from Seattle at the end of 1969 to Milwaukee (to become the Brewers we all know and wonder about).

And now the inevitable and deserved paragraph on the Yankees. The New York Yankees are a phenomenon and phenomenal. The only surprise, looking at the last 36 years, conditioned by the past six, is that it took them so long to find dominance again. They found it under Torre in 1996. The feeling of relief you get when you look at a list of World Series winners and not see New York AL between 1978 and 1996 is also gratifying. Then you look at their complete absence from the Series for 14 years after '78 and marvel that it actually happened. This is the club, remember, that won 13 of 16 between 1947 and 1962 and 9 of the previous 24. Over the whole period there, they competed in 5 more, where the thing is this: once they got to a Series, they normally stuffed you. Three of those five defeats came in '55, '57 and '60; before that the Yankee machine was almost completely unstoppable when they had a pennant winning team. Furthermore, the first ten times they won the World Series, not once did they allow their opponents to win three games. Only twice did they even concede two games. That is dominance on drugs (not literally, you understand). That is practically an obscene exhibition of power and sporting prowess.

At the time of writing – November 2004 – we are either in the midst or the end of a period of the dragon sleeping: no set of rings since for four seasons. To win in 2005 they will have to almost completely rebuild their pitching staff. Looking at recent Yankee history, even with that vast war chest of cash, there is no certainty of anything for them. They have only won 6 times in 36 years. After a slow start, the first 36 seasons where a World Series was played saw them winning 8 times. The worst 36-year period in their history – 1963-1998 – saw 4 wins. So look at it this way: if you're British (or European) and have just come to baseball in the last year, you have arrived at almost the worst period in their entire history, yet they can still say they have been the best team in baseball for 4 of the past 9 years.

Finally, it's time to look at the 30 clubs performance over the whole major league period, 1901-2004 in the attempt to get to some sort of true order of merit. Of course, there's no such thing as "true" because, as stated earlier, these decisions about how to arrive at such a thing is made up of fallible human decision making. Here's a shot at it anyway, and here is the system. Firstly, I took six performance indicators: league/division position, World Series record, Play Offs record, winning percentage, games won per season and regular season + post-season ranking points per season and rank-ordered the clubs 1-30 in each. Second and finally, I averaged the six 1-30 positions for a final national (note the small 'n') league table. Here it is.

Regular & Post-Season Performance of the 30 Franchises 1901-2004

Pos	Franchise	Ave Pos.	WS Pts	Play Offs	W%	GWo	Pts Per Seas	Final
1	New York Yankees	1	1	1	1	1	2	1.17
2	St Louis Cardinals	4	2	4	4	4	4	3.67
3	Brooklyn/LA Dodgers	3	4	6	3	3	6	4.33
4	New York/SanFran Giants	2	5	11	2	2	9	4.83
5	Boston Red Sox	8	6	9	5	6	10	7.33
6	Pittsburgh Pirates	6	8	14	6	5	13	8.67
7	Cincinnati Reds	11	7	8	11	9	11	9.5
8	Philadelphia/Oakland A's	15=	3	3	16	19	5	10.17
9	Cleveland Indians	9	13	10	7	7	17=	10.5
10	Detroit Tigers	5	9	22	9	8	16	11.5
11	Boston/Mil./Atlanta Braves	14	10	2	17	22	12	12.5
12	Chicago Cubs	10	12	25	12	10	17=	14.33
13	St Louis/Baltimore Orioles	15=	11	5	19	24	14	14.67
14	Toronto Blue Jays	19	18=	16	13	16	8	15
15=	New York Mets	24	15	7	20	20	7	15.33
15=	Arizona Diamondbacks	21	22=	21	8	17	3	15.33
17	Chicago White Sox	7	14	27	10	11	25	15.67
18	Florida Marlins	26	17=	12=	24	28	1	17.17
19	WashingtonS/MinnTwins	13	16	15	18	21	22	17.5
20	Kansas City Royals	12	21	19	26	13	15	17.67
21	Anaheim Angels	18	22=	20	14	15	20	18.17
22	Philadelphia Phillies	20	20	12=	27	26	23	21.33
23	Houston Astros	17	30	24	29	12	26	23
24	Montreal Expos	23	30	26	15	18	27	23.17
25=	Milwaukee Brewers	27	24	23	22	23	24	23.83
25=	Seattle Mariners	29	30	17=	21	25	21	23.83
27	San Diego Padres	28	25	17=	28	29	19	24.33
28	Texas Rangers	22	30	28=	25	14	29	24.67
29	Colorado Rockies	25	30	28=	23	27	28	26.83
30	Tampa Bay Devil Rays	30	30	30	30	30	30	30

Before you give yourself a sore throat shouting, I know, how do you reconcile the fact that the gaps between 2nd and 3rd and 14th and 15th place might be considerable? Or if you didn't get that, in each of the six categories, each team is the same distance apart from each other, when in truth, the Oakland A's World Series record is arguably a hundred times better than that of the Milwaukee Brewers. My only answer is, "I didn't have the time to refine it any better than this, leave me alone! Next time I'll do better!"

At least here there is some balance between record over a long period of time – the '16 franchises have had a lot longer to win post-season ranking points factor – and striking performance over in a short history. So I don't think the table is without interest because the methodology is without merit. As for a laying out of who's come where, I'll leave that to you.

For desert, or something to look at as you file out of the exit with the crowd, here's a table showing the relative performances of the mobile franchises, separated. I don't want to say much to finish this chapter off, because the figures suggest clear conclusions, but boy, I do feel sorry for the people of Milwaukee, Wisconsin who had a terrifically successful baseball franchise land in their laps in 1953 only to see it disappear on them 13 years later.

Franchise	Dates	Reg. Seas Ave Pts	Wins Per Season	WS Wins	Pennants /Div Wins
St Louis Browns	1901-1953	3.22	63.6 (154)	0	1
Baltimore Orioles	1954-2004	4.27	82.47	3	9
Philadelphia A's	1901-1954	4.04	71.96 (154)	5/3	8
Kansas City A's	1955-1967	1.69	63.76	0/0	0 (hi of 6th)
Oakland A's	1968-2004	3.84	82.86	4/2	11 + '81 tie
Boston Braves	1901-1952	3.19	66.38 (154)	1/1	2
Milwaukee Braves	1953-1965	6.54	88.15	1/1	2
Atlanta Braves	1966-2004	3.74	81.51	1/2	15
New York Giants	1901-1957	5.74	84.08 (154)	5/9	14
San Francisco Giants	1958-2004	4.53	82.87	0/3	5
Brooklyn Dodgers	1901-1957	4.29	77.38 (154)	1/8	9
Los Angeles Dodgers	1958-2004	4.77	85.34	5/4	12+ '81 tie
Washington Senators	1901-1960	3.58	70.38 (154)	1/1	3
Minnesota Twins	1961-2004	4.02	77.37	2	8
Washington Senators II	1961-1971	2.18	67.27	0	0
Texas Rangers	1972-2004	3.18	74.02	0	4

Note on Games Per Season. Do note that both leagues switched from a 154-game season to a 162-game one in 1961. Also, in many seasons teams do not end up the season making up "meaningless" games that were earlier postponed, so have seasons where only 161 or 153 games were completed.

You can quote me on that . . .

When asked whether the fact that he was missing the index finger of his pitching hand explained his great curveball, Mordecai Brown replied,

"To know for sure, I'd have to throw with a normal hand, and I've never tried it."

Mordecai "Three-Finger" Brown

4
SAVING TELEVISION IN THE DEAD OF NIGHT

"..But I want to talk about the Expos: they're three games above five hundred, they've just played twenty out of twenty-three games on the road; they've been all over the continent; their fans have been misled and abused for over a decade...and I got news for you: they're not done."

David Lengel, on the Montreal Expos, August 2003

If there's one thing you and I have in common it's that we watch Channel 5's *Baseball On 5*. It's a fair bet too that we both love it. This chapter is devoted to the respect and, dammit, love I feel for this humble TV programme that unfolds through the Sunday and Wednesday nights of the long season that chases summer through to the edge of winter. It's much more than televised baseball from the United States of America. It's even more than Erik's Stompers, bad shirts, great action montages, great punditry, World Series tuxedos and National Anthem ratings, the problems with David Lengel's armpits and the ability to keep firing up tremendous enthusiasm for baseball right through to dawn.

To watch the show is to be more than a baseball fan, more than feeling part of a community; it's to feel part of a family. This makes *Bo5* pretty much unique television. A lot of this, maybe most of it, is Jonny Gould's doing. The man has a gift for leading the crew of professionals who make the show happen and an uncanny ability to bring you the viewer right through the screen into the studio with them. This intimacy is a media phenomenon more usually associated with radio, where, in the absence of pictures, the broadcaster unconsciously (perhaps) reaches out to the also unseen listener while we in turn, if we like the person we hear, automatically respond. Think of John Peel, a guy who genuinely cared not only for his music but for his audience too. Television, on the other hand, is a shallow, plastic medium compared with radio. The pictures immediately make it a "Show!", a performance, which encourages artifice; Jonny Gould has managed to make a nonsense of the idea in the seven years he's been fronting the UK's sole baseball programme.

By tradition, the first night of the World Series sees presenter Jonny Gould (left) and 2003 & 2004 pundit David Lengel (right) decked out in tuxedos. Much is made of this. Last season, Lengel was down to wear a kilt on his bottom half but bottled it, allegedly. We see here even in this fragment, Gould donning the soup and fish as if to the manner born, looking like a cross between James Bond and Barbie's Ken. Lengel appears to be taking the move into formal garb completely in his stride as is his hip, languorous wont.

Gould has done this by smashing the rules. Television's unwritten Book Of Professional Tele-visual Conduct insists that a wooden barrier is put up between presenter and viewer. In the world of the perfectly and expensively constructed set, of the coiffed and made up presenter who under the glare of a stark and unnatural light must never make a mistake or at least admit to one, everything must run with smooth, lacquered precision. Every second must be logged and accounted for; each change of item and shift of emphasis precisely planned and pre-conceived. Well bollocks to that, I say, and in

---

* It's "Jonny" Gould, not Jonathan. As he later told me, when he had long established himself on the show, Talk Sport/LBC's own Jonny Gould wrote an allegedly obnoxious letter to our Jonny Gould's London televison station (LNN) claiming he (our JG) was trying to cash in on his fame and demanded that he change his (our JG's) own name! The other JG was trying to break into televison at the time. Our JG subsequently told the agent of the other JG to take a hike and the storm blew over. Quite by the by, it's been said of Talk Sport's Jonny Gould that he has "the perfect face for radio," which I always think is a nice compliment. Because of the name dispute, "in the papers and on the credits I'm Jonathan Gould. But though I was christened 'Jonathan' everyone has always called me Jonny."

effect, so does Jonny Gould*, aided and abetted with yankee alacrity at the moment by David Lengel. An example. Game 1 of the 2004 World Series, opening montage fades to the expected shot of Gould and Lengel in spankingly sharp tuxedos behind the studio desk. Gould opens with his now customary, perfectly paced spiel, all enthusiasm and friendly grin. He looks every bit The Presenter part, with the chiselled good looks and the full head of brush-backed hair. He ought to be wooden, but in moments he's mentioning a female acquaintance he knows will be tuning in:

"Sue is having a 40th birthday party and a World Series party tonight and if I know Sue, she'll be behind the sofa already, rat-arsed."

'Steady, Jonny,' you think and look behind Lengel's smile to camera to see if he's thinking. 'Jonny, you wouldn't be getting away with this if we were doing this in America.'

There's the show right there. Jonny Gould, shining in the glory of the opening night Tux and he's almost gone too far. But this is why we love it. It isn't just the baseball. It's his enjoyment of sport and the presenting of it that comes pouring into the room, because Jonny just thinks, 'to hell with what I'm supposed to do and be, I'm going to have some fun and the hell with you if you don't like it.' Jonny is lucky. He knows he couldn't get away with this if this went out at 8 in the evening. Every night is the middle of the night and he imagines no one with a suit mentality at Channel 5, if there is such a thing at Channel 5, is watching him. And eight years down the line, no one at the station has called him in to tear his face off.

Released from the normal bonds of the trade – he couldn't do this at the BBC by the way even during night owl time – he is free to give full rein to his inclination that the show's audience are happy with his approach to sports broadcasting. Later on in the week, during Game 3, he is caught eating chocolate as an inning ends in St Louis and the director in the control room pulls the show out of America and back to London. This season they've almost become a comedy duo. It would be terrible if it were true. Happily as Gould, no doubt exhausted by other work commitments at the end of another anaconda season that twists his body clock so out of shape its starting to resemble a Dali masterpiece, defends himself against the charge of sloppy professionalism, Lengel cuts past him into an explanation of the depth of the St Louis fall from grace, which consists mostly of the Cardinals' hitters having developed a helpless palsy at the plate in the face of Boston pitching. He does it passionately and expertly, tugging the programme back to the central reason it exists: because there is a big 'we' out here who have come to love baseball with a similar passion. David Lengel, a graduate in History and Political Science and who wants one day to work in that field, for the moment gives the strong impression that he lives and breathes baseball. You listen, his intensity sucks you in and you learn. And you love the programme because it's so real. Lengel's love of baseball is real, Jonny's enjoyment in presenting is real; the whole programme is an exercise in transforming television from plasticity into humanity. Thank God for baseball. Thank God for these people.

Another of "these people" is Erik Janssen, the show's producer. He is also a major reason why Jonny is Jonny on the TV. Erik, as aficionados of the show are no doubt keenly aware, is the butt of constant jibes and verbal harassment from Jonny Gould. He never answers the hammering back. I don't have to ask him whether he minds, because I think I know he doesn't. If he did, Gould wouldn't do it. This is Janssen for you. Loose, relaxed, phlegmatic, personable. You meet him and you think he wouldn't have been flustered by having to die on the Titanic. 'You've got to go sometime,' he says in my imagination. A television producer is in a powerful position. He (in this case) makes the decisions that mould the programme into its shape. If he thought Gould and Lengel joked around too much, he could tell them to cut it out. If he wanted a change of personnel at the desk, he couldn't perhaps get it immediately, but whoever he wanted out could be very seriously undermined.

Erik, in case you want to know, and I suspect you do, is exactly as a nice a person as you hope and want him to be. I first met him when I went to see the show live back in April 2004, Oakland against the Anaheim Angels second week of the season, I hadn't yet spoken to him; Jonny had set the thing up, knowing I was writing this book. He came to ITN reception, sometime past 11 o'clock Sunday night, and was as friendly and welcoming as any stranger could want. He takes me round, introduces me to people, fills me in on what I want to know. I look at my watch and there's about 45 minutes to go before show time. Is he rushing, is he tense? Is he barking instructions or checking in a loud voice that everything is all set to go? Is he hell. Admittedly, this is an unusual night because he isn't officially producing, Mike Hussey is doing that as well as directing.

"He can do that okay?"

"Oh, sure," says Erik.

Even on a night off (he was at the studio this night to work on the hockey show that he also produces, and it's Stanley Cup time – "heaven," he later tells me, as the season of his two favourite sports overlap for a sweet month) he still exuded something of the proprietor, talking to me, but watching everyone and everything going on smoothly around him. We're sitting at *the* desk now, he in the Lengel position, me in the Gould, the lighting director using us to test his hardware, and I'm thinking that I don't care if this is night off, this fellow is amazingly relaxed, as cool and easy as a man who has just been told he's never going to die. It's no wonder Gould and the pundits look so laid back they might slide on to the floor at any moment or eat a bowl of spaghetti while they're talking.

We go into the control room where the director is talking loudly and showing signs of having a trial to face shortly, but Erik watches, satisfied. He stands there with me while a quartet of heads get on with their job, hands in jacket pockets, cap on head (was it the Expos? I forget), and tells me one of the things I'd came to find out even before I directly asked about it.

"Well, y'know, the thing is, it's really a family, all the people that work here."

This all sounds very cutesy pie and roses growing up the cottage window, but like the bad shirts the boys occasionally wear and the klunky, naff feature on British baseball last season that didn't exactly form any of the most fluid moments in the recent history of television, with Baseball On 5, what you get is what you see. There is no smoke, no mirrors and no bull.

"So how did you get to work for the programme," I asked.

"I watched the show when it was on in its first year," he begins.

He speaks very, very quickly, his words sliding at you like a snow sliding down a mountainside. Sorry, but Canada always makes me think of snow.

". . . and it was terrible. They were doing everything wrong. The presenter would say 'okay here's the Thome home run' and it would be someone being struckout. And no one seemed to know anything about baseball. It was just awful. So I did something I'd never done: I rang up and complained. And I'd written out a list of things I was going to say; and I went through them. And they said, 'you seem to know what you're talking about, will you come in and give us some advice while we're doing the show?' So I said, 'sure.' So when I got there, and I introduced myself to Toddo, he put his arms around me and hugged me; he was so relieved; he'd been going crazy."

Janssen fairly quickly made himself indispensable with his ability to explain to the producer, the director and the technicians, none of them who knew anything about the game apart from the fact that some guy with a cap on threw a white ball at a guy wearing a helmet and carrying a bat, what was going on and what needed re-playing. When an opportunity to move into the production chair in 1998, he took it. I was about to be knocked down with a feather until Erik told me about his film school degree in Britain, and his experience in television behind the camera whilst he came in initially as an advisor to the show. He understood all the processes involved in stitching and piecing a programme like this together.

Ah, the days of Toddo (1997-2001), the Canadian Todd Macklin. Many viewers are won over by people who manage to convey a supercharged level of enthusiasm whilst combining it with prodigious knowledge of their subject. Toddo had that. It seems to pour out of the set like some mysterious miasma and work you over to the point where you become enslaved to the subject. It could be Rick Stein with fish cookery, Danny Baker with football or in this case TM with baseball.

"And presumably you like doing it," I said, just to be on hand with a nit-wit question.

"It's a dream job. If I'd have written down on a piece of paper what job I wanted to do, this would be it."

While the director Pete Hussey talks down a mike to a cameraman, striving to lock down the ship so that technically the craft is unsinkable, outside the control room the whole scene is one of unhurried calm, with everyone seeming to know exactly what they have to do and when. I imagined that with this TV show being in effect a live performance, there would be tension, anxiety, taut expressions, but it's not at all like that. I should have realised that most of these people have been doing the show for at least three seasons, so the whole operation is bound to run on tramlines from soup to nuts, but I'm too tired, having come straight from the airport after a knackering four day race up and down the north-east coast of America. I only think about this later. I've worked in enough organisations myself also, I figure out back home, to realise that the show also works so smoothly because no one is getting hassled from above. No one is getting management stress dumped on their head; Erik just trusts that each member of the team knows his or her job and how to do it effectively, so they just get on and do it. And no one, I smile to myself later, looks like they're burdened by the dead weight of bureaucracy. In this much better world of work than a lot of us now know in this daft age, all that matters is output.

Much later on in the year I was to meet Erik again when I'd thought about the show a lot more. I put it to him that the reason for its being so real, loose and informal was simply a reflection of him. Erik looked at me with a slightly enigmatic, but essentially puzzled expression, in workaday jeans, soft shirt and Detroit Tigers baseball cap. "You think so?" he says. I also think that lack of self-interest and aggrandizement is also a crucial factor in creating the chemistry that makes this illusion of sound and light waves so great. This ability to set aside personal needs came through time and again in the time I spent talking to the people who give its special shape, texture and tone.

Suddenly I hear a voice to my right and David Lengel has arrived in a Mets shirt. He got into town off a plane from New York about twenty-four hours ago so looks pretty fresh. He's taller than I imagined, and slimmer and younger. On screen he could be 32, 33; in the flesh he's very boyish for 29. I only know him from his friendly emails, but he's immediately helpful, answering my questions.

"I really wanted this gig," he confides. He was passed over twice before he got the pundit seat in mid-2003, temping for Josh Chetwynd. He sits in a swivel chair in front of a computer fixed on a baseball website and stares vacantly across the room. "I *really* wanted to do it."

"Well I think you're doing a great job," I tell him but he makes a face, scoffing at the notion.

"No, I'm not. I can't analyse baseball anything as well as Josh. He brings an insight to the game that I can't, especially as he's played the game."

I spent months afterwards watching and listening to his work, through to the World Series of 2004, and studied Josh carefully when he sat in for six weeks mid-season. He was right. Josh has the same infectious enthusiasm, but doesn't do the joking around that David Lengel enjoys like crazy. Josh always cuts right to the heart of the inning just over, or the key at bats before a pitching change. He uses a phrase, 'dead-red' maybe, and immediately responds to Jonny's "what do you mean?" with a fast, sharp, clear definition before making his point without a pause for breath. I always liked JC, but dug Lengel's New York street angle jive more. After four shows of '04 Josh, I decide I like them equally. As the regular season slide by into post-season play, I notice how David has improved over the previous twelve months. He's still funny and suss and metropolitan, but his ability to preview, then deconstruct the unfolding of a game of modern baseball has jumped forward. He is a tremendous foil for Jonny also, though in a different way to Josh. When JG and JC get together it's a love-fest, which, you know, is nice and it's real: the two are very firm friends. When it's the Gould-Lengel partnership, there's a ton of mutual respect but there's the mock conflict which is cool because one, you don't see it on TV normally and two, it's warm and funny.

Back here in April on the second Sunday of the season, Lengel is unwrapping presents for people: a surprise baseball memento for Erik and American candy for someone who put in an order. Janssen later tells me that what Lengel was doing here in the 2004 season, commuting the Atlantic Ocean was "an absolute miracle." He was flying from JFK on a Saturday overnight flight, getting to a friend's by about nine, sleeping until five, then researching the show until it was time to go to the studio. From there he'd be driven to Heathrow for the first flight back to New York, alighting there six hours later only to go straight to work at ESPN for another week of making 25th anniversary sporting documentaries. He did this for ten weeks. Quite how he coped is a mystery.

Away from the actual set which is about as large, or as small, as a medium sized living room, the studio is eerily empty, save the eight or so people milling and toiling around its periphery. Five or six small offices adjacent to the main open plan area of a dozen or more desks lie empty. It's way past midnight now before a one a.m. start and the strip lighting is beginning to make my eyes ache. We're like oversized Borrowers, coming out to play after everyone else has gone home. Then Jonny Gould arrives, who I've actually met face-to-face once before, and I play nosy journalist, standing back to observe his interaction with colleagues and crew. I notice how he doesn't make a b-line for David, or Erik, but is quickly yakking about something and nothing with one of the backroom gang with easy familiarity. You hope, as a fanatical supporter of the programme that you aren't going to be disappointed with anyone; and with Jonny being the human flagship of the operation, the face of American Baseball In The UK, you don't want him to be a jerk, or as they say over there, an asshole. I give an inward grunt of satisfaction as I notice straight away that Erik's point about family is accurate. Gould is family alright, on equal terms with the whole gang. At no stage in the slow march to dawn does this change. There is no star treatment, no special Jonny perks or space, apart from a car that picks him up from home and takes him back at five in the morning; there are no dressing rooms at all in fact, in case you were wondering. As the bare white light seems to strip layers of protection off my cornea, it's clear there is no glamour at all to doing the actual work of putting baseball on the television. If there is any glitz or stardust attached to this construction, it's in our own heads on our own sofas. In a way we get the best of the deal on offer.

Everyone is very nice to me, and you know, there's no obvious reason why they should be. The floor manager Ivor Ramsay somehow finds the time to make me a cup of coffee. The assistant producers take great pains to tell me what they

---

Another Jonny footnote. Apparently, he only got his opportunity to present *Baseball On 5* because ex-Magpie and well-known radio presenter Tommy Boyd,, the show's first front man, came in one night, told the producer he was ill and walked off never to be heard of again (allegedly). Apparently he hated the show (and Toddo) from day one and often referred to it, on air as "glorified rounders." You won't be surprised to know that he is not spoken of with great fondness by people surrounding the show. I do think, however, that it would be excellent for Erik to consider showing us clips of the first year of the programme showing Tommy in full flight. For the sake of history, and all that.

do, and talk to me as if I somehow belong, when clearly I don't, through the whole night. I even get away with giving Georges, the tape editor, stick about his proclivity for supporting Satan's own football team, the Arsenal. I was impressed by George. He has to take requests for slo-mo playbacks from the control room, find the strikeout or the home run in about a minute and have it cued up and ready to go the second the director wants it. Each time tonight, and from what I can tell back in my living room, and every night, he never misses. He stands by his rack of machines all night long and flicks his switches like it's nothing and nothing is at stake. Then near the end, fuses together a crisp and excellent montage of home runs and catches from the night's game with all the show and palaver of someone politely and quickly blowing their nose.

No one at any stage looks at me as if to say, 'are you still here?' I pass five hours with and around the crew and I leave in a state of exhaustion for my train back north, which rules out proper thought. There was a sense of the surreal to the event I just passed through. I'm just a huge fan of the show and there I was, between innings, watching and hearing Jonny and David doing what I love from three feet away, peering through gaps in the set. I keep on doing this. It's like a delicious form of cheating, like climbing out of reality and looking back through from the other side.

After the game had finished and the set was packed up, and Nick the assistant producer gathered up the caps and pennants and other baseball knick-knacks to take back to the Sackille Street office next day, the show people gradually filtered away to their homes across London and out into the suburbs. Strange jobs they have, nothing like mine. Jobs you never normally see or even think about for a second. Ordinary and good people making their way through life same as everyone else that wonders what to do for a living, for a career; looking for promotion one day maybe, and annoyed no doubt by the things that bug everyone else at work. But the folk I saw tonight making *Baseball On 5* happen, prodding the programme through this scientific illusion of light, seemed pretty much okay with their lot, and the guys from Sunset And Vine, the ones concerned with the actual baseball, had a glint in their eye, at managing to escape a nightmare workaday fate where you live for Friday and look at the clock far too many times than is good for your physical and mental well-being.

One problem the programme seems to have is getting it and its representatives taken seriously by United States television. Here one of the stalkers of the game's upper echelon Pete Gammons looks at Josh Chetwynd during the Boston stage of the 2004 World Series as if to say 'who the fuck are you and why am I standing here wasting my time?' We of course, know better.

I walk out of the building last with David Lengel just as his people carrier arrives to whisk him back to the airport and another week's work at ESPN, producing shows himself. It's past five o'clock and daylight is moving steadily through London as an ITN newsreader whose face I recognise but whose name I can't remember strides into the start of his working day, smiling. I walk around the corner with my travel bags too smashed up with tiredness to think any more about what I've just seen. All I can think about is a 6 o'clock train back to my bed.

The pundit's chair of *Baseball On 5* is much like the drum chair of the fictional hard rock outfit Spinal Tap. In the film, they keep dying. In the reality of *BO5* they don't die, they just come and go. There have been over six pundits alongside first Tommy Boyd, then Jonny Gould on the show since it first went on air in 1997. Of the three that have attained semi-permanent status, first there was Todd Macklin, "Toddo," a cult-hero to new British baseball fans, all enthusiasm and compendious knowledge of the game, and now there is David Lengel. In between, there was Josh Chetwynd. A chapter committed to Baseball On 5 would obviously not be competent, never mind complete, without the fruit of some sort of communication with this man. Not long after a couple of weeks after meeting Erik, I spoke to him over the telephone. As aficionados will doubtless know, I found him in Arizona studying for a law degree, the reason he left the show as Pundit In Situ back at the mid-point of the 2003 season.

The start of our talk had me on the ropes immediately. "You're writing a baseball book for UK fans? Are you related to Andy Thomas, who wrote a book that came out in 1987?" Erm... "And Mike Ross, of SABR, wrote one that came out in 1987 through Marks & Spencer. Have you been in contact with him?" There's nothing like someone firing information at you that you think you should know to unsettle the stomach. After all, to write a book is immediately to set yourself up as an expert. Unrelated to Andy, I stared hard at the Beatles postcard on my office wall and concentrated on not being overwhelmed by knowledge.

And enthusiasm; Josh Chetwynd is the most enthusiastic and impressively authoritative person I have ever spoken to. He's the guy you know from the screen but without the boyish innocence. This is the guy who worked has worked in print journalism with USA Today, on the subject of movies, through which he appeared a number of times as a talking head on US television, the Communications Executive in Major League Baseball's London office, and who is now studying Law. Earlier he was a graduate of Northwestern University in Evanston and was once paid money to play baseball in the USA. Back in the recent times, he has experience as a baseball pundit in this country as we know, has played baseball professionally in Sweden and represented Great Britain in the same sport from 1996 to 2003. He is 33 years of age and I decide a couple of hours later that this guy is not quite the sweet and somewhat green lad off the telly; he is, I can tell you, a very considerable gentleman indeed: strong, driven and imbued with a savvy only acquired through engagement with the tough, grown up world that is America For Achievers.

He's a force of nature, practically. He buzzes with information that practically overflows amid the conversation. He loves talking I think because he loves information and loves life. He is doing a Law degree, he tells me, not as I assume, because he has serious intentions of making a career out of a sober and steady profession but "to expand my horizons." Fucking hell. And there was me thinking I was doing a lot pecking at a keyboard writing a book or two.

I'm pleased about this fresh daylight spilling into his story because the thought of Josh bedding himself down somewhere in the stomach of corporate America doesn't sit well with the image I have of him as an eternally youthful media dude, a bit like Lengel only more the sort of fellow my mum would have wanted to marry my sister, if I'd had one (I don't think she would have taken to David L, with his dark threatening looks; she'd have accused him behind his back of taking a lot of drugs and being generally a bit shifty).

"The future is an open book," he tells me before we quit, me to cook and him to get back to studying.

The past for Chetwynd has this country more closely connected to his personal history than I had hitherto suspected.

"My father was English," he says, in such a thick, chocolate cake American accent you think 'what? you're kidding? You can't be!"

Trying to re-gather professionalism, I ask him where he was from, "St John's Wood."

The penny then drops 'chink!' in the back of dopey author's head. 'So that's how you came to play for Great Britain...' I say out loud.

Josh spins back to his early baseball playing days and tells me the full story, of how he played in college for four years at a high level, in the Big 10 Conference, as a catcher.

"I was quite a good hitter – I hit .297 at Evanston and I'm quite proud of that, but really what I wasn't that good. But catching is a specialism."

Not many people go for that...

"Exactly. I wasn't going to be a great hitter, but I figured I could make myself into a good catcher. And I was pretty smart and I could call the game for the pitcher"

Another click. The guy who began the conversation as if he were auditioning for Brainiac of the Year was attracted to it from a cerebral point of view. Obviously.

He went on from good standard college ball to actually get paid to play, in Zanesville, Ohio in low class 'A' ball. He takes me through the levels.

"At the bottom there's the Rookie League, then low class 'A,' high class 'A,' then 'AA' then 'AAA.' I played one season of pro-ball in the Frontier League. For the "Greys" in Zanesville.

So were you disappointed not to have made it further? An obvious question that was met with a burst of enthusiastic modesty.

"Oh," he gushed across about 5 000 miles of distance, "I was just proud to have made it as far as I did, to actually get paid to play baseball was something."

The thing that surprised my about Josh to this point, about 75 per cent the way through the fifty minute call (I could have gone on listening to him all night, frankly), was his self-confidence. He told me about his achievements in his professional life in a style that we in England mistake for big-headedness. I did this and I did that and I was pretty smart and so on. We can all take a lesson from JC here. If I have this right, here is a guy with brains, fine. A lot of us have that. But he has this, I think, typically American energy and drive that comes with a determination to go out and do, rather than a British 'sit on my arse and hope for the best.' A lot of us would do well to copy that instead of being unnerved, as a lot of Brits are by Americans who are forthright and confident.

If I had any doubts about how genuine and safely modest the man is, they were utterly dismissed by our talk about his role in the *Baseball On 5* show. He got into it via his work with MLB in London and its connection to the show. Here he was, with his drive, determination and television experience at a moment in time, February 2002, when the UK's only baseball show was floundering a little after the loss of Todd Macklin. His two successors, though they had their baseball knowledge, didn't have the 'It' factor for the screen.

"I did a screen test at Sunset + Vine; there were about eight or nine of us. We sat on stools in a mock-up of a studio, Jonny and me, and we talked about baseball and straightaway I made him laugh; we had this chemistry.

And I got the job; it was a great opportunity."

How was the first show?

"I was pretty scared; it was the Cleveland Indians against the Anaheim Angels and I was really nervous. Erik was wonderful. He came over after the first inning and said 'this is the best first show we've ever had.' I don't know if he was being serious.

"It was tough trying to replace Todd," he later confided, but when all's said and done, one of the miracles of the show is that through seven years, the audience has lucky to have spent most of that time revelling in glorious television, in a programme they can genuinely call their own. Josh has his explanation for that and offers it without the slightest bit of prompting from me.

"Jonny Gould is the heart and soul of the show. He has this energy and creates a wonderful tone. He's what makes it."

This is exactly what Erik had told me, again out of sheer admiration and perhaps gratitude for a colleague. Tell Chetwynd how good he is at his job and you can almost hear his feet shuffle with semi-embarrassment. Tell him how his work is viewed by a fellow pundit and he practically goes into complete collapse out of humility.

"Well, it's the work that has given me more enjoyment than anything I've ever done," he says.

Though I would like to talk to Mike Carlson, a lesser-known substitute in the Lengel/Chetwynd chair, for I admire his own contribution of sound baseball knowledge last season, the circle is now complete. Though I saw Toddo in his pomp in 2000, to me he feels long gone, from a different era almost. I have met those who count the most: Gould, Lengel, Janssen and as good as, Chetwynd. I have felt very special feelings towards few media shows: I would go to the wall to defend Danny Baker's morning show on another 5, Radio 5, when it began in 1993, the most brilliant jewel in media history for this author who loves irreverence, comedy and expert love of music more than practically everything else in life. I would also chip in for a Baker statue in my town square for his original 606 from the same era. And after that there is Baseball On 5, which I have cherished for only three seasons, so far and which has given me an opportunity to fall in love with baseball in a way that to me is special practically beyond words. However, just as I used to listen to Baker back in the mid-90s every morning thinking, 'make the most of this because this is the best there will ever be and it won't be around forever,' so one might do well to carry around the same caution about Bo5. At time of writing, the Channel 5 contract with MLB is up for renewal and parties, possibly more than two, are around the negotiating table. If another channel makes a deal with MLB for UK baseball coverage, say Sky or Channel 4, how is it possible, even if it was to let the Sunset and Vine production company continue to make the programme, that it will allow Jonny and David to have the freedom do what they do and be what they are: natural and loose and glorious in their freedom of expression.

At the end of my conversation with Josh, I questioned him, naturally, about the future. Earlier he'd disturbingly used the past tense to describe his association with Bo5 and it was time to follow this up.

"It's David's job now. I wouldn't presume to think that I should do any of the shows."

But if asked?

"Well, of course that would be wonderful."

It's not a nice thought, much as one tries to successfully and philosophically wrestle with the idea that nothing in life has 'permanent' truly written into the contract, that we've seen JC in the punditry chair for the last time. There's also the strong possibility that David will be far too busy with ESPN or some other outfit in another field for him to continue. Last season's transatlantic commute was itself absolutely extraordinary – he must surely have almost been paying Channel 5 for the privilege of broadcasting to a smallish British baseball audience in the middle of the night – no one can expect that to last indefinitely. Would Josh come back to work in Britain?

"Anything is possible," he says.

The lack of fixity to our Baseball on 5 is something we'll all have to accept. One thing at least appears clear: that Jonny Gould's commitment and enthusiasm for the show is as strong if not stronger than ever and is going nowhere. If one of the walls was to fall in: Lengel and Chetwynd both to be lost, then maybe our luck will hold and a fourth great pundit will emerge seemingly from nowhere with the same charisma, chemistry and love of baseball to save the day.

I came across a great article on t'Internet this morning on my electric travels. It was from May 2000, is entitled "Montréal Behind The Scenes" and if I may say so, very nicely written. Here's an excerpt from the penultimate paragraph:

"Great fans in a great city. A jewel of a new stadium in the heart of downtown. A new owner with vision and enthusiasm. Altogether the future of baseball has never been brighter in Montréal!"

I'm no Expos fan but I feel reading that half ready to fall over in a dead faint. Then when you realise you're going to stay upright, you're left with a residual taste of the bitter, cruel irony of the words, now we all know that the Montreal Expos are nothing but a dead ball club and a bag of memories for their suffering fans. I met with Erik Janssen again one warm October afternoon of 2004 in London near the Sunset + Vine production office to talk again about the continued success of the show but also for me to find out what in heaven's name happened to the Expos: tantalisingly in 2003, Lengel made a short impassioned speech on behalf of Expos and I thought all sports fans, at how a bunch of suits could play with a beloved institution of the people could play games with it as small boys do to flies and Gods to Lear and Tess, but ninety seconds of air time didn't give him room to say much more than something rotten was abroad in the state of Baseball and that we should all be worried about it.

The year 2004 brought the long, slow death of the Montreal Expos but I hadn't had time or the access to the details of this travesty of natural sporting justice; now meeting Erik again game me the chance.

Here's where caption writers come up with inane imaginary "things we're going to pretend they were saying at the time" like "And another thing about Jeffrey Loria.." or "Get me another hot dog, I'm the goddam producer, for Christ's sake!" But instead we just say, here's Erik Janssen in a depressingly near-empty Olympic Stadium, Montreal, in an Expos cap, August 2004, looking the wrong way.

I have spent my own life too much emotionally connected to football clubs not to feel a sense of loss at the end of baseball in Montréal. They say we all die a little when someone we love or admire exits the planet; the same is true for us as fans. The departure of baseball from French Canada, and in such brutal fashion, represents for us all a very real danger, even here in Britain. North America and Britain are so tied as cousins that strange and distant events and trends 'there' sooner or later can easily become present realities 'here.' Just ask Wimbledon fans.

I don't know whether it was painful or cathartic for Erik to walk me through what happened to his team, but he did anyway.

"So where did it all start to go wrong," I asked, as we drank a four o'clock cuppa in a pretty swish Mayfair cake and coffee shop, and Erik began:

"Expos had lost a lot of money because of the strike."

For those who like a good tragedy, a perfect beginning is a glimpse at the year 1994. The battered franchise, ten years before their death, were riding high in the National League East with a win-loss record of 74-40, six games ahead of the Braves and, without sentiment, looking good for a first World Series when on August 12, the players struck. The most immediate cause was the owners' demand for a salary cap. Empathizing with Expos fans at the time isn't hard: indeed, a knot in the stomach starts to form just considering the position they here found themselves in: twenty-five years into a franchise history which had seen only one previous successful campaign – 1981, victory in the first Division Series over the Phillies before defeat in the Championship Series against the Dodgers – here was The Big One looming ecstatically into view. Then this dispute showed up. Well no need to worry, because labor disputes and baseball had always gone together like nuts on an ice cream sundae, but never had a post-season been lost, or anything close to that. Then a month and two days later, crisis into calamity: the rest of the season is cancelled; the end of the world for the Expos. Ah, well, maybe next year, eh? Pedro Martinez, Larry Walker, Moises Alou and Cliff Floyd were Montreal Expos that year.

Erik: "The team sort of hobbled along. People say 'the fans never came back,' but people forget that for four years, before the McGwyre-Sosa thing [the 1998 chase of Roger Maris' 1961 61 home run record], no one went back to any ballpark; fans were disillusioned with all the teams. Attendance was down all across the major leagues because fans were fed up, were pissed off, they didn't want to put any money in. The good thing about it was that ticket prices went down because owners were worried that the fans were leaving."

The franchise, boning up on its short history, seems to have been forever mired in ownership instability. For instance, back in 1991, Charles Bronfman, who it was widely thought, had rescued the franchise in its very infancy, announced that he wanted to get out of baseball. There followed a scrabbling around while local French-Canadian Claude Brochu, who had been granted the presidency by Bronfman back in 1986, managed to bring together the city government with thirteen private investors to buy the franchise. Back in Bronfman's days, the threat was always that the franchise would survive, but up and leave Canada for the home country: as if baseball doesn't properly, validly in the poor relation country. Somehow emblematically, that same season ended with the team spending the last month on the road after a chunk of concrete fell from Olympic Stadium roof. It also finished last in the NL East 71 wins and 90 losses.

Erik's account of things after the '94 strike now becomes more and more accusing:

"The team were just a terrible team. Then slowly they were making a comeback. So Claude Brochu was scared because the Expos were losing money and because all the stockholders were going to pull out of the Expos. So instead of buying players he in effect lined the pockets of the shareholders. But it just wasn't working so he had to sell. He was trying to find any buyer: 'help me out here, this is a losing cause, does anybody want to buy this losing cause?' No one would buy it except this guy called Jeffrey Loria, an art dealer from New York."

We're skating rapidly forward in time here. November 1999 was the month and year of Loria's move into baseball mogulhood in Quebec. Pedro meanwhile has become a Cy Young winner, finishing 1998 with 24 wins, an ERA of 1.90, and been traded away to Boston, not so much unrequired as unaffordable.

"Pedro cried when he left Montreal," says Erik Janssen with pride. "He didn't want to leave Felipe Alou. Didn't want to leave this team."

So what of Loria?

"He came in with promises of maintaining plans to build a spanking new downtown ballpark, didn't he? "He comes up and he's supposed to be the Knight in Shining Armour, the guy that was going to save the Expos. And he came up with this slogan: 'Why not us? Why not now?' First thing he did when he came over, he went to all the broadcasters, who'd been with the Expos since day one, since the inception, and kicked them all out of the stadium and said, 'if you want to come back and broadcast Expos games, this is how much it'll cost you. And they said, 'what are you talking about? We've been doing the Expos for years, you can't just kick us out.' They were in-house broadcasters, broadcasting across Montreal and across Canada as well. They'd been doing it for a nominal fee. So they brought in such a ridiculous price tag that anyone broadcasting Expos games would be losing like $300 a day. They wouldn't be making any profits. For two whole years, no one was listening to them on radio. Television, forget about it. For two years I couldn't talk to a cab driver, hear them say 'Did you hear about the Expos? I listened to it on the radio – I can't believe they let that home run in the bottom of the ninth.' So all that was gone. So if you went up to any ten year old kid and said, 'Vladimir Guerrero.,' it was 'who?' Attendance went down. No one knew who the players were any more. It had a devastating affect."

It's of course intriguing, or laughable, how this tale of woe contrasts with the more formal accounts available of the same events. For example, "November 29, 1999, proved to be a historic day, as the League approved the change in the team's control person. Following the buy-back of Claude Brochu's shares, Jeffrey Loria was introduced to the media as the team's Chairman, Chief Executive Officer and Managing General Partner on December 9th."

Then again, Loria appears to be the sort of guy not even the pussy press can present in a positive light, at least not all the time, one who just cannot help upsetting people. Here's one report from a most respectable source:

"Cynics suggested that Loria had no intention of keeping the Expos in Montreal; speculation that was fuelled in June 2001 by his tactless response to an Air Canada flight attendant who asked him to turn off his cellphone before takeoff. 'No wonder everybody wants to leave Canada,' Loria grumbled."

Some British football fans may recognise the chairman of their nightmares in the next snippet:

"Loria made waves on the field, as well. He invited Maury Wills and Jeff Torborg to spring training as instructors in 2000 without consulting manager Felipe Alou, and a year later he hired Torborg to replace the popular skipper."

Alou was the Expos' manager in the now disappeared years of near glory of the early 90s: two seconds in the run up to the 'posthumously' awarded first place in '94, and another second in '96. His successor didn't last long in Montreal either, but he wasn't sacked: Loria was about to pack the club's key personnel up and take it with him to Florida. On February 12th 2002, the National League owners approved the ownership of the Montreal club by Major League Baseball. Extraordinary. Said the Commissioner of Baseball, Bud Selig at the time, "I am very pleased with the management team that we have assembled. They have long experience in the game and they are first rate in every way. Now that they are in place, they will have the authority to operate the club with complete autonomy." Selig, who the previous year had announced his express determination to contract the whole major leagues by two clubs, a move supported, it should be said, by twenty-eight of thirty owners, is part of the legend of the betrayal of the people of Montreal, but not according to Erik:

"I'll give Bud Selig his due. Some people have said he was just as big an asshole as Loria. Selig tried for two years to try to help Montreal. He said 'baseball in Canada is very important to the major leagues' and for two years he tried to find a buyer for the Expos."

Erik's view of Loria's exit to the Sunshine & Constant Air-Con State is a lot less charitable, as you might expect.

"Then slowly radio came back, but only one French-Canadian channel did about ten games. There's a conspiracy theory that he [Loria] was trying to create a dud team, so he could bring them to another city of his choice and make his money there. I've seen it alleged that Major League Baseball even believed that and actually said to them, 'we know what you're trying to do. We're taking the team off you, we'll pay you off.' And he was supposed to have said, 'Let's do it this way: I'll sell the Expos to you, but give me another team.' So they gave him the Florida Marlins."

Not quite give: it cost Loria $120 million to take control of the Marlins, but point taken. As part of the same deal, the then Marlins' owner was given leave to buy into the Boston Red Sox: one John Henry, with the whiff of the national pastime as a giant chess board for giant entrepreneurs.

Loria's reputation appears to have nosedived further with his move to Florida. When three key members of the Expos' staff decided to remain – he apparently tried to take the front office, coaching and scouting strength in its entirety – he immediately announced a $5 000 bonus for the movers, which elicited this response from 'a baseball official:'

"No matter how you slice it, the ownership is pure evil. There are a lot of good people in the organization, and it's a shame they've been put through this."

Jeffrey didn't quite see it that way. This was his assessment of 'Loria, The Canada Years':

"I'm very proud of what we tried to accomplish, I think it was a wonderful experience and we enjoyed the people in Canada. Unfortunately the market just didn't seem to be there."

In Florida, in 2003, the art expert had the last laugh. More pain for Erik:

"And in his first year he wins the World Series. It was like a knife through Montreal's heart. And we pretty much never recovered from that."

The story from there has been dismal. I couldn't understand why, when then the United States is not exactly a country without a bunch of billionaires, none of them wanted to buy up one of the mere thirty major league baseball clubs and lavish it with financial attention.

"It was damaged goods," according to Erik, "it was already an unattractive product; it had already passed the point of no return."

The downtown stadium never got built, due to the local government's unpreparedness to put up the necessary money.

"I agree, maybe taxes should go to hospitals rather than building baseball stadiums. But..."

But when you see local taxpayers' money funding beautiful new baseball stadia in the States, it breaks your heart when you think of your own team playing in a "concrete toilet bowl" (Erik's words).

World Series ring or no, fans of baseball still poked fun at Loria. Driving down costs, Marlins' office workers according to reports, were told they were not allowed to send faxes with cover sheets. This drew some inspired help from the minders of the *jerkoftheweek.com* website: they organised a charity drive to send reams of fresh white printer paper to St Petersburg. The way their Steve Hofstetter saw things in 2003,

"the Marlins are a young team with a lot of potential. They look really good on paper right now so we're just trying to send them the paper for them to look good on."

Funny as this all may be, it's doubtless no comfort for Montreal diehards. Finally, MLB decided that the future of the joint twentieth franchise in their history belonged to another city, another country and the end of Montreal baseball for Erik Janssen,

"I go home every year. There hasn't been a year when I haven't seen an Expos game. And now I won't be doing that any more; it's sad."

I told him that all things considered, he was holding up amazingly well.

"Well, it's been coming for the last five years. I'm used to it. I went back in 2001 for four games thinking that this was going to be the last time. It was grim. At the end of the last game of the season, the announcer didn't say, 'See you next year,' so I thought 'maybe this is it.' Then I went back in 2002 thinking it was going to be the last time. At the end I thought, 'let's just get it over with.'"

But did he not feel any fondness for the old concrete crapper?

"I used to say: 'when they detonate it, I want to be the one to pull the plug,' but now when I think of it, it's like a council house where you look at it and say, 'I used to live there.'"

Oh. And there was I half expecting Erik to still hold some feelings of nostalgic warmth for the old Montreal home despite everything. Then he takes me down a hole and tells me some of the grisly tale that is the history of the Olympic Stadium, Montreal. It was never designed for baseball, having been built for the 1976 Games and if that wasn't bad enough, had a roof that was so disastrous you have to laugh.

"It had a retractable roof," used for the first time in 1988, supposedly to protect les citoyens from vicious early Aprils and biting mid-Octobers, "but one time after it closed, it got stuck and they couldn't get it open. And it stayed that way. It was too expensive to fix it.

"The Olympic Stadium was a concrete toilet bowl. Winters are long, you had this ugly roof on top of the stadium, it was damp, it wasn't even a nice place to sit in. It was fine for what it was. Summers are short, when you go to a ball game you want to go outdoors. October, you need a roof. The fans would rather have a rainout than sit inside."

That roof was, the books tell you, the first ever retractable one in the world. In 1998 it was finally removed. In the year 2001, the average gate over 81 games was a shade over 7 500. And as if it all couldn't get any worse, Erik goes on, "Montreal taxpayers are still paying for it."

He was there for the last ever Expos game at Olympic Stadium where, projecting how I would feel if this was happening to my football team, I suspected it was a terrible experience.

"It should have been, and I should have cried, but, but I just wanted to yell at the extra 21 000, 'where were you?'"

Tony Batista (b. 1973, Puerta Plata, Dominican Republic, Oakland Athletics, Arizona Diamondbacks, Toronto Blue Jays, Baltimore Orioles, Montreal Expos)

Of all the 2004 roster Expos, Tony Batista is the one who most connected with the fans. He averaged .241 in Montreal's last season in the majors, more than ten points below his career record at the end of '03, but hit 32 homers and batted in 110 RBIs. A real journeyman pro, he came up in '96 with Oakland.

Here Tony Batista makes his final exit from Olympic Stadium, September 28th 2004, fans reluctant to let him go.

For any sports fan with any sense of what it is to be emotionally engaged with your team, what has happened to the Montreal Expos is way beyond sad. And as you may already know, if you saw the feature-ette he did to camera in September when he changed his Montreal cap for another, he still has a place of refuge, the Tigers. I was going to say, 'fortunate guy,' but then again...and his English football team of choice is West Ham United. Maybe Erik was just born to lose.

Nothing in the world of television is permanent except for two things: Coronation Street and the fundamental instability of all other programmes. We have *Baseball on 5* now but for how long, no one knows. The show has outlasted every other show the channel has put on since it began broadcasting in 1997. It has become a cherished thing in many, many British people's lives, as well as saving the lives of exiled Americans, of whom there are many in this country, who thought that to work here was to lose touch with their home summer game. Like Francis Ford Coppola, for example, who emailed the show a few seasons ago saying just that when he came to London to make a film. It gets better every season – although the start times seem to get ever more bizarre and insulting – and so ever more precious. So let us cross everything and hope that it stays with us. John Arlott said of cricket when the Kerry Packer revolution hit in 1978, "it'll never be the same again." This will equally be so if televised baseball lost Jonny Gould and the other key to the way the programme has become and is right now, the quiet, strong, guiding influence behind the scenes, Erik Janssen.

5

ANOTHER BASEBALL ESSENTIAL - CLOSING THE LITERATURE GAP

It's almost an insult to recommend books to people, as if they haven't got the brains or taste to go find good stuff for themselves. The excuse for the author is time: I've made it or got it and you haven't. So in the following pages, consider your cards marked for you and if you go out and buy something on the strength of what follows, I urge you to write a strong letter to The Times about the scandal of modern reviewing, I really do. As good a start to make is with **Bernard Malamud's *The Natural*. (Farrar, Straus & Giroux, 231 pages, $13 full price).** That is, if you're attracted to baseball because of the romantic mythology that goes with the game and its history and want to get your education really up and going.

The last thing you want to do is commit hours of your brain time to scooping up a pile of sentimental bilge. Attractive though Barry Levinson's heroic and perfectly monikered Roy Hobbs is, and as warmly and immaculately portrayed as he is by Robert Redford, the film isn't the book.

Without screwing things irreparably for you, Levinson's re-arranging of the narrative ending almost completely destroys Malamud's creation. I'm sure Bernard enjoyed the money, but must have beaten his brains out to see what had been done to his recreation of something approaching a real baseball of the middle of the 20th century. One can only hope that his death in 1986 at 72 had no material connection to the arrival of the movie in the world two years earlier.

The book isn't exactly brilliantly wrought: much of the writing is clumsily executed, but in among the flaws is the well-worked character of Roy and a cast of baseball characters chipped out of authentic 30s, 40s stone rather than cardboard. The morally warped who set up much of the slightly obvious - to us in the early twenty-first century at any rate (the book was first published in 1952) - are archetypes, but judging from the pile of non-fiction print I've happily waded through this past year, aren't remotely far-fetched. The background baseball detail is authentic too, so a read of this fast-tracks you entertainingly through the baseball rites and rituals of the time: the pitcher shagging of flies; the wonder of flood light; the crazy crowd rooters; the bird dog scouts in love with their protégés; the locker room grime and much, much else.

Aside from the absence of literary style, Malamud probably leaned too heavily on the staging posts of baseball history to that point: the emergence of Ruth and the 1919 Black Sox scandal for example, for his own good. But aside from the innocent pleasure of a decent yarn, the author's serious attempt to reach for the depth of the professional sportsman's psychological existence and the reality of his pain makes *The Natural*'s continued availability important and the book very worthwhile. His portrait painting of a ballplayer's existential struggle is also a handy lesson to you of how important baseball is to the (male) American psyche. You

have to know that about the game almost as badly as you got to know about Ruth, Gehrig, Johnson, Bonds, Shoeless Joe and.........

● ● ● ● ● ● ● ● ● ● ● ● ● ● ● ● ● ● ●

Cobb A Biography – Al Stump
Algonquin Books of Chapel Hill
1994
420 pages
Rating ⊘⊘⊘⊘⊘

If as a new fan of baseball you want to start making inroads into the vast outfield of knowledge waiting to be consumed, you could do a lot worse than choose to begin here. For not only will you learn much of baseball history in the early part of the century, from around 1900 to 1930, but you will meet one of the most extraordinary men in the history of sport on this planet.

If you think Al Stump is a pseudonym, forget it. My friend on the east coast of America tells me he knew a number of Stumps growing up in West Virginia, and there are scores of 'em in the Boston phonebook right now. Al was plying his trade as sports journalist when in 1960 he was approached, or rather selected to ghost the dying Cobb's autobiography. At this point in his life, not far from the end, the subject was violent, unpredictable and awful: as bearable as acid on the skin. But the remarkable thing is that this was the same Cobb who played out his whole existence on the earth, only slightly more so. He carried a gun for most of his life, the things he did caused almost everyone he came into contact with to hate his guts and he would, as one observer somewhere said, run to the top of a mountain just to fight with his echo. He was also a ballplayer of such magnitude that to many, he is the greatest player of all time, even greater than Babe Ruth.

I won't spoil the book for you by telling you more Cobb stories (apart from one) for they need to be approached and savoured freshly and alone, but I will try to give you more of the outline sketch. He was born in 1897 in a rural backwater in the state of Georgia and came into baseball from a wealthy middle class southern family. He came early enough in baseball history not to break records but to establish them, especially the batting average. This is the man who batted .300 minimum twenty-four consecutive seasons, most of them in an era when the ball seemed impossible to hit because it was scuffed, dirty and dark in the late afternoons. Where even talented others struggled against the odds at the plate, Cobb carved out hits by the hundred, spraying the ball seemingly at will to all parts of the field, and perfected what is known as "scientific baseball." He was absolute master of the bunt, the stolen base and the slide into safety at the base. The Cobb speciality was something that has died from the game: stealing home plate. For the uninitiated, this means running from third base to home while the pitcher hurls the ball at the batter. It should be impossible:

the catcher catches the ball if it's not hit (it normally isn't) and simply touches the runner with the gloved ball before he can get any part of his body on to the plate. However, in the Cobbian age when a certain amount of physicality was enjoyed by the public and indulged by the authorities, the art of stealing home was to either to be so fast and to slide so elusively that the catcher couldn't touch you in time or to smash into the catcher with the violence of a savage gladiator such that the ball fell from the catcher's grasp as he was sent sprawling across the dirt. Cobb could do both. Yet he was not a large man. He was just over six feet and slim; but he his thighs rippled with muscle and he was fuelled with an anger that was scarcely human, which, added to the competitiveness of a jungle animal, made him a foe (he was always your enemy) only the bravest would tangle with.

Here is a baseball plainly unrecognisable from that which we see on our TV screens today. Not only was Cobb allowed to make baseball the nearest sport has ever come to war this side of Rollerball,

The anger made him plain, stinking nasty. The source of it (I won't spoil that for you either) makes Cobb explicable, but troublingly, he was a mean little bastard before the event which undoubtedly changed his life forever. So here we have one of the world's greatest and most gifted sportsmen who was also one of its most cruel. On the park he played with psychotic desperation and fought men physically: players, umpires, fans. His spikes tore at fielders' bodies, not just their legs, his fists flew and his tongue was a vicious razor. The word 'extreme' only hints at what this man was like. Why, for those of a spiritual bent, did God endow such a man with such extravagant gifts? Tyrus James Cobb's story is one that reaches way beyond sport into the philosophy of man. For the story is more complex yet: Ty was famously mean with his vast wealth - not earned from baseball, not either by endorsements a la Ruth, but through his startling business acumen, accumulated *while* he was still playing - but this is a man who sent regular cheques to many ailing ballplayers he respected, year after year. Who endowed scholarships for poor Georgia children to attend college. What his rich, relentless and remarkable life teaches us is that we humans are anything but simple: that in the end we are not merely advanced animals.

Al Stump did a brilliant job (he died in 1994, just after publication). In telling a story like Cobb's, it's best to get out of the way and let the Man's actions and words do the talking, which the writer does. This is not easy. The subject is a gift, because the story is better than fiction and there is loads of it. So the art is in selecting episodes carefully and skilfully and laying them out on the page the same. Stump did it exceptionally well. And while many a book like this wilts at the end as the writer tires of the job, this isn't the case here. True, the Peach's later years rush past, but this looks more like commercial editing at work, not Stump boredom. The book is still a wonder near the end. At the conclusion of a fight at Cobb's house over a row at the dinner table, which sees Ty calling a guest's wife "a whore," the husband smashes a chair over our subject's head. The police are telephoned. "I think I just killed a man," the guest tells a deputy. "What's his name?" "Ty Cobb." "Yes," says the officer, "we know about that sonofabitch. It's a wonder someone hasn't killed him a long time ago."

Babe – The Legend Comes To Life
Robert W. Creamer
Fireside (Simon & Schuster) 1974
420 pages
Rating ⊘⊘⊘⊘

Another biography with a title there's no excuse for (If "Cobb – A Biography" was an attempt at clever understatement, it didn't work). "The Legend Comes To Life" sounds like third- rate promo copy for "The Babe," a terrible biopic, of which more later on other pages, which is unfortunate because this is an extremely worthwhile book. Creamer is a stalwart of the long established *Sports Illustrated*, is one of those old geezers who have more knowledge of baseball than they quite know what to do with, which is quite a wonderful thing when you're standing with your tongue hanging out for as much of the stuff as you can gets you can get it.

Like Ty Cobb, George Herman Ruth, aka Babe Ruth, was a magnificent ballplayer. Culturally, he was a phenomenon, swallowed up by America's beautiful desire to exalt itself. Like Cobb he was a man of extraordinary appetites: "Jidge" for food, sex, drink and the big hit, the Peach for mortal combat with his fellow man. For those wanting to know Ruth the ballplayer, this does the job pretty admirably. Creamer's full account of his rise from neglected son of a dissolute Baltimore bartender to uncrowned King Of Popular America is sober and steers clear of serious analysis. Or rather, like Stump, he just says "here's Babe Ruth" to the reader and leaves you to make up your own mind about the man you find.

There's a lot to be said for the clear-eyed, no nonsense narrative approach to a subject, especially where Babe Ruth is concerned. For the Babe is so famous even strangers to baseball in the UK know roughly who is. It's a good idea then to strip him down to facts and a few figures. In present day Britain where a culture of rampant speculation and swatting facts out of the way so they don't get in the way of a sensation or scandal, a quite hour in the evening with a restrained account of the man who revolutionised baseball is a fine thing.

One of the wonderful surprises of a fully sketched-in Ruth is to come across the facts of his pitching career. At the end of his Boston Red Sox career in 1920 he had a 93-36 win-loss record and left them on a run of 23 scoreless innings in World Series games. It's hard to imagine this when you know the distant Himalayan heights he achieved as a batter: the populariser of the home run - he hit a ridiculous 714 career long balls - 13 seasons with slugging averages taken to monstrous levels, batting champion in 1924 (highest batting average), eight times highest run scorer, 12 times scorer of the highest number of homers (2 of those tied, admittedly), highest total bases six times, RBI king six times and the highest number of walks eleven times (because hardly any pitcher wanted to pitch to him for fear of getting smashed out of sight). In 1921 Ruth hit 59 home runs with his new club the Yankees. The previous year, the National League home run champion had hit eight! Almost in a trice, the terms of the game were changed. Purists were horrified (Cobb at the forefront of them) as a new breed of batters came to the plate to wallop the baseball into the stands and bleachers. And they did. America was swept up in a vortex of extravagant baseball power (when you see your first live home run in a stadium, you'll know exactly what I'm talking about). Yet Ruth had been on the way to a career as a great pitcher? It seems that way.

Another scarcely believable fact about Ruth was his lifestyle. Times many he went out in the afternoon to play professional baseball, often against great pitchers, having been drinking and whoring 'til three or four in the morning. Sometimes he hadn't been to bed at all. He lived life like a man in a mad hurry to consume a record amount of material pleasure; he revelled in the limelight; he spent money as if Armageddon was around the corner and tipped like an Emperor. He was often overweight. He fought umpires with much the same gusto as he ate and drank. He was a walking metaphor for that optimistic, free-living America – ironically in the age of Prohibition – and oh how the crowd loved him for it.

The shame of Creamer's book is the fact that he doesn't take the risk of revelling in the life in authorial sympathy just a little. His writing lacks colour and warmth, and if any sportsman ever deserved a biographer to live a little in the writing of his life, it's George Herman. Much as Creamer is a competent man, he (or again, his editor) gets to the finish line with indecent speed. One minute Babe is hitting the ball out of Forbes Field, Pittsburgh over the left field stands in the dim twilight of his eighteen-season career (he was 42 when he left the game), the first time this had ever been done, the next he's dead of cancer in 1947. Creamer also leaves us with no summation, no conclusions, like the actor who dashes off the stage before the final soliloquy to go to the toilet. For a writer as experienced as he is it's highly peculiar and very disappointing. You have to go back to the introductory chapter – in what would have been the best part of the book if Ruth's life wasn't do damned fascinating – for a deeper sense of what Ruth meant to and for baseball and America. It's not as if the author is trying to be clever, trying to match the sudden demise of his subject: the last twelve years of his life dragged miserably as pro-baseball, the world he had dwarfed like Gulliver, kept the door shut on his managerial ambitions.

This said, there does not appear to be a better or more thorough biography of George Herman Ruth on the shelves, which leaves *The Legend Comes To Life* as a book that requires collecting and reading with care and, to be fair, no little enjoyment.

● ● ● ● ● ● ● ● ● ● ● ● ● ● ● ● ● ●

Eight Men Out – The Black Sox and the 1919 World Series
Eliot Asinof
Owl Books 1964
293 pages
Rating ◯◯◯◯

Baseball history covers only a short period of time: from about 1865 to the present. Just as you soon run up against Ruth and Cobb when you begin to cover (and uncover) its past, you won't get far before the name Shoeless Joe Jackson looms out of the mist at you.

Actually, he has loomed through a misty cornfield in Iowa toward you already if you've seen *Field Of Dreams* as many a casual or non-baseball fan has by accident (it's strange that in supposedly non-baseball interested Britain you get a lot of baseball films repeated on the box). This is a nifty little film that can slide past you comfortably without you being aware that it has anything to do with the real history of baseball. As we shall see later on, it's a book of a novel, but one which contains real players from a bygone age. And not any: specifically, we have Shoeless Joe and his anonymous colleagues. Collectively they form the eight outcasts of baseball history. They became known as the Black Sox, firstly because their tight-fisted owner Charles Comiskey refused to "waste" money having his team, the Chicago *White* Sox's uniforms cleaned regularly then secondly, devastatingly, because they threw the 1919 World Series.

Now here's one of the key differences between baseball and football – our football, not Gridiron: what do you know about English football in 1919? Who do you know that played the game then? Did league football continue during the war? Who won the league title in 1919? The FA Cup? I class myself a dyed-in-the-wool footer fan but I can't answer those last two questions. I can only answer the first and third. It has struck me hard over and over again studying baseball that we in this country haven't looked after the game, certainly not in terms of its history. English football history is dead and dying. Or remote and fading further through the eternal mists of time into nothingness. Yet go to baseball and thanks to books like this the events of the Black Sox Scandal of 1919 are as fresh and vivid as last year's Cup Final. More so. Books like this are almost ten a penny in the States, and in them, the History Of Baseball is lovingly polished like the old aristocracy's silver. And what a joy that is for the likes of us.

Asinof's terrific piece of work was published in 1964 but hasn't remotely dated (contrast that with Arthur Hopcraft's *The Football Man*). It is *the* book on the Black Sox. The author has painstakingly recreated a highly detailed narrative of events from the voluminous amount of newsprint devoted to the matter at the time and the Grand Jury and subsequent criminal trials of the eight men who supposedly sold out the Series to the gamblers. The story is involved enough to have you re-reading the odd chapter or two near the beginning to get a handle on the names of the dramatic personae, but this is no hardship as the text reads fast, don't worry. Indeed, the whole book flashes by. It's a gripping, grisly, awful story. The players are either filthy rotten cheats or naïve, country-boy victims, depending on your point of view. Expertly, Asinof pretty much disengages himself emotionally from the tale, which one can't help admire strongly, and you're struck in thinking about that how many really good baseball writers there are or have been in America.

My favourite thing about the book is the fact that giant of American sporting mythology, Shoeless Joe Jackson emerges into the light of reality a fallible and actually rather ugly looking man. There is a photograph in the book in the midst of the legal wrangles of 1920 of a scared, creepy looking man of about 40 with a thin face, a beaky nose and eyebrows so heavy they must have been pencilled in afterwards by a mischievous schoolboy. This is Joe Jackson. It's shattering but pleasingly so. *Field Of Dreams* has endangered the man's real past existence. He's in danger of becoming a sporting Father Christmas. Patently, he was one of the greatest hitters of all time. "Natural" is the word that crops up again and again. "The greatest natural hitter I have seen," said none other than Ty Cobb. Babe Ruth actually modelled his swing on the fellow leftie. Shoeless Joe hit .375 in the fateful Series without fully extending himself, deliberately. Despite the whitewash job that *Field Of Dreams* tries to inflict on us, the great man was in on the alleged conspiracy and so was run out of the game permanently.

It is virtually impossible to keep strongly felt sentiment out of the story, however. Awful though the thought of professional ballplayers being bent is – and they were as bent as the proverbial nine bob note – it's almost impossible to leave the book feeling as though these guys were victims. They didn't make much money from the scam, though gamblers made fat fortunes, and they were practically driven to their fate by the revolting curmudgeon that was Comiskey, the man that paid world-class athletes and sportsmen not a lot more than factory wages. By 1919 vast crowds were out watching the games – gates went on to double in 1920 – and the men of the 1919 White Sox were as loved and revered as any of our heroes in this country now. More so, in fact. Immorality might well be an absolute but for those who want to debate otherwise the Black Sox Scandal is a perfect crucible for argument. Weren't Gandil, Cicotte ("See-cot"), Jackson, Williams, Felsch, Risberg and McMullin driven to corruption by the miserly rewards offered by a greedy fool who treated these stars as serfs? And didn't the appalling Reserve Clause system which imprisoned them and the Ten Day Rule which meant the White Sox could terminate their contracts in the event of career-ending injury virtually plead with them to make this doomed attempt to wrest some of the rewards from America's Pastime? Because after all, was it not governed by an arrogant, class-bound bunch of Sonsobitches who lacked even the basic threads of humanity?

The tragic hero of the saga is not Shoeless Joe, but poor Buck Weaver, a working class man made Prince Of Third Base by his manager Kid Gleason, then crushed underfoot by not one bastard-bastion of new Baseball Commission authority but three. The lump in the throat is not just for Buck though, but for SJJ. Asinof, as if finally moved by his own unemotional storytelling, signs off by sharing with us the poetry of Nelson Algren,

"...Shoeless Joe is gone, long gone,
A yellow grass-blade between his teeth
And the bleacher shadows beneath...."

This touches the awful innocence of these men. Their leader Gandil was perhaps the only hardened proto-criminal, the man who tried to activate a deal with the moneymen initially, but most of the rest stepped into the corruption zone casually, with the opposite of street wisdom, as if years of professional baseball had separated them tragically from the working class streets and fields they grew up in. The Series lasts a long time too: they had time to lose heart, interest even, as the dollar bags failed to arrive. They were regretful and confused even before they'd gone down 3-5 to an inferior team, suckered by the real baddies: hard-bitten liars and cheats who they helped make rich who, when the law went looking for them, disappeared into America like vapour. Except the man who bankrolled the money the Black Sox did get, Arthur Rothstein, whose brazen self-righteousness upon his visit to a Chicago courtroom is utterly breathtaking. This is much better than CSI and all those other TV morality plays down the decades

where the baddies always get it. This is practically the stuff of Shakespearian tragedy, and it's probably the fact that There But For The Want Of A Different Place In Time go ourselves. We could so easily, in the same or similar situation, be Black Sox ourselves.

Back at the authorship of the book, this is essential reading, pure and simple.

● ●

The New Bill James Historical Baseball Abstract
Bill James
Free Press (Simon & Schuster) 2001
983 pages
Rating ✇✇✇/✇✇✇✇✇

So enough of biography for the time being; in a different literary world is this tome from the researcher-author Bill James. Now then: if you're coming fresh to the subject of Bill James, sit up and concentrate. I'll do my best to put this simply: Bill James deals primarily by using statistics to measure baseball performance, past and present. He covers the historical waterfront, right back to the days when pitchers threw sidearm and fielders stopped and caught the ball barehanded. This is before the birth of the modern majors in 1901 – well before. He is an authority on baseball statistics of sufficient magnitude for the Boston Red Sox to have him on salary giving both the front office and playing management Team advice.

The front office of an organisation does the trading for and of players. James will tell them exactly how useful anyone the Red Sox want to acquire is, has been and was. If they're interested in a 28 year old left-handed pitcher, James can tell them exactly how much they can expect from him in terms of performance, based on the average performance of 28-40 year old leftie hurlers over whatever time period the General Manager wants: last twenty years? 1950-2004? 1880-2004? Pitchers from the American League compared with the National, pitchers from organisations east of the Mississippi compared with west of the Mississippi, pitchers born in north of the Mason-Dixon Line compared with south, pitchers married compared with those who are single, those who went to college compared to those who didn't. You want any sort of data on players' past performance, Bill James will either have it or will get it.

This statistical approach was revolutionary: the tactics used by managers and coaches since the dawn of organised ball was entirely based on gut instincts – which most of the time means prejudices – and tradition: how to play the game was a body of unwritten rules or laws passed down the generations. In the 1970s James began to question some of these assumptions. Then he began to test them using hard statistics. What he found was that some completely entrenched views on how baseball should be played were based on fallacies: on thinking that was utterly incorrect. This meant that, in effect, most, if not all managers and coaches didn't know what they were doing. His key move, as I understand it, was to investigate the central question of what tactics produced most runs, a good idea when this is how you will ball games (true, you win by stopping the other side with great pitching too, but bare with me). In doing this, he tested one of the conventional wisdoms of the game, which said that the bunt is a useful tool to move a runner over from first to second base. This is good because it puts him in "scoring position" (see the Dictionary for meanings of these phrases if you don't know them), which is supposed to increase the team's chances of scoring a run. A sacrifice fly (high hit to the back of the outfield) was also deemed a good move. James tested the notion and couldn't find evidence to justify it. Neither could he find any support the completely cemented view that lefty hitters aren't very good against lefty pitchers. James found he couldn't support the notion that the batting average was the most important hitting statistic. Instead he discovered that the best thing a manager could do if they wanted to win ball games was to tell batters that they had to do their utmost best to get on base – anyhow. And once there, not risk a precious out by trying to steal a base. This elevated the importance of the walk. And not striking out.

Fascinating stuff. Well it is to me, and it was to a few others, but here's what makes this subject even more engrossing: here we are thirty-seven years later and James is still only in the early stages of getting people inside the game to believe that he is anything other than an idiot. James has won over almost nobody to his views and indeed, his whole statistical approach to the game of baseball. The bunt is still, in the game where the home run is more or less king, pretty sacred and "must" be used in certain situations, and the stolen base has made something of a comeback since 1977. The resistance is based on one assumption made by 99.9% of all managers, coaches and scouts across Baseball America: if you've never played in the majors, you don't know shit about how to play the game. And that being so, shut up, we're not interested in your opinions. The conflict here cuts across all professional sports in all countries. The same is true in football over here.

There is one gigantic exception to the near-totality of anti-Jamesness, who I'll come to in the next review.

James became famous and arguably important because his ideas spread among fans who were interested in statistics and to put it more importantly, interested in using a logical and rational approach to understanding baseball, mostly guys in universities and other arenas where stats were considered vitally important, like the world of high finance. This led to the setting up of a body of enthusiasts called the Society For the Advancement of Baseball Research and from this, the word "Sabermetrics," which means trying to unlock the mysteries of the game using numbers and a laptop (SABR is the acronym from the Society's full name).

But to get to this book itself: Bill James was also interested in evaluating players. So he came up with a piece of calculation for every game since the beginning of the major leagues: he calls it the "Win Shares" system. He has split the result of every game ever played into three and awarded a share of the win to three players in that game. By doing so, he has calculated every major league players' win shares in their career. He makes this assumption: the player with the most win shares is the best. The guy with the second most is the second best, and so on. It sounds dry, yes? The man isn't a fool, for he has allowed himself room for subjective judgement. His Win Shares Book covers the subject in immense detail: The Baseball Abstract also covers the subject of Win Shares too. It's a remarkable book and you must get it if you decide baseball's got you in its pouch and you can't get out. Don't worry about the number of pages; it's cheap (the paper's sooo cheap, darling).

So it is, but don't let this put you off either (I bought it via Amazon new for about fourteen quid and the postage was free).

My only quibble with the work is its unwieldy structure: it's actually two books in one. The first, of 328 pages, is a quirky decade-by-decade history of the game. This isn't your regular narrative: its laid out in a neo-fanzine style. The tone is light while James takes us through areas such as "How The Game Was Played," "Where The Game Was Played" and "Who The Game Was Played By" before delivering history "In A Box." This lays out each ten year chunk in magazine categories: Most Home Runs; Most Strikeouts By Pitcher; Best Win/Loss Record By Team; Percentage of Regulars Hitting .300 and many, many more. Here he strays perilously close to tabloid culture – "Most Admirable Superstar," "Least Admirable," "Slowest Player," "Iron Man" and "Most Handsome Player," not much use to anyone at all apart from weirdos who get off on sepia photos of ballplayers from the 1890s. The "Clint Hartung" and "Ozzie Guillen" Awards didn't mean a thing to me either, given that I hadn't the faintest idea what this duo were famous for when I first consulted the book in 2003 and still don't now. Ditto the "Odd Couple" category is lost on me. For a grasp of something called "Retrobermanisms" you would appear to need to be American, though judging by some of them, "Socks (If I May Be) Sobould," "Jim (Citizen) Kane" it seems to be an attempt to construct humour around the (punnish) similarity of old baseball players to famous books, films and sayings. They only go to serve – as does the likeness of baseball names to those Charles Dickens was fond of using – that Bill is to comedy as Thora Hird was to running the bases in major league baseball in the 1960s.

In embarrassing himself in this way, I can only imagine James is trying to act against type to try to lay waste the accusation that he's a boring anus who uses baseball statistics as a refuge from real life. As far as I can see this was totally unnecessary in the construction of the Abstract. If you want to know about baseball players past and present, you have to have this book. Two reasons: one, there's at least two paragraphs about the top 900 (in his view) to have played the game. So you're going to find out something about all the greats and some of those playing now. However, what James isn't here is thorough. He doesn't take the approach that you need to know all the basics about Ty Cobb or Cy Young for he assumes you already know it. A somewhat unfortunate state of affairs for the new Brit student of the game is this, obviously. What he delivers however is hundreds of wonderful baseball anecdotes. These are usually exquisitely quirky and colourful. Some examples: here he gives you a quote from Keith Hernandez on fellow Met Lenny Dykstra: " There's so much tobacco juice out there you can get cancer from just playing centre field. It's like a toxic waste dump." From Alvin Dark, Shortstop #27: "The Lord taught me to love everyone...I'm still working on the sportswriters." Ken McMullen's entry - Third Base #73 - is an example of typical Jamesian understatement: he just tells us about his (McMullen's) reaction to his wife's death from cancer: "'I took off a few weeks to get the kids straightened away...then I went back to work; I had to make a living; there was nothing else I could do." Nothing about Hoak and baseball per se, only this poignant little glimpse into a ball player's life.

The hotchpotch nature of the player sections: you never know what you're going to get from each to the next: a page of stats, a lifestyle insight, a nugget of analysis or a glib throwaway assessment: this: "Did everything well, but nothing spectacularly well, and was only as real good player for about four-five years" forms his entire entry for Pete O'Brien, First Base #96), is intensely frustrating. You know this guy could tell you most of what you need to know about everyone who's ever played in the majors, or feel he could, but he'll go, "90-RBI guy, trying to come back from his first off-season" and that's *it*! (for Travis Fryman, in this instance) And you wonder whether you can summon up the will to see the thing through. You do, I did, either because James has a way of delivering something fascinating in the very next entry (the Fryman entry is followed immediately by the McMullen one) or because I'm a sports nerd who should get out more.

Ultimately, I'd suggest that 1) the book is essential on your journey towards baseball-enlightenment and 2) if you meet James in person, you should administer the man a swift kick up the kilt.

● ● ● ● ● ● ● ● ● ● ● ● ● ● ● ● ● ●

Moneyball
Michael Lewis
Norton 2003
304 pages
Rating ⚾⚾⚾⚾⚾

The reason I'd gladly pick Bill up off the floor and take him out for dinner, or one of them, is that without Bill James there probably would have been no *Moneyball*. *Moneyball* is easily one of the best sports books of all time.

"*Moneyball*" is, as you may already have said to yourself, is a shockingly bad title for this book: it sounds like you're in for a truly terrible novel about God Knows What sport, or a volume of advice on how to predict the outcome of some national lottery. However, that's the only thing about it that isn't brilliant, absorbing or inspiring. This though, will depend upon your temperament. Your reviewer is a sucker for anything that's going to attack people who are a) rich, b) powerful and c) stupid. This is the heart of *Moneyball*.

Its hero is one Billy Beane. No, this is not a made up name. For those of who are unaware, this man is the GM (General Manager, see Dictionary) of the Oakland Athletics. He is in the process right now of proving an alleged fact which, for those who accept its validity, drives a titanically proportioned iceberg into the good ship Modern Baseball, to wit: you win by spending bank-loads of money. In 2003, the A's had the 27th highest (or 5th lowest) payrolls in the game, yet they won their division easily, for the second time in a row and third time in four seasons. Beane set the trend when he took up the GM job in 1999, employed to pull of the impossible: playing success on a small budget. Guess what: it's worked. For the past four seasons, they've made the play offs. The story is not so much this as how Beane has done it. I won't spoil the yarn for you too much: suffice to say it's been done by overturning whole swathes of the coaching manual, ideas so deeply entrenched in baseball culture and its history that they are more like sacred laws from the holy book.

However, they have only been overturned in Oakland (and to some extent Boston): the rest of the baseball world still rejects Beane and his co-theorists. Completely. Commissioner Bud Selig regards the Athletics' reign as Team Number One in the American League East as "an aberration." The rest have trashed *Moneyball* the book and the ideas it faithfully records since its publication in 2003. One might say that have good reason: Beane is in the process of making clubs realise that the way things have been done in baseball for the last century in terms of playing strategy are complete bullshit. Wrong. Seeing as baseball cultural history is partly about men of great wisdom managing and coaching teams on to victory Beane is a terrorist. So profound are the implications of what he's done in Oakland are so great as to virtually make the need for a manager completely unnecessary. Technical coaches for hitters and pitchers, yes. Motivators and psychologists: not required (we might violently disagree with this one). Managers? Well, though neither Beane nor author Lewis come out and say it, we might say on the evidence of BB's work in Oakland in the past five years, what's the point, they only get in the way of the team winning.

I apologise if I'm being wilfully obscure, here: read *Moneyball* and find out what I'm talking about.

What I like about it especially is that it's made me think about all the rules I live by: all the ideas and nostrums we take for granted. It's got me examining each one and holding it up to the light of reason and thinking, does this make sense? Why have we always done things this way? Is it because it works? Reason is the heart and soul of Beane's philosophy. He's taken Bill James and Sabermetrics, applied them to modern baseball and scared the shit out of the big wigs who own the game. He's upset Joe Morgan, the guy we hear on ESPN all the time (Morgan comes in for a lot of stick in the book). If this were the 1950s, Beane would be charged with being un-American. What he's done however is opened the door of baseball to fresh wind. He's going to cause more organisations to take up his ideas and baseball will change, or so it would appear, with the Boston Red Sox having been more or less converted to the Billy Beane stratagems.

As a piece of writing, *Moneyball* is admirably slick extended journalism. Michael Lewis is effortlessly competent, finding a clean spot for his tone somewhere between emotional and science-dry: he's detached without being bloodless. The text is so tight and well paced it's a very fast read. Lewis's decision to give you a story makes the pages fly by too. I like that he doesn't manipulate you by setting up false plot moments. He has fantastic material but he could have over-egged the pudding: he pretty much gets out of the way as an author and lets Billy Beane, his fellow religionists and his situation drive the narrative. So, in short, this book is absolutely indispensable for someone trying to get a baseball education.

● ● ● ● ● ● ● ● ● ● ● ● ● ● ● ● ● ●

Ball Four
Jim Bouton
1971
455 pages
Rating ⚾⚾⚾⚾⚾

I went into Sportspages in London's Charing Cross Road in 2001 when I first discovered baseball and asked a guy who worked in there what I should read to start off my baseball education. He said get a stats book, which I didn't, Creamer's biography of Babe

Ruth, which I did and Ball Four by Jim Bouton. Most of it went over my head because I understood almost none of the terminology. Furthermore, all I knew of baseball then was that blokes threw, fielded and hit and the team that scored the most runs won; and that there was a World Series to decide which was the best team every year. I was a first year infant baseball fan. But I still thought *Ball Four* was great. For this, like *Moneyball*, is a story of one guy against the baseball establishment.

Bouton is another iconoclast. Freak is how he was viewed by the baseball fraternity in his playing days – roughly 1960 to 1978. The ballplayer then (and it isn't very different now) was a guy who despised intellectual activity. A ballplayer was tough, macho, chased chicks (whether married or not) and could punch his way out of an argument when required. The establishment liked it this way, because an uneducated ballplayer could be exploited like a milked cow. A guy without education was one who didn't have the confidence to make a stand over his wages. Ballplayers *now* get paid vast sums of money, but in 1969 they didn't. They were trapped by the reserve clause that didn't allow them to sell their labour to the highest bidder like every other American and as a mob, didn't have the confidence or the gumption to unionise themselves effectively. The organisation held them down as little more than serfs. Bouton's book isn't about his fight against the establishment. *Ball Four* is Bouton's baseball diary for the 1969 season and it only begins with his holding out for more money. This just sets the tone. For the book is as more about the stupidity of baseball and its establishment, and their relentless desire to exploit ballplayers than it is about a washed up pitcher's struggle to stay in the majors by converting to the knuckleball.

In this book we also get a horrifying glimpse of baseball as Disneyland playing sports. The game is presented to the people of America via a media that colludes with the owners to sell it as an apple-pie nice, safe product. The athletes are all good, hard working people with great talent, heroes to be looked up to by all American boys (and some girls). They're an essential part of what makes America not just great but what makes America "America:" the greatest and most morally enriched country on the planet. Then along comes Bouton who writes a book telling everyone that ballplayers spend a lot of their time when not actually engaged in a sporting contest, not analysing their at bats but looking up mini skirts at the ballpark, spying on half-dressed or better still, naked chicks through motel windows with telescopes (when they can't get in there and fuck 'em) and taking amphetamines to get them to play better. He tells the world that guess what: ballplayers are just what you'd be if you were in your 20s or early 30s in an increasingly permissive age if you got the chance: a young guy full of the lifeblood looking for a good time. And Baseball went berserk when it came out, the public buying it in gleeful droves. Bouton was summoned by the Commissioner who demanded that he sign a statement to say that he made it all up: that *Ball Four* was all fairy stories. Just about every baseball writer in the country tore him (Bouton) to shreds for being a mischief-maker, a self publicist and unpatriotic liar when they knew damned well that every word the author had written was true.

It's pretty astonishing that at a time when its President was sending the fruit of American manhood off to maiming, mental illness and death while dropping vast amounts of napalm around

them on an imaginary threat to American way of life, the sporting establishment could work themselves up into a frenzy about a book that reveals professional baseball players as normal human beings. But twentieth century American Government and Big Business was obsessed with its own power, and keeping the masses in either held down in a state of cowed weakness or a state of ignorant bliss about the reality of that power always seemed like a pretty good idea. The irony of Bouton's problems with *Ball Four* is that as any student of baseball will tell you, the game for the first 50 years of the century was absolutely red in tooth and claw, played by guys who could fight like nobody's business, spat tobacco juice in the faces of umpires and who shouted obscenities at each other as a matter of course. The 1934 World Series winners were known to be almost ragged men who played in dirty uniforms. By 1968 every baseball professional was expected to keep up a cartoon pretence that he had the moral values of Superman. What happened?

Television and an increased fear of a world Communist conspiracy is what. Marvellous as TV can be, by the 50s, situation comedy and serial drama was, probably for financial reasons, keen to promote a fictional America where life was sweet, harmless and safe and where the baddie always got his just deserts. When baseball hit the screens its presentation had to marry with this image of America. Somewhere along the line, baseball writing, which at least until 1940s was often tough, honest and brilliant, had fallen into line. The McCarthyist 50s – you can tell I haven't studied this enough – no doubt helped cow the press into serving the power elites. In war, truth is always the first casualty – Britain is no exception until perhaps recently where the press barons rather like the idea of keeping a Labour government at the very least, honest – and after 1963, the United States was again at war. Seven years later, Jim Bouton gently pulls the lid off Baseball as I Love Lucy and the establishment, now used to control, can't hack it. Their thinking went like this: "America needs heroes: it needs its ballplayers to be heroes. Therefore they must be believed in as good American boys, loving their moms, being faithful to their wives and having a good honest run around the ballpark every day in summer. So Bouton, admit you made it all up to make money." Contrast this with the reaction of Baseball to the Black Sox Scandal: only a half-hearted attempt was made at a cover up, and by 1920, a Commissioner of Baseball had been appointed by the owners to clean up the game. True, the establishment was afraid or too contaminated by corruption itself to convict the real villains, the gamblers, but at least it was prepared to admit that the game needed fixing, so to speak.

Let me not suggest here that Bouton's book is remotely serious, preaching or grim. It's a lot of fun. However, he does tell a serious story. His is a season-long tale of the pressures and stresses of the ballplayer's life, which are considerable. The tendency of the major-leaguer to commit suicide had fallen away by the late 60s, perhaps because of the cushion of material gain and comfort for him, but it was still then a tough life. Bouton is trying to reinvent himself as a knuckleball pitcher at a brand new expansion club: the Seattle Pilots. His chief problem is not his arm or his ability to master the difficult new pitch, but that of the real scandal of baseball in 1969: the baseball ignorance purveyed and displayed by the manager and coaches. Not just Joe Schultz and the once great

Giants pitcher (now pitching coach) Sal Maglie, but, as Bouton trawls through his baseball past for us, those at most every other club also. The players, it is revealed, are taught the game according to the Book of Orthodoxy, a set of sacred informal rules, processes and habits which must be followed at all times and at all costs or else. Or else you fall out of favour with the skipper who doesn't call you out of the bullpen to pitch, or if you're a hitter, doesn't put you in the line up, not even to pinch-hit. Or you get effectively executed: sent down to the minor leagues, a place of oblivion from which the major leaguer expects never to return. The lack of sense in the Book, its lack of logic, of common sense, of science is something that startles us, thirty-five years down the line in the age of the sports psychologist, the dietician and the dominance of management as intricate planning, much more than it startles Bouton. The undoubted hero of Ball Four seems only confused or bemused by the lack of proper explanation for the management decisions which decide his fate and therefore dictate his daily state of mind. Though what passes for baseball expertise is utterly laughable for us in 2004, Bouton, nurtured in a world of The Orthodoxy along with every other ballplayer of his time, seems still to be emerging from his chrysalis of innocence.

Bouton's has a couple of acute difficulties with The Orthodoxy: his attempt to ditch his flamethrowing past in favour of the knuck is not so much not-understood by his manager as viewed with contempt. Real pitchers don't mess with a form of pitching considered by the coaching establishment as a form of witchcraft, not to say Communism: Real Pitchers Throw The Fastball. Then there is the debate regarding how much the relief pitchers should throw on a daily basis. The Orthodoxy has it in 1969 that as far as possible, the relievers should save their arms for the fray. Two issues here: one, the relievers often didn't pitch in the game at all so could hardly wear their arms out through over use. Two, when relievers did get into a game, they usually threw for an inning, tops. So why wrap them in cotton wool? A further point that Jim B. tried repeatedly to make to his coach Maglie was that the knuckleball takes nothing out of the arm as it's a fairly slowly thrown pitch (perfectly true); so he should be able to practice it every day without fear. Usual result? a look of complete befuddlement on the face of Maglie, the ex-Giant pennant winner.

Reading this constantly recurring problem, one is reminded of the madness in 1950s football in England where it was established in the coaching manual that players should train all week without the ball so that they're hungry for it on when a match starts on the Saturday. This seems about as clever as an idea as pouring petrol over one's own head and setting alight to it.

One of the best things about reading sports books is the way the best of them send out bolts of light which illuminate the connectedness of things. Baseball coaching in 1969 reminds us directly of Billy Beane's showing humiliation of establishment thinking in *Moneyball*, right now. So it that we gather an awareness of the awkward, not to say sometimes downright pathetic flow of history. In this case, its flow is like an awful treacle, with Bouton and Beane either trying to unstuck his boots from it (the former) or skating over the top of it in triumph (the latter).

So good is baseball literature that you can't help your mind tackling a number of highly important sports issues. For example,

the idea that sport can be somehow be separated from politics is hilarious. Bouton and *Ball Four* also proves that sportsmen can affect the way we think and the way we live as a society. The book is, was, an important act of rebellion. It may not have saved a life in Vietnam, but its huge audience was exposed to a vital lesson on free-thinking.

● ●

Boys of Summer
Roger Kahn
Harper and Row 1971
442 pages
Rating ⬭⬭⬭

This is one for the nostalgia hounds and for anyone who loves or is intrigued by the Brooklyn Dodgers. The book is constructed in three stages: first, the Brooklyn upbringing of the author mostly in the context of baseball with which he was obsessed, then his progress into the plum-est job in his world, covering the Dodgers for a New York daily newspaper and finally, his search for the team that won the World Series of 1951 in what was then 'today,' in 1975. The best thing about it is Kahn's childhood, where he tells his childhood story with delightful deftness and admirable elegance. We follow him into the adult world with a lot of enthusiasm because, basically, that's us crossing America with his (our) heroes being paid to watch baseball (football, cricket, whatever). The third and final section is disappointing simply because old baseball players aren't very interesting. When you consider that one of the old Dodgers he spent time with was Jackie Robinson, then you can only scratch your head and wonder what went wrong, unless you re-circle your way back to the original point that although Duke Snider might have been a glorious hitter boys at the time fell platonically in love with, as a retired sportsman he is no longer sprinkled in magic dust.

It's worth reading though and I can't say it wasn't enjoyable because it was. And the best pages of writing are very good indeed.

● ●

Once More Around The Park
Roger Angell
Ivan R. Dee 1991
£13.95 (import, Sportspages)
351 pages
Rating ⬭⬭⬭⬭

The guy who can take nothing and make it effortlessly interesting is Roger Angell. Most of the time anyway. Angell is one of baseball writing's institutions and his long end of season summaries are much awaited each autumn. This is not surprising when you read him because he is a writer with a big range. He knows the game but doesn't claim to be an expert. He loves the game very, very deeply, but isn't blind to its faults. His writing has little ego, but he is not afraid to make an opinion. He loves detail but his fondness and ear for a succulent anecdote means his work is far from dry. That's a lot going for you as a writer as far as I can see.

His style is gentle and loving for most of the time. He reveres baseball, worships it, and of course this rubs off. He also has a great eye for a subject. In this one of several collection of what are essentially essays, we are treated to, among other pieces, his superb reflection on the brilliant Afro-American pitcher from the late 60s, Bob Gibson, his accidental meeting in 1981 with an aged star of the early 20th century and my favourite, *Three For The Tigers*, an account of time spent with three middle-aged fans of the Detroit club.

Angell at his best produces writing that flows like a wide, beautiful, absorbing river. Like so many of his time – he's now in his 80s but still working – baseball is essentially a subject of romance, where the game has assumed gigantic proportions, reverberating and resonating with various layers and shades of enjoyment and meaning.

The only problem with an Angell is not his fault: if publishers wish to place his more factual accounts of the season just ended, it's not for us to carp at his letting them. But close play by play recordings of World Series that weren't particularly memorable are not so interesting, not for this reader anyway. They still have one benefit however: they're good tests of your knowledge of the terminology, and the placement of a dictionary nearby will be handy in helping you to use them to further your linguistic baseball education.

Also read by Roger Angell: **Five Summers** (Simon and Schuster, 1978, 411 pp, via Amazon 2nd Hand), which includes winter accounts of five World Series in the Seventies: 1972-76 as well as the usual inimitable Angell vibe. **Game Time** (Harcourt, 2003, 398 pp), another excellent collection to sit alongside *OMATP*, but watch out for overlaps: *Distance* and *The Web Of The Game* appear here as they do in *Park*. *Summers* has *On The Ball, Gone For Good* and *Three For The Tigers* which all appear in *Park* also, and it has *Scout, Sunny Side Of The Street* and *The Companions of the Game* from *Game Time*.

Annoying though this is, if you are or become a fan of his writing, it shouldn't be too much of a penance having to pick up all three and his other listed baseball works, **Late Innings** and **Season Ticket** and **A Pitcher's Story** (*Innings With David Cone*).

● ● ● ● ● ● ● ● ● ● ● ● ● ● ● ● ● ● ●

The New Dickson Baseball Dictionary
Harcourt & Brace 1999
579 pages
$20 (via Amazon)

I don't think I would have written this book without it including a dictionary, and I don't think I would have attempted a completely fresh and original dictionary if I had seen Dickson's effort. So I would like here and now to thank the booksellers of Britain for signally failing to place baseball books on their shelves thinking that there is not a constituency of Brit baseball fans out here gagging for stuff to read.

If you're looking for an outstandingly thorough work on the arcane language of baseball from the mid-19th century through to more or less now, this is it, according to one of my sources at Cooperstown. On the plus side it has over 7 000 terms, according to the blurb, but more than that, it has detailed etymology on each phrase where Dickson has found it or thought such a study worthy of the term. This is detail you cannot beat; the guy isn't messing. I also love the photographs, cartoons and posters. For these alone it's worth paying at least half the asking price. A

magnificent Ted Williams swing in 1948, an old Louisville pitcher wearing two gloves, a 1905 Giants scorecard, a shot of an unnamed team in clown outfits looking bemused and annoyed at having to promote the game in this stupid way, and so on and so on.

Where the book does fall down is its failure to record the language of the present day television broadcaster; many phrases in every night usage are missing here. It was first published in 1988 and by the look of it, Dickson has not been concerned about chasing up the organic development of arcane usages on the box. He may well have been more concerned with literary developments, I wouldn't know. But still, for anyone looking to build a baseball bookshelf this is indispensable – it's a magnificent work of reference one cannot but sit back from time to time and marvel at. And for anyone particularly interested in the origin of baseball terminology, you'll be creaming your jeans in no time when you get your hands on it.

● ● ● ● ● ● ● ● ● ● ● ● ● ● ● ● ● ● ●

Summer of '49
David Halberstam
Avon Paperback
336 pages
Rating ⚾⚾⚾⚾⚾

Notwithstanding the fact that this guy once wrote that foreigners were unlikely to understand baseball properly because you had to play it as a child as grow playing it, his famous *Summer of '49* gets a good review here and rightly so, I think. This was the first baseball book I read, about five years ago and I enjoyed it as I went along very much. Now I wonder why, seeing as I realise that I hardly understood what he was talking about. *So'49* is a detailed account of the Red Sox-Yankees fight for the American League pennant that year, so you get a lot of game description. So on page 250 where the author tells us, "Doerr dropped an almost perfect squeeze bunt" I hadn't the remotest idea what he was talking about, not having a baseball dictionary to hand (at the time), but anyway I didn't care. To be honest, back then, I was just as happy as a pig in shit to be reading a real live American book about baseball.

If you don't like re-reading books then, you're better off leaving *So'49* until you've watched a lot of games on TV and have done some reading to support that (you have to do that, I'm telling you). When you do feel like you have a pretty good grip on the game, then you will probably find it to be a gem. It's beautifully detailed and lovingly researched. It's slow, because Halberstam gives you masses of background biographical detail to the key men on each side, the likes of Casey Stengel and Joe McCarthy, the two skippers for example, and of course Joe DiMaggio, but it gives you much to savour.

Actually it's a remarkable book because of the depth of detail and the unflagging energy that the author sustains right through to the last page. Treacly waters they may be if, like me, you are using this as a starting off point for your baseball educational journey via the written word, but if you've grasped the basics and a bit more when you open this small, modest looking item, you're going to be able to savour a beautiful set of history lessons on the 1940s game.

● ● ● ● ● ● ● ● ● ● ● ● ● ● ● ● ● ● ●

Take Me Out To The Ballpark
Josh Leventhal
Black Dog & Leventhal Publishers Inc. 2000
128 pages
£24.95 (on import from Sportspages)
Rating ⚾⚾⚾⚾

When I clept eyes on this it was sitting upon a high shelf in Sportspages in Charing Cross Road (London) one afternoon whist I was on a raid. I thought at first I may have been stupidly extravagant shelling out twenty-five of the best for the thing, but a year has passed and this is one of my favourite books. Don't be fooled by the small number of pages: they're large and it doesn't feel, when you're leafing through at a leisurely pace at whatever time of day it happens to be, that you're reading a slight volume.

The physicality of it precludes such thinking: it's tall and wide, has pleasantly thick covers and is shaped like a baseball field – home plate in bottom left-hand corner – giving it a somewhat bulbous shape that doesn't go well with reading it on a train; you need to spread out for it.

For me, this is primarily a book of photographs, but what photographs! There are superb colour shots of present ballparks by the lapful, Three Rivers (Pittsburgh) looking gorgeous and Comiskey II ecstatic in a Chicago twilight, for examples, and tremendous images in monochrome of parks gone by.

Need I say more before you splash out or resolve to put away a coin a week until you have enough?

I suppose you have to love pictures of ballparks to want it and appreciate it and I do. I've loved football grounds deeply and possibly stupidly since the age of 5, so this book is tailor made for the way I look pitifully out on to life; it may not be your thing. But then again, an hour in its company may convert you completely. There is killer shot after killer shot in here: to open it at random, I landed on Sportsman's Park, St Louis, pages 84 and 85, and right here before me are three smashers: a black and white aerial shot, standard but great; a reprinted postcard painting from the 20s (probably) showing the bunting lined double decker stands in their best bib and tucker above home plate and third base line and a luscious zoom lens 60s colour shot from the bleachers of sundown over packed night stands. Additionally Leventhal provides facts, figures and stories a-plenty as standard: a no-hitter record from Browns days (it was originally theirs before it was shared with the Cards from '20-'66; the Browns left for Baltimore and became the Orioles after '53), Earl Combs crashing into a concrete wall in 1934 and the essential knowledge that a one-armed player, Pete Gray, played here and elsewhere 77 times in '45.

And here's the thing about this book: while typing the above paragraph I just noticed for the first time a small but beautiful b/w photo of the park from outside the empty stadium. Tiny but still remarkable and ravishing. So how could you not want fall in love with this book?

I suppose you could carp at the lack of critical tone. The Olympic Stadium, for example, gets off scot-free, as does the Vet in Philadelphia. The latter he dams with faint praise: one page coverage including only 81 words of text; and most of that is hopeful padding about special ceremonial first pitches. And then again, you see, with magnificent visual material at his disposal,

even the Vet page is a bit of a triumph with the selection of a nighttime colour image full of excitement and interest.

The other problem for Leventhal is the fact that park building is racing forward at a stiff march, leaving an attempt like this to definitively capture the sport's architecture imperfect. Conversely, it opens the way for volume 2 around 2007 if he can be bothered. Though developments in San Diego, Philadelphia and St Louis (not to mention those soon to arrive in Miami and possibly Boston and New York) are not recorded here, it shouldn't put you off a purchase; Josh has done the baseball fan a vast service in pouring several tons of love and a terrific eye for a telling image into this superb work. If you want to give a baseball friend a gift that keeps on giving, this is it.

● ● ● ● ● ● ● ● ● ● ● ● ● ● ● ● ● ●

The Politics of Glory
Bill James
Macmillan 1994
452 pages
$4 (Amazon second hand)

Whilst wading through the statistical details of the Hall of Fame players on the Hall's own website some time ago, I kept making this puzzled expression on account of the numbers of some of the players appearing to be somewhat unremarkable. Yes, so hitting .300 for eight consecutive seasons is excellent stuff, but a lot of these fellows' grinning faces didn't seem to be all that special in terms of their achievements. A year ago I was sufficiently in awe of everything to do with baseball in America it didn't ruffle my feathers unduly. I just assumed they must have had some magic about them that I, being a neophyte foreigner-Brit, wasn't aware of. There didn't appear to be room for very much detail about their baseball lives on the site so I assumed that their stirring deeds of brilliance were reposing in various books and in the memories of the octa- and nonagenarians still knocking about across the United States of America. It didn't occur to me that there could be anything controversial about their inclusion in the Hall.

One of the great things about Bill James is that he doesn't care in the slightest about using sledgehammers to break up the outer crust of baseball knowledge past. You feel that a wrecking ball wouldn't quite do as it wouldn't place the destructive implement right there in his palm. This isn't to suggest that he has a big ego but that his love of baseball and directness would mean that he would have to feel the dust in his face as fusty reputations go crashing down into oblivion.

I love Bill James. He's one of life's rebels who comes along looking like a harmless geek (you should see the picture of him on the book jacket here) but who in his search for truth throws down the establishment. Books are not guns though, or pieces of television coverage on prime time TV. I can't see James on a podium amid dozens of media microphones and flashing cameras brandishing a flaming draft copy of his latest book screaming "Down with the Shibboleths of baseball history! Away with the sham wisdom of managers and third base coaches! A pox on scouting lore!"

James, as you may well know, is one of the reasons for the Red Sox victory of 2004, so his statistical ideas: in simplistic brevity, that games are won by scoring runs which are scored by hitters getting on base as much as possible, so don't underestimate the walk! and that you can use the stats of the past to predict who is likely in your team to be successful and for how long (and how much longer), have marched along pretty well in the ten years since he published *The Politics of Glory*. Back then he wasn't so well known in baseball but had already been dubbed "The Mozart of baseball statisticians" (by the Chicago Sun). He was a plumpish-faced, bearded fellow who had self-published something called a *Baseball Abstract* back in 1977 and who had patiently made a name for himself through the clear-brained force of his own logic. He uses it in spectacular abundance here in this utterly splendid book that respectfully tears to pieces many of the choices of Cooperstown judges whose job it was after 1936 to bestow the status of immortality upon the greatest athletes ever to play baseball.

The Hall, as everyone knows, is the virtually untouchable cathedral of the game. Thus its Hall of Famer panel form a veritable if not absolute Sanhedrin of the sport. Bowing respectfully, James takes us through the history of the institution step by step, explaining that for various reasons, some right old mediocrities have been chosen by the various selection committees down the decades. Most tellingly of all, he accuses them of consistently failing to develop a sensible, never mind failsafe, set of criteria with which to operate their indisputably vitally important system. In fact, it would appear that up to 1994, the men who sat down each year to consider the weighty matter of Hall of Fame entry, the Veterans Committee and the Baseball Writers Association, were given a system to operate that didn't work (the latter) or worked with no plan at all; which inevitably meant that they depended upon anecdote, memory and reputation, not to mention prejudice, to enable them to make their decision. Some of the Hall of Famers, I won't say who, according to James, owe their places to the simple fact that the wise and sagacious heads had played with them. As in "He's great; you should have seen the way he pitched one time against the Pirates..." Apparently at times they made their deliberations wholly without the use of statistics; or that the stats that were made available were not considered to be of any great importance.

James does not describe the system as corrupt, just unorganised and unplanned. He just seems to think that at certain times in Hall history, the institution has been run by a bunch of stupid morons. For example, during the 60s he describes some of the decisions made as "appalling," particularly when Frankie Frisch, the ex-Giants and Cardinals stalwart apparently led the Veterans Committee into a policy of picking team mates, blinded by the prejudice of their own warm experiences of playing with the guys, instead of being logical and rigorous. The lack of sensible thinking on even a basic level must have driven such a clear and rational thinker as James to the brink of insanity whilst writing the book. He doesn't call Frisch et al as morons, but he implies it right enough.

The great thing about the author is the way he writes. He loves stats but loves a juicy, funny or otherwise illuminating anecdote just as much. He is a great writer in the sense of having an absolute command of his subject and laying out his words with a wonderful sense of enjoyment. It's easy reading, but the intelligence of the writer is huge and impressive. It's joyous reading, whether he's regaling with you with his depth of knowledge of the characters, some obscure, who have made up baseball history or slipping it across the powers that be at Cooperstown years ago by quipping that they changed the rules "more often than a hooker changes her underwear."

Just as you should not be put off James by fearing that you're going to be in you're your head in a sea of formulae, neither should you be put off by the age of the book The only problem here is that it may well be out of print so will only be available used.

So once again, here is a book that will add considerable amounts of flesh to the skeleton of your baseball ignorance. If you like a book to move at breakneck pace it'll annoy you, but if you're looking for something to soak up the long winter evening hours, this is the baby. I'm reading it again at the moment and I'm loving every line.

● ● ● ● ● ● ● ● ● ● ● ● ● ● ● ● ● ● ●

The Glory of Their Times
Laurence Ritter
Perennial/Harper Collins Enlarged 1992 edition,
originally published in 1966.
360 pages
$14.95
Rating ⦰⦰⦰⦰⦰

This is arguably the most popular baseball book ever written and definitely one of the most important. It's sold around half a million copies since it first arrived in the mid-60s, but more than that, it was so influential that it is argued – by Bill James and many others – that it caused a number of the players featured in it to be voted into the Hall of Fame by the Veterans Committee. The book penetrated the national consciousness as deeply as a book could possibly go.

It is also credited with giving birth to the love affair with baseball through nostalgia for the monochrome gladiators of the long past that more and more seems to drive 21st century baseball forward. Fine, but is it good to read?

Oh, yes. *Times* is good stuff alright. Here are names from a time way, way gone, real again in real and present words. Their emotions and memories have a sharpness to them that breaks up time to pieces. There is no commentary from Ritter, just yards of authentic oral baseball history. You can almost taste the dusty grass and touch the grubby bleacher bums in their haze of cigarette smoke. Above all, you can feel the love all these guys have of it all and perhaps, tellingly, above all, the glorious relief and joy in being asked, usually more than forty years afterwards, to bring it all back home to the baseball public through a 22lb tape recorder he lugged around the United States for six years and 75 000 miles.

One of the immense attractions of this book and baseball too, I think, is that its history is so intoxicating. Here is a book of 26 personal "how I made it and this is what it was like" stories but by some trick of the mind, though they're all very similar, the absorbing of them isn't boring, unless I am (quite possible). When each one starts, almost invariably with childhood after Ritter's dramatic editing (more of which in a minute), you begin afresh with the youth on the Oklahoma farm or growing up in the heart of Detroit, we're right there with the kid, wanting to make it. And when he gets his break in the big leagues and has to start mixing with Honus Wagner or Ty Cobb or John McGraw, this us too. These are all small dramas in which it's all too easy to take on their fears, their hopes, their struggles.

In one respect Ritter is lucky or careful with his editing, because all these stories are of baseball joy as opposed to tragedy. These ballplayers, to a man, made the grade and loved every minute of their time in the impossibly glamorous Big Time. These are all happy, life-affirming stories.

Ritter is famous for this book and won huge praise for it. Yet aside from the forward, he doesn't write a word. His editing though (if it is his) is acutely intelligent in terms of dealing with the potential difficulty of repetition. Take Stan Coveleski's opening:

"Had four brothers, all ballplayers. Oldest was Jacob, a pitcher. Killed in the Spanish-American War in 1898." It's very hard not to be gripped by that." Or the great Hank Greenberg's: "Lots of people were surprised when they heard I'd signed up to play professional baseball. Most people never considered me that good a ballplayer." You want to keep reading that, don't you. And Harry Hooper's: "Sure, I still follow baseball. *Of course* I do. What a question to ask!" Ritter realised or took on board somebody's suggestion to start like this so the reader would be immediately pitched into the middle of a conversation already flowing.

I would say further, that if you want to start a baseball collection from scratch, you could hardly do better than pencil this in as your number one.

● ● ● ● ● ● ● ● ● ● ● ● ● ● ● ● ● ●

When The Grass Was Real
Donald Honig
Bison Books
£13.95 from Sportspages (import)
320 pages
Rating ✪✪✪

This is "Son of *The Glory of Their Times*" only it isn't remotely as good. It has some big names: Cool Papa Bell; Wes Ferrell; Babe Herman; Johnny Mize; Lefty Grove and Bob Feller, but somehow it lacks the energy of its direct predecessor (Honig dedicates the book to Ritter and carried through the project with his blessing). Perhaps it only emphasizes what a tremendous job Ritter did, with a format that superficially looks as easy as floating on the Dead Sea: just find an old ballplayer, fire some questions at 'em which they reply to into a microphone, copy it down on a keyboard and hey presto! A sure fire winner!

Only it isn't as easy.

This *is* an interesting book, however and like *Times,* it has some lovely pictures, so I'll read it again. It just doesn't have the magic of its father.

● ● ● ● ● ● ● ● ● ● ● ● ● ● ● ● ● ●

Line Drives – 100 Contemporary Baseball Poems
Edited by Tim Horvath and Tim Wiles Southern Illinois
University Press
£7.57 via Amazon
207 pages
Rating ✪✪✪✪✪

Let us not end the book section with carping and moaning but with something beautiful and baseball: poetry. Come on now,

men: it's time for some of us to recognize our feminine side and enjoy another of life's many joys.

Anyone out there scarred for life by tortuous sessions on Shelley and Keats from schoolday English lessons can quit worrying immediately, for the American approach to the poetic muse is emphatically not prissy or pretentious. Most of the time, anyway.

I have to tell you: this is one of my favourite books, period. I was sent this as a freebie after I met one of the editors, Tim Wiles, when I beetled off to Cooperstown from Boston one day on a research trip for *Redemption*. I was more than happy to review it before I saw it, but having had to time to pick it up in those odd moments between everything else, I just love it and urge you to go and buy it.

How can I persuade you? Let me tell you about some of the poems I like. Here are the first couple of stanzas from Keith Eisner's *Shall I Compare Thee To A Triple Play?*

Yes, they cut down the flowers in the outfield, and the
*   flowers grow again.*
A miracle under out feet, every day, every game.
And the power that grows in the green grass grows in
*   you.*

Yes, the infield rests with power.
* On the clean dirt and over the base paths*
the air is sweet vibrancy.
You are tender and kind and hard when you need to be
*   – and I really like your thighs –*
and this has nothing to do with the baseball poem except
*   it's true.*

I like the sudden switch from the poetic to the everyday, just when you think you're going to get an overblown "baseball is America is life is everything that is true and good, etc" lecture. I like the unorthodoxy and the looseness of it and I love, actually, the way the whole poem develops from there.

Shall I Compare Thee... is very typical of the collection. As a breed the works here deal with and present the depth of importance baseball carries in America. Most of the poems manage that difficult trick: to be deadly serious whilst avoiding the crime of taking themselves too seriously. Instead they chronicle the weight of this love affair the country has with this game. Many do the job with a marvellous eye for detail, whether it's

My father, on the day he died,
watched baseball
Tigers at the White Sox, WGN,
as they wheeled him into ICU
*   (My Father On The Day He Died,* Michelle Jones)

or

In the first game
* of a twi-night*
double-header,
July 10 1947,
Recovering alcoholic
Donald P Black
of the Cleveland Indians,

only moments before
I slid safely into
the world,
fired a final
belt-high heater
that rookie
Ferris Burrhead Fain
waved goodbye to....

(From *Biographical Note,* by Jeff Worley)

The almost banal use of the everyday seems to run through modern American poetry just as the classical allusion, marvellous or utterly pointless depending on your point of view, runs through verse from olde England like blue veins through Stilton, and I have to say I like this fact very, very much indeed. The conditions of service the poets are able to work under, complete liberation from the constraints of traditional form and diction, seem so archetypically American and are used time and again in *Line Drives* to deliver absolute belters. Mary Kennan Herbert's *Night Baseball 1947* is a tiny poem but the image of her fluttering dress is as large and as beautiful as a mid-Western summer sky. Jim Daniels *Polish-American Night, Tiger Stadium* is reminiscent of *American Graffiti* but is deeper and more poignant and with its reference to Karen Carpenter, wonderfully free and open. Modern poetry has no apparent rules, the use of the sacred and profane side by side a handy tool used to new classic effect among the pages. There's

> *While we walked the wet streets we knew, the game was*
> *holy and the rain was sacred. We turned chairs facing*
> *the Travel Lodge window....*

from Mark J. Mitchell's *Minor League Rainout,* and

> *From an adoring, pink,*
> *intoxicated face,*
> *love shimmered, love radiated*
> *like equatorial sunshine,*
> *the way a lover's face*
> *illuminates the lover,*
> *the loved and the dark world*
> *in one strange, lucent moment:*
> *satisfied and thrilled, intense*
> *and effortless – as God*
> *regards us every moment.*
> *I couldn't bear it, I left*
> *in the fifth inning....*

from *In The Red Seats* by Andrew Hudgins

These excerpts don't do justice to the poems, not least because so many of them are beautifully finished off, meanings often left hanging, leaving us thinking in empty spaces, dwelling on the weight of what we've just read; of baseball, of life - the end-moods often heavy and threatening. If you want light, frothy, sunny poems, don't buy this book.

Baseball is displayed here as object of love and as a natural remedy for the ills and travails of modern life. What with poets often seeming to belong as if by right to the class of the educational

faithless intellectual, baseball appears as object of worship too: if you can no longer trust God to help you through, then turn to baseball, that eternally mystical sanctuary. The individual poems are beautifully confessional, usually dark and thoughtful, taking us deep into ourselves, as well as baseball. The climax of the final section deals directly with a poet's (Richard Behm's *Looking For A Baseball*) loss of religious faith and fear of death. That he finds solace of a sort in the American pastime will come as no surprise.

We expect, having seen *Field of Dreams* and *The Natural* and even *Bull Durham,* nostalgia and romanticism when Americans come to baseball. What is great here is the absence of it in its ghastly, *Mills And Boon-*cum-*Daily Express* form. Instead in comes with a clarity and simplicity of expression that hits the spot time after time. Here's just a tiny sample:

> *I let her drink real Coke,*
> *Eat Milky Ways and dance with strangers*
> *At 11.30 on a school night and still*
> *Ninety minutes from home*
> *(Karen Zaborowski, World Series Game 5)*

> *Jimmy Foxx died an alcoholic*
> *in a skidrow hotel*
> *room.*
> *Beau Jack ended up shining*
> *shoes,*
> *just where he*
> *began.*
> *(Charles Bukowski, Betting On The Muse)*

> *Somebody should drop*
> *a cold mountain on the car*
> *right now, bury me*
> *with the shutout.*
> *(Maj Ragain, Blyleven's Fourth Shutout, June 1985)*

The above excerpts represent a mere fraction of what's on offer. Poetry shorn of the ornate and the fussy may be too plain for you, but for me it has a cleanliness I find irresistible.

I suppose precise, sharply defined verse can become plain dull, but the editors have a great ear for picking the best. So there are a couple of poems here where the clarity of wordplay is well in evidence, but the meaning memorably unclear. Richard Brautigan's *A Baseball Game* starts like this:

> *Baudelaire went*
> *to a baseball game*
> *and bought a hot dog*
> *and lit up a pipe*
> *of opium.*

This might be a real Cooperstown poem: the winters are long in upstate New York and to endure them, flights into fancy via the mystery of substance use may be one of the local verities, for all I know. Whatever, Brautigan's short poem continues and ends brilliantly, and gives me the opportunity of making the point that the variety within the collection is considerable. There is a tedious and tenuous link from Mitchell to the gravest poem here, Dale Ritterbusch's *World Series 1968, South-East Asia.* Among other

6

THE MAJOR LEAGUE BASEBALL CLUBS

When I first started following baseball, getting to grips with the thirty clubs (I was soon to learn that I should have been saying "organisations" or "franchises" and that it should be "ballclub," never "club") and their names seemed nigh on impossible. The Sunday night highlights would sweep through the Florida Marlins, the Tampa Bay Devil Rays, the San Diego Padres and the rest so quickly that by the end of the night I was sure that the San Marlin Sharks had earlier beaten the Baltimore Brewing Devils 8-3. If you're anything like I was and your baseball obsession is just in its infancy, I hope this section will help. For the more advanced and for those with geeky tendencies (that I share, don't fret), I hope you'll find this part of the book handy too. The thirty ball clubs are placed in alphabetical order. I just thought it better that way.

Notes:
1. 2004 Statistics. All 1-30 positions worked out by the author. All "At Bat per" and figures calculated by the author from the widely available base sources of information available on the Internet.
2. All statements of opinion must be blamed on the author.
3. All Hall of Fame summaries are the original work of the author.
4. All rankings and ratings ditto, except where stated.
5. Attendance increase/decreases expressed as change to average attendance, not aggregate.
6. Hall of Fame Player Ratings: BJ = Bill James, arguably the best, certainly the most interesting stats analyst around. In paragraph entry, ratings are those in his Baseball Abstract 2001 edition, as are his Top 100 ratings. In the "Top 100" Ratings info, "BJ10" means the player is 10th in Bill James' top 100 players of all time in the Abstract. "SN10" is the Sporting News version and "SABR10" is the Society For The Advancement of Baseball Research's version of same.
7. In counting the number of Division titles won, the four 1981 Division Series winners have each been awarded a division.
8. The American spelling for our centre, 'center' has been used where relevant to ball parks. I recently heard a British sports hack on Radio 5 taking exception to the 'Boston Red Sox' not being called the 'Boston Red Socks' in a typical display of arrogance and ignorance.
9. See separate chapter "Some Sort Of Pecking Order" for details of how "Total Historical Rating" was worked out.
10. All pitchers and batters are right-handed except where an 'L' appears.

• •

Continued from page 91 . . .

directions of thought, this takes you down the one that most blokes with a rack of educational qualifications as well as an obsession with team sports have travelled - those who haven't wiped half their brain cells away through drinking – the one about sport essentially being a complete waste of time. Happily most of us don't have to worry about the matter of returning from the trauma of jungle combat. It's bad enough that one can find oneself waking in a cold sweat in the dark hour before a winter dawn with the sudden realisation that our tribal love for the favourite club is essentially a completely fruitless waste of time.

On the other side of the world
he begins,
it don't mean nothin' –
the slow tedium of the pitcher
holding the ball in both hands

This is such a beautiful and disturbing poem that committing yourself to a year or two of meaningless absorption in baseball (or football) suddenly seems absolutely the only thing to do. There are demons out there after all that need to be constantly kept at a safe distance.

The virtue of making poetry real and rooted in the everyday is a lesson driven home throughout the book. Such cleaning and polishing as has been done by these poets serve only to present their great thoughtfulness, their love - of people, of things and of words, as well as baseball – and their endless search for meaning in the world. So it's not true to say that this is a great book of baseball poetry, but that it's a great book of poetry with baseball as the leading common denominator. It's such a good book I could go on and on for pages. So good that I've easily written this revue without being able to get around to mentioning my favourite five or six poems at all: the one about the woman on the beach; the one called *How To Hit A Home Run* and the one about Geronimo.

ANAHEIM ANGELS

Anaheim, California

SINCE 1961

AMERICAN LEAGUE   WEST DIVISION

NAME CHANGE HISTORY

California Angels 1961-64- Los Angeles Angels 1965-96 Anaheim Angels 1996-2005

Honours

World Series Champions	2002
Division Winners	1979, 1982, 1986 & 2004
Division Series Winners	2002 (via Wild Card)
Championship Winners	2002
World Series Win	**Manager**
2002 – v. San Francisco Giants 4-3	Mike Scioscia

"Grantland Rice, the great sportswriter once said, 'It's not whether you win or lose, it's how you play the game.'
Well Grantland Rice can go to hell as far as I'm concerned."

Gene Autry, owner of the Anaheim Angels.

Season   2004

American League MVP Award Winner: Vladimir Guerrero

Payroll 2003/2004	$83m (13)/ $102m (3)
Highest Paid Players	**Starter**
Vladimir Guerrero (OF)	$11m
Bartolo Colon (P)	$11m
Kevin Appier (P)*	$10.5m
Troy Glaus (3B)	$10.45m
Tim Salmon (OF)	$9.9m
Aaron Sele (P)	$8.66m
Troy Percival (P)	$8m
Garret Anderson (OF)	$6.25m
Kelvim Escobar (P)	$5.75m
Jarrod Washburn (P)	$5.45m

*Traded to Royals 2003

2004 Team Statistics

Position in Div	1st of 5
Record	92-70
Games Back	+ 1
% Record	.568 (6th=)
Split	45-36 **H**; 47-34 **R**
Last 10 Seasons	2422433221
Runs per game	**5.16** (10th)
Staff ERA	**4.28** (13th)
Ave ERA Starters	**4.70** (16th)
Ave ERA Relievers	**3.47** (4th)
Batting ave.	**.282** (1=)
Slugging ave.	**.429** (17th)
On Base %:	**.341** (13th)
AB per Hit	**3.54** (2nd)

Total/Net Homers	162/170 (**-8** 19th)
AB per HR	**35.03** (20th)
AB per SO	**6.02** (4th)
Runs For/Against	**836** (10) **734** (10)
Net Runs	**102** (6th)
Net BB/BB p AB	**-52/12.70** (29th)
Total Steals	**143** (1st)
Total Errors	**90** (7th)
Unearned Runs Given	**42** (4th)
Record Attendance:	See 2004
Attendance. 2003	3 061 090 **Ave** 37 791
Attendance 2004	3 375 677 **Ave** 41 675
	(3rd) 10,27% increase

2004 Starting Rotation:

Starter	Starter
Bartolo Colon	34: 18-12, 5.01 ERA
Kelvin Escobar	33: 11-12, 3.93 ERA
John Lackey	32: 14-13, 4.67 ERA
Jarrod Washburn	25: 11-8, 4.64 ERA
Aaron Sele	24: 9-4, 5.04 ERA
Russ Ortiz	14: 5-7, 4.43 ERA
Closer	
Troy Percival	33/38 SV, 2.90 ERA
Bullpen Star	
Francisco Rodriguez	('K-Rod' 12/19 SV,
1.82 ERA 133 K's	
Catcher	
Benji Molina* 97g	.276, 10HR, 54 RBI
Jose Molina 73g	.261, 3HR, 21 RBI

*Allegedly the 'slowest runner in baseball'.

Briefly ... The "Halos" were one of the first two expansion franchises in tandem with the Minnesota Twins in 1961. Their name has shifted uncomfortably, but "Anaheim" seems to be permanent (though you never know). Their playing record is mediocre to poor but they won a Series from a Wild Card position in 2002. The owner for years was actor Gene Autry whose "baby" the club originally was. Sadly before he could see his team win a Series: he died, in 1998.

2004 A magnificent second half for the boys saw them overhauling a strangely off-colour Oakland A's in the final weeks of the season, only for the Red Sox to then maul them 0-3 in the AL Division Series. Soundly beaten in the first two on home turf by big pitching and bigger hitting, a Guerrero grand slam comeback in the third, squaring things at 6-6 in the seventh came to nought as the Sox bullpen silenced the Angel bats again. This enabled David Ortiz to hit a 10th inning walk-off homer from Washburn's first pitch. Scoscia had just pulled K-Rod immediately after striking out Ramirez – claiming his man was tiring. Had K-Rod stayed in and the Angels made it 1-2, would they have taken two more?

Optimists will have been gnawing on that thought all winter, especially in the light of what the Sox later did to the Yanks. The suspension of Jose Guillen in the last week of the regular season for attitude problems will also nag at the brain. Would his bat have made the difference against the Beantown Mob or was the ballclub better off without him? We'll never know. In the end, despite all that money spent, the pitchers didn't do a good enough job.

Uniforms: Home – White shirts with red "Angels" lettering, red number under heart, red undershirts, white pants with red side stripe, red caps with halo logo (Alt: White sleeveless shirts with red sleeve inside edging). **Road –** Same configuration in grey.

Owners(s): Arturo Moreno **GM:** Bill Stoneman. **Manager: Mike Scioscia** has been manager of the Angels since 2000. He wears 14 and was 46 in November 2004. Has an overall 425/385 record (.525). This is his first major league managerial job and he has made a tremendous start, what with the unexpected 2002 triumph. He was a shoe-in for a Manager of the Year that season. He became the 17th man to win a World Series as both player and manager. After thirteen years catching for the Dodgers, he came up through their coaching ranks as a third base and bench guy before piloting their triple-A outfit, the Albuquerque Dukes. (Own career: 1441 games. Lifetime .259, 68 homers. Retired 1992).

Home - Angel Stadium (Gr) (recently 'Edison Field' until Dec. '03) is a renamed Anaheim Stadium, which opened in 1966 with the team named the California Angels (Result: loss to the White Sox 1-3 on April 19 in front of 31 360). The Angels previously played at Wrigley Field (Los Angeles) for one year, then shared Dodger Stadium 1962 through 1965 (First game at Wrigley on April 11: 2-7 to the Baltimore Orioles 7-2). **Capacity is 45 050.**

The present park is asymmetrical. Dimensions: 330' to the left and right field poles and 400 dead to center. Left-center is 387 compared to 370 in center-right, so the park is a little better for left-handed hitters. **Pitcher's Park (slight advantage).**

"Fancy That": Angel Jarrod Washburn sent Mariner Ichiro Suzuki a package of deer meat mid-September as a gift in return for an autographed bat Ichiro supplied for JW earlier in the season.

World Series And Post-Season Ratings	Position	Points/Occasions/%	
Full Playing Record 1961-2004	**14**	3412-3586: .487	
Total Historical Rating	21	N/A	
World Series Rating	22=	32 Ranking Points	
Play Offs Rating	20	41 Ranking Points	
Pennant Wins (pre-69)	17 (& last)	0	
Division Wins (post-69)	20=	3	
World Series Wins/Appearances/Games Won	19=/22=/21=	1/1/4	
Level Of Recent Success		**Won/Lost**	
Games Won Per Season Post-69	17	75.2	
Seasons Since A World Series Appearance	2	2002 beat SF Giants 4-3	
Seasons Since A Division Series	0	2004 Lost to Boston 0-3 2002 Beat NYY 3-1	
Seasons Since A Championship Series	2	2002 Beat Twins 4-1	
Since A Division Win	19	1986 – Won ALW by 5 games	

RATINGS

Most Home Runs Hit For The Angels	Most Games Won By A Pitcher
Season: 47 Troy Glaus 2000	Season: 22 Clyde Wright 1970; Nolan Ryan 1974
Career: 269 Tim Salmon	Career: 165 Chuck Findlay
Highest Batting Average	**Most Strikeouts**
Season: .355 Darin Erstad 2000	Season: 383 Nolan Ryan 1973
Career: .314 Rod Carew	Career: 2 416 Nolan Ryan

RECORDS

Best Batting Ave. 2004 Vladimir Guerrero .337	**Most Home Runs 2004** Vladimir Guerrero 39
RBI Leader Guerrero 126	**Most Bases** Guerrero 366
Most K's Kelvim Escobar 191	**Most HR Given Up** Bartolo Colon 38
Most Innings Pitched Escobar/Colon 208.1	**Most Walks** Escobar 76
Other Top Bats: Chone Figgins, .296, 171h, Jose Guillen, .294, 104 RBI. Garret Anderson, .301	

2004

Angels Hall Of Famers

Officially there are no Angels Hall Of Famers in the gallery wearing an Angels cap, but it would be churlish not to write something about Nolan Ryan right here seeing as he played 8 winning seasons with the franchise. He was here from 1972 to '79 and won twenty games twice. His overall record was 138-121. That said he had a similar record with the Astros, with whom he spent eleven seasons (106-94). He went only 51-39 as a Ranger over his final five seasons in a career remarkable for its longevity – 28 seasons – but it is that club's hat he wears in the gallery at Cooperstown.

Retired Uniform Numbers

11 Jim Fregosi	26 Gene Autry	29 Rod Carew
30 Nolan Ryan		50 Jimmie Reese

AAA Salt Lake Stingers   **Spring Training Venue:** Tempe Diablo Stadium, Tempe, Arizona

Randy Johnson
b. 1963, Walnut Creek, California. (Montreal Expos, Seattle Mariners, Arizona Diamondbacks & New York Yankees) Here The Big Unit is pointing to The Boss to thank him for arriving in the 4000 strikeout club, there to join Nolan Ryan, Steve Carlton and Roger Clemens. Last season he pitched only the 17th perfect game in baseball history, at 41 years of age. A true phenomenon. He memorably took the Diamondbacks to a World Series victory in 2001 in tandem with Curt Schilling.

ARIZONA DIAMONDBACKS

Phoenix, Arizona

SINCE 1998
NATIONAL LEAGUE WEST DIVISION

Honours

World Series Champions	2001
Division Winners	1999, 2001 & 2002
Division Series Winners	2001
Championship Winners	2001*

*Qualified for Play Offs via Wild Card

World Series Win	Manager
2001 – v. New York Yankees 4-3	Bob Brenly

"A baseball manager is a necessary evil."

Sparky Anderson.

Season 2004

Payroll 2003/2004	$93m(10) $70m (13)
Highest Paid	**Salary**
Randy Johnson	$16.5 m
Richie Sexson (1B)	$8.72m
Luis Gonzalez	$8.25m
Matt Mantei (P)	
(injured after May);	$7m
Steve Finlay	
(To Dodgers July '04)	$7m
Elmer Dessens (P)	
(To Dodgers mid-season);	$4m
Danny Bautista (OF)	$4m
% 25 Roster on less than $1m: 52.	

2004 Team Statistics

Position in Div	5th of 5
Record	51-111
Games Back	42
% Record	.315 (30th)
Split	29-52 **H**; 22-59 **R**
Last 7 Seasons	5131135
Runs per game	**3.18** (30th)
Staff ERA	**4.98** (27th)
Ave ERA Starters	**5.15** (24th)
Ave ERA Relievers	**4.68** (25th)
Batting ave	**.253** (26th)
Slugging ave.	**.393** (28th)
On Base %:	**.310** (30th)
Hits per AB	**3.95** (26th)
Total/Net Homers	135/197 (*-62* 29th)
AB per HR	**41.06** (29th)

S'out/At Bat Ratio	**5.42** (13th)
Runs For/Against	**615** (30) **899** (27)
Net Runs	**-274** (30th)
Net BB/BB p AB	**-247/12.57** (29th)
Total Steals	**53** (26th)
Total Errors	**139** (29th)
Unearned Runs Given	**105** (30th)
Record Attendance	1998: 3,600,412.
Finished 5th. 1st season in majors.	**Ave:** 44 450.
Attendance. 2003	2 805 542 **Ave** 34 636
Attendance 2004	2 519 560 **Ave** 31 105 (14th)
10.2% decrease	

2004 Starting Rotation:

Starter	Record
Randy Johnson	35: 16-14, 2.60 ERA
Brandon Webb	35: 7-16, 3.59 ERA
Casey Fossum	27: 4-15, 6.65 ERA
Steve Sparks	18: 3-7, 6.04 ERA
Jeff Fassero	12: 12-4, 3.44 ERA
Casey Daigle	10: 2-3, 7.16 ERA
Edgar Gonzalez	10: 0-9, 9.32 ERA
Closer	
Greg Aquino	15/18 SV 3.06 ERA
Jose Valverde	8/10 SV 4.25 ERA
Bullpen Star	
Elmer Dessens	2.03 ERA*,
*but traded to Dodgers.	Then Greg Aquino
Catcher	
Robby Hammock 62g	.241, 4HR, 18 RBI
Juan Brito 54g	.205, 3HR, 12 RBI

Briefly... Baseball in the desert. Huge early success: World Series winners in 2001 over the Yankees, led by the fabulous pitching of Curt Schilling and Randy Johnson; three first places in first seven seasons, unusual and remarkable. Budget cuts cost competitiveness in 2004, but the mooted July trade of the Big Unit to the Yankees failed to materialise, allowing Johnson to give D'backs fans another marvellous season, including his perfect game on 18th May, the 17th in baseball history against the Atlanta Braves in Turner Field. At 40, he became the oldest pitcher ever to make this achievement.

Uniforms: Home - White sleeveless jersey with purple pinstripe, purple undershirts. 'A' Diamondback logo on left breast, no lettering; white pants with purple pinstripe; purple caps with jade 'A' D'back logo in the form of a diamondback snake. **Road** - Grey sleeveless pinstripe shirts with purple undershirt, grey pinstripe pants, "Arizona" letters. **Alt -** Black short-sleeved shirts with "Arizona" letters in purple with white surround and snake pattern sleeve edging.

GM: Joe Garagiola Jr. **Previous Manager:** Bob Brenley began the '04 season as skipper but was fired July 2nd with a 29-50 record. He'd taken the D'backs to a fabulous World Series victory in his first season, and parted company with a 303-262 Record (.536).Venezuelan **Al Pedrique**, third base coach, took over for the remainder of the season. He went 22-61, which means there was nothing he could do with the injury ravaged and talent depleted team either. **Present Manager** is **Bob Melvin**, who fairly bizarrely was looked over for the job after an interview in late October in favour of Wally Backman, before being offered the job four days into the Backman era on account of some murky legal stuff concerning the Wallster. Huh? Exactly. Anyhow, Melvin was bench coach during the successful Brenly regime and is back as skip following two years without glory in Seattle. Will it work? We'll see soon enough. So long then, Bob Brenly, now ex-D'back legend. There's a great story about him I just read in Roger Angell's magnificent book, *"Once More Around The Park"*, where in a game for the Giants against the Braves at Candlestick Park in September 1986 he made four fielding errors in one inning, the fifth, costing his side four runs. This mostly involved his standing at his post, third base, experimenting with a new hybrid sport that crosses baseball with our football. But he then went up to the plate with the bat and hit two home runs and a single that brought in a couple of runners. It should be noted too that his second homer was in the bottom of the ninth with the scores tied, two men out and with the count at 3 and 2.

Home: Bank One Ballpark (Gr-Ret Roof) - Situated in the city of Phoenix out in the western desert, since March 31 1998 this has been the one home of expansion team the Arizona Diamondbacks. The inaugural game was played in front of 50 179 fans. **Capacity: 48 500.** The colossal, cathedral of a park is almost perfectly symmetrical, shaped in straight angled lines, in from the foul poles at 328' and 335' respectively to form a flat head in center at a 407' distance. At the angles in center-left and center-right, the distances are 412' and 414'. Known as 'The Bob,' this is the second highest park above sea level in the majors (behind Colorado). Cost of the whole shebang was $354 million. The turf is Bull's Eye Bermuda, which is also the name of a lethal cocktail beloved of thrash metal crowd surfers out of the Seattle area. **Hitter's Park.(clear advantage).**

World Series And Post-Season Ratings	Position	Points/Occasions/%
Full Playing Record 1998-2004	**8**	575-559: .507
Total Historical Rating	15=	N/A
World Series Rating	21=	70 Ranking Points
Play Offs Rating	21	29 Ranking Points
Division Wins	20=	3
World Series Wins/Appearances/Games Won	19=/22=/21=	1/1/4
World Series Wins	11=	1
World Series Appearances	28=	1
Level Of Recent Success		**Won/Lost/Games**
Games Won Per Season Post-69	**18=**	75
Seasons Since A World Series Appearance	3	2001 beat NYY 4-3
Seasons Since A Division Series	2	2002 lost to St Louis 0-3
Seasons Since A Championship Series	3	2001 beat Atlanta 4-1
Seasons Since A Division Win	2	2002 won NLW by 2.5 games

RATINGS

Most Home Runs Hit For The Diamondbacks:
Season: 57 Luis Gonzalez 2001 (162 games)
Career: 185 Luis Gonzalez
Highest Batting Average:
Season: .336 Luis Gonzalez 1999
Career: .317 Greg Colbrun

Most Games Won By A Pitcher:
Season: 24 Randy Johnson 2002
Career: 103 Randy Johnson
Most Strikeouts:
Season: 372 Randy Johnson 2001
Career: 1 832 Randy Johnson

RECORDS

Best Batting Ave. 2004 Shea Hillenbrand .309
RBI Leader Shea Hillenbrand 80
Most K's Randy Johnson 290
Most HR Given Up Casey Fossum 31
Other Top Bats: Danny Bautista , .286, 65 RBI; Chad Tracy (rookie), .285, 53 RBI.

Most Home Runs 2004 Luis Gonzalez 17
Most Bases Hillenbrand 261
Most Innings Pitched Johnson 245.2
Most Walks Brandon Webb 119

2004

Hall Of Famers

None, but obviously, the Big Unit, Randy Johnson, is a racing certainty as soon as the required five years has expired after retirement. Chances are he'll go in as a D'back (rather than a Mariner). The other pitching hero of 2001, Curt Schilling will also make it, of course.

AAA Tucson Sidewinders   **Spring Training Venue:** Tucson Electric Park, Tucson, Arizona

ATLANTA BRAVES

Atlanta, Georgia

SINCE 1966
NATIONAL LEAGUE
WEST DIVISION 1969-93;
EAST DIVISION 1994-2005

NAME CHANGE HISTORY

Boston Red Caps 1876-1882; Boston Beaneaters 1883-1906; Boston Doves 1907-1910; Boston Rustlers 1911;
Boston Braves 1912-1935; Boston Bees 1936-1940; Boston Braves 1941-1952; Milwaukee Braves 1953-1965;
Atlanta Braves 1966-2005

Honours

World Series Champions	1995
Division Winners West	1969, 1982, 1991, 1992 & 1993. East: 1995, 1996, 1997, 1998, 1999, 2000, 2001, 2002, 2003 & 2004
Division Series Winners	1995, 1996, 1997, 1998, 1999 & 2001
Championship Winners	1991, 1992, 1995, 1996 & 1999
World Series Losses	1991 v Minnesota Twins 3-4; 1992 v Toronto Blue Jays 2-4; 1996 v New York Yankees 2-4; 1999 v New York Yankees 0-4

World Series Win	Manager
1995 – v. Cleveland Indians 4-2	Bobby Cox

"I bought the Braves for two reasons. To get an autographed baseball without pleading for it and to get good seats."
Ted Turner, sometime owner of the Atlanta Braves, famous for, among other things, field managing
the team for one game during a losing streak in 1977, before being ordered from
the dugout by National League President Chub Feeney.

Season   2004

National League Manager of the year: Bobby Cox

Payroll 2003/2004	$104m(6)/$89m(8).
Highest Paid	**Starter**
Chipper Jones (3B/OF)	$15.33m
Andruw Jones (OF)	$12.5m
Mike Hampton (P)	$12.95m
John Smoltz (Cl)	$11.66
Russ Ortiz (P)	$6.2m
Paul Byrd (P)	$7m
JD Drew (RF)	$4.2m
Rafael Furcal (SS)	$3.7m
Eli Marrero (OF)	$3m

2004 Team Statistics

Position in Div	1st of 5
Record	96-66
Games Back	+10
% Record	.593 (4th)
Split	49-32 **H**; 47-34 **R**
Last 10 Seasons	1111111111
Runs per game	**4.96** (13th=)
Staff ERA	**3.74** (1st)
Ave ERA Starters	**3.84** (2nd)
Ave ERA Relievers	**3.55** (5th)
Batting ave	**.270** (9th=)
Slugging ave.	**.434** (13th)
On Base %:	**.343** (6th)
Hits per AB	**3.70** (11th=)

Total/Net Homers	**178/157** (**21** 11th)
AB per HR	**31.29** (18th)
AB per SO	**4.81** (25th=)
Runs For/Against	**803** (13) **668** (4)
Net Runs	**135** (3rd)
Net BB/BB p AB	**64/9.49** (9th)
Total Steals	**86** (15th =)
Total Errors	**116** (22nd)
Unearned Runs Con	**65** (18th)
Record Attendance	1993: 3 884 725.
Finished 1st	**Ave: 42 771.**
Attendance 2003	2 401 082 **Ave** 30 393.
Attendance 2004	3.27% decrease. 2 322 565 (79) **Ave** 29 399 (16th)

2004 Starting Rotation

Starter	Starter
Russ Ortiz	34: 15-9, 4.13 ERA
John Thomson	33: 14-8, 3.72 ERA
Jaret Wright	32: 15-8, 3.28 ERA
Mike Hampton	29: 13-9, 4.28 ERA
Paul Byrd	19: 8-7, 3.94 ERA
Horatio Ramirez	9: 2-4, 2.39 ERA
until injured.	
Bullpen Star	
A Alfonseca	2.57 ERA (79 games)
Closer	
John Smoltz	44/49 SV, 2.76 ERA*
Catcher	
John Estrada 134g	.314, 9HR, 76 RBI

*45 saves from 49 in 2003, with Gagne became the second to score 100+ saves in two seasons. 1.12 ERA 2003. **in '04 became the first switch-hitting catcher to hit .300.

98

Briefly... The only major league franchise from the Deep South.; a mobile organisation having begun in Boston and moved, bewilderingly, to Milwaukee in the 50s before settling in Georgia. Huge ball club in recent times, but underachieving in World Series terms. Despite boasting huge stars such as, Chipper Jones, Andru Jones, Gary Sheffield, Greg Maddux and Tom Glavine in recent years, and having won the Eastern Division for the last eight years straight, they have not won the World Series since 1995. Odd. Like a relay team of the fastest runners in the world that keeps dropping the baton at the crucial moment. No wonder Bobby Cox is always coming out of the dugout to argue with umpires. You then have to go back to 1957 and the days of Hank Aaron to get to the next set of Braves that won divisions, in Milwaukee (1953-65).

2004. Their relentless grip on the National League Eastern Division looked busted last season after a terrible start, having lost Maddux, Lopez and Sheffield from 2003. However, with great pitching they did it again. But their defeat in the Division Series to the mighty Cardinals was not remotely unexpected. 2004 was a triumph for Cox for making tremendous baseball capital out of relatively meagre resources.

Uniforms: Home - White shirts with red lettered 'Braves' and red tomahawk logo, red 'Y' and sleeve piping, blue undershirts, blue caps with red brim and white "A" script logo. **Road** – Grey shirt and pants. Season 2004, wore "21" home plate white and black patch on left sleeve in honour of Warren Spahn who died the previous off-season.

Owner(s): AOL Time Warner. **GM:** John Schuerholtz. **Manager: Bobby Cox** (6). Now 64 (May '05), he spent four years as Braves skipper from 1978 to 1981 before returning again part-way through the 1990 season and has been in situ ever since. First time around he could do nothing and it took the arrival of one Joe Torre in 1982 to take the Atlanta Braves to their first place. Cox the player was a nondescript two-year major leaguer with the Yankees in 1968 and 9, hitting .225 with 9 homers. Present record: 2002-1531 (.567). Now a crusty, immovable legend.

Home: Turner Field (Gr). Home of the Atlanta Braves since only 1997. First game, April 4th where the Braves beat the Cubs 5-4. Turner is a purpose built ballpark, or as good as – it was built for the 1996 Olympics, then turned over to the Braves thereafter. It's another of the post-modern parks, somewhat asymmetrical but lacking the design panache of Camden Yards and the new San Diego park. It's less than a mile from the downtown, though (which is nice). Cost was $235m. **Capacity: now 50 062.** Dimensions: 335' to left field, 401' to center field and 330' to right field. **Pitcher's Park (very slight advantage).**

This is their second Atlanta home, the franchise having moved from Milwaukee in 1965. For thirty-one seasons the Braves played in the **Atlanta-Fulton County Stadium**, a spectacular perfect circle of a venue but a "creaking albatross" according to one smart Oriole observer. However, it was a place to see a home run, being known locally known as "The Launching Pad. " It was also the site of Hank Aaron's Ruth-breaking 715th home run, on April 8th 1974. This vastly awaited event brought about the stadium's record crowd of 53 774.

How 'bout that: Bobby Cox is now in his 14th consecutive season as Braves manager; in only one year have they not won the NL East: 1994 when the Expos pipped them under Felipe Alou.

World Series And Post-Season Ratings	Position	Points/Occasions/%	
Full Playing Record 1901-2004	**17**	7757-8309: .479	
Total Historical Rating	11	N/A	
World Series Rating	10	330 Ranking Points	
Play Offs Rating	2	138 Ranking Points	
Pennant Wins (Pre-'69)	11=	4 (2 Boston, 2 Milwaukee)	
First Place Division Finishes	1	15	
World Series Wins/Appearances/Games Won	10=/8=/9	3/9/24	
Level Of Recent Success		**Won/Lost**	
Games Won Per Season Post-69	7=	78.9	
Seasons Since A World Series Appearance	5	1999 Lost to NYY 0-4	
Seasons Since A Division Series	0	Lost to Marlins 2-3	
Seasons Since A Championship Series	3	2001 lost to Arizona 1-4	
Seasons Since A Division Win	0	Won NLE by 10 games	RATINGS

Most Home Runs Hit For The Braves	Most Games Won By A Pitcher:	
Season: 47 Hank Aaron 1971	Season: 24 John Smoltz 1996	
Career: 371 Dale Murphy (left hander: David Justice 160)	Career: 266 Phil Niekro	
Highest Batting Average:	**Most Strikeouts**	
Season: .366 Rico Carty 1970	Season: 976 John Smoltz 1996	
Career: .317 Ralph Garr	Career: 2 855 Phil Niekro	RECORDS

Best Batting Ave. 2004 Johnny Estrada .314	Most Home Runs 2004 JD Drew 31	
RBI Leader Chipper Jones 96	**Most Bases** JD Drew 295 (158h)	
Most K's Jaret Wright 159	**Most Walks** Russ Ortiz 112	
Most HR Given Up Ortiz 23	**Most Innings Pitched** Ortiz 204.2	
Other Top Bats: Marcus Giles .311. 48 RBI.	Julio Franco, .309, 99h.	2004

Braves Hall of Famers

Henry Aaron 1954-76 ('54-75): The hitter of the most home runs in the history of major league baseball with 755. 24 All-Star games, MVP in 1957, 40 homers in 8 seasons (the first in 1957, the last in 1973), 3 771 hits (3ʳᵈ), 2297 RBIs (1ˢᵗ), 100 RBIs 11 times, .300 average 14 times (A/A). Played first 12 seasons as a Milwaukee Brave. "Hammerin' Hank's" record-breaking year was 1974. Also Milwaukee Brewers. (BJ2) **1982.** Top 100: **BJ12- SN5 – SABR4**

Phil Niekro P 1964-87, 318-274, 3.35 ERA: Huge longevity from the most famous of the knuckleballers. His wins total is AT13, he's AT4 in innings pitched (5403.2) and AT4 in games started (716) Won 121 games after reaching 40 (AT1) (BJ96) Also Yankees, Indians, Blue Jays. "Knucksie." **1997**

As Boston Braves and Beaneaters

Charles "Old Hoss" Radbourn P 1881-91, 310-196: No ERA stats at that date, so how do we assess a pitcher like this? In 1884 he won 60 games (AT1) and achieved 441 strikeouts and threw 73 complete games. These are crazy numbers in the context of the game's entire history; thus how good he was compared to the modern greats is exceptionally hard. In his own time however, he was a leader, which is most important, I suppose. (BJ45) **1939**

Billy Hamilton: CF 1888-'01 (Bos '96-'01) L: A 12-time .300 batter and his lifetime .344 average is the 9ᵗʰ highest of all-time. He was a short, speeding lead off man, known as "Sliding" Billy Hamilton. A hugely successful base stealer, he once set a record of stealing 7 bases in a game. Also KC Cowboys and Philly NL. (BJ9) **1961**

Tommy McCarthy RF 1884-96 (Bos '84-'5 & '92-'96): Lifetime .294 hitter and born and bred Bostonian, one of the so-called "Heavenly Twins" – the other was fellow Beaneater Hugh Duffy. An old photo has him looking as dashing as hell, all dark good looks and a stripey blazer. Also St Louis (AA) and Philly NL. (BJ88) **1946**

Rabbit Maranville SS 1912-35, ('12-'20; '29-'35) LT .258: Perhaps baseball's greatest clown, in the best sense of the word. Apparently there are a million stories of his larks and eccentricities; the ones I've read are all great (see Bill James's Baseball Abstract pp615-17. Also Pirates, Cubs, Browns and Cardinals. (BJ38) **1954**

Charles "Kid" Nicols P 1890-1906, ('90-'01) 360-205: The best 19ᵗʰ century pitcher, perhaps even better than Cy Young, as according to Bill James he out pitched Young for the first 9 seasons of their careers. Young had a much longer career. A small guy but dominated batters mostly with fastballs. Also Cardinals and P. Phillies. (BJ9)

Vic Willis P 1898-1910 248-208 2.63 ERA: Tall mainstay of the Boston Beaneaters who won 89 games in four seasons. A notable purveyor of the curve ball. His 45 complete games in 1902 is an NL 20ᵗʰ century record. No cap worn on plaque. Also Pirates and Cards. (BJ84) **1995.**

As Milwaukee Braves

Eddie Mathews 3B 1952-68 ('53-'65) L: A brilliant player, especially in his early 20s, he had totals of 135 RBI and league leader with 47 home runs in '53 and was HR leader again in '59. His career 512 homer record is AT15 and his 45 multiple homer games is AT9. He played for all 3 Braves incarnations. Also Astros and Tigers (BJ3) **1978.**
Top 100: **BJ31- SN63 – SABR31**

Warren Spahn P 1942-65, 363-245, 3.09 ERA L: One of the most outstanding pitchers in history was this Boston/Milwaukee Brave. A 20-game winner13 times his 363 wins is a southpaw record. He won a Cy Young in 1957 and is the winningest left-handed pitcher in history. (BJ5) **1973.** Top 100: **BJ36- SN21 – SABR15**

Braves Retired Uniform Numbers

3 Dale Murphy	21 Warren Spahn	35 Phil Niekro
	41 Eddie Mathews	44 Hank Aaron

"I used to love to come to the ballpark. Now I hate it. Every day becomes a little tougher because of all this. Writers, tape recorders, microphones, cameras, questions and more questions. Roger Maris lost his hair the season he hit sixty-one. I still have all my hair, but when it's over, I'm going home to Mobile and fish for a long time."

Hank Aaron, as he closed in on Babe Ruth's career home run record in 1974.

AAA Richmond Braves **Spring Training Venue:** Disney's Wide World Sports Baseball Stadium, Kissimmee, Florida

BALTIMORE ORIOLES

Baltimore, Maryland

SINCE 1954

AMERICAN LEAGUE EAST DIVISION 1969-2005

NAME CHANGE HISTORY

Milwaukee Brewers 1901; St Louis Browns 1902-53; Baltimore Orioles 1954-2005

Honours

World Series Champions	1966, 1970 & 1983
League Pennant Winners	1969 & 1971
Division Winners	1968, 1969, 1971, 1973, 1974, 1979, 1983 & 1997
Division Scries Winners	1996* & 1997
Championship Winners	1969, 1970, 1979 & 1983
World Series Losses	1969 v New York Mets 1-4; 1971 v Pittsburgh Pirates 3-4; 1979 v Pittsburgh Pirates 3-4

*Qualified for post-season via Wild Card position

World Series Wins	Managers
1966 – v. Los Angeles Dodgers 4-0	Hank Bauer
1970 – v Cincinnati Reds 4-1	Earl Weaver
1983 – v. Philadelphia Phillies 4-1	Joe Altobelli

"I keep my eyes clear and I hit them where they ain't."
Wee Willie Keeler, one time Baltimore Oriole and inventor of the Baltimore Chop (you don't eat it).

Season 2004

Payroll 2003/2004	$76m (16) $49m (22)
Highest	**Salaries**
David Segui (1B)	$6.81m
Javier Lopez I	$6m
Miguel Tejada (SS)	$4.78m
Omar Daal (P)	$4.5m
Rafael Palmeiro (1B)	$4m
Marty Cordova (LF)	$3.5m
(injured for entire '04 season)	
Jay Gibbons (RF)	$3m
Buddy Groom (P)	$3m
Sidney Ponson (P)	$3m

2004 Team Statistics

Position in Div	3rd of 5
Record	78-84
Games Back	23
% Record	.481 (18th)
Split	38-43 **H**; 40-41 **R**
Last 10 Seasons	3214444443
Runs per game	5.20 (8th)
Staff ERA	4.70 (20th)
Ave ERA Starters	5.05 (23rd)
Ave ERA Relievers	4.11 (17th)
Batting ave	.281 (3rd)
Slugging ave.	.432 (15th)
On Base %:	.345 (5th)
AB/Hits Ratio	3.55 (3rd)

Total/Net Homers	169/159 (*10* 15th)
AB per HR	33,94 (19th)
S'out/At Bat Ratio	6.04 (3rd)
Runs For/Against	842 (8) 830 (22)
Net Runs	12 (17th)
Total Steals	101 (10th)
Net BB/BB p AB	41/10.86 (18th)
Total Errors	110 (19th)
Unearned Runs Given	70 (19th)
Record Attendance:	1997: 3 711 132.
Finished 1st.	**Ave:** 45 816.
Attendance. 2003	2 454 523 **Ave** 30 303
Attendance 2004	2 744 013 (80) **Ave** 34
13.2% increase.	300 (12th)

2004 Starting Rotation:

Starter	Starter
Sidney Ponson	33: 11-15, 5.30 ERA
Daniel Cabrera	27: 12-8, 5.00 ERA
Erik Bedard	26: 6-10, 4.59 ERA
Rodrigo Lopez	23: 13-8, 3.77 ERA
Eric DuBose	14: 4-6, 6.39 ERA
Matt Riley	13: 3-4, 5.63 ERA
Bullpen Star	
BJ Ryan	2.28 ERA
Closer	
Jorge Julio	12/22 SV 4.57 ERA
Catcher	
Javy Lopez 150g	.316, 23HR, 86 RBI

Briefly... In terms of history, successful newcomers (relatively) from the city just south of Washington DC Currently unable to make headway in the appallingly competitive American League East. The Baltimore Orioles were the 1901 and 1902 forerunners of the New York Highlanders who went on to become the New York Yankees; the present Baltimore Orioles club has different antecedents.

2004: Some spectacular hitting from Miguel Tejada (MLB top RBI man with 150, newly acquired from Oakland), Melvin Mora (.340, 27HR, 104 RBI), with support from ex-Brave catcher Javy Lopez, gave the faithful something substantial to cling on to but weak pitching cost the team game after game. All in all, still not truly competitive, and in this Group Of Death, permanently barb-wired up to the Yankees and the Red Sox, the outlook is still grim. And for good measure, Baltimore is wondering whether new D.C. ball is going to steal a chunk of the Orioles fan and therefore dollar base.

Uniforms: **Home:** white shirts with "Orioles" script lettering in black with orange edge, "Y" black piping. Black caps with oriole bird motif; orange bills.**– Road –**Grey shirts with orange "Orioles" letters (fans want "BALTIMORE"), Last season, a "50" patch was worn on left sleeve to denote the fiftieth anniversary of the club's arrival in the major leagues. **Alt –** Black jersey with orange letters, black undershirts.

Owner: Peter Angelos. **Joint GM:** Jim Beattie/Mike Flanagan. **Manager: Lee Mazzili** (since 2004). Former Mets, Pirates, Yankees, Rangers, Blue Jays; lifetime .259 and 93 homers. Retired 1989. 45 years old. He was picked up from his job as the Yankees' first base coach. A "Torre disciple" he spent 1997-1999 in the Yankee organisation. A quiet presence on the bench with undertones of menace, but too quiet for some diehards. Record:78-84 (.481).

Home: **Camden Yards (Gr),** officially **Oriole Park at Camden Yards,** beautiful home of the Baltimore Orioles. First game April 6, 1992, **Capacity 48 876**. Dimensions: 333' to left field, 400' to center field, 318' to right field. The former railway depot location is only two blocks from the birthplace of one George Herman Ruth. The late nineteenth century Orioles were hugely dominant but were not included in the two major leagues system established in 1901. The new club has sprinkled pennants and World Series since the mid-60s. The stadium is owned by the state of Maryland and was built at a cost of $110 m (around £68m). Its asymmetrical playing field is a direct attempt at a move away from post-60s modernism back towards the feel of the old Ebbets Field-Fenway style of ballpark. As such the arrival of Camden Yards on the scene signaled the beginning of the 'new' retro ballpark. **Pitcher's Park (slight advantage).**

World Series And Post-Season Ratings	Position	Points/Occasions/%	
Full Playing Record 1901-2004	**19**	7668-8399: .477	
Total Historical Rating	18	N/A	
World Series Rating	12	265 Ranking Points	
Play Offs Rating	5	114 Ranking Points	
Pennant Wins (pre-'69)	15=	1 (+ 1 as St Louis Browns)	
Division Wins (post-'69)	7=	8	
World Series Wins/Appearances/Games Won	10=/13/11=	3/6/19	
Level Of Recent Success	**Pos/S'ons**	**Won/Lost**	
Games Won Per Season Post-69	**24**	73.3	
Seasons Since A World Series Appearance	21	1983 beat Phillies 4-1	
Seasons Since A Division Series	7	1997 Bt Seattle 3-1	
Seasons Since A Championship Series	7	1997 Lost to Cleveland 2-4	
Since A Division Win	7	1997: won by 2 games	

Most Home Runs Hit For The Orioles	Most Games Won By A Pitcher
Season: 50 Brady Anderson 1996	Season: 25 Steve Stone 1980
Career: 431 Cal Ripken Jr	Career: 268 Jim Palmer
Highest Batting Average	**Most Strikeouts**
Season: .328 Ken Singleton 1977; Roberto Alomar 1996	Season: 218 Mike Mussina 1997
Career: .303 Bob Nieman	Career: 2 212 Jim Palmer

Best Batting Ave. 2004 Melvin Mora .342	**Most Home Runs 2004** Miguel Tejada 34
RBI Leader Tejada 150	**Most Bases** Tejada 349
Most K's BJ Ryan 122 (2.28 RBI)	**Most Walks** Daniel Cabrera 89
Most HR Given Up Sidney Ponson 23	**Most Innings Pitched** Ponson 215.2
Other Top Bats: Javy Lopez, .316, 183h; David Newhan, .311, 54 RBI.	

St Louis Browns Pennant Win	1944
St Louis Browns World Series	Loss & Losing Manager
1944 lost to St Louis Cardinals 2-4	Luke Sewell

Oriole Hall of Famers

Ned Hanlon: Manager of the hugely successful Baltimore Orioles in 1890s prior to the formation of the modern majors. He won three pennants in the mid-90s before going on to Brooklyn to win two more in 1899 and 1900. Invented the hit and run and Baltimore Chop. **1996**

Joe Kelley LF 1891-1908 ('02-'06): Lifetime .321 batting average for this extremely successful star of the late century. He was noted for vanity, carrying a mirror onto the field to check his appearance during games. This must be worse even than Manny fielding with the back-pocket water bottle. (BJ28) **1971**

Eddie Murray: 1B 1977-97 L/R: This lifetime .287 and 504 homer hitter was inducted at the first opportunity in 2003. A hugely consistent driver-in of runs and hitter of long balls, year after year. Also Indians, Mets, Dodgers and Angels. (BJ5) RoY 1977 **2003. Top 100: BJ61- SN77 – SABR82**

Jim Palmer P 1965-84, 268-152, 2.86 ERA: The typical all-American boy athlete in terms of looks, but was an ego-loaded sourpuss, allegedly, when things went against him. "Most pitchers are too smart to manage," he once said. Pick out the meaning for yourself. Fact: none of the present 30 major league managers are ex-pitchers. (17BJ) CY 1973 **1990. Top 100: BJ00- SN64 – SABR57**

Brooks Robinson 3B 1955-77 LT.257: "Fifty years from now I'll be just three inches of type in a record book," said this man once, but he underestimated himself. One of the all-time best defensive third basemen if not *the* best. One of nature's great people too, apparently. (7BJ) MVP 1964. **1983. Top 100: BJ91- SN80 – SABR32**

Frank Robinson RF 1956-76 (O66-71, CR '56-65): Easily the best ex-player now managing. I very much like the way Bill James deals with him in the *Baseball Abstract*, laying out four reminiscences of him containing completely contradictory opinions of him as a man. What's clear from them is that he more than held his position down defensively and that with a lifetime average of .294 in an era that was not good for hitters, he was great at the plate too. His 586 home run total is AT5. He once said of his playing days, "I had no trouble communicating, the player's just didn't like what I had to say." Unsurprisingly, he became a manager, the first black manager of all time, in fact. (BJ3) Also Dodgers, Angels and Indians. RoY 1956. MVP 1961, 1966. **1982. Top 100: BJ24- SN22 – SABR24**

Earl Weaver: 1968-82; 1985. Manager: Two great Earl Weaver quotes: "On my tombstone just write, 'the sorest loser that ever lived'" and "It's what you learn after you know it all that counts." He was one of the old school alright. Oh and a third I really like: "There should be bad blood between all clubs." It describes how I feel about (UK) football. Weaver won six pennants with the O's, the first in his first full season, and the one World Series. The year after he left they won another series, in '83, under Joe Altobelli. **1996**

Outside The Hall

Cal Ripken MVP 1983, 1991. RoY 1982 and holder of the record for the most consecutive games played, 2 632.

Retired Numbers		
4 Earl Weaver	5 Brooks Robinson	8 Cal Ripken Jr
20 Frank Robinson	22 Jim Palmer	33 Eddie Murray

Great Orioles website: birdsinthebelfry.com.

AAA Ottawa Lynx   **Spring Training Venue:** Fort Lauderdale Stadium, Ft. Lauderdale, Florida

• •

Quotes that couldn't find a proper home . . .

"

"The only thing my father & I have in common is that our similarities are different."

Dale Berra, Pittsburgh shortstop and son of Yogi, King of the Malapropists

"Yogi, you're from St. Louis, we live in New Jersey, and you played ball in New York. If you go before I do, where would you like me to have you buried?" Carmen Berra to husband.
"Surprise me."
Yogi Berra, New York Yankees "

BOSTON RED SOX

Boston, Massachusetts

SINCE 1901
AMERICAN LEAGUE EAST DIVISION (SINCE 1969)

NAME CHANGE HISTORY
Boston Americans 1901-07; Boston Red Sox 1908-2005

Honours

World Series Champions	1903, 1912, 1915, 1916, 1918 & 2004
League Pennant Winners	1903, 1912, 1915, 1916, 1918, 1946 & 1967
Division Winners	1988, 1990, 1995 (Lost division play off 1978)
Division Series Winners	2003* & 2004*
Championship Series Winners	1975, 1986, 2004
World Series Losses	1946 v St Louis Cardinals 3-4 1967 v St Louis Cardinals 3-4
	1975 v Cincinnati Reds 3-4 1986 v New York Mets 3-4

*Qualified via Wild Card Spot

World Series Wins And	Managers
1903 – v. Pittsburgh Pirates 5-3	Jimmy Collins
1912 – v. New York Giants 4-3	Jake Stahl
1915 – v. Philadelphia Phillies 4-1	Bill Carrigan
1916 – v. Brooklyn Dodgers 4-1	Bill Carrigan
1918 – v. Chicago Cubs 4-2	Ed Barrow
2004 – v. St Louis Cardinals 4-0	Terry Francona

"Did you ever see me play? If you did, you'll know why there's no chance of my being over-confident."

Terry Francona before Game 4 of the 2004 World Series.

Season 2004

Payroll 2003 & 2004:	$105m (5) $125m (2)
Highest Paid Players	Starter
Manny Ramirez (LF)	$20.4m
Pedro Martinez (P)	$17.5m
Curt Schilling (P)	**$12m**
Johnny Damon (OF)	$8m
Jason Varitek I	$6.9m
Orlando Cabrera (SS)	$6m, acquired from Montreal, July '04
David Ortiz (DH)	$4.6m (rising to $6 + 2005)
Derek Lowe (P)	$4.5m
Trot Nixon (OF)	$4.5m
Tim Wakefield (P)	$4.3m
Ramiro Mendoza (P)	$3.6m
Keith Foulke (Cl)	$3.5m
Kevin Millar (1B)	$3.3m
Byung Yung Kim (P)	$3.42m
Scott Williamson (P)	$3.17m

2004 Team Statistics

Position in Div	2nd of 5
Record	98-64
Games Back	3
% Record	.608 (3rd)
Split	55-26 **H**; 43-38 **R**
Last 10 Seasons	1342222222
Runs per game	5.86 (1st)
Staff ERA	4.18 (11th)
Ave ERA Starters	4.31 (11th)
Ave ERA Relievers	3.87 (9th=)

Batting ave	.282 (1st=)
Slugging ave.	.472 (1st)
On Base %:	.360 (1st)
AB/Hits Ratio	3.54 (1st)
Total/Net Homers	222/159 (*63* 2nd)
AB per HR	25.76 (5TH)
AB per SO	4.81 (25th=)
Runs For/Against	949 (1) 768 (14)
Net Runs	181 (2nd)
Total Steals	68 (21st)
Net BB/BB p AB T	212/8.67 (3rd)
Total Errors	118 (24th)
Unearned Runs Given	94 (29th)
Record Attendance	2004 (see below)
Attendance. 2003	2 724 165 **Ave**: 33 632
Attendance 2004	2 837 304 **Ave** 35 028 (11th)
4.15% increase	

2004 Starter   Record

Pedro Martinez	33:16-9, 3.90 ERA
Kurt Schilling	32: 21-6, 3.26 ERA
Derek Lowe	32: 14-12, 5.42 ERA
Tim Wakefield	32: 12-10, 4.87 ERA
Bronson Arroyo	32: 10-9, 4.03 ERA
Bullpen Star	
Scott Williamson	1.26 ERA
Closer	
Keith Foulke	32/39 SV, 2.17 ERA
Catcher	
Jason Varitek 137g	.296, 18HR, 137 hits
Doug Mirabelli 59g	.289, 9HR, 37 RBI

Briefly... one of the great historical franchises, famous intriguingly or tiresomely for their "Curse of the Bambino," which supposedly fell upon them for the crime of trading the greatest baseball player of the 20th century, one George Herman Ruth in 1919 to the New York Yankees because the owner was short of readies. The club has never truly prospered since; until, of course, the year 2003 (why 2003? See the World Series section). Decades of rust and misery were brightened only by their acquisition of arguably the most stylish and best hitter of all time, Ted Williams (1939-60) and four major attempts to slay the beast, in 1946, 1967, 1975 and 1986. They are now deep in revival however.

Uniforms: Home - White shirts with 'Y' red piping, red "Red Sox" letters, red undershirts and plain white trews. Blue caps with red 'B' logo. A pair of red socks forms sleeve and back cap logo. **Road –** Plain grey shirts with 'Boston' lettering and red inside-edge sleeve stripe, grey pants. Otherwise, as home. Unfortunately, the home kit is, for me, the most unimpressive in the major leagues. I wouldn't wear one for $29.99 never mind the MLB asking price of $149.99.

Owner: John W. Henry. **GM:** Theo Epstein. **Manager: Terry "Tito" Francona.** The gobbing maestro expels three-quarters of the water content of his body per game. His playing record, as with so, so many managers of the recent past, amounted to nothing compared with what he has just achieved in Boston. Now in his second managerial appointment, his first came with the Phillies from 1997 to 2000 where he and his team failed to post a winning record each year. He re-graduated to a skippering position via Oakland, where his experience with Sabermetrics formed a period of grooming or acclimatisation for Boston where GM Theo Epstein and now employed advisor Bill James are fully committed to statistics over ineffective tradition. Such modernism is ironic given their . . .

Home: Fenway Park (Gr), home of Boston Red Sox. Opened April 20, 1912, before 27 000. v. New York Highlanders (won 7-6 in 11 innings). The **Capacity is 33, 871**, easily the smallest in the majors. Dimensions: 310' to the Green Monster in left field, 420' to center field and only 302' to right field. Along with the Chicago Cubs' Wrigley Field, this is the most romanticized ballpark in America. The reason is because it has a tremendous atmosphere and why? because it is now sold out for every game. And under field lights or on a sunny afternoon it is beautiful. The Green Monster isn't, but the red "Fenway Park" graphic that stands up on the deep, broad fascia above the press and broadcasting boxes behind home plate is; it forms a towering monument. Further, the park manages to combine ancient structures and modern neon to form a visual American feast. It's real and it's rough, but it isn't scruffy. Hitter's Park. (Decent advantage).

"Do they leave it there during a game?"

Pitcher Bill Lee on first sighting the Green Monster.

World Series And Post-Season Ratings	Pos.	Points/Occasions/%	
Full Playing Record 1901-2004	5	8263-7814: .514	**R**
Total Historical Rating	5	N/A	**A**
World Series Rating	6	455 Ranking Points	**T**
Play Offs Rating	9	85 Ranking Points	**I**
Pennant Wins (pre-'69)	7=	8	**N**
Division Wins (post-'69)	13=	5	**G**
World Series Wins/Appearances/Games Won	4=/6=/6	6/10/37	**S**
Level Of Recent Success	**S'ons/Pos**	**Won/Lost/Games**	
Games Won Per Season Post-69	2	82.6	
Seasons Since A World Series Appearance	0	St Louis Cardinals (1986 Lost to Mets 3-4)	
Seasons Since A Division Series	0	2004 Beat Angels 3-0 2003 Beat Oakland 3-2	
Seasons Since A Championship Series	0	2004 Beat NYY 4-3 2003 Lost to NYY 3-4	
Since A Division Win	9	1995: won by 7 games	

Most Home Runs Hit For The Red Sox	Most Games Won By A Pitcher	
Season: 149 Jimmy Foxx 1938	Season: 34 Smokey Joe Wood 1912	**R**
Career: 521 Ted Williams	Career: 192 Cy Young & Roger Clemens	**E**
Highest Batting Average	**Most Strikeouts**	**C**
Season: .406 Ted Williams 1941	Season: 313 Pedro Martinez 1999	**O**
Career: .344 Ted Williams	Career: 2 590 Roger Clemens	**R**
		D
		S

Best Batting Ave. 2004 Manny Ramirez .314	**Most Home Runs 2004** Ramirez 43 (Ortiz 41)	
RBI Leader David Ortiz 139 (Ramirez 130)	**Most Bases** Ortiz 351 (Ramirez 348)	**2**
Most K's Pedro Martinez 227	**Most Walks** Derek Lowe 71	**0**
Most HR Given Up Tim Wakefield 29	**Most Innings Pitched** Curt Schilling 226.2	**0**
Other Top Batters: Damon: .304, 189h, 94 RBI.	Varitek: .296, 137h, 73h	**4**

Red Sox Hall of Famers

"All I want out of life is when I walk down the street, people say, 'there goes the greatest hitter that ever lived.'"

Ted Williams
105

Wade Boggs 3B 1982-99 ('82-'92): As the guy with the best 20th century third baseman batting average, and rated as BJ's 4th best A-T in that position, it's no surprise that he crashed through the minimum requirement for the Hall with 474 votes, the third highest ever. The only player ever to have had 7 straight 200 hit seasons. A hitting machine also known for a prodigious commitment to pre-game and in-game superstitions. BJ60 SN95 SABR80 2005

Jimmy Collins 3B 1895-1908 ('01-'08): Was player-manager of the club's win in the first World Series of 1903. A regular +.300 hitter and brilliant gloveman at third base. Wears no hat in the Hall Of Fame. (BJ17) Also Beaneaters, A's, Louisville Colonels. 1945

Joe Cronin SS/M 1926-45 ('35-'45): A brilliant shortstop (BJ8) who was a 7-time All-Star and who batted .302 lifetime. Was only 26 when he won a pennant with the Senators as player-manager in 1933. A record trade to the Red Sox in '34 for a reputed $250 000. Also Pirates and Senators. 1956 Top 100: BJ00- SN29 – SABR84

Bobby Doerr 2B 1937-51: A lifetime .288 hitter of real quality and superb in defense. A major influence in the late 40s Sox team (as captain) that threatened to win the World Series but failed. Six times he drove in 100 runs and hit .406 in the .46 World Series. (BJ18) 1986

Rick Ferrell C 1929-47 ('33-'37): Batted .300 with the Red Sox: these were his best years. Brother of Wes who is not in the Hall Of Fame, despite being one of the best hitting pitchers of all time as well as being a great at his number one job. Rick hit LT.281. (BJ29). Also Browns and Senators. 1984.

Carlton Fisk C 1969-94 ('69-'80): A huge career of 25 seasons. Famous in Boston for the game-winning run in Game 6 of the 1975 World Series against the Reds. LY .269. Holds the records – for a catcher – of most total bases and most runs scored in a career. Also Chicago White Sox. (BJ6) RoY 1972. 2000. Top 100: BJ97- SN00 – SABR92

Jimmy Foxx 1B 1925-45 ('36-'42) "The Beast": A Philli 'A' before joining the Red Sox, he is one of the best hitters of all time. So strong he was said to have had 'muscles on his hair.' Appears all over the record books: 534 homers (AT11); 55 multiple home run games (AT7); 17 Grand Slams (AT4); 4,956 total bases (AT17); 1,117 long hits (AT12 with Ted Williams); 1,921 RBI (AT6) and a slugging average of .609 (AT4). He was only the second player (after Ruth) to hit 500 homers. We'll have to forgive him for not being much of a baserunner (AT nowhere). MVP 1932, 1933, 1938 (BJ2) 1951. Top 100: BJ29- SN15 – SABR14

Robert Moses 'Lefty' Grove P 1925-41 ('34-41): Also an 'A' in Philly, from '25-'33. For only two patches of their history were the A's remotely competitive. The second one coincided directly with their discovery of this Marylander. After his appearance, they jumped from 10 years in the second division to 2nd – 3rd – 2nd – 2nd and then three pennants. He left for Boston in '34, at the end of which season the A's finished 5th, then 8th, then 8th and it was mostly the same until they left Washington for Kansas City in '61. No wonder James has this aggressive son of a bitch from a local coalfield at number two all-time. To be the second most highly rated pitcher in the history of baseball by the uncrowned King of Sabermetrics is almost like being Pele. Maradona, then. MVP 1931 (BJ2) 1947 . Top 100: BJ19- SN23 – SABR33

Harry Hooper RF (L) 1909-25 ('09-'20): Star of four World Championship winning teams. Batted .300 in 4 of his first 5 seasons after the start of the Lively Ball Era. Stole 375 bases. Still holds record assists for a right fielder. Does not wear any insignia on his Hall Of Fame cap, but his principal club was the Red Sox. (BJ43) Also Chicago White Sox 1971

Ted Williams LF (L) 1939-60: Famously the last player to hit .400 for the season (.406 in 1942) and one of the all-time great hitters. A San Diegan who was signed to the Boston Red Sox in 1939 and stayed put until he retired in 1962. Was .344 lifetime, won 2 MVPs and 6 batting championships. Won 2 Triple Crowns. Called himself "Teddy Ballgame" and was a famously arrogant youth. 13= in the all-time home run list with 521. Achieved all this despite losing 5 years of his career to two wars as a pilot. His last at bat was at Fenway Park and he hit a home run. (BJ1) MVP 1946, 1949 1966. Top 100: BJ7- SN8 – SABR3

Carl Yastrzemski: LF 1961-83 LT .285: "Yaz," after Williams and Ruth, is perhaps the Red Sox most renowned player locally. Accused of being not totally committed at all times. Won the '67 MVP and holds the record for the number of AL games played (3 308). Achieved a .400 slugging average in all but one of his last eleven seasons. Said, "I loved the game. I loved the competition. But I never had any fun. I never enjoyed it. All hard work all the time." (BJ5) 1989. Top 100: BJ37- SN72 – SABR45

Outside The Hall Of Fame

Roger Clemens SN53 – SABR34 BJ11. Clemens won't be entering the Hall with a Boston cap as everyone knows, but he deserves a mention here for his feats with the Red Sox in the 80s.

Retired Shirt Numbers		
1 Bobby Doerr	4 Joe Cronin	8 Carl Yastrzemski
	9 Ted Williams	27 Carlton Fisk

AAA Pawtucket Red Sox   **Spring Training Venue:** Spring Palms Stadium, Fort Myers, Florida

CHICAGO CUBS

Chicago, Ohio

SINCE 1876

NATIONAL LEAGUE   EAST DIVISION 1969-93;

CENTRAL DIVISION 1994-2005

NAME CHANGE HISTORY

Chicago White Stockings 1876-1889; Chicago Colts 1890-1897;
Chicago Orphans 1898-1901; Chicago Cubs 1902-2005

Honours

World Series Champions	1907 & 1908
League Pennant Winners	1906, 1907, 1908, 1910, 1918, 1929, 1932, 1935, 1938 & 1945
Division Winners	1984, 1989 & 2003
Division Series Winners	2003
Championship Winners	0
World Series Losses	1932 v New York Yankees 0-4; 1935 v Detroit Tigers 2-4; 1938 v New York Yankees 0-4;
	1945 v Detroit Tigers 3-4; 1906 v Chicago White Sox 2-4; 1910 v Philadelphia A's 1-4;
	1918 v Boston Red Sox 2-4; 1929 v Philadelphia A's 1-4

World Series Wins	Manager
1907 – v. Detroit Tigers 4-0	Frank Chance
1908 – v. Detroit Tigers 4-1	Frank Chance

"You must try to generate happiness within yourself. If you aren't happy in one place, chances are you won't be happy anyplace."

Philosopher and fabulous Cubs hitting legend, Ernie Banks.

Philosophy is what you need to be associated with the Chicago Cubs.

"At the end of the day boys, don't tell me how rough the water is, you bring in the ship."

Controversial Cubs broadcaster Steve Stone on the end of season slump disaster.

Season 2004

Payroll 2003/2004:	$87m(12) $91m(6)
Highest Paid Players	**Starter**
Sammy Sosa (RF)	$16.8m
Nomar Garciaparra (SS)	$11.5m*
Moises Alou (OF)	$9.5m
Kerry Wood (P)	$8m
Derek Lee (1B)	$6.1m
Aramis Ramirez (SS)	$6m
Greg Maddux (P)	$6m
Matt Clement (P)	$6m
Mike Remlinger (P)	$3.98m
Mark Prior (P)	$3.15m

*acquired from Red Sox July '04

2004 Team Statistics

Position in Div	3rd of 6
Record	89-73
Games Back	16
% Record	.549 (11th=)
Split	45-37 **H**; 44-36 **R**
Last 10 Seasons	3452663513
Runs per game	**4.87** (16th)
Staff ERA	**3.81** (3rd)
Ave ERA Starters	**3.72** (1st)
Ave ERA Relievers	**4.03** (15th)
Batting ave	**.268** (13th=)
Slugging ave.	**.458** (4th)

On Base %:	.328 (22nd)
AB/Hits Ratio	3.73 (15th)
Total/Net Homers	235/169 (*66* 1st)
AB per HR	23.94 (3rd)
S'out/At Bat Ratio	5.47 (11th)
Runs For/Against	789 (16) 665 (2)
Net Runs	124 (4th)
Total Steals	66 (23rd)
Net BB/BB p AB	-56/11.50 (24th)
Total Errors	86 (3rd)
Unearned Runs Given	44 (5th)
Record Attendance	2003 (see below)
Attendance 2003	2 962 630 **Ave** 37 033.
Attendance 2004 5.68% increase.	3 170 184 **Ave** 39 138 (6th)

Starting Rotation   Starter

Greg Maddux	33: 16-11, 4.02 ERA
Carlos Zambrano	31: 16-8, 2.75 ERA
Matt Clement	30: 9-13, 3.68 ERA
Kerry Wood	22: 8-9, 3.72 ERA
Mark Prior	21: 6-4, 4.02 ERA
Glendon Rusch	16: 6-2, 3.47 ERA
Bullpen Star	
Kent Mercker	2.55 ERA
Closer	
LaTroy Hawkins	25/34 SV, 2.63 ERA
Catcher	
Michael Barratt 134g	.287, 16HR, 65 RBI.

Briefly... The poor Cubbies: after being immensely strong in the first part of the 20th century, the club and its fans have lived off shamefully meagre rations ever since. The recent upswing amounts to its second period of revival since the Second World War. And now America looks to this ballclub to be the next one to lay to rest the ghosts of the past. The Cubs even own their own curse, the Curse of the Goat, laid supposedly on the team for all time by one Sam Gianis, for the simple reason that his goat was not allowed entry to home stadium to watch the World Series of 1945. He'd been a regular for donkey's years, and so had his billy goat, but the big occasion had brought out the jobsworth mentality of the Cubs management who said no to goats. "You'll never win another pennant" said Sam. He probably snarled that, actually. No one is sure whether he could see the future quality of Cubs teams or whether he was trying to lay a curse on one half of Chicago baseball. Cynics who don't believe in such things would do well to consider the notion that the curse was so strong that it has affected the other half of the city as well.

2004. After a highly successful 2003 – let's put aside losing a Championship Series in seven games after being 3-2 ahead of the Marlins – where they won their first Division title for 14 years, 2004 was both triumph and disaster. Yes, the team established itself again as a real force in modern baseball. However, poised to win the NL play off Wild Card spot behind a rampant, out of sight Cardinals, they were blasted out of the way by the Houston Astros. Or rather, the team imploded in the last week of the season, losing five or their last six while Houston won their last seven. Result? an unmitigated meltdown disaster. Where was slugging superstar Slammin' Sammy Sosa when he was needed to lead the offence? Nowhere; he didn't even hit .260 on the season. Is he now in permanent decline? This isn't a Cubs problem any more.

Uniforms: Home: Blue shirts with large right breast badge: blue bear cub with large red 'C' curled around. Numbers on front. Blue caps with red bill. **Alt –** White shirt and pants with blue pinstripe. **Road:** Grey shirts with "Chicago" letters, grey pants.

Owner: Chicago Tribune Co. **GM:** Jim Hendry **Manager:** Johnnie B. Jr, a.k.a. **Dusty Baker** (12), since 2003, spent 19 years in the majors with the Braves, Giants, Dodgers and the A's, hitting a lifetime .278 with 242 homers in 2039 games. He was a successful manager with the Giants, scoring two firsts and six seconds in ten seasons. The World Series remained out of reach, however. In 2003 with profound managerial skills and exceptional young pitching talent in Mark Prior and Kerry Wood, he resurrected a losing team and took them to within five outs of competing for the big one. Dusty was 56 in June '04, but after his team's spectacular end of season inexplicable fall of the mountain, he probably feels 86. Still he has three NL Manager of the Year awards to comfort him at home. Record: 1017-862 (.541).

Home: Wrigley Field (Gr) home of the Chicago Cubs. The first professional game there was played on April 23, 1914 when the Chicago Federals defeated Kansas City 7-1. The Cubs first played there on April 20 1916, beating the Cincinnati Reds 7-6 in 11 innings. Wrigley is considered to be one of the two best ballparks in the country for the neutral looking for the quintessential baseball experience. It's old and lovely and highly distinctive with its ivy covering the outfield fence. It's also one of the biggest fields in the National League. Dimensions: 355' to left field, 400' to center field, 353' to right field, making this one of the biggest fields in the majors. And it's so famously symbolical of what baseball stands for in America, that it's now a fatuous cliché to say that it's a place you "gotta go." **Capacity: 38 902. Pitcher's Park (Slight advantage)**

World Series And Post-Season Ratings	Position	Points/Occasions/%	
Full Playing Record 1901-2004	**12**	8135-7969: .502	
Total Historical Rating	12	N/A	
World Series Rating	13	245 Ranking Points	
Play Offs Rating	25	18 Ranking Points	
Pennant Wins (pre-'69)	5	10	
Division Wins (post-'69)	20=	3	**RATINGS**
World Series Wins/Appearances/Games Won	13=/6=/12=	2/10/19	
Level Of Recent Success	**S'ons/Pos**	**Won/Lost/Games**	
Games Won Per Season Post-69	22	73.9	
Seasons Since A World Series Appearance	59	1945 Lost to Detroit 3-4	
Seasons Since A Division Series	1	2003 Beat Atlanta 3-2 -	
Seasons Since A Championship Series	1	2003 Lost to Marlins 3-4 -	
Since a Division win	1	2003 Won NL Central by 3 games over Houston	

Most Home Runs Hit For The Cubs	Most Games Won By A Pitcher	
Season: 66 Sammy Sosa 1998	Season: 29 Mordecai Brown 1908	
Career: 512 Ernie Banks	Career: 201 Charlie Root	
Highest Batting Average (since 1900)	**Most Strikeouts**	**RECORDS**
Season: .380 Rogers Hornsby 1926	Season: 274 Ferguson Jenkins 1970	
Career: .336 Riggs Stephenson	Career: 2 036 Ferguson Jenkins	

Cubs Hall of Famers

Adrian "Cap" Anson 1B 1876-97: One of the early 'superstars.' Had 19 seasons batting over .300. in late 19th century. Is credited, not least by Bill James, of saving baseball in 1879 as player-manager of the Cubs (or White Stockings, as the White Sox then were known) by stealing the best players from other leagues, forcing other National League clubs to do the same. This, it is argued, caused the league to have the muscular strength to be now regarded as a 'major' league. As a player, he held a spread of records in his 1876-97 career, including 19 times a .300 hitter and a .336 lifetime average. (BJ11) **1939**

Ernie Banks SS 1953-71: One of the all-time great sluggers who only hit .300 three times in a long career but who hit 512 career homers (AT15) (Slugging ave. of .555 – AT10). He also won consecutive MVPs, in 1958 and 1959. His five grand slams in '55 is a record. (BJ5) **1977. Top 100: BJ77- SN38 – SABR27**

Mordecai Brown P 1903-16 (1904-12; 1916); One of the greats of early 20th century pitching, toe to toe rival of the great Mathewson. Won three pennants with the Cubs and won a career 239 games. His 29-9 record in 1908 has only been bettered in the NL ten times. Note: in the gallery at the Hall Of Fame, "Three Fingers'" cap is turned to an angle where no insignia is visible. Also Cards and Reds. (BJ20) **1949. Top 100: BJ83- SN00 – SABR75**

Frank Chance 1B 1898-1914 ('98-'12): Achieved Hall of Fame-worthy recognition as player-manager from 1906-10 winning four pennants in five seasons and two World Championships. (BJ25) Also Yankees. **1946**

John Clarkson P 1882-94 ('85-'87): huge pitching star of his day, when the Cubs were the White Stockings, a rival of Kid Nicols. Recorded 53 wins (this is no mistake) in 1885, which poses legitimate questions about the quality of 19th century batters as well as the conditions in which they had to hit. Also a Boston Beaneater for one season more than he was a CWS. (BJ42) **1963**

Hazen Shirley Cuyler RF 1921-38: High quality, high average batter and base stealer. Hit over .300 ten times and hit .357 in 1925 for the Pirates when he drove in the winning World Series run. As a Cub, hit .360 and .355 in 1929-30 knocking in 236 runs. 'Kiki,' because of a stutter as a young man. (BJ39) **1968**

Johnny Evers 2B 1902-29 ('02-13): Lifetime .270 hitter; also hit over .350 in three of four World Series. One of the "$100 000 Infield" Fantastic quote from BJ: "Evers was a screamer and a fighter; he got on everyone's nerves almost every day, apparently including his own, as he had a nervous breakdown in 1911." Perhaps he had a complex about being unable to hit like a man: his career total of 12 is the second lowest of all the Hall Of Famers. (BJ25). **1946**

Clark Griffith P/Manager 1891-'14: Though he made the Hall Of Fame as a manager, Griffith won 20 games 7 times with the Cubs in the '90s: not spectacular, but good. He player managed the team to a pennant in 1901. He helped Christy Mathewson invent the screwball during this period also. Also Reds, White Sox, Yankees and Senators as manager. (BJ70) **1946**

Gabby Hartnett C 1922-41 ('22-'40): An all-time great catcher with an ironic name from his rookie year, he was the NL MVP in 1935. .297 lifetime hitter with high of .344 in 1935. (BJ9) Also Giants. **1955**

Billy Herman 2B 1931-47 ('31-'41): Hit and run specialist, excellent defensively and a .304 lifetime hitter. Also Dodgers, Braves and Pirates. (BJ14) **1975**

Ferguson Jenkins: P 1965-83 ('66-'73; '82-'83), 284-226, 3.34 ERA: Extremely highly rated Canadian born Cubs ace, 6 times a 20 games winner consecutively from '67-72. Also Phillies, Rangers and Red Sox. (BJ23) CY 1971 **1991. Top 100: BJ00- SN00 – SABR96**

Frank Selee: Manager Superlative early manager of the Cubs (after the Boston Beaneaters) for 16 years, from 1890 to 1905 and transformed them into a formidable outfit. Architect of the Tinkers-Evans-Chance double play. **1999**

Ryne Sandberg: 2B: 1981-97 ('82-'94; '96-7): One of the best second basemen of all time and likened to Gwynn in gentlemanship. Holds NL record for consecutive errorless games (123) and went 4 years without a throwing error. A very fine hitter, his 282 homers is second A-T behind Jeff Kent's 302. (BJ7) **Top 100: BJ58- SN00 – SABR98. 2005**

Joe Tinker SS 1902-16: Shortstop and .262 hitter. Came up with the Cubs in 1902 – left in 1913. Another with turned head in the gallery, so we can't see the club of his cap. Instead, he stares out at us from the Hall Of Fame 2003 yearbook in a state of rugged magnificence, resplendent in tailored ball-shirt, itself a work of art. (BJ33) **1946**

Hack Wilson: CF a Cub from 1927-31, batting over .307 lifetime. Holds the RBI record for one season, 191, in 1930 (The next highest in the NL, incidentally, is Sammy Sosa's 160 in 2001). His 57 homers that year was a NL record for fully 68 years. Hit 244 lifetime homers. (BJ19) **1979**

Billy Williams: LF 1959-76 LT.290: For a former rookie of the year (in 1961), a hitter of 426 career homers, a six time All Star and 1972 NL batting champion (.333), this guy is an unknown to this writer.. Why? I suppose it didn't help that for most of his career, the Cubs were a poor outfit, and when they improved in the early 70s under Leo Durocher, they still didn't win a pennant. His 1 117 consecutive games is AT5 (BJ11) RoY 1961. **1987**

Outside The Hall Of Fame

Ron Santo: Cubs one club stalwart from '60-'74. Power hitter with 100 RBIs four times, 342 career homers, .464 slugging average and 2254 hits in 2243 games. (BJ6) Retired aged 34. **Top 100: BJ90.**

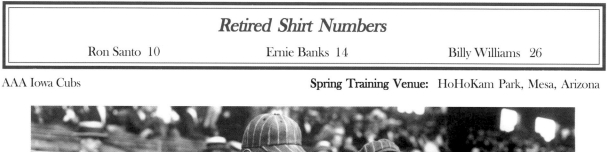

Retired Shirt Numbers		
Ron Santo 10	Ernie Banks 14	Billy Williams 26

AAA Iowa Cubs   **Spring Training Venue:** HoHoKam Park, Mesa, Arizona

Chief (Charles Albert) Bender - 1884-1954 b. Brainerd, Crow Wing County, Minnesota - and **Eddie Collins 1887-1951** b. Millerton, New York (Chicago White Sox, Second Baseman). Some uniform, eh? This was worn by the Chicago White Sox and the year here is 1925. Collins was a great all round player, one of the famous $100 000 Infield when an Athletic and the ninth member of the 3 000 hit club. Bender played only one game this season for the Sox. By then he was 41. He was a considerable pitcher in the 1910s and among his achievements, threw a complete game shutout in the 1905. His biography is extremely interesting: his father was German, his mother from the Chippewa tribe. He always signed his name, "Charley Bender."

CHICAGO WHITE SOX

Chicago, Ohio

SINCE 1901
AMERICAN LEAGUE   WEST DIVISION 1969-93;
CENTRAL DIVISION 1994-2005

NAME CHANGE HISTORY
Chicago White Stockings 1901-1903; Chicago White Sox 1904-2005

Honours

World Series Champions 1906 & 1917
League Pennant Winners 1901, 1906, 1919 & 1959
Division Winners   1983, 1993 & 1994* & 2000
Division Series Winners 0
Championship Winners N/a
World Series Losses   1919 v Cincinnati Reds 3-5; 1959 v Los Angeles Dodgers 2-4

*No post-season in 1994. The White Sox 0-3 loss in the 2000 Division Series to Seattle means that they have never won a modern post-series game.

World Series Wins	Manager
1906 v Chicago Cubs 4-2	Fielder Jones
1917 v New York Giants 4-2	Pants Rowland

"A Louisiville Slugger bat signed by the ex-White Sox slugger 'Shoeless' Joe Jackson sold for $137 000 at auction Saturday...a bat used by Ty Cobb fetched $132 000."

USA newspaper report, Nov 2004

Season   2004

Payroll 2003/2004	$71m (17) $68m (15).
Highest Paid Players	Starter
Magglio Ordonez	$14m
Jose Contreras	$9m
Paul Konerko	$8m
Freddie Garcia	$6.85m
Carlos Lee	$6.5m
Frank Thomas	$6m
Jose Valentin (SS)	$5m
Mark Buerhle	$3.5m
Carl Everett	$3m

2004 Team Statistics

Position in Div	2nd of 5
Record	83-79
Games Back	9
% Record	.512 (15th=)
Split	46-35 H; 37-44 R
Last 10 Seasons	3222213222
Runs per game	5.34 (3rd)
Staff ERA	4.91 (24th=)
Ave ERA Starters	5.17 (26th)
Ave ERA Relievers	4.31 (20th)
Batting ave	.268 (13th=)
Slugging ave.	.457 (6th)
On Base %:	.333 (15th)

AB/Hits Ratio	3.73 (14th)
Total/Net Homers	242/224 (*18* 12th)
AB per HR	22.86 (2nd)
S'out/At Bat Ratio	5.37 (16th)
Runs For/Against	865 (3) 831 (23)
Net Runs	34 (15th)
Total Steals	78 (18th)
Net BB/BB p AB	172/11.09 (22nd)
Total Errors	100 (12th=)
Unearned R's Given	49 (10th)
Record Attendance	1991: 2 934 154.
Finished 2nd	**Ave: 36 224**
Attendance. 2003	1 939 611 **Ave** 23 946
Attendance 2004	1 930 537 (79)
2% increase.	**Ave** 24 437 (21st)

2004 Rotation   Starter

Mark Buehrle	35: 16-10, 3.89 ERA
Freddy Garcia	31: 13-11, 3.81 ERA
John Garland	33: 12-11, 4.89 ERA
Jose Contreras	31: 13-9, 5.50 ERA
Scott Shoeneweis	19: 6-9, 5.59 ERA
Bullpen Star	See 'Closer'
Closer	
Shingo Takatsu	19/20 SV 2.31 ERA
Catcher	
Ben Davis 68g	.207, 6HR, 18 RBI
S. Alomar/ J.Burke	.240/.333 14/15 RBI

Briefly... Famously strong in the first decade of the 20th century, then supreme at the latter part of the 10s until the Black Sox Scandal of 1919. Decades of misery have only recently been lifted by competitive seasons in the 1990s. Which completely understates the position, doesn't it: so they haven't won a World Series since 1917? Only 4 'old' pennants in 69 seasons, after having a crack team at the end of the 1910s? I mean, there were only eight teams in the National League almost all of that time. Add it to the Cubs's record and man, what a completely dismal story of failure. Let's move on, quickly.

2004. Though expected to be competitive, last season was a write off thanks not so much to the injuries to sluggers Frank Thomas and Magglio Ordonez, but to the sub-standard pitching. There were also severe doubts about the wisdom of the Loaiza-Contreras trade with the Yankees as the season ended. The overall failure is easily spotted: just look at the pitching stats. More runs may have been scored also by the batters looking for timely controlled hitting rather than a daily assault on the fences. 22nd in walks represents a well below-average level of patience.

Uniforms: Home – White pinstripes top and bottom with black "Sox" letter logo on breast, number underneath, black undershirts, black caps with white "Sox" logo. Left sleeve has a pair of white sox inside a diamond. Road- plain grey with white "Chicago" script letters in black edged with white. Alt – Plain black shirt (and under) with white "Sox" letters, white sleeve edging, number on left at rib height.

Owners(s): Jerry Reinsdorf **GM:** Ken Williams. **Manager:** Ozzie Guillen (13) The first Venezuelan manager in major league baseball, coming in for Jerry Manuel for the start of 2004. Record so far: 83-79 (.512) (obviously). Ozzie was once a flashy, fizzing, quality White Sox shortstop, coming in as a 21 year-old in 1985 and took the Rookie of The Year. His batting was never great though his fielding was, until a serious knee injury reduced his mobility and speed on the bases. He went on to play for the Orioles, the Braves and finally the Devil Rays, as a utility player rather than SS.

Home: U.S. Cellular Field (Gr) (Comiskey Park II), present home of the Chicago White Sox since 1991. First game played in front of 42 191. This is a balanced, almost exactly symmetrical park, 330' to the left field pole, 335' to the right. The slight advantage here for right-handed hitters is mitigated by a five feet disadvantage to right-center (377-372). The 400' distance to center- field is standard. **Pitcher's Park (Clear advantage) Present capacity is 44 321.** The stadium is considered dismal by 5 pundit Josh Chetwynd; the viewing is supposed to be great though. **Previously,** the original **Comiskey Park** was the Sox homestead, opening July 1 1910, replacing 39th Street Grounds, home since 1900. Lost to St Louis 0-2 on that day. When it went into disuse in 1990 it was the oldest park in continuous use, having had its inaugural game in 1910 in front of 28 000. Comiskey II was built right alongside this piece of history, and in the magnificent photo in Josh Leverthal's indispensable book, it looks like a toy copy of a real stadium. Still, it was impressive, with its double-decker stands enclosing the field in a classic diamond shape.

World Series And Post-Season Ratings	Position	Points/Occasions/%
Full Playing Record 1901-2004	10	8111-7957: .505
Total Historical Rating	17	N/A
World Series Rating	14	205 Ranking Points
Play Offs Points	27	6 Ranking Points
Pennant Wins (pre-'69)	10	5
Division Wins (post-'69)	17=	4
World Series Wins/Appearances/Games Won	13=/16/14	2/4/13

Level Of Recent Success	S'ons/Pos	Won/Lost/Games
Games Won Per Season	13=	76
Seasons Since A World Series Appearance	45	1959 lost to LA 2-4
Seasons Since A Division Series	4	2000 lost to Seattle 0-3
Seasons Since A Championship Series	11	1993 lost to Toronto 2-4
Since a Division win	4	Won in 2000 by 5 games

RATINGS

Most Home Runs Hit For The White Sox	Most Games Won By A Pitcher
Season: 49 Albert Belle 1998	Season: 40 Ed A Walsh 1908
Career: 436 Frank Thomas	Career: 260 Ted Lyons
Highest Batting Average	**Most Strikeouts**
Season: .388 Luke Appling 1936	Season: 269 Ed A Walsh 190
Career: .340 Joe Jackson	Career: 1 796 Billy Pierce

RECORDS

Best Batting Ave. 2004 Aaron Rowland .310	**Most Home Runs 2004** Paul Konerko 41 (Lee 31)
RBI Leader Konerko 117 (.277)	**Most Bases** Carlos Lee 310 (.305)
Most K's Freddie Garcia 184	**Most HR Given Up** John Garland 34
Most Innings Pitched Mark Buehrle 245.1	**Most Walks** Jose Contreras 84
Other top bats: Ross Gload: .321, 44 RBI (234AB); Frank Thomas .271 (74g), Mag. Ordonez .292 (52g)	

2004

White Sox Hall Of Famers

Luis Aparicio SS 1956-73 ('56-'62; '68-'70): One of the first Latin greats, an exceptional shortstop, revived the stolen base (506 l'time – best 57). Rookie of the Year in 1956 and 9 time Gold Glove winner. Lifetime .343 hitter. (13BJ) **1984.**
Top 100: BJ00- SN00 – SABR88

Luke Appling SS 1930-50: Contact hitting White Sox leader in many categories in a 20 year career. A .300 hitter 14 times and twice AL batting champion. "Old Aches and Pains." (BJ11) **1964. Top 100: BJ00 - SN00 – SABR86**

Eddie Collins: 2B 1906-30 L: A man of superstar numbers and amazing longevity: he hit .340 for ten seasons, is 9th all-time with 3 309 hits and was exceptionally quick on the base paths. Hit over .300 18 times (LT .333). His 25-year career is a record for a position player. No insignia on Hall Of Fame cap. Originally part of the famous Philadelphia $100 000 infield. (BJ2) **1939. Top 100: BJ18- SN24 – SABR49**

Charlie Comiskey: Owner of the club for 31 years from 1900 and built Comiskey Park in 1910. Player-managed the St Louis Browns and won four pennants from 1885-88. **1939**

George Davis SS 1890-1909 (1904-09): An unknown, plain old name from the distant past like this - a "superior batsman" it says on Davis's Hall Of Fame plaque, which distances us from that past, with its echoes of late 19th century aristocratic politeness - doesn't do anything for the mind when you're stumbling up that old (or new) learning curve except to emphasize how much you don't know and how dead the past can sometimes feel. Then you pick up a book which has something about the guy in it and right in front of your eyes history springs to life. George Davis: was traded to the Giants for Buck Ewing, a major star of the period (we're in 1892 now); was about to become the second highest paid player in the game after Nap Lajoie, no less, when a snatch from the NL Giants to the rising AL league's Chicago team, the White Sox was imminent for a while: heroically saved some women from death in their burning apartment building one day in 1900. Suddenly you feel that you half know the guy. He could be placed with the New York Giants or the Cincinnati Reds – there are no initials on his Hall Of Fame cap - but I'm placing him with the White Sox in honour of his 6 RBI in the club's 1906 World Series win over the Cubs, this moustachioed switch hitter with the lifetime, 297 average. (BJ14) 1998 (why did it take so long?)

Urban 'Red' Faber: P 1914-33, 254-213, 3.15 ERA: After a struggle to make it to the majors from inside the White Sox organisation he stayed around until well into his 40s. Won three World Series games against the New York Giants in 1917. He was one of the chosen few still allowed to use the spitball after the 1920 ban. (BJ56). **1964**

Nellie Fox 2B 1947-65 ('50-'63) L: A 12 time All-Star and 1959 MVP, a prolific singles hitter and influential second baseman. (BJ15) **1997**

Al Lopez (Alfonso Ramon) Manager 1957-69: Successful skipper of both the "Go Go!" White Sox and Cleveland Indians in the 50s. The '59 pennant win for the Sox was their first for 40 years. The first Latino skipper elected to the Hall. **1977**

Ted Lyons: P 1923-46 260-230 3.67 ERA: Another of the pitchers who worked into their 40s. Bill James makes the interesting point that Lyons was one of the "Sunday" pitchers. In the days before night games, weekend double headers were the norm. The extra game therefore had room, indeed a need for an extra pitcher in the starting rotation. With the decline of the double header has gone that of the once-a-week Sunday pitcher: too old or beat to pitch twice a week but able to do sterling work if allowed just the one outing. Won 260 games for the White Sox in 21 seasons and went 16-4 at the age of 41. (BJ43) **1955**

Ray Schalk C 1912-29 ('29 NYG): One of the first catchers to play 100 games a season regularly, he was a small man but an expert base stealer. His 1916 30 steals record for a catcher lasted until 1982. No cap insignia, but his principal club was clearly the White Sox. Of all the Hall Of Famers, Schalk has the lowest number of career home runs, 11. Exonerated from all suspicions of involvement in the Black Sox Scandal 1919. (BJ35) **1955**

Ed Walsh P 1904-17, 195-126, 1.82 ERA: A spitballing man, magnificently captured in the yearbook in rakish pose on the field in the tiny gloves worn by pitchers in the early century. Has the lowest ERA of all the Hall Of Fame pitchers, a .607 percentage and pitched almost 3000 innings in 459 games. Had 40-15 record in 1908, one of the reasons for his very high James rating, 19th among his top 100 pitchers. **1946. Top 100: BJ00- SN82 – SABR85**

Outside The Hall Of Fame

Shoeless Joe Jackson SN35 SABR52 It isn't hard to find opinions about Joe Jackson and the Hall of Fame, so this is a short one: with racists and nasty bastards among the Hall of Famers, the requirement of "good standing" should be waived to include the Shoeless one. It isn't about to happen in the next five or ten years, though. I think one day though, some visionary is going to lever the decision-makers into a fairer assessment of 1919: that the crooked players were driven to their moral fall through the sheer meanness of the owners of their day.

Frank Thomas BJ75 A great hitter with perhaps good enough numbers. It would help if the now 39 year old Big Hurt could end his career with a couple of really good years though.

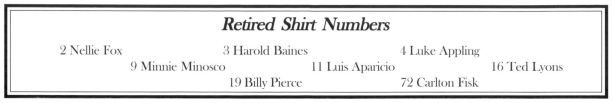

Retired Shirt Numbers

2 Nellie Fox	3 Harold Baines	4 Luke Appling
9 Minnie Minosco	11 Luis Aparicio	16 Ted Lyons
19 Billy Pierce	72 Carlton Fisk	

AAA Charlotte Knights   **Spring Training Venue:** Tucson Electric Park, Tucson, Arizona

Joe Jackson   1889-1951
b. Pickens County, South Carolina. (Cleveland Naps, Chicago White Sox). This is Shoeless Joe Jackson, ballplayer of legend.
His final batting average, when he was kicked out of organised baseball in 1920, is almost a legend in itself: .356.
If his story is not a tragic one, it has been made so through the haze of dreams projected upon it.

CINCINNATI REDS

Cincinnati, Missouri

SINCE 1882

NATIONAL LEAGUE   WEST DIVISION 1969-93;
CENTRAL DIVISION 1994-2005

NAME CHANGE HISTORY

Cincinnati Red Stockings 1882-1889 (AA); Cincinnati Reds 1890-1952
Cincinnati Redlegs 1953-58; Cincinnati Reds 1959-2005

Honours

World Series Champions	1919, 1940, 1975, 1976 & 1990
League Pennant Winners	1919, 1939, 1940 & 1961
Division Winners	1970, 1972, 1973, 1975, 1976, 1979, 1990, 1994 & 1995
Division Series Winners	1995
Championship Series Winners	1970, 1972, 1975, 1976 & 1990
World Series Losses	1939 v New York Yankees 0-4 1961 v New York Yankees 1-4

1970 v Baltimore Orioles 1-4 1972 v Oakland A's 3-4

World Series Wins	Managers
1919 - v. Chicago White Sox 5-3	Pat Moran
1940 - v. Detroit Tigers 4-3	Bill McKechnie
1975 - v. Boston Red Sox 4-3	Sparky Anderson
1976 – v. New York Yankees 4-0	Sparky Anderson
1990 - v. Oakland As 4-0	Lou Piniella

"People who live in the past generally are afraid to compete in the present. I've got my faults but living in the past is not one of them; there's no future in it."

Sparky Anderson, Reds Manager 1970-78.

Season 2004

Payroll 2003/2004	$65m(19) $43m(25)
Ken Griffey Jr	$9.1m
Sean Casey	$6.8m
Danny Graves	$6m
Paul Wilson	$3.5m

2004 Team Stats

Position in Div	4th of 6
Record	76-86
Games Back	29
% Record	.469 (19th)
Split	40-41 **H**; 33-49 **R**
Last 10 Seasons	1334225354
Runs per game	**4.63** (20th)
Staff ERA	**5.19** (29th)
Ave ERA Starters	**5.23** (27th)
Ave ERA Relievers	**5.12** (29th)
Batting ave	**.250** (27th)
Slugging ave.	**.418** (19th)
On Base %:	**.331** (18th)
AB/Hits Ratio	4.00 (27th)
Total/Net Homers	194/236 (*-42* 24th)
AB per HR	28.44 (11th)
AB per SO	4.13 (30th)
Runs For/Against	**750** (20) **907** (29)

Net Runs	-157 (28th)
Total Steals	77 (19th)
Net BB/BB p AB	27/9.21 (5th)
Total Errors	113 (20th=)
Unearned R's Given	75 (23rd)
Record Attendance	1976. 2 629 708
Finished 1st	**Ave:** 32 465
Attendance. 2003	2 335 160 **Ave** 29 076
Attendance 2004	2 287 250
2.78% decrease.	**Ave** 28 237 (18th)

2004 Starting Rotation

Starter	Record
Paul Wilson	29: 11-6, 4.32 ERA
Jose Acevedo	27: 5-12.5.97 ERA
Aaron Harang	28: 10-9, 4.86 ERA
Todd Van Poppel	11: 4-6, 6.09 ERA
Brandon Claussen	14: 2-8, 6.14 ERA
Josh Hancock	11: 5-2, 5.09 ERA
Bullpen Star	
Didn't Have One.	Lowest ERA 3.79
Closer	
Danny Graves	41/50 SV, 3.95 ERA
Catcher:	
Jason LaRue 114g	.251,14HR, 55 RBI
Javier Valentin 82g	.233, 6HR, 20 RBIe

Briefly: One of the 1901 originals, but one with a meagre record of success over this long period, despite their infamous defeat of the Black Sox in 1919 and the "Big Red Machine" of the '70s. Those days are long gone. Presently the club is very uncompetitive, not least because of the recently slashed payroll figure. Aside from a fading Ken Griffey Jr, who hit his 500th home run early last season, it has no stars, unless you include Sean Casey. In short: help desperately wanted to restore old dilapidated house to former glory.

2004 The Reds are in a hole in terms of playing performance: no second place since 2000. They've no payroll and no pitching. The two of course are linked. A glance at the pitching stats is horrifying: 29th in runs against, staff ERA and ERA relief. If a large influx of finance cannot be produced, then the Reds are doomed to mediocrity or worse for the foreseeable future. **2004 Extra Note:** Sean Casey struck out a mere 36 times in 571 at bats. That's one per 15.86.

Uniforms: Home – White sleeveless jerseys with red pinstripe and red "Cincinnati" printed letters, large red 'C' badge with 'Reds' in white on blue inside, red numbers over left breast, red undershirts, white pants with pinstripe. **Road:** grey sleeveless shirts with same lettering, but numbers under heart, black undershirts, grey pants with red side-stripe. No pinstripes.

Owners(s): Carl Lindner Jr **GM:** Dan O'Brien. **Manager: Dave Miley** (12) since 2003. Born Tampa, Florida in April 1962. He is one of the managers who didn't play in the Bigs, but who got there through 24 years service to the Cincinnati Reds organisation. He was made interim skipper after father of many Boones, Bob Boone got the pink slip in mid-2003 along with GM Jim Bowden. After the latter's philosophy of building success upon creaking knees (aka trading in veterans), new guy O'Brien has switched to something of a youth policy, one into which Miley, previously AAA manager in Kentucky (since 2000) seems to fit. Record: 98-121 (.447)

Home: Cinergy Field (Gr) (formerly the elegantly named Riverfront Stadium) is a 1970 cookie cutter job, the scene of the Big Red Machine's dominance of mid-70s baseball. This was thanks to Pete Rose, Johnny Bench, Tony Perez and ESPN's own Joe Morgan. **Capacity is 52 953**, which must make a visit for present home fans somewhat depressing and can't do that much for the players either. In their previous home, **Crosley Field**, the first night game in the majors was played, on May 24th, 1935, 8.35pm start. GM Larry McPhail managed the considerable propaganda coup of persuading President Roosevelt to push a gold key into a slot set up in the White House to begin this revolution in the way the game is played. Cynics said either wouldn't catch on (NYY's Ed Barrow) or would actually destroy the game (Messrs Navin of the Tigers and Wrigley of the Cubs). Bloody old curmudgeons. **Pitcher's Park** (Slight advantage)

"Every ballpark used to be unique. Now, it's like women's breasts - if you've seen one, you've seen 'em both."
Jim Kaat, former pitcher. He could have been talking about the Riverfront.

Historical Note. Just in case you thought it was possible to separate politics from sport, notice the name change of this club during the fiercest years of the McCarthyite anti-Communist witch hunt. 'Reds' being as good as calling your club the Cincinnati Communists Out To Destroy The American Way Of Life, those at the helm of the club saw fit to alter the name to a more respectable 'Redlegs.' Only it made the team sound like a pack of union schizophrenics and therefore more rabidly political than a team named simply for a colour. Eventually sanity prevailed.

World Series And Post-Season Ratings	Position	Points/Occasions/%
Full Playing Record 1901-2004	11	8107-8003: .503
Total Historical Rating	7=	N/A
World Series Rating	8	370 Ranking Points
Play Offs Rating	8	97 Ranking Points
Pennant Wins (pre-'69)	11=	4
Division Wins (post-'69)	5=	9
World Series Wins/Appearances/Games Won	6=/8=/7=	5/9/26
Level Of Recent Success	**S'ons/Pos**	**Won/Lost/Games**
Games Won Per Season	4	81.3
Seasons Since A World Series Appearance	14	1990 bt Oakland 4-0
Seasons Since A Division Series	9	1995 bt Dodgers 3-0
Seasons Since A Championship Series	9	1995 Lost to Atlanta 0-4
Since A Division Win	9	1995 Won NLC by 9 games

RATINGS

Most Home Runs Hit For The Reds:	Most Games Won By A Pitcher:
Season: 52 George Foster 1977	Season: 27 Dolf Luque 1923; Bucky Walters 1939.
Career: 389 Johnny Bench	Career: 179 Eppa Rixey
Highest Batting Average (since 1900):	**Most Strikeouts**
Season: .377 Cy Seymour 1905	Season: 274 Mario Soto 1982
Career: .332 Cy Seymour	Career: 1 592 Jim Maloney

RECORDS

Best Batting Ave. 2004 Sean Casey .323	**Most Home Runs 2004** Adam Dunn 46
RBI Leader Dunn 102 (ave. .266)	**Most Bases** Dunn 323 (Slg ave .569)
Most K's Aaron Harang 125	**Most HR Given Up** Jose Acevedo 30
Most Innings Pitched Paul Wilson 183.2	**Most Walks** Wilson 63
Other Top Bats: Sean Casey, 185 hits, 99 RBI, +Dunn 1st in strikeouts in major leagues w/ 195.	

2004

Reds Hall of Famers

Sparky Anderson 1970-95 ('70-'78): Has third best manager's winning record. A two-time Manager of the Year. Is the only manager to have won the World Series with a team in each league: with the Reds and the Detroit Tigers. **2000**

Johnny Bench C 1967-1983: *The* modern catching great. He established one-handed catching whilst winning 10 Gold Gloves; he also hit 389 home runs. Also snagged two MVPs in 1970 & 1972, hitting 40 homers in those years. No wonder that both Sporting News and SABR have him in their top 20 players of all time. James rates him at 44, however but has him at 2 in the catcher category. RoY 1968 **1989. Top 100: BJ44- SN16 – SABR19**

Ernie Lombardi C 1931-47 ('32-'41): Huge man who caught and threw with distinction and skill and who smacked his way to 10 .300 seasons. Couldn't run for toffee, especially late in his career when he carried a sizeable midriff bulge. Also Dodgers (his 1st season), Braves and Giants. (BJ22) **1986**

Bill McKechnie 1938-46: Manager of the 1940 World Champions. "Deacon" also skippered the 1925 Pittsburgh Pirates to Series victory. **1962**

Bid McPhee 2B 1882-99: The last barehanded second baseman. I hope for his sake that the ball was softer than the modern ones like they say. Try playing catch with one these days for ten minutes without a mitt and you realise cricketers have it easy. McFee was a decent hitter as well as being a 19th century defensive player of the highest order, apparently. (BJ30). **2000**

Joe Morgan: 2B 1963-84 L: The AL MVP '75 & '76, this is Bill James's best second baseman of all time. The leader of the Big Red Machine of the mid-70s. Brilliant eye, ace base-stealer and clutch guy. At .677 his record in percentages is the highest of all time since the required data became available. James has him 15th in his top 100, compared to SN's 60th and SABR's 37th. (BJ1) MVP 1975, 1976 **1990. Top 100: BJ15- SN60 – SABR37**

Tony Pérez (Antanasio Pérez Rigal) 1B 1964-86 ('64-'76; '84-'86): LT .279. One of the nicest men of his era. His escape from poverty in early revolutionary Cuba to major league fame is inimitable. The skinny kid grew to become one of the major components of the Big Red Machine and hit crucial homers in the famous 1975 Fall Classic against the Red Sox. "The Big Dog" Also Red Sox, Expos and Phillies. (BJ13) **2000**

Eppa Rixey P 1912-33 ('21-'33) 3.15 ERA L: Time that he played and with a name like that, he ought to have been a crusted old geezer pitching spitters 'til he was about 43, his origins from the good ol' south. He came out of the University of Virginia in 1912 and threw reliably for over twenty years, amassing wins. So most of it was right. Except his photograph in the HoF yearbook shows a bright, young fellow with a sensitive kind of face. He was 6' 5" tall and an ex-college basketball as well as baseball star. Okay, so only some of it. (BJ75) **1963**

Edd Roush CF 1913-31 ('16-'26; '31) L: How about this: Edd once lay down on the outfield during a prolonged manager-umpire spat: and fell asleep. He was woken up to be ejected from the field for delaying the game! Statistics pall against such facts. He was a brilliant defensive outfielder and .323 lifetime hitter. (BJ15) **1962**

Outside The Hall

Pete Rose. RoY 1963

Retired Uniform Numbers

1 Fred Hutchinson	5 Johnny Bench	8 Joe Morgan
	Ted Kluszewski	20 Frank Robinson

AAA Louisville Bats   **Spring Training Venue:** Ed Smith Stadium, Sarasota, Florida

• •

" Quotes that couldn't find a proper home. . .

"How do you say, "Adios" in Spanish?"

Clay Carrol, former Reds reliever "

CLEVELAND INDIANS

Cleveland, Michigan

SINCE 1901
AMERICAN LEAGUE   EAST DIVISION 1969-1993;
CENTRAL DIVISION 1994-2005

NAME CHANGE HISTORY

Cleveland Spiders- Cleveland Blues 1901-1904; Cleveland Naps 1905-14
Cleveland Indians 1915-2005

Honours

World Series Champions	1920 & 1948
League Pennant Winners	1920, 1948 & 1954
Division Winners	1995 & 1997
Division Series Winners	1996, 1997, 1998, 1999 & 2001
Championship Winners	1995 & 1997
World Series Losses	1954 v New York Giants 0-4; 1995 v Atlanta Braves 2-4 ; 1997 v Florida Marlins 3-4

World Series Wins	Managers
1920 – v. Brooklyn Dodgers 5-2	Tris Speaker
1948 – v. Boston Braves 4-2	Lou Boudreau

"I felt I was duty-bound under contract to stick with Cleveland, and I can truthfully say, in all my playing days there and everywhere, I never shirked a duty to baseball."

Shoeless Joe Jackson, an Indian before he was a Black Sox.

Season 2004

Payroll 2003/2004	$65m(24) $35m (28)
Matt Lawton (LF)	$7.25m
Omar Vizquel (SS)	$6.25m
Bob Wickman (P)	$6m
CC Sabathia (P)	$2.7m
Ron Belliard (2B)*	$1.1m

*All-Star 2004

2004 Team Statistics

Position in Div	3rd of 5
Record	80-82
Games Back	12
% Record	.494 (17th)
Split	44-37 H; 36-45 R
Last 10 Seasons	1111121343
Runs per game	5.26 (6th)
Staff ERA	4.81 (22nd=)
Ave ERA Starters	4.77 (17th)
Ave ERA Relievers	4.88 (26th)
Batting ave	.276 (5th)
Slugging ave.	.444 (9th)
On Base %:	.351 (4th)
AB/Hits Ratio	3.62 (5th)
Total/Net Homers	184/201 (-17 20th)
AB per HR	30.84 (17th)

AB per SO	5.62 (10th)
Runs For/Against	858 (5) 857 (26)
Net Runs	1 (18th)
Total Steals	94 (13th)
Net BB/BB p AB	27/9.36 (7th)
Total Errors	106 (15th=)
Unearned Runs Giv	73 (25th)
Record Attendance	1999: 3 468 456
Finished 1st	Ave: 42 820.
Attendance. 2003	1 730 001 Ave 21 358.
Attendance 2004	1 814 401 Ave 22 400 (25th)

2004 Starting Rotation

Starter	Starter
CC Sabathia	30: 11-10, 4.12 ERA
Jake Westbrook	30:14-9, 3.38 ERA
Cliff Lee	33: 14-8, 5.43 ERA
Jason Davis	19: 2-7, 5.51 ERA
Scott Elarton	21: 3-5, 4.53 ERA.
Bullpen Star	
Bob Howry	2.74 ERA
Closer	
By Committee:	32/60 SV 5.56 ERA
Catcher	
Victor Martinez 141g	.283, 23HR, 108 RBI.

* acquired from Rockies July '04

Briefly... Despite the awful and allegedly be-littling grinning Indian club emblem, the club's name came as a mark of respect for one Louis Sockalexis, a Penobscot Indian who had wonderful natural ability as an arm in the outfield as a hitter. Sadly alcohol ruined his career almost as soon as he made the majors in the late 1890s; he played only two seasons, hitting .313 despite proving unable not to drink. When he died in 1913 at the age of 43, Cleveland fans voted for the change of name from

Naps to Indians. The use of the name 'Naps' appears to be unique. The club was so dominated by the brilliance of hitter Napoleon Lajoie that a club nickname – 'Naps' became official in 1905.

2004. After six divisional firsts in the seven seasons between 1995 and 2001, the Indians have struggled. 2003's showing was the club's worst showing since 1993, but last season saw recovery. A young ballclub, their hitting was and on base percentage was impressive. Five players made the All-Star game for the American League (Westbrook, Martinez, Belliard, Lawton & Sabathia). Depth of pitching was the team's major downfall and the defence was suspect, giving up the 6th highest number of unearned runs. The fact that in August the club threatened to be genuinely competitive before falling back dramatically – on August 15 they were 63-55 having just beaten the Twins twice, then immediately lost 9 straight - caused the season to end with predictions of 2005 being a year of winning baseball. How far the team might go this time is a very interesting question, especially when one remembers the fact that they beat the Yankees 22-0 on the last day of August. As you can see from the stats, they did not have enough starting pitching to mount a really serious challenge at the top of the division.

Uniforms: Home – White shirts with red letters and blue sleeve trim. Blue and red caps with Chief Wahoo logo on heart, numbers below left. **Road –** Grey shirts with 'Cleveland' script and scimitar underline, blue 'Y' piping, blue undershirts, blue caps with Chief Wahoo logo. Tres chic, man.

Owner: Lawrence J. Dolan **GM:** Mark Shapiro. **Manager: Eric Wedge** (22) was born as recently as 1968. His career consisted of only 39 games over four seasons (1991-94), mostly with the Red Sox. He is one of many major league managers who, remarkably for this dyed-in-the-wool British football fan, are vulnerable to easy dismissal because of a lack of a track record. Only Torre, LaRussa, Cox, Scoscia, Piniella, McKeon and now Francona among existing manages have won a World Series and below this shallow stratum of experienced guys with a track record (excepting the latter) there seems to be a sea of unproven strugglers thrashing around for a bunch of answers to the all-important question: how do you produce a team that wins five and a half games out of six? Career Record: 148-176 (.457).

Home: Jacobs Field (Gr) has been the home of the Cleveland Indians since 1994 is set in the heart of the downtown. This is one of the "new" classic retro parks: asymmetrical in shape with the open part sitting in left field: the double-decker grandstand which stretches down the right field line bends in at a sharp angle and gives way in center field (the Leventhal book has a fantastic illustration of this). Opening day was April 4 v Seattle Mariners before 41 459. Indians won 4-3 in 11 innings. The capacity now is: 43 368. The dimensions: 325' to left field, 405' to center field and 325' to right field. Usually, a **Pitcher's park (Clear advantage)**, falling back in 2004 towards neutral. **Capacity 43 368.**

Previously the team played in the vastness of **Municipal Stadium, Cleveland** (also 'Cleveland Stadium'), the so-called "mistake by the lake." The first game there was on July 31 1932 1-0 over the Philadelphia A's, where the fence in center field was fully 470 feet away from home plate. Bill Veeck, buying the franchise in 1947, brought in the fences that year. The capacity of Municipal was 78 000, which must have felt like playing tiddly-winks in an empty Concorde hangar. Small wonder they moved. **League Park**, also known as Dunn Field, had a left-center field fence 505 feet away from home.

World Series And Post-Season Ratings	Position	Points/Occasions/%	
Full Playing Record 1901-2004	**7**	8209-7877: .510	
Total Historical Rating	9	N/A	
World Series Rating	15	200 Ranking Points	
Play Offs Rating	10	83 Ranking Points	
Pennant Wins (pre-'69)	14	3	
Division Wins (post-'69)	10=	6	
World Series Wins/Appearances/Games Won	13=/14=/14	2/5/14	
Level Of Recent Success	**S'ons/Pos**	**Won/Lost/Games**	**RATINGS**
Games Won Per Season	23	73.8	
Seasons Since A World Series Appearance	7	1997 lost to Marlins 3-4	
Seasons Since A Division Series	3	2001 lost to Seattle 2-3	
Seasons Since A Championship Series	6	1998 lost to NYY 2-4	
Since A Division Win	3	2001 Won ALC by 6 games	

Most Home Runs Hit For The Indians	Most Games Won By A Pitcher	
Season: 52 Jim Thome 2002	Season: 31 Jim Bagby Jr 1920	
Career: 334 Jim Thome	Career: 266 Bob Feller	
Highest Batting Average	**Most Strikeouts**	**RECORDS**
Season: .408 Joe Jackson 1911	Season: 348 Bob Feller 1941	
Career: .375 Joe Jackson	Career: 2 581 Bob Feller	

Best Batting Ave. 2004 Travis Hafner .311	**Most Home Runs 2004** Hafner/Casey Blake 28
RBI Leader Hafner 109 (150h)	**Most Bases** Blake 285 (88 RBI, 159h)
Most K's Cliff Lee 161	**Most HR Given Up** Lee 30
Most Innings Pitched Jake Westbrook 215.2	**Most Walks** Lee 81
Other Top Batters: Omar Vizquel .291, 165h.	Ron Belliard: .282, 70 RBI, 169h.

Indians Hall of Famers

Earl Averill CF 1929-41 ('29-'39) L: A fairly sublime set of numbers here after sublimely homering in his first at bat in the big leagues: batted .318 lifetime, eight times + .300 in his first ten years, .378 in 1936, five times 100 RBIs. At times labelled "The Earl of Snohomish" after his birthplace in Washington state. (BJ14) **1975**

Lou Boudreau SS: Manager of the last Indians to win a World Series in 1948. Came up from a University education (Illinois) where, like Eppa Rixey was a jock in a basketball kind of way. Skipper at 24 (24!), he won a batting title in 1944. His big year of '48 saw him batting .355, netting 106 RBIs and making 6 hits in a play off for the pennant. Devised the infield shift to cope with Ted Williams's prowess. (BJ12) **1970**

Stan Coveleski: P 1912-28 215-142, 2.89 ERA (1916-24): Pitcher who rose to fame on the back of a spitball in the legal days. Won 215 games in 17 seasons, including 3 in the 1920 World Series, all complete games, surrendering only 2 runs. (BJ58) **1969**

Larry Doby: CF 1947-59 ('47-55) L: The first black player in the American league, to state the obvious. He hit 253 homers and 959 RBIs in 13 major league seasons. A six time All-Star, ring winner in 1948 and pennant winner in 1954. (A/A) LT .283 (BJ11) **1998**

Bob Feller P 1936-56 266-162, 3.25 ERA: Almost certainly the greatest fastball pitcher in the first years after WW2 and one of the fastest throwers of all-time. Struck out 15 in his first start as a mere 17 year old. Few ballplayers start this early, never mind this successfully. Played his whole career with the Indians. (BJ12) **1962. Top 100: BJ56- SN36 – SABR22**

Elmer Flick RF 1898-1910 ('02-'10) L: Came up with the Phillies but was traded after just over 4 seasons. A great player, winning batting titles and putting up tremendous numbers initially: .344 in 1899, then .378 (with 11 homers, a high figure in the Dead Ball era), then .336. His average fell but he still averaged 160 hits a season from '03-'07. (BJ23) No insignia on Hall Of Fame cap. **1963**

Addie Joss P 1902-1910: A one-club control pitcher with a very low ERA (1.89). James however rates him as low as 80, adjusting his ERA downwards because he threw in pitchers' parks in the Dead Ball era when ERAs were generally much lower than today. James places a lot of stress on career longevity in his ratings too, which counts against Joss, who died tragically young of tubercular meningitis in 1911. He was considered to be one of the very best pitchers of his day, however. (BJ80). **1978. Top 100: BJ00- SN00 – SABR99**

Napoleon Lajoie: 2B 1896-1916 "Larrie": So good they named the whole ball club after him. Even in the Dead Ball Era, he still hit over .300 in 16 of 21 seasons, was a triple crowner and was batting champion in 1905 with .422, a record still never bettered. Began his career with the Phillies. Napoleon wears a Naps cap in the Hall Of Fame. His name, by the way, is pronounced, 'La-jou-way,' with a soft 'J' in the middle as in the French word for 'play,' 'Jouer.' The stress is on the first syllable. (BJ6) **1937. Top 100: BJ40- SN29 – SABR38**

Bob Lemon P 1946-58 207-128 3.23 ERA: Won 20 games seven times, led the AL in wins thrice. Career ERA of 3.23. Also one of the rare successful hitters, hitting .264 lifetime. (BJ48) (BJ48) **1976**

Satchel Paige: 'Negro pitching legend' hardly does justice to the guy's achievements and astounding fame and reputation among blacks and whites alike. He was 42 when he finally got to pitch in the major leagues, and had long suffered from severe arm problems. He still had a 6 and 1 record in a short first season for the Indians, pitching 73 innings and striking out 43 batters. **Top 100: BJ17- SN19 – SABR00**

Joe Sewell SS 1920-33 ('20-30) L: Not a name you hear in the UK but this guy from the 20s and 30s is the hardest batter to strikeout in the history of baseball. His 1 in 63 strikeouts is by a distance the best in history as is his record low of 3Ks for the entire 1932 season. (BJ23) **1977**

Tris Speaker: CF, 1907-28 L: Outstanding .345 lifetime hitter and shallow defensive center fielder. All time leader in doubles (793). Hit record three 20 games in one season, 1912. (BJ4) **1937. Top 100: BJ11- SN27 – SABR23**

Early Wynn: P 1939-63, 300-244, 3.54 ERA His longevity is a still an AL record; this is an old-style bullet-nosed hurler famous for keeping batters off the plate. He also played for the Senators from rookie year to '48, though he missed 2 war seasons, and the White Sox from '58-'62 where he won a Cy Young in '59. (BJ47) **1972. Top 100: BJ00- SN100 – SABR97**

Cy Young: P 1890 –11, 511-315, 2.63 ERA: Denton True Young pitched 818 games (AT1) in 22 seasons winning 511 of them (AT1). He won 20 games 16 times (AT1) and won 30 games 7 times (AT4=). He hit 18 homers too. He is the earliest legend of pitching and his win total is the highest in the history of the game by 94 (over Walter Johnson). Small wonder then that the annual pitching awards is named in his honour. Cy is for "Cyclone." Though much known as a Red Sox, Young wears a Cleveland Naps hat in the Hall Of Fame gallery. (BJ4) **1937. Top 100: BJ23- SN14 – SABR18**

Retired Uniform Numbers

Bob Feller 19	Mel Harder 18	Earl Averill 3
Lou Boudreau 5	Larry Doby 14	Bob Lemon 21

AAA Buffalo Bisons **Spring Training Venue:** Chain of Lakes, Winter Haven, Florida

Bob Feller – b. 1918
Van Meter, Iowa (Cleveland Indians) Seen here with his father, he broke into the majors with the Indians aged 17, though here he looks more like 12. His career is full of spectacular numbers and achievements, which establishes him as the greatest pitcher of his day. Remarkably, the Second World War, in which he served with distinction, didn't hurt his career: he was phenomenally good before and he was still great in the years immediately after.

COLORADO ROCKIES

Denig, Colorado

Denver, Colorado

SINCE 1993

NATIONAL LEAGUE WEST DIVISION

Honours		
World Series Wins	None	
Play Off Seasons	None	

Season 2004

Payroll 2003/2004	$79m (15) $69m(14)
Top Earners	Starter
Todd Helton	$11.6m
Larry Walker*	$12.67
Denny Neagle	$9m
Charles Johnson (C)	$9m
Preston Wilson (OF)	$9m

*traded to Cardinals, July '04

2004 Team Statistics

Position in Div	4th of 5
Record	68-94
Games Back	25
% Record	.420 (24th)
Split	38-43 H; 30-51 R
Last 10 Seasons	2334545444
Runs per game	5.14 (11th)
Staff ERA	5.54 (30th)
Ave ERA Starters	5.54 (30th)
Ave ERA Relievers	5.53 (30th)
Batting ave	.276 (6th)
Slugging ave.	.455 (7th)
On Base %:	.345 (7th=)
AB/Hits Ratio	3.64 (6th)
Total/Net Homers	202/198 (4 17th)

AB per HR	27.60 (9th)
AB per SO	4.72 (28th)
Runs For/Against	833 (11) 923 (30)
Net Runs	-90 (22nd)
Total Steals	44 (29th)
Net BB & BB/AB	-129/9.81 (10th)
Total Errors	89 (6th)
Total Unearned Giv	40 (2nd)
Record Attendance	1993 4, 483, 350
	Ave: 55 350
Attendance. 2003	2 334 085 Ave 28 816.
Attendance 2004	2 338 069 (79)
	Ave 29 595 (15th)

2004 Starting Rotation

Starter	Starter
Sean Estes	34: 15-8, 5.84 ERA
Jason Jennings	33: 11-12, 5.51 ERA
Joe Kennedy	27: 9-7, 3.66 ERA
Aaron Cook	16:6-4, 4.28 ERA
Jamie Wright	13: 2-3, 4.12 ERA
Bullpen Star	
Steve Reed	3.68 ERA
Closer	
Shawn Chacon	35/44 SV 7.11 ERA
Catchers	109g/75g
Charles Johnson /	.236 13HR, 47 RBI/
Todd Greene	.282, 10HR, 35 RBI

Briefly... An expansion franchise of 1993 vintage which has yet to find a winning formula. Their short history has been notable for the highest stadium in the leagues, and thus the place where doubles go to fly out of the stadium on wings. The hugely gifted left-handed hitter Larry Walker, one of two banner guys here for some time (along with Helton), was off-loaded in mid-season to save money. What Walker gave this franchise was only too evident in the St Louis Cardinals' play off drive to the Series. On 5's show, pundit Lengel expressed the organisation's frustration for them: "I don't know what the answer is." The problem? Pitching as well as a lack of payroll cash. Which stellar pitchers are going to want to come and perform in the mountains and watch their career ERA figures go south? You would think that with the Caribbean and Central American baseball hot beds producing so many great or just very talented players, and with the game still being played by huge organisations in the States themselves, there would be enough truly high class players to go around. It doesn't seem unreasonable for a collective world baseball population of over 500 000 million (I'm including Japan here) to produce the 450 pitchers required by 30 major league franchises. They're out there somewhere, so it must be a failure of management or the coaching system, to get them onto the field.

The franchise has to hold on to Todd Helton (b. 20/8/73), a prolific hitter who has put up Hall of Fame numbers in an 8 season career: 251 homers, 1372 hits and a .339 average thus far.

Uniforms: Home - Navy jersey or white with navy pinstripe, grey and navy 'Rockies' letters, white trews with navy pinstripes, navy undershirts. **Road:** Grey suit with pinstripes, "Colorado" letters, numbers under heart.

Chairman & CEO: Charles K. Monfort. **GM:** Dan O'Dowd. **Manager:** Clint Hurdle (13) since part-way through 2002. He averaged 50 games a season with the Royals, Reds and Mets over ten years. Has achieved only two fourth places so far with the youthful franchise in a tough division. Fans last season were not optimistic about Clint's position here: the team clearly lacked the quality required to compete and everyone knew it. It's thought that this season is one where a lot of younger players will come up from the minors and show their worth, but the perhaps cynical (perhaps realistic) view among the diehards is that Hurdle will be dropped faster than a piece of hot metal by the mid-point if the team do significantly better than they did in 2004. Record: 209-255 (.450).

Home: Coors Field (Gr), Denver home of the Colorado Rockies since the opening day of the 1995 season, April 26th, after two seasons at Mile High Stadium. The Rockies beat the Mets 11-9. The Capacity at that time was 50, 200. **Capacity is** now a fraction higher at **50 381.** Dimensions: 347' to left field, 415' to center field, 350' to right field. Even in this largish field, Coors is a hitter's paradise, hits carrying further in the thin mountain air there. And a jet stream carries the ball out of the park in left-center to make the nightmare worse for visiting and home pitchers alike. The spectacular stadium is 5, 280 feet above sea level. Still a mile high. **Batter's Park (Big advantage).**

World Series And Post-Season Ratings	Position	Points/Occasions/%	
Full Playing Record 1993-2004	**23**	882-999: .469	**RATINGS**
Total Historical Rating	29	N/A	
World Series Rating	30=	0 Ranking Points	
Play Offs Rating	28=	2 Ranking Points	
Division Wins (post-'69)	30=	0	
World Series Wins/Appearances/Games Won	30=/30=/30=	0/0/0	
Level Of Recent Success	**S'ons/Pos**	**Won/Lost/Games**	
Games Won Per Season	28	67.8	
No Play Off Record. The Colorado Rockies have never won a division title			

Most Home Runs Hit For The Rockies	**Most Games Won By A Pitcher**	**RECORDS**
Season: 49 Larry Walker 1997; Todd Helton 2001	Season: 17 Kevin Ritz 1996; Pedro Astacio 1999	
Career: 236 Larry Walker	Career: 53 Pedro Astacio	
Highest Batting Average	**Most Strikeouts**	
Season: .379 Larry Walker 1999	Season: 210 Pedro Astacio 1999	
Career: .341 Larry Walker	Career: 749 Pedro Astacio	

Best Batting Ave. 2004 Todd Helton .347	**Most Home Runs 2004** Jeremy Burnitz 37 (110RB)	**2004**
RBI Leader Vinny Castilla 131 (34 HR)	**Most Bases** Helton 339 (32 HR)	
Most K's Jason Jennings 133	**Most HR Given Up** Sean Estes 30	
Most Innings Pitched Estes 202	**Most Walks** Estes 105	
Other Top Bats: Aaron Miles: .292, 47 RBI, 153h.; Royce Clayton: 160h, .279, 54 RBI.		

Retired Uniforms

None

Hall of Famers

None, but it is distinctly possible that 1. Larry Walker one day makes it and 2. That he chooses to go in wearing a Rockies cap.

AAA Colorado Springs Sky Sox   **Spring Training Venue:** Hi Corbett Field, Tucson, Arizona

● ●

" Quotes that couldn't find a proper home . . .

"If I ever find a pitcher who has heat, a good curve, and a slider, I might seriously consider
marrying him, or at least proposing."
Sparky Anderson, Inaugural Manager of the Year (NL) 1984 **"**

DETROIT TIGERS

Detroit, Michigan

SINCE 1901

AMERICAN LEAGUE EAST DIVISION 1969-97;
CENTRAL DIVISION 1998-2005

Honours

World Series Champions	1935, 1945, 1968 & 1984
League Pennant Winners	1907, 1908, 1909, 1934, 1940 & 1968
Division Winners	1972, 1984 & 1987
Division Series Wins	N/R.
Championship Series Winners	1984
World Series Losses	1907 v Chicago Cubs 0-4; 1908 v Chicago Cubs 1-4; 1909 v Pittsburgh Pirates 3-4; 1934 v St Louis Cardinals 3-4 ; 1940 v Cincinnati Reds 3-4

World Series Wins	Managers
1935 - v. Chicago Cubs 4-2	Mickey Cochrane
1945 - v. Chicago Cubs 4-3	Steve O'Neill
1968 - v. St Louis Cardinals 4-3	Mayo Smith
1984 - v. San Diego Padres 4-1	Sparky Anderson

"Let him sleep, if he will. If you get him riled up, he will annihilate us."
Connie Mack, A's skipper, on the Detroit Tigers greatest ever player, Tyrus Cobb.

Season 2004

Payroll 2003/2004	$59m(23) $50m (21)
Highest Paid Players:	Salary
Bobby Higginson	$8.85m
Dmitri Young	$7.75m
Ivan Rodriguez	$6.5m
Matt Anderson (P)	$4.3m
Urbina (Cl)	$3.5m
Jason Johnson (P)	$3m
Fernando Vina (2B)	$3m

2004 Team Statistics

Position in Div	4th of 5
Record	72-90
Games Back	20
% Record	.444 (21st)
Split	38-43 II; 34-47 R
Last 10 Seasons	4535334454
Runs per game	5.10 (12th)
Staff ERA	4.93 (26th)
Ave ERA Starters	4.93 (22nd)
Ave ERA Relievers	4.91 (27th)
Batting ave	.272 (8th)
Slugging ave.	.449 (8th)
On Base %:	.337 (14th)
AB/Hits Ratio	3.67 (8th)
Total/Net Homers	201/190 (11 14th)

AB per HR	27.97 (10th)
AB per SO	4.91 (24th)
Runs For/Against	827 (12) 844 (25)
Net Runs	-17 (19th)
Total Steals	86 (15th=)
Net BB/BB p AB	-12/10.85 (17th)
Total Errors	144 (30th)
Unearned Runs Giv	56 (14th)
Record Attendance	2000: 2 533 752.
Finished 3rd.	Ave: 31 281.
Attendance. 2003	1 368 285 Ave 17 104
Attendance 2004	1 917 004 (80) Ave 23 962
(22nd)	

2004 Starting Rotation

Starter	Starter
Mike Maroth	33: 11-13, 4.31 ERA
Jason Johnson	33: 8-15, 5.13 ERA
Nate Robertson	32: 12-10, 4.90 ERA
Jeremy Bonderman	32: 11-13, 4.89 ERA
Gary Knotts	19: 7-6, 5.25 ERA
Bullpen Star	
Jamie Walker	3.20 ERA
Closers	
Ugueth Urbina	21/24 SV, 4.50 ERA. Esteban
Yan	7/17 SV, 3.83 ERA
Catcher	
Ivan Rodriguez	.334, 19HR, 176 hits

Briefly... One of the original 16 of the modern majors, the Tigers' initial history in the 20th century majors seems at first glance to have been a rich and illustrious one. However, closer inspection reveals a club of great players: Cobb, Crawford, Cochrane and so on, not a club that actually won very much. Recent years has seen very slim pickings indeed. The 2003 team lost a record 119 games, but last year, with the arrival of the magnificent Pudge Rodriguez (c) from the Marlins, some improvement, predictably, was made. With a falling payroll in 2004, the team, also predictably, failed to hoist a winning record; they just didn't have the pitching to do better. However, at the least the club has lifted itself out of an abyss. Still, the club has not had a second place since 1991 and a first since 1987.

Uniforms: Home – White shirts with navy 'Y' piping, gothic 'D' logo on heart only, navy undershirts; navy caps with gothic 'D' logo. Road –Grey jerseys with 'Y' piping, black "Detroit" letters with orange edge, numbers below heart.

Owners(s): Mike Illitch. **GM/CEO:** David Dombrowski **Manager: Alan Trammell (3)** (b. 1958) was a one-club twenty season Tiger and genuine club great and one of the best shortstops of all time (James has him at no. 9). He hit a (then) record 9 hits in the '84 World Series, in which he was MVP. His other stellar year was 1987 when he hit .343, 28 homers and knocked in 105 on 208 hits. 2005 will be his 3rd season in charge of the Tigers. Record: 115-209 (.355)

Home: Comerica Park (Gr). Home of the Detroit Tigers since April 11 2000. The home team beat the Mariners 5-2. The Tigers had played in Tiger Stadium since 1912 (previously named Navin Field, then Briggs Stadium) and played 6,783 games there. **Capacity: 40 000.** Dimensions: 346' to left field, 422' to center field and 330' to right field. The furthest distance to the center field wall makes it the biggest playing field in the American League.
Pitcher's Park (Slight-Clear advantage)

Previously, Tigers Stadium was one of the great old homes of baseball. By the time the team left there at the end of the 1999 season, it could house 43 000 spectators, but in surroundings something akin to St James Park or Maine Road in the sixties. In other words, this almost biblical baseball home had to go, I suppose. This had been the home of Hughie Jennings, Sam Crawford, Hank Greenberg, Al Kaline and of course, Ty Cobb. So if there isn't a plaque there to commemorate its place in history when I eventually get there, I might have to call in all my gangster connections to sort the problem out.

World Series And Post-Season Ratings	Position	Points/Occasions/%	
Full Playing Record 1901-2004	9	8150-7959: .506	
Total Historical Rating	10	10.6	
World Series Rating	7	380 Ranking Points	**RATINGS**
Play Offs Rating	22	22 Ranking Points	
Pennant Wins (pre-'69)	7=	8	
Division Wins (post '69)	20=	3	
World Series Wins/Appearances/Games Won	9/8=/7=	4/9/26	
Level Of Recent Success	**S'ons/Pos**	**Won/Lost/Games**	
Games Won Per Season	21	74	
Seasons Since A World Series Appearance	21	1984 bt San Diego 4-1	
Seasons Since A Division Series	N/A	-	
Seasons Since A Championship Series	17	1987 lost to Minnesto 1-4	
Seasons Since A Division Win	17	1987 Won ALC by 2 games	

Most Home Runs Hit For The Tigers	Most Games Won By A Pitcher	
Season: 58 Hank Greenberg 1938	Season: 31 Denny MacLain 1968	**RECORDS**
Career: 399 Al Kaline	Career: 223 Hooks Dauss	
Highest Batting Average	**Most Strikeouts**	
Season: .420 Ty Cobb	Season: 308 Mickey Lolich	
Career: .368 Ty Cobb	Career: 2 679 Mickey Lolich	

Best Batting Ave. 2004 Ivan Rodriguez .337	**Most Home Runs 2004** Carlos Pena 27 (Irod 19)	
RBI Leader Carlos Guillen 97 (.318)	**Most Bases** Guillen 283 (Irod 269)	**2004**
Most K's Jeremy Bonderman 168	**Most HR Given Up** Nate Robertson 30	
Most Innings Pitched Mark Maroth 217	**Most Walks** Bonderman 73	
Other Top Batters: Alex Sanchez .322, 107h (79g) ; Craig Monroe: .293, 131h, 72 RBI.		

Tigers Hall of Famers

Sparky Anderson 1970-95 ('79-'95): Uniquely a successful World Series manager in both leagues, here with the Tigers and also with the Cincinnati Reds. Presided over four 100 game-winning seasons.

Ty Cobb CF 1905-28 ('05-'26): 24 years an outfielder; a legendary but hated figure of the early 20th century game: 12 batting titles, a record; hits leader 8 times, a record; lifetime .367; 4 191 hits; 23 .300 seasons and 3 of .400; 23 seasons consecutively hit above .300. His record of 16 bases in a single game in 1925 in the AL has yet to be broken. "The Georgia Peach" played nasty, pummelling opponents on the slide into bases with body and spikes; he was arrogant and friendless, but arguably an even greater talent than Ruth. Also Philadelphia A's (at end of career) (BJ2) **1937. Top 100: BJ5- SN3 – SABR7**

Mickey Cochrane: C, 1925-37: Huge figure in hitting history who led the club from 1934-37, taking them to two World Series in 1934 and 1935, victoriously in the latter. He batted .320, .319, .290 and .306 in his 4 seasons. Also Philadelphia A's. (BJ4) MVP 1934 **1947**. Top 100: BJ72- SN65 – SABR50

Sam Crawford: RF, 1899-1917 L: Played a major role in the three time pennant winning team in the 1910s. This is the record holder for triples (in the Deadball Era where homers were rare), with 312. Stole 393 bases. Lifetime .309 with 2 964 hits, 27th all-time. "Wahoo Sam:" he hailed from Wahoo, Nebraska. Just three other HoFs come from the same state: Bob Gibson, Pete Alexander and Richie Ashburn (not many people know that). (BJ10) **1957**. Top 100: BJ89- SN84 – SABR90

Charlie Gehringer: 2B, 1924-42 L: 13 seasons a +.300 hitter, lifetime .320 average. League RBI leader in '35, '37, '40 and '46. For the record, his Hall Of Fame plaque has him turning his head, rendering his cap insignia invisible. (BJ8) MVP 1937 **1949**. Top 100: BJ59- SN46– SABR46

Hank Greenberg 1B 1930-47,: Superb hitter: LT .313 (AT68);1,276 RBI (AT80); 331 homers (AT78) and 35 multiple HR games (AT29). He was an inspiration and hugely important figure for America's Jewish community. He later managed the Indians in the 50s to a mixture of acclaim and criticism. (BJ8) MVP 1935, 1940 **1956**. Top 100: BJ68- SN37 – SABR35

Harry Heilmann RF 1914-32 ('14-'29): 3rd best right-hander average of all-time at .342. AL batting champ 4 times with huge averages: .394; .403; .393 & .398. (BJ16) **1952**. Top 100: BJ400 SN54 – SABR91

Hughie Jennings SS 1891-1918: Huge figure in this period of baseball, for both the colourful nature of his career – his nickname was "Ee-Yah" after his mid-game battle cry – and for his excellence as a hitter and fielder: he was a lifetime .311 hitter and played the most innings at shortstop of any in that position. Add in the red hair and the raw proletarian coal mining background, tremendous success as a manager with the Orioles and Tigers (not to mention coaching the Giants to four pennants) and you have a man who leaps off the pages of baseball history right at you. (BJ18) **1945**

Al Kaline RF 1953-74: LT .297. 1980. "Mr Tiger" was the club no. 1 star of his day, a fifteen –time All-Star and batting champion in '55. Played 2834 times as a one-clubman, a franchise record. Ended his career one shy of 400 homers and a .297 career average after having been over .300 for almost all of it. Also won 10 Gold Gloves. Graceful and great player all-round. (BJ11). Top 100: BJ90- SN76 – SABR59

George Kell 3B 1943-57 ('46-'52): A great batter, biggest star to emerge from the latter war years. Was 1949's batting champion, thwarting a second Triple Crown for Ted Williams. Hit .300 for eight consecutive seasons after '46. Was also a brilliant third baseman. (BJ30) **1983**

Heinie Manush LF 1923-39 ('23-'27) L: Won a batting title in 1926, his breakthrough Tiger season. Hits league leader twice, in '28 (241!) and '33. Had a lifetime .330 average. Was traded to the Browns, then the Senators where he had a 33-game hit streak in 1933, the year of their last World Series appearance. A tremendously effective hitter with year-on-year consistency. (BJ30) **1964**

Hal Newhouser P 1939-55, 207-150, 3.06 ERA L: Top class pro of the mid-late 40s and got very little run support. He is still the only pitcher in major league history to win back-to-back MVPs (1944, 1945). Was a six-time All-Star. The standard of play declined during the war years, so caution required in assessing 'Prince Hal.' Had heart ailment that kept him out of service. Still very successful post-war until shoulder problems. (BJ36) **1992**

Retired Shirt Numbers

Al Kaline 6	Charlie Gehringer 2	Hank Greenberg 5
Hal Newhouser 16	Willie Horton 23	

AAA Toledo Mud Hens   **Spring Training Venue:** Joker Marchant Stadium, Lakeland, Florida

● ●

" Casey quotes that couldn't find a proper home . . .

"Good pitching will always stop good hitting and vice-versa."

Casey Stengel

"The secret of managing is to keep the guys who hate you away from the guys who are undecided."

Casey Stengel "

FLORIDA MARLINS

Miami, Florida

<small>SINCE 1993</small>

<small>NATIONAL LEAGUE   EAST DIVISION</small>

Honours

World Series Champions	1997 & 2003
League Pennant Winners	N/A
Division Winners	0
Division Series Winners	1997* & 2003*
Championship Series Winners	1997 & 2003

*Qualified for post-season via Wild Card position

World Series Wins	Managers
1997 – v. Cleveland Indians 4-2	Jim Leyland
2003 – V. New York Yankees 4-2	Jack McKeon

"I am elated; I didn't have any idea that we would win in the playoffs or win the Wild Card. I had no idea we would get to the World Series and I had no idea we would win the World Series."

Jack McKeon, the only World Series skipper with 9 grandchildren to his credit, tries to come to terms with the Marlins 2003 triumph in the immediate aftermath.

Season 2004

Payroll 2003/2004	$63.28m (20)
	$42m (26)

Highest Paid Players	Salary
Mike Hampton (P)	$10m to Braves
Mike Lowell (3B)	$6.5m
Billy Koch (P)	$6m
Luis Castillo (2B)	$4.66m
Paul LoDuca (C)	$4.06m
(from Dodgers, July '04)	
David Weathers (P)	$3.9m
Carl Pavano (P)	$3.8m
Brad Penny (P)	$3,73
(traded to Dodgers mid),	
Juan Encarnacion (RF)	$3.56m
Armando Benitez (Cl)	$3.5m
Jeff Conine (LF)	$3m

2004 Team Statistics

Position in Div	3rd of 5
Record	83-79
Games Back	13
% Record	.512 (15th=)
Split	42-38 H; 41-41 R
Last 10 Seasons	4325534423
Runs per game	4.43 (23rd)
Staff ERA	4.10 (9th)
Ave. ERA Starters	4.08 (4th=)
Ave ERA Relievers	4.13 (18th)
Batting ave	.264 (20th)
Slugging ave.	.329 (22nd)
On Base %:	.406 (21st)

AB/Hits Ratio	3.79 (20th)
Total/Net Homers	148/166 (-18 21st)
AB per HR	37.06 (23rd)
AB per SO	5.66 (8th)
Runs For/Against	718 (23) 700 (6)
Net Runs	18 (16th)
Total Steals	96 (12th)
Net BB/BB p AB	-14/10.99 (20th)
Total Errors	86 (3rd)
Unearned Runs Giv	45 (7th)
Record Attendance.	1993: 3 064 847.
First season in the major leagues	Ave: 37 837
Finished 6th.	
Attendance. 2003	1 303 214
(62.3% increase on 2002).	Ave 16 290.
Attendance 2004	1 723 105 (78)
35.6% increase.	Ave 22 091 (26th).

2004 Starting Rotation

Starter	Record
Josh Beckett	26: 9-9, 3.79 ERA
Dontrelle Willis	32: 10-11, 4.02 ERA
Carl Pavano	31: 18-8, 3.00 ERA
Ismael Valdez	31: 14-9, 5.19 ERA
Andy Burnett	19: 7-6, 3.74 ERA
Closer & Bullpen Star	
Armando Benitez	47/51, 1.29 ERA
Also Rudy Seanez	2.74 ERA
Catcher	
Paul LoDuca* 52g Fl.	.258, 31 RBI, 3HR
Mike Redmond. 81g	.256. 25 RBI, 2HR

*traded at the July deadline from the Dodgers

Briefly... The playing record in just 12 seasons is undeniably fantastic. The word after 2003's spectacular success under owner Jeffrey Loria was that a break up of the World Champions would be inevitable but it hasn't quite happened. However, official sources claim that owner Loria is coughing up $20m a season to support the Marlins and to bridge the gap, the organisation ended the 2004 season negotiating with the City of Miami and Miami-Dade County for a $350 million purpose built stadium adjacent to the Orange Bowl, with a retractable roof to keep out that Florida heat. From a business perspective the stadium is a necessity to enable the franchise to stand on its own two feet financially. Thus is it now the case that having financed a World Championship ring for himself (and McKeon and the players, of course), Jeffrey is no longer going to play Sugar Daddy with bottomless pockets?

2004 Pudge Rodriquez left to join the Tigers, but otherwise, McKeon's side remained competitive. The pitching, with Beckett, Pavano and Willis remained strong, but the team was deficient in hitting. Note the 30% slash in the payroll figure. In 2005, it's going to be impossible to dislodge the Braves from the top of the division, and still a mountain to beat out the Giants, the Cubs and the Astros (or the Cards) for the Wild Card spot. Surely.

Uniforms: Home - Black shirts with aqua green and white 'Marlins' letters. White pants. **Road -** White sleeveless shirts. Black caps with aqua green marlin fish shaped 'F.'x

Owners(s): Jeffrey Loria. **GM:** Larry Beinfest. Manager: **Jack McKeon**, who took over a struggling Fish in May of 2003, only to drive them to an outstanding World Series victory. Jack did not have a major league career. The Bobby Robson of his profession, he turned 74, last November ('04). Ended 2004 with a .552 record as the Marlin skip, 158-128. Previously McKeon managed Kansas City, Oakland, San Diego and Cincinnati and has never won a division. Record: 928-861 (.519).

Home: Pro Player Stadium, first and only (Miami) home of the Florida Marlins since April 5 1993. Marlins beat the Los Angeles Dodgers 6-3 in front of 42, 334. The stadium is shared with the NFL outfit, the Miami Dolphins. And therefore, seriously lacks true baseball atmosphere. **Capacity: 42 531.** Dimensions: 335' to left field, 410' to center field, 345' to right field. **Neutral Park** (From Pitcher to Hitter, 2003 to 2004, though this depends on whose reading of the stats you take).

World Series And Post-Season Ratings	Position	Points/No. of times...	
Full Playing Record 1993-2004	**24**	880-997: .469	
Total Historical Rating	18	21.4	
World Series Rating	17	240 Ranking Points	**RATINGS**
Play Offs Rating	12=	58 Ranking Points	
Division Wins (post-'69)	30=	0	
World Series Wins/Appearances/Games Won	13=/18=/17=	2/2/8	
Level Of Recent Success	**S'ons/Pos**	**Won/Lost/Games**	
Games Won Per Season	29	66.6	
Seasons Since A World Series Appearance	1	2003 beat NYY 4-2	
Seasons Since A Division Series	1	Beat San Francisco 3-2	
Seasons Since A Championship Series	1	Beat Chicago Cubs 4-3	
The Florida Marlins have never won a division title			

Most Home Runs Hit For The Marlins	Most Games Won By A Pitcher	
Season: 42 Gary Sheffield 1996	Season: 18 Carl Pavano, 2004*	
Career: 122 Gary Sheffield	Career: 42 Ryan Dempster	**RECORDS**
Highest Batting Average	**Most Strikeouts**	
Season: .334 Luis Castillo 2000	Season: 209 Ryan Dempster 2000	
Career: .296 Kevin Millar	Career: 628 Ryan Dempster	

*Beating the previous record: 17 Kevin Brown 1996; Alex Fernandez 1997

Best Batting Ave. Juan Pierre .326	**Most Home Runs** Miguel Cabrera 33	
RBI Leader Cabrera 112	**Most Bases** Cabrera 309 (.294)	
Most K's Josh Beckett 162	**Most HR Given Up** Ismael Valdez 33	**2004**
Most Innings Pitched Pavano 222.1	**Most Walks** Dontrelle Willis 61	
Other Top Bats: M. Lowell: .293, 27HR, 85 RBI	L. Castillo: .291, 164h, 47 RBI.	

Marlin Hall of Famers

None

Outside The Hall Of Fame

There's a good chance that Ivan 'Pudge' Rodriguez will one day make the grade – interesting to see how he immediately lifted the Tigers last year and hit with exceptional consistency– and I daresay he will never be forgotten by the Marlin fans of 2003, for his unforgettable leadership through the second half of the season and into the heart of the play offs. where he was magnificent.

1997: The World Series winning Marlins featured Gary Sheffield, Moises Alou, Kevin Brown, Edgar Renteria and Luis Castillo. Only the latter is still with the organisation. It's a good example of baseball club as revolving door or players as highly paid wondering slaves.

Marlin Retired Shirt Numbers

None

AAA Albuquerque Isotopes   **Spring Training Venue:** Roger Dean Stadium, Jupiter, Florida

---

EMERGENCY BASEBALL RECORDS - MISPLACED APPENDIX 1

Hitting

Most Home Runs:	Hank Aaron	755	Est. 1974
Most Seasons + .300	Ty Cobb	23	Est. 1928
Highest Lifetime Average	Ty Cobb	.367	1905-1928
Highest Slugging Average (career)	Babe Ruth	.690	1914-34
Most At Bats (Career)	Pete Rose	14, 053	1963-86
Most Runs Scored (Career)	Rickey Henderson	2,295	1979-03
Most Hits (Career)	Pete Rose	4,256	1963-86
Most Consecutive Games	Cal Ripken Jr	2, 632	1982-95
Most 200 Hit Seasons	Pete Rose	10	Est. 1979
Most Singles (Career)	Pete Rose	3,215	1963-86
Most Doubles (Career)	Tris Speaker	793	Est. 1928
Most Triples (Career)	Sam Crawford	312	Est. 1916
Most Multiple HR Games	Babe Ruth	72	Est. 1935
Most Grand Slams (Car)	Lou Gehrig	23	1923-39
Highest Career Total Bases	Hank Aaron	6,856	1954-76
Most Long Hits	Hank Aaron	1,477	1954-76
Most Runs Batted In	Hank Aaron	2,297	1954-76
Most Walks	Barry Bonds	2,179	1979-2003
Most Strikeouts (Batter- Career)	Reggie Jackson	2,597	1967-87
Most Stolen Bases (Career)	Rickey Henderson	1,406	1979-2003
Most Steals Of Home Plate (Career)	Ty Cobb	50	Est. 1928
Most Home Runs (Game)	14 players: 1st Bobby Lowe 1894	4	14th – Shawn Green, 2002

Most Home Runs All Time			Most Home Runs In A Season			
1.	Hank Aaron	755	1.	Barry Bonds	2001	73
2.	Babe Ruth	714	2.	Mark McGwire	1998	70
3.	Barry Bonds	703	3.	Sammy Sosa	1998	66
4.	Willie Mays	660	4.	Mark McGwire	1999	65
5.	Frank Robinson	586	5.	Sammy Sosa	2001	64
6.	Mark McGwire	583	6.	Sammy Sosa	1999	63
7.	Sammy Sosa	574	7.	Roger Maris	1961	61
8.	Harmon Killibrew	573	8.	Babe Ruth	1927	60
9.	Reggie Jackson	563				
10.	Raphael Palmeiro	551				

HOUSTON ASTROS

Houston, Texas

SINCE 1962

NATIONAL LEAGUE   WEST DIVISION 1969-93;

CENTRAL DIVISION 1994-2005

NAME CHANGE HISTORY

Houston Colt .45s 1962-64;

Houston Astros 1965-2005

Honours

World Series Wins	None
League Pennant Winners	N/R
Division Winners	1980, 1986, 1997, 1998, 1999
Division Series Winners	0
Championship Winners	N/R

"I just told my players that without question this is one of the greatest runs in the history of the game."
Phil Garner after Game 7, NLCS 2004, makes his point about the Astros post-All-Star Game run;
he may only have been exaggerating a little.

Season 2004

National League Cy Young Award Winner: Roger Clemens

Payroll 2003/2004	$90m(14) $7.5m(12)
Highest Paid Players	**Salary**
Jeff Bagwell	$17m
Andy Pettite	$10.5
Jeff Kent	$9.1
Hidalgo (OF)	$8,
Clemens,	$5
Biggio (OF)	$4,
Berkman (OF)	$3.5
Wade (P)	$3.4
Oswalt (P)	$3.25.

Team Statistics

Position in Div	2nd of 6
Record	92-70
Games Back	13
% Record	.568 (6th=)
Split	48-33 H; 44-37 R
Last 10 Seasons	2211141222
Runs per game	4.96 (13th=)
Staff ERA	4.05 (7th)
Ave ERA Starters	4.03 (3rd)
Ave ERA Relievers	4.10 (16th)
Batting Average	.267 (16th=)
Slugging ave.	.436 (12th)
On Base %:	.342 (11th)
AB/Hits Ratio	3.75 (7th)
Total/Net Homers	187/174 (*13* 13th)

AB per HR	29.24 (12th)
S'out/At Bat Ratio	5.47 (11th=)
Runs For/Against	803 (14) 698 (5)
Net Runs	105 (5th)
Net BB/BB p AB	65/9.26 (6th)
Total Steals	89 (14th)
Total Errors	101 (13th)
Unearned Runs Giv	48 (6th)
Record Attendance	2000: 3 056 139.
First season in Enron Field	**Ave**: 37 730.
Finished 4th.	
Attendance. 2003	2 454 038 **Ave** 30 297
Attendance 2004	3 087 872
25.82% increase	**Ave** 38 121 (7TH)

2004 Starting Rotation

Starter	Record
Roy Oswalt	35: 20-10, 3.49 ERA
Roger Clemens	34: 18-4, 2.98 ERA
Pete Munro	19: 4-7, 5.15 ERA.
Tim Redding	17: 5-7, 5.72 ERA
Wade Miller	15: 7-7, 3.35 ERA
Andy Pettite	15: 6-4, 3.90 ERA
Closer & Bullpen Star	28/32 SV 1.93 ERA B r a d
Lidge	
2nd Closer	14/17 SV 3.12 ERA
Octavio Dotel	
Catcher	
Brad Ausmus 129g	.248, 5HR, 31 RBI
Raul Chavez	.210, 0HR, 23 RBI

Briefly... The franchise of future Hall of Famers Jeff Bagwell and Craig Biggio, but to history first. n '62 huge, brash Texas won major league ball. Here is the club that gave us Astroturf and a vision of sports future: synthetic grass, air con stadiums and rapid consumer greed pandered to at the concession stand. Amazingly, the future has become the past: the Astros left the awful Astrodome for an old style ballpark in 2000 and hey presto! the future became a return to the past and a respect for history. In playing terms, the Astros did nothing until the late 80s: the dearth of Hall of Famers here tells a tale. However, the very recent past reveals "third pennant" wins and a feeling of the imminence of huge success.

2004 Despite a poor start to the season, the ditching of skipper Jimy Williams with a record of .500 in 88 games was the catalyst for great, if not ultimate success. Phil Garner was riding his Harley and playing a lot of golf when he got the call out of the blue from the Astros front office asking if he fancied taking over from Jimy Williams who was leading a bunch of talented guys to a life of .500 ball. By all accounts, the lack of pressure caused this firy little guy to manage without fear of failure. Making them more of a devilish "to hell with" it outfit enabled the huge talents of Clemens, Kent, Biggio, Bagwell, Berkman and the freshly aquired Beltran to breathe. The result was a spectacular run at the NL Wild Card spot, defeat of the Atlanta Braves in five in the NLDS and a last gasp loss under the daunting pressure of a Game 7 in the pennant round after leading them 4 games to 3. All is set for another tilt at the Big One in 2005.

Owner: Drayton McLane. **GM:** Tim Purpura **Manager: Phil Garner** (b. April 1949). "Scrap Iron" toiled for almost all 8 years of his time skippering the Brewers (beginning in 1992), before having two rough years with the Tigers. The third, 2003, opened up with 6 straight defeats and the push for Phil. Golf and professional wilderness was his lot until offered a slot gaffering in Houston. Record: 756-828 (.477).

Uniforms: Home - White jerseys and pants with black pinstripe; navy letters with sand and maroon 'Astros' letters; navy caps with star logo in club colours of sand and maroon with black edging. **Alt –** Maroon shirts with sand "Astros" lettering, navy undershirts, navy caps, white pants. Last season the team wore an All-Star Game patch on right sleeve.

Home: Minute Maid Park. This is the Astros's second home: they left the infamous Houston Astrodome, original home since 1962, in 1999. The Astrodome was a hitter's graveyard, with deep hits dying in the airless atmosphere thanks to the roof. It should be noted that the new ballpark was initially named Enron Field, but the title was dropped like a red hot poker after the Enron Scandal broke the following year. **Capacity is 42 000,** as opposed to the Dome's 53 370. Dimensions: 315' to left field, 435' to center field, 326' to right field. Although this means that hitters in this park have the longest hit to make for a homer in the country, this is balanced by the fact that the distances to the outer fields are the smallest in the majors. The park is often described as a "band box," a tiny park ripe for homers. First Game: The first regular season game was played here on April 7 2000 against the Philiadelphia Philies. Astros; won 4-1. **Hitter's Park (Slight advantage).**

The original home of the Astros was **The Astrodome.** In its time, the Astrodome - named after the state's space technology fame - was a wonder. It was considered an indoor circular marvel when it was opened, pointing the way to the future. The roof was considered essential for warding off the summer Texas heat - the interior would be air-conditioned - and summer bugs. But real grass does not grow well under a roof. Thus a new synthetic turf was invented for the Astrodome and it was named, guess what: Astroturf.

World Series And Post-Season Ratings	Position	Points/Occasions/%
Full Playing Record 1962-2004	29	3408-4430: .435
Total Historical Rating	23	22.4
World Series Rating	30=	0 Ranking Points
Play Offs Rating	24	19 Ranking Points
Pennant Wins (pre-'69)	17= (=last)	0
Division Wins (post-'69)	10=	6
World Series Wins/Appearances/Games Won	30=/30=/30=	0/0/0

Level Of Recent Success	S'ons/Pos	Won/Lost/Games
Games Won Per Season	6	79
Seasons Since A World Series Appearance	N/A	N/a
Seasons Since A Division Series	0	2004 beat Atlanta 3-2 (2001 lost to Atlanta 0-3)
Seasons Since A Championship Series	0	Lost to St Louis –2-4 (1986 lost to Mets 2-4)
Seasons Since A Division Win	3	Tied NLC with St Louis

RATINGS

Most Home Runs Hit For The Astros	Most Games Won By A Pitcher
Season: 47 Jeff Bagwell 2000	Season: 22 Mike Hampton 1999
Career: 380 Jeff Bagwell	Career: 144 Joe Niekro
Highest Batting Average	**Most Strikeouts**
Season: .355 Moises Alou 2000	Season: 313 J.R. Richards 319
Career: .302 Jeff Bagwell	Career: 1 886 Nolan Ryan

RECORDS

Best Batting Ave. 2004 Lance Berkman .316	Most Home Runs 2004 Berkman 30
RBI Leader Jeff Kent 107 (Berkman 106)	**Most Bases** Berkman 308
Most K's Clemens 218 (Oswalt 206)	**Most HR Given Up** Roy Oswalt 17
Most Innings Pitched Oswalt 237	**Most Walks** Clemens 79
Other Top Bats: Jeff Bagwell: .266, 89 RBI, 152h Craig Biggio: .281, 178h, 63 RBI.	

2004

Astros Hall of Famers

None, but Bagwell and Biggio are, like current colleague Clemens (see below), both shoe-ins for Cooperstown after they retire.

Retired Uniform Numbers

25 Jose Cruz	32 Jim Umbricht	33 Mike Scott
34 Nolan Ryan	40 Don Wilson	49 Larry Dierker

AAA Round Rock Express   **Spring Training Venue:** Osceola Stadium, Kissimmee, Florida

You can quote me on that . . .

"I would have jumped off a tall building. But the way I'm batting, I wouldn't have hit the ground."

Phil Garner

William Roger Clemens – "The Rocket" - (b. 1962, Dayton, Ohio, Boston Red Sox, Toronto Blue Jays, New York Yankees, Houston Astros). Here on June 2, 2004, Clemens is out of self-proclaimed retirement pushing 42, a second away from releasing another pitch in another win (against the Cubs, 5-1). He finished '04 with 328 career wins (10th= AT) and 4,317 strikeouts (2nd AT). With Randy Johnson, the greatest active pitcher alive for longevity and numbers.

KANSAS CITY ROYALS

Kansas City, Missouri

SINCE 1969

AMERICAN LEAGUE WEST DIVISION 1969-93;
CENTRAL DIVISION 1994-2005

Honours

World Series Champions	1985
Division Winners	1976; 1977; 1978; 1984 & 1985
Division Series Winners	0
Championship Winners	1980 & 1985
World Series Losses	1980 v Philadelphia Phillies 2-4

World Series Win	Manager
1985 - v. St Louis Cardinals 4-3	Dick Howser

*"I could have played another year, but I would have been playing for the money,
and baseball deserves better than that."*

A touch of nobility from the Royals' best ever player, George Brett.

Season 2004

Payroll 2003/2004	$48.47 (27) $48 (23)
Highest	Salaries
Mike Sweeney	$11m
Juan Gonzalez	$4m*
Carlos Beltran	$4.03*
Brian Anderson (P)	$3.25m
Joe Randa (3B)	$3.25m
*to Houston June '04	

2004 Team Statistics

Position in Div	5th of 5
Record	58-104
Games Back	34
% Record	.358 (29th)
Split	33-47 H; 25-57 R
Last 10 Seasons	2553445435
Runs per game	4.44
Staff ERA	5.15 (28th)
Ave ERA Starters	5.50 (29th)
Ave ERA Relievers	4.50 (22nd)
Batting ave	.259 (24th)
Slugging ave.	.397 (26th)
On Base %:	.322 (24th)
AB/Hits Ratio	3.86 (24th)
Total/Net Homers	150/208 (-58 28th)
AB per HR	36.92 (22nd)
S'out/At Bat Ratio	5.24 (17th)

Runs For/Against	720 (21) 905 (28)
Net Runs	-185 (29th)
Total Steals	67 (22nd)
Net BB/BB p AB	-57/12.01 (27th)
Total Errors	131 (27th)
Unearned Runs Giv	92 (28th)
Record Attendance	1989: 2 477 700.
Finished 2nd	Ave 30 589.
Attendance. 2003	1 779 895
	Ave 22 819
Attendance 2004	1 661 478 (79)
7.83% decrease.	Ave 21 031 (28th)

Starting Rotation 2004

Starter	Record
Darrell May	31: 9-19, 5.61 ERA
Brian Anderson	26:6-12, 5.64 ERA
Jimmy Gobble	24: 9-8, 5.35 ERA
Zack Greinke	24: 8-11; 3.97 ERA
Mike Wood	17: 3-8, 5.94 ERA
Dennys Reyes	12 4-8, 4.78 ERA
Closer	
Jeremy Affeldt	13/17 SV 5.02 ERA
Best Of The Bullpen	
Jaime Cerda	3.15 ERA
Catcher	
Benito Santiago 49g	.274, 23 RBI, 6 HR
John Buck 71g	.256 30 RBI, 12 HR

Briefly... This is the notable mid-western city that hungered after major league baseball, got it in the 50s when the Braves left Boston, lost it when the owners took the whole thing south to Atlanta, but got their own club as part of the '69 expansion which also gave us the Expos. As you can see from the table below, they have had their glorious years already, but at the moment, despite the predictions for play off work in 2004 from the Channel 5 studio after a promising 2003, it didn't happen for them. In fact, it was an complete disaster. The trading of star slugger Carlos Beltran (27) to Houston as early as June 24 said it all: a losing franchise drastically shedding payroll too frightened, financially or otherwise, to compete with the big boys. Grim. That said, there were a couple of bright points of light: John Buck and Abraham Nunez became the first pair of rookies in major league history to hit grand slams in the same game and on September 9th the teams smashed the Tigers 26-5 with Joe Randa becoming the first in the AL to score 6 hits and 6 runs in a game.

Uniforms: Home - Royal blue with black trim and white 'Royals' letters. Royal blue caps with black peak. 'KC' logo, white pants. **Alt:** white shirt with blue sleeve edging and blue letters. Further alternative: beige jersey with black sleeves with blue 'Kansas City' letters. Beige pants. **Road –** Grey sleeveless shirts with "Kansas City" letters in blue with white edge, numbers under heart, black undershirts. **Alt –** Black shirts with blue 'Y' piping and sleeve edging.

Owners: David Glass. **GM:** Allard Baird. **Manager: Tony Pena** (b. June 1957, Dominican Republic) was voted NL Manager of the Year by the Baseball Writers of America in 2003 because he seemed able to mould the Royals into a group of contenders after 2002 had seen 100 losses. Finishing third they were nevertheless only 7 games out and led the division for a portion of the early season, to everyone's surprise. However, it all went south again last year. The loss of '03 .307/100 RBI man Carlos Beltran to Houston added to an injury ravaged roster to create an unmitigated disaster. That Beltran put up Hall of Fame numbers in the crucible of play off baseball (.417 & 4 homers in the NLCS, etc) only serves to underline the current plight. To move forward, it's not much use giving up your superstar. Regardless, TP struggles on, trying to smile through the frustration.

Home: Kauffman Stadium..Originally named Royals Stadium, this has been the home of the Kansas City Royals, since April 10 1973. Inaugural game was played in front of 39 464 as KCR mashed the Texas Rangers 12-1. The present name emanates from original Royals owner . Ewing Kauffman. **Capacity: 40 625.** Dimensions: 330' to both left and right fields, 400' to centre field. **Neutral Park (From Hitter to Pitcher, 2003-2004)** Kauffman is usually very much a **hitters park** but runs were much more scarce than usual in 2004. Former home was the **Municipal Stadium, Kansas City.** First game April 12 1955 6-2 winners over Detroit.

World Series And Post-Season Ratings	Position	Points/Occasions/%	
Full Playing Record 1969-2004	26	2816-2877: .464	
Total Historical Rating	20	18	
World Series Rating	20	95 Ranking Points	
Play Offs Rating	19	44 Ranking Points	
Division Wins (post-'69)	10=	6	
World Series Wins/Appearances/Games Won	19=/18=/20	1/2/6	
Level Of Recent Success	**S'ons/Pos**	**Won/Lost/Games**	**RATINGS**
Games Won Per Season	12	76.6	
Seasons Since A World Series Appearance	19	1985 bt Cards 4-3	
Seasons Since A Division Series	23	1981 lost to Oakland 0-3	
Seasons Since A Championship Series	19	1985 Beat Toronto 4-3	
Seasons Since A Division Win	19	1985 Won ALW by 1 game	

Most Home Runs Hit For The Royals	Most Games Won By A Pitcher	
Season: 36 Steve Balboni 1985	Season: 23 Bret Saberhagen 1989	
Career: 317 George Brett	Career: 166 Paul Splittorff	
Highest Batting Average	**Most Strikeouts**	**RECORDS**
Season: .390 George Brett 1980	Season: 244 Dennis Leonard 1977	
Career: .305 George Brett	Career: 1 451 Kevin Appier	

Best Batting Ave: Joe Randa, Ken Harvey, Mike Sweeney, David Dejesus .287	**Most Home Runs:** Sweeney 22	
	Most Bases Sweeney 207	**2004**
RBI Leader Sweeney 79 (next highest 66, Stairs)	**Most HR Given Up** May 38 (Anderson 33)	
Most K's Darrell May 207 (Greinke 100)	**Most Walks** May 55 (Anderson 53)	
Most Innings Pitched May 186		

Royals Hall of Famers

George Brett 3B, 1973-93, LT .305 L: A left-handed hitter of tremendous accomplishment: has 3,154 hits (AT14), 319 home runs, three batting titles (in 3 decades) to his name, as well as a .390 average in 1980.13 times an All-Star. (BJ2) MVP 1980 1999. Top 100: **BJ30*- SN55 – SABR29** James thus rates Brett as the 24th best hitter of all time.

Retired Uniform Numbers		
5 George Brett	10 Dick Howser	20 Frank White

AAA Omaha Royals   **Spring Training Venue:** Surprise Stadium, Surprise, Florida

LOS ANGELES DODGERS

Los Angeles, California

Since 1958

National League

West Division 1969-2005

Name Change History

1884-88 Brooklyn Trolley Dodgers; 889-98 Brooklyn Bridegrooms; 1899-1910 Brooklyn Superbas; 1911-13 Brooklyn Dodgers; 1914-31 Brooklyn Robins; 1932-1957 Brooklyn Dodgers; 1958-2005 Los Angeles Dodgers

Honours

World Series Champions	1959, 1963, 1965, 1981 & 1988
League Pennant Winners	1959, 1963, 1965 & 1966
Division Winners	1974; 1977; 1978; 1983, 1988, 1994, 1995 & 2004
Division Series Winners	0
Championship Winners	1974, 1977, 1978, 1981 & 1988
World Series Losses	1966 v Baltimore Orioles 0-4 1974 v Oakland A's 1-4; 1977 v New York Yankees 2-4 1978 v New York Yankees 2-4

World Series Wins	Managers
1959 - v. Chicago White Sox 4-2	Walter Alston
1963 - V. New York Yankees 4-0	Walter Alston
1965 - v. Minnesota Twins 4-3	Walter Alston
1981 - V. New York Yankees 4-2	Tommy Lasorda
1988 - v. Oakland As 4-1	Tommy Lasorda

"I say this from the bottom of my heart: that if you don't root for the Dodgers, you may not get into heaven."

Tommy Lasorda.

Season 2004

Payroll 2003/2004	$109.24 (3) $90 (7)
Highest	Salaries
Shawn Green (OF)	$16.67m
Darren Dreifort (P)	$11.4m
Hideo Nomo (P)	$9m
Todd Hundley (C)	$7m (DL – 2004)
Derek Weaver (P)	$6.25m
Adrian Beltre (3B)	$5m
Eric Gagne (Cl)	$5m
Odalis Perez (P),	$5m
Acquired 2004	$4,
Steve Finley (CF)	$7m
from Arizona	

2004 Team Statistics

Position in Div	1st of 5
Record	93-69
Games Back	+ 2
% Record	.574 (5th)
Split	49-32 H; 44-37 R
Last 10 seasons	1223323321
Runs per game	4.70 (19th)
Staff ERA	4.01 (4th)
Ave ERA Starters	4.53 (13th=)
Ave ERA Relievers	3.06 (2nd)
Batting ave	.262 (21st)
Slugging ave.	.423 (18th)
On Base %	.332 (16th)

AB/Hits Ratio	3.82 (21st)
Total/Net Homers	203/178 (*25* 6th)
AB per HR	27.30 (8th)
S'out/At Bat Ratio	5.07 (22nd)
Runs For/Against	761 (19) 684 (3)
Net Runs	76 (9th)
Net BB/BB p AB	15/10.34 (14th)
Total Steals	102 (9th)
Total Errors	73 (1st)
Unearned Runs Giv	37 (1st)
Record Attendance	1982 3 608 881.
Finished 2nd	Ave 44 554
Attendance 2003	3 138 626 Ave: 38 748
Attendance 2004	3 488 283 Ave 43 065 (2nd)

2004 Starting Rotation

Starter	Record
Jeff Weaver	34: 13-13, 4.01 ERA
Odalis Perez	31: 7-6, 3.25 ERA
Jose Lima	24: 13-5, 4.07 ERA
Kazuhisa Ishii	31: 13-8, 4.71 ERA
Brad Penny	24: 9-10, 3.15 ERA
Wilson Alvarez	14: 7-6, 4.03 ERA
Hideo Nomo	18: 4-11, 8.25 ERA
Closer: Eric Gagne	45/47 SV, 2.19 ERA
Bullpen Stars: G. Mota	2.14 ERA
G. Carrara	2.18 ERA
Catchers*: Bret Mayne 83g	.221, 0HR, 15 RBI
David Ross 70g	.170, 5HR, 15RBI

*Catcher Paul LoDuca traded at deadline to Marlins. .301, 10HR, 41 RBI in 90 games forLA before the July trade.e

Briefly... If you like the glory but don't want to be so predictable as to follow the Yankees, go for the Dodgers. Their history is dirty and gloriously urban from their days as the poor relation in the five boroughs of New York, scandalous and for many tragic with the move to LA in 1957, becoming a story of modern competitive winning of the big prize. It's a long way to go for a home game, mind.

2004 was a great season, not withstanding the early play off departure to St Louis in four games. 93 wins was the most since '91, 53 of them comeback wins, which spoke volumes for the team's character. It's interesting to see how many national pundits will agree that the exciting Division victory was down to DePodesta, the Moneyball disciple of Beane. Whatever the reason, the Dodgers hit much better in '04 than in their milky '03 season, with great results. And of course, there was Gagne.

Uniforms: Home – Plain white shirts with royal blue "Dodgers" letters in script, white pants. Red numbers under heart. Blue under shirts. **Road -** Grey jerseys with blue 'Y' piping,'Los Angeles' letters or 'Dodgers' in script. Grey pants. 'LA' logo on left sleeve. Blue caps withwhite 'LA' logo. Immaculately clean look. Blue under shirts.

Owner: Frank McCourt. **GM:** Paul DePodesta. **Manager:** 48 year-old **Jim Tracy** is the Dodgers skipper, wearing 12. As a player, he had just a two-year career with the Cubs, 1981 and 82, hitting 3 homers and .249 in 87 games in the outfield. Seems to be doing an okay job, but under the Billy Beane model followed by GM acolyte DePodesta, what's to do when the stats are right in front of the field manager to tell him whether to bring a reliever in for the seventh or not, and which bullpen guy is most likely to get the outs required? At the time of going to press the GM was looking to extend Tracy's contract, which might just suggest that he knows how to operate the system and with a successful 2004 under everyone's belt, rocking the boat would have to be the wrong move. Record: 356-292 (.549).

Gagne... Closer Eric Gagne won his first Cy Young in 2003. His 55 saves from 55 opportunities was simply sensational. "This guy is incredible," said Dennis Eckersley at the Baseball Writers of America awards ceremony in January. He also became the first pitcher to achieve 50 saves in two consecutive seasons. Last season he took the "art" of the save to a new level, recording a record of 95 consecutive successes. Despite the trepidation his arrival, accompanied by the words, "Game Over" being flashed all around Dodgers Stadium, for batters, the pressure his growing consecutive save total must have put on him makes his achievement extremely impressive. His 2003 salary was $550 000 for 2003 (he was essentially a failed starter at this point, relegated to the bullpen). He wanted $8 for 2004 but was offered $5.

Home: Dodger Stadium began its existence as home of the LA Dodgers in April 1962, five years after the Walter O'Malley moved the Dodgers to California from a heartbroken Brooklyn. The LA franchise began life in front of 78 672 spectators at the Los Angeles Coliseum. Dodger Stadium held 56 000 on opening day v. the Cincinnati Reds. **Capacity: 56 000** officially, but as in G4 of the Division Series against St Louis last October the ground record was broken with 56 368 paying spectators, that has to be out the window. Dimensions: 330' to left field, 395' to center field, 330' to right field. The venue is also known as "Chavez Ravine." **Pitcher's Park (Very clear advantage).** Former Home: **Ebbett's Field,** Brooklyn, now semi-mystical home of the Dodgers, First game, April 9 1913. Philies NL 1 Brooklyn 0.

World Series And Post-Season Ratings	Position	Points/Occasions/%
Full Playing Record 1901-2004	3	8421-7675: .520
Total Historical Rating	3	N/A
World Series Rating (Dodgers Franchise)	4=	255 Ranking Points
Play Offs Rating	6	101 Ranking Points
Pennant Wins (pre-'69)	3	13 (9 Brooklyn, 4 LA)
Division Wins (post-'69)	4	10
World Series Wins/Appearances/Games Won	4=/2/3=	6/18/45
Level Of Recent Success	**S'ons/Pos**	**Won/Lost/Games**
Games Per Season	3	82.3
Seasons Since A World Series Appearance	16	1988 bt Oakland 4-1
Seasons Since A Division Series	0	2004 lost to Houston 1-3 (1996 lost to Atlanta 0-3)
Seasons Since A Championship Series	16	1988 bt Mets 4-3
Seasons Since A Division Win	0	Won NLW by 1 game (1995 Won NLW by 2 games)

Most Home Runs Hit For The LA Dodgers	Most Games Won By A Pitcher
Season: 49 Shawn Green 2001	Season: 27 Sandy Koufax 1966
Career: 257 Eric Karros	Career: 233 Don Sutton
Highest Batting Average:	**Most Strikeouts**
Season: .362 Mike Piazza 1997	Season: 382 Sandy Koufax 1965

Best Batting Ave. 2004 Adrian Beltre .334	**Most Home Runs 2004** Beltre 48
RBI Leader Beltre 121 (Finley 94)	**Most Bases** Beltre 376 (200h)
Most K's Jeff Weaver 153	**Most HR Given Up** Jose Lima 33
Most Innings Pitched Weaver 220	**Most Walks** Kazuhisa Ishii 98
Other Top Bats: Ces. Izturis: .288, 193h, 62 RBI	Shawn Green: 266, 157h, 86 RBI.

RATINGS

RECORDS

2004

Brooklyn Dodgers World Series Wins   1955
League Pennant Winners: 1916, 1920, 1941, 1947, 1949, 1952, 1953, 1955 & 1956.
World Series losses: 1-4 to Boston Red Sox in 1916 2-5 to Cleveland Indians in 1920 1-4 to New York Yankees
in 1941 3-4 to New   York Yankees in 1947 1-4 to New York Yankees in 1949 3-4 to
New York Yankees in 1952 2-4 to Washington Senators in 1953 3-4 to New York Yankees in 1956

Dodgers Hall of Famers

"Jackie was the greatest competitor I ever saw. He didn't win. He triumphed."

Ralph Branca, Dodger pitcher, 1947

"Rex Barney could throw a baseball through a brick wall if he could hit the brick wall."
Unknown comment on the Brooklyn Dodgers '40s fastballer of whom it was also said by an unknown observer
He would be the greatest of all-time if the strike zone was high and outside."

Roy Campanella C 1948-57: This catcher and hitter came through in the wake of Jackie Robinson and was a three time NL MVP. In 1953 he hit a record 41 home runs for a catcher and knocked in 142 RBIs. He batted over .300 three times. His 10 year 242 HR career was cut short by a car crash in 1958. .276 LT. (BJ3) MVP 1951 **1969.** Top 100: BJ53- SN50 – SABR47

Don Drysdale P 1956-69 209-166 2.95 ERA.: Fiercely competitive pitcher, making exceptionally formidable combo with Koufax (3 WS wins during this pairing's time). 12th all time ERA. CY 1962 (BJ33) **1984**

Burleigh Grimes P 1916-34 ('18-'26) 270-212 3.53 ERA: One of the 9 pitchers allowed to use the spitball after 1919. 5-time 20 game winner. His absence from the Top 100 lists is attributable no doubt to his being able to use the questionable ball throughout the whole of his career at a time when almost all his contemporaries couldn't use this formidable weapon. (BJ62) **1964**

Willie Keeler RF 1892-1910 L: hit over .300 13 times in consecutive seasons. 'Wee Willie.' One of the all time nice guys of the game, spending a lot of time, during games even, talking to fans. Famous for his saying, "I hit them where they ain't." Entered the Hall Of Fame with a Brooklyn Superbas hat. (BJ35) **1939 BJ00 SN75 SABR00**

Pee Wee Reese: SS, 1940-58: Exceptional fielder and more than useful lead off hitter. One of the great names of the pennant and Series winning Brooklyn Dodgers, playing over 2000 games. (BJ10) **1984**

Jackie Robinson: 2B, 1947-56: 311 lifetime hitter and brilliant second baseman, leading NL batter and MVP in 1949, two years after breaking into the majors from the Negro leagues in 1947 with the Dodgers. Was the first Rookie of the Year in 1947. His number, 42, was retired by Commissioner of Baseball Bud Selig in 1997. MVP '49 (BJ4) **1962.** Top 100: BJ32- SN44 – SABR36

Wilbert Robinson 1914-31: Manager in the two pennant winning teams of 1916 and 1920.

Duke Snider: CF 1947-64 ('47-'57) L: prodigious 1950s hitter with brilliant World Series record: 11 homers and 26 RBIs. Hit Ebbets Field's last ever home run in September 1957. Hit 40 homers five consecutive seasons. (BJ6) **1980.** Top 100: BJ50- SN83 – SABR68

Dazzy Vance P 1915-35 197-140, 3.24 ERA: 1922-32 with Brooklyn Robins, then Dodgers (in '32), 197 career wins. Highly unusual career for hitting great form for the first time at 31 after a freak arm accident caused the solution to a long-term sore arm problem. Real old fashioned fastball pitcher with surely one of the great names. Peers out from his plaque wearing a Robins cap. (BJ35) **1955**

Zack Wheat: LF 1909-27 L: Spanned Brooklyn Superbas, Dodgers and Robins, hitting lifetime .317. An immensely popular man and player and one of the few big league players with Native American blood. Also wears a Robins hat in the gallery. (BJ23) **1959**

Los Angeles Dodgers Hall of Famers

Sandy Koufax: P 1955-66 165-187 2.76 ERA L: Supremely dominant pitcher of the early 60s, one of the greatest, even working in a pitcher's park for much of his career (after the '62 to Dodgers Stadium especially). Retired early through injury from being overworked. Pronounced "Ko-fax." CY '63, '65, '66, (BJ10) **1972.** Top 100: BJ51- SN26 – SABR21

Tommy Lasorda M.: Led the Dodgers to their 2 World Series wins in the 80s. Stills works for the franchise as legend.

Don Sutton P 1966-88 324-256, 3.26 ERA: His victories figure in 11th of all time, his ERA 26th. However, he was helped by pitching in hitter-unfriendly Dodgers Stadium. His 3,574 strikeouts tell their own tale, however. Also Astros, Brewers, Athletics and Angels in a career of great longevity. Starred in four teams that made in to the Series. (BJ31) **1998**

Retired Uniform Numbers

2 Tommy Lasorda	4 Duke Snider	1 Pee Wee Reese
19 Jim Gilliam	24 Walter Alston	32 Sandy Koufax
39 Roy Campanella	20 Don Sutton	

Brooklyn Dodgers attendance record: **1947: 1 807 526. Average: 23 474. Finished 1st.**

AAA Las Vegas 51s   **Spring Training Venue:** Holman Stadium, Vero Beach, Florida

Two tough-looking bastards here, alright. **Leo Durocher** (pronounced "Du-row-sher", known as "The Lip") - **1905-91** b. West Springfield, Massachusetts - was an ultra, ultra competitive player and manager to the point of utter ruthlessness; as arrogant as he was charismatic; a turbulent, conflict-seeking big mouth. He was Shortstop on the 1934 Gashouse Gang in St Louis and managed the Dodgers with success in from 1939-46, organising and motivating them to their first pennant win (in 1941) for 21 years. **Joe McCarthy – 1887-1978** b. Philadelphia, Pennsylvania - managed both the Yankees and the Red Sox, winning eight pennants with the latter and challenging his old team hard in the late 40s with the Sox. This is the man who took the Yankee job when Ruth wanted it. They never got along because of it.

MILWAUKEE BREWERS

Milwaukee, Wisconsin

SINCE 1969
AMERICAN LEAGUE
WEST DIVISION 1969-71;
EAST DIVISION 1972-1993
CENTRAL DIVISION 1993-1997;
NATIONAL LEAGUE; CENTRAL DIVISION 1998-2005

NAME CHANGE HISTORY

Seattle Pilots 1969; Milwaukee Brewers 1970-2005

"The team was purchased on April 1, 1970 by an ownership group headed by Milwaukee auto dealer Bud Selig. The team was still in spring training as the Seattle Pilots. The trucks carrying the team's equipment were sent to Salt Lake City, Utah from Arizona, where they were to receive instruction whether to continue to Seattle or Milwaukee. The team had six days to remove the Pilots logos from team uniforms and replace them with Brewers logos."
From online encyclopedia Nationmaster.com; just an interesting tit-bit or apt franchise metaphor 1970-2005?

Honours

World Series Wins	None
League Pennant Winners	N/a
Division Winners	1982
Division Series Winners	()
Championship Series Winners	1982 bt California Angels 3-2; 1982 v St Louis Cardinals 3-4

Season — 2004

Payroll 2003/2004	$47m (28) $28m (30)
Highest	Salaries
Geoff Jenkins ()	$8.7m
Ben Sheets	$2.45m
Danny Kolb (Cl)	$1.5m
Craig Counsell (SS)	$2.42m

2004 Team Statistics

Position in Div	6th of 6
Record	67-94
Games Back	37.5
% Record	.416 (25th=)
Split	36-45 H; 31-49 R
Last 10 seasons	4335534666
Runs per game	3.91 (29th)
Staff ERA	4.24 (12th)
Ave ERA Starters	4.21 (9th=)
Ave ERA Relievers	4.28 (19th)
Batting ave	.248 (30th)
Slugging ave.	.387 (30th)
On Base %:	.321 (25th)
AB/Hits Ratio	4.03 (30th)
Total/Net Homers	135/164 (-29 22nd)
AB per HR	40.61 (28th)

AB per SO	4.18 (29th)
Runs For/Against	634 (29) 757 (13)
Net Runs	-123 (25th)
Net BB/BB p AB	64/10.15 (13th)
Total Steals	138 (2nd)
Total Errors	117 (24th)
Unearned Runs Giv	78 (26th)
Record Attendance	2001: 2 811 041.
New stadium	Ave: 34 704.
	Finished 4th.
Attendance. 2003	1 685 049 Ave: 20 803
Attendance 2004	2 062 383 Ave 25 461 (20th)

2004 Starting Rotation

Starter	Record
Ben Sheets	34: 12-14, 2.70 ERA
Doug Davis	34: 12-12, 3.39 ERA
Victor Santos	28: 11-12, 4.97 ERA
Wes Obermueller	20: 6-8, 5.80 ERA
Chris Capuano	17:6-8, 4.99 ERA
Closer	
Dan Kolb	39/44 SV 2.98 ERA
Bullpen Stars	
Kolb & Matt Kinney	3.13 ERA
Catcher	
Chad Moeller 101g	.208, 5HR, 27 RBI
Gary Bennett. 75g	.224, 3HR, 20 RBI

Briefly... The franchise, as they would say in the States, was set up in 1969 and played in Seattle as the Pilots for one season (See Book Review section, Ball Four). The following year they were in Milwaukee, Wisconsin competing in the AL as the Brewers, a reflection of the trade of their owners. In terms of winning pennants and so on, the Brewers are the modern St Louis

Browns and Boston Braves: they can't get arrested. Despite a surge of winningness at the back end of '81 and the 1982 season, they have only been able to manage second place in their division twice. However, under new owner Los Angeles investor Mark Attanasio who bought the franchise from the Selig family in September, new and very different times could be ahead. According to local professor and fan James Baughman, what the Brewers need is "somebody with deep pockets and he has deep pockets. The problem with the Brewers is that they have been reluctant to spend money, but Attanasio will change that." As of early November '04, we await news from Wisconsin.

Uniforms: Home - White jerseys with superb navy blue 'Brewers' letters in script with yellow edging. 'M' on sleeve and numbers on jersey front. White pants with blue and yellow side stripes, blue caps with 'M' logo in white with beige edging. **Alt:** Blue shirts with white "Brewers" letters and white sleeve edge. **Road –** Grey shirts with blue "Brewers" script letters with fine yellow edge, double blue thin sleeve stripe middled with yellow, blue undershirts.

Owner: Mark Attanasio **GM:** Doug Melvin. **Manager: Ned Yost** (b. Aug 1954) is a team boss in his second season. Had a brief major league career, spending six seasons mostly with the Brewers (and one with the Rangers). Hit just .212 in 219 games, and 12 homers. Another last place in 2004, the Brewers have not had a season over .500 since 1992. Previous to his present job, Edgar Yost spent 12 seasons in a variety of coaching roles with the Atlanta Braves - bullpen coach and third base coach over his last 10 years there. Doubtless the front office trusted the notion that old Bobby Cox wouldn't have a fool in such positions and that some of that Coxness and fairy dust of constant winning would bound to rub off on Milwaukee teams sooner or later. At the moment we're heading for later, but realistically, without a payroll to speak of, no one is expecting Ned to lead the Brewers to a winning record this season. Record: 135-188 (.418)

Home: Miller Park. 'State of the art' home of the Milwaukee Brewers since April 6 2001, upon which occasion, the Brewers beat the Reds 5-4. The franchise began its playing history in 1970 at County Stadium. On April 7th the Brewers lost to the California (later Anaheim) Angels 12-0. **Capacity: 43 000.** Dimensions: 342' to left field, 400' to center field, 345' to right field. Pitcher's Park (Clear advantage).

World Series And Post-Season Ratings	Position	Points/Occasions/%	
Full Playing Record 1969-2004	22	2680-3019: .470	
Total Historical Rating	25=	N/A	
World Series Rating	23	25 Ranking Points	
Play Offs Rating	23	20 Ranking Points	
Division Wins (post-'69)	26	1	
World Series Wins/Appearances/Games Won	30=/22=/23	0/1/3	**RATINGS**
Level Of Recent Success	**S'ons/Pos**	**Won/Lost/Games**	
Games Won Per Season	25	72.5	
Seasons Since A World Series Appearance	22	1982 lost 3-4 to St Louis	
Seasons Since A Division Series	11	1981 lost to NYY 2-3*	
Seasons Since A Championship Series	22	1982 beat California Angels 3-2	
Seasons Since A Division Win	10	1982 Won ALE by 1 game	

*In 1981, the Brewers qualified for the play offs from 3rd place in their division. They lost their division series to the Yankees 2-3. Don't ask me to explain it. It might be like Arsenal getting promoted to Division 1 after the First World War after finishing 8th or something in Division 2 in 1914.

Most Home Runs Hit For The Brewers	Most Games Won By A Pitcher	
Season: 45 Gorman Thomas 1979; Richie Sexson 2001.	Season: 22 Mike Caldwell 1978	
Career: 251 Robin Yount	Career: 117 Jim Slaton	
Highest Batting Average	**Most Strikeouts**	**RECORDS**
Season: .353 Paul Molitor	Season: *264 Ben Sheets 2004*	
Career: .307 Jeff Cirillo	Career: 1 081 Teddy Higuera	

Best Batting Ave. 2004 Lyle Overbay .301	Most Home Runs 2004 Geoff Jenkins 27	
RBI Leader Jenkins 93 (Overrbay 87)	**Most Bases** Jenkins 292	
Most K's Ben Sheets 264	**Most HR Given Up** Sheets 25	**2004**
Most Innings Pitched Sheets 237	**Most Walks** Doug Davis 79	

Brewers Hall of Famers

Robin Yount: SS 1974-93: Absolutely exceptional player of 2 856 career games. Batted .293 lifetime and hit 251 home runs. He was almost a pro golfer instead of ball player, four years into a career that began at 18. His slugging ave. of .430 is AT55. His 11,008 at bats AT7. MVP 1982, 1989 (BJ4) **1999.** Top 100: BJ55- SN00 – SABR79

Paul Molitor Inf: 2004 entrant and hugely deserved for a long and hugely successful career in which he - in 1982, broke the World Series record for hits in a game, making 6. Made 3,319 hits (AT8) 2003 but was a great outfielder also. Now hitting coach to the Seattle Mariners. **Top 100: BJ00- SN99 – SABR81**

Retired Uniform Numbers

Robin Yount 19		Paul Molitor 4
	34　Rollie Fingers	44 - Hank Aaron

AAA Nashville Sounds

Spring Training Venue: Maryvale Baseball Park, Phoenix, Arizona

You can quote me on that . . .

"There'll be two buses leaving the hotel for the park tomorrow. The two o'clock bus will be for those of you who need a little extra work. The empty bus will leave at five o'clock."

David Bristol, Milwaukee Brewers manager

EMERGENCY BASEBALL RECORDS - MISPLACED APPENDIX 2

Best ERA of Active Pitchers @October 2004

	Name	ERA	W-L	Name	ERA	W-L
1.	P. Martinez	2.71	182-76	E Walsh	1.82	195-126
2.	J. Franco	2.84	90-86	A Joss	1.89	160-97
3.	G. Maddux	2.95	305-174	A Spalding	2.04	252-65
4.	R. Johnson	3.07	246-128	M Brown	2.06	239-130
5.	J. Orosco	3.16	87-80	J Ward	2.10	164-102
6.	R. Clemens	3.18	328-164	C Mathewson	2.13	373-188
7.	K. Brown	3.20	207-137	T Bond	2.14	234-163
8.	J. Rijo	3.24	116-91	R Waddell	2.16	193-143
9.	J. Smoltz	3.27	163-121	W Johnson	2.17	417-279
10.	T. Hudson	3.30	92-39	E Ruelbach	2.28	182-106

EMERGENCY BASEBALL RECORDS - MISPLACED APPENDIX 3
TRIPLE CROWN WINNERS

American League

Year	Player	Average	Home Runs	RBI
1901	Nap Lajoie	.422	14	125
1909	Ty Cobb	.377	9	115
1933	Jimmy Foxx	.356	48	163
1934	Lou Gehrig	.363	49	165
1942	Ted Williams	.356	36	137
1947	Ted Williams	.343	32	114
1956	Mickey Mantle	.353	52	130
1966	Frank Robinson	.316	49	122
1967	Carl Yastrzemski	.326	44	121

National League

Year	Player	Average	Home Runs	RBI
1912	Heinie Zimmerman	.372	14	98
1922	Rogers Hornsby	.401	42	152
1925	Rogers Hornsby	.403	39	143
1933	Chuck Klein	.368	28	120
1937	Joe Medwick	.374	31	154

MINNESOTA TWINS

Minneapolis, Minnesota

SINCE 1961
AMERICAN LEAGUE   WEST DIVISION 1969-93;
CENTRAL DIVISION 1994-2005

NAME CHANGE HISTORY

1901-1960 Washington Senators; 1961-2005 Minnesota Twins

Honours

World Series Champions	1987 & 1991
League Pennant Winners	1965
Division Winners	1969, 1970, 1987, 1991, 2002, 2003 & 2004
Division Series Winners	2002
Championship Series Winners	1987 & 1991
World Series Losses	1965 (3-4 to Los Angeles Dodgers)
Division Series Losses	2003
World Series Losses	1965 v Los Angeles Dodgers 3-4

World Series Wins	Manager
1987 – v. St Louis Cardinals 4-3	Tom Kelly
1991 – v. Atlanta Braves 4-3	Tom Kelly

Season 2004

American League Cy Young Award Winner: Johan Santana

Payroll 2003/2004	$65m (18) $54m (19)
Highest	Salaries
Brad Radke	$10.75m
Torri Hunter	$6.5m
Joe Mays (P)	$5.75m
Shannon Stewart	$5.5m
Corie Koskie (3B)	$4.5m,
Jacque Jones (OF)	$4.35m
Cristian Guzman (SS)	$3.72m

2004 Team Statistics

Position in Div	1st of 5
Record	92-70
Games Back	+9
% Record	.568 (6th=)
Split	49-32 **H**; 43-38 **R**
Last 10 Seasons	5444552111
Runs per game	4.81 (17th)
Staff ERA	4.03 (5th=)
Ave ERA Starters	4.08 (4th=)
Ave ERA Relievers	3.93 (12th)
Batting ave	.266 (18th)
Slugging ave.	.431 (16th)
On Base %:	.332 (17th)
AB/Hits Ratio	3.76 (18th)

Total/Net Homers	191/167 (*24* 8th)
AB per HR	29.43 (13th)
AB per SO	5.72 (7th)
Runs For/Against	780(17) 715(8)
Net Runs	65 (11th)
Net BB/BB p AB	82/10.96 (19th)
Total Steals	116 (4th)
Total Errors	88 (5th)
Unearned Runs Giv	55 (12th)
Record Attendance	1992 2 482 428.
Finished 2nd.	**Ave** 30 647.
Attendance 2003	1 946 011 **Ave**: 24 025
Attendance 2004	1 879 222 (80)
	Ave 23 490 (23rd)

2004 Starting Rotation

Starter	Record
Johan Santana	34: 20-6, 2.61 ERA
Brad Radke	34: 11-8, 3.48 ERA
Carlos Silva	33: 14-8, 3.48 ERA
Kyle Lohse	33: 8-12, 5.33 ERA
Terry Mulholland	15: 5-9, 5.18 ERA
Closer	
Joe Nathan	44/47 SV, 1.62 ERA
Bullpen Stars	
Nathan & Juan Rincon	2.63 ERA
Catcher	
Henry Blanco 114g	.206, 10HR, 37 RBI

Briefly... The Twins are now beautifully competitive having just completed three consecutive Division wins, but who keep getting stuck in the first round of the play offs. Their horrendous regular season record against the Yankees seems to have wedged a psychological crowbar against the door to true glory. Take 2004: this time, having recently won a series against the Yankees for the first time in ages, they were expected to take the creaking dinosaur. But no, they went down to another 1-3 reverse after winning the first game. So they're becoming a real "Wait 'til next year" team. What the GM and the manager are doing on baseball's 19th highest payroll is sensational though. They may be only a couple of big bats short of a real threat this time. The big question is still, "will someone produce the cash for a hungry marquee hitter and another great starting pitcher to keep Santana company?"

Uniforms: Home - Blue shirts with red 'Twins' letters and red piping, red number below left. Blue undershirts. Pants are white with blue pinstripes. Caps are blue caps with TC logo, "twin cities" (of Minneapolis and St Paul) or large 'M'. **Road –** Grey jerseys and pants both with pinstripe. "Minnesota" college print lettering. "M" cap logo.

Owners(s): Carl Pohlad. **GM:** Terry Ryan. **Manager:** The sumptuously named **Ron Gardenhire** has now had three firsts in his first three years here, the first for the club in nine (the since 1991 and following eight losing seasons Twins were actually second in Tom Kelly's last year). Yet another manager with not much of a major league record, he spent five seasons with the Mets in the 80s, averaging 57 games and .232 with the bat. Hit 3 homers. He'll be 47 on the 24th of October and he wears 35. Record: 276-209 (.569)

Home: The indoor **Metrodome** (carpet), but the team started life in the majors in 1961 in the Metropolitan (Met) Stadium, also in Minneapolis. It was demolished in 1985. The franchise's official website is cagey about the crowd on the Metrodome's opening day; we'll assume it was a disappointing crowd then. The place looks awful, from outside and in, with its roof held up by air-pressure resembling a plastic pillow. The lack of grass on the deck gives you plastic looking baseball. That's the author's, but by no means a minority view. The Twins are stuck with this whilst they share the premises with the local football team who have to contend with the vicious Minnesota winters. The joint is known as the 'Homerdome' because of the dingers struck there. Something about *this* indoor air causes the ball to travel when airborne, especially, for some reason, when the air-con is off. **Capacity 48 678. Hitter's Park (Clear advantage).**

World Series And Post-Season Ratings	Position	Points/Occasions/%	
Full Historical Record	18	7705-8369: .476	**RATINGS**
Total Historical Rating	19	N/A	
World Series Rating	11	285 Ranking Points	
Play Offs Rating	15	53 Ranking Points	
Pennant Wins (pre-'69)	11=	4 (3 as Wash. Senators)	
Division Wins (post-'69)	9	7	
World Series Wins/Appearances/Games Won	10=/11=/12=	3/7/19	
Level Of Recent Success	**S'ons/Pos**	**Won/Lost/Games**	
Games Won Per Season	18=	75	
Seasons Since A World Series Appearance	13	1991 bt Atlanta 4-3	
Seasons Since A Division Series	0	2004 lost to NYY 1-3 (2003 lost to NYY 1-3)	
Seasons Since A Championship Series	2	2002 lost to Anaheim 1-4	
Seasons Since A Division Win	0	2004 Won ALC by 9 games (2003 Won ALC by	

Most Home Runs Hit For The Twins	Most Games Won By A Pitcher	
Season: 49 Harmon Killebrew 1964 & 1969	Season: 25 Jim Kaat 1966	**RECORDS**
Career: 475 Harmon Killebrew	Career: 189 Jim Kaat	
Highest Batting Average	**Most Strikeouts**	
Season: .388 Rod Carew 1977	Season: Johan Santana 265 2004 (258 Bert Blyleven '73)	
Career: .334 Rod Carew	Career: 2 035 Bert Blyleven	

Best Batting Ave. 2004 Shannon Stewart .304	**Most Home Runs 2004** Corey Koske 25	**2004**
RBI Leader Torri Hunter 81	**Most Bases** Lew Ford 254	
Most K's Johan Santana 265	**Most HR Given Up** Kyle Lohse 28	
Most Innings Pitched Santana 228	**Most Walks** Lohse 76	
Other Top Bats: Jacques Jones: .254, 141h, 24HR	Cr. Guzman: .274, 158h, 46 RBI.	

Washington Senators Pennant Wins	1924, 1925 & 1933
World Series Losses	1925 lost to Pittsburgh 3-4; 1933 lost to New York Giants 1-4
Senators World Series Win	**Winning Manager**
1924 v. New York Giants 4 3	Bucky Harris

Twins/Senators Hall of Famers

"He has an uncanny ability to move the ball around as if the bat were some kind of magic wand."

Ken Holtzman *on . .*

...Rod Carew 2B, 1967-85 L: This brilliant Panamanian was an 18 straight year All-Star, won 7 batting titles and hit over .300 for 15 consecutive seasons. Stole 353 bases and made 3 053 hits. Indifferent fielder. LT .328. RoY 1967, MVP 1977. (BJ9) **1991.** Top 100: BJ64- SN29 – SABR51

Harmon Killebrew 1B, 1954-75: The hugely successful slugger of the 60s and 70s with the big bald head and the athleticism of a large Yorkshire pudding. 573 homers (AT7) and a lifetime average of .256 tell the tale: an all or nothing banger. MVP 1969 (BJ7) **1984.** Top 100: BJ63- SN69 – SABR69

Kirby Puckett CF 1984-95: .318 lifetime average and '91 World Series saviour with Game 6 catch and winning home run. Hit with power too, eventually slamming 207 homers in a shortish career of 12 seasons. Won 6 GGs and was a 10-time All-Star. His career was cut short by a fast ball which crashed into his eye, causing permanent damage. (BJ8) **2001** Top 100: BJ98- SN86 – SABR95

As Senators

Leon "Goose" Goslin LF 1921-38, LT .316 (AT57) L: Hit better than .300 eleven times and had a slugging average of .500 (AT24), from an unusual one-eyed stance. RBI leader in '24 with 129 while a Senator. Had a superb arm too. Nickname derives from his outsized conk. (BJ16) **1968.** Top 100: BJ00- SN89 – SABR38

Walter Johnson P, 1907-27, 2.17 ERA: Widely credited as the best pitcher of all time. "The Big Train." A colossus of early 20th century baseball. Pitched 531 complete games (AT4=), pitched 5,923 innings (AT3), 417 victories (AT2) and was a 12 time 20 game winner (AT4). Add those to these: 38 1-0 complete game victories (AT1, 21 ahead of 2nd); 110 shutouts (AT1) and an LT ERA of 2.37 (AT1). We're also talking about a man who pitched almost all his career for a lousy team. (BJ1) **1936.** Top 100: BJ8- SN4 – SABR11

Sam Rice RF, 1915-34 L: Despite starting his career late, at 27, he holds a raft of franchise records: most career games, at bats, hits, doubles, RBIs and total bases. A lifetime average of .322 and 6 seasons where he made more than 200 hits made sure of his place in the Hall. (BJ33) **1963**

Note: Harmon Killebrew spent the first 8 seasons of his career a Senator.

Retired Uniform Numbers

3 Harmon Killebrew	6 Tony Oliva	29 Rod Carew
14 Kent Hrbek	34 Kirby Puckett	

AAA Rochester Red Wings   **Spring Training Venue:** Lee County Sports Complex, Fort Myers, Florida

---

EMERGENCY BASEBALL RECORDS - MISPLACED APPENDIX 4

Highest Career Average All Time

1.	Ty Cobb	.367	1905-28
2.	Rogers Hornsby	.358	1915-37
3.	Joe Jackson	.356	1900-19

Highest Season Average - Last 25 Years

Tony Gwynn (San Diego P)	1994	.394
George Brett (Kansas CR)	1980	.390
Nomar Garciapparra (BoSox)	2000	.372
Tony Gwynn (SDP) .372	1997	.372
Todd Helton (Col R) .372 2000	2000	.372
Ichiro Suzuki (Sea) .372	2004	.372

MONTREAL EXPOS

Montreal, Quebec, Canada

SINCE 1969
NATIONAL LEAGUE
EAST DIVISION 1969-2005

Honours

World Series Wins	None
League Pennant Winners	N/A
Division Winners	1994
Division Series Winners	N/A
Championship Series Winners	N/A: no post-season in 1994

It was an enjoyable time in Montreal. It was a relaxing time and a very good time."

Manager Frank Robinson, October 2004.

Season 2004

Payroll 2003/2004	$46m(29) $43m (24)
Highest	Salaries
Jose Vidro (2B)	$9m
Livan Hernandez (P)	$6m
Orlando Cabrera	$6m*
Carl Everett (OF)	$3.75m**
Einar Diaz	$2.5m
Okha (P)	$2.34

* traded to Red Sox July '04
** traded to White Sox July '04

2004 Team Statistics

Position in Div	5th of 5
Record	67-95
Games Back	29
% Record	.404 (27th)
Split	35-45 **H**; 32-50 **R**
Last 10 Seasons	5244445245
Runs per game	3.93 (28th)
Staff ERA	4.33 (16th)
Ave ERA Starters	4.53 (13th=)
Ave ERA Relievers	4.00 (13th=)
Batting ave	.249 (28th)
Slugging ave.	.392 (29th)
On Base %:	.313 (29th)
AB Per Hit	4.02 (28th)
Total/Net Homers	151/191 (-40 26th)
AB Per HR	36.25 (21st)

At Bats Per S'out	5.91 (5th)
Runs For/Against	635(28) 769(15)
Net Runs	-134 (27th)
Total Steals	109 (7th)
Net BB/BB p AB	-86/11.03 (21st)
Total Errors	97 (11th)
Unearned Runs Giv	73 (21st=)
Record Attendance	1982: 2 318 292.
	Ave: 28 617. 3rd/1st.
2003 Attendance	1 023 680 **Ave:** 12 638
2004 Attendance	748 550 (80)
	Ave 9 356 (30th)

2004 Starting Rotation

Starter	Record
Livan Hernandez	35: 11-15, 3.60 ERA
Zack Day	19: 5-10, 3.93 ERA
John Patterson	19: 4-7, 5.03 ERA
Sunny Kim	17: 4-5, 4.51 ERA
Tony Armas	16: 2-4, 4.88 ERA
Tomo Ohka	15: 3-7, 3.40 ERA
Claudio Vargas	14: 5-5, 5.09 ERA
Scott Downs	12: 3-6, 5.14 ERA
Closers	
Chad Cordero	14/18 SV, 2.94 ERA
Rocky Biddle	11/15 SV, 6.92 ERA
Bullpen Star	
Luis Ayala	2.69 ERA
Catcher	
Brian Schneider 135g	.247, 12HR, 49 RBI

Briefly... The Montreal Expos are no more. 2004 was their last season of major league baseball. When you look above the box in which I'm typing, you could be forgiven for getting depressed. And the weather outside is grey and lousy to boot. Here is a team who had one great season out of thirty-five; and just as destiny beckoned, ball players across the United States went on strike, causing the play offs and World Series to be cancelled. To an outsider, that seems to sum up the Expos, though I'm sure it doesn't..

2004. On the playing front last year, the loss of Vladimir Guerrero, slugger extraordinaire, was in the event, devastating. His supposed replacements, Carl Everett and Nick Johnson, were soon on the DL and only managed 110 games between them, both only hitting .250. Only Batista and Wilkerson's 32 homers (each) added a spark to a season more dismal than any sports fans in the west (at least we have them and they're not usually corrupt) can ever have had to deal with.

Uniforms: Home - White jerseys and pants with pinstripe (no colour "Y" or sleeve edging), royal blue "Expos" letters in script with fine red edge; blue numbers below heart; blue undershirts; blue caps with "M" logo. **Road –** Grey shirts with red "Montreal" letters with fine blue edge, blue and red sleeve stripe, red heart numbers with blue edge; grey pants with blue and red side stripe; blue undershirts and caps as home.

Club President: Tony Tavares. **GM:** Omar Minaya **Manager:** The Expos are one of the few clubs in the majors to be managed by a man who is a legendary Hall Of Famer: **Frank Robinson.** 586 homers and a lifetime average of .290. He was 69 on 25th September (2004). He came up with Cincinnati in 1956 when they were the Redlegs and hit 35 homers. Stole 20 bases four times. In the circumstances of a club with an identity crisis, his second .512 record on the bounce in 2003 was considered highly creditable. "The worrying thing for the Expos with Frank must be the fact that his managerial career with the Orioles, the Indians and the Giants has not even seen a second place." When I typed this, months ago, there were still two baseball organisations in Canada, and now there is only one. At the time of writing here, whether Frank Robinson's failure to win anything as a skipper is going to be a bother to anyone in Washington D.C. is anyone's guess. Record: 913-1004 (.476).

Home: Olympic Stadium (carpet) was the vast home of the Montreal Expos. The team originally played in wide-open Jarry Park for the first 7 seasons of its history (beginning in 1969). They played in the new stadium for the first time on April 15 in front of 57,592 fans. They lost 7-2 to the Phillies. It has a synthetic surface. **Capacity: 46,500.** Dimensions: 325' to left field, 404' to center field, 325' to right field. Dead air, pretty capacious outfield: **Pitcher's Park (Very clear advantage).** **Note.** In their last season in the majors, the Expos played on the synthetic field turf at the Olympic Stadium only 59 times, the rest being played in the Hiram Bithorn Stadium in Puerto Rico. This fiasco began in 2003 and can now be viewed historically as the middle of the end.

World Series And Post-Season Ratings	Position	Points/Occasions/%	
Full Historical Record	15	2755-2943: .483	
Total Historical Rating	24	N/A	
World Series Rating	30=	0 Ranking Points	
Play Offs Rating	26	11 Ranking Points	
Division Wins (post"69)	25	2	
World Series Wins/Appearances/Games Won	30=/30=/30=	0/0/0	**RATINGS**
Level Of Recent Success	**S'ons/Pos**	**Won/Lost/Games**	
Games Won Per Season	20	74.7	
No Play Off Record	-	-	
Seasons Since A Division Win	9	1994 Won NLE by 6 games.	

Most Home Runs Hit For The Expos:	Most Games Won By A Pitcher:	
Season: 44 Vladimir Guerrero 2000	Season: 20 Ross Grimsley 1978	
Career: 225 Andre Dawson	Career: 158 Steve Rogers	
Highest Batting Average:	**Most Strikeouts**	**RECORDS**
Season: .345 Vladimir Guerrero	Season: 305 Pedro Martinez 1997	
Career: .322 Vladimir Guerrero	Career: 1,621 Steve Rogers	

Best Batting Ave. Juan Rivera .307	**Most Home Runs** Tony Batista 32	
RBI Leader Batista 110	**Most Bases** Brad Wilkerson 285	**2004**
Most K's Livan Hernandez 186	**Most HR Given Up** Hernandez/Vargas 26	
Most Innings Pitched Hernandez 255	**Most Walks** Hernandez 83	
Other Top Batters: Jose Vidro: .294, 121h, 60 RBI; Endy Chavez .277, 139h, 34 RBI.		

Expos Hall of Famers

Gary Carter C 1974-92: 'The Kid' was a hugely successful catcher with infectious attitude. Winner of 3 Gold Gloves, he was often described as 'rock like.' Hit 324 home runs in 18 seasons and hold the record for 12,988 chances accepted behind the plate. Hit expeditious single in dramatic 1986 World Series win for the Mets over the Red Sox. LT .262. (BJ8). **2002**

Retired Uniform Numbers

8 - Gary Carter	10 Rusty Staub	10 Andre Dawson

AAA New Orleans Zephyrs   **Spring Training Venue:** Space Coast Stadium, Melbourne, Florida

NEW YORK METS

Forest Hills, New York

SINCE 1962

NATIONAL LEAGUE   EAST DIVISION 1969-2005

Honours

World Series Champions	1969 & 1986
League Pennant Winners	0
Division Winners	1969, 1973, 1983, 1986
Division Series Winners	1999* & 2000*.
Championship Series Winners	1969, 1973, 1986 & 2000.
World Series Losses	1973 to Oakland A's 3-4 2000 to New York Yankees 1-4

*Qualified for post-season from Wild Card position

World Series Wins	Managers
1969 – Baltimore Orioles 4-1	Gil Hodges – The 'Miracle Mets'
1986 – Boston Red Sox 4-3	Dave Johnson

"There's only one thing worse than a Mets game and that's a Mets double header."

Mets manager Casey Stengel during the bad old days non pareil of 1962.

Season 2004

Payroll 2003/2004	$116m (2) $96m (4)
Highest	Salaries
Mo Vaughan	$17.66m
Mike Piazza	$16.07m
Richard Hidalgo	$12.50m
Tom Glavine	$10.76m
Al Leiter	$10.23m
Cliff Floyd (OF)	$6.5m
Kris Benson	$6.15m*
Kaz Matsui (SS)	$5m
Steve Trachsel (P)	$5m
Mike Cameron (OF)	$4.3m
Mike Stanton (P)	$3

*to Mets July '04

Team Statistics

Position in Div	4th of 5
Record	71-91
Games Back	25
% Record	.438 (22nd)
Split	38-43 H; 33-48 R
Last 10 seasons	2432223554
Runs per game	4.22 (26th)
Staff ERA	4.09 (8th)
Ave ERA Starters	4.21 (9th=)
Ave ERA Relievers	3.87 (9th=)
Batting ave	.249 (29th)
Slugging ave.	.409 (21st)
On Base %:	.317 (28th)

At Bats Per Hit	4.02 (9th)
Total/Net Homers	178/156 (22 9th)
AB Per HR	29.9 (14th)
AB per SO	4.76 (27th)
Runs For/Against	684(26) 731(9)
Net Runs	-47 (20th)
Total Steals	107 (8th)
Net BB/BB p AB	-80/10.80 (16th)
Total Errors	137 (28th)
Unearned Runs Giv	73 (21st)
Record Attendance	1988 3 3 055 445
Finished 1st	Ave 37 721
2003 Attendance	2 140 599 Ave 28 165
2004 Attendance	2 318 321 (80)
	Ave 28 979 (18th)

2004 Starting Rotation

Starter	Record
Tom Glavine	33: 11-14, 3.60 ERA
Steve Trachsel	33: 12-13, 4.00 ERA
Al Leiter	30: 10-8, 3.21 ERA
Jae Weong Seo	21: 5-10, 4.90 ERA
Kris Benson	31: 12-12, 4.31 ERA
Matt Ginter	14: 1-3, 4.54 ERA
Closer	
Braden Looper	34/29 SV 2.70 ERA
Bullpen Star	
Mike DeJean	1.69 ERA
Catchers	
Jason Phillips 128g	.218, 7HR, 34 RBI
Vance Wilson 75g	.274, 4HR, 21 RBI

Briefly... The New York Metropolitan club, or New York Mets as they are now universally known, has its genesis in the 1957 move of the Brooklyn Dodgers and New York Giants to California. The colours incorporated into the club emblem are both Giant orange and Dodger blue. The Mets are notable partly for being unremittingly dreadful when they started out in 1962. They weren't much better two years later when ex-Yankee supremo Casey Stengel who'd skippered them for that first expansion season, just about said it all: "He (Lydon Johnson, the then US President) wants to see poverty? He should come and see my team.!"

Uniforms: Home – White shirts with blue "Y" centre piping and inner edge sleeve stripe, blue "Mets" letters with orange edge, black undershirt, black caps with 'NY' logo in orange, blue and white. Numbers on shirt front under heart in blue (w/ orange edging). **Alt:** Black shirts with blue, orange and white letters and blue piping trim. White trews. Also, white pinstripe jersey. **Road –** Grey jerseys with blue "Y" piping, blue inside edge on sleeves, circus print "New York" letters in blue with orange edge, blue pants stripe.

Owners(s): Fred Wilpon (principal owner) Son Jeff is chief operating officer. **GM:** Omar Minaya/Jim Duquette. **Manager:** following Bobby Valentine's eight years leading the Mets, **Art Howe** (18) took over for 2003, a disastrous year: .410 and last place. He came over from a successful period with Oakland where he, or Billy Beane, more realistically, took them to two firsts and two seconds in his last four seasons, but also two Division series defeats. Record: 1129-1137 (.498). His replacement on November 7th 2004 was Willie Randolph. He became the fifth Afro-American manager in the major leagues. The Mets then, kept it in the city with the appointment: Randolph comes to Shea Stadium after 11 years on the Yankees coaching staff. He was a player with the Bombers after coming up with the Pirates where Willie Stargell was his mentor. After three seasons of losing baseball, the fan base looks for a saviour in this boyhood Mets fan who "danced in the streets" the day the Miracle Mets brought home the 1969 World Series.

Home: Polo Grounds. Former home to both the New York Yankees and the New York Mets (1962-63). First game after fire, June 28 1911, New York Giants 3 Boston 0. **Shea Stadium,** in Flushing Meadow, Queens, this has been home to the New York Metropolitans since April 17, 1964, in front of 48 736 fans. In the UK it's still better known as one of the venues on The Beatles's two tours of the States in 1965 and 1966. The Mets played their inaugural season at the Polo Grounds, the old oval-shaped home of the New York Giants, which by 1962 was becoming very dilapidated. It's capacity was 55 777. Dimensions: 338' to left field, 410' to center field, 338' to right field. The Polo Grounds had always been a vast park, and even with the fences having been brought in towards home plate in recent years, it was still a hard place to hit home runs. In their first seven years, in the old pre-divisional National League, the Mets finished in last place five times, and 9th twice, and of course, their opening season record still stands as one of the worst of all time: Played 162: Won 40; Lost 120.

World Series And Post-Season Ratings	Position	Points/Occasions	
Full Historical Record	20	3228-3598 .473	**R**
Total Historical Rating	15	N/A	**A**
World Series Rating	16	180 Ranking Points	**T**
Play Offs Rating	7	100 Ranking Points	**I**
Pennant Wins (pre-'69)	17= (& last)	0	**N**
Division Wins (post-'69)	17=	4	**G**
World Series Wins/Appearances/Games Won	13=/16=/15	2/4/12	**S**
Level Of Recent Success	**S'ons/Pos**	**Won/Lost/Games**	
Games Won Per Season	11	76.8	
Seasons Since A World Series Appearance	4	2000 Lost to NYY 1-4	
Seasons Since A Division Series	4	2000 Beat Giants 3-1	
Seasons Since A Championship Series	4	2000 Beat St Louis 4-1	
Seasons Since A Division Win	16	1988 Won NLE by 15 games	

Most Home Runs Hit For The Mets	Most Games Won By A Pitcher	
Season: 40 Mike Piazza 1999	Season: 25 Tom Seaver 1969	**R**
Career: 252 Daryl Strawberry	Career: 198 Tom Seaver	**E**
Highest Batting Average:	**Most Strikeouts**	**C**
Season: .354 John Olerud 1998	Season: 289 Tom Seaver 1971	**O**
Career: .301 Mike Piazza	Career: 2 541 Tom Seaver	**R**

Best Batting Ave. 2004 Kazuo Matsui .272	**Most Home Runs 2004** Mike Cameron 30	**2**
RBI Leader Richard Hidalgo 82	**Most Bases** Cameron 236 (.231)	**0**
Most K's Kris Benson 134	**Most HR Given Up** Steve Traschel 25	**0**
Most Innings Pitched Tom Glavine 212.2	**Most Walks** Al Leiter 97	**4**
Other Top Bats: Mike Piazza: .266, 121h, 20HR	David Wright: .293, 14HR, 40 RBI. (rookie 69g)	

Mets Hall of Famers

Tom Seaver 1967-86 ('67-'77; '83): His biography is a blur of power pitching statistics: NL record strikeouts (3 272), 311 wins, 200 fans in a season a record ten times. Paved the way to the 1969 World Series victory. One of the greats. (BJ6) RoY 1967 **1992.** Top 100: BJ38- SN32 – SABR28

Outside The Hall

The best thing about 2004 was **Mike Piazza** passing Carlton Fisk's record for the most homers by a catcher when he hit his 352nd on May 5th. This brilliant hitter with a lusciously aesthetic swing is a dead-cert for the Hall. RoY 1993.

Retired Uniform Numbers		
14 Gil Hodges	37 Casey Stengel	41 Tom Seaver

AAA Norfolk Tides   **Spring Training Venue:** Thomas J White Stadium, Port St Lucie, Florida

Casey Stengel 1889-1975
b. Kansas City, Missouri. *"Does anybody here know how to play this game?"*
Baseball Legend. Manager of the New York Yankees from 1949 to 1960 (10 pennants, 7 World Series wins)
and of the New York Mets from 1962 t0 1965.

NEW YORK YANKEES

Bronx, New York

SINCE 1901

AMERICAN LEAGUE EAST DIVISION 1969-2004

NAME CHANGE HISTORY

Baltimore Orioles 1901-02; New York Highlanders 1903-1912;
New York Yankees 1913-2005

"The more self-centered and egotistical a guy is, the better ballplayer he's going to be. You take a team with twenty-five assholes and I'll show you a pennant. I'll show you the New York Yankees."

Bill Lee, Boston Red Sox

Honours

World Series Champions	1923; 1927; 1928; 1932; 1936; 1937; 1938; 1939; 1941; 1943; 1947; 1950; 1951; 1952; 1953; 1956; 1958; 1961; 1962; 1977; 1978; 1996; 1998; 1999 & 2000 (26)
League Pennant Winners	1921; 1922, 1926, 1942, 1955; 1957; 1960; 1963 &. 1964 (+ all of the WSC years)
Division Winners	1976, 1977, 1978; 1996, 1998, 1999, 2000, 2001, 2002, 2003 & 2004
Division Series Winners	1981, 1996, 1998, 1999, 2000 & 2003
Championship Series Winners	1976, 1977, 1978, 1981, 1996, 1998, 1999, 2000, 2001 & 2003
World Series Losses	1921 v New York Giants 3-5; 1922 v New York Giants 0-4 ; 1926 v St Louis Cardinals 3-4; 1942 v St Louis Cardinals 1-4 ; 1955 v Brooklyn Dodgers 3-4; 1957 v Milwaukee Braves 3-4 ; 1960 v Pittsburgh Pirates 3-4; 1963 v Los Angeles Dodgers 0-4 ; 1964 v St Louis Cardinals 3-4; 1976 v Cincinnati Reds 0-4; 1981 v Los Angeles Dodgers 2-4; 2001 v Arizona Diamondbacks 3-4 ; 2003 v Florida Marlins 2-4

World Series Wins...

Miller Huggins
1923 - v. New York Giants 4-2
1927 - v. Pittsburgh Pirates 4-0
1928 - v. St Louis Cardinals 4-0

Joe McCarthy:
1932 - v. Chicago Cubs 4-0
1936 - v. New York Giants 4-2
1937 - v. New York Giants 4-1
1938 - v. Chicago Cubs 4-0
1939 - v. Cincinnati Reds 4-0
1941 - v. Brooklyn Dodgers 4-1
1943 - v. St Louis Cardinals 4-1

Ralph Houk
1961 - v. Cincinnati Reds 4-1
1962 - v. San Francisco Giants 4-3

Billy Martin
1977 - v. Los Angeles Dodgers 4-2
1978 - v. Los Angeles Dodgers 4-2

...And Managers

Bucky Harris
1947 - v. Brooklyn Dodgers 4-3

Casey Stengel
1949 – v. Brooklyn Dodgers 4-1
1950 - v. Philadelphia Phillies 4-0
1951 - v. New York Giants 4-2
1952 - v. Brooklyn Dodgers 4-3
1953 - v. Brooklyn Dodgers 4-2
1956 – v. Brooklyn Dodgers 4-3
1958 - v. Milwaukee Brewers 4-3

Joe Torre
1996 - v. Atlanta Braves 4-2
1998 - v. San Diego Padres 4-0
1999 - v. Atlanta Braves 4-0
2000 - v. New York Mets 4-1

Season 2004

Payroll 2003/2004:	$180m (1) $183m (1).
Highest Paid Players	**Salary**
Alex Rodriguez (3B)	$21.7m
Derek Jeter (SS)	$18.6m
Mike Mussina (P)	$16m.
Kevin Brown (P)	$15.7m
Jason Giambi (DH/1B)	$12.4m
Bernie Williams (OF/DH)	$12.3m
Gary Sheffield (OF)	$12
Mariano Rivera (Cl)	$10.9m

Javier Vasquez (P)	$9m
Jorge Posada (Ca)	$9m
John Olerud (1B)	$7.7m
Hideki Matsui (LF)	$7m
Steve Karsay (P)	$6m
Esteban Loaiza (P)	$4m
Tom Gordon (P)	$3.5m
Paul Quantrill (P)	$3m

Team Statistics

Position in Div	1st of 5
Record	101-61

Games Back	+ 3
Percentage	.623 (2nd)
Split	57-24 H; 44-37 R
Last 10 Seasons	2121111111
Runs per Game	5.54 (2nd)
Staff ERA	4.69 (19th)
Ave ERA starters	4.82 (18th)
Ave ERA relievers	4.43 (21st)
Batting ave.	.268 (15th)
Slugging ave.	.458 (3rd =)
On Base %	.353 (3rd)
AB/Hits Ratio	3,72 (13th)
Total/Net Homers	242/182 (60 3rd)
AB per HR	22,83 (1st)
AB per SO	5.63 (9th)
Runs For/Against	897 (2) 808 (19)
Net Runs	89 (7th)
Net BB/BB p AB	225/8.25 (2nd)
Total Steals	84 (17th)
Total Errors	109 (18th)

Unearned Runs Giv	56 (13th)
Record Attendance	2004 (see below)
Finished 1st	
Attendance 2003	3 465 585 Ave 42 785.
Attendance 2004	3 775 838 (79)
	Ave 47 778 (1st)

2004 Starting Rotation

Starter	Record
Javier Vazquez	32: 14-10, 4.91 ERA
Jon Lieber	27: 14-8; 4.33 ERA
Mike Mussina	27: 12-9, 4.59 ERA
Estaban Loiza*	27: 10-7; 5.70 ERA
Kevin Brown	22: 10-6, 4.09 ERA
Orlando Hernandez	15: 8-2, 3.30 ERA
Closer & Bullpen Star	
Mariano Rivera	53/57 SV, 1.94 ERA
Catchers:	
Jorge Posada 137g	.272, 21HR, 81 RBI
John Flaherty 47g	.252, 6HR, 16RBI
*traded from White Sox	

Briefly... The towering monolith of American baseball, the Damn' Yankees. Loathed for their supremely ultra-professional image and an arrogance that has paid handsome dividends since the great Babe Ruth breakthrough in the 1920s. Things have to be done "a certain way" with this team and above all, they have to win; because owner George Steinbrenner (since 1973) and Yankee tradition says they have to, they do. Signs of creakage at the game's achievement pinnacle exist now however, for they have not won a World Series for four years, an unthinkable state of affairs for the club that prides itself on lordly dominance of the scene. And as for the quote at the top: if you're a Yankee fan, don't take it hard; for this must be the culture the ballplayer is imbued with when he becomes a Yankee. This is surely how and why the Yankees are the Yankees.

Uniforms: Home – White shirts and pants with blue Yankee pinstripe, no player names and small traditional numbering on back; "Yankees" script lettering in blue, navy undershirts, ubiquitous navy caps with white "NY" logo. **Road –** Plain grey with "New York" capital lettering; navy caps with white 'NY' logo.

Owners(s): George Steinbrenner **GM:** Brian Cashman. **Manager: Joe Torre**, wearing 6, has been the skipper here with enormous success since 1996: first place every year bar one (in 1997); four World Series wins and two defeats. He was 64 in July. He managed the Mets for four seasons from 1978 to 1981 with no success whatsoever to show for it but took the Braves to first place in the NL West in 1982. He left in 1985 after two more second places. As a catcher he was a very highly rated player indeed and, if it weren't for the fact that his managerial record is going to get him there sooner or later, he may well have made it eventually as a player. Record: 1781-1570 (.531).

Home: Yankee Stadium. "The House That Ruth Built" or simply "The Stadium," to fanatics, the "Bronx Zoo" to phobes on account of its raucous fans. "Home Of Champions" is the self-appointed title (much as Old Trafford has been ludicrously touted as the "Theatre Of Dreams" by its propagandist owners and feeble commentators - and I like Manchester United!). First game, April 18 1923. Yankees beat the Red Sox - who else - 4-0 in front of an officially declared 74 200. Previous to this, since 1913 the Yankees had shared the Polo Grounds across the Harlem River, a venue owned by rivals the New York Giants. This is probably the most famous baseball park in America, never mind the UK where this is perhaps the only US baseball stadium of which the average sports fan has heard, though Wrigley Field and Fenway Park are equally well known. Perhaps 'most notorious' would be a better description. That said, any trip to the Big Apple must include a stadium tour for every baseball fan, to see the immaculately presented Monument Park and to stand in the place where Babe Ruth made the game what it has become. **Capacity: 57 478,** the largest in the AL by almost 9 000. The field is roughly symmetrical, as if a child was trying to draw a symmetrical ballpark but just missed: it's 399 to left-center, but 385 to right-center; 318 to the left field foul pole, but 314 the right, one of the smallest carries in the league. **Pitcher's Park** (Clear advantage with mitigating short-porch in right helping left-handed hitters).

"I didn't come to New York to be a star. I brought my own star with me."

Reggie Jackson

"I became a major league manager in several cities and was discharged, we call it "discharged," because there is no question I had to leave. (Laughter)."

Casey Stengel testifying before the Senate Anti-Trust and Monopoly Sub-Committee hearings in 1958

World Series And Post-Season Ratings	Position	Points/Occasions/%	
Full Historical Record 1901-2004	1	9097-6970 :.563	
Total Historical Rating	1	N/A	
World Series Rating	1	2080 Ranking Points	
Play Offs Rating	1	276 Ranking Points	
Pennant Wins (Pre-69)	1	29	
Division Wins (Post-69)	2	14	
World Series Wins/Appearances/Games Won	1/1/1	26/39/130	**RATINGS**
Level Of Recent Success		**Won/Lost**	
Games Won Per Season Post-69	1	85	
Seasons Since A World Series Appearance	1	2003 Lost to Marlins 2-4	
Seasons Since A Division Series	0	2004 Beat Minnesota 3-1	
Seasons Since A Championship Series	0	2004 Lost to Boston 3-4	
Seasons Since A Division Win	0	Won ALE by 3 games	

Most Home Runs Hit For The Yankees	Highest Batting Average	
Season: 61 Roger Maris 1961	Season: .393 Babe Ruth 1923	
Career: 659 Babe Ruth	Career: .349 Babe Ruth	
Most Games Won By A Pitcher	**Most Strikeouts**	**RECORDS**
Season: 41 Jack Chesbro 1904	Season: 248 Ron Guidry 1978	
Career: 236 Whitey Ford	Career: 1 956 Whitey Ford	

Best Batting Ave. 2004 H. Matsui .298 (108 RBI)	**Most Home Runs 2004** Sheffield & Rodriguez 36	
RBI Leader Sheffield 121 (121 RBI)	**Most Bases** Rodriguez 308 (106 RBI)	
Most K's Javier Vazquez 150	**Most Walks** Estoban Loiaza 71	**2004**
Most HR's Given Up Vazquez 33	**Most Innings Pitched** Vazquez 198	
Other Bat Stats: Posada: .272, 21 HR, 81 RBI.	**Jeter:** .292, 188h, 23HR;	

Yankee Hall Of Famers

Yogi Berra C,1946-1965 (1946-63) L: Huge figure in Yankee history: All-Star continuously from 1948 to 1962; 3-time MVP; five 100 RBI seasons(c) and lifetime .295. Probably the greatest catcher in baseball history. Record number of appearances in WS play: 14 series, 75 games, 259 at bats and 71 hits. He is also famous for malapropisms such as, "when you come to a fork in the road, take it" and "it ain't over 'til it's over."(BJ1) His cap insignia is not visible on his plaque, but if it were, it would of course be a Yankee one. **1972. Top 100: BJ41- SN40 – SABR26**

Jack Chesbro P, 1899-1909: was a pitching ace of the Highlanders who achieved a remarkable record in 1904: started 51 games, completed 48 and won 41 in 455 innings. Won 70 games with the Pirates in the first part of his career. "Happy Jack"'s Hall Of Fame cap has no insignia. **1946**

Earle Combs CF 1924-35 L: This lead off hitter in 3 World Championship teams hit a lifetime .325 and was a 3-time 200+ hits per season man. Career ended by fractured skull. (BJ34) **1970**

Bill Dickey C 1928-46 L: An immensity: a catcher in seven World Series wins and a .313 lifetime hitter. In his pomp he hit 102 homers and 460 RBIs in 4 seasons – from 1936-39 – peaking at .362 (.617 slug.) in 1936. (BJ7) **1954. Top 100: BJ57- SN57 – SABR63**

Bucky Harris, Manager 1947-48: Manager for just two seasons in his 50s, Bucky was a 27-year-old rookie player-manager who captured a World Series with his team, the Washington Senators.

Miller Huggins, Manager 1918-29: This is the guy who made the Yankees the Yankees, if it wasn't Babe Ruth on his own: the first six pennants the ball club won were under him, in 2 hat tricks, '21-3 and '26-8. He once said, "any ballplayers that played for me on either the Cardinals or the Yankees could come to me if he were in need and I would give him a helping hand. I made only two exceptions, Carl Mays and Joe Bush. If they were in a gutter, I'd kick them." Why he felt this way about these two I'm still trying to find out.

Joe DiMaggio CF 1936-51: a stylist as well as one with beautiful numbers: .325 lifetime; 3 MVPs; the record hitting streak of 56 games, compiled in 1941 and an average haul of 118 RBIs. Add immortalisation in song and a marriage to Marilyn Monroe to become an entrenched part of the American myth and you have a legend among legends. (BJ5). **1955. Top 100: BJ13- SN11 – SABR6**

Whitey Ford P 1950-67 236-106 2.75 ERA L: the 'Chairman Of The Board' or 'My Bandy Rooster' as Stengel called him. He was one of the post-war greats in anyone's book. '61 Cy Young winner (25-4) A decent Ford quote: "I never threw the spitter, well maybe once or twice when I really needed to get a guy out real bad." And another: "Sooner or later the arm goes bad. It has to...Sooner or later you have to start pitching in pain." (BJ22) **1974. Top 100: BJ00- SN52 – SABR54**

Lou Gehrig: 1B 1923-39: the genius in the Babe's shadow: bloody-mindedly played 2 130 consecutive games to carve out his own unique record (until overtaken by Cal Ripken Jr). Hit 493 home runs and had a lifetime average of .360, which would have been even higher had he not played on with the disease that killed him in 1941. The photographs of him on his own day in Yankee Stadium in '39 are some of the most heartbreaking in sports history: at the time, this guy did not know what was happening to him, that he was soon going to die. (BJ1) **1939. Top 100: BJ14- SN6 – SABR2**

Vernon "Lefty" Gomez: P, 1930-43, 189-102, 3.34 ERA, L: Red Ruffing's partner in the great team of the 30s which won 5 World Series. Led the league in strikeouts and ERA three times. (BJ64) **1972. Top 100: BJ00- SN73 – SABR00**

Waite Hoyt P, 1918-38, 237-182, 3.59 ERA: Spotted pitching batting practice by Giants manager John McGraw and signed at 15 years of age. Thence nicknamed "The Boy Wonder." After two seasons at the Red Sox he moved on to the Yankees where he pitched for his best 10 seasons. He pitched superbly and reliably in several World Series. Finished in the NL as a successful relief pitcher, then went on to become a fine broadcaster for 24 years for the Cincinnati Reds. (BJ78) **1969**

Reggie Jackson: "Mr October." See **Oakland A's.**

Tony Lazzeri 2B, 1926-39 ('26-'37), L: One of the notorious members of Murderer's Row, and good enough to be in James's top 20 second basemen of all time. An epileptic, a quiet man, a Californian and a great player by a great many accounts. Was the first player to hit two grand slams in one game. Also Cubs, Dodgers, Giants. (BJ19) **1991**

Joe McCarthy: Manager: Got the job in 1931, to the dismay of Babe Ruth who, aged 36, wanted to player-manage. By the time McCarthy was done, 15 years, 8 pennants and 7 World Series wins later, Ruth already had the cancer that would kill him in the summer of 1948.

Mickey Mantle: CF, 1951-68 LT.298 Sw: "The Mick." One of the true legends of (modern) baseball history, a superstar slugger of tremendous effectiveness and skill. BJ3 behind Mays and Cobb. When that puts him ahead of Joe DiMaggio, it tells you that his significance in the game and to the Yankees of the late 50s and 60s is an absolute. Honoured with a headstone in Memorial Park. From a poor Oklahoman background, check out Kahn's *Memories of Summer* for a great portrait. Died in 1995 of liver cancer. **1974. Top 100: BJ6- SN17 – SABR12**

Herb Pennock P 1912-34 ('23-'33) L: "The Knight Of Kennett Square." A good pitcher, but not a great one, evidently. Only twice figures in the list of 20 game winners at a time when lots of pitchers were doing it (53 times in the 10s, 42 times in the 20s). Has no cap insignia in the gallery, but he seems to belong here with the other Yankees. **1948**

Phil Rizzuto: SS 1941-56 LT .273.: MVP winner in '50. Fantastic early career but halted by war service in 1943. Said Yankee manager Casey Stengel to him, "Kid, you're too small: you should go out and shine shoes." (BJ15) **1994**

Red "Chuck" Ruffing: P 1924-47: 273-225 3.80 ERA: Had only 1 toe on his left foot after a coal mining accident, but converted from the outfield to a true major league pitcher. His career stats are a blaze of 20 game seasons and leads in winning percentage and strikeouts. (BJ51). He was also easily one of the best hitting pitchers of all time, batting for .300 no less than eight times. His .364 average for 1930 is bettered only by Walter Johnson, who batted .433 in 1925. **1967**

George Herman Ruth L: a colossus the like of which no British sport has ever seen. He transformed the game by making the home run fashionable and for all future baseball times, necessary. The crowds were awed by his power of his hits and by their frequency. Hit 714 homers, was the first to hit 20, 30, 40, 50 and 60 home runs. His figure of 60 in 1927 was held for 34 years until beaten by another Yankee, Roger Maris. An American giant as much as he is a baseball legend. "Babe," "The Bambino," "The Sultan Of Swat," "Nigger Lips" to opponents who tried to razz him. (BJ1) Also Boston Red Sox and Boston Braves. **1936. Top 100: BJ1- SN1 – SABR1**

Casey Stengel: Was one of the game's greatest legends for his brilliant tactical deeds with the Yankees and his way with words. He won 12 pennants and seven world titles from 1949 to 1960. Also batted .283 and won a couple of World Series with the Giants making crucial homers. A master of the hoary quote that makes you think the old bustard had only half a finger on the tiller of life, he once said: "There's three things you can do in a game of baseball: you can win, you can lose or it can rain."

Retired Uniform Numbers

1 Billy Martin   3 Babe Ruth   4 Lou Gehrig   5 Joe DiMaggio   7 Mickey Mantle   8 Bill Dickey

8 Yogi Berra   9 Roger Maris   10 Phil Rizzuto   15 Thurman Munson   16 Whitey Ford

23 Don Mattingley   32 Elston Howard   37 Casey Stengel   44 Reggie Jackson

AAA Portland Beavers   **Spring Training Venue:** Legends Field, Tampa, Florida

Joe DiMaggio

The Yankee Clipper again, in close up. Not only was he, is he, perhaps the most celebrated, even revered player of baseball after Babe Ruth, but he is one of the most complex. A man of shyness but not of depth. A man who was so brilliant that he set a mark of 56 consecutive games with a hit that may never be beaten in our lifetimes, yet one who was so stressed by his job that he suffered stomach pains and ulcers fairly constantly. Say "361" to a true baseball fan and they'll all tell you it's Joe DiMaggio's career home run total.

OAKLAND A'S

Oakland, California

<small>SINCE 1968</small>

<small>AMERICAN LEAGUE WEST DIVISION 1969-2004</small>

NAME CHANGE HISTORY

Philadelphia Athletics 1901-54; Kansas City Athletics 1955-67;
Oakland Athletics 1968 2005

Honours

World Series Champions 1972, 1973, 1974 & 1989
League Pennant Winners See CSWs
Division Winners   1971, 1972, 1973, 1974, 1975, 1988, 1989, 1990, 2000, 2002 & 2003
Division Series Winners 1981*
Championship Series Winners   1972, 1973, 1974, 1988, 1989 & 1990
World Series Losses   1988 - Lost to LA Dodgers 1-4; 1990 – Lost to Cincinnati Reds 0-4

World Series Wins	Managers
1972 - v. Cincinnati Reds 4-3	Dick Williams
1973 - v. New York Mets 4-3	Dick Williams
1974 - v. Los Angeles Dodgers 4-1	Alvin Dark
1989 - v. San Francisco Giants 4-0	Tony LaRussa

Season   2004

American League Rookie of the Year: Bobby Crosby

Payroll 2003/2004:	$57m (26)-$60m (18)
Starter	**Starter**
Jermaine Dye (OF)	$11.6m
Mark Kotsay (OF)	$6.5m
Eric Chavez (3B)	$5.3m
Tim Hudson (P)	$5m
Mark Mulder (P)	$4.4m
Jim Mecir (P)	$3.3m
Barry Zito (P)	$3m

2004 Team Stats

Position in Div	2nd of 5
Record	91-71
Games Back	1 (7 from WC)
Percentage	.562 (9th=)
Split	33-49 **H**; 33-49 **R**
Last 10 Seasons	4344212112
Runs per Game:	**4.89** (15th)
Staff ERA	**4.17** (10th)
Ave ERA starters	**4.82** (12th)
Ave ERA relievers	**4.43** (13th=)
Batting ave:	**.270** (9th=)
Slugging ave.	**.433** (14th)
On Base %:	**.343** (9th)
ABS Per Hit	**3.70** (10th)
Total/Net Homers	**189/164** (*25* 6th=)

AB per HR	30.30 (15th)
AB Per SO	5.40 (15th)
Runs For/Against	793 (15) 742 (11)
Net Runs	51 (14th)
Net BB/BB p AB	66/9.42 (8th)
Total Steals:	45 (28th)
Total Errors	91 (8th)
Unearned Runs Giv	60 (16th)
Record Attendance	1990 2 900 217
Finished 1st	**Ave:** 35 805
Attendance 2003	2 216 596 **Ave** 27 365.
Attendance 2004	2 201 516 **Ave** 27 179 (20th)

2004 Starting Rotation

Starter	Record
Tim Hudson	27: 12-6; 3.53 ERA
Barry Zito	34: 11-11; 4.48 ERA
Mark Mulder	33: 12-12; 4.43 ERA
Mark Redman	32: 11-12; 4.71 ERA
Rich Harden	31: 11-7; 3.99 ERA
Closer	
Octavio Dotel	22/28 SV, 4.09 ERA
Arthur Rhodes	9/14 SV, 5.12 ERA
Bullpen Star	
Chris Hammond	ERA 2.69
Catchers	
Damian Miller 110g	.272, 9HR, 58 RBI
Adrian Melhuse. 69g	.257, 11HR, 31 RBI

Briefly... Oakland is the home of the exciting and controversial "Moneyball" style of baseball, originated by Billy Beane, the organisation's General Manager (see dictionary). This has resulted in the A's having tremendous regular season success, "against the odds" resulting from a relatively small payroll and the absence of stars. Nickname – Back in 1901, New York Giants Manager John McGraw dismissed the A's with contempt, calling them "The White Elephants*," Mack defiantly adopted the White Elephant as the team insignia, and in 1902, the A's won the American League pennant. The players still wear the White Elephant patch on their shirt sleeves today. (*a "white elephant" is any large organisation which is reckoned or reckons itself to be capable of great things, but fails).

Uniform: Home – White shirts with "Athletics" script letters in green and yellow, white pants, green undershirts, green caps with yellow 'A's' logo. **Road -** Grey uniform with green 'Oakland' letters edged in yellow. Green undershirts. Green stockings. Unofficially, the team have habit of playing in white or light grey shoes.

Owners(s): Steve Schott   **GM:** Billy Beane   **Manager:** Assisting Beane the As to another first place in the AL West in 2003 was 53 year old (54 on) **Ken Macha.** Macha became skipper on October 29th 2002 after being his predecessor Art Howe's bench coach for three seasons. He seems to fit the bill for Beane: Macha played only 180 games in the majors over seven years ('74-'81) as a catcher. His system requires only a field manager to make calls during a game. However, although Oakland's recent regular season record has been immensely impressive, the policy of filling in the pilot hole with little more than a nodding dog risks depriving the team of a motivating leader. The answer is to find that leader among the players, as in days of old. Record: 187-137 (.577)

Home: Network Associates Coliseum. This horrifically named ballpark belongs to the Oakland Athletics' association. Originally the Almeida County Coliseum, it has housed every A's game since the franchise moved from Kansas City after the 1967 season. The A's played in Philly from 1901 to 1954, then in Kansas from 1955 to 1967. **Capacity: 43 662**. From the air, the park looks like a water or wine carrier from ancient times, with the flat top in centre field, then a gentle symmetrical slope at both sides to form gently curving shoulders. They lines angle in again then hit foul poles to bring us out of history and into modern baseball. In terms of distance, the Coliseum is not a big challenge for the hitter: the poles are an almost reasonable 330 feet away, and the alleys a fair 367-388 and centre field 400. **Pitcher's Park** (Clear advantage)

World Series And Post-Season Ratings	Position	Points/Occasions/%	
Full Historical Record	16	7782-8269: .482	
Total Historical Rating	8	N/A	
World Series Rating (Franchise)	3	705 Ranking Points (inc. Phil)	
Play Offs Rating	3	133 Ranking Points	
Pennant Wins (pre-'69)	6	9 (all Philadelphia)	
Division Wins (post-'69)	3	13	
World Series Wins/Appearances/Games Won	2=/5/5	9/14/41	**RATINGS**
Level Of Recent Success		**Won/Lost**	
Games Won Per Season Post-69	5	80.4	
Seasons Since A World Series Appearance	14	1990 Lost to Cincinnati 0-4	
Seasons Since A Division Series	1	2003 Lost to Boston 2-3*	
Seasons Since A Championship Series	12	1992 Lost to Toronto 2-4	
Seasons Since A Division Win	1	2003 Won ALW by 2 games	

*Lost to Boston Red Sox in Division Series 2-3 after leading 2-0. This was the third consecutive 3-2 loss in the Division Series first round.

Most Home Runs Hit For The Athletics	Most Games Won By A Pitcher	
Season: 52 Mark McGwire 1996	Season: 27 Bob Welch 1990	
Career: 363 Mark McGwire	Career: 131 Catfish Hunter	
Highest Batting Average	**Most Strikeouts**	**RECORDS**
Season: .342 Jason Giambi 2001	Season: 301 Vida Blue 1971	
Career: .308 Jason Giambi	Career: 1 315 Vida Blue	

Best Batting Ave. 2004 Erubiel Durazo .321	**Most Homers 2004** Eric Chavez 29 (.276, 77 RBI)	
RBI Leader Durazo 88	**Most Bases** Mark Kotsay 278 (.314, 78 RBI, 190 h)	
Most K's Rich Harden 167	**Most Walks** Mark Mulder 83	**2004**
Most HR Given Up Zito/Redman 28	**Most Innings Pitched** Mulder 225.2	
Other Top Bats: Eric Byrnes: .283, 161h,73 RBI.	Scott Hatteberg, .284, 82 RBI, 156h.	

"Humanity is the keystone that holds nations and men together. When that collapses, the whole structure crumbles. This is as true of baseball teams as any other pursuit in life."

Cornelius McGillicuddy, "Connie Mack", field manager of the
Philadelphia Athletics for just a short amount of time: 1901-1950.

I wonder whether in this quote lies the key to why he only won 9 pennants in that time, six of them between 1901 and 1914. He sold a lot of stars to simply balance the books too.

Philadelphia A's World Series Wins	1910, 1911, 1913, 1929 & 1930
League Pennant Wins	All of the above plus 1905, 1914 & 1931
World Series Losses	1905 lost to New York Giants 1-4
	1914 lost to Boston Braves 0-4
	1931 lost to St Louis Cardinals 3-4

Philadelphia A's World Series Wins	Manager
1910 v Chicago Cubs 4-1	Connie Mack
1911 v New York Giants 4-2	Connie Mack
1913 v New York Giants 4-1	Connie Mack
1929 v Chicago Cubs 4-1	Connie Mack
1930 v St Louis Cardinals 4-2	Connie Mack

Philadelphia A's Hall Of Famers

Frank 'Home Run' Baker 3B L: Brilliant third baseman, one of the all-time best. One of Mack's famous $100, 000 infield, he scored two home runs in the victorious 1911 World Series for the A's, thus earning his nickname. Later played for the Yankees in two losing World Series after three rings with Philadelphia. Scored 96 career homers, lifetime .307 ave.. No cap insignia but there's a photo showing him in a magnificent striped A's cap and a bat over his shoulder which is enough to make the lover of history drool. (BJ5) **1955. Top 100: BJ70- SN00 – SABR00**

Dave Bancroft SS, 1915-30 (1915-20) Sw: made his name with the Giants as one of the great short stops of all time but came up with the Phillies and played there for six seasons.
No insignia (BJ28) **1971**

Charles Albert 'Chief' Bender P, 1903-25 (1903-14) 212- 127, 2.97 ERA: Pitcher from the Chippewa tribe who won six World Series games with the A's. Won 212 games in 16 seasons. No insignia on cap. **1953**

Mickey Cochrane C 1925-37 (25-33) L: A true leader from behind the plate of the conquering A's of 1929-31. Batted over .300 in 9 of 13 seasons with a lifetime average of .320. Then led the Tigers to victory in the 1935 World Series as player-manager after a league pennant in 1934. (BJ4) **1947. Top 100: BJ72- SN00 – SABR97**

Eddie Collins 2B 1906-30 L: Supremely good infielder. A Philly A for his first 9 of 25 seasons, this legend from the 1906 to 1930 period batted over .300 in his last 6 seasons before a move to the White Sox. (BJ2). **Top 100: BJ18-**

George Kell: 3B, 1943-57, LT .306: A contact hitter with low secondary average (.208), but the tenth third basemen of all-time in terms of lifetime average. Later an inspiration for another third baseman, Brooks Robinson of the Orioles. (30BJ) **1983**

Connie Mack: Managed the As of Philly for a scarcely believable 50 seasons (this is not a misprint). Retired at 88 (!) with 5 World Series crowns notched and four pennants with two distinct teams, that of 1910-13 and 1929-31. "The Tall Tactician."

Eddie Plank P (L), 1901-17 ('01-'14), 326-194, 2.35 ERA L: Eddie is 3rd all-time in wins for left-handers. A finesse guy and a key to the club's major successes of the early century. Born, educated and died in Gettysburg, Pennsylvania. No cap insignia on plaque. (BJ34) Photographs of him and his team reveal an extraordinary amount of daring for its time: a fancy striped cap, billowing shirt with huge 'A,' baggy trews and big striped socks. Cool fancy dress gear in 2004: you'd be certain to get a reaction. **1946. Top 100: BJ00- SN68 – SABR94**

Al Simmons LF, 1924-44 ('24-'32; '40-'41; '44): Was a Philly 'A's' hitter with a brilliant 307 HR total and a lifetime .334 average. Had 11 consecutive seasons as .300 and 100 RBI man. A great. Called "Buckfoot Al" on account of his unorthodox hitting style. (BJ7) **1953. Top 100: BJ71- SN43 – SABR66**

Rube Waddell P, 1897-1910, 193-143, 2.16 ERA L: Six years with the Phillies, this is a 193 game winner from 408 games. Famously thought to be somewhat simple minded, he nevertheless was smart enough to out pitch Cy Young in 1905, giving up just 2 runs (in the first) in 20 innings! (BJ53). Insignia out of sight due to turned head. **1946. Top 100: BJ00- SN00 – SABR97**

Oakland A's

"The sun don't shine on the same dog's ass all the time."

Catfish Hunter. Philosophy is not a requirement of a Hall of Famer

Dennis Eckersley: P, 1975-98: One of the two inductees from 2003 and one of a tiny number of relief pitchers to have made the Hall. Elected after the minimum period possible. Made 390 (AT3) saves in a long career. (BJ32) **2003. Top 100: BJ00-SN98 – SABR64**

Rollie Fingers: P, 2.90 ERA, 341 Career Saves: A rarity, a relief Hall Of Fame pitcher. Won 2 and saved 6 World Series games. 341 career saves, 1981 MVP and Cy Young award winner and a waxed moustache unique to modern baseball. However, not even included in the BJ top 100 pitchers. **1992. Top 100: BJ00- SN96 – SABR76**

Catfish Hunter P, 224-166, 3.26 ERA: Big game pitcher. Real name Jim, nickname a fiction dreamed up owner Charlie Finley for a gullible media. Posted 5-3 World Series record, won a '74 Cy Young and won 20 games five straight years from 1971-75. (BJ64) No cap insignia. Died aged 53 of Lou Gehrig's Disease. **1987**

Reggie Jackson RF, 1967-87, ('68-'75; '87) L: The bespectacled 'Mr October,' so-called for his 3 homers in 3 consecutive at bats in the '78 World Series. Has a WS record of .755 slugging average in 30 games, and in the '77 and '78 series with the Yankees hit 7 home runs, including 4 in 2 consecutive games in '77. An out and out slugger; anything but a stylist. (BJ7) **1993. Top 100: BJ57- SN48 – SABR67**

Outside The Hall...

Rickey Henderson: Oakland A's player from '79-'84. Went to Yankees for four and a half seasons before heading back to Oakland for six more (with a spell in the middle at Toronto). Spent nearly two seasons with the Padres before a third spell with the A's in '98 for 152 games where he still stole 66 bases at the age of 39, his highest for eight years. He then pinballed around: the Mets; the Mariners; the Padres (again); the Red Sox and finally, aged 44, he had 72 at bats with the Dodgers. His career totals: 3 081 games (AT4); 10 961 at bats (AT10); 3 055 hits (AT20); 1 115 RBIs (not high, not his job); 510 doubles (ditto); 66 triples (ditto); 297 home runs (not so bad); stolen bases 1 406 (AT1 – 468 ahead of 2nd place Lou Brock); 2 190 walks (AT1 – 128 ahead of 2nd place Babe Ruth); 25 years service (almost, AT2=). At this point in time all Henderson is to your correspondent is a mass of figures. Plus the knowledge that everyone says he's sure to be in the Hall Of Fame by 2010. What these stats help to reveal once more is the greatness of The Babe. His career walks total seems huge to me, though obvious no doubt to a long time baseball fan: it just struck me how he must have gone through what Bonds is going through in this season 2004: he was so good, no one wanted to pitch to him. Barry, by the way, will soon overtake Henderson's walk record. Tonight – 28th April – he stands on 2012, only 9 behind Ted Williams in 3rd place. By October 1st, at the present rate (after 20 games), he'll be past Henderson, having smashed the record for walks in a season with about 240. And he's not getting enough exercise to get injured. (BJ4). **Top 100: BJ26- SN51 – SABR60**

Retired Uniform Numbers

27 Catfish Hunter   34 Rollie Fingers

AAA Portland Beavers   **Spring Training Venue:** Phoenix Stadium, Phoenix, Arizona

---

EMERGENCY BASEBALL RECORDS - MISPLACED APPENDIX 5

Pitching: Most Career Wins

Player	Wins	Career
Cy Young	511	1890-1911
Walter Johnson	417	1907-27
Christy Mathewson	373	1900-16
Pete Alexander	373	1919-30
Pud Galvin	364	1875-92
Warren Spahn	363	1942-65
Kid Nichols	361	1890-1906
Tim Keefe	342	1880-93
Steve Carlton	329	1965-88
Roger Clemens	328	1984-2004
John Clarkson	328	1882-94

Reggie Jackson – 1946-
b. Wyncote, Pennsylvania. (Oakland Athletics, New York Yankees)
His "Mr October" is one of the most famous nicknames in baseball history. His most remembered feat
was his hitting three home runs in one World Series game, in 1978, on only three pitches. A man never
short on self-confidence. His other name, "Reggie," is instantly known in America as belonging to this unique
character and player. His low career average didn't stop him entering the Hall or his becoming one of
the supreme modern legends of the game.

PHILADELPHIA PHILLIES

Philadelphia, Pennsylvania

SINCE 1901

NATIONAL LEAGUE

EAST DIVISION 1969-2004

NAME CHANGE HISTORY

Philadelphia Quakers 1883-89; Philadelphia Phillies 1890-2005

Honours

World Series Champions	1980
League Pennant Winners	1915 & 1950
Division Winners	1983; 1993; 1994; 2000
Division Series Winners	1976, 1977, 1978, 1980, 1981, 1983 & 1993
Championship Series Winners	1980, 1983 & 1993
Losing World Series	1915, 1950, 1983 & 1993

World Series Wins	Manager
1980 – v. Kansas City Royals 4-2	Dallas Green

Season 2004

Payroll 2003/2004	$9.5m (9) $93m (5)
Highest Paid Players	Starter
Jim Thome (1B)	$12.2m
Kevin Millward (P)	$11m
Bobby Abreu (OF)	$10.6m
Eric Milton (P)	$9m
Billie Wagner (P)	$8m
Mike Lieberthal (C)	$7.5m
Randy Wolf (P)	$4.4m
Jay Bell (3B)	$4.4m

2004 Team Stats

Position in Div	2nd of 5
Record	86-76
Games Back	10 (6 from WC)
Percentage	.531 (14th)
Split	42-39 H; 44-37 R
Last 10 Seasons	2553352332
Runs per Game:	5.18 (9th)
Staff ERA	4.45 (17th)
Ave ERA starters:	4.91 (21st)
Ave ERA relievers	3.68 (7th)
Batting ave:	.267 (16th=)
Slugging ave.	.443 (10th)
On Base %:	.345 (7th=)
ABS Per Hit	3,75 (16th)
Total/Net Homers	215/214 (1 16th)

AB per HR	26.24 (7th)
ABS Per SO	4.98 (23rd)
Runs For/Against	840 (9) 781 (17)
Net Runs	59 (13th)
Net BB/BB p AB	143/8.75 (4th)
Total Steals:	100 (11th)
Total Errors	81 (2nd)
Unearned Runs Giv	57 (15th)
Record Attendance	1993 3 137 674
	Ave 38 736
Attendance 2003	2 223 353 Ave 28 505.
Attendance 2004	3 206 532 (79)
	Ave 40 589 (5th)

2004 Starting Rotation

Starter	Record
Cory Lidle	34:12-12; 4.90 ERA
Eric Milton	34: 14-6; 4.75 ERA
Brett Myers	31: 11-11, 4.90 ERA
Kevin Millwood	25: 9-6; 4.85 ERA
Randy Wolf	23: 5-8; 4.28 ERA
Vicente Padilla	20: 7-7; 4.53 ERA
Closer	
Billy Wagner	21-25; SV 2.42 ERA
Tim Worrell	19-27; SV 3.68 ERA
Bullpen Star	
Ryan Madson	1.65 ERA
Catcher	
Mike Lieberthal 131g	.271, 17HR, 61RBI

Briefly... Historically the club was more ugly sister than Cinderella, having the worst historical rating of all the original 1901 set, but the last quarter of the 20th century saw a big turnaround with seven division titles between '76 and '93. The last ten have been drought years, however. Much was expected in 2004 of this club in their new ballpark with their big payroll and power hitting line up- Thome et al, but it all failed to deliver.

Uniforms: Home – White shirts and pants with red pinstripe, 'Phillies' script lettering with blue star dots, player number on right sleeve in red, red undershirts. Red caps with white 'P'. **Road –** plain grey shirts with same 'Phillies' script (edged in white), red undershirts. White sleeve edging split by red middle stripe. Superb.

Owners: Bunch of four faceless corporations, according to the Philadelphia Daily News. President (who makes big decisions): Dave Montgomery. GM: Ed Wade Ex-Manager: Larry Bowa was bombed out one day before the end of the 2004 season, but seeing as he seemed to be feuding with his players in the second half of 2003, its' amazing he held the post for that long. Record: 418-435 (.490). New Manager @ 5 November 2004 is Charlie Manuel, successful skipper of the Cleveland Indians in the 90s. Was "special adviser" to the club from 2003 and was expected to take over from Bowa well before he in fact did.

Home: Citizen Bank Park. A shamefully dull name for the terrific new stadium that opened in April 2004, especially when you consider that this is one of the venerable American League clubs (that's what you get, however, with sponsorship). This is balanced by the fact that CBP is yet another of the modish retro ballparks, with their emphasis upon irregularity of design shape and a little quirkiness. **Pitcher's Park** (Very clear advantage)

The recent old home for the Phillies was **Veterans Stadium** ("The Vet") The now 'old' home was itself a 'new' park in 1971. **Capacity: 62 409.** Dimensions: 330' to left field, 408' to center field, 330' to right field. First game was on April 10th 1971. The Vet's unpopularity was revealed on the programme by Mr Lengel in August 2003: it was an unlovely huge, circular concrete bowl of a stadium much in vogue when it was first built back in 1971 with an unkind synthetic surface. Talk on the commentary the same night about rats and other 'critters' fleeing into nearby neighbourhoods on implosion day didn't do much to help the image for the distant observer. It still didn't look bad under lights through a camera lens mind. The club's seasonal attendance record was set in 1993 when the Phillies won their division. It was broken last season, however.

World Series And Post-Season Ratings	Position	Points/Occasions/%	
Full Historical Record 1901-2004	**27**	7383-8688: .457	
Total Historical Rating	22	N/A	
World Series Rating	19	130 Ranking Points	
Play Offs Rating	12=	58 Ranking Points	
Pennant Wins (pre-'69)	15=	2	
Division Wins (post-'69)	13=	5	
World Series Wins/Appearances/Games Won	19=/14=/17=	1/5/8	
Level Of Recent Success		**Won/Lost**	RATINGS
Games Won Per Season Post-69	16	75.2	
Seasons Since A World Series Appearance	11	1993 Lost to Toronto 2-4	
Seasons Since A Division Series	23	1981 lost to Montreal 4-2	
Seasons Since A Championship Series	11	1993 Beat Atlanta 4-2	
Seasons Since A Division Win	11	1993 Won NLE by 3 games	

Most Home Runs Hit For The Phillies	Most Games Won By A Pitcher	
Season: 48 Mike Schmidt 1980	Season: 33 Grover Alexander 1916	
Career: 548 Mike Schmidt	Career: 241 Steve Carlton	
Highest Batting Average	**Most Strikeouts**	RECORDS
Season: .398 Lefty O'Doul	Season: 319 Curt Schilling 1997	
Career: .362 Billy Hamilton	Career: 3 031 Steve Carlton	

Best Batting Ave. 2004 Bobby Abreu .301	**Most Home Runs 2004** Jim Thome 42 (105 RBI)	
RBI Leader Abreu 105	**Most Bases** Abreu 312 (105 RBI)	
Most K's Eric Milton 161	**Most Walks** Milton 75	2004
Most HR Given Up Milton 43	**Most Innings Pitched** Corey Lidle 211.1	
Other Top Bats: Jimmy Rollins: .289; 190h, 73 RBI. David Bell: .295, 155h, 77 RBI.		

Phillies Hall Of Famers

"After fifteen years of facing them you don't really get over them. They're devious. They're the only players in the game allowed to cheat." Richie Ashburn on the most serious daily problem for the 50s hitter: pitchers.

Grover Cleveland Pete Alexander P, 1911-30 ('11-17; 30), 373-208, 2.56 ERA: One of the colossal quartet of early 20th century pitchers, he notched 373 wins, 3rd = all-time behind Young and Johnson (and level with Mathewson). Won 190 games in his 7 Philly seasons and won 20 games 9 times. The facts of his life are dramatic, a man who became great despite being an epileptic, an alcoholic and a man who faced real combat in World War One. No cap insignia in the Hall plaque. (BJ3) **1938.** **Top 100: BJ20- SN12 – SABR25**

Richie Ashburn: CF, 1948-62 ('48-59) L: Twice batting champion (in '55 and '58 with .338 and .350 respectively), a rookie All-Star. Holds club record for putouts. Batted .300 nine times. Hustling lead off hitter, not a slugger – only 29 homers in 2 189 games. .308 lifetime average. (BJ16) **1995**

Jim Bunning: P, 1955-71 (1955-63), 224-184, 3.27 ERA: 2 855 strikeouts, 40 shutouts and 3.27 ERA in 3759 innings pitched in a distinguished 17 season career. An extremely interesting player who after winning 224 games and winning 100 games and achieving 1 000 strikeouts in each league as a pitcher went on to the Senate representing the state of Kentucky via a vital role in establishing the power of the Player's Union. Scourge of batters and front offices alike. (BJ30) **1996**

Steve Carlton P 1965-88 329-244 3.22 ERA: One of the modern greats and with huge longevity. 3 Cy Young's in the 70s. Reading some accounts of him, his total dedication to his job and preparation for it is suggestive of 'Kevin Keegan' in his playing days. Yet this quote suggests he was more than that. "Lefty was a craftsman, an artist. He was a perfectionist. He painted a ballgame. Stroke, stroke, stroke, and when he got through (pitching a game) it was a masterpiece." – Richie Ashburn (BJ15). **1994. Top 100: BJ78- SN30 – SABR30**

Roger Connor 1B, 1880-97, L: A Philly for just one season, 1892, but it's the only one of the 30 present major leaguers who is able to claim the home run king before Babe Ruth wiped him. Roger hit a record 138 homers in 19 seasons in an era where the homer was a vulgarity. He wears no cap insignia in the Hall Of Fame but I've put him here. (BJ22) **1976**

Ed Delahanty: LF, 1888-1903 (1888-89; 1891-01): This excellent hitter's last season was the first of the World Series era, played with Washington, but with the Phillies he made over 2 000 hits and hit .400 twice. Finished with a lifetime .346 average. (BJ12) **1945. Top 100: BJ99- SN00 – SABR00**

Hugh Duffy CF 1888-1906 (1904-06): The Phillies might try to claim this .330 lifetime hitter and superb outfielder, but he won 4 pennants in 9 seasons with the Boston Beaneaters, forerunners of the Braves organisation. Played only 34 games for the Phillies. (BJ20) **1945**

Chuck Klein: RF, 1928-44 L: Lifetime .320 (.359 and 139 RBI in first 5 seasons). Career 300 homers and first in 'modern' era to hit 4 in one game, in 1936. (BJ40) **1980. Top 100: BJ00- SN92 – SABR00**

Robin Roberts: P, 1948-66, 286-245, 3.40 ERA: A fastball hurler with wicked movement, he was a 20-game winner 1950-55 and NL leader in 4. Went on a streak of 28 complete games in 1952-3 that is inconceivable in terms of the modern game. 7 straight All-Star games with 5 equal record starts. The Cy Young did not begin until '56, but Bill James has him winning 5 between '50 and '55. Is now one of the Hall Of Fame's Board Of Directors. (BJ16) **1955. Top 100: BJ96- SN74 – SABR83**

Mike Schmidt 3B, 1972-89: Phenomenal one clubman, winner of 12 Gold Gloves at third base and 10 All Star accolades. A powerhouse who hit 548 home runs, 9th all time at the start of 2004. (BJ1) **1995. Top 100: BJ21- SN28 – SABR16**

Sam Thompson RF, 1885-1906, L: To me, his mug shot in my Hall Of Fame yearbook looks to be that of a typical late 19th century ballplayer: he looks as though for two pins he'd punch you from here to next week. A bony face, a sharp looking moustache and altogether a look of suppressed violence. Then I read about him in a book and he apparently was a popular, cheerful soul and a brilliantly productive hitter. He leads the all-time record of RBI's per game with .923. He was a lifetime .331.hitter with 127 career homers when hardly anyone hit them; when the ball was constantly smeared, and was soft and dark. This must have been some player. (BJ37) **1974**

Outside The Hall Of Fame...

Pete Rose: he stands outside the door on account of being found supposedly guilty by the baseball – not Federal or state – authorities of betting on games of baseball as a player.

Retired Uniform Numbers

P Grover Alexander*	1 Richie Ashburn	14 Jim Bunning
3 Steve Carlton	P Chuck Klein	36 Robin Roberts
	20 Mike Schmidt	

---

*(numbers not worn during his era)

AAA Portland Beavers   **Spring Training Venue:** Clearwater Community Sports Complex, Clearwater, Florida

Pittsburgh, Pennsylvania

SINCE 1901
NATIONAL LEAGUE EAST DIVISION 1969-1993;
CENTRAL DIVISION 1994-2004

NAME CHANGE HISTORY
Pittsburgh Alleghenys 1882-1890;
Pittsburgh Pirates 1891-2005

Honours

World Series Champions	1909, 1925, 1960, 1971 & 1979
League Pennant Winners	1901, 1902, 1903, 1909, 1925, 1927, 1960.
Division Winners	1970, 1971, 1972, 1974, 1975, 1979, 1990, 1991 & 1992
Division Series	1970, 1971, 1972, 1974, 1975, 1979, 1990, 1991, 1992
Championship Series Winners	1971, 1979
World Series Losses	1903, 1927

World Series Wins	Managers
1909 - v. Detroit Tigers 4-3	Fred Clarke
1925 - v. Washington Senators 4-3	Bill McKechnie
1960 - v. New York Yankees 4-3	Danny Murtaugh
1971 - v. Baltimore Orioles 4-3	Danny Murtaugh
1979 - v. Baltimore Orioles 4-3	Chuck Tanner

Season 2004

National League Rookie of the Year: Jason Bay

Payroll 2003/2004	$62m (21)-$40m (27).
Top Paid Players:	Salary
Jason Kendall (C	$8.5m
Rick Reed	$8m
Kris Benson (P)*	$3.45
Jack Wilson (SS)	$1.85m,
Craig Wilson (OF)	$1.15m.

*traded to Mets mid-season

2004 Team Stats

Position in Div	5th of 6
Record	72-89
Games Back	32.5
Percentage	.447 (20th)
Split	39-41 H; 33-48 R
Last 10 Seasons	5526356445
Runs per Game:	4.20 (27th)
Staff ERA	4.29 (14th=)
Ave ERA starters:	4.68 (15th)
Ave ERA relievers:	3.57 (6th)
Batting ave:	.260 (22nd=)
Slugging ave. .	.401 (25th)
On Base %:	.321 (25th=)
ABS Per Hit	3.84 (22nd)

Total/Net Homers	142/149 (-7 18th)
ABS per HR	38.61 (26th)
ABS Per SO	5.14 (18th)
Runs For/Against	680 (27) 744 (12)
Net Runs	-64 (21st)
Net BB/BB p AB	-161/13.21 (30th)
Total Steals:	63 (24th)
Total Errors	113 (20th)
Unearned Runs Giv	64 (17th)
Record Attendance	2001 2 436 126
	Ave: 30 075
Attendance 2003	1 636 761 **Ave** 20 984
Attendance 2004	1 583 031 (75)
	Ave 21 107 (28)

2004 Starting Rotation

Starter	Record
Oliver Perez	30: 12-10; 2.98 ERA
Josh Fogg	32: 11-10, 4.64 ERA
Kip Wells	24: 5-7, 4.55 ERA
Ryan Vogelson	26: 6-13, 6.50 ERA
Sean Burnett	13: 5-5, 5.02 ERA
Bullpen Star	
Mike Gonzalez	1.25 ERA
Closer	
Jose Mesa	43/48 SV, 3.25 ERA
Catchers	
Jason Kendall 147g	.319, 3HR, 51 RBI

Briefly... Small market team albeit with long history and some success, now struggling to compete with a small payroll of $62 million. The Pirates have not had a first place since 1992 and only one season since then where they have been competitive: in 1997 when they finished five games out of top spot. They have a great modern ballpark and some promising talent in starter Oliver Perez and last season's star rookie Jason Bay but the organisation is still very much in slow re-building mode. It seems that there are two ways to win in modern baseball: you either get star players who cost tremendous amounts of cash or you invent a whole new philosophy like Beane's *Moneyball*. There are no signs of either in Pittsburgh.

Uniforms: White sleeveless jerseys with "Pirates" letters in black with yellow edge, yellow and black armpit edge stripe, black undershirts, black caps with yellow "P" logo. **Road** – Grey sleeveless jerseys with black "Pittsburgh" lettering with yellow edge, black and yellow numbers below heart. Yellow and black double stripe on grey pants.

Nicknames: Bucs' (abb.Buccaneers)

Owners(s): Kevin S. McClachy **GM:** Dave Littlefield **Manager:** Lloyd McClendon (b. Jan 1959) has now completed four seasons with the organisation as skipper after four as hitting coach. As a player with the Reds, Cubs and Pirates he was no great shakes as a player, not playing every day, but he exhibited excellent leadership skills which caused his GM to say upon his appointment in 2001, the first Afro-American skipper in Pirates history, incidentally, to say that "he got the job simply because he was the best guy available." According to the stats - record: 281-365 (.435) – this sounds like major league bull, but with the raw material at his disposal on a shrinking payroll, it's hard to say how good a leader Lloyd is.

Home: **PNC Park**, home of the Pittsburgh Pirates since 2001. Is it any wonder they never win anything with a name like this. I bet the fans can really get emotional about it. They've been on the shores of the Allegheny River since April 9 2001, when the home team was pasted by the Reds, 9-2. The crowd was 36,954. A statue of Roberto Clemente stands outside the park. Previously, the franchise had inhabited **Three Rivers Stadium** (from 1970) and before that, **Forbes Field** (from 1909), which had been the nation's first stadium made entirely of poured concrete and steel. This was the park where the Babe hit his last three home runs (in 1935). **Capacity: 38,127.** Dimensions: 325' to left field, 399' to center field, 320' to right field.

Three Rivers Stadium, the most beautifully named baseball stadium of all time (I've decided) was built on top of Exposition Stadium at the point where the Allegheny and Monongahela rivers meet the Ohio. The original plans for what is now RS was for it to span the Monongahela with boats going by underneath. For that fact alone I would immediately make myself a Pirates fan, but for the stumbling block that I'm already stone committed to the Red Sox through an accident of friendship geography. So it goes. *Pitcher's Park (Very clear advantage).*

World Series And Post-Season Ratings	Position	Points/Occasions/%
Full Historical Record 1901-2004	6	8276-7814: .511
Total Historical Rating	6	N/A
World Series Rating	9	365 Ranking Points
Play Offs Rating	14	54 Ranking Points
Pennant Wins (pre-'69)	9	7
Division Wins (post-'69)	5=	9
World Series Wins/Appearances/Games Won	6=/11=/10	5/7/23

Level Of Recent Success		Won/Lost
Games Won Per Season Post-69	10	77.4
Seasons Since A World Series Appearance	25	1979 Beat Baltimore 4-3
Seasons Since A Division Series	N/A	Div. Series began in 1995
Seasons Since A Championship Series	N/A	Ch. Series began in 1995
Seasons Since A Division Win	12	1992 Won NLE by 9 games (for the 3rd consecutive year)

RATINGS

Most Home Runs Hit For The Pirates	Most Games Won By A Pitcher
Season: 54 Ralph Kiner HF 1949	Season: 28 Jack Chesbro 1902
Career: 301 Ralph Kiner	Career: 202 Wilbur Cooper
Highest Batting Average	**Most Strikeouts**
Season: .385 Arky Vaughan HF 1935	Season: 276 Bob Veale 1965
Career: .340 Paul Vaner	Career: 1,682 Bob Friend

RECORDS

Best Batting Ave. 2004 Jason Kendall .319	**Most Home Runs 2004** Jack Wilson 29
RBI Leader Jason Bay & Craig Wilson 82	**Most Bases** J. Wilson 299 (201h, .308)
Most K's Oliver Perez 239	**Most Walks** Perez 81
Most HR's Given Up Perez/Vogelsong 22	**Most Innings Pitched** Perez 196
Other Stats: Craig Wilson was 3rd in strikeouts in	the majors, Jason Bay 23rd.

2004

Pirates Hall Of Famers

"Chuck the ball as hard as you can at him and pray."
John McGraw on how to cope with Honus Wagner's arrival at the plate.

Max Carey CF, 1910-29 Sw: Base-stealer (51 from 53 attempts in 1922 and a high of 63 in 1916), above-average hitter (six times over .300 and .458 in 1925 World Series) and excellent outfielder. (BJ23) **1961**

Fred Clarke LF, 1894-1915, L: A lifetime .315 hitter who was player manager in 16 of 19 seasons, winning 14 first place finishes. Ten times batted over .300. No insignia on cap in hall. (BJ22) **1945**

Roberto Clemente RF 19-'72: Star of 1960 and 1971 World Series Pirates wins and series MVP in second. A superb right-outfielder with spectacularly good arm, he died in a tragic air crash taking overloaded relief supplies to earthquake-struck Nicaraguans in 1972. Cuban. (BJ28) (BJ8) **1973. Top 100: BJ74- SN20 – SABR20**

Ralph Kiner LF: A Pirate from 1946 (as rookie) to 1952. A considerable home run hitter: 51-40-54-47-42 from 1947 through 1951 and thus the biggest crowd puller in Pirates history. 14.1 at bats per homer, second only to Babe Ruth's 11.8. (BJ18) **1975 Top 100: BJ00- SN90 – SABR89**

Freddie Lindstrom 3B 1924-36 ('24-'32): Though here in the Pirates section due to his hat, this guy came up with the Giants and within months was the youngest player ever to appear in a Series, at 18, where he had four hits in one game off none other than Walter Johnson. In a neutral ballpark, he hit .358 with 231 hits in 1928 and bettered than in 1930 with .379. Not a prolific home run hitter, but finished a fairly short career .311 lifetime. Looked somewhat like Jeff Bridges. (BJ43) **1976**

Bill McKechnie 1922-26: Manager of the '25 World Champions. See Cincinnati.

Bill Maseroski 2B 1956-72: Defensive king of the second base. The first man to win a World Series with a walk-off home run, in 1960, a photo of which can be found in the Ken Burns book of the epic TV documentary series. (BJ29). **2001**

Willie Stargell LF, 1962-82, L: "Pops" hit 475 career homers, was NL MVP in 1979, the oldest in history and led NL in homers twice. A slugger of huge power, he is only one of two players to hit a ball out of Dodgers Stadium. Had an award winning comeback year in '78 after bad knee trouble, then swept all before him in '79, leading the club to World Series victory with his clubhouse charisma and great hitting. A true leader, his statue stands outside PNC Park. A/A. (BJ9) **1988. Top 100: BJ82- SN81 – SABR93**

Harold "Pie" Traynor 3B, 1920-37: A one-club .320 lifetime hitter widely regarded as the greatest of all third basemen. He certainly batted better than .300 with ease: he did it ten times. He also 200 hits per 162 games, an achievement only matched by three other players. His doubles and triples numbers are far superior to his homers total, his playing in the vast depths of Forbes Field. It was a park made for contact hitting and bunting. The child Pie eater was an expert. (BJ15) **1948. Top 100: BJ00- SN70 – SABR70**

Joseph "Arky" Vaughan SS 1932-1948, L; .318 hitter in 14-year career and brilliant shortstop. His talent was in its fullest flower during the '34-'36 period where he dominated the stats of those years. In '35 he won The Sporting News Player Of The Year award after being 3rd in the MVP stakes the year before. He was an All-Star in all the years between '34 and '42. It says something of the times the game was played when this "quiet, gentlemanly" player, when on the receiving end of threats of a revenge attack from one Dick Bartell after a game clash, approached the latter before the game the next time the two teams met and offered him out "under the stands" as was the phrase at the time. He also led a principled stand against the managerial methods of Leo Durocher. An admirable, superlative player. (BJ2) **1985. Top 100: BJ39- SN00 – SABR00**

Honus Wagner SS 1897-1917: One of the all time great players, period, and the best ever shortstop in most people's reckoning. Superb hitter, despite being stuck in the Dead Ball era. An 18 season Pirate, batting .327 over a 10,430 at bat career. Said John McGraw of trying to cope with him, "just chuck him the ball as hard as you can and pray." Head turned so no Pirates insignia visible on cap. (BJ1) **1936. Top 100: BJ2- SN13 – SABR10**

Lloyd Waner CF, 1927-45, L: .316 lifetime batting average in a long career, seventeen seasons a Pirate. With his older brother he amassed big stats in terms of average, hits and runs in the 30s. Not a power hitter, he hit over 200 hits a season 4 times. Hit only 27 career home runs. Not noted for fielding. "Little Poison." (BJ50) **1967**

Paul Waner RF, 1926-45, L: had a 2 549 game career batting .333. 16 years a Pirate and a *prodigious* drinker, by all accounts. He and brother Lloyd together were key in the pennant winning team of, 27. He hit .380 that year and won the NL MVP. He led the league again in average twice more, in '34 and '36. Also Dodgers, Braves, Yankees, during the war years. "Big Poison." (BJ9). **1952. Top 100: BJ84- SN00 – SABR71**

> *"The way to get a ball past Wagner is to hit it eight feet over his head."*
>
> John McGraw on the greatest third baseman of his day

Retired Uniform Numbers

1 Billy Meyer (manager)	4 Ralph Kiner	8 Willie Stargell
9 Bill Mazeroski	20 Pie Traynor	21 Roberto Clemente
	33 Honus Wagner	

AAA Portland Beavers **Spring Training Venue:** McKechnie Field, Bradenton, Florida

ST LOUIS CARDINALS

St Louis, Missouri

SINCE 1901

NATIONAL LEAGUE EAST DIVISION 1969-93;
CENTRAL DIVISION 1994-2004

NAME CHANGE HISTORY

St Louis Brown Stockings 1882; St Louis Browns 1883-1898; St Louis Perfectos 1899;
St Louis Cardinals 1900-2005

Honours

World Series Winners	1926, 1931, 1934, 1942, 1944, 1946, 1964, 1967 & 1982
Division Winners	1985, 1987, 1996, 2000, 2001, 2002 & 2004
Division Series Winners	1996, 2000, 2002 & 2004
Championship Series Winners	1982, 1985, 1987 & 2004
League Pennant Winners	1926, 1928, 1930, 1931, 1934, 1942, 1943, 1944, 1946, 1964, 1966 & 1968
World Series Losses	0-4 to the New York Yankees in 1928; 2-4 to the Philadelphia As in 1930; 1-4 to the New York Yankees in 1943; 0-4 to the Boston Red Sox 2004; 3-4 to the Detroit Tigers in 1968; 3-4 to the Kansas City Royals in 1985; 3-4 to the Minnesota Twins in 1987

Winning World Series Wins	Managers
1926 v. New York Yankees 4-3	Rogers Hornsby
1931 v. Philadelphia As 4-3	Gabby Street
1934 v. Detroit Tigers 4-3	Frankie Frisch
1942 - v. New York Yankees 4-3	Billy Southworth
1944 - v. St Louis Browns 4-2	Billy Southworth.
1946 v. Boston Red Sox 4-3	Eddie Dyer
1964 - v. New York Yankees 4-3	Johnny Keane
1967 - v. Boston Red Sox 4-3	Red Schoendienst
1982 - v. Milwaukee Brewers 4-3	Whitey Herzog

Season   2004

Payroll 2003/2004	$102m(7) $81 (10)
Highest	**Salaries**
Albert Pujols	$14.28m
Larry Walker	$12.67m (from Colorado July '04)
Matt Morris (P)	$12.5m
Jim Edmonds (OF)	$9.3m
Scott Rolen (3B)	$7.78m
Jason Isringhausen (Cl)	$7.7m
Edgar Renteria (SS)	$7.25m
Woody Williams (P)	$6.5m
Roger Cedeno (RF)	$5.37m
Mike Matheny (C)	$4m

*Note that Dugout Dollars gives Pujols' salary as double this figure.

2004 Team Stats

Position in Div	1st of 6
Record	105-57
Games Back	+13
Percentage	.648 (1st)
Split	53-28 H; 52-29 R
Last 10 Seasons	4143411131
Runs per Game:	5.28
Staff ERA	3.75 (2nd)
Ave ERA starters:	4.08 (4th=)
Ave ERA relievers:	3.01 (1st)
Batting ave:	.278 (4th)
Slugging ave.	.460 (2nd)

On Base %:	.344 (10th)
ABS Per Hit	3.59 (4th)
Total/Net Homers	214/169 (45 4th=)
AB per HR	25.95 (6th)
AB Per SO	5.12 (19th)
Runs For/Against	855 (6) 659 (1)
Net Runs	196 (1st)
Net BB/BB p AB	108/10.13 (12th)
Total Steals:	111 (5th)
Total Errors	93 (10th)
Unearned Runs Giv	54 (11th)
Record Attendance	2000 3 336 493; **Ave:** 41 191
2003 Attendance	2 910 371 ; **Ave** 35 931
2004 Attendance	

2004 Starting Rotation

Starter	Record
Matt Morris	32: 15-10; 4.72 ERA
Chris Carpenter	28: 15-5; 3.46 ERA
Jason Marquis	32: 15-7; 3.71 ERA
Woody Williams	31: 11-8; 4.18 ERA
Jeff Suppan	31: 16-9; 4.16 ERA
Bullpen Star	
Steve Kline	1.69 ERA
Closer	
Jason Isringhausen	47/54 SV, 2.78 ERA
Catchers	
Mike Matheny 122g	.247, 5HR, 50 RBI

Briefly... Extremely venerable original major league club - they contested the first World Series in 1903, losing to the Boston Beaneaters 3-5 - and home of the farm system first deployed by Branch Rickey. It has become fashionable again to describe them as the New York Yankees of the National League what with their exploits last season. They have won 9 World Series, 4 more than the next most successful NL franchise, but they haven't, as you can readily see here, won one for 22 years.

The modern Cardinals have been consistently threatening but it wasn't until last 2004 season that Tony LaRussa's team truly found itself, with a hitting line up of exceptional power and talent, stacked up through a huge payroll, monstering the opposition. See elsewhere in this book for what happened when they met the Boston Red Sox.

Uniforms: Home - Immaculate white shirts with 2 Cardinal birds perched on sloping yellow bat and dominating "Cardinals" script in red; Crimson/cardinal red numbers under heart, red undershirts and cardinal red caps with interlocking St L logo. White pants. All in all, a modern-traditional classic, un 'omage to supposedly glorious baseball past. **Road** - Grey version of home.

Owners: "The Owners of the St Louis Cardinals" as they seem to be known in a hundred articles.

GM: Walter Jocketty. **Manager:** Tony LaRussa, b. October 4th 1944, a man whose managerial longevity threatens to make him a modern institution, has had five first places in his division in nine seasons with the Cards, but has been unable to snag the big prize. The 2004 meltdown in the face of the surging Red Sox tide will have come as an immense shock, but he is still in place for another run at the thing with a much-changed roster. His Cardinals story continues for another season at the very least.

LaRussa had no sort of major league career, failing fractionally to meet the Mendoza line in six seasons where he only managed to get 176 at bats with the Atlanta Braves and the Athletics of both Kansas City and Oakland. His management career began in 1979 with the Chicago White Sox in the AL West, where he stayed eight seasons and earned one first place, in 1983. The Sox lost that championship series to the Orioles 1-3. At Oakland from 1986 to 1995 he was even more successful: four first place finishes, two championships and a World Series in 1989. He has had four Manager Of The Year awards: 1983; 1988; 1992 and 2002. Record: 2114-1846 (.534)

Home: Busch Stadium, which is soon to be known as Busch Stadium I, as from the beginning of the 2006 season, the Cardinals are going to be performing in yet another state-of-the-art retro ballpark. And magnificent it looks as a figment of a computer's imagination: 50 000 + capacity, great sightlines, a million ways to chomp yourself through the night or weekend afternoon.

The present Busch is a 1966 cookie cutter affair **(capacity 50 345)** but made distinctive by high concrete arches with encircle the whole concrete shebang. However, because of said building substance, a recent observer opined that the place had all the character of the Olympic Stadium in Montreal, that monument to Space Age dehumanising fundamentalism. Still, under lights, Busch looks pretty enough, at least in photographs and on the box, which isn't the point. It's the opinion of those in Missouri who pay the entrance money that counts. **Pitcher's Park** (But moving towards neutral).

The naming of the new Busch Stadium which is, if I haven't made this quite clear, is going to be called "Busch Stadium" is to be done in honour of the money that Anaheuser-Busch, the local brewing giant, has put up to help offset the $400m cost.

World Series And Post-Season Ratings	Position	Points/Occasions/%
Full Historical Record 1901-2004	4	8336-7757: .515
Total Historical Rating	2	N/A
World Series Rating	2	750 Ranking Points
Play Offs Rating	4	128 Ranking Points
Pennant Wins (pre-'69)	4=	12
Division Wins (post-'69)	7=	8
World Series Wins/Appearances/Games Won	2=/4/2	9/16/48
Level Of Recent Success		**Won/Lost**
Games Won Per Season Post-69	7=	78.9
Seasons Since A World Series Appearance	15	2004 lost to Red Sox 0-4
Seasons Since A Division Series	0	2004 beat LA Dodgers 3-1
	(2002 lost to Arizona 3-0)	
Seasons Since A Championship Series	0	2004 beat Houston 4-2
		(2002 lost to Giants 1-4)
Seasons Since A Division Win	0	2004 Won NLE by 13 games

RATINGS

*World Series Rating would be 2nd if Brooklyn and Los Angeles Dodgers are treated as separate clubs.

Most Home Runs Hit For The Cardinals Season: 70 Mark McGwire 1998 Career: 475 Stan Musial HF **Highest Batting Average** Season: .424 Rogers Hornsby HF 1924 Career: .359 Rogers Hornsby	**Most Games Won By A Pitcher** Season: 30 Dizzy Dean HF 1930 Career: 251 Bob Gibson HF **Most Strikeouts** Season: 274 Bob Gibson 1970 Career: 3 117 Bob Gibson

RECORDS

Best Batting Ave. 2004 Albert Pujols .331 **RBI Leader** Scott Rolen 124 (Pujols 123) **Most K's** Chris Carpenter 152 **Most HR's Given Up** Matt Morris 35 **Other Top Bats:** Edmonds .301, 111RBI.	**Most Home Runs 2004** Pujols 46 (Edmonds 42) **Most Bases** Pujols 389 **Most Walks** Jason Marquis 70 **Most Innings Pitched** Morris 202 Womack: .307, 170h/Walker .298, 17HR in 82g

2004

Cardinals Hall of Famers

"People ask me what I do in winter when there's no baseball. I'll tell you what I do. I stare out the window and wait for spring." - Rogers Hornsby

Jake Beckley 1B, 1888-1907 (1904-07) L: Distinguished hitter who ended his career in the early years of the 'modern' majors. .325 average in his first season. 2, 930 hits and .308 lifetime. (BJ52) **1971**

Jim Bottomley 1B, 1922-37 (1922-32; 36-7), L: 1928 MVP and lifetime .310 hitter, famously good in the clutch. 100 RBIs consecutively from 1925-29. Also a Red. No insignia on Hall Of Fame plaque cap. (BJ36) **1974**

Lou Brock LF, 1961-79 (1964-79) L: 2nd all-time in total base steals and good enough to bat over .300 8 times (lifetime .293 & 149 HR). In 1967, became the first player to steal 50 bases and hit 20 homers. Stole 50 bases 12 times – 118 in 1974. (A/A). (BJ15) **1985. Top 100: BJ00- SN58 – SABR73**

Jesse Burkett LF, 1890-1905 (1899-1904) L: hitter who ended his career in the early majors. Ended his career with .342 ave. and 2nd place in all-time hits to that point with 2872. (BJ14) **1946**

Dizzy Dean P 1930-47 ('30-37; '47) 3.02 ERA : Texan Jay Dean, original member of the 'Gas House Gang'. 30 wins and MVP in 1934 and won the World Series of that year pitching a shutout in Game 7. All-Star 1934 through '37, his career was ruined by broken toe he never allowed to heal properly. Was a famed raconteur after he retired not least for his quotes such as this to a young batter: "Son, which kind of pitch would you like to miss?" and "I ain't who I used to be, but who the hell is?" (BJ25) **1953. Top 100: BJ00- SN85 – SABR74**

Frankie Frisch 2B, 1919-37 Sw: Player-manager of the Cards from '34-'38 his team's uncompromising style gave birth to the nickname for the World Champions of '34, the 'Gashouse Gang.' Was a .316 career switch hitter and played with 8 pennant winners in 18 seasons. "The Fordham Flash," so-named for being from the Fordham Road area of the Bronx, Steely Dan fans take note. No insignia visible on cap. (BJ11) **1947. Top 100: BJ88- SN88 – SABR72**

Bob Gibson P 1959-75, 251-174, 2.91 ERA: Widely regarded as best ever Cardinals pitcher. Absolutely brilliant in two World Series: 1964 & 1967, the latter after a mid-season broken leg. Pitched 2 complete game victories in '64 and 3 complete games with 1.00 ERA in '67. An immensely interesting character study of him appears in *Once More Around The Park* by Roger Angel. (BJ8) **1981. Top 100: BJ46- SN31 – SABR17**

Chick Hafey LF 1924-37 ('32-37): Shy and weak-eyed, he played in spectacles in the second part of his career. Holds an NL record of 10 consecutive hits over three games. Lifetime .317 average. Supposedly couldn't read street signs *with* glasses, which casts doubt on his deserving his place in the gallery, according to statisticians. (BJ59) **1971**

Jesse Haines P, 210-158, 3.64 ERA: 2 World Series victories against the Yankees in 1926 form the highlight of his career. The adjectives "durable" and "tough" suggest that his inclusion in the venerable Hall owes something to a Chick Hafey-like myopia. Or maybe I'm just too big a Bill James fan. **1970**
No insignia visible.

Rogers Hornsby 2B, 1915-37: Vastly important figure of the game between the wars. A lifetime .358 hitter, in 1922 he had the best season of any second baseman of all time according to the Baseball Abstract. He was NL batting champion from '20 right through to '25 and again in '28. He topped the slugging averages in those years and '29 also. His .424 in '24 is a 20th century major league record and may never be beaten. He was a fascinating man, a complex blend of characteristics. Was player-manager of the World Series winning '26 Cardinals. Sensationally he was then traded to the Giants. A consensus of observers since the '20s would probably place him as the third best hitter of all time, behind Cobb and Ruth (or Ruth and Cobb). Managed for many years while and after he played, but his cold personality and inability to motivate players constantly dogged his steps. Also, Giants, Braves, Cubs and Browns. Turned head, no visible insignia. (BJ3)**1942. Top 100: BJ22- SN9 – SABR9**

Joe Medwick LF 1932-48 ('32-'40; '47-'48): 'Ducky' and 'Ducky Wucky.' A great bad-ball hitter with a lot of excellent numbers. Hit .358 in the victorious Gashouse '34 Series. Check out the ejection story of that year wherever you can find it. He was a truly dominant hitter of this period: league leading 227 & 223 hits respectively in '36 and '37, for example. He won the last NL Triple Crown in '37, so the fee for his trade to the Dodgers was unsurprisingly huge - $125,000. He then assisted his new club to their first pennant in 20 years. Also Dodgers, Giants and Braves. No insignia. (BJ13) **1968. Top 100: BJ00- SN79 – SABR100**

Johnny Mize 1B, 1936-53 L: A superlative slugger, he was home run King in the NL four times (max. 51 in '47). He was also batting champion in '39 with .349. Led in slugging 3 seasons running, '38-'40. You're getting the picture. "The Big Cat" also played for the Giants and the Yankees (as effective pinch-hitter at the end of his career). Missed 3 prime seasons due to war service also. (BJ6) No insignia. **1981. Top 100: BJ62- SN00 – SABR87**

Stan Musial LF 1941-63, L: 'The Man,' a massive baseball star. 24 All-Star games, from 1942 hit +.300 for 16 straight seasons. 4th all-time in hits. MVP in 1943, 1946 & 1949. Honoured with statue outside Busch Stadium. Threw out ceremonial first pitch in G4 WS 2004. (BJ2) **1971. Top 100: BJ10- SN10 – SABR5**

Kid Nicols P, 1890-1906 ('04-'05), 360-205: 21-13 record in his one full season. Made his name with the Boston Beaneaters. His completion rate is huge: 531 of 561 starts. Won 5 pennants with Boston and at BJ9 and T100-47, he must have been brilliant. **Top 100: BJ47- SN00 – SABR00**

Red Schoendienst 2B, 1945-63 Sw: Superb second baseman with brilliant defensive numbers and +.300 hitter five times. 10 time All-Star. Successfully managed the Cardinals too, to two World Series, in 1967 – victorious - and 1968 (not). Real name 'Albert.' (BJ28). **1989**

George Sisler 1B, 1915-30 L: All-time great first baseman (although this is latterly disputed by Sabermetrics) with .341 lifetime batting average and a number of records: twice batting champion with average above .400, highest hits 1920 & 1922 and highest runs in '22. Six times had more than 200 hits. Had a batting streak of 41 in 1922. Also St Louis Browns. (BJ24). **1971. Top 100: BJ00*- SN33 – SABR55**
*Sisler is James's highest ranked player outside his top 100.

Enos Slaughter RF, 1938-59 L: Famous for the 'home from first run' to win the 1946 World Series against the Red Sox, but also an excellent .300 lifetime hitter. He became a hustling leftie, brilliant in clutch situations. "Country" Slaughter, he was known as. (BJ12) **1985**

Ozzie Smith SS Sw, Inducted in 2002, he was unusual in being a brilliant 13 Gold Gloves winning short stop but mediocre hitter who improved considerably over time. Hit .303 in 1987 and in 1985 hit a World Series winning home run against the Dodgers in Game 5. He made 2 400 hits and stole 500 bases. (BJ7) **2002. Top 100: BJ00 - SN87 – SABR56**

Bobby Wallace SS, 1894-1918: "Mr Shortstop" played for both St Louis Clubs. .268 lifetime hitter. 25-year career. Also Browns and Reds. (BJ36) **1953**

Outside The Hall Of Fame

Mark McGwire: A 583 home run career and the breaking of the Maris record in 1998 means he's a shoe-in as long as he is not sucked into the steroid controversy vortex in a most unfortunate way.

Retired Uniform Numbers

1 Ozzie Smith	2 Red Schoendienst	6 Stan Musial
9 Enos Slaughter	14 Ken Boyer	7 Dizzy Dean
20 Lou Brock	45 Bob Gibson	85 August Busch

AAA Portland Beavers   **Spring Training Venue:** Roger Dean Stadium, Jupiter, Florida

San Diego, California

SINCE 1969

NATIONAL LEAGUE WEST DIVISION 1969-2005

Honours

World Series Wins	None
Division Winners	1984, 1996 & 1998
Division Series Winners	1998
Division Championship Winners	1984; 1998
World Series Losers	1984 & 1998
Seasons Since A World Series Appearance	5
World Series Losses	1-4 to the Detroit Tigers in 1984; 0-4 to the Yankees in 1998

Season 2004

Payroll 2003/2004	$58m (26) $64m (16)
Highest Paid Players	Salary
Brian Giles (OF)	$8.56m
Phil Nevin (3B)	$8.5m;
Andy Ashby (P)	$8.5m
(from LA Sept '04)	
Jeff Cirillo (3B)	$7.1m
Ryan Klesco (OF)	$6m.
Alex S. Gonzalez	$5.7m
(from Cubs Sept '04)	
Terence Long (OF)	$3.57m
Rich Aurilia (SS)	$3.1m
(acquired from Seattle July '04)	
David Wells	$1.25m

2004 Team Stats

Position in Div	3rd of 5
Record	87-75
Games Back	6 (5 from WC)
Percentage	.537 (13th)
Split	42-39 H; 45-36 R
Last 10 Seasons	3141454553
Runs per Game:	4.74 (18th)
Staff ERA	4.03 (5th)
Ave ERA starters	4.17 (7th)
Ave ERA relievers:	3.75 (8th)
Batting ave:	.273 (7th)
Slugging ave.	.414 (20th)

On Base %:	.342 (12th)
ABS Per Hit	3.66 (7th)
Total/Net Homers	139/184 (-45 25th)
AB per HR	40.09 (27th)
ABS Per SO	6.12 (2nd)
Runs For/Against	768 (18) 705 (7)
Net Runs	63 (12th)
Net BB/BB p AB	108/9.84 (11th)
Total Steals:	52 (27th)
Total Errors	108 (17th)
Unearned Runs Giv	48 (8th=)
Record Attendance	1998: 2 555 901
Finished 1st (At Qualcom)	Ave: 31 554
Attendance 2003	2 030 064 Ave 25 063
Attendance 2004	3 040 046 Ave 37 531 (10th)

2004 Starting Rotation

Starter		Record
Jason Peavy	27:	15-6; 2.27 ERA
David Wells	31:	12-8, 3.73 ERA
Brian Lawrence	34:	15-14, 4.12 ERA
Adam Eaton	33:	11-14, 4.61 ERA
Bullpen Star		
Akinori Otsuka (32)		1.75 ERA
Closer		
Trevor Hoffman 4		1/45 SV, 2.30 ERA
Catcher		
Ramon Hernandez 111g		.276, 18HR, 63 RBI
Miguel Orjeda 62g		.256, 8HR, 26 RBI

Briefly... The Padres is a middling franchise but with perhaps the potential for more success on the most recent evidence. This thought is sobered by the fact that they have to compete in a viciously competitive environment: the NL West division, which contains the presently dominant Dodgers and Giants. They have a low-middle payroll but a delightful "old-modern" stadium. One superstar, soon to enter the Hall of Fame dominates their short history: Tony Gwynn. Their grand 1998 season where they made the World Series suggests that all is not lost; and indeed, 2004's 3rd place winning record was much better than many pundits expected.

Uniform: Home – White shirt with navy script "Padres" lettering with scimitar underlining, navy and white sleeve and v-neck thin edging. **Road** – Magnificent and clean, beige shirt with large 'San Diego' college print lettering (w/ white edging), thin navy edging on neck and sleeve, grey pants with double blue side stripe. **Alt** – Blue shirt with beige edging, "Padres" lettering in beige with white edge.

Owners(s): John Moores **GM:** Kevin Towers **Manager:** Bruce Bochy (pronounced "Bow" – as in violin – "Chee") has been skipper for almost ten seasons. He has two division titles to his name but an overall .488 record. Last season's record was the club's best performance since 1998, so Bochy may well be around for still longer. Had a meagre playing record in the majors but made his mark through apparently having a huge head. When called up to the Mets in '82 they couldn't find a helmet big enough to fit him.Bruce was a catcher with a mediocre hitting record: lifetime .239 with 26 homers. He came up with the Astros in 1978 and also played with the Mets before finishing with the Padres in 1987. He was 49 in April. Record: 781-821 (.488).

Home: Petco Park, is the much-admired new waterfront home of the San Diego Padres as of April 8 2004. The Padres left the huge Qualcom (formerly the Jack Murphy and before that the San Diego Stadium), their home since they began life in the majors in 1969. One old stadium, 2,774 regular season games: three different names. The new ballpark was featured on the second Sunday of the new 2004 season in a game against the Giants (where Bonds was still reaching to tie Willie Mays) and in the evening sun looked an absolute picture. Baseball really is now moving away completely from the "cookie cutter" symmetry of the 70s and 80s; Petco is a glorious mess of irregularly shaped corners and edges. It also has the splendid old warehouse building of the Western Metal Supply Company at the end of the left field line. The foul pole is painted on the side of the building. Thus it really is a case of "bye-bye faceless corporate regularity" and "hello, let's get back to Mom and Pop and Blueberry Pies cooling on the windowsill." Its downtown position is also a signifier of the new modernity. Here its part of a revitalisation programme of the old inner city. Capacity: 42 500. Pitcher's Park (slight advantage).

World Series And Post-Season Ratings	Position	Points/Occasions/%	
Full Historical Record 1969-2004	**28**	2611-3094: .457	**RATINGS**
Total Historical Rating	27	N/A	
World Series Rating	23	3 Ranking Points	
Play Offs Rating	17=	45 Ranking Points	
Division Wins (post-'69)	20=	3	
World Series Wins/Appearances/Games Won	30=/18=/24	0/2/1	
World Series Wins	0	0	
World Series Appearances	20=	2	
Level Of Recent Success		**Won/Lost**	
Games Won Per Season Post-69	27	70	
Seasons Since A World Series Appearance	6	1998 Lost to NYY 0-4	
Seasons Since A Division Series	6	1998 Beat Houston 3-1	
Seasons Since A Championship Series	6	1998 Beat Atlanta 4-2	
Seasons Since A Division Win	6	Won NLW by 9.5 games	

Most Home Runs Hit For The Padres	Most Games Won By A Pitcher	
Season: 50 Greg Vaughn 1998	Season: 22 Randy Jones 1976	**RECORDS**
Career: 163 Nate Colbert	Career: 100 Eric Show	
Highest Batting Average:	**Most Strikeouts**	
Season: .372 Tony Gwynn	Season: 257 Kevin Brown 1998	
Career: .338 Tony Gwynn	Career: 1 036 Andy Benes	

Best Batting Ave. 2004 Mark Loretta .335	**Most Home Runs 2004** Phil Nevin 26	**2004**
RBI Leader Nevin 105	**Most Bases** Loretta 307	
Most K's Jake Peavy 173	**Most Walks** Brian Lawrence 55	
Most HR's Given Up Adam Eaton 28	**Most Innings Pitched** Lawrence 203	
Other Top Batters: Brian Giles: 94 RBI, .284	Sean Burroughs, 156 hits, .298.	

Padres Hall Of Famers

Dave Winfield RF, 1973-95: 3110 hits and 465 homers. A/A (BJ13) **2001. Top 100: BJ00- SN94 – SABR00**

Outside The Hall Of Fame

Tony Gwynne: Not a slugger (138 career homers), but a fantastic contact hitter with 3141 hits. In batting average he was the NL champion eight times and posted four of the best ten post-war records. He retired in 2001 with a phenomenal career batting average of .338. In the 1998 World Series he hit .500 in 16 at bats and had one home run. A certain first ballot Hall of Famer in 2006, he is now a very decent co-commentator on TV. **Top 100: BJ54- SN49 – SABR38**

Retired Uniform Numbers			
6 Steve Garvey	19 Tony Gwynn	31 Dave Winfield	35 Randy Jones

AAA Portland Beavers **Spring Training Venue:** Peoria Stadium, Peoria, Arizo

SAN FRANCISCO GIANTS

San Francisco, California

SINCE 1958

NATIONAL LEAGUE WEST DIVISION 1969-2

NAME CHANGE HISTORY
New York Gothams 1883-84; New York Giants 1885-1957; San Francisco Giants 1958-2004

Honours

San Francisco Giants World Series Wins	None
League Pennant Winners	1962
Division Winners	1971, 1989, 1997, 2000 & 2003
Division Winners	1971, 1987 & 2000
Division Series Winners	2002
Championship Series Winners	1989 & 2002
World Series Losers	1962, 1989 & 2002
Wild Card League Winners	2002
World Series losses	3-4 to the Yankees in 1962; 0-4 to Oakland in 1989; 3-4 to Anaheim in 2002

Season 2004

National League MVP Award Winner: Barry Bonds

Payroll 2003/2004	$100m(8) $82m (9)
Highest Paid	**Salary**
Barry Bonds (OF)	$18m
Robb Nen (P)	$9.1m*
Jason Schmidt (P)	$7.93m
Durham (2B)	$7.2m
Edgardo Alfonzo (3B)	$6.5m
Kirk Reuter (P)	$6m
A.J. Pierzinski (C)	$3.5m

* (shoulder injured since 2002, closer w/ more than 300 career saves)

2004 Team Stats

Position in Div	2nd of 5
Record	91-71
Games Back	2
Percentage	.562 (9th=)
Split	47-34 **H**; 44-36 **R**
Last 10 Seasons	4412212212
Runs per Game:	**5.25** (7th)
Staff Era	**4.29** (14th=)
Ave ERA starters	**4.18** (8th)
Ave ERA relievers	**4.53** (24th)
Batting ave:	**.270** (9th=)
Slugging ave.	**.438** (11th)
On Base %:	**.357** (2nd)
AB Per Hit	**3.69** (9th)
Total/Net Homers	183/161 (**22** 9th=)
AB per HR	**30.30** (16th)

AB Per SO	6.34 (1st)
Runs For/Against	850 (7) 770 (16)
Net Runs	80 (8th)
Net BB/BB p AB	157/7.86 (1st)*
Total Steals	43 (30th)
Total Errors	101 (13th)
Unearned Runs Giv	75 (23rd=)
Record Attendance	2000: 3 315 330
Finished 1st	**Ave** 40 930. First season at present park.
Attendance 2003	3 264 903 **Ave** 40 307.
Attendance 2004	3 258 864 **Ave** 40 232

*The Bonds Effect

2004 Starting Rotation

Starter	Starter
Jason Schmidt	32: 18-7, 3.20 ERA
Kirk Rueter	33: 9-12, 4.73 ERA
Brett Tomko	31: 11-7, 4.04 ERA
Dustin Hermanson	18: 6-9, 4.53 ERA
Noah Lowry	14: 6-0, 3.82 ERA
Jerome Williams	22: 10-7, 4.24 ERA
Closers	
Matt Herges	23/31 SV, 5.23 ERA
Dustin Hermanson	17/20 SV, 4.53 ERA
Bullpen "Star"	
Jim Brower	3.29 ERA
Catcher	
A.J. Pierzynski 131g	.272, 11HR, 77 RBI
Yorvit Torrealba 64g	.227, 6HR, 23 RBI

Briefly... After having been one of the earliest professional baseball clubs, the Giants smashed their way into the history of the 'Majors As We Know Them' by appointing a manager who stopped a World Series: that of 1904. Manager John McGraw refused to play the winners of the young upstart American League because of his feud with president and founder Ban Johnson. The latter, wanting 'clean baseball' as opposed to the brawling roughhouse approach of McGraw enforced the rule of law (the Umpires), thus incurring the unending bile of the then skipper of the Baltimore Orioles. They only won 5 World Series through 1954, being overshadowed by their Yankee rivals across the Harlem River. Still, 13 pennants in the other league assured them of monumental status historically, at least.

Sensation was caused in 1957 with their departure for the west coast at the same time as the Dodgers. This can only be fully explained by the desire of the then owner Horace Stoneham to get away from the grim shadow of the Pinstripe Monster.

Uniforms: Home – Cream shirts with black "Giants" print letters in black with orange edging, black sleeve and v-neck edging. Cream pants, black undershirts. **Road** - Grey jerseys with orange 'San Francisco' printed lettering in black with orange edge, plus sleeve and collar orange and black edging, black undershirts. Black caps with orange 'SF' logo. The Giants are one of three clubs that do not feature player identification lettering on rear of shirts because of "tradition."

Owners(s): Peter A Magowan **GM:** Brian R. Sabean **Manager:** An almost excellent first season for the venerable Felipe Alou (b. 1935 and father of Moises at the Cubs) in 2003 where the divisional first place position of Dusty Baker's last season was retained, but frustratingly the team were busted by the Marlins in the first round of the play offs. As a player Alou was a quality hitter with a variety of clubs. He came up with the Giants in '58 and stayed six years before going on to the Braves for another six. He played out his career with the A's, the Expos, the Yankees and finally the Brewers. In his best year, 1966, he hit .327 and 31 in the Braves first major league year in Atlanta. Wears 23. Record: 882-849 (.510).

Home: Was **Pacific Bell Park**, the 'Pac Bell', until the start of the '04 season, when it became the **SBC Park**. First game was on April 11 2000 where the home team lost to the Dodgers 6-5. Ouch! The Pac Bell is famous for McCovey Cove, the water into which Barry Bonds often deposits home runs when he isn't being walked – as did Willy McCovey before him – and an 80 foot long Coke bottle. The team moved here from Candlestick Park (famous not least for being the venue for The Beatles last ever gig). **Capacity: 55 777. SBC Park :** From directly above, its shape is a head which has been smashed on the right side by a heavy frying pan. But where a sharp pull by a leftie or a good contact the other way is only 309 feet away, a slightly pulled hit for a leftie has to travel 421 feet to get out of the park (and into the Pacific Ocean). The top of the head has also been bashed precisely flat 399 feet away from home plate. The left field wall cuts down to the 339 foul pole in a straight line. Was *Pitcher's Park* but high home run volume in 2004 has tilted it clearly the other way: **Hitter's Park (clear advantage).**

World Series And Post-Season Ratings	Position	Points/Occasions/%	
Full Historical Record 1901-2004	2	8688-7407: .537	
Total Historical Rating	4	N/A	
World Series Rating	4=	.595 Ranking Points	
Play Offs Rating	11	.59 Ranking Points	
Pennant Wins (pre-'69)	2	16 (15 New York, 1 San Fran.)	**RATINGS**
Division Wins (post-'69)	13=	5	
World Series Wins/Appearances/Games Won	6=/3/3=	5/17/45	
Level Of Recent Success		**Won/Lost**	
Games Won Per Season Post-69	9	78.6	
Seasons Since A World Series Appearance	2	2002 Lost to Angels 3-4	
Seasons Since A Division Series	1	2003 Lost to Cubs 2-3	
Seasons Since A Championship Series	2	2002 Beat St Louis 4-1	

Most Home Runs Hit For Giants	Most Games Won By A Pitcher	
Season: 73 Barry Bonds 2001	Season: 26 Juan Marichal 1968	
(Major League Record)	Career: 238 Juan Marichal	
Career: 469 Willie McCovey		**RECORDS**
Highest Batting Average	**Most Strikeouts**	
Season: .370 Barry Bonds 2002	Season: Jason Schmidt 251 2004, beating 248 Juan Marichal 1963	
Career: .316 Barry Bonds	Career: 2 281 Juan Marichal	

Best Batting Ave. 2004 Barry Bonds .362*	**Most Home Runs 2004** Bonds 45	
RBI Leader Bonds 101	**Most Bases** Bonds 303	
Most K's Jason Schmidt 251	**Most Walks** Schmidt 77	**2004**
Most HR's Given Up Kirk Rueter 21	**Most Innings Pitched** Schmidt 22	
Other Top Batters: JT Snow .327, 12h, 60 RBI.	Marquis Grissom. .279, 90 RBI, 157 h.	
*NL Batting Champion		

"Buy a steak for a player on another club after the game, but don't even speak to him on the field. Get out there and beat them to death."

Leo Durocher, New York Giants manager, 1948-55.

New York Giants World Series Wins	1905,1921, 1922, 1933 & 1954.
League Pennant Winners:	1904, 1905, 1911, 1912, 1913, 1917, 1921, 1922, 1923, 1924, 1933, 1936, 1937, 1951 & 1954.
World Series Losses:	2-4 to Philadelphia A's in 1911; 3-4 to Boston Red Sox in 1912; 1-4 to Philadelphia A's in 1913; 2-4 to Chicago White Sox in 1917; 2-4 to New York Yankees in 1923; 3-4 to Washington Senators in 1924; 2-4 to New York Yankees in 1936; 1-4 to New York Yankees in 1937; 2-4 to New York Yankees in 1951

Giants World Series Wins	Winning Managers
1905 v. Philadelphia Athletics 4-1	John McGraw
1921 v. New York Yankees 5-3	John McGraw
1922 v. New York Yankees 4-0	John McGraw
1933 v. Washington Senators 4-1	Bill Terry
1954 v. Cleveland Indians 4-0	Leo Durocher

Hall of Famers

As a New York Giant

Dave Bancroft SS 1915-30 (1920-23) Sw: "Beauty" came up with the Phillies but batted over .300 in his four seasons at the Polo Grounds – well, .299 in 1920 – and established himself as one of the great short stops of all time. Also Braves, Dodgers and Phillies. **1971**

Did You Know? I'm not sure I like publications that give you "Did You Know" sections, but can I use this ruse to tell you that all the Shortstops in the Hall Of Fame are right-handed batters? Some long-held prejudice against left-handed infielders on the part of generations of managers, apparently.

Roger Bresnahan C 1897-1915 (1902-08): Part of the 1905 World Series winning team. A superlative catcher, he was also a headgear and shin guard innovator. From Ireland, he was known as the "Duke Of Tralee." No insignia. **1945**

Did You Know? All the catchers are right-handed too, for the same reason.

Roger Connor 1B 1880-97 L: (BJ22) This is the guy whose figures Babe Ruth overtook in 1921. A career total of 138 wasn't a big one to beat, as it turned out, but Connor was the Home Run King of his day. One of a tiny few in the history of the game to go 6 for 6, he batted .300 in 12 of his 18 seasons in the roughhouse game that was the '90s. **1976**

Leo Durocher 1948-55: "The Lip." Larger than life figure, a viciously abrasive but brilliant manager of the Giants who won the Fall Classic in 1954 and a pennant in 1951. Ex-Cardinals short stop who couldn't hit much, so made the Hall as a skipper. He was so mediocre a SS in fact, that James doesn't have him in the top 125 of all time. Played with the Yankees, the Reds, the Cardinals and the Dodgers where he began his managerial career in 1939. Brooklyn. Here he immediately took them out of the second division, finishing 3rd. In 1941 he won their first pennant since 1916. Managed the Cubs and Astros after leaving the Giants in '55. **1994**

Carl Hubbell P 1928-43 L: 'The Meal Ticket.' Such a great nickname, I think. Was at the heart of the team that won three pennants in the 30s. One of the few who hurled the arm-ruining screwball. Won 20 games four times and went an astonishing 46 1/3 innings without conceding a run in 1933. His famous fanning of Ruth, Gehrig, Foxx, Simmons and Cronin in the '34 All-Star game makes the James rating below look unsound, as in fact, do these other stats. (BJ13) **1947. Top 100: BJ94- SN45 – SABR41**

Monte Irvin LF, 1949-55: In his big year, 1951 (aged 32), he batted .458 in the World Series, and made 174 hits, 24 homers and batted in 121, but made his name in the Negro League previous to following Jackie Robinson's crossing of the colour line. Hit 99 homers with the Giants in 7 seasons. (A/A). (No BJ rating, which is odd, it seems to me). **1973.**

Travis Jackson SS 1922-36 "Stonewall." Immaculate defence and key clutch hitting were among his strengths. John McGraw's buzzing, hustling captain of the side that won a pennant in '22 and '23, and later in '33 and '36. LT .291. (BJ40) **1982**

George Kelly 1B 1915-32 ('15-'26): Apparently fine hitting first baseman. Despite John McGraw's high praise about making more important hits for him than any other of his players, a low win shares rating suggests he's lucky to have made the Hall. Mind, he did hit 7 homers in 6 consecutive games, which is still a NL record. James's system sets a high premium on longevity of career and Kelly only had six really good full seasons. (BJ65) **1973.**

John McGraw Manager 1902-32: 'Little Napoleon.' History records this man to have been the meanest, nastiest son of a bitch in the whole of baseball. He made a virtue of umpire and opponent intimidation to the point where he was "as welcome as a man with black smallpox." The point of it all was to win and this his team did. He won six pennants and one Series, the 1905. This said, those who played under him loved him to pieces and would have gone to the wall for him. Whatever his fibre as a man, he is one of the monumental figures of baseball history. **1937**

Joe McGinnity P, 1899-1908 ('02-'08) 246-141, No ERA available: Different times: he was known as "Iron Man" not because of his immense strength but because he worked in an iron foundry in the winters. Different times: in 1903 he pitched both ends of a doubleheader in a single month and won all six. Perfect illustration of the term "Dead Ball Era"? Joe retired at 54 from the minors, so he may have had the original rubber arm. No hat. (BJ41) **1946**

Rube Marquard P, 1908-25 ('08-'15), 201-177, 3.13 ERA L: Named for his pitching likeness to the more famous Rube Waddell, Richard was a record signing to the 1908 Giants at $11 000. I love the story (thanks Baseball Library.Com) of his throwing the pitch that enabled Frank Baker to win game 2 of the 1911 World Series for the A's, thus inadvertently giving birth to a very famous nickname. I love too the fact that after Christy Mathewson criticised his pitch in the papers next day, Baker hit a game-tying homer off him (Christy) next day. (BJNo Rating) No insignia. **1971**

Christy Mathewson P, 1900-16, 373-166, 2.62 ERA: "...But the saddest words of all to a pitcher are three: 'Take him out.'" So said Christy. This virtually never happened to this all-time great, though. Connie Mack (see Philadelphia/Oakland A's) described him as "wonderful to watch unless he's pitching against you" and also regarded him as the greatest pitcher who ever lived. Died prematurely of TB in 1925 aged 45 after copping several lungfuls of gas in a training exercise (!) alongside Ty Cobb in France in 1918. One of baseball's tragedies. (BJ7) **1936. Top 100: BJ42- SN7 – SABR13**

Willie Mays – CF, 1951-73, ('51-'72), 3000 H – The "Say Hey Kid." His 660 home run total, 3rd behind the Babe and Aaron was brought to the fore once again last year as his Godchild bust past him. A titan of the post-WW2 era. He was the first ballplayer to be mentioned in a Dylan song (the second was Catfish Hunter). A/A (BJ1) **1979. Top 100: BJ3- SN2 – SABR8**

Jim O'Rourke LF/C 1876-93 & '04: According to the Spalding Guide 1885, he was a brilliant all-round player of his time, having speed, great hitting ability and superb agility and hands in the outfield. He was known as "Orator" Jim for his extraordinary use of language, which was extravagantly verbose. Lifetime .310 (51HR). (BJ34) **1945**

Mel Ott RF 1926-47 L: Power hitter of 22 seasons who slammed a record breaking (in its time) 511 homers, so clearly one of the best. No hat on plaque. (BJ4) **1951. Top 100: BJ28- SN42 – SABR42**

Amos Rusie P, 1889-01, 248-171, No ERA stats at that date: A hurler who spanned the 50 feet and 60 feet, 6 inches eras. Won masses of games with his fastball and was also a considerable curveball merchant. (BJ28). **1977**

Bill Terry 1B 1923-36 L: A colossus of Giants history, a one club man who was the last NL .400 hitter .401 in 1930, the year he won the MVP. He batted not .300 but .320 nine times consecutively and regularly had 200 hits. His lifetime .341 average is a modern left-hander's record. (154 HR) He then went on to manage the team to three pennants, (BJ26) **1954. Top 100: BJ00- SN59 – SABR78**

John Montgomery Ward P/SS, 1878-94 L: Led the National League in wins in 1879 and ERA in '78, but Monte converted to shortstop and it is under this classification that he is listed in the Hall. He played a major role in the Giants' first two pennant wins in '88 and '89. He had 2 104 hits in a 17 season career, with a .275 lifetime average. He went on from there to form an early union, the Players' Brotherhood that was temporarily successful. (BJ35) **1964**

Mickey Welch P, 1880-92, 307-210 No ERA: Won 307 games in a 13-season career, eight with the Giants. This period of the game may be obscure, but Welch holds a major league record, for striking out the first nine batters he faced in a game in August 1884. He was no mean hitter either, with almost 500 career hits and 92 doubles. His 1.66 ERA in 1885 perhaps reflects the dominance of pitching in this period, given that Bill James does not rate him in his top 100 hurlers of all time. **1973**

Hoyt Wilhelm P 1952-72, 143-122, 2.52 ERA: One of the best knuckleball pitchers of all time and one who was used as a relief pitcher for much of his career, hence the low win total. 227 career saves. (BJ27) Also Chicago White Sox. (27 BJ) **1985. Top 100: BJ00- SN00 – SABR77**

Ross Youngs RF 1917-26 L: 'Pep' was ten years a Giant, batting .322 lifetime, he was one of the stellar hitters of the 20s in a short career. Died tragically young, at 30, of Bright's Disease, a terminal kidney ailment. Perhaps because of this loss, John McGraw kept his picture in his office with only one other, Christy Mathewson. (BJ46) **1972**

As a San Francisco Giant

Orlando Cepeda 1B 1958-74. Hit 225 homers in seven seasons. Hit .312 as a rookie in 1958 and 142 RBIs in 1961. (H). See also St Louis. A potentially historic career was seriously compromised by a bad knee injury in 1965. Still had a great career though, hitting 379 homers, led the league in doubles in his rookie year with the Giants in their first year out west. Had a great '61 too, leading the NL in dingers (46) and RBI (142), no mean feat with the likes of Banks and Aaron around. (BJ17). As a Cardinal, was unanimous MVP in the 1967 World Championship winning club. Hit 111 RBIs and 25 homers that year. (H). "The Baby Bull." **1999**

Willie McCovey 1B 1959-80 ('59-'73; '78-80) L: The only Famer to have a piece of water named after them (as far as I know), the famous McCovey Cove just beyond the narrow centre field end of the Giant's ballpark. He hit 521 homers all told, and a number them in the stretch of water now shelled by Le Bonds. Ten years apart were his Rookie Of The Year award and MVP ('59 and '69). "Stretch" played 18 seasons with San Fran, and also with Oakland and The Padres. **1986. Top 100: BJ69-SN56 – SABR62**

Juan Marichal (Sanchez) P, 1960-75 ('60-'73), 243-142, 2.89 ERA: "The Dominican Dandy" of the high leg kick. Had command of a range of great pitches as well as a damaging fastball. A consistent 20 game winner, he fell away in 1971 after a bad reaction to penicillin gave him chronic arthritis. Later Dominica's Minister Of Sport. Post-Giants: Red Sox, Dodgers. (BJ21). **1983. Top 100: BJ00- SN71 – SABR58**

Gaylord Perry P 1962-83 ('62-'71) 314-265 3.11 ERA: Came up as a Giant but won Cy Youngs with two other teams, the Indians and the Padres. (BJ18). Won a Cy Young in '78 with the Padres, but his win-loss record was allegedly won off the back of a great offence. Pronounced 'Gaylerd' or 'Gayl'rd.' **1991. Top 100: BJ00- SN97 – SABR00**

Outside The Hall Of Fame

Barry Bonds. Featured on page.58.

<table>
<tr><td colspan="3" align="center">*Retired Uniform Numbers*</td></tr>
<tr><td>NY – Christy Matthewson</td><td>NY – John McGraw</td><td>3 Bill Terry</td></tr>
<tr><td>4 Mel Ott</td><td>11 Carl Hubbell</td><td>24 Willie Mays</td></tr>
<tr><td>27 Juan Marichal</td><td>30 Orlando Cepeda</td><td></td></tr>
</table>

AAA Fresno Grizzlies   **Spring Training Venue:** Scottsdale Stadium, Scottsdale, Arizona

Willie Mays
The young tyro ready to let go one of his arrowhead throws from deep. His 1954 catch in the World Series is part of baseball legend, though he claimed without a shred of ego to have made catches like it on a regular basis. This was a time before TV cameras captured every single game. Note the empty midweek afternoon seats; baseball had yet to move these games to night time to attract bigger crowds.

SEATTLE MARINERS

Seattle, Washington

SINCE 1977

AMERICAN LEAGUE   WEST DIVISION 1977-2004

Honours

World Series Wins	None
League Pennant Winners	N/A
Division Winners	1995; 1997 & 2001
Division Series Winners	1995, 2000* & 2001
Championship Series Winners	0

*Qualified for play offs through Wild Card system.

Season   2004

Payroll 2003/2004	$92m (11) $78m (11)
Highest Paid Players:	**Salary**
Brett Boone (2B)	$8m
Jamie Moyer (P)	$7m
Ichiro Suzuki (OF)	$6.52m
Eddie Guardado (Cl)	$4m
Raul Ibanez (OF)	$3.9m
Randy Winn	$3.5m
Dan Wilson	$3.5m
Joel Pineiro	$3m
Edgar Martinez	$3m

2004 Team Stats

Position in Div	4th of 4
Record	63-99
Games Back	29
Percentage	.389 (28th)
Split	38-44 **H**; 25-55 **R**
Last 10 Seasons	1213321324
Runs per Game:	4.31 (25th)
Staff ERA	4.76 (21st)
Ave ERA starters:	4.88 (20th)
Ave ERA relievers:	4.51 (23rd)
Batting ave:	.270 (9th=)
Slugging ave. .	.396 (27th)
On Base %:	.331 (19th)
AB per Hit	3.70 (11th=)

Total Home Runs	136/212 (*-76* 30th)
AB per HR	-125 (30th)
AB per SO	42.07 (14th)
Runs For/Against	698 (25) 823 (20)
Net Runs	-125 (26th)
Net BB/AB p BB	-83/11.63 (25th)
Total Steals:	110 (6th)
Total Errors	103 (15th)
Unearned Runs Giv	41 (3rd)
Record Attendance	2002: 3 540 482
Finished 3rd.	**Ave:** 43 709
Attendance 2003	3 268 864 **Ave** 40 356.
Attendance 2004	2 940 731 **Ave** 36 305 (11th)

*Withhout Ichiro, the top 7 hitters averaged only 122 hits.

2004 Starting Rotation

Starter	Starter
Jamie Moyer	33:7-13, 5.21 ERA
Ryan Franklin	32: 4-16, 4.90 ERA
Joel Pineiro	21: 6-11, 4.67 ERA
Gil Meche	23: 7-7, 5.01 ERA
Ron Villone	10: 8-6, 4.08 ERA
Bobby Madritsch	11: 6-3 3.27 ERA
Closer & Bullpen Star	
Eddie Guardado	18/25 SV, 2.78 ERA
JJPutz	9/13 SV, 4.71 ERA
Catchers	
Dan Wilson 103g	.251, 2HR, 33 RBI
Miguel Olivo. 96g	.233, 13HR, 40 RBI

Briefly... A disastrously uncompetitive season became a story of Ichiro Suzuki's fabulous (word used advisedly) pursuit of George Sisler's hit-in-a-season record from 1924. On the night of Friday October 1st, Ichiro smashed the all-time singles record established in 1898 by Willie Keeler and went further towards baseball immortality by demolishing the Sisler mark, laying to rest the notion that there exists in the game's hall of history, a group of records that sit there fossilized (to some extent anyway). 2004 was also the retirement year of Mariners stalwart Edgar Martinez of 18 seasons. He batted .312 over that time, making 2247 hits and 309 home runs. A possible Hall of Famer – depends on whether the powers in Cooperstown are going to be prepared to waive the ten year minimum season rule currently in place - and a loved legend in Seattle.

Uniforms: Home - White shirts and pants, both with blue pinstripe, blue caps with 'S' compass logo. **Road** – Grey shirts and pants with 'Y' and outside leg teal piping. 'Seattle' lettering with star and compass logo through 'S.' Alt - Black shirts and undershirts, with off-white 'Mariners' edged in teal with star and compass logo above 'M'. Navy caps with 'S' and compass logo.

Owners(s): George Argyros **GM:** Bill Bavasi **Manager:** Mike Hargrove, on Oct 20. 2004 was announced as replacement for Bob Melvin. Records: Melvin: 156-168 (.481). Hargrove: 996-963 (.508). The latter's winning record is an attractive feature when so few managers in the major leagues have them. He won four division titles in Cleveland before spending four much less successful seasons with the Orioles, leaving at the end of the 2003 campaign.

His nickname as a player (with the Rangers, the Padres and the Indians) was The Human Rain Delay, because of his laborious preparations for receiving each pitch, which has already endeared me to him. What a great name. He batted a career .290, but with only 79 homers in 12 seasons, he never quite made it, seeing that he was the AL Rookie of the Year in 1974.

World Series And Post-Season Ratings	Position	Points/Occasions/%	
Full Historical Record 1977-2004	21	2080-2331: .471	
Total Historical Rating	25	N/A	
World Series Rating	30=	0 Ranking Points	
Play Offs Rating	17=	45 Ranking Points	RATINGS
Division Wins (post-'69)	20=	3	
World Series Wins/Appearances/Games Won	30=/30=/30=	0/0/0	
Level Of Recent Success		**Won/Lost**	
Games Won Per Season Post-69	26	72	
Seasons Since A Division Series	3	2001 Bt Cleveland 3-2	
Seasons Since A Championship Series	3	2001 Lost to NYY 1-4	
Seasons Since A Division Win	3	2001 Won ALW by 14 games	

Most Home Runs Hit For The Mariners	Most Games Won By A Pitcher	
Season: 56 Ken Griffey Jr 1997 & 1998	Season: 20 Randy Johnson 1995 & Jamie Moyer 2001	
Career: 398 Ken Griffey Jr	Career: 130 Randy Johnson	
Highest Batting Average	**Most Strikeouts**	RECORDS
Season: .358 Alex Rodriguez 1996	Season: 308 Randy Johnson 1993	
Career: .317 Edgar Martinez	Career: 2 162 Randy Johnson	

Best Batting Ave. 2004 Ichiro Suzuki .372*	**Most Home Runs 2004** Bret Boone 24	
RBI Leader Boone 83	**Most Bases** Ichiro 320 & 262 hits	
Most K's Jamie Moyer 125	**Most Walks** Ron Villone 64	2004
Most HR's Given Up Moyer 44	**Most Innings Pitched** Moyer 202	
Other Top Batters: Randy Winn, .286, 81 RBI.	Raul Ibanez, .304, 62 RBI.	
*AL Batting Champion		

Home: Safeco Field (Gr. Retractable Roof) July 15 1999 saw the inaugural game at this new home of the 1977 born Seattle Mariners, versus the San Diego Padres of the National League West. The attendance was 47 000, a full house. This is still the capacity. A slightly better park for left-handed hitters in a quirkily shaped field (the trip along the wall from centre to the right foul pole demands a right turn half way, not the case in left field. The hit to right-center is 3 feet shorter at 387 than the 390 to left-center and the left foul pole is 4 feet further away (331) than the right (327). A challenging park for the hitter with center field 405 feet away and considered to be a big park anyway. **Capacity: 47 772. Pitcher's Park (clear advantage -** the most challenging in the majors according to present stats).

"I have a good feeling about this club. But that could be gas." - Mike Hargrove, when Cleveland Indians manager, on the Indians' advance to the 1998 ALCS. They lost to the Yankees 2-4.

Hall of Fame Mariners

None have gone into the form in a Mariners cap and only one Hall of Famer has ever played for the club, Gaylord Perry (former Giant and A's pitcher), in 1982 and 1983.

Retired Uniform Numbers

None, though by the time you read this, Edgar Martinez's number 11 may well have become the first. And one day of course, Ichiro's 51, unless he leaves Seattle soon for a club likely to win.

"You stay out of the way of a moving train."
Team hitting coach Paul Molitor on whether he coached Ichiro to the record.

AAA Tacoma Rainiers   **Spring Training Venue:** Peoria Stadium, Peoria, Arizona

TAMPA BAY DEVIL RAYS

Tampa, Florida

SINCE 1998

AMERICAN LEAGUE EAST DIVISION 1998-2004

Season	2004
Payroll 2003/2004	$32m (30) $28m (29)
Highest Paid Players	Salary
Tino Martinez (SS)	$7.5m
Aubrey Huff (OF)	$2.66m
Jose Cruz Jnr (OF)	$2.5m

2004 Team Stats

Position in Div	4th of 5
Record	70-91
Games Back	30.5
Percentage	.435 (23rd)
Split	41-39 H; 29-52 R
Last 7 Seasons	5555554
Runs per Game	4.40 (24th)
Staff ERA	4.81 (22nd=)
Ave ERA starters	5.40 (28th)
Ave ERA relievers	3.87 (9th=)
Batting ave.	.258 (25th)
Slugging ave.	.405 (23rd)
On Base %:	.320 (27th)
AB Per Hit	3.87 (25th)
Total/Net Homers	145/192 (-47 27th)
AB per HR	37.81 (24th)
AB per SO	5.81 (6th)
Runs For/Against	714(24) 842(24)

Net Runs	-128 (24th)
Net BB/AB p BB	-121 (26th)
Total Steals	132 (3rd)
Total Errors	119 (26th)
Unearned Runs Giv	85 (27th)
Record Attendance	1998 2 506 023
Finished 5th	Ave 30 938
Attendance 2003	1 058 622 Ave 13 069.
Attendance 2004	1 275 011 (79)
	Ave 16 139 (30th)

2004 Starting Rotation

Starter	Record
Victor Zambrano*	22: 9-7, 4.43 ERA
Mark Hendrickson	30: 10-15, 4.81 ERA
Rob Bell	19: 8-8, 4.46 ERA
John Halama	13: 6-6, 4.75 ERA
Dewon Brazelton	21: 12-12; 2.22 ERA
Doug Waechter	14: 5-7, 6.01 ERA
Bullpen Star	
John Halama	2.45 ERA
Closer	
Danys Baez	30/33SV, 3.57 ERA
Catcher	
Toby Hall 119g	.255, 8HR, 60 RBI
* to Mets July 2004.	

Briefly... This new franchise – still – was making a bid for growth and development in 2004 and by the measure of games won and position in the standings, they did it. They play in the town of St Petersburg, for many years a heartland of spring training baseball. The organisation, because of its lack of financial clout, has promoted many young players to the majors arguably before their time. This is at least partially offset by the piloting of the project on the field of Lou Piniella, a man of huge baseball experience. Overall verdict: moving forward. Purple mid—season patch of 27-6 proved this conclusively.

Uniforms - Home - White jerseys with green 'Rays' modern lettering (printed with 'Y's' stem turning at 90 degree angle to underline 'A' and 'Y.' Green 'Y' double line piping on shirt front and shoulder top behind. Green double sleeve edging. White pants with double thin green piping, green belt. Green undershirts with 'TB' logo on neck roll. Numbers on shirt front below heart. Green caps with 'TB' logo underscored by outline of one devil ray (fish). **Road** - Same, mostly, in grey, but with 'Devil Rays' on shirt front. Tremendously stylish.

Owner: Consortium of individuals. **GM:** Chuck LaMar. **Manager:** Lou Piniella (b. 1943) had ten great seasons skippering the Mariners from the outset of their time as a major league ball club. Prior to that he had a colourful time at the helm of the Yankees and the Reds, where he won a World Series win in 1990 with the Cincinnati Reds in his first season. He went to Tampa in 2003 to resurrect their dreadful fortunes – five consecutive 5th place finishes – the same challenge he faced in Seattle, and began to work the oracle. Fifth again they may have been in 2003, but most are agreed that despite losing 99 games the club was more difficult to beat and had some good wins. Record: 1019-949 (.518).

2004 Key Hitters: Carl Crawford and Aubrey Huff were the two stars of an indecently young hitting side. Elder statesman was Tino Martinez, the ex-90s Yankees star. Crawford (22) led the league in stolen bases (61) and hit .294 while power hitter Huff hit .291 with 25 homers. Martinez (36) hit only .262 (and 24 homers) but then he has never hit .300. Rocco Baldelli, just 23, showed great promise with super center field work and a .270 average.

Home: Tropicana Field, St Petersburg (carpet). Formerly known as the Florida Sun coast Dome and the Thunderdome, it 'features' artificial turf but "all dirt base paths" as the franchise website proudly tells you. **Capacity** is now **45 200**. Roof height is 225', the 3rd highest of the five domes in history.

Dramatically misshapen perimeter in a ballpark stretched out away from the batter in centre field. Dead centre is 404, but this is pushed to 410 towards left-centre. It's still 404 about 20 feet to right-centre before the park cuts "south-east" very sharply to only 322 at the right foul pole. Same thing to left where the foul pole is a juicy 315 feet away for the right handed hitter. The perimeter in left particularly has quirkly angles, especially in the left field corner. This park should be bad for fly ball hitters because of the roof being non-retractable – so they can't ever benefit from a wind blowing out from the plate – but the outfield is small, so things are balanced out. The quirkiness was deliberate in the design of what is otherwise an ultra-modern, domed ballpark. **First Game:** March 31 1998, first game played by new franchise Tampa Bay Devil Rays. They lost to the Tigers 11-6 in front of a capacity 43 369. **Pitcher's Park (clear advantage).**

World Series And Post-Season Ratings	Position	Points/Occasions/%	
Full Playing Record 1998-2004	**30**	451-680: .399	**RATINGS**
Total Historical Rating	30	N/A	
World Series Rating	30=	0 Ranking Points	
Play Offs Rating	30	0 Ranking Points	
Division Wins (post-'69)	30=	0	
World Series Wins/Appearances/Games Won	30=/30=/30=	0/0/0	
Level Of Recent Success		No Play Off record as yet.	
Games Won Per Season Post-69	30	54.4	

Most Home Runs Hit For The Devil Rays	Most Games Won By A Pitcher	
Season: 34 Jose Canseco 1999	Season: 14 Rolando Orrojo 1998	**RECORDS**
Career: 97 Fred McGriff	Career: 26 Albie Lopez & Estaban Yan	
Highest Batting Average	**Most Strikeouts**	
Season: .310 Fred McGriff 1999	Season: 172 Tony Saunders 1998	
Career: .295 Fred McGriff	Career: 351 Estaban Yan	

Best Batting Ave Aubrey Huff .297	**Most Home Runs** Huff 29	**2004**
RBI Leader Huff 104	**Most Bases** Huff 296	
Most K's Victor Zambrano 109	**Most Walks** Zambrano 96	
Most HR's Given Up Mark Hendrickson 21	**Most Innings Pitched** Hendrickson 183.1	
Other Top Batters: Carl Crawford 185 h, .296.	Rocco Baldelli, .280, 74 RBI, 145 h.	

Hall Of Fame Devil Rays

None

Retired Uniform Numbers

12 Wade Boggs

AAA Durham Bulls   **Spring Training Venue:** Progress Energy Park, Home of Al Lang Field, St Petersburg, Florida

• •

66 The last quote that couldn't find a proper home . . .

When asked whether the fact that he was missing the index finger of his pitching hand explained his great curveball, Mordecai Brown replied,

"To know for sure, I'd have to throw with a normal hand, and I've never tried it." **99**

Mordecai "Three-Finger" Brown

TEXAS RANGERS

Arlington, Texas

SINCE 1972

AMERICAN LEAGUE WEST DIVISION 1972-2004

NAME CHANGE HISTORY

Washington Senators 1961-71 Texas Rangers 1972-2004

Honours

No World Series Record	-
Division Winners	1994, 1996, 1998 & 1999
Division Series Wins	0
Championship Series Appearances	0

Season   2004

American League Manager of the Year: Buck Showalter

Totals 2003/2004	$106m (4) $60m (17).
Highest	**Salaries**
Chan Ho Park (P)	$13.87m
Alex Rodriguez	$8m

(as part of agreement that sent ARod to the Yankees)

Rusty Greer (OF)	$7.4*
Alfonso Soriano (2B)	$7.4m
Jeff Zimmerman	$4.46m

*Greer has not played since 2002 due to elbow, shoulder, neck, hip and knee injuries, all requiring surgery!).

2004 Team Stats

Position in Div	3rd of 4
Record	89-73
Games Back	3 (9 from WC)
Percentage	.549 (11th=)
Split	51-30 **H**; 38-43 **R**
Last 10 Seasons	3131144443
Runs per Game	5.31 (4th)
Staff ERA	4.53 (18th)
Ave ERA starters	5.16 (25th)
Ave ERA relievers	3.46 (3rd)
Batting Average	.266 (19th)
Slugging Ave	.457 (5th)
On Base %	.329 (20th)
AB Per Hit	3.76 (19th)

Total/Net Homers	227/182 (45 4th=)
AB per HR	24.73 (4th)
AB Per SO	5.11 (20th)
Runs For/Against	860 (4) 794 (18)
Net Runs	66 (10th)
Net BB/AB p BB	-47/11.23 (23rd)
Total Steals	69 (20th)
Total Errors	116 (22nd)
Unearned Runs Giv	70 (19th=)
Record Attendance Finished 3rd	1997: 2 945 228. **Ave:** 36 360.
Attendance 2003	2 095 630 **Ave** 25 866
Attendance 2004	2 513 685 (79)
	Ave 31 818 (14th)

2004 Starting Rotation

Starter	Record
Ryan Drese	33: 14-10, 4.20 ERA
Kenny Rodgers	35: 18-9, 4.76 ERA
R.A. Dickey	15: 6-7, 5.61 ERA
Javier Benoit	15: 3-5, 5.68 ERA
Chan Ho Park	15: 4-7, 5.46 ERA
John Wasdin	10: 2-4, 6.78 ERA
Bullpen Stars	
Cordero and Brian Shouse 2.23 ERA	
Closer:	
Francisco Cordero	49/54 SV, 2.13 ERA
Catcher:	
Rod Barajas 108g	.249, 15HR, 58 RBI

Briefly... Very strong showing indeed this first post-ARod season when they were expected to do nothing. Until late August the team was in contention for the division title but lack of pitching did for them, as expected. The addition of Soriano from the Yankees was huge, but even more so was the knitting together of team spirit.

The powering forward of the organisation on the field was marred, or enlivened, depending on your point of view by the September 14th quasi-brawl with Oakland fans and chair throwing incident which broke a woman's nose. Classy.

In the bandbox that the home ballpark is supposed to be, the batters seemed to go all out for the fences, resulting in good slugging, but poor averages and on base percentage. Whether this will result in a more canny approach this season, we shall see. The starting pitching was not, with an ERA of 5.31, considered good enough to take the side to the play offs, and so it proved.

Uniforms: Home Royal Blue shirts with white sleeve edging and waving Texas Lone Star flag on left sleeve; white "Texas" letters on shirt-centre with red shadow; blue long sleeve under-t-shirt. Blue caps with white "T" logo with red shadow. *Road*: white sleeveless jerseys over blue undershirt with red 'T' on left breast. 'Rangers' lettering in blue with red shadow edge. Blue 'Y' central edging. White pants with blue side-stripe. Blue caps with white 'T.'

Owners(s): Thomas O. Hicks. **GM:** John Hart. **Manager:** Buck Showalter (b. 1956) AL Manager of the Year in 1994 with the New York Yankees and last season this Good Ol' Boy did it again. During four seasons with the Yankees from 1991, the strike of that late year possibly deprived him of a rookie World Series and it would have been the club's first win since 1978. He quit in 1995 because he refused to follow owner George Steinbrenner's orders to fire two coaches. In 1998 he led the expansion D'backs and took them to first place in 1999. In his time there he was known to sleep in his office. He was dismissed after the 2000 season, which paved the way for a conquering Bob Brenly in 2001. Buck – 49 in May 2005 – had a bad first year in Texas. He is renowned as a disciplinarian: he handed out a 300 page organisational manual to the players in his first year in Arizona. As a player, he was most notably a successful minor league player with the New York Yankees organisation, but didn't play a single game in the majors. Record: 478-423 (.528)

Home: Ameriquest Field In Arlington (Gr.). Yes, appalling, is it not. Before 2004 it was simply "The Ballpark In Arlington," a charming name. According to experts, this ought to be an easy hitter's park, what with its fairly small dimensions, but in its short history it has baffled sluggers, apparently, who have struggled here. That said the rock hard ground, baked by the constant Texas sun, is a nightmare for fielders as groundballs hustle along on the bounce and bobble and the ball flies in the dry Texas air. By 1994, some retro philosophy was beginning to leak into the minds of the powers that be here in Texas, so the park was built to an asymmetrical design to approximate the traditional USA ballpark of the early 20th Century. Some southern style wrought iron work behind center field is particularly attractive. This philosophy, so at odds with much architectural thinking in the States in the second half of the twentieth century, has taken a firm hold. For those who like the sound of something technical, the Ballpark is laid with Bermuda Tifway419, some name for grass: grown in Texas. This is a fact that makes a great conversation piece. **Capacity: 49 166**. Dimensions: 332' to left field, 400' to center field, 327' to right field. First Game: 11 April 1994 saw the first regular season game here against the Brewers. **Hitter's Park (Strong advantage).**

World Series And Post-Season Ratings	Position	Points/Occasions/%	
Full Historical Record	**25**	3257-3724: .466	
Total Historical Rating	28	N/A	
World Series Rating	30=	0 Ranking Points	
Play Offs Rating	28=	2 Ranking Points	
Division Wins (post-'69)	17=	4	**R**
World Series Wins/Appearances/Games Won	30=/30=/30=	0/0/0	**A**
			T
Level Of Recent Success		**Won/Lost**	**I**
Games Won Per Season Post-69	13=	76	**N**
Seasons Since A Division Series	5*	1999 – Lost to NYY 0-3	**G**
Seasons Since A Championship Series	-	None Competed	**S**
Seasons Since A Division Win	5	1999 Won ALW by 5 games	

*There were no post-season games in 1994. The Texas Rangers have lost all three of their division series in the play offs: 1-3 to the Yankees in 1996, 0-3 to the Yankees in 1998 and by the same score to the same team the following year.

Most Home Runs Hit For The Rangers	Most Games Won By A Pitcher	
Season: 57 Alex Rodriguez 2002	Season: 25 Ferguson Jenkins 1974	
Career: 348 Juan Gonzalez	Career: 139 Charlie Hough (knuckleballer)	**R**
Highest Batting Average	**Most Strikeouts**	**E**
Season: .341 Julio Franco 1991	Season: 301 Nolan Ryan 1989	**C**
Career: .291 Al Oliver	Career: 1 452 Charlie Hough	**O**

Best Batting Ave Mark Young .313**	Most Home Runs Mark Teixera 38	
RBI Leader Teixera 112	**Most Bases** Young 333	
Most K's Kenny Rogers 126	**Most Walks** Rogers 66	**2**
Most HR's Given Up Rogers 24	**Most Innings Pitched** Rogers 211.2	**0**
Other Top Batters: Alfonso Soriano.280, 91 RBI.	Hank Blalock, .276, 110 RBI.	**0 4**

**Young broke the club record for hits last season, with 216, beating Randy Winn's 186 in 2002.

Hall Of Fame Rangers

Nolan Ryan – Ryan struckout 9.55 batters per 9 innings and allowed them an average of .204. **1999**
Top 100: BJ00- SN41 – SABR44

Retired Uniform Numbers

"Ryan's the only guy to put fear in me. You just hoped to mix in a walk so you could have a good night and go 0-for-3."
Reggie Jackson, on Nolan Ryan

34 Nolan Ryan*

---

*Nolan Ryan is the only player to have his number retired by three teams: the other two are the Astros (34) and the Angels (30).

AAA Okahoma Redhawks   **Spring Training Venue:** Surprise Stadium, Surprise, Arizona

---

MAJOR OFF SEASON TRADES AND FREE AGENTS MOVES

Position Players

1. Carlos Beltran, Houston Astros to New York Mets
2. Adrian Beltre, Los Angeles Dodgers to Seattle Mariners
3. Shawn Green, Los Angeles Dodgers to Arizona Diamondbacks
4. Carlos Delgado, Toronto Blue Jays to Florida Marlins
5. Sammy Sosa, Chicago Cubs to Baltimore Orioles
6. Jeff Kent, Houston Astros to Los Angeles Dodgers
7. Magglio Ordonez, Chicago White Sox to Detroit Tigers
8. Edgar Renteria, St Louis Cardinals to Boston Red Sox
9. Troy Glaus, Anaheim Angels to Arizona Diamondbacks
10. Jose Guillen, Anaheim Angels to Washington Nationals
11. Steve Finlay, Los Angeles Dodgers to Anaheim Angels
12. Richie Sexson, Arizona Diamondbacks to Seattle Mariners
13. Orlando Cabrera, Boston Red Sox to Anaheim Angels
14. Omar Vizquel, Cleveland Indians to San Francisco Giants
15. Vinny Castilla, Colorado Rockies to Washington Nationals
16. Matt Lawton, Cleveland Indians to Pittsburgh Pirates
17. Jermaine Dye, Oakland Athletics to Chicago White Sox
18. Tony Womack, St Louis Cardinals to New York Yankees
19. Orlando Cabrera, Boston Red Sox to Anaheim Angels
20. JD Drew, Atlanta Braves to Los Angeles Dodgers
21. Jose Valentin Chicago White Sox to Los Angeles Dodgers
22. Carlos Lee, Chicago White Sox to Milwaukee Brewers
23. Benito Santiago, Kansas City Royals to Pittsburgh Pirates
24. David Eckstein, Anaheim Angels to St Louis Cardinals
25. Dave Roberts, Boston Red Sox to San Diego Padres
26. Kenny Lofton, New York Yankees to Philadelphia Phillies
27. Roberto Alomar, Chicago White Sox to Tampa Bay Devil Rays
28. Doug Mientkiewitcz, Boston Red Sox to New York Mets

Pitchers

1. Randy Johnson, Arizona Diamondbacks to New York Yankees
2. Pedro Martinez, Boston Red Sox to New York Mets
3. Derek Lowe, Boston Red Sox to Los Angeles Dodgers
4. Matt Clement, Chicago Cubs to Boston Red Sox
5. Carl Pavano, Florida Marlins to New York Yankees
6. Mark Mulder, Oakland Athletics to St Louis Cardinals
7. David Wells, San Diego Padres to Boston Red Sox
8. Tim Hudson, Oakland Athletics to Atlanta Braves
9. Al Leiter, New York Mets to Florida Marlins
10. Jon Lieber, New York Yankees to Philadelphia Phillies
11. Troy Percival, Anaheim Angels to Detroit Tigers
12. Woody Williams, St Louis Cardinals to San Diego Padres
13. Kevin Millwood, Philadelphia Phillies to Cleveland Indians
14. Jose Lima, Los Angeles Dodgers to Kansas City Royals
15. Jaret Wright Atlanta Braves to New York Yankees
16. Orlando Hernandez, New York Yankees to Chicago White Sox
17. Danny Kolb, Milwaukee Brewers to Atlanta Braves
18. Russ Ortiz, Atlanta Braves to Arizona Diamondbacks
19. Armando Benitez, Florida Marlins to San Francisco Giants
20. Dustin Hermanson, San Francisco Giants to Chicago White Sox

The off-season 2004-5 has seen a winter of spectacular trading of a raft of future Hall of Famers and near-miss stars. You have doubts about that? Just listen to the names: Sammy Sosa, Pedro Martinez, Randy Johnson, Carlos Delgado, Shawn Green, Jeff Kent, Magglio Ordonez, Roberto Alomar. If that's not enough to make you wonder how much grease it takes to stop the revolving doors of the thirty major league franchises seizing up, how about the fact of the surprise Home Run King of 2004 Adrian Beltre moving on, along with the surprise monster hitting star of the post-season, Carlos Beltran? Feed in the names of others just below top rank: Mulder and Hudson; Pavano and Clement; World Series hero Derek Lowe of course; Renteria; Guillen and Glaus, and you might, as a Brit used to the goings-on of the football scene, confess to complete bewilderment. The merry-go-round took a huge spin and you wonder whether it's all nothing but a whole lot of madness. Where is the stability? Here is commerce – the insatiable dollar-lust of the ballplayer saying "super-size me" to their agents – making its grand statement to the gazing, cynical or amazed hundreds of millions fans across the globe. The sport-as-business ethic just pummelled North American ice hockey into the frozen ground, a complete season lost. Meanwhile, baseball plunges forward once more into the future, hoping that the gargantuan pile of cash pumped into the game won't release some noxious gas that'll kill everyone and everything that's still good in the game.

TORONTO BLUE JAYS

Toronto, Canada

SINCE 1977
AMERICAN LEAGUE
EAST DIVISION 1977-2004

Honours

World Series Champions	1992 & 1993
Division Winners	1985, 1989, 1991, 1992 & 1993
Division Series Wins	N/A
Championship Series Wins	1992 and 1993
Championship Series Losses	1985 3-4 to Kansas City 1989 1-4 to Oakland 1991; 1-4 to Minnesota
World Series Losses	0

World Series Wins	Managers
1992	Cito Gaston
1993	Cito Gaston

Season 2004

Payroll 2003/2004:	$61m (20)/$50m (20)
Highest Paid	**Salary**
Carlos Delgado (1B)	$19.7m
Roy Halliday (SP)	$6m
Miguel Batista (SS)	$3.6m
Ted Lilly (SP)	$1.9m

2004 Team Stats

Position in Div	5th of 5
Record	67-94
Games Back	33.5
Percentage	.416 (25th=)
Split	40-41 H; 27-53 R
Last 10 Seasons	5453333335
Runs per Game	4.44 (22nd)
Staff ERA	4.91 (24th=)
Ave ERA Starters:	4.85 (19th)
Ave ERA Re'ver	5.02 (28th)
Batting ave:	.260 (22nd=)
Slugging ave.	.403 (24th)
On Base %: .	.328 (23rd)
AB Per Hit	3.84 (23rd)
Total/Net Homers	145/181 (-36 23rd)
AB per HR	38.14 (25th)
AB per SO	5.10 (21st)
Runs For/Against	719 (22) 823 (21)

Net Runs	-104 (23rd)
Net BB/BB p AB	-95/10.78 (15th)
Total Steals:	58 (25th)
Total Errors	91 (8th=)
Unearned Runs Giv	48 (8th=)
Record Attendance	1993: 4 057 947
Finished 1st	**Ave:** 50 098
Attendance 2003	1 799 458 **Ave** 22 216
Attendance 2004	1 900 041 **Ave** 23 457 (25th)

2004 Starting Rotation

Starter	Record
Miguel Batista	31: 10-13, 4.80 ERA
Ted Lilly	32: 12-10, 4.06 ERA
Roy Halliday	21: 8-8, 4.20 ERA
Josh Towers	21: 9-9, 5.11 ERA
Pat Hentgen	16: 2-9, 6.95 ERA
Dave Bush	16: 5-4, 3.69 ERA
Justin Miller	15: 3-4, 6.06 ERA
Bullpen Star	
None: Speier has lowest bullpen ERA	
Closer	
Jason Frasor	17/19 SV, 4.08 ERA
Justin Speier	7/11 SV, 3.91 ERA
Catcher	
Gregg Zaun 107g	.269, 6HR, 36 RBI
Kevin Cash 60g	.193, 4HR, 21 RBI

Briefly... Now Canada's only ball club, this expansion team has won the World Series twice, in 1992 and 1993. They are one of only eight ball clubs to retain the Fall Classic. In the tough playground of the AL East, they've finished third in each of the past six seasons. The resurgence of the Red Sox and the presence of the Damn Yankees make the post-season a tremendously difficult proposition at the moment and with a reduced payroll in 2004, they sunk even below the Tampa Bay Devil Rays, hitherto regarded as a no-hope franchise.

Their decline last season had much to do with the fact that the hitters just didn't hit. Carlos Delgado had his worst season in ten years, Vernon Wells, the other franchise marquee player had his worst in five. 2003 Cy Young winner Roy Haliday had an injury scarred season, but that can't be an excuse. No pitcher had an ERA below 4, so in short, the whole season was a disaster..

Uniforms: Home - White shirts (plain) with 'Toronto' in modern print design, blue caps with 'J' and bird-head logo. White pants with blue side piping. **Road** – Same in grey. Also black shirts with black undershirts., black caps with 'J' and bird-head logo.

Owner: Rogers Communications Inc. **General Manager:** J.P. Ricciardi **Manager:** John Gibbons, who took over from Cuban Carlos Tosca, after 111 games last season. The latter's 47-64 (.423) record – team in toilet and going round the u-bend – was considered unacceptable. With Gibbons, the same players went 20-30, so excitement about 2005 in Toronto may well be unwise unless some pretty amazing trades get made in the off-season.. Tosca had never appeared in the majors but Gibbons did. However, he failed to climb any trees, his career falling apart with the Mets after breaking a cheekbone in a collision. Ricciardi is a Moneyball guy and it could be that like Beane, he needs a guy without a strong personality who will simply execute baseball common sense and the Sabermetrical plan. That said Gibbons began his slide up Toronto's greasy pole after a couple of manager of the year awards in the minors. In his playing days he was a team mate of Ricciardi in 1981 at Shelby in the South Atlantic League. **Tosca 's TBJ record: 191-191 (.500)**

How 'bout That: Braves manager Bobby Cox skippered the Blue Jays from 1982-5, winning the AL East in his final year.
How 'bout That - 2: For four years straight, from 1990 to 1993, the stadium saw its total attendance record for a season smashed.

Home: The SkyDome (Carpet-retractable roof)**.** Now somewhat unfashionable, the enclosed park on artificial turf was still 'the future' when it opened. Size is the big deal here. State of the art in June 1989 when the club moved into these new premises with retractable roof and over 150 private boxes and probably as many places where you can joyously stuff your face full of junk food. They play on Astroturf, a groundball pitcher's graveyard. Their Jumbotron is apparently the biggest on the continent of North America and the second biggest in the world.(woo!).The Skydome is supposed to be hard for hitters. The wind, when the roof is open, blows in hard towards home plate. At least the fences aren't far away which may have accounted for the larger number of homers hit here than normal. Indeed, in 2004 it was the fourth best park for runs scored.

At 310' the Skydome has the highest of all the domes. Capacity: 50 516. The park is perfectly and boringly symmetrical with a smooth, rounded perimeter. It's 328' at the poles, 375' in the power alleys and 400' to dead centre. First game: June 5 1989: Toronto Blue Jays 3 Milwaukee Brewers 5. (att: 48 378). The Blue Jays' previous home was Exhibition Stadium (first game April 7 1977: TBJ 9 Chicago WS 5. Att: 44 649). This was my first visit to a baseball stadium (in 1983) and it was not a pretty place.

World Series And Post-Season Ratings	Position	Points/Occasions/%	
Full Historical Record 1977-2004	**13**	2187-2233: .494	
Total Historical Rating	14	N/A	
World Series Rating	17=	140 Ranking Points	
Play Offs Rating	16	46 Ranking Points	
Division Wins (post-'69)	13=	5	
World Series Wins/Appearances/Games Won	13=/18=/17=	2/2/8	**RATINGS**
Level Of Recent Success		**Won/Lost**	
Games Won Per Season Post-69	15	75.4	
Seasons Since A World Series Appearance	11	1993 Beat Phillies 4-2	
Seasons Since A Division Series	N/A	-	
Seasons Since A Championship Series	11	1993 beat Chicago White Sox 4-2	
Seasons Since A Division Win	11	Won ALE by 7 games (for the third consecutive year)	

Most Home Runs Hit For The Blue Jays	Most Games Won By A Pitcher:	
Season: 47 George Bell 1987	Season: 21 Jack Morris 1992 & Roger Clemens 1997	
Career: 262 Carlos Delgado	Career: 175 Dave Stieb	
Highest Batting Average:	**Most Strikeouts:**	**RECORDS**
Season: .363 John Olerud 1993	Season: 292 Roger Clemens 1997	
Career: .307 Roberto Alomar	Career: 1 658 Dave Stieb	

Best Batting Ave. Vernon Wells .275	**Most Home Runs** Carlos Delgado 32	
RBI Leader Delgado 99	**Most Bases** Wells 253	
Most K's Ted Lilly 168	**Most Walks Miguel** Batista 96	**2004**
Most HR's Given Up Lilly 26	**Most Innings Pitched** Batista 198.2	
Other Top Batters: Orlando Hudson, .270, 132 h	Alex Rios, .286, 122 h, C Gomez .282, 96 h	

Hall Of Fame Blue Jays

None

Retired Uniform Numbers

None As Yet

AAA Club Syracus Skychiefs   **Spring Training Venue:** Dunedin Stadium at Grant Field, Dunedin, Florida.
Making the final score, Arizona (desert) 11, Florida (seaside) 19

7

A DICTIONARY OF BASEBALL IN 1000 WORDS AND PHRASES

A

Aboard - When a batter is 'aboard' he's made it to first base: the team now has a chance of scoring a run.

Ace – A reference to a club's number one starting pitcher. At a stretch, a team can have as many as four, or five, I suppose, if they're good enough. Most clubs would be lucky to have two aces.

Aces - Sometimes used for 'runs.'

Adjustments – This refers most often to a hitter coming up against a pitcher who has got him out his first time up at the plate, and altering his stance or his position in the batter's box or the speed at which he needs to bring the bat through to make contact. He adjusts to the pitcher. Quite often he may not have faced the pitcher before, so may need an at bat or two to get used to his motion, his speed, his trajectory and his use of different pitches. Similarly, pitchers may need to make adjustments to different hitters, changing strategy and location. Plus "adjustments" was *the* word of the 2004 season, it seemed to me, being used over and over and over again by the commentators ad nauseam. Even the hot dog vendors were making adjustments after sluggish early sales.

Advance the Runner– An important concept where a man on base (see 'base runner' and 'runner') tries to move forward to the next base or indeed more than one base. Linguistically, he doesn't 'move forward' or 'progress,' he 'advances'. So a team looks to 'advance the runner' once he's on base to home plate to score a run.

Ahead In The Count – When there are clearly more strikes than balls during the pitch count, or clearly more balls than strikes, either the pitcher or the batter is "ahead."[See also, **'The Count (Pitch)'**]

Alleys - Gaps between the outfielders, between left field and centre, and centre-field and right fielder.

All Fields – This means the whole ballpark. When a guy hits to all fields it's a big compliment, meaning he's not a limited pull hitter.

Allowing Four Hits – Each pitcher is quickly measured against how many hit he concedes: only in the everyday language of the game he "allows" hits of "gives them up." Note how the accent is on the pitcher failing rather than hitter succeeding, reflecting the early history of the major league game, before the changes in the wake of the 1919 Black Sox scandal, when pitchers dominated, often throwing shutouts.

All-Star - If you're an ace, you're certain to already be an All-Star. Though the USA now sends a baseball team to compete in the Olympic Games, there is no national baseball team that equates to our English (or Scottish, Welsh or Northern Irish) football team or the England football team. Thus there is no accolade for the best ball players in the country equivalent to 'playing for England.' The nearest thing is to be an All-Star. Each year since 1933, two 'best of' teams, one from each of by now established major leagues, American and National, have competed against each other in a single game. It is a signal honour for a player to be chosen as an All-Star and the greater the number of years he gets selected, the greater the honour and the greater the player, give or take. You will hear players being referred to as being a 'three time All-Star,' indicating to us that such and such has been elected that number of times for his league team.

All-Star Game - This is the game mentioned above, played each July at a different ball park each year, played by all the normal rules and stipulations of baseball. Peculiarly, it seems to me, the players play not in National and American League uniforms (not 'kit,' you'll notice) but in those of their own teams. Strange.

All-Star Break - For this game there is a break from the intensity and sheer slog of the regular baseball season. It lasts at the moment for three days.

All-Star Winning Team - Controversy in the game was caused in the off-season of 2002-03 when it was decided that from 2003 until further notice, home advantage in the World Series, four games at home for the American League championship winners to the National League Championship winners' three, or vice versa, depending on which League won the All- Star Game each July. The idea behind the move was to inject a little competition, not to say meaning, into the All-Star Game, which was in danger of becoming little more than an exhibition game and the opportunity for the big US Corporations to let loose some more advertising dollars with the assistant of the TV company which has the honour of the coverage (ESPN).

Angels' Sixth, The – (or the Royals' or the Devil Rays'...) Refers to a particular team's turn at bat in whatever inning.

Around The Horn - Specific type of double play which goes from third to second to first bases. Also known as a 6-4-3 double play. See '**fielding positions.'**

Artificial Turf - A dying commodity in baseball, thankfully according to the purists who think that only a grass surface befits America's greatest game (how can anyone disagree?). Four artificial surfaces are left: at the homes of the Milwaukee Brewers, the Minnesota Twins, The Montreal Expos and the Toronto Blue Jays.

Assignment (Designated for) – Term for a player being sent to a specific minor league team in an organization's farm system: can be the same as being "sent down" from the majors, in which case this is dreaded news for the ballplayer, or the beginning of the dream's realization if you're being taken on by a club for the very first time.

Assists - Assists are made by fielders in putting out or forcing out batters. The assist is made by the act of throwing a batted ball to a baseman. Though not much commented upon in games, statisticians faithfully record them.

Astroturf – This is the most well known of the artificial playing surfaces still in use in major league baseball. The term comes from the Houston Astros ball club. When they build their first purpose built ballpark, the Astrodome, just after they entered the major leagues in 1962 they decided that grass wouldn't work as they wanted a roof over the top to keep out summer bugs and so they could use air conditioning to cool the crowd on those hot Texas nights. The artificial grass that a bunch of scientists came up with for them – the owners weren't short of a bob or two, you can tell – they named after the team.

At Bat – n, Each time a player comes up "to bat," he has an additional plate appearance to his statistical record. An "at bat" is a plate appearance where the hitter either strikes out, hits the ball into the air and is caught out (though this phrase is unknown: he's simply "put out" - "*Chavez makes the catch for the put out*"), is thrown out at a base after hitting the ball into fair territory or hits the ball successfully in to fair territory for a hit of some kind. A player can make an out and not have an at bat charged to his record (an at bat without a hit brings down his batting average): if his out results in a run being scored (see '*sacrifice bunt*' and '*sacrifice fly*'). The exception to this is when putting the ball in play results in a run being scored and a double play (when two men are out on the same pitch).

The term is key: baseball is made of at bats just as we could say that it's made up of pitches.

At Bat 2 – When a player is "at bat" he's up in the batter's box receiving pitches.

At Home – As in our football - team playing at.... - used only occasionally. "*Home field advantage*" is much more common.

Awards – Baseball has more annual performance awards than the film industry, let me tell you. The most important are as follows: the Cy Young Award for the best pitcher in each league. The Most Valuable Player in each league. Rookie of the Year is the next most important, but some way behind the first two. Manager of the Year in each league gets some coverage too, but not that much. Further down the priority list is Comeback Player of the Year.

Away - This refers to the part of the strike zone farthest away from the batter's reach. To 'pitch away' is for the pitcher to pursue a perceived weakness in a batter. All batters like the ball straight down the middle where they can take a nice huge comfy swing at the ball, but if they can't get that, some prefer the ball to come to them either slightly more towards the body – 'in' – but few like an away pitch. Pitchers commonly 'pitch away' to get a batter to '*chase one out of the zone:*' to reach for a ball that's not in an ideal to hit, being a little too far from the body. 'Low and away' are even better, presenting two difficulties to the batter: it works because hitters will still sometimes chase it, especially on two strikes.

B

Back Door Slider - The term 'back door' is used for a pitch that creeps into the strike zone in the last part-second of its journey from the pitcher's hand. A *slider* that does this is one of these.

Back Him Off The Plate - Some batters like to position themselves in the batter's box close to the plate. This is especially useful to be able to reach a pitch on or near the outer corner of the strike zone. If this doesn't suit the pitcher whose preferred site line is one without the batter being that close to the plate, he may well throw a pitch or two close to the batter. This physical endangerment is likely to cause him to 'back off' the plate.

Backstop 1 - A term for the catcher, somewhat gone out of usage.

Backstop 2 – The other meaning of backstop is in the naming of any piece of boarding some way behind the catcher and umpire to stop the ball running into the crowd. Also called the 'screen.'

Back-To-Back Jacks - Frequently used term in television coverage to describe home runs hit in two consecutive at bats.

Bag, The - The actual bases, now made of a rubber-like substance so they don't injure base runners, used to be bags of stuffed canvas. Home plate, used in the at-bat as the umpire's guide to the width of the strike zone, becomes the "bag" at home when a runner is trying to score. The bases are described and named as "bags" in the official Laws of The Game and were introduced in 1877, 15 inches square. They still are.

Balata Ball - Type of ball used in the majors during the Second World War, made from substitute juices of tropical trees instead of the real thing normally found at the centre of a baseball: rubber. At the time, precious rubber was needed for military purposes as the Western democracies (and the Soviet Union) fought back Nazi tyranny. The balata core was softer and so balls failed to travel the normal distance, reducing batter extra base hits considerably during this period. At the start of the 1943 season, eleven of the first twenty-nine games were shutouts.

Balk - A rule to prevent a pitcher deceiving a runner, i.e., getting into his wind up then turning and throwing to first base (or a.n. other) thus putting out the runner who is already on his way to second or who is ready to scoot there on a ball hit fair by the batter. This strengthens the legitimacy of the principle of runners being able to steal bases and take off early for the next base. A balk is called by the home plate umpire with the result that the hitter and any runners already on base advance by one base to punish the pitcher for, essentially, cheating.

Ball – When a pitcher makes his pitch, one of four things can happen to the baseball: it's hit by the batter; it's swung at and missed by the batter; it's deliberately let go by the batter; it hits the batter. When not hitting the batter or being hit by him, the status of the baseball divides into three possibilities: if the batter swings and misses, a 'strike' is immediately called against him by the home plate umpire; if the batter chooses not to hit the pitch and if the pitch arrives in the immediate vicinity of the batter within the designated strike zone, a strike is also called. However, if the pitch arrives at a point level with the batter outside the strike zone, it is said to be a 'ball' and is called as such by the home plate umpire.

This is of crucial importance because four balls before three strikes will mean the batter then proceeds to first base. When following the game, the fan takes close and constant note, mental or on paper of the number of balls relative to the number of strikes. It might be useful at this point to go to 'the count.'

Ball Club - Another term for baseball club. In fact, the latter is rarely used: it's pretty much always 'ball club.' The term originates from mid-19th century baseball when the first teams were played by the US equivalent of the upper class.

Ball Four - Equals a walk to first base for the batter. See also "***Base on Balls.***" At one time a pitcher was allowed seven balls, before the number dropped over time to six, five, then four in 1889, where it has stayed ever since. 'Ball Four' is called aloud by the umpire, signaling the walk.

Ballgame - Somewhat stupidly it seems to me, broadcasters on Radio 5 began last season to refer to a game of football continually as 'this football match' as if we might suddenly forget and think it was netball. Perhaps this has been acquired from baseball where a lot of the time a game of baseball is often referred to as 'the ballgame' instead of just 'the game.'

Ball One (1-0) - The first pitch during an at bat, if it misses the strike zone is labeled 'ball one,' often aloud by the umpire when he's not shouting "*bauugghhh!*"

Base On Balls - A base on balls is the noun used for a batter receiving four balls and getting a walk or ***free pass*** to first base. Good for the offensive team and bad for the defensive team unless the batter is likely to made an extra base hit or home run, in which case he may be ***intentionally walked*** or ***pitched around***.

Ball, On The Inside - Means that the pitch (that has been left by the batter) is not a strike because it was out of the strike zone to the right as we look behind the camera, inside because the ball passes wide on the batter side of the plate. It's 'inside' from the batter's point of view (the opposite is 'away').

Ball, On The Inside Corner – This describes a pitch which misses the strike zone on the side nearest the batter at the top or bottom of the zone. Peculiarly, the 'corners' are the outer edges of the strike zone, whatever height the ball passes through the edge of it.

Ball, On The Outside - Means a pitch that misses the strike zone on the left hand edge as we look over the pitcher's arm.

Ball On The Outside Corner – The opposite, obviously, of a ball on the inside corner. This ball has missed the strike zone on the portion furthest away from the batter.

Ballpark - Not 'the ground,' sometimes 'the stadium,' but mostly, 'the ballpark.'

Ballplayer – A cricketer to cricket, a footballer to football and a 'ballplayer' to baseball.

Baltimore Chop - When the batter hits the pitch straight into the ground causing it to bounce up high, often over the top of the pitcher on the mound and the infield. Actually a technique for getting on base developed by the Baltimore Orioles in the late 19th century, well before they became the major league ball club we know today (in 1954). Note: yes, in between, they played in the majors for two years before they became the New York Highlanders (then later Yankees).

Bandbox – A term for a small ballpark, one good for hitters, of course, not pitchers. The Rangers' Ballpark in Arlington is an example, as is Fenway Park or the Minute Maid Park in Houston...

Bang-Bang Play – When a throw to first base hits the glove of the fielder there (bang 1) followed immediately by the front foot of the batter hitting the base (bang 2).

Banner Day – When a player has a great game, usually a batter having a multiple home run day or going 5 for 5 and bringing home a lot of runs. For a pitcher, something like a two-hit complete game. A no hitter goes beyond Banner Day.

Barehanded - One of the things that surprises the new British baseball fan is the sense of difficulty for the fielders if they ever have to or decide to handle the baseball without their glove on, i.e., barehanded. I'm immediately reminded of the catch Jonty Rhodes once took in England at short mid off where he dived full length to grab a lofted drive that was hit like a shell barely ten yards away, and I wonder what the hell everyone in baseball would make of it. That said, the gloved fielder adds something special to the spectacle of the sport, no doubt. **Note.** Since writing this first draft I got hold of a real major league baseball, and for those cynics who think Americans are all Jessies, a cricket ball is appreciably softer on the hands; even when thrown at a short distance a baseball can give you a nasty surprise.

Barnstorming – A team on tour, going from town to town to play resident nines, is 'barnstorming.' In short, traveling, touring. Most all the Negro teams before the beginning of integrated baseball in 1946 (Robinson in Montreal AAA in the Dodgers organization) had to make their living by playing on the move, constantly barnstorming around the nation. In the off-season, white major leaguers organized traveling teams to go barnstorming to supplement their often meagre summertime wages. Babe Ruth, on the other hand, went barnstorming to capitalize on his enormous fame. Fairly often, the black teams would play 'exhibition' matches (they were fiercely contested) against the major leaguers, giving crowds (and history) dramatically fascinating glimpses of what might have been had the likes of Paige, Gibson and Charleston been allowed to play in the majors. Very often, the black stars proved embarrassingly conclusively how well they would have fared in the majors.

Barrel- Though it has to come, by the official rules, in one long continuous piece, there are two 'parts' to a bat: the slim *handle*, which then broadens out gradually to the *barrel* with which the hitter is supposed to make contact.

Base – There are four bases in the game, forming the poetic "diamond." The actual bases or "bags" must be 15 inches square, according to the laws of the game. Getting to first, then around the rest is the object of the game. The bases are 90 feet apart.

Baseball, The - The company Rawlins sends something in excess of 600 000 baseballs for use in major league play each season. Nice contract. All of these are manufactured in Costa Rica. On average, a major league baseball has a lifespan of six pitches. The ball is covered in animal hide: cowhide since 1976, horsehide before that. They were running short of horses.

Baseball, The 2 – Baseball is what it is because of the ball. Or more to the point, the fact that it has red-stitch seams running all over it. Because of this, when thrown in certain ways by pitchers, it changes direction in mid-flight. If it didn't, it would have declined as a professional sport long ago through every game being a tedious procession of balls smashed out of every park in America. So, a batter at the plate has a projectile hurled at him at about 88 miles an hour – bad enough, you might think – which might swerve to the left, swerve to the right, come in to him straight and then swerve away from him at the last fraction of a second, come in to him straight then drop down at the last fraction of a second or come towards him starting at head height before dropping in on him at the knees. If this combo of difficulties isn't hard enough, the pitcher may well fool him by thrashing the arm through at normal speed whilst releasing the ball early so that he's swung through the ball before it's even arrived. There's worse to come. Just when the starting pitcher is tiring, the opposition's manager can pass the ball along to one, two, three or even four fresh guys who can do their worst to you with energetic abandon. And get this, right at the end of the game, the batter might have to face a guy whose specialism, *specialism,* if you please, it to chuck the ball toward you at about 95 miles an hour snorting fire and manic, super-professional purpose.

Admittedly these last two problems have nothing directly to do with the seams on the ball, but I couldn't resist completing the picture of trouble for our daily batter at his place of work, the plate. Of course, this all only serves to tell you what an amazing feat of organization and composition the human being is. Because there are, believe it or not, people out there in America who can deal with these problems to the extent of being able to produce hits which have fans out of their seats, goggling, and critics salivating at the stats which bear comparison with all the greats bar Babe Ruth, who, like Bradman, is out there on his own.

Baseball, The 3 – There is still some controversy over whether or not the inside of the sphere is exactly the same year on year. The more tightly wound the thread around the hard inner core is, the faster and further it travels off the bat. Barry Bonds complained after the 2003 season that the ball was softer that year, which explained the falling off of his number of home runs. Could say more about Barry Bonds than the baseball though.

Baseball - was invented we don't know where. It used to be thought that a man called Abner Doubleday laid out a diamond and most of the rules we still have in 1845 in a place called Cooperstown at the end of a big lake in up state New York, but now we know this myth was only a good reason to put the hallowed Hall Of Fame right out of the way so that it's a bugger to get to (no planes, no trains...) Baseball became a nine innings game in 1857. Before this, the first team to score 21 runs was the winner. Run scoring was very heavy at that time due to the ball weighing a mere 3 ounces. The standard weight of the ball became 5-5.25 ounces by 1872 and remains so to this day.

Baseball Annie – This is a term for a baseball groupie, of which there have been plenty for a very long time. Eddie Waitkus, a Philadelphia Philly first baseman, was shot by one in 1949 though not quite killed. So we're talking that far back and further. Favourite BA: Susan Sarandon in *Bull Durham.*

Baseball Ground – This is one of the peculiarities of the history of football, how one of the original 12 of the 1888 football league, Derby County, came to name their home "The Baseball Ground," which they did after they left the Racecourse Ground in 1895. Fact is, it already was baseball ground. A local industrialist, Francis Ley had set aside some land for his workers to let off steam at some point in his firm's history. By 1890, the playing of baseball was so well established there that "the Derby club," as it was known to the Derby Mercury at the time, was in the process of being one of the founder members of a small English baseball league. Some 36 clubs were reckoned to be playing the game seriously around the country at the time. Ley it seems, was the spearhead of this development. What happened next in Derby is shrouded in mystery, but presumably, when the football club moved across to the south of the town to the Peartree inner suburb, the name "Baseball Ground" was well established. Indeed, the baseball club at some point became an arm of the football club, star Steve Bloomer being known to have played the nine-man game regularly, for example. So Baseball Ground it was and Baseball Ground it stayed until the club moved to Pride Park in 1999. (4BB)

Base Hit - A base hit is one where the batter hits the ball into fair territory and is able to get to first base. If the batter gets to second base, it's still a hit, but it's now called a 'double.' The term 'base hit' is normally shortened to 'hit.'

Base On Balls – Long hand for a walk: reaching base on four balls thrown before the batter hit the ball into play or went down on strikes. Abb. **BB.**

Base Paths - These are the expansive, gravely, sandy strips between the two grassy areas of the baseball field, the infield and the outfield, connecting all the bases, there for the base runners to run along. All four infielders position themselves on the base paths, save when one or more comes in close in anticipation of a bunt, especially with a man on third. (See also *squeeze* play). The material underfoot on the base paths prevents slippage in wet conditions for both fielder and base runner. Though now the extent of the dirt is institutionalized: it forms the space between the inner grass diamond and the line formed by a line taken between first and third bases in the form of part of a perfect circle, I suspect that in the early days of the game, the paths were grass and this was worn away by base runners in no time. Similarly, the grass behind the paths where the infielders take up their positions would have been worn away to dirt by their constant foot scratching, running and diving. When these non-grass areas of play became standardized I couldn't tell you.

Base Runner - Once the batter has got onto base by whatever means, he is now a 'base runner' or 'runner' for short. 'Runner' is the much more common usage.

Base Running - Term for what the batters do when they run around the base paths. Something some teams are strong in, others less so. Players also. There is much to it. Joe Morgan's worthwhile *Baseball For Dummies* has an entire chapter devoted to this, entitled *The Science Of Baserunning.*

Bases Clean – Same as *bases empty*; phrase suddenly appearing during the World Series thanks to sportscaster Dave O'Brien: there are no men on base.

Bases Loaded - Inimitable expression to describe the offensive team having a man on each of the first three bases, a moment pregnant with possibility for the offensive team. That said it's very, very common for an offence to fail to score in this situation. Thus on occasions, with men on second and third, a defensive team manager will choose to intentionally walk a guy and you're thinking, "what kind of madness is this?" But if there's two out, in only takes one batted ball to the infield to end the inning, and if the guy *behind* the man you're going to intentionally walk is a much inferior hitter, you're better off pitching to him. And with one out, you're one ground ball away from a **double play.** Also "*bases jammed.*"

Basket Catch – A style of catching in the outfield where the glove is held at the centre of the waistline to pouch a hit fly ball. Initiated in the majors by one Willie Mays. (See San Francisco Hall of Famers) Normally you'll see players catch the high (fly) ball above their heads.

Bat, The - The rules of baseball are strict about the bat. It has to be made of one continuous piece of wood and must be no more than 42 inches long and two and three-quarter inches in diameter. Where bats used predominantly to be made of ash, maple is more often used in present times. This is because the wood is harder and it is less porous, so absorbs less moisture. The drier bat gives the hitter a higher 'coefficient of restitution,' say the theorists: the wood springs back faster after being struck causing it to go further. This is one explanation of the increasing number of home runs being hit in the modern age. In terms of weight, Barry Bonds, who uses a Canadian bat of sugar maple called the Sam Bat, uses a bat of 30 ounces. The lighter bat, though the difference is only three or four ounces, enables the modern player to develop greater bat speed. This may also account for more effective hitting. Bat size was first regulated in 1863. There are no weight rules about the bat.

Bat Boy – A tradition in the game is for each team in the course of play to have a youth carrying and picking up the bats discarded immediately after a hitter is done at the plate. He picks 'em up and runs them back to their place in the dug out bat racks, wears full uniform of the team and has a name: bat boy.

Bat Speed - Commonly heard term for the speed at which the batter swings the bat through the air at the ball. The faster the bat speed, the more fastball pitches the batter will get to, given the merest fraction of a second of reaction time the batter has at the plate. So a major league hitter needs tremendous bat speed to be successful.

Bat(tted) Around – When all 9 offensive players come to the plate for an at bat in a single inning. This is not all that common, thankfully pitchers. If this happens, a fair amount of mayhem will probably be going on: there'll be at least one pitching change, hits, walks, possibly a home run or two, and either the home fans going nuts or booing, depending on which team's filling their boots (*not* an Americanism).

Batted Ball – When a batter makes contact with a pitch, the ball is now "batted." This is merely a matter of baseball semantics.

Batter - In baseball, the player going in to attempt to score runs by hitting the baseball to parts of the ballpark various, is known as the 'batter' (as opposed to batsman in cricket, though incidentally, the tendency of cricketers to use the baseball term emerged in the 1980s)

Batter's Box – There is nothing in the official rules about the size of the batter's box, which is odd as legally, he has to stand within it when up at bat. However, there is a diagram in the rules of every detail of the playing field, so if someone has obviously measured the length and breadth of the lines on the (scale) drawing and passed the news on to all the clubs, because all batter's boxes have the same dimension. Why have batter's boxes? So no one can make a spectacle of themselves taking a flying run at a 96mph fastball or stand behind the catcher giving himself more time to see the pitch and confusing hell out of everyone; not least the catcher, who knows he has to stand behind the batter to get a strike call. No, the whole game is predicated upon everyone's body describing a defined set of movements from precisely designated places.

Battery – The collective term for the pitcher-catcher combo.

Batting Average - A player's batting average records his ability to make hits. If Barry Bonds in his first ten at bats of the season makes a hit - any form of hit - five times, then his average is .500. This is verbalized always, as 'five hundred 'not' point five In terms of what to expect from hitters from the start of a new season, though some may have a hot streak when they make a hit half the times they go to the plate, or better than that, no one has ever finished the season batting five hundred. Indeed, no one in the American has topped the averages batting four hundred since Ted Williams in 1941 and no one in the National League has done it since Bill Terry of the New York Giants in 1930. Thus, as it is often said, baseball is a game based on failure – or batting failure, anyway, which is a quite arresting thought. Even the greatest hitters in the game's history fail at least six times out of ten to get a hit.

When a batter is hit or gets a walk, the at bat is void in terms of his average. Neither does he gain anything from the compliment of being intentionally walked, which doesn't seem quite fair when a walk often occurs through the excellence of the batter's judgment and patience. If he manages to deliberately manoevre the pitcher into throwing four balls and getting a walk to first base, he gets no credit for that either. Batters making sacrifice outs: the deeply hit fly ball and the sac bunt that brings in a run, do not count as failed at bats against him. In a single game, then, a hitter may have only a couple of at bats on his *line*. He can expect around 5 plate appearances in a game, but if he draws two walks, hits a sac fly, gets hit by a pitch and hits a double, only one at bat will be logged on to his record. This would be a rarity though. Batting average, recorded from 1865 onwards, is still the number one measure of a batter's ability. Arguably it shouldn't be, when there is a range of other available measures: home runs; on base percentage; slugging percentage and secondary average, but it is.

Batting Cage – Mobile ballpark stage-scenery, always three sides of netting, placed behind the home plate area to 'catch' balls that get past batters in batting practice. Players on both teams take batting practice about an hour before games to get themselves loose and used to seeing the ball.

Batting Champion – The hitter with the highest end of season batting average in each league is its batting champion. This is illustrative of how much is placed on one single statistic. AL 2004 Champion: AL Champion: Suzuki (Sea) .372, NL Champion: Bonds (SF) .362. Note the high numbers now, by comparison with the late-60s and 70s. Suspiciously high? We'll see in the next year or so, I guess.

(AL 2003 Champion: Bill Mueller, (Bos), .326; NL 2003 Champion: Albert Pujols, (St L), .359. Note that four other NL players had a better batting average than Mueller: Todd Helton (Col) .358; Barry Bonds (SanF) .341; Edgar Renteria (St L) .330 & Gary Sheffield (Atl) .330.)

Batting Crown – If you win a batting crown, you win one of three main seasonal titles: most home runs; highest batting average and most Runs Batted In. See *Triple Crown*.

Batting Gloves - Most players wear protective gloves but they are nowhere near as thick as cricketers' gloves, as they would reduce bat speed. Some protection from the fastball is required by almost all these days. See **'Protection.'**

Batting Practice (Take) – Time-honoured ritual before each game, *taken*, not *had*. It happens an hour or so before first pitch, and if you can be bothered or sufficiently organized, you can get to the game early enough to see it for yourself.

Batting Title - The batting title is the competition for the highest batting average, a calculation of the number of hits per at bat the batters make at the end of the season.

Bat Weights – That strange hollow object sheathing the middle part of the hitter's bat when he's in the on-deck circle is a weight. Long used in the game, the idea is for the hitter to get used to swinging the heavier bat, so that when grasping the lighter weapon a few moments later it feels like he's holding a pencil. So, thus psychologically elevated, he can whip it through the next few pitches and make good. Previously hitters would swing two or three bats to gain the same effect.

Bay Bridge Series. This is a term which describes any series played between the two clubs either side of San Francisco Bay: the San Francisco Giants and the Oakland As. Seeing as they play in different leagues, these have only occurred since the start of Inter- League play.

Beaning - If you get 'beaned' you get hit on the head with the baseball by the pitcher.

Bear Down – To try your hardest. Or sometimes, 'don't bear down!' The journey through baseball history contains many dismal (though if you're in the right sort of mood, colourful) stories of bribery and attempted bribery where players have been tempted into throwing ball games. One way of ensuring the result goes the right way for the gamblers is to persuade the pitcher not to 'bear down' against the batters: in other words, not to try to hard or indeed, throw too hard. I thought this phrase was facing complete obsolescence until one of the Boston players used it about four times in a post 2004 Game 7 interview.

Beat out (a bunt/a throw) – To "beat out" means to get to the bag safely before you're thrown out.

Behind In The Count - If a pitcher gets behind in the count the number of strikes is fewer than the number of balls. This is not the place to be. It's an extremely strong tradition that behind in the count, the pitcher has to throw the ball over the plate, in which case the batter is much more likely now to make good contact. The pitcher is more likely to be more predictable, most particularly to throw a fastball, the pitch a lot of guys really like to get more than any other type of pitch because it generally doesn't swerve in the air.

Belt High – A pitch and a bad one. It's bad because it's a convenient height for the batter: its level with the belt often worn by batters. It's used approximately. Anywhere an inch or two either way is still 'belt high.' Unless it's got a lot of movement on it, it should be jam for the batter.

Bench - The bench is literally where the players, coaches and manager sit during the game. The term also means the players the manager has in reserve from whom he can choose pinch hitters and runners or players for the next day. If you're on the bench you're not in the team. If you're 'benched,' you're a normally a regular player who has not been selected. The bench, these days, is in the dugout. Even as late as the 30s, some ballparks had benches just back from the foul lines unprotected from crowds who often chucked rubbish at visitors, especially when things got a little rowdy.

Bench Coach – The manager's number two; the equivalent of the assistant manager in football. In terms of other coaches, generally only two others from the coaching staff sit on the bench with the manager and the players, the pitching coach and the hitting coach.

Bench Jockey – Someone who tries to wind up players and officials from the other team from the dug out. This was much, much more prevalent in days gone by than it is now, though it does happen. It used to be the done thing, absolutely.

Bench Manager – This is an old term from the days when most managers were player-managers. This describes the alternative, the team boss who doesn't play on the field, but directs operations from the dugout.

Bench Player - This is one who cannot command a place in the first choice nine. He will play as a pinch hitter or runner, or when one of the top guys in injured.

Bench Warmer – A player on the roster who doesn't get to play; all he does is sit in the dug out with his ass stuck in one place. There are more of these guys around when the rosters expand from 25 to 40 each September.

Big Bats - Term for a group of sluggers/and or run producers. A player might be said to "carry a big bat" in a game, meaning he's made a lot of hits for extra bases, esp. homers.

Big Leagues - A commonly used term for the two major leagues.

Bigs, The - Short for the 'big leagues.'

Bill – The peak of a ball player's cap.

Bird Dog – Scout who works independently looking for talent, often in obscure parts of the country (traditionally, mythically?), only getting paid when one of his finds is signed on. Not on salary.

Blast - A 'two-run blast' is a big hit that went out of the park for a home run.

Bleachers - These are the cheap seats at the ballpark, always the furthest away from the diamond, normally in center field. These are normally bench seats, or used to be in the older ballparks.

Bleeder - A softly, weakly or otherwise under-hit ball that becomes a base hit.

Blocked Ball (In The Dirt) – A blocked ball merely describes a pitch which passes through the strike zone on the floor in front of the catcher so he has to do some work to block it. Reveals his skill, I suppose.

Block The Plate – This is what fielders do, catchers especially at home, to stop a base runner getting safely to a base. If they do it without the ball in their hands, it's interference and illegal and the runner will almost certainly be awarded the base. With the ball in glove or hand, the fielder will try to tag (touch) the runner with it, thus forcing him out. In the old days of rough, tough baseball, runners would try to smash into the fielder knocking the fielder sideways and the ball flying away, making them safe. These days, things are somewhat more sedate, though robust physical contact is still allowed. Runners now are more likely to use finesse, speed and guile to avoid the tag rather than brute force, or in one case, to try to slap the ball out of the fielder's hand like a pantomime fairy.

Bloop Hit - The blooper can embarrass fielders as they scoot helplessly after this silly looping mis-hit, sometimes colliding providing much entertainment in the process, and fail to catch it. Meanwhile, the perhaps also embarrassed batter has sprinted to first base safely. He's got himself a 'bloop hit' and it counts just as much on his batting average as a sweetly struck line drive that goes straight to an outfielder on the bounce.

Bloop Single - Same as a bloop hit, and **blooper,** the more common name for a mis-hit by a batter that struggles into the air slowly before landing safely for a hit.

Blowout – Is a term for a one-sided game of baseball. By the time we get to a team being 6-1 ahead, we're talking blowout.

Blows That One By Him - Term used to describe what a pitcher does when he sends a fastball tearing past the bat of the hitter for a strike.

Blown Save - This goes down on the record of the closer (the pitcher brought in to finish off the game when his team is ahead in [normally] the ninth inning) who fails to hold on to the lead. The closer has become a glory position if he's successful, but a closer who doesn't do the job is in a very exposed position and is easily blamed for the defeat. Whether that constitutes quality analysis or not is another matter.

Bomb - ('...Bonds smashed a two run bomb in the seventh...') is a home run hit with considerable power, clearing the fences comfortably.

Bonus Baby – The Bonus Baby rule was brought in 1953 to stop organizations signing up college and high school kids and burying them in their minor league system for years and years. The new rule said that if a club signed a young prospect with a $10,000 signing on bonus, they had to put him on the active roster immediately and keep him there for two years. The rule was to discourage clubs from spending large wads of cash on young players as it was thought to be bad for the game. The rule only lasted until 1957.

Bottom of the first - The inning is split into two parts: first the away team goes into bat - this is called the top of the inning. Then, the team with home field advantage takes its turn; this is the 'bottom' of the inning. This second part of the inning is also called the "bottom half."

Box, The – This is not the batter's box but oddly the pitcher's mound. The word is used very specifically here, in terms of a batter "hitting the ball back through the box," meaning straight at and past the pitcher. The term dates from a time when the pitcher threw from flat ground, his place marked by a box painted in a white line.

Box Score(s) - The first box scores appeared in newspapers around the year 1876. The concept was the invention of an exiled Brit, Henry Chadwick, though both facts are disputed. A box score is a detailed statistical re-telling of that particular game. It includes each batter and each pitcher's personal performance statistics, plus a range of other information such as when runs were scored, how many men each team left on base, who made errors and more besides.

E.g. here, a hitter's box from an everyday newspaper and the official MLB website:

Player	AB	R	H	HR	BB	SO	RBI	LOB	AVE
Ramirez	4	1	3	1	1	0	4	3	.32

Where AB = at bat; R = run scored; H = Hits; HR = Home runs; BB = walks; SO = strikeouts; RBI = runs batter in; LOB = runners left on base after an at bat and AVE = batting average for the season, not the game.

Box Seats - the best seats in the ballpark, but specifically also refers to the fact that in the late 19th century the closest seats to the action were laid out in groups of two or four and boxed in by a rail for a sense of seclusion and privacy. The term has become metaphorical, of course.

Breaking A Game Open – When the scores are tied, either at 0-0 or after a bout of scoring, it becomes tied at 2-2, or whatever, and this goes on for an inning or more, if a hitter finally breaks the deadlock by scoring a run, then the game is said to have been 'broken open.'

Breaking Ball - Any pitch that isn't a fastball and isn't a change up is a breaking ball: one, which has a significant amount of movement on it through the air. After trying to master pitch labeling for the last 12 months, I have to say I am still confused about whether a curve ball is a type of breaking ball or a type all to itself. I have to do some more digging, I think.

Breakout Season/Year – A breakout season is one where a player goes from mediocrity or anonymity to establishing themselves as a credible, useful member of the team or even as a star.

Break Up The Double Play – When one of the base runners stymie the double play attempt, through the runner leaving first and arriving at second getting there quickly enough and with sufficient physical presence to delay the throw from second to first. Thus only one out will have been made.

Broken Bat – Broken bats are very common, given the velocity of the baseball and the speed at which the bat is thrown at the ball. Often this causes the ball to bloop off the bat inconveniently for fielders and pitcher. Play continues as normal when this occurs - the ball is not declared dead. It's a not unspectacular event and was certainly this in game two of the World Series played in 2001 between the two New York clubs, the Mets and the Yankees. The fearsome (and loathsome, as far as many Mets fans were concerned) Roger Clemens was pitching for the Yankees at the talismanic Mike Piazza of the Mets when his bat broke, sending a sizeable chunk of it in the direction of the pitcher. Clemens then chucked it, casually or deliberately, depending on your point of view and perhaps fan affiliation, about two feet from Piazza as he vainly ran towards first base. Cue Piazza taking great exception and twenty-four hours media hysteria. No punches were thrown, no blood was spilt, but in the context of this so-called Subway Series within American sport this was a huge event. The following season when the two teams met (see 'inter-league play') and Clemens was due to pitch in Shea Stadium (home of the Mets), he was pulled out of the rotation by Yankees manager Joe Torre, such was the depth of controversy still surrounding Piazza v Clemens.

Bronx Bombers - Nickname of the New York Yankees: they play in the Bronx suburb of New York City. Often shortened to just 'the Bombers.'

Bronx Cheer - A boo or hoot of derision. This is a gentle swipe at those ruffian Yankee fans.

Bronx Zoo - Derisive appellation for the home of the New York Yankees. Their Yankee Stadium is situated in the Bronx and the fans are often raucous and vociferous.

Brushing back (the batter) - A term for the pitcher throwing close to the batter to get him to back off the plate. See *'Crowding the plate.'*

Bullpen - This is where the relief pitchers and closers warm up. It's a penned off area of the park – its placement varies from park to park, but it's almost always adjacent to the distant outfield. The origin of the term probably comes from the fact that the pitchers are confined to their area of limited space and for the moment, of somewhat diminished value. They move around until let out like a bunch of cattle. The theory that the term derives from the huge Bull Durham advertising signs in the early part of the 20th century is also very popular, but less likely, I think. The relievers often warmed up near to or under the signs (for shade). Nice thought, but unlikely. Note. *Bull Durham* was a brand of chewing tobacco.

Bullpen By Committee - In modern baseball, all teams have a designated closer, the man whose specific job it is to close out the game in the ninth inning when his team is in the lead. Well, almost all. One or two, most especially the Red Sox in the first part of the 2003 season used a much-derided system called 'bullpen by committee' where from one day to the next, manager Grady Little decided which pitcher to call on from the bullpen to relieve a tired starter or hold on to a lead.

Bullpen Catcher - Someone has to catch for those warm-up relievers and closers. As two pitchers may be warming up together, you need two in there at least.

Bunt - A bunt is at the opposite end of the spectrum of the home run. A bunt is executed by a batter in order to drop the baseball down within around ten or twenty feet from the bat, slowly. Ideally this should be far enough away from both the pitcher and the catcher so prevent them throwing out the batter at first base. However, this scarcely matters when for much of the time, the attempt to put down a bunt is made so as to move a base runner along by one base. The tactic is more associated with the National League than the American: the NL has an immensely strong tradition of using **small ball** tactics as opposed to try to smash the ball deep for extra base hits. (See *'Sacrifice Bunt* and *Squeeze Play')*. Note: you don't bunt with two outs and as a bunt that goes foul counts as a third strike.

'Bush' /"Busher" - Nickname for a rookie, a player just come up to the majors from the minors.

Bush Leagues - A generic term for the minor leagues: i.e., out in the bush, the Styx, Nowheresville, not the Bigs, baby. Also 'busher.'

Butchered – A fielder 'butchers one' when he misfields a hit ball badly or sloppily.

Butterfly Pitch – Term for a knuckleball pitch, which often darts up and down in flight like a butterfly on the wing. On a show last season, the Rangers' skipper Buck Showalter spoke during the game of how his hitters were having difficulty in hitting "Wake's (Tim Wakefield, Boston Red Sox) butterflies."

C

Caddy - Relief pitcher who comes in the seventh or eighth inning to hold on to the lead so the closer can finish things off in the ninth. Same as a '*set up man'*

Called Ball – A ball, not a strike, called aloud by the umpire, not being hit foul by batter.

Called Strike – A strike, not where the batter has swung and missed but where the pitch has passed through the strike zone without the batter having swung at it. Thus the ump has to make a judgment as to whether the pitch crossed the SZ and call this aloud while also signaling it with his hand and other body parts.

Called Strike On the Outside – This tells us the location of the strike in terms of the geography of the strike zone. 'On the outside' means that it has crossed the zone on the furthest edge from the batter. A strike **on the inside** crossed zone on the edge nearest the batter.

Called Up - This is what a minor league player is if he's wanted by his major league club. '*...called up from the minors.*'

Calling (off) In The Field – Important in baseball as in cricket. In the outfield, the center fielder is the captain and has the right to take control of fly balls, '**calling off**' the other fielder(s). Collisions are rare, but do happen.

Canned - Used to describe the removal of a player from the game for misconduct.

Cannon - Term for a fielder with a really hard throw. 'Rolen has a cannon for a throw.'

Captains - In general, baseball teams do not have captains, although the Yankees do, but only at certain times. Derek Jeter became only the eleventh captain of the ball club in June of last season, suddenly or finally being dubbed worthy of the accolade by owner George Steinbrenner. "He believes as I do that there is no substitute for victory," said George of Derek. Babe Ruth lost the captaincy of the Yankees in 1922 after only five days after he threw dirt in the face of an umpire and attacked the crowd in the stands who shouted insults, after disputing an out at second base.

Carom – Ubiquitous phrase used in America where we would say 'canon' or 'bounced.' It's used in baseball terms almost invariably to describe the cannoning of a baseball off a wall.

Catch - There is no 'catches win matches' saying in baseball, but they can make huge outs, especially of the outfield wall leaping to keep out a home run kind. Many spectacular ones are made, showing the agility of most of the players, and very few bungled. Indeed, it's a shock to see a drop when it does occur. Rightly so, you might say, thinking of the fact that fielders wear a huge glove to assist them.

Catcher – The catcher is the fulcrum of the fielding side. He has the broadest and most complex fielding job. His job requires not only that he catch the ball with unfailing reliability but also that he select – "call" - all the pitches for his pitcher. Sometimes the pitcher disagrees and shakes him off, but most all the time he doesn't and accepts what the catcher thinks he should throw. A whole lot of finger signs have to be created by the catcher for this. He also needs to be able to come out to the mound to advise his pitcher and to help his frame of mind; he's as good as a pitching coach out there. He also will be expected to have strong words with the home plate umpire if he thinks the ump isn't calling strikes (is calling balls when the pitcher/catcher thinks they crossed the plate in the strike zone). These days he is also expected to bat well. The catcher is also expected to take a pounding. These days they have a large amount of protective gear on, but in days gone by when gloves weren't so thick and protective helmets were not so comprehensive in dimension, they used to get a lot of injuries and bumps. Teams normally have three or four catchers on a forty-man roster, two on a twenty-five. Some pitchers have their own specialist catcher, particularly knuckleball pitchers such as Tim Wakefield of the Red Sox, who is caught by second-string guy Doug Mirabelli.

Catch Up With It (Couldn't) – When a hitter can't swing the bat through fast enough to make contact on a fastball.

Caught Looking - When a batter is called out on strikes. He should have swung at that third!

Cellar – This is the US form what we know as being 'bottom of the table.'

Center Field - The geographical expression for the middle part of the outfield. The curvature of each ballpark perimeter makes center field the furthest part of the field from home plate, over 400 feet away. Thus it's the longest way for a hitter to go to get a homer. It's no wonder then that most batters try to pull the ball where the distance to the outfield wall or fence is much, much shorter.

Center Fielder - The center fielder is normally the fastest of the three outfielders and is normally considered to be the leader of the outfielders. His territory overlaps with the other two and they will are expected to defer to his seniority out there.

Ceremonial First Pitch - In most games a local or national luminary (politician, film or TV star, model, ex-player, rock singer) will come out and make a ceremonial pitch to a catcher from the mound, part of the almost sacred group of rituals that have accompanied baseball for a long time. From the President downwards, it's an honour widely accepted and gratefully received.

Challenging (the hitter) – This is code for a pitcher throwing a fastball. It emanates from the essential macho culture of the game, going way back, that a *real* pitcher throws fearsomely fast pitches and a *real* hitter can hit the fastball, proving that both are *men*. Oh, yes.

Championship Series - Second set of play off games in each league where the two victorious Division Series winners play off for the League Pennant over seven games for the honour of that and playing in the World Series.

Chances Accepted – Fairly obscure fielding statistic that measures an infielder's efficiency, expressed as a percentage. The perfect infielder catches every throw to force or put out every runner. Every major league infielder's CA figure is in the nineties.

Change Up - This is to baseball as slower ball is to cricket but in this case the art of bowling has been way, way behind the art of pitching. The idea is to deceive the batter by delivering the baseball more slowly from the hand without a reduction in arm speed visible to the batter. He thinks the pitch is going to come through the air as fast as the last ball but it doesn't, causing him to swing early and miss or mis-connect for a simple out on a grounder or bloop. In common parlance, the pitch is designed to 'throw off the hitter's timing.' The change up is a vital part of the pitcher's armoury and all pitchers use it except for a few fastball specialists. Also called a "slow ball." See '***Off Speed Pitch.***'

'Charges The Ball' - This is when a fielder runs in quickly towards the ball when fielding it rather than waiting for it to arrive. This is the way it should be done, cutting the time in getting the ball to the base for the force out.

Charley Horse - When a player gets a 'Charley Horse' he has painful leg cramps from severe muscle fatigue. The name comes from the Hall Of Fame pitcher from the nineteenth century, one Charles "Old Hoss" Radbourn. Seeing as in 1884 he pitched 72 games (winning 60), it's no wonder he went down with the affliction on enough occasions to bequeath baseball a name for this particular pain.

Since typing the above in the winter of 2004, I have read Dickson's encyclopedia which gives 6 alternative explanations of the term's origin, none of which is the above one.

Checked Swing – Often, in response to the change up particularly, the batter starts to make a swing then thinks better of it. If the bat is out in front of his body it is called a swing and a strike called by the home plate umpire. The fielders often have to appeal for what is called the 'checked swing.'

Cheese - Interesting, not to say intriguing term for a baseball huzzed at the catcher very fast indeed. See **'high cheese'** for a little more on this.

Chin Music - A series of high pitches near the face of the batter, used to unsettle or intimidate him.

Choke Up (on the bat) – As experienced wielders of a cricket bat will know, if you want to hit the ball high and hard, your best bet is to grip the handle with both hands at the top: the bat then makes a larger arc through the air and generates more bat speed in the process. The problem with the bigger swing is that you've more chance of moving your head, which causes you to take your eye of the ball, which considerably increases your chances of missing the ball or hitting it straight up in the air. If, on the other hand, you are a hitter who just wants to make good contact with the ball and reduce your chances of the swinging strike and the miscue, you should grip the bat further down the "handle" (strictly speaking the baseball bat has a "top of the bat" not a handle). The arc of your swing will be smaller, but you are now going to be much more in control of it, thus your chances of clean contact are much increased. Ty Cobb, still the holder of the highest career batting average of all time - .368 – swore by choking up on the bat. He loathed the big swing, thinking it cheap, vulgar and unintelligent. Instead he was content to be the best ***contact hitter*** of all his and all time.

Chopper - This is a batted ball that bounces within a metre or so of the batter's box into play.

Circle Change – Type of Change Up where the ball is gripped with the whole hand plus the first finger and thumb forming a circle on the side of the ball. Apparently. If anybody out there's tried it, let me know how it feels to throw it.

Clean Up – Classic term for a classic position in the batting line up: the man who hits the double, triple or home run to send home runners already on base (***the table setters***). As you'll know, to 'clean up' is to collect, in this case in runs batted in rather than money. The glamour position on the team, he traditionally bats in the fourth spot (in the line up) and will be the team's best slugger.

Clean Up Hitter. See immediately above. Present day clean up hitters: Manny Ramirez for the Red Sox, Jim Thome for the Phillies, Sosa for the Cubs and of course, Barry Bonds for the Giants.

Clearing Benches - There is a tradition in baseball of players brawling on the turf or at least, squaring up to each other. This never happens in terms of a rogue individual bursting out of the dug out to confront a pitcher, say, but involves the impressive spectacle of participating athletes, potential replacements and resting pitchers emerging en masse to make a macho stand against an offending enemy, thus emptying or 'clearing' the bench upon which the players sit watching the game (or chatting or spitting or whatever). This usually occurs when a pitcher appears to be deliberately trying to maim a hitter with a head-high fastball. Most likely to occur in a Red Sox-Yankee game at present.

Cleats - UK football fans call them 'studs,' though I believe that at one time this was in usage in posh footer circles.

Closer - Each team has at least one of these and needs one, for he can be one of the most important members of a baseball team. The theory surrounding the role of the closer is that this is the man who comes in to pitch when the team is one run (or more) ahead at the beginning of the ninth (and hopefully last) inning and is so powerful and accurate that the opposing batters find him impossible to score against. It's a beautiful theory and in Manny Rivera and Eric Gagne respectively, the Yankees and the Dodgers have a mighty weapon each at their disposal. Closers have, as their chief weapon, the fastball. Batters, now well warmed up and loose, are expected to struggle much more against speed that a pitcher of artistry, accuracy and guile. See **The Save**.

Clout - Home run.

Clubhouse - This word describes the physical area where the players change and prepare for games and clean up afterwards - what we'd call the changing rooms basically, plus recreation rooms and additional places like the manager's office and the room a lot of clubs have for watching videotapes of games past or actually in progress.

Clutch, The - Another unique expression we could do with appropriating in British circles. 'The clutch' situation is the US equivalent of a team being one-nil down in injury time, or describes a situation in which a goalkeeper faces a penalty at a critical time. 'The Clutch' is when a hitter needs to make a hit to level the score or win the game or a pitcher needs to strike a batter out: when the bases are loaded, for example.

Clutch Hit - So a clutch hit is one made in a clutch situation and, obviously, is so important that it has this little phrase all to itself. Some players who respond well at desperate or crucial times in games develop reputations as being "good in the clutch." This is disputed hotly by **Sabermetricians**.

Coaches - A ball club has a whole raft of coaches, some of whom actually stand on the field during play. Sitting beside the manager in the dug out will be the pitching coach. He is on hand to give running advice to the starting pitcher when the team is batting and to send signs to all the pitchers whist pitching if necessary. He is also expected to ready with advice or an opinion when the manager is considering the issue of bringing in some pitching relief. He will often be the guy who gets on the phone to the bullpen to tell a reliever or the closer to warm up and a little later, to get his ass on to the field to pitch. Not only that, he can come on to the field when he sees fit, with the say-so of the manager, naturally, to give some encouragement or some advice to the pitcher on the mound. So he always has to look spruce and well turned out. In fact, he has to wear the whole team uniform in the dug out because it's an old rule in baseball that no one is allowed onto the field of play without a uniform apart from the umpires. The dug out will contain the hitting coach too, to give batters running advice, as and when. The assistant coaches, both hitting and pitching, may well be in the dug out too, if there's room, though at least one pitching coach or assistant coach is required in the bullpen throughout the game to receive phone calls and supervise the warming up process for the relievers and closer.

On the field at all times are a first base coach and a third base coach. These stand adjacent to the bases (but in **foul territory**). The **First Base Coach** advises on whether a runner on first should advance to second, though in terms of stealing, the sign will be given by the manager from the dug out. **Third Base Coach** has the job of advising, not to say instructing, base runners at second and third in terms of when to run and when not. On a hit to the outfield, the third base coach has to advise on whether a runner from first or second should hold at third or carry on and try to make it home. Note that there is no second base coach. Not enough room out there, presumably. These coaches jobs used to be just sinecures for old pros and pals of the manager. This is in the process of dying out.

Comebacker – Ball hit by a batter straight back to the pitcher.

Command – This refers to a pitcher's control, his ability to throw the ball where he wants to. *"Hudson's command got worse as his outing went on."*

Commissioner of Baseball – The game's nominal Big Boss, with technically unlimited jurisdiction over the clubs. The power reality is somewhat different now compared to the first man in situ. one Kennesaw Mountain Landis, given jurisdiction over the game in 1920 after the Black Sox debacle. Present incumbent, Bud Selig, is seen in some quarters as a tool of the big gun franchise owners such as Steinbrenner of New York, but given his apparent, alleged role in the demise of the Expos and his desire to contract the majors of up to three clubs including his own, the Milwaukee Brewers (!!), he has proved himself to be capable of wielding a very big stick in the primary school playground himself. Is supposedly responsible for the introduction of the Wild Card system in 1995 and inter-league play in 1997.

Complete Game - This describes a pitcher who pitches in every inning of the game through to its completion. The more complete games he pitches, the better the pitcher as a starter only stays in the game if he's not getting hit. With the advance of the reliever in the game in the second half of the 20th century, the number of complete games has fallen drastically, almost completely. However, as late as the mid-seventies, the starter was completing around one third of his games. Now, even the best pitchers will rarely pitch a complete game: the manager has an army of relievers in the bullpen and will be thinking of saving his precious starter's arm.

Complete Game Shut Out - The *shut out* is where no runs are scored against the pitcher so one of these is where the pitcher not only completes the game, but also does not concede any runs. Very rare now.

Contact Hitter - This is a term which describes a perhaps unspectacular hitter, one not given to smashing home runs but who is excellent at getting bat on ball and therefore one who has a highly respectable (or better) on base percentage. Time for '*On- base percentage*,' perhaps?

Contraction - This refers to the belief of some administrators, including Commissioner Selig that the major leagues would benefit from a reduction in the number of franchises due to their supposed economic unsustainability. Since expansion began in 1961, however, there has been no contraction.

Control Pitcher - This kind of guy doesn't throw fast stuff, but wins games by a mix of pitches: change ups, curves and other types of breaking balls, and above all, is accurate: he *throws strikes.*

Cookie Cutter (Stadium) – This is a name for a dull circle of grey concrete masquerading as a ballpark. These monuments to faceless symmetry were built between the 60s and the 80s and were multi-purpose jobs, needing to host football games too. Hence seats were required all the way around the stadium. And if that was the case, the old ballpark stands ending at the end of the left and right foul lines, giving way to an open-ended stadium simply wouldn't do. The Philadelphia Phillies's old Veteran's Stadium was a prime example of the ugly breed (along with the Braves' Turner Field which still stands) and was razed in February 2004. Happily now wildly out of fashion.

Cooperstown - See '*Hall Of Fame.*'

Corked Bats – There was huge controversy early in June of the 2003 season when the Chicago Cubs' uber-star Sammy Sosa broke a bat during a game against Tampa Bay whilst at the plate. It rapidly transpired upon umpirical inspection that the centre of the bat had a tube of cork in it. The inserted material, being lighter than wood, makes the bat easier to swing fast through the air; in other words, Slammin' Sammy was found guilty of cheating and was temporarily suspended by the Commissioner. This was one of the events of 2003. Sammy, in a slump at the time, was assumed to have given himself some extra help in breaking out of it, though he protested vehemently that it was a mistake. In fairness to him, all his 76 other bats were impounded on the same night, inspected, and found to have been fashioned from solid wood. Some players keep corked bats for practice to show off their slugging skills to early attendees at the ballpark – or so they say. Others found in the past using corked bats include Albert Belle (suspended in 1994) and Wilton Guerrero (suspended in 1997). For Sosa, a permanent cloud of doubt has been cast on his achievements: he's the only guy with three 60-homer seasons in history, for instance.

Corner(s) - One of the meanings of the word 'corner' in baseball refers to the two vertical edges of the strike zone close to the batter - the 'inside corner' - and away from the batter - the 'outside corner.' Even the middle of each edge, half way up (or down) the zone, is the corner. The outside corner is also 'away.'

Count, The (Pitch) – If baseball consists of at bats, then in each at bat, the pitch count is crucial. You don't have to watch much baseball to realize that the pitcher v batter duel is one of careful and detailed strategy. The pitcher can afford to miss the strike zone 3 times and still have the batter there in front of him. Fourth time, it's a walk. The batter can, if he wants, watch ('take') two pitches that cross the strike zone, as he waits for a juice pitch to hit. Third time, it's Strike 3 and he's gone. During each at bat, the number of balls and strikes is counted, and is shown on the stadium scoreboard as it goes along (this has been the case for 100 years and more). During an at bat, there might be a "pitcher's count." This is when there are more strikes than balls. At 0-1 (strikes always shown second), the pitcher is already 'ahead.' Another strike and the batter is on the verge of being out. At this point the pitcher might waste a pitch, throwing one wide to see if the hitter will stupidly chase it. At 0-2, the batter pretty much has to swing at the next pitch. Ideally he wants to wait for a good pitch but now he can't. Conversely, a 2-0 count favours the batter and is known as a "hitter's count." He can now wait dead-eyed for something in the strike zone without chasing something, because now the pitcher has to throw a strike. Another ball and it's 3 and 0 and then he's one inaccurate pitch away from the batter getting on base. Even more so now, the pitcher has to come in and pitch in the zone. Thus the hitter is now at a greater advantage, as he knows at least roughly where the next pitch is likely to be aimed. Doesn't mean he's going to hit it though.

Cracker Jacks - Ballpark snack of the ages. Over to my close associate Josh Alexander, resident of Boston, Ma. "Aahhh, Crackerjacks. Such memories. Haven't seen a box in 30 yrs I bet. Highly overrated as a snack. It's a mix of peanuts and popcorn all coated in a caramel sugar sauce substance that hardens and congeals the whole mix together into nibble sized bits. Its big selling point was that every box contained a 'prize,' also highly overrated." My last time in America, I felt I had to check out this phenomenon for myself, so, overlooking the bags which at Fenway Park costs an innocent punter about four and a half dollars, ventured out to a nearby gas station after the game where I bought the same sized bag for 99c. Verdict? They're okay, but no big deal. See, '*Take Me Out To The Ball Game.*'

Crowding The Plate - This is a term that describes a hitter positioning himself in the batter's box rather close to the plate (new fans may need to note that a hitter needs to stand a little distance away from home plate to be able to make a good full swing at a pitch). There is an issue of ownership here, disputed by pitcher and hitter. Some hitters like to stand at a comfortable distance from the plate, but others like to crowd it. A lot of pitchers don't like the latter because it interrupts their view of the strike zone and the catcher and thus disturbs their concentration. There may be a little macho thing going on too – or may have been in times gone past. A batter standing close to the plate might not only be able to reach the "away" pitch more easily, but is carrying out an act of bravado, invading the pitcher's territory. If a batter crowds the plate, he obviously has no fear, because he's asking to get hit. Fifty years ago and back from there, throwing at batters was common and they got away with it; these days '**brushing back the hitter**' by pitching at him is much more likely to get the pitcher thrown out of the game. Today, the forces seem to be equally balanced. Not many men crowd the plate because, I would guess, millionaires don't like getting hurt.

Crushes It! - A batter who 'crushes' the ball makes great contact, hits it hard, most likely for a homer.

Cup Of Coffee – This is a phrase to describe a minor leagues player who comes up to the majors for just a few games before being sent back down. He didn't get the full meal......

Curtain Call – When a batter hits a home run, he may well come back out from the dugout to salute the crowd if the hit is getting a particularly rousing ovation. This is a curtain call. The batter will take off his helmet or cap (if he's already got it back on) and salute the crowd from the top of the dugout steps or a pace or two towards the infield grass. Ted Williams, who basically had a hate-hate-sort of love relationship with the Boston crowd, refused after he got booed early in his career at Fenway Park never to come out for a curtain call. In his final game at Fenway, at his last ever at bat as a ballplayer, guess what: yep, he hit a home run. The crowd wasn't very big, but it went nuts, and applauded so long it was begging Ol' Teddy Ballgame to come out and give the time-honoured salute. And did he let sentiment get the better of him on this occasion? (the Boston Red Sox was his only club, remember, and he played for them for 22 seasons)? No, he didn't.

Curve Ball – The traditional, indeed historical alternative pitch to the fastball. It is a gruesome pitch from the batter's perspective it is night on impossible to hit. It comes in much more slowly than the fastball yet is thrown with similar arm speed, so it is effectively a change up too. To make the pitch, overspin is imparted on the ball with a so-called 'snap' of the wrist – hence the term to 'snap' the curve. It's still very much used in the modern game and has a number of synonyms such as 'Uncle Charlie.' Candy Cummins is reckoned to have invented the pitch in 1863-4 and owes his place in the Hall of Fame to it. To throw the pitch your fingers and wrist have to pull down hard on the ball clockwise (for a right-hander) – the wrist has to be cocked. This imparts the overspin that causes the ball to drop. Excuse me while I go out to the park with my kid to see if I can do it...

Cut ('He takes a big cut at that and misses') - A neat term for a swing at the ball by a batter. After a back injury in 2004 spring training, Barry Bonds was said to be back 'taking some cuts in the batting cage yesterday.

Cut Fast Ball - This is a fastball with some late movement away from the right-handed batter because the pitcher uses a *cutter* grip. Looks very similar to a slider, curving away from the r-h batter.

Cut Off Man - See immediately below.

Cut Off Throw - The distance from home plate to the most distant part of the outfield in center being usually well in excess of 130 yards, and with specialist hitters not necessarily having great arms, some help is often required to get the ball to a particular base to make an out or prevent a runner attempting to get to the next base. The ball hurled from deep then is often intercepted and relayed to its intended destination by another fielder. This first throw is always termed the 'cut off throw.' The fielder making the interception and second throw is known as the 'cut off man.'

Cutter – Short for '**Cut Fast Ball**,' a hard pitch that breaks into the left-handed batter from the right-handed pitcher. This is Mariano Rivera's bread and butter pitch. .

Cycle, The - The cycle is a batting achievement in a single game of baseball. They player 'hits for the cycle' by hitting a single, a double, a triple and a home run all in the same game. First player to hit for the cycle was Curry Foley in the National League for Buffalo in 1882. A measure of the difficulty of achieving this feat can be appreciated by the fact that the first player to break the American League's duck was nineteen years later when Harry Davis did it for the Phillies.

Cy Young – (n) The Cy Young award, the premier annual award for pitchers. It's exceptionally prestigious, given to one pitcher from each league each year. Named after Cy Young, the best pitcher from his era (with Cleveland, the Cards and both Boston teams) the 1890-1911, who won 511 games with an ERA of 2.63, setting the standard for all who have followed in his wake.

D

Day To Day - A player is not fit or unfit, he is either 'healthy,' 'on the **DL**' or 'Day To Day.' If he's on the DL he's on the disabled list it means that the player has an injury that will keep him out for quite a spell and another player can be brought on to the roster in his place until he is fit again. This is very significant, however, because going on the DL means a mandatory absence of 15 days. Therefore, once on it, he can't go back on the roster for two weeks plus one. The rules are a little more flexible than this might sound, as a player deemed sufficiently unfit to be put on the DL, can have the 15 day absence back-dated to the day when the injury occurred. If he's day to day it means the injury is minor and that he might be back in any time. In this situation a player is not brought in from the minor leagues in his place on the roster.

Dead Ball Era – In short, the period in baseball from 1901-1920, when the ball was softer than it is now, so it wouldn't travel far when hit; it was "dead." At the time, pitchers were also able to scuff, spit on and smear the ball with any kind of crap they could lay their hands on: dirt; tobacco juice; Vaseline; an emery board; making it fly all over the place. Plus, it was dirty so the batters could hardly see it, especially in the latter part of afternoons at either end of the season. So, runs in this period were scarce. The game could in a sense be described as 'dead' in another sense. Except that baseball writers, considering themselves as purists, fell in love with the "pitching duel," the battle between the pitchers for supremacy in a game. They gave us the image of the sporting duelists, men of supreme nobility and craft battling out full nine innings of athletic chess. The fate of each game lay in their hands. Personally, I think this was the only way they could make the game sound interesting to readers or to actually enjoy the game in real time. I mean, here's a game, played with bat and ball, and the bat hardly saw any real action: 1-0 games were extremely common. How interesting is that to watch? I'm either a philistine Brit who knows nothing or absolutely correct. Whatever, in 1920, it all came to an end. (See '*Lively Ball Era*')

Dead-Red – A fairly rare term (I heard it for the first time used by Josh Chetwynd on Baseball On 5 (21/6/04) over a replay of a Shawn Green home run). "Dead-red" describes a fastball. Dickson tells us that to "sit dead-red" is to wait for a fastball. "Dead red" also implies the fastball arriving over the plate, but not derogatively.

Decision – Each ball game has a winning and a losing pitcher. "The decision" is simply the question of who gets the win and who the loss. It used to be easy when starting pitchers went the distance, but it's complicated sometimes now because of all the relievers who come into the game. Sometimes a manager will use as many as seven. If a pitcher is taken out in the eighth inning with the team ahead 2-1, he will get the decision if the team goes on to win, even if the final score is 9-1. If he leaves at 2-1 but the team goes on to lose, then self-evidently, he doesn't get the win because there isn't one (this explanation is simplified for those who may be reading this with flu or with too much alcohol in their system). But he doesn't get the loss. The guy pitching when the lead was lost is stuck with the loss. If the starter leaves at 2-2 or 1-2 and the team goes on to win, then it is the reliever who is pitching when the team gets the go-ahead run who is awarded the win. Similarly, in the case of a loss, the pitcher pitching when the go-behind run is conceded is the guy who picks up the loss. Just to complicate things a little more: if a reliever ends the eighth inning for the home team with the score at 4-4, but is replaced for the ninth and gets taken out of the game. However, the starter has to go five innings before he can claim the win. (See also '*No Decision*.')

Deep - The back third, roughly, of the outfield.

Deep In The Count – 2-2 or 3-2 is deep in the pitcher's count of strikes and balls.

Defensive Swing – The eye of the major league hitter is so good that it's reckoned that he has time to adjust his reaction to a 90 mph pitch. He's always looking for a good pitch to hit, something out over the plate and not too quick. Especially with two strikes on him, he's looking to avoid being struck out and may just make sure that he gets some bat on a difficult pitch to foul it off and stay alive. This is a defensive swing.

Deliberate Walks - The deliberate walk is a strategy used by the pitching side to avoid a top class hitter making a hit or a home run. It's also used to try to get two outs on one pitch, the **double play** (you can only work a double play if there is a man on first). To execute this, the pitcher lobs four consecutive balls to a catcher who stands well wide of the batter at home plate. The batter cannot leave the batter's box so the spectacle of the batter leaping wide waggling a bat frantically at the ball is unknown. To be 'walked' is both a compliment to the skill of the batter (unless the man behind you is a batter in the most wretched form or the pitcher - See **National League** or **Designated Hitter**) and an annoyance.

"Dem Bums" – Slang term for the Brooklyn Dodgers, especially in their losing years before Robinson, Snider et al. Means, "those idiots" out there on the field and at the plate, 'dem' being the local vernacular for 'them' and 'bums' being local v. for useless prat. The settlement of Brooklyn, immediately across the East River to the east of the southern tip of Manhattan Island, increasingly became a working class community as the 20th century progressed.

Designated Hitter or 'DH' - This is a place in the batting line up only for teams in the American League. Whereas in the National League each team's pitcher is one of the batting line up of nine whether he's useless or not, the ninth place in the AL is taken by a 'designated hitter' whose sole job is to bat: he doesn't field. This adds hitting power to all the AL clubs and you will find that as a fairly obvious result, there are more hits, homers and runs scored in the AL each season. The NL pitching records are a fraction better than the AL for this reason also. The 'DH,' as it is often abbreviated, is a modern phenomenon, being experimentally introduced in 1973. It stuck in the AL, but hasn't caught on in the National League and probably never will, the leagues enjoying their independence.

Deuce - A Curveball. There's a great scene in Bull Durham where Tim Robbins's Nuke Lalooshe wants to throw one when catcher Crash Davis (Kevin Costner) calls for a fastball. But Nuke doesn't call it a curveball: keeps calling it a d'uce. He shakes off his catcher and the pitch gets mashed.

Diamond, The - The mystical diamond, the beautiful shape made by the joining together the four bases, ninety feet apart, in your imagination or by using the actual lines made by the base paths. It's actually a square stood on one of its four ends, but it is still 'the diamond' in all baseball circles. The whole field, in and out, is sometimes referred to as the diamond, oddly, as the whole thing is fan shaped.

Digging In – The sight of a hitter making the scraping sound with his feet at the plate to get himself set to deal with the pitcher is "digging in" and it's traditionally a red rag to the hurler's bull. Tradition has it that the fellow on the mound will be a flinging fastballs and the batter should not, under any circumstances, do anything that suggests that he's comfortable at the plate. So the sight of a batter "digging in" used to lead directly to the next pitch being aimed somewhere around his ears.

Dinger - Home run.

Disabled List ('The DL') – See **'Day to Day.'**

Dish - Home plate.

Dope – The 'dope' means information, especially when referring to opposition players or the team as a whole. Old-fashioned usage, one would say these days. **Dope Sheets** are pages of information about opposition players (and team collectively, perhaps), detailing their strengths and weaknesses. These days, whole dossiers are compiled by managers and coaches on the 'oppo,' including each batter's/hitter's record against each pitcher/hitter on the enemy team. Many players keep their own notebooks on hitters and pitchers they're likely to face.

Double - A hit that takes a batter around first base and successfully into second is a 'double.'

Double 'A' (AA) - Second most prestigious minor league, one below triple A. All AA teams are fully professional.

Doubles 1 - If a batter "doubles home a run" it means he hits a double, which enables a base runner to score a run.

Doubles 2 – As in "doubles him off the bag for the third out." The word 'double' as a verb connects to the noun that is the 'double play.' If a fielder "doubles" the runner, it means that this out forms the second part of this play that removes two guys on one pitch. 'Off the bag' means that the runner hadn't left the base he started at.

Double Header - This describes two games played between two teams on the same day. In days gone by the second would start almost as soon as the first was over and even now some will say that this is the only real double header and the ones these days with a few hours gap between the bottom of the first ninth and the second top of the first don't count. Floodlit games have made this pause possible. Doubleheaders are much less frequent in the modern age than once was the case when Sunday was the traditional day for the doubleheader. See **'Matinee'** and **'Night-cap.'**

Double Play - This is a beautiful occurrence for the pitching side, often disastrous for the batting side, as it describes a play where two base runners are forced out on one pitch. This normally occurs when a batter hits a grounder straight to an infielder (very often the shortstop to whom the pitch is pulled, by a right-handed batter). If no one is on first base, one out will usually be the result (the batter on a fruitless chase to first base). However, if there is a man on first, he now has to run towards second base, where the shortstop will have thrown to the second baseman already, it being a short distance, for out number one. The second baseman then throws hard and flat to first base before the batter can arrive there for the second out. If this occurs when a batting side has one out, the inning will suddenly and dramatically therefore be over in a matter of about two seconds. A team 'turns' a double play, rather than makes a double play. Very common is the phrase, "turn it over," as in "the guys turned it over nicely there" ('it' being the double play). See also '***Turn it over***' for a second meaning.

Double Steal – This is where two runners on base steal the next base simultaneously. This is an unusual play now, but was very common in the late 19th and the first half of the 20th centuries.

Double Switch – This describes a player substitution where a pitcher and a fielder are replaced at the same time, enabling the new fielder to bat in front of the pitcher in the batting order.

Down And In(side) - This describes a ball, which is both too low and too close to the batter to be a strike.

Down Low (For A Ball) - Means that the pitch wasn't high enough to be in the strike zone.

Down The Middle - Means what it says on the tin. It's always, but always a ***mistake*** when the pitcher delivers a ball to the middle of the plate. 'Down the middle' also implies a nice height for the batter too, level with the stomach or 'belt high.'

Down The Stretch - The last, crucial games of the season. The stretch can consist of say, thirty, though, so the stretch can be....stretched to whatever size the talker wants it, within reason.

Down The Pipe - Means exactly the same as down the middle.

Downtowner – Home run.

Down 2 and 0/Down 0 and 2 – Both a pitcher and a batter can be 'down' in terms of the pitch count. It's the same as being 'behind.' See "**The Count (Pitch)**"

Draft System – Every June, the major league organizations pick up several hundred college and high school baseball wannabes in an organized way. Linked together by phone to the Commissioner of Baseball's office, they each take their turn over many rounds to take their picks. The team with the worst playing record from the previous season gets to go first, as is now traditional in North American sports, the second worst second, and so on, until they get to the New York Yankees. The system is complicated somewhat by the rule whereby a team losing a free agent gets a compensation draft pick from the club he goes to. For a superb and vivid picture of the system, go to Chapter 5 of Michael Lewis's *Moneyball*.

Drag Bunt – This is a term for a bunt laid down along the first base line while setting off for first base, so that the horizontal bat is almost behind the hitter when contact with the ball is made. A genuine attempt is being made here to get to first base.

Draws A Walk – The hitter doesn't 'get' or 'make' a walk, he 'draws' it from the pitcher.

Drills The Ball – Hits it very hard.

Drive- Batters are often described as 'driving' the ball or 'driving a home run.' The term 'drive' describes a hitter making good contact on the ball with a full swing.

Drives Him In – ...hence we'll often hear broadcasters using the term as a verb to describe a hit enabling a base runner to come in to score a run. From this we also have to 'drive in a run.'

Dropped (a doubleheader) - Team losing both games of a doubleheader.

Duck Snort – A looping (I should probably say 'blooping') mis-hit that drops over the heads of the frantic infielders but short of the flailing outfielders.

Dugout - Where the players sit when not out there on the field. It has to be covered with a roof according to the rules and it's covered in all kinds of crap by about the sixth inning.

Duster – A ball aimed at a batsman by a pitcher with the intention of intimidating or hurting.

Dying Quail Shot - This describes a poorly hit ball by the batter, where he just about manages to get enough bat on it to make it loop pathetically in the air before falling to earth (lucky) or being caught by a fielder.

E

Earned Run – Runs debited to the pitcher's good reputation have to be earned. This term is nice and contradictory. An earned run counts against him because, theoretically, he conceded the hit that got the hitter on base, whether it was a lucky bloop hit off a beautiful pitch or a home run shot off a belt high fastball. Hence in box scores you'll see "ER" in a pitcher's *line* in a box score. It's only these, which make up a pitcher's ERA. See ***Unearned Run***.

Eephus Pitch - Slang for a high, slow lob of a pitch. It was developed by Rip Sewell in the 40s. Ted Williams is the only major leaguer to have hit a homer from an Eephus Pitch and did so memorably in the 1946 All Star Game at Fenway Park. He came at a run out of the batter's box towards the ball before whacking it out. It's died out of course and unfortunately so, variety being the source of practically endless entertainment for you, the spectator.

Eight Pitches – This is the number of pitches a relief pitcher is allowed to throw to the catcher when he comes to the mound, and the number a pitcher is allowed to throw before the start of an inning. The throwing of these must not exceed a minute.

Emery Ball – This is a baseball that has been tampered with, in this case had its surface roughed up with a nail-filing emery board. The roughness will give the ball much more movement through the air. Even fairly recently, players have occasionally been found to have or been suspected of having an emery board sewn into his mitt, his belt or the peak of his cap.

ERA (Earned Run Average) – All pitchers are measured by their ERA (though closers more by the number of blown saves). This is the number of runs they concede or 'give up' per nine innings. It is also the standard by which pitchers are compared with each other and ultimately valued in the context of the game's history. You might expect an 'average number of hits given up per game or inning' statistic to be used as well as the ERA but you won't see it. Neither is an 'average hits per batter faced' stat used which might tell us much about the effectiveness of a pitcher. So, on the TV screen when a pitcher's record is displayed, you'll always see his running ERA for the season alongside his win-loss record, the second of the two big measurements of his prowess (supposedly).

For a starting pitcher, a stat of three point something is today considered acceptable, whilst four-plus begins to run towards mediocrity. An ERA of more than five and he's a liability or a guy having a bad season. The best starting pitchers may have an ERA of more than two but less than two. At the time of writing here in the early-mid 2004 season, Al Leiter has the best ERA in either league with 2.52. Seven other pitchers have an ERA of less than three. Relievers, guys who now only go for an inning late in the game, little more, need an ERA below of between two and three to be judged totally successful. Excellent closers will be looking at an ERA of between one and two.

In the American League, only twice since the Second World War has the pitcher with the lowest ERA for the year gone above three (most recently Freddy Garcia of the Mariners with 3.05 in 2002 - the other was Early Winn in 1950 with Cleveland). Ten times since the war the winner of the accolade has had an ERA below two, only three times in the last 31. Generally, the emphasis in modern times is on the big hit and to support that change in tactical emphasis, hitters are doing more work on their upper body strength and are fitter and more prepared than ever before. In the National League where the hitting strength of the opposing line up is diluted by the pitcher having to hit, ERA figures are lower. No one since 1961 (Warren Spahn of Milwaukee) has the leading ERA man gone over the three mark.

The best ERA record last season is owned by Jake Peavy of the Padres with 2.27, some way above Bob Gibson's record 1.12 in 1968. (2003 leader was Pedro Martinez with 2.22)

Error - Unlike any other sport, errors are charged to fielders in baseball. A running log of these is kept, they are logged on scorecards and in newspaper box scores and totals for seasons and careers appear in books of baseball records. Because hitters getting on base don't count against the pitcher in his stats (and because stats are everything in this game), marginal calls by the official scorer are crucial.

Expanding the zone - Term referring to a pitcher throwing some of his pitches wide to the outside corner of the plate hoping the hitter is going to be tempted into an injudicious swing. If the pitcher can continually make the hitter feel he has to swing at these marginal pitches, it has the effect of making the strike zone bigger for him. Conversely, the patient hitter who swings the bat only at strikes (balls passing directly through the official strike zone) will have the effect of shrinking the zone.

Expansion Team - Any team that has joined the major leagues since the 16 major league franchises were increased since 1961 can be (and is often) described as an expansion team. The complete list is as follows: Houston Astros (1961); Los Angeles Angels (1961); New York Mets (1962); Kansas City Royals (1969); San Diego Padres (1969); Seattle Pilots (1969) who after one season became the Brewers in Milwaukee the following season; Texas Rangers (1972); Toronto Blue Jays (1977), Montreal Expos (1977); Seattle Mariners (1977), Florida Marlins (1993); Colorado Rockies (1993); Arizona Diamondbacks (1998) and the Tampa Bay Devil Rays (1998).

Extra Base Hit - This is a hit that enables a runner to reach second, third or home base (via a home run); any hit that's more than a single.

Extra Bases - Thus, a hit for 'extra bases' is any hit beyond first base.

Extra Innings - The word 'draw' is unknown in American sport. In football, hockey and baseball there isn't even the word the Americans use for the same thing, the 'tie' (though there is now in the North American Soccer League, though as all footer fans of a certain age know, isn't how it used to be). In football and hockey there is 'overtime' until one team scores an extra goal or points. In baseball there are extra innings, which are played until after a completed inning, one team has scored one more run than their opponents. So the game goes on indefinitely, even unto one in the morning or whatever (G5 of the ALCS '04 ended at 1.25am). Until the advent of electric light in the 1930s, however, ties were known and were caused simply by failing light. Games were played in the late afternoons so a crowd could show up.

Eyes – A ground ball "with eyes" is a ball that skates along the floor and somehow makes it through for a single even though it doesn't look as though it will, through not being hit properly. It seems to have eyes, enabling it to avoid the fielders' despairing attempts to grab it.

F

Fadeaway Pitch – Invented by maestro Walter Johnson. It became known as a screwball. The pitch moves or 'fades' away from the batter, the opposite direction to the natural lateral curve, which is thrown with a clockwise (if a right-hander) twist of the fingers and wrist. The twisting of the arm in an anti-clockwise direction that is demanded – hence the term 'screwball,' the arm is twisting like a screw, is damaging to the arm if overused. Johnson used it sparingly for this reason.

Fake Bunt - This is where the batter chokes up on the bat, showing bunt, but swings just as the pitcher is about to release, thus trying to fool the infield. Also known as a **'slug bunt.'**

Fair Ball - Once a ball is struck by the batter it's either a fair ball or a foul ball. The ball is in play, a fair ball, if it travels and lands inside the foul lines that extend from home plate at an angle of 90 degrees in a dead straight line through first and third bases to the perimeter of the field. A batted ball that travels through the line of one of the bases is fair. See *foul ball*.

Fair Territory – The fair ball lands in fair territory.

Fall Classic, The - A much used generic term for the World Series.

Fan - When a hitter is "fanned," he's struck out, especially by a fastball.

Fan Interference 1 - The 2003 NL Championship Series saw a spectacular row over a 'was it-wasn't it?' fan interference incident. It occurred during Game 7 of the titanic Cubs-Marlins struggle at Wrigley Field, Chicago when, a mere five outs away from World Series glory in the eighth inning – their first since 1945 - and leading to boot, a foul fly was knocked high into the air slightly behind the third base foul line. Cubs' left fielder Moises Alou raced in and with the ball about to drop into the overhanging fans, was apparently thwarted by one of them, Steve Bartman by name, who clawed at the ball before it dropped into the waiting glove. This issue of whether the catch would have been made is moot. Point is, the fan had beer and other sources of refreshment thrown at him and buffeted by jeers, had to be escorted from the park by a couple of Chicago's finest. The poor guy couldn't leave his house for days. You may remember the excellent exchange between Gould and Lengel on the programme, with the latter adamant on one issue at least: that he should accept the offer from the victorious Marlins of a free ball game vacation in Miami. An unfortunate incident produced one of the televisual highlights of the season.

"I am so truly sorry from the bottom of this Cubs fan's broken heart," Bartman said later in his apology to Cubworld. Some are still waiting for an apology from the other half dozen or so fans who also made a grab for the considerable prize of a Game 7, eighth inning NLCS Cubs On The Way To Glory souvenir baseball, but failed.

Fan Interference 2 - At the time of the Bartman incident, the name of Jeffrey Maier reared into prominence again. This is because in October 1996 the 12-year-old schoolboy Jeffrey may also have interfered with the manifest destiny of the sport. Derek Jeter's deep hit to right field in Yankee Stadium was about to thud into the padding at the top of the wall above the glove of the Orioles' Tony Tarasco and back into play, when the youngster, there at the game armed with mitt, snaffled the ball. Whilst the rules could have seen Jeter called out under the rule covering fan interference, the umpire mistakenly ruled the play a homer. The run was crucial: bottom of the eighth, Yankees 5-4 down. The game went to extra innings. The Orioles lost. And the game happened to be an AL Championship Series play off. It was only Game 1, but even so. If that wasn't enough to secure Jeffrey's place in history, a frantic media follow up ensured it. Talk shows and journalists virtually ate each other to get their hands on this new Yankee hero.

All very interesting, but it begs questions to the sober minded about the lack of security at games: so fans are *allowed* to reach over the top of the wall with the opportunity to rob teams of home runs, or in this case, trip an umpire up into handing one over? Technically it isn't allowed, but the failure of clubs to ban fans for this misdemeanor means that in many parks, ground balls hit near low fences are too often are snaffled by selfish idiots who think that their quest for a souvenir is more important the mere game.

Farm Team - A minor league team that's used by a major league ball club to nurture and develop talented youngsters who may one day make it to the big leagues. The team will not have the same name as the team in the major leagues, playing single, double and triple 'A' ball. The first farm system was set up by the 1930s owner of the St Louis Cardinals, Branch Rickey (an exec- Hall of Famer, in fact).

Fastball – The traditional chief weapon of the baseball pitcher. Orthodoxy demands every pitcher to have one and use it as the basis of his armoury: there is still a strong element of macho culture in baseball. As may be obvious, this is the pitch that is thrown mostly to beat the hitter through sheer velocity, though the greats all have movement 'on' it also, at least some of the time. There are several types of fastball. See '*Split-fingered Fastball,*' '*Two-Seam and Four-Seam Fastball.*'

Fastball Hitters – Since the dawn of professional baseball, some hitters actually like the fastball, even one with velocity in the 90 mph range and more. Why? It travels in the opposite direction faster and if you have no fear up at the plate, you may make score very heavily and spectacularly from it. Obviously these guys have fantastic eyes - they pick up the pitch a fraction of a second earlier than lesser mortals - and wonderful hand-eye co-ordination (in other words, you wouldn't catch a coward like me getting anywhere near one).

Fielder's Choice- When an infielder collects a batted ball and has a choice of runner to throw out - imagine a ball hit to the second baseman who can throw out a runner advancing from first to second or the batter trying to make it to first – the out he makes (assuming he does, because he should) is described and scored officially as a "fielder's choice." An offensive player can be out on a fielder's choice or make it to first base on a fielder's choice. If a batter makes it to first base on a fielder's choice – the infielder choosing to throw out the guy most advanced around the bases, as is the norm - he is not credited with a hit because without the base runner he would not have made it to first base safely. See *Hit, Scoring a.*

Fielding Average - With leaders for seasons recording 100 per cent records, it could be that this is the baseball statistician's answer to men in fawn jackets keeping records of coach numbers in Blackpool car parks, but it could be something is missing in me. The thing is if you want to know whether the best career average for failure to make a mistake is higher in the first baseman category than the third baseman, it's all there for you. The stat is calculated by dividing his total number of completed *put outs* and assists by his total number of chances to make put outs and assists (or putouts, assists and errors)

Fielding Positions - The fielders have numbers unofficially, for scoring purposes. They are as follows: 1. Pitcher. 2. Catcher. 3. First Baseman 4. Second Baseman 5. Third Baseman 6. Short Stop 7. Left Fielder 8. Center Fielder. 9. Right fielder.

These are most used for communicating easily how a double play was executed. See '*6-4-3 Double Play.*'

Field Lights –AKA floodlights in this country (also lights along grandstand roofs).

Fights It Off - If a pitcher is pushing for that third strike, the batter now in danger of imminent demise, as it were, the latter may well be desperate just to get some part of the bat on the ball while he waits, perhaps in vain, for a good pitch to hit. When he does so, expect the sportscaster to use this expression just after a ball hurtles towards the spectators behind the third base line. Good job spectators are so mad keen on collecting foul balls as souvenirs, otherwise spectator injuries would be more common, no doubt.

Field Manager – Manager of the team as it actually plays the game. Used to distinguish this role from the administrational management of the ball club.

Finesse Pitcher - This is a term used to describe a pitcher who relies on variety of pitch and pitches with a lot of movement on the ball rather than pure speed. His fastball might not be in excess of 85mph (in other words, not that fast). Through the history of baseball, it is much harder for the finesse pitcher to be highly successful than those with a lightning fastball.

Fireballer – Old alternative for a predominantly fastball pitcher.

Fireman – Your fireman comes out of the bullpen to snuff out danger: when there are men in scoring position on the bases. Your fireman throws hard; hence this has a double layer of meaning.

First Base - The first base is ninety feet away from the batter's box and is where or what the batter must try to reach upon putting the baseball in play before a throw arrives there from a fielder.

First Base Coach – See **Coaches**.

First Base Line - Line of white 'paint' that extends at ninety degrees to the third base line towards the perimeter fence, dividing fair territory from foul. Down this line is a handy place to hit the ball past or over the first baseman. The right outfielder may have some work to do to run and gather the ball, enabling a runner on first to easily make it to third. A runner in scoring position on second may well get home from such a hit too. At the end of the line is a *foul pole*.

First Baseman – Infielder stationed at or very close to first base. Most put outs are made here, so the first baseman needs to be close to the bag. With no throwing to do, the man with the weakest arm may be put here or the slowest runner. This job is one of catching and being able to stretch your body to catch the ball keeping one foot on the bag (if your foot lifts off the bag even one centimetre, the put out is lost). Your nearest thing to a duffer is put here as there is little athletic to do here. However, the ideal is to have an athletic guy here who is supple and can catch the inaccurate throws that will come in from time to time (or regularly if you're the Red Sox first baseman). He will receive far more throws than any other infielder too, so the position is very important.

First Base Umpire – Stands a short way behind the bag at first to make in/out calls, punching the air in front of him to signal 'out' or spreading both arms wide for 'in.'

First Division – When the two big leagues began in tandem in 1901, there were eight clubs in each. The top four in each at the end of the season were said to be the 'First Division' and the bottom four the **'Second Division.'** Not used now that divisions consist only of four, five or six clubs.

First Of The Seventh - The first half of the complete inning which consists of both teams taking at bats until they make three outs.

Five Hundred. (.500) (Teams). Teams are measured most often in terms of performance not in terms of how many games they have won but by what their winning percentage is. Reference to the equilibrium five hundred is most common. "The Yankees are thirty games over five hundred again!" for example. Five hundred, or more properly .500, is considered to be the starting point of a decent record on the season, but normally, a team with a record of around .500 most seasons, will be out of contention.

Flag - Alternative for a 'pennant', and used in baseball lit. to denote a team vying for or winning the National or the American League before the play offs began in 1969, or one of the divisions thereafter. The term derives for the fact that teams who won the league weren't given trophies, they were given pennants or flags to fly proudly from flagpoles at their stadiums stating their achievement and year.

Flagged Down – This refers to a fly ball being caught in the outfield, as in "Jones flagged down two fly balls in the seventh inning."

Flare – Same as a blooper: a short mis-hit that loops into the air over the infield and lands on the turf in front of the in-rushing outfielders.

'Flashed Some Leather (on that play)' - An excellent piece of fielding is known as 'flashing some leather.'

Flies Out - When you hit the ball in the air, sometimes cleanly, sometimes not, but you're caught, you've 'flied out.'

Flies out to left - Describes the geography of the out – in this case to left field. Could be 'to shallow right' or 'deep center,' etc.

Fluttering - The knuckleball pitch, the one where the ball does not rotate in flight, often appears to wobble from side to side in flight, or 'flutter.' Common usage.

Fly Ball - This describes any ball hit into the air but with distance, as opposed to the pop up which goes more or less straight up in the air.

Forkball - Type of split-fingered fastball that has a little less speed and tends to drop as it arrives at the plate. So-called because the first and middle fingers are spread to make a 'V' or fork shape on top of the ball. This ball was in its heyday in the 60s, before being more or less superceded by the *splitter* (split-fingered fast ball which does the same thing to the ball). It was invented, or at least, first put into effective usage by relief pitcher Elroy Face around 1959 and, now reinvented, so dramatic was the effect of the pitch, went 18-1 with it that year.

Force Out - A 'force out' is made by the fielding side when they throw out or tag a runner.

Force Play - This describes the act of forcing out a runner by the fielders.

Forfeited Game – If a game is forfeited to another team, because of chronic player indiscipline or whatever, a score of 9-0 is recorded. One run per inning, I suppose.

Forty Game Season. This has been done once since 1901, by the New York Yankee's Jack Chesbro in 1907. You can imagine, if you're already aware of how good a pitcher is if he wins twenty games in a season, how good a forty game pitcher is. Although Jack is in the Hall Of Fame, games were shorter a hundred years ago, so pitchers made fewer pitches and didn't wear out their arms because they more easily dominated batters. So they were able to pitch much more often. Starting pitchers these days don't pitch forty times a season, never mind win forty times.

Forty Steals and Forty Home Runs/40-40 Club - Only thrice has this feat been achieved in baseball history, first by Jose Canseco of the Oakland As in 1988 before being emulated by Barry Bonds of the Giants in 1996. Alex Rodriguez, then with Seattle sped and hit into this exclusive club two years later. Its rarity is down to the fact that not many hitters are good enough to hit forty homers in the first place. Still less is a champion slugger expected to execute one of the arts of small ball at the same time. Another mention for Bonds: in 1990 he made fifty steals and twenty homers (52-23).

Foul – A ball hit 'foul' is one that lands in '*foul territory.*' A hitter is out if he hits a ball into foul territory which is caught.

Foul Ball – A foul ball is a pitch hit into foul territory. A pitch hit into the foot, leg or body is also a foul ball, even if it rolls into fair territory.

'Fouled Back' - 'Fouls that back' says the commentator very often when a takes a cut at the ball sending it flying off the 'edge' of the bat behind him.

Foul Pole - At the point where both the first and third base lines meet the perimeter of the field is a foul pole. This is simply to determine whether a struck ball is in fair or foul territory. The rule is that if it hits the pole, no matter which side of the pole it thence drops, is deemed fair, it being considered to have crossed the perimeter boundary touching some part of the line. Most famous foul pole is at Boston's Fenway Park where there stands Pesky's Pole, named after Johnny Pesky who actually didn't hit many home runs near the first base line foul pole.

Foul Line - Term for either the first or third base line.

Foul Out – A foul out is an out made when a batter pops a batted ball up into the air which would fall into foul territory were it not caught by a fielder.

Foul Pop Fly - A struck baseball which flies or loops into the air behind either base line is one of these. See *'Pop Up.'* A 'Foul Pop Up' is virtually the same as above only the ball doesn't lift so high in the air.

'Fouls That Off' – Same as 'fights that off' from earlier.

Foul Territory - Only when a pitch is hit in play, in fair territory, can bases be reached and runs scored. However, foul territory is important as a batter can be caught out there (Note. If there is a 'throw out' and a 'force out' why is there not a 'catch out'? It's simply 'Rodriguez makes the catch for the out.').

Foul Tip - You don't have 'edge' in baseball as you do in cricket when the ball skims off the outer part of the bat. You have a *foul tip* if the ball is edged behind the first base and third base lines past the catcher. It counts as a strike against the batter if the tip is caught.

4-4 – A night a hitter might have only once a season. He's in heaven.

Four Games Back/Four Games Out - The words 'back' and 'out' are used to express how far behind a team is from the one at the top of the division. The leaders are always a certain number of games 'ahead.' To go a whole game ahead, the first placed Twins have to win while the second place Indians have to lose.

Four-Seam Fastball - This is your basic fastball. The grip is the thing that distinguishes it from the two-seamer: for the four, the first two fingers are placed on the ball, across the seam at one of the two widest areas (grab a tennis ball to see for yourself, it has the same seam structure as a baseball). To generate some movement, the pitcher (apparently) needs to place these two fingers on one side of the ball or the other. Pulling down with the fingers to one side of the ball or other, with some wrist rotation, imparts spin, which causes the ball to deviate through the air.

Frame – n ...is half an inning: one team's at bats while they make three outs.

Framing (The Ball) – This describes the position of the catcher's mitt a split second after he catches the pitch. One of the catcher's jobs is to catch a pitch on the edge of the strike zone or just outside it and to subtly shift the glove into the strike zone to make the umpire think he should call a strike rather than a ball. The swiftness of the mitt is intended to deceive the eye. Given the fuzzy, or shall we say, negotiable location of the strike zone, framing the ball can help the pitcher a lot. If it's done too crudely it winds up the umpire, so this form of cheating has to be done with some aplomb and care.

Franchise - Universal term in the game for a baseball 'club.' 'It's a business,' this seems to stress.

Free Agent/Agency - A player who is out of contract at the end of the season and free to sell his labour to the highest bidder.

Free Pass - Slang term for a walk/base on balls. The batter hasn't hat to make a hit to get there so he gets a 'free pass'.

Front Office – Term for the business and administrational part of a baseball organization.

Full Count - When the count stands at three balls and two strikes (3 and 2) you have a 'full count.' In terms of base running, at this point, any men on the bases will probably get the sign from the manager to "go:" to break for the next base; if it's a ball it's a walk and so they can't be thrown out by the catcher, and if it's a strike, the at bat is over, so there is no risk attached to breaking for the next bag.

Full Swing Bunt – This describes a peculiar mis-hit where a batter takes a full swing of the bat, but only achieves the dribbling of the ball a few yards out of the batter's box a few yards. Thus the effect is that of a (perhaps) good bunt. Whether this will be enough to get the batter to first base safely is decidedly moot – probably not. Same as "**Swinging Bunt.**"

Fungos - At practice sessions, balls are hit with a bat to fielders for catching or scooping up off the ground. These hits are called 'fungos.' They are sometimes hit with a bat with a slim barrel called, guess what: a fungo bat.

G

Game - Never 'match,' it's always a 'game' that's played. See **'*match up.*'**

Game Called - Term for a game being abandoned due to rain or for any other reason.

Gameday – The live service on MLB.com, where by clicking on the green field symbol you can watch, statistically, the game unfold live, pitch by pitch. It's truly wonderful.

Games Out - We're now talking how well your team is doing during the season. If your team is the Indians, straight away you know that you're not at the top of the division (not 'top of the table', you'll note). However, if you're only 'two games out' you're not far behind and very much in contention.

How is it measured? If the Tribe is two games out on the Chicago White Sox, the top may look like this:

Chicago   12-8
Cleveland 10-10 +2

The '+2' denotes the 'two games out' and it means that the White Sox have won two more games than the Indians. Or that it will take the Indians winning two games whilst the White Sox loses two to put the Indians level. Note that the Indians aren't 'two games behind' but 'two games out.' Always.

If two games isn't a big gap, then five games out is. Teams in this situation have famously hauled themselves to the top of the division plenty of times in the past, but if a quality team like the Atlanta Braves or New York Yankees build up a five game lead during a season then they're in a pretty commanding position: expect them to move further ahead. When measuring the distance between the teams in the standings in this way, half-games are used when two teams have played a different number of games.

In this situation:

Chicago   13-8
Cleveland 10-10

where the Sox have played one game more than Cleveland and won it, they are +2 ½, games out or back. Another way to calculate the 2 ½ is to add the two differences in their games won then halve them: 13-10= 3. plus 10-8 = 2, which makes 5, divided by 2, which = 2 ½.

So, when assessing how well your team's doing, it's how they're doing relative to five hundred and how many games out they are. Or games ahead, of course. And don't forget to take note of the ***wild card*** situation.

Gap(s), The - Space between the outfielders and center fielders which will turn a single into a double, possibly triple.

General Manager – Or "GM," this is one of the most important men at a ball club. His job is to build a team of pitchers and position players to take on all-comers. It is and it isn't an administrational job. He works with the team owner (or owners) who may be hands on guys like Steinbrenner of the Yankees and Chuck O Finlay, ex-owner of the Oakland A's as part of the front office team, but as he is in charge of player buying and selling, he also resembles our familiar football manager. A unique present day GM is Billy Beane of the Oakland Athletics.

Get It Goin' - When a team is losing and needs to pull its finger out before it gets worse or too late, this is the phrase you'll usually hear. Always used in terms of offence, it means the batters need to start getting some bat on ball. Also 'get somethin' goin'.'

Get Out Of The Inning - Used to describe the pitcher or defense, under pressure, bringing an inning to a conclusion, or wanting/trying to.

'Getting Giambi Looking' – Means the hitter was struck out by the pitcher whose third strike crossed the plate without the hitter taking a swing. He was 'looking' at the ball.

Giddy Up – A fastball with 'extra' speed on it.

Giving Up A Home Run - When a pitcher gets hit, he is almost always said to have 'given up' a home run or a single or whatever. This is standard parlance. He rarely 'concedes' a home run.

Glove, The - Gloves have been worn by fielders since the 1880s. There are strict rules regarding its dimensions and colour and further, the dimensions are different for different positions. The catcher's mitt must not exceed 38 inches in circumference and 15 1/2 from top to bottom; plus, the webbing must be no more than 7 inches across. The first baseman's mitt must be no more than 12 inches from bottom to top and no more than 8 wide across the center of the palm of the hand. The webbing must not exceed five high, four across. Pitcher and other fielders: 12 inches high and only 7 wide. The colour for pitchers must not be light and not grey, as it must not be used to camouflage the ball so he has an extra trick. If all this seems finicky, it stops fielders going out with gloves the size of buckets. These latest legal stipulations were put in place in 1973.

Go Ahead Run – The run that puts one team ahead of the other when the scores are tied is the 'go ahead run.'

Go Ahead Run Comes To The Plate - This refers to the potential of the man coming up to bat with the scores tied. If he later makes it home, the team will go ahead. See also '*Tying Run (is at the plate).*'

Goat - It's a cliché of the big game build up for pundits to opine that whatever happens, there's bound to be either a 'hero or goat by the end of it'. The 'goat' in US sports generally, is the one who makes the mistake(s) that decide the outcome. The fool, the idiot, the poor sod.

Goes Deep – Another euphemism for the home run. The hitter "goes deep," not the pitcher.

Goes Down Swinging – When a hitter's third and fatal strike is a swing and a miss.

Goes/Went Fishing – Hitter swings and misses at a wide pitch. Pitchers ahead in the count like to place a pitch or two here just for this purpose: to temp him into a mistake.

Goes The Other Way - If a batter doesn't pull the ball as is natural but keeps his shoulders open and the bat on a more parallel plane to the plate, especially on a pitch on the outside half of the plate, he will send the ball into center or right field (if he connects well). This is called 'going the other way.' The norm for a right-hander is to pull the ball into left field, into right if you're a left-hander. Being able to hit the ball the other way is considered an accomplishment, though this rather patronizes all hitters throughout history, as if they're all morons who can only think of wrenching every pitch for the glory of a home run, or before the Ruthian home run revolution of 1918, just plain morons.

Goes Yard – Yet another code term for the home run.

Going For The A's – The use of the verb "to go" here is to tell you who is pitching for a team in a particular game. "Zito will be going for the A's Thursday night."

Going Out To The Mound - When a pitcher is in trouble, expect to see the pitching coach or the manager to out to the mound. When it's the manager, expect a pitching change. It's always the manager who goes out to the mound to tell the pitcher, 'that's enough,' or words to that effect. Officially, when he takes the ball from the pitcher's hand, the night is over for the pitcher at that moment.

Gold Glove – Each league gives a Gold Glove award at the end of each season to the best fielder in each position. They're awarded by the baseball writers. There is a tendency to pass over statistics and award them to 'stars' or for them to be awarded on reputation, according to Sabermetricians. The award has a lot of prestige in the game among players and media alike.

Got A Piece Of It - A hitter being unable to make good contact on the ball, slicing it off into foul territory; but he didn't miss it completely, he got a piece of it.

Got It All – If a batter gets all of it, expect it to have already disappeared over the fence.

'Got Around On The Fastball'– The basic problem presented by the fastball for the hitter is that it too easily goes by them. To make good contact when attempting to pull the ball, you have to be quick enough, or produce enough bat speed to "get around on it."

Grand Slam – In one sense the ultimate for a hitter: a home run hit with a man on each base: four runs scored on one swing of the bat. In 2003, 63 grand slams were hit by AL hitters, 60 by NL hitters. Lou Gehrig is the record holder for career GSs with 23.

Green Light - This is something the manager gives the batter at the plate, meaning he says, 'okay, go on, smash the next pitch into oblivion if you want to try.' As the mighty swipe is the strategy of highest risk, there may well be times when the manager wants the batter just to make good contact on the pitch maximizing the chances of the batter getting on base and advancing any base runners. A runner waits for a green light to steal a base also.

Ground ball - A batted ball that travels along the ground or very close to it.

Grounder - Shorter alternative to groundball. Means exactly the same thing.

Grounding Into Double Play - To effect the double play, the fielding side needs a groundball (or maybe a *hopper*) to be struck by the batter. The batter who hits a groundball to an infielder causing two outs with one stroke is said to have 'grounded into a double play.' What the manager says he's done might be something quite different. Abb: GIDP

Groundout – When a batter is thrown out on a groundball.

Grounded Out To First - Use of the above as a verb.

Ground Rule Double - It's not uncommon to see a long arcing hit over the head of an outfielder take one bounce on the hard gravel 'warning track' in between grass and perimeter fence and go into the crowd (some ball parks don't have high fences all the way round the perimeter). A "ground rule double" is immediately awarded to the hitter/batting team, meaning that the batter goes to second base and no further. This is often a relief to the fielding side and a downer for the batter as with a higher fence a triple may well have been in the offing. It also means though that any runners at second or third base can trot in easily to score a run or a runner on first coming round to third, so it's not all bad news for the offensive team. So-called because each park has its own rules: its 'ground rules.'

Grounds Crew - These are the people who rake the base paths between innings and bring on the tarpaulins and other turf protecting gear when it rains. Not to be confused with Groundskeeper Willie.

Grubber - Is the same as a ground ball, one that really holds to the turf and doesn't travel further than the infield.

Gunned Down – When a base runner is forced out at a base or home plate by a hard throw from a fielder. The fielder can be said to do the gunning down.

H

Had No Play To Make - Describes a fielder who collects the ball cleanly but can't put out any of the runners because they've all made it safely to their bases. It emphasizes a situation where it isn't the infielder's fault he couldn't make an assist to a putout: he just didn't have a play to make.

Hall Of Fame - Baseball has a literal and metaphorical place of honour for its great players in history: the Hall Of Fame. The buildings are in Cooperstown, New York State and a maximum of three new players are inducted to it each year by the Baseball Writers of America and every other year by the Veterans Committee. Two were inducted in 2004, relief pitcher Dennis Eckersley and outfielder Paul Molitor. The first players were inducted on February 2 1936 and they were: Honus Wagner, Babe Ruth, Ty Cobb, Christy Matthewson and Walter Johnson.

Handcuffed – When a hard hit ball bounces or flicks off a glove or wrist of a fielder unable to gather in the ball.

Hang - The verb here refers to what a pitcher needs to avoid: throwing a pitch across the plate that is so straight and without sufficient speed to beat the batter, so it seems to the naked eye to 'hang' there begging for a Ruthian blow. That said, Clem Labine, in Kahn's *Boys Of Summer*, long after his playing days tells someone that he "used to hang some curves" and didn't mean that he gave hitters easy balls. So it also stands as a substitute verb for throwing pitches.

Hanging Breaking Ball - A breaking ball is any pitch that produces some curvature on the ball; a hanging one is when it seems to sit up and beg for the batter to send over the wall. Hence the phrase, 'hanging curve' also: a curve ball that sits up and begs.

Heads Up Play – Term for an intelligent (piece of) play, a clever piece of fielding perhaps, or baserunning.

Healthy - Players are never 'fit' or 'fit to play,' they're 'healthy.' I still haven't quite got used to this yet. Joe Morgan saying, 'he might get to 50 home runs if he stays healthy' still sounds distinctly odd.

Heartbreaker – Game where a team loses narrowly and dramatically, usually after holding a lead.

Heavy Bats - Same as '**big bats**,' the term describes a team having a group of dangerous big hitters.

Heat - Heat is sheer speed from the pitcher.

Heater - The same concept as above only this is a noun describing a very fast fastball.

Helmets- Protective headgear worn by batters. It became compulsory to don them in 1971.

Herky Jerky (Motion) - A pitcher who goes through his wind up and delivery in a fashion that lacks a certain smoothness of movement and continuity of rhythm is usually, if commented upon, described as having a 'herky-jerky' delivery or motion.

Hesitation Pitch - The hesitation pitch was named by the fantastic 20s and 30s Negro League pitcher Satchell Paige and is where the pitcher hesitates dramatically between his wind up and his release, so as to try to throw the timing of the batter off. His 'bow tie' was a pitch around the batter's throat.

High and Tight - This describes a pitch that comes in too high and is too close to the batter for a strike.

High Ball Hitter – A player who likes the ball pitched to him somewhere between the belt and the letters.

High For A Ball - A value for money expression to denote the fact that pitch you just saw wasn't a strike because it was too high.

High Cheese - This is a hard fastball that comes in high over the plate

High Hard One - A high fastball, crossing the plate above the strike zone.

High Heat - 'Some high heat!' describes a rapid fastball that passes the batter too high for a strike.

Hill - Slang term for pitcher's mound.

Hit - To make a 'hit' in baseball you have to do more than make contact with the ball with the bat: it's only a 'hit' if you manage to run safely to first base without a fielder helping you by making an error. If you get to second or third base on your contact it's still a hit, but it's a hit for extra bases.

Hit and Run - This is an offensive strategy where a base runner, usually at first base, sets off for second in anticipation of the batter putting the ball in play. A sign from the manager in the dugout will be sent to both batter and runner before the play is attempted. The job of the hitter in this situation is not to hit a home run but just to make good contact. Missing the ball will increase the chances of the runner being thrown out by the catcher. An example of typical National League strategy.

Hit Batter - A hit batter describes not an injured one but one who has just had the ball touch his uniform or any part of his anatomy. This means he goes immediately to first base.

Hit Safely - When a player 'hit safely in 12 of his last 20 games of the season' it simply means that he got at least one hit in 12 of those 20 games.

Hit, Scoring a – The making or scoring of a hit is quite a complicated thing. If a batter hits the ball to the shortstop, who juggles it by mistake, allowing him to make it safely to first base, is it a hit? No it is not. The play is scored as error. Is an at bat charged to him (so that he's 0 for 1 if it's his first plate appearance of the night)? No it is not; he remains 0 for 0. If the batter hits a ball in play to the shortstop with a man having to run from first and the SS throws out the lead runner at second, but the throw from second to first isn't fast enough to stop the runner making it to first base does he get a hit? No he does not. He is scored as getting on base on a "fielder's choice." If on the same play a man on third comes in to score, does the batter get credited with an RBI? Yes he does. If a batter hits a pitch to the deep outfield where he is caught for the second out of the inning, but a man on third comes home to score, does the fact that he enabled his team to score a run mean he gets a hit? No, he does not, but he is credited with the **RBI**. If a batter hits the ball to right field for a single, but because the fielder's throw to third base is wild and runs away, a runner advancing from second to third now comes in to score and the batter goes around to second, is the batter credited with a double and an RBI? No he is not. A batter may in reality on the diamond make it to second but he isn't credited with a double because his hit, without the fielding error, was only ever going to get him to first base. With two out, if a batter scores a base hit to left field, but as a result of a baserunning mistake**,** a runner is tagged out, does the fact that the inning has ended take away the hit? No it does not.

Hitter - A word that is usually interchangeable with 'batter.'

Hitter's Ballpark – A park in which an above average number of home runs are hit. This is due normally to less than great acreage or in the case of Denver and Arizona, through high, thin air.

Hitter's Count – The count when there are more balls than strikes. See **"The Count (Pitch)."**

Hitter's Team – Term to describe a club with much better hitting than pitching.

Hitting For The Cycle - This suggests that a player aims consciously, chooses, to try to hit a single, double, triple and home run in a single game (see '**Cycle**'). He doesn't: he either achieves the feat or gets close. But in terms of semantics, he always 'hits *for* the cycle.' when he achieves it.

Hitting Streak - When a hitter has racked up a number of consecutive games where he makes at least one hit per game he is said to be on a hitting streak. The record belongs to Joe DiMaggio, who in 1941 went on a 56 game streak.

"Hitting .300" – The benchmark of the top class hitter, a standard which is generally applied by 'experts' to all baseball history. This is the case despite the fact that at different times it has been easier, or more difficult, depending on certain factors, to make three hits in ten throughout a season. In this present age of high volume hits and home runs, .300 may be less of an achievement than it was twenty years ago, but it's still the yardstick of the quality hitter. Last season, 33 hitters hit .300.

Hitting .223 Against Loaiza This Season – A note to you how much more thorough baseball is compared to our football and cricket in its statistical analysis. It's normal during a broadcast to see or hear what a hitter's record is against a particular pitcher. Why on earth can't TV football give us Henry's career rate of scoring against each Premiership club? A team's penalty taker's percentage success rate against every goalkeeper in the Premiership? And our newspapers, come to that.

Hit Worth A Lick, Can't - This is a batter whose form is really terrible.

Hold – A 'hold,' a pitching statistic, is when a reliever comes into the game with a man (or men) on base and manages to prevent him/them scoring.

Hold, (The Runners) – The runner(s) hold when they are on base but are unable to advance on a pitch, especially one where the ball is hit into play. They are normally said to have been held by a fielder able to get to the ball smartly, pick it up cleanly and threaten to throw (at least) one of them out. *'...Garciaparra makes the pick up and is able to hold the runners.'* To 'hold the runner close' means for a fielder, on a base with a base runner there on the bag next to him, to keep that runner from attempting to get to the next base. With no one on base, all the infielders can play as shallow or as deep as they want; generally they play behind the bases, often by some yards. But as soon as there is a base runner, both the first and second basemen will play close to the first and second base bags to be there to make a force out.

Hole, The - This refers to any of the three gaps between the infielders, especially that between third and shortstop.

Hole + Number – *"Morneau is hitting in the number* **two hole** *tonight for the Twins."* Spot in the batting line up. Two spot means he comes up straight after the lead off hitter.

Home - Ubiquitous term used as short for 'home plate.' Home is also where the player gets when he crosses home plate to bring in a run.

Home Alone Shot - Of recent derivation (obviously): a home run hit when there are no runners on base, for one run, so the trip around the bases is made alone.

Home Field - Teams don't have a 'home ground' they have this.

Home Field Advantage - Effortlessly effective terms for a team having the advantage of playing a game in the familiar surroundings of their own ball park. Also *Home Plate Advantage.*

Home Plate - There is no fourth base, there is home plate, the place the runner has to reach to score a run. He has not only to arrive there but also touch the 'bag' (which the plate just used to judge a pitch for its status as ball or strike has now become) with some (any) part of his anatomy. So fundamental is home plate that when a ball club moves stadium, the home plate is taken, oft times with impressive ceremonial procedure, to the new stadium where its use will signify some sort of continuity. It confers upon the piece of metal a near mystical significance.

Home Plate Umpire - The chief of umpires with the power to overrule the others. He stands behind the catcher where his principle job is to decide whether a pitch crosses the plate in the strike zone or not. He can overrule any call by one of his colleagues, within reason: he may decide on whether a fly ball was fair or a home run, but not a close call on a slide into a base unless he had clearly the best view.

Homer - Most common piece of slang for 'home run.'

Home Run – What all but the die-hard baseball purist most wants to see: the ball being hit beyond the perimeter fence or wall (or more prosaically sometimes, being hit above the white line painted on to the perimeter wall in some ball parks). It's always spectacular, the ball arcing sometimes hugely, sometimes absolutely majestically high in the air on its way into the crowd, or out of the stadium completely (as at Wrigley Field, home of the Cubs where the bleachers on the third base side and beyond center field are by no means deep) or in the case of SBC Park, San Francisco, into the Pacific Ocean behind center field.

The home run, however, is only worth one run if there are no base runners, but is worth an extra run for each man on base. The seasonal home run record is currently held by Barry Bonds with 73 in 2001 and in career terms, by Henry Aaron with 755.

Home Run Derby - This is an All-Star Break event, a competition between some of the games best sluggers, selected for the All-Star Game for a trophy. Each hitter has a limited amount of time in which to hit as many homers as possible. Played off like a cup competition in pairs.

Home Stand - When a team plays a number of games together it's called a 'home stand.' This can be over one series of games or more. It's normal for a team to play ten or eleven consecutive games on their home field during the season at least a couple of times.

Hook: This describes the big curve of a big curve ball.

Hop 1 – Bounce, as in the bounce of the ball after it's been struck by the batter.

Hop 2 – 'Hop' on a fastball is one with real speed.

Hopper – This describes a hit that bounces a number of times before it reaches an infielder.

Horse – Pitcher who has stamina as well as talent and pitches a lot of innings in a lot of games.

Hot Buttered Popcorn – What a pitcher throws when in devastating form, with just power or a mix of power and breaking stuff. Used by David Lengel on the 5-Show in September 2004.

Hot Corner - The third base fielding position, so-called because of the tendency of most hitters to pull the ball with power. This makes it a notoriously difficult place to field.

Hot Dog – A 'hot dog' is a big head, a player who thinks he's it. A term much applied to Reggie Jackson, for example: huge ego, huge bat Hall of Famer who played for the A's, the Orioles and the Yankees.

Hot Stove League – Not a league at all, but a superb image, meaning baseball talk during the off-season winter. Why 'hot stove?' Back in the origination of the phrase, the men, more often than not the old and retired, would congregate at the dry goods store in town's stove to chew the fat, keep warm and talk.

Hundred Wins - In this is the established mark of the very good team. In 2003 in the American League, only the New York Yankees won a hundred games (101). In the National League, both the Atlanta Braves and the San Francisco Giants hit the century. (Braves 101, Giants 100). 116 is the record number of wins in one season, held by the 1906 Chicago Cubs and the 2001 Seattle Mariners. The Cubs played fewer games however, so theirs is obviously the better record.

Hurler - Another name for a pitcher, especially of fastballs.

Hustle - Hustle in baseball is about batters getting on base with small ball tactics which harry and bother the infielders into mistakes. It takes some bunting, some stealing and it takes some athletes at the bottom of your line up. A hustler is often labeled a "Charlie Hustle," the greatest of who was probably Pete Rose, the all-time leader in career hits, singles, games and at bats.

I

Infield - The infield consists of the playing field more or less inside the base paths. The term also refers to the four infielders who together form a ring of defense against the batter.

Infielder - There are four of these: first baseman, second baseman, short stop and third baseman, in that order travelling anti-clockwise around the bases from first

Infield Fly - A pitch mis-hit skywards by the batter within the confines of the diamond, for which the **Infield Fly Rule** (see below) is invoked.

Infield Fly Rule – If a player hits the ball into the air within reach of an infielder who is almost certain to catch it, and there are runners on first or second, the umpire automatically calls the Infield Fly Rule into operation. This means that the batter is out, even before the ball is caught. Odd perhaps, but this prevents the fielding side from cheating. If the relevant infielder were to let the ball drop to the floor, he would be able to turn one out – the catching out of the hitter – into two: a double play. This is so because if a catch is made, the man on first has the choice of whether to attempt to reach second or stay safe at his initial base. However, if the fielder allows the ball to drop in fair territory, the man at first has to run toward second (and second towards third), and could be an easy force out. Also called the "infield rule."

Infield Hit - A fumble on a groundball or dropped catch to an infielder can allow a batter to scramble in to first base safely (and frequently does). This will invariably mean an error being charged to the fielder as only Superman can run the 90 feet to first quickly enough to beat a well-fielded groundball.

Infield Out - An out executed by one of the infielders.

Infield Playing In - The infielders may choose to play 'in,' for two main reasons: one, if the batter looks like he's going to bunt (if you've no idea what I'm talking about, go to the 'Bs' without further ado), because the ball is only going to drop a few metres from the bat, and two, if there is a runner on third base – with a lead taken by the base runner, the ball *must* be fielded and thrown to the catcher rapidly if a run is not to be conceded. Playing in will also narrow the space between the four infielders making it harder for the groundball to get through. It of course increases the chances of a fumble and anything in the air will more easily clear the infield.

Infield Shift - Sounds complicated, but it simply means that for a left handed hitter, the infielders move ('shift') around clockwise to that there is a fielder, the second baseman, between first and second base. This is because the left-handed hitter is most likely to pull the ball (this is why the short stop stands between second and third base for the right handed hitter, as you may already have gathered). This was allegedly first used to combat the threat from the Boston great Ted Williams. Often abbreviated to *'the shift.'*

Infield Single – Practically the same as an infield hit, but clarifies the fact that only one base was gained by a batted ball not clearing the infield. The error may be awarded harshly if the ball traveled at great speed.

In On The Hands – Describes a pitch that is aimed or curves towards the batter's hands as he stands in the batter's box. A useful pitch as the hitter may well not be able to avoid making a swing. It's also used to unsettle the batter: 90 miles and hour pitch coming towards your essentially unprotected bare hands is a serious matter, especially when you need them in good nick to play the game six days a week for seven months. The phrase is used when the pitch was not directed there deliberately.

Inside - The inside part of the plate or strike zone is the part nearest the batter. It's normally termed 'inside' instead of the long version, 'inside part of the plate' though you hear that too. A pitch anywhere close to the batter is also 'inside.'

Inside Corner - Imagining the strike zone as your fridge again, the inside corner is right 20% of it: a pitch here is a great one because it's in the channel where the batter might think he can leave it for a ball. It's also hard to hit, period and for the more skilled hitter, hard to hit with power.

Inside Move - When the pitcher throws out - "picks off" a runner trying to get a lead or a steal at second base, not first.

'Inside Outs The Ball' - The swing on a pulled ball sees the bat descending from ten o'clock towards roughly four. When a batter wants to direct the ball more centrally or into the opposite field, he needs to swing from 'inside to out.' This time the swing will begin from closer to eleven o'clock, and instead of the bat being pulled across the body, it is rather more pushed out in front and away from the body. He *'stays on it'* (the pitch).

Inside The Park Home Run - You don't have to hit the baseball over the outfield wall to get a home run. But to get around three bases to home on a hit that's going to hit the wall and bounce back or clear the head of the relevant outfielder and dribble into a corner, you're going to need a fielding error to do it. Or two outfielders will have to collide or slide to make a catch and miss the pill. These are almost extinct now in the age of the smaller park but they were once not at all unusual.

Insurance Run - If a team is one run ahead they want an extra one (at least) for 'insurance,' which makes keeping the lead more likely.

Intentional Pass - See below, 'Intentional Walk.'

Intentional Walk – When four consecutive pitches are thrown deliberately wide. The idea here is to prevent the hitter doing damage to the defensive team by getting him out of the way to first base as a kind of least-worst option. Though it's normally used when a slugger comes to the plate (especially one in good form or who has hit a homer in a previous inning in the game), it's a tactic sometimes used against a not especially dangerous batter to get to one who is weak. Thus it's used in the National League it might be used to get to the pitcher who has to bat who is often easy to strike out. The first intentional walk took place with the bases loaded was Hall of Farmer Nap Lahore of the Philadelphia As in 1901. As he batted a massive .426 that season it's not surprising. See *'pitch out.'*

Interference - If a fielder obstructs the batter in any way in the opinion of the umpire, the runner will be 'awarded the base:' will be allowed to go to the one he was running to.

Inter-League Play - In recent years only, the regular season has included series of games between teams from different leagues. So inter-league play is any series played between an American and a National league one. Several series are played for a mid-season couple of weeks before the All-Star Game only. It was a controversial move and is still opposed by some in the game.

In Order – When a side is retired 'in order' it means that in that inning, none of the hitters got on base. Same as '***Three Up-Three Down.***'

In The Dirt - This describes a pitch that lands on the floor near or at the feet of the catcher, a nightmare for him. If the ball goes through him it may be scored against him as a ***passed ball,*** an error against him in effect... The 'dirt' is the orange gravel used to cover the surface of the base paths.

In The Gap - A pitch hit 'in the gap' is one hit in either of the two channels between the center fielder and his two flanking outfielders. An excellent place to hit it; it should be worth a double.

In The Hole- Batter who is due up (to bat) after the man in the on deck circle. Its origin is from the dug out being below ground level.

Irrevocable Waivers - Put on irrevocable waivers, the ball club wants rid of the ball player. He is made publicly available for a trade. See also ***waivers.***

J

Jack – Home run.

Jam - A 'jam' is a tough or tight spot for the pitcher; when he gets behind in the count of allows some batters to get on base and has a tough job now to prevent a run being scored.

"Jammed 'im" – One part of a pitcher's pitching strategy is the pitch inside which cramps the hitter for room. If it's located accurately it 'jams 'im': he hasn't the room to make a good swing of the bat. An easy groundout often results.

Jerk The Ball (out of the park) – Hit the ball for a home run.

Jersey- Players do not wear baseball shirts, but baseball 'jerseys.' See '***Uniforms.***'

Jockey - Name for a big mouth on the team who shouts abuse at umpires and opposing players from the bench. Hence the oft-used term, '***bench jockey.***'

Jolt - A player may be heard to have 'jolted' a home run out of the park. Hence Joe DiMaggio was known as 'Joltin' Joe, as all Simon And Garfunkel fans will be aware.

Jumps On That - This is a term for a batter energetically making good contact with the pitch so getting a hit.

Junkball Pitcher – 'Junk' is a slang term for non-fastball pitches. The knuckleballer is the ultimate junkball pitcher, his work being just throwing soft pitches that flutter on the breeze. The need to abuse knuckleballers stems, I'm sure, from the inability of a large number of batters to hit them successfully.

$9 + 427 = 436$

K

'Ks' - Fans like to tape A4 size pieces of paper on the walls of the stands with big 'Ks' drawn and shaded on them for each strikeout their pitching ace gets during their time on the mound. 'K' as in 'KO' as in 'knockout.'

Kitchen, In His - The hitter's kitchen is the area adjacent to his midriff area. Traditionally, this pitch "sets up" an outside pitch to follow.

Knock – Alternative for (base) hit.

Knockdown Pitch - From days gone by, this pitch is not so much to hit the batter – though it might – but to intimidate him: he's put on the floor by having to avoid it.

Knocked Out (of the box) – When a pitcher gets taken for a lot of hits early in the game. The box part refers to the early period of the game where what we now know as the mound was a chalk painted box on the infield.

Knuckle Ball - The knuckleball isn't so much a type of pitch as a whole slab of baseball history and mythology. This subject alone is one that can stand as a major reason for falling in love with baseball. The knuckleball (or 'knuck') is a pitch more pushed out of the hand than thrown. It travels at a sedate pace to the plate and should be easy to hit, but if thrown correctly, the ball darts and dives in the air making it extremely hard for the batter to make well-timed contact. The reason for the huge and unpredictable movement is the fact that when pushed from the hand, the ball does not rotate. Or rather, when it travels through the air without rotating in flight, the stitches on the ball cause more movement, presumably because the air meets more resistance from that when pitched without rotation.

Like the leg spinner, the knuckleballer has almost become an extinct species. Though he was to be found in the persons of Hoyt Wilhelm and Warren Spahn in earlier times, only Tim Wakefield of the Boston Red Sox throws it in the Bigs. Given that he bamboozled and defeated the Yankees in the 2003 the play offs not once but twice in two outings, one would think ball clubs would be frantically trying to rescue this dying art. However, even if the knuckleball could come back into fashion, there aren't many, if any coaches around to school young prospects.

The pitch is so called because 1) supposedly, the ball is gripped by the knuckles. This takes some believing if you've ever tried to throw a baseball just gripping it by the knuckles. Knucklers also grip the ball with their fingertips or nails. 2) It may well have got this appellation because of the way the pitcher's knuckles clearly stick up and point at the batter as the ball leaves the hand. I'm not sure which is right: possibly both.

Knuckle Ball Pitcher - This is a pitcher who mostly pitches knuckleballs. He may throw other pitches for variation to surprise the batter, but the knuckleball is essentially what he throws. As Jim Bouton makes clear in his great book '*Ball Four*,' at least up until the late 60s, the knuckleball pitcher wasn't trusted by most managers in the game. This is because when it's not fluttering, moving in the air a lot, it's an easy ball to hit. They're seen as unreliable and if we're being psychological, not manly enough for baseball. The old style manager preferred the big steak of the fastball.

See **Junkball pitcher.**

Knuckle Curve – The knuckleballer traditionally can pitch a ball that has a predictable curve to it, with the same vertical drop of the orthodox curve ball. It's a bit of a misnomer, however. "The knuckle curve, thrown today by the Yankees' Mike Mussina, is released with topspin, or overspin, and so does not even belong in the flutterball's extended low-spin family." I've lost the source of this quote, so I hope whoever said this will forgive me for using it here in the name of baseball education.

K-Zone - This is a televisual aid and a joy, as it is a 'painted' outer edge of the strike zone superimposed in over a slo-mo of any pitch the director chooses. Thus we can see with perfect clarity how good the pitch was and whether the home plate umpire made a correct call. Hated by umpires, naturally.

L

Last Lick - Term for the last inning for each team, the ninth.

Last (of the third) – Each inning has two 'frames,' sets of three outs. The 'last' of the inning is the second team going in to bat (always the home team).

Late Inning Reliever - Post-starting pitcher whose job it is to come into the game for the eighth inning or ninth inning – from the seventh is pushing it - when the team is behind. Same as the 'set up man.'

Laugher – A game won very easily by one team or the other: 12-1 or 10-1, say.

Lay Down A Bunt- See 'Bunt' for details of this batting manoevre. In the vernacular a bunt is 'put down' or 'laid down.'

Laying Off The Pitch - Refers to a batter leaving a pitch rather than being tempted to swing.

Lead/Big Lead - Means a base runner moving a few strides from his base towards the next when looking to **steal**, as the pitcher is going into his windup. The lead is also taken so that the next base (at least) can be reached in the event of the hitter making contact.

Leaders – Short for 'clubhouse leader,' an extremely important aspect of the baseball team. It is known and expected that all aspiring teams will have not one but several "leaders" in the clubhouse who will be key influential figures who the younger, the less-assertive and the fainter-hearted players on the roster will look to for inspiration, guidance and motivation in addition to what's coming from the manager and coaches.

Leading Off - '*Soriano then, leading off.*' See '**lead off man.**'

Leading Off Second – Usage as verb of the lead taken by base runners to get closer to the next base.

Lead Off Hitter/Lead Off Man 1 - The first man in the batting team in each inning is universally known as the lead off hitter or man.

Lead Off Hitter/Man 2 – This is also the label for the number one batter in the line up as written. It is in the written rules of the game that before the game can start the manager of each team (and no one else) has to present the home plate umpire with the line up on the field of play. The LOM may only come to the plate first in an inning in the first but we can still call him the 'lead off hitter.' This is a specialist position. In baseball theory his job is to get on base in any way possible. Classically he is a **slap** hitter or **singles hitter**, because this approach to hitting is that of lowest risk. Classically too he is also a fast runner so he can steal bases. So his job is to get on base then steal second, and even third, so that one of the sluggers can *drive him home.* By no means all teams have these, though Juan Pierre of the Marlins is a lead off man in the traditional mould.

Lead Off Single/ Double/ Home Run - These terms describe a hit by the first man up at the plate in an inning. It doesn't have to have been made by the lead off man, the first man in the official batting line up. It's used to denote the fact that the hit was made with none out.

Lead Runner - He is the runner furthest round the bases at any time there is more than one man on base; the nearest to home and to scoring a run.

Leaving It Out Over The Plate - Phrase for a pitch being thrown over the middle of the plate as opposed to 'inside' or 'away.' Always used to denote a **mistake**, it doesn't always get **smoked** but arguably it always should.

Left - Short for left field, as in, *'Thome flies out to left.'*

Left-Center – Another geographical expression that describes the area which comprises roughly of the right hand portion of center field and the left hand portion of right field.

Left-Center Gap – Space between the left and center fielders in the outfield, good for a double.

Left Field – Also a matter of field geography: the sector that makes up the left third of the outfield as the batter looks out towards the pitcher.

Left Field Corner - Where left (out)field ends at the left field line foul pole. In some ballparks the corner is oddly shaped making it difficult for the right fielder to collect the ball quickly and cleanly.

Left Fielder - This man patrols the left hand third of the outfield though he is usually referred to as 'in left field.' Where he stands depends on how powerful the hitter at the plate is and whether or not he tends to pull the ball or not. Generally the left fielder gives himself thirty metres of space or so behind him as he will have time to retreat towards the wall to try to catch a towering fly ball that seems to be going over his head. He doesn't want to be too deep as a **pop up** might easily fall between him and the retreating infielder (and frequently does).

Left Field Line - The painted white line dividing fair from foul territory that extends from home plate to the perimeter fence at a ninety-degree angle to the third base line. This is a great place for a batter to hit the ball. As the third baseman usually plays a little towards the infield of the bag, the ball often scoots low into the outfield corner; the outfielder in left field has to run back and across to fetch the ball, often waiting for it to bounce off at least one part of the wall, followed by a slow dribble, by which time the hitter may be on second and anyone in scoring position may well be able to make home. Also the required place to lay down a drag bunt, where you seriously want to have a chance to get on base and for a man on first to get across to second, or from second to third. Not the place for a **squeeze play**, as the man on third can easily be **tagged out**.

Left Field Umpire - In the World Series only, the outfield umpire with responsibility for left field and left-center. He must stand in foul territory. He is there to be certain about catches made near the turf and calls concerning hits to the foul pole.

Left Hander – This always means a left-handed pitcher, not batter.

Left On (base) - *'The Twins leave two on at the bottom of the fifth.'* In this case, the Minnesota Twins have ended their half of the inning with two men on base. The fact is pointed out by sportscasters to tell you how near they were to scoring (more) runs. Frustrating if you're following your team on the Internet or reading about the game next day, like your football team hitting the post. The statistic of how many men a team leaves on in the entire game can be found in the box scores (**Abb: LOB**).

Lefty - Shorthand for a left-handed pitcher or hitter, but especially pitcher.

Lights Out - *'When he's getting that low strike, he's pretty much lights out,'* said pundit David Justice in 2003 of pitcher Derek Lowe. Meaning it was 'lights out' time for practically each batter coming to the plate, an almost certain out. Pitcher in top form and very hard to hit.

Line – (n) Baseball statistics are displayed in horizontal lines of numbers (and codes above). Thus, a player's "line" is his stats for the given period.

Line Drive - Term for the striking of the baseball through the air by the batter. It's a trajectory thing, between the fly ball hit high in the air and the grounder that skims or bounces across the turf.

Line Drive Swing - A swing of the bat that looks to hit the ball in the flattish arc of the line drive.

Lines It - Describes the batter hitting a line drive.

Lines Out (*'Alou lines out to left'*) **-** A line drive that ends in an out, caught by a fielder.

Line Up - The list of nine batters in a team is known as the line up. Not, note, the 'team.'

Little League Home Run – Same as '**Inside the park home run.**'

Lit Up - You don't want to be 'lit up' if you're a pitcher. '*And Hammond, who had given up just one home run in 43 games this year, has been lit up twice in one inning*' said John Miller during a Bo-Sox-Yankee game in July 2003. He'd just been hit for two homers in consecutive at bats.

Live Fastball – If a pitcher has one of these, its particularly quick (see '***mustard,*** ' '**cheese,**' '**heat**' '***something on it***' and '**giddy up.**')

Lively Ball Era – This is the period of baseball history immediately after the instatement of a new harder type of ball in 1921 to combat the utter dominance of the pitcher since the modern majors began in 1901 (with the acceptance of the equality of the new American League by the National). The harder ball traveled further off the bat and this, with the addition of the banning of the spitball and more frequent changes of ball, led to the huge increase in home runs and batting average during the 20s, which continued through the 30s.

Location – This is the Holy Grail for pitchers. 'Location' means a pitcher throwing the ball exactly where he wants it to go, when he wants it to go there. Sometimes a pitcher, however well he has been throwing in practice or pitching in recent games, can't put it (*spot it*) on the corners, inside, low and away or temptingly high; he's said to have 'lost his location.' Same as '**command.**'

Locker Room - The part of the clubhouse where the players change and shower after every game. It's absolutely normal for them to conduct interviews there immediately after play. Unlike the football dressing room, baseball's equivalent has lockers, cubicles, separating the players from each other somewhat and giving them more space to stow their stuff.

Lone Star Series – Any series played by the two Texas ball clubs, the Houston Astros and the Texas Rangers.

Long Ball - Another term for home run. Formerly a term for a long hit in the age when outfield fences were pretty much too distant for home runs to be hit.

Long Hit - Anything better than a single is a long hit: i.e., a hit that gets the runner to second, third or home. Babe Ruth holds the record for the most long hits in a season: 119 in 1921.

Long Relief/Long Reliever – A long reliever comes to the mound when the starting pitcher has been knocked out of the game early on. The trend before 1980-ish was for starters to be yanked as early as the first inning if they're giving up runs, so long relief would start there. These days he may be given a little more time to settle down and get in the groove. If a reliever comes in this early, he may usually be expected to pitch as a second starter: go for four or five more innings. Managers are reluctant to spread the nine innings out between the seven or eight relievers as present theory has it relievers should not be pitching every night because of the wear and tear on the arm.

Looks - '*Snider looked at a fast ball*' **–** Means the batter let it go for a strike, rarely deliberately.

Looking Inside/Looking Away – A batter hoping the ball will come to him in this area because he likes this type of pitch.

Losingest - Language purists in the UK will no doubt consider this an absolute abomination, but a team or manager with the worst record for that season is known as the 'losingest' manager. For me, this economy of language beats "I suppose the Devil Rays' manager must have the worst record in the American League this season." over the head with a large mallet. Then you're being asked for clarification: "what do you mean by 'the worst?'" and then having to reply, "I mean he's lost the most games." At this point, you may still be pressed for further elucidation. "You mean he's lost the most games?" "That's exactly what I mean." While the conversation is being batted across like an intense game of table tennis, you might easily miss a Bonds home run. Much easier just to say "he's the losingest in the AL this season." Do that and you'll miss nothing. See '**winningest**' for...well I won't insult your intelligence by explaining that one further.

Loss, The – Every game, one pitcher must take the loss on to his record. Win-loss records being more precious than money to them, insult and ignominy awaits the bearer of the loss each night of the summer. To reiterate on '**The**

Decision' entry, the loss is incurred by the pitcher who concedes the run or runs that decide the game. If a starting pitcher gives up all five runs in a 3-5 reverse, obviously he takes the loss. If the score is 5-6 and it isn't he who concedes the sixth run, then he escapes and the reliever who conceded that sixth is the man who incurs the loss. The Win-Loss record of the pitcher is shown or described thus: 'Mussina is 8 and 2 this season.' This means that in his first ten decisions Mike Mussina (currently of the Yankees) has won eight and lost two games. This is a fine record, even on the Yankees who generally win around six out of every ten games. Comparing pitching records in this way has to take account of who the pitcher plays for. Eight and two might be very fine work for Mussina but miraculous if he's playing for the Padres or the Expos. The pitcher is said to 'get' or 'take' the loss. See **'Win, The.'**

Louisville Slugger - Type of bat very widely used in the majors, the "official bat of the major leagues" in fact. Made by Hillerich and Bradsby. This is the dominant bat maker of the past. Ruth and just about all the greats from the 20s onwards used the ubiquitous Louisville Slugger bats. The raw material is ash.

Low Ball Hitter – Left-handers are said to be basically low ball hitters: in other words, they like the ball to arrive at around knee height.

Low Field - Joe Morgan talked about the Braves hitters "using the low field," broadcasting on a play off game in 2003, meaning hitting flat line drives as opposed to looking to knock the ball out of the park.

Lumber – The bat or bats. I read just now of a player who "showcased his lumber" in a game: made some important and big hits.

Luxury Tax – Introduced through an agreement made between the clubs and the Commissioner in 2002 in an arguably limp attempt to maintain some semblance of equal competitiveness of the ballclubs. The following season the Yankees paid $11.82m on a $171m payroll (at a rate of 17½% above a threshold of $l17m). The rate increased to 22½ % in 2004. The present agreement runs to 2006 and is the second of its kind. The first ran from 1997-99.

M

Major League, The - There is a pecking order of professional baseball leagues: at the top of the pyramidal structure are the American and the National Leagues. When the term 'major league' is used, the two leagues combined are being referred to. The plural is not usually used, but the term 'big leagues,' often used, also describes both leagues combined.

Majors, The - Much used shorthand for the two major leagues.

Make Some Pitches - Throw a variety of pitches or a number of good ones. Joe Torre said after a defeat against the Blue Jays last season, *"you have to make some pitches on them or they're going to put the ball in play."*

Makes The Play - A 'play' - an opportunity to put out a hitter or a runner, or keep bases earned down to a minimum in the field - is there to be made every time a ball goes into fair territory and sometimes foul territory too when there is the possibility of a caught batter. If a fielder *makes the play* he successfully catches the ball, tags the runner, puts out the runner at the plate with a catch, makes a successful relay throw and so on.

Manager - The manager is as important a figure in baseball as he is in football: he is the master tactician and motivator. It is his job to make all of the important decisions that need to be made during each and every ball game: deciding who pitches and when; choosing when to green light a steal and a swing at the plate as opposed to leaving it for a ball; deciding whether and when to bring in pinch hitters and pinch runners. He can win and lose ball games much more than a football manager can win and lose matches. In baseball he hasn't got the excuse that "once the players cross the white line, it's up to them." True, the manager can't pitch, hit and throw but his decisions will affect the outcome of a game more than in any other sport. The manager wears the uniform too, because he is the guy who comes out of the dug out to tell a pitcher he's finished or to give him some advice, and to have a blazing row with the home plate umpire any time he feels aggrieved about something. No one is allowed to enter the field of play without wearing a baseball uniform.

Manufactured a run – If home runs or deep hits for doubles and triples are "easy" way to score runs, manufacturing a run is the harder way. It's also the traditional way. These days, it's what an offense might need to do when it can't get to grips with a pitcher. Manufacturing means to manoeuvre men around the bases without a big hit, starting perhaps with a bunt, then stealing a base or two and maybe using the hit and run to do it. A bunt and a steal will put a man in scoring position and from there just puncturing the infield may well be able to bring home the runner. A sacrifice fly might also be used too, with no outs or one. A pitcher might be so good on a particular night that you can't hit him out, but someone might be able to loft the ball to the deep part of the outfield. It may be an easy out for the defense, but a man on third will be able to score on a fly ball to deep center or deep right. This sort of baseball without the sacrifice fly is known as **"*small ball.*"** It's also much more associated with the National League than with the American League.

Mark – Where we would tend to talk about a new record in a sport being "set," in the States you're more likely to hear of a player establishing a new "mark." It means the same thing.

Marquee Player - Used in US sports generally to note a superstar: a Jeter, a Pujols or a Bonds, one who in Hollywood terms has his or her name up in lights outside the theatre on the 'marquee.'

Mashes It! - What a slugger does to a baseball when it goes for a big home run.

Masterpiece – Literary writers on the game do like to depict the game poetically and many writers, be they hacks or esteemed authors moonlighting on baseball pieces, have enjoyed likening the pitcher to a painter. He '*paints the outside corner*' with a curve ball or '*spots a fastball on the inside corner*' like a Rembrandt dabbing his canvas carefully with a spot of yellow ochre. Thus a brilliant pitching performance is sometimes described as a 'masterpiece.' This one word is a high-speed lesson in the way the game is viewed in America: it is in fact more revered by its intelligentsia than cricket is in this country.

Match Up – One of the phrases that takes a little getting used to. A match up is the pairing or meeting of two teams for a game of baseball. So instead of hearing *"Tonight's game is between...."* we hear *"Tonight's match-up is between the Indians and the Cards."* Similarly, the two pitchers are usually seen as opponents – this was especially so in the past when they would tend to go the full nine innings if they weren't getting hit – so we might hear of a *"match-up between Clemens and Johnson."*

Matinee – The first game of a double header.

Meatball - An easy pitch to hit, straight down the middle.

Meat Zone - Center of the strike zone, a pitch that should be 'easy meat' for the hitter.

Mechanics - This describes the technique of the pitcher. The pitch is made up of a series of physical processes or moves: the windup, the leg kick, the pivot and the release of the ball. How a pitcher does these things, the way he does things, from a purely physical point of view, makes up his mechanics.

Medium Right Field – If short right field is the grass just beyond the infield in right, then medium is a bit further towards the fences, but not as far as deep right field.

Mendoza Line – The Mendoza Line is batting .200. A worse batting average than this is considered to be unacceptable for a hitter in the majors. This standard of base mediocrity stems from the career of one Mario Mendoza of the late 70s Pittsburgh Pirates. There is some dispute as to whether The Line should be .215, which was his career average with the Pirates, or .200, which is the figure which seems to be the standard set when his colleagues in Seattle, then George Brett began to bandy the term around, but Mendoza Line it is.

Middle Inning Reliever – About the same as a long reliever, a guy who comes in to replace the starting pitcher earlier than is desirable for the defensive manager at around the fourth or fifth inning.

Middle Of The First - At this point of the game, the visiting team has completed their (first) inning and the home team is about to start theirs. We have 'middle of the second, middle of the third,' and so on.

Midsummer Classic - A very common term for the All Star Game (it's played in July). It is not by any means always a classic.

Minor Leagues - All baseball leagues below the majors are the minor leagues.

Minors - Simply short for 'minor leagues.'

Misplay - Means a mis-field or any other mistake made by a fielder.

Misses On The Inside/Outside Corner - Terminology used to tell you which part of the strike zone the pitch just missed on its journey to becoming a ball.

Missing His Spots – If a pitcher is doing this his location is not good: he's not putting the ball where he's intending to put it (which usually means he's getting hit or giving up a lot of walks).

Mistake – A mistake is a poor pitch, to wit, one that should be hit by the batter for a couple of bases at least. It isn't always, of course.

Mitt - Another word for the glove worn by the fielders. The catcher wears a mitt usually, rather than a glove.

Mix His Pitches - Refers to the pitcher having a range of different pitches to choose from during each at bat: sliders, splitters and change ups and so on. These days all pitchers are expected to have a range of pitches rather than rely on just the fastball, and his prowess may depend on his ability to mix well.

Moneyball Philosophy – "*Moneyball, The Art Of Winning an Unfair Game*" is a successful book by author Michael Lewis. It's about the 2002 Oakland Athletics and their General Manager Billy Beane, whose job it is to produce a successful ball club without a limitless pot of cash to spend on superstar salaries. The books tells of Beane's ability to develop players via the college draft system and practice of buying lesser known players and nurturing them to a place where they are extremely effective in helping the team to win a lot of ball games – under Beane, the A's keep reaching the play offs. The approach has confounded the traditional orthodoxy of the supposed wise acres. Commissioner Selig (also owner of the Milwaukee Brewers) has described the Oakland phenomenon as "an aberration." Imagine if Beane and the A's could win a Series, thus "proving" that all this time owners have been in effect setting fire to millions of dollars each year. The Oakland 2003 salary bill for ballplayers was around $56 ½ million, the 5th lowest in the majors, yet they won the American League West.

Money – A player who is great at his job, whether hitter or pitcher, can be said to be 'money.' It's used to stress reliability also: when you need a performance from him, he'll do it: he's money.

Money Pitch – A pitcher's 'money pitch' is the one he throws best and gets most of his batters out with, be it a fastball, a slider or curve.

Motion - The pitcher's motion is the same as the bowler's action in cricket. It's how he delivers the pitch.

Mound, The - The pitcher does not pitch from the same level as the batter but on a raised mound of earth called 'the mound' or the pitcher's mound. The mound has also been treated as having almost mystical significance, the lonely place where the pitcher is either triumphant or lost. The songwriters Paul Simon and Neil Young have both added to the myth with excellent music about the mound and the loneliness of the pitcher there. The mound is now ten inches in height. It was lowered to this for the 1969 season from the previous fifteen because of the apparent development in the game of rather dull low-scoring games. The previous season the St Louis ace Bob Gibson finished the season with an ERA of 1.12 and 13 shutouts. It was dubbed 'the year of the pitcher' in the press. Many around the game believed that the height of mounds was gradually creeping up and up to aid the pitcher. It was thought that the higher mound was giving pitcher's an advantage as it appeared to be harder for batters to make a true hit with the ball arriving further away from the horizontal plane. However, figures in terms of hits and averages are inconclusive. The '68 bad year for batters may simply have reflected a temporary edging off of quality hitting.

On the top of the mound in the middle is a rectangular strip of rubber, 24" by 12"against or on which the pitcher must put his foot when he makes his pitch. There is only six inches of flat surface on the top of the mound.

Movement - The same as the term in cricket. A baseball is like a cricket ball: it moves in the air (swerves, to the uninitiated). This is because of the seam on the ball, a more complex pattern than the single equatorial ridge on cricket's red orb. Pitchers do not shine the ball, indeed they are not allowed by law to tamper with it in any way at all. They don't need to because of the winding river of the seam. All pitchers look for some movement, even fastball specialists, because it is so devastating. Or put another way, without it games would end 32-30. One of the unique things about the game is the balance between pitcher and batter: without movement the hitter can hit even a 94 miles per hour fastball with frightening reliability. It is the ability of the pitcher to make the ball deviate that creates the tension upon which the game depends.

Move The Runner(s) Up/Move The Runner(s) Over - The two phrases mean the same thing: the manager, with the help of his hitters, getting one or more base runners from one base to the next. Most commonly, a runner will need to move over from first to second. Once there, in **scoring position**, a single will often be enough to get the runner home (for a run). To move the runner over, two tactics are normally employed apart from this obvious, the hit: a **sacrifice bunt,** a tap to the ground along or near one of the base lines or a **sacrifice fly** where the ball is batted to the deep outfield giving a runner time to run safely across from one base to the next.

Mud Ball – One of the many ways pitchers used, before the game was cleaned up somewhat after the Black Sox Scandal in 1919-20, to doctor a ball so it moved in the air so much it was next to un-hittable, was to put dirt or mud on it; hence 'Mud Ball' here. Smearing the ball with muck also had the virtue, as far as pitchers were concerned, of darkening the colour of it so as to make it hard to see out of the his hand. In those days there was no baseball version of a sightscreen, a block of seats left empty covered in a light 'tarp' (tarpaulin).

Mudville – Part of the lore, history, and mythology of the game is a poem, Casey At The Bat, by Ernest L. Thayer and published in 1888. It's excellent, I think. Casey plays for Mudville. The town has, over the passing decades, been endowed with symbolical status as the "Everytown" all Americans come from, where everyone wants to grow up to be Johnson, Cobb, Ruth, Musial or Koufax. But the writers don't (or they wouldn't be writing, they'd be playing).

So they're all Caseys from Mudville. 'Mudville' also has a pejorative meaning too: an insulting term for the world of major league baseball.

"Muscles (The Ball Out of the Yard)" – When a hitter manages to hit a home run (or double or triple) by using brute strength rather than good timing.

Mustard – If a pitcher throws a fastball with mustard on it, it means it was fast (had some heat*)*.

MVP – 'MVP' is short for the Most Valuable Player Award, given to one player from each league each year. Because the Cy Young Award for best pitcher has so much importance in the game, the MVP winners are usually hitters. Championship Series also see MVP awards being given out. The two MVPs from 2003, Barry Bonds of the Giants and Alex Rodriguez, then of Texas, were replaced at the end of last season by... Barry Bonds of the Giants and

N

Nasty – Adjective to describe a great pitch, especially a huge curve, or a slider or a change-up with big movement. Meant as a compliment to the pitch and pitcher.

Natural Cycle - When a batter achieves hitting for the cycle in ascending sequence of hit: a single, then a double, then a triple, then a home run. Exceptionally rare.

Negro National League - The most famous of the Negro Leagues, founded in 1920 by Rube Foster (a Hall of Famer) and containing great future Hall of Famers such as Cool Papa Bell, Satchel Paige and Josh Gibson. The standard of play was at least as high among the top teams as in the white majors, according to many observers. Games were often played in major league stadiums. The league was very successful but fell away after major league clubs finally started to ditch their racist practices after 1947.

Nickel Curve - Allegedly invented by Chief Bender, this is another name for the slider. It's a term of derision: a cheap curve, not a proper curve. Probably some defeated and disgruntled batter invented the term, or a manager whose team just got mashed by one with a pitcher throwing this new-fangled pitch. As Chief Bender pitched from 1903 to 1925, there seems to be a mysterious time lapse between his invention of this pitch and the advent of the slider in the big leagues, which didn't really happen until the late 1950s or early '60s.

Nightcap – The second game of a double-header.

Nine – **(n)** A team used often to be referred to as a 'nine.' It's far less used these days. I've not heard a modern team referred to as a 'nine' on the TV or in the press since I started following the game.

90 Feet - is the distance that separates each base from the next. Ninety feet and six inches is the distance between the pitcher and the batter (between the mound and the plate).

No Decision – When a starting pitcher is taken out of the game with the scores close, the decision in terms of which pitcher gets the win or loss on his record will often go to a reliever: the ones pitching when the balance of the game changes. If this is the case, the starter gets a "no decision." This is not generally recorded. (See '**Decision**')

No Hitter – Almost the ultimate for a starting pitcher: where he does not give up a single hit in a game. The team will thus almost certainly win the game, so long as their offence manages to bat in at least one run. It is a given that a starter, even if tiring, will be allowed to go the distance to the end of the ninth inning if he has not given up a hit, even now in the age of relievers coming in every night as the norm. But you don't take out a starter in the eighth inning if he's on for the no hitter, unless it's in a must-win game (say in the play offs) because so much prestige is still attached to the feat.

The rarity of the achievement is such that the record for most no hit games in a season is two in both the American and National Leagues. The record for most No Hitters Pitched In A Whole Career is owned by fastballing legend Nolan Ryan (California Angels and Texas Rangers, 70s-early 90s) who threw seven. Only one pitching feat in a game of baseball supercedes the no hitter: the ***Perfect Game***.

Non-tenders - When a player is non-tendered in the off-season, he is officially no longer required by the ball club and becomes a free agent.

Nubber – A poorly hit groundball mis-timed off the bat.

Numbered Uniforms – First appeared in the National League in Cincinnati in 1883, and in the American League not until 1929 in: New York. Numbered sleeves first appeared in the game between, Cleveland v Chicago on June 26 1916.

Numbers - You'll often hear pundits and commentators talking about a player's 'numbers.' These are his stats: ERA probably if he's pitcher; batting average and number of home runs hit if a hitter is the subject of conversation.

Nursery Team - All major league clubs have nursery teams in the minors where they try to produce future stars. Concept mooted in UK football but has been considered too controversial to be experimented with. Almost all minor league teams are now a part of one of the 30 major league franchises which all function as nurseries for growing future big leaguers.

O

Offence - A term used in all American sports including baseball to describe a team's run scoring capability and run scoring record.

Off Season - This is a term that simply describes the time between the last game of the World Series, played in October, and the first game of the next season, usually on or around April 1st.

Off Speed Pitch - Any sort of pitch that comes through the air more slowly than expected as part of an organised pitching strategy. Usually the **change up**, but the splitter can be used as an off speed pitch too.

0 for 4 - This stat is given to you to let you know how a batter is doing in this particular game or how he went. In this case, 0 or 4 is bad and means that the batter has had no hits in four at bats. The four tells you he probably had a walk or was hit, as a hitter can normally expect five plate appearances in a game. He may get six if the team scores a lot of runs and if he's somewhere at the top of the order. He'll get more if there are extra innings, obviously.

Oh And One – The pitching count at no balls, one strike. Nice start for the pitcher.

Oh And One Delivery, The - This refers to the next pitch when the count is at Oh and One. "Here comes the oh and one delivery..."

Oh And Two - No balls, two strikes - one strike away from the batter being struck out: a pitcher's count.

Oh And Three - *Trick entry.* There is no 'Oh and Three' as at this point the batter is simply described as having 'struck out.' I'm just checking you're still awake.

On - Short for 'on base.'

On Base - A player at any of the bases is on base, but it's principally used to tell you that a batter is now a runner on first, or as a measure of a player or team's level success, e.g. *'The Brewers had only four men on base the entire night.'*

On Base Percentage - The game being in a sense all about each team getting as many men on base as they can each inning, the frequency with which each hitter gets on base is understandably important. This is especially so when one appreciates the fact that baseball is a sport obsessed with measuring the value of every participant's performance statistically. This percentage then, records how often the batter reaches first base. Making it four times in ten at bats will give him an OBP of .400 which incidentally is considered very good. His OBP should be higher than his batting average, as it includes walks and being hit. The current rise to importance of Sabermetrics and the success of Billy Beane's so-called 'Moneyball' philosophy at Oakland is raising the profile and significance of on base percentage. The value of a batter getting on base as a key to scoring runs is gradually percolating through the game. Anything over .350 is very good. .400 will get you in the Top 10 every year. Bonds had an on base % of .609, but hardly anyone wanted to pitch to him so he ended the year with a record breaking 232 walks.

On Deck - When a hitter is up at the plate for an at bat, the next player up is already out of the dug out waiting for his turn at the plate. He is said to be 'on deck.' There's a little nautical thing going on here I'll leave you to work out.

On Deck Circle - Whilst on deck, the waiting batter is supposed to wait in a designated white painted box. This is known as the 'on deck circle.' It's about ten feet from the batter's box and there are two: one for the home team, one for the away team. The waiting hitter is not compelled to inhabit it.

One Away - When the first batter is out in an inning, expect to hear the commentator say 'and there's 'one away:' there's one out. Also 'two away,' but not 'three away.' Rather you'll hear, 'and that's the inning.'

One Down - Similar to above, it means the first out of the inning has just been executed by the defense (also again, 'two down' but not 'three,' but see '*Three Up, Three Down.*'

1-4 – Not a good night, but at least your favourite batter got a hit.

One Left On - When an inning is over, it is noted how many men have been left on the bases (on base). It's considered to be somewhere between careless and inept for a batting side to keep getting men on base successfully but being unable to bring them home to score runs. 'One left on' then, records the fact that this team has left one man on base - he could be at first, second or third, it doesn't matter - at the end of this inning.

One On - This means that an offensive team has one man on one of the bases.

One Out, One On - No need to go to 'two out, two on' or 'three out, one man on:' you get the idea.

One Out Double - Used to denote the part of the inning where a double, in this case, though it could be any kind of hit, has been scored by a hitter. Also 'one run single' and 'one run triple.' Also 'two run' or 'three run double, etc.'

One Run Double - A 'one run double' tells us that one run has been scored as a result of ('on') a double. Also 'one run single' and 'one run triple' and 'two run/three run double/triple.' You're not going to hear a 'four run' anything because only a homer can bring in four runs and if this occurs, it's always called a '**Grand Slam**' and everyone knows that brings in four runs.

On The Fists – Geographical expression to describe a pitch inside that lands near the batter's hands as he swings at it. See also '**in on the hands.**'

On The Letters - This one is used to describe a pitch thrown high and in on the batter, at chest height level with the place on the shirt where the team letters are printed. (also an *inside pitch*)

"On" the Padres, Plays – In US sports, players don't play 'for' a team; they play 'on' it.

On The Road - Perennially used to describe a team when they're playing a series 'away from home,' as we'd say in football. It's often used in terms of statistics: "*The Expos are 15 and 23 on the road this year.*"

On The Screws - This means that the batter has hit the baseball on the thick part of the bat - the 'sweet spot' - and timed it really well, hitting it hard and true.

On Three Pitches – "Vizquel struck out swinging on three pitches" means that his at bat only lasted three pitches. In this case, while we're about it, each one would have been a strike.

Opener - Games are played in series of three and four, occasionally two. The first one is called the 'opener.'

Opposite Field - The natural thing for a hitter is to pull the ball. For a right-hander this obviously means hitting the baseball into left field. If however he connects a little earlier he will hit the ball much straighter. Or, if he is pitched away he may not be able to pull the bat round on the ball sufficiently to pull it. If for either reason he actually hits it into right field, he's hit it to the 'opposite field,' the opposite of what you'd expect a hitter to do. See '**Goes The Other Way.**'

Optioned – Looks like a positive statement about a player if he's "optioned," but it isn't: he's just been dropped off the roster, sent down to the minors (to a farm team).

Order, The - The order of the batters in a team. The 'line up.'

Organisation - Euphemism for 'club,' in the total sense. Implied is the importance of the power-wielders: the owner: the CEO (chief executive officer) and the General Manager. It is used just to mean 'the club,' though.

Other Way, The - See '**Goes The Other Way**' and '**Opposite Field.**'

Out (1) - This word is used in noun form in baseball, 'the out.' "*... Furcal throws to first base for the out.*"

Out (2) - This refers to a batter hitting a pitch out of the park for a home run. If you hit it out, it's a homer. "*Keller hit a couple out*"

Out At Home – This is when a runner is tagged out at home plate. When a runner is on base going to the next (or further), it isn't enough for a fielder to step on the base unless an easy out is being made on a double (or triple) play attempt. So at home, the catcher has to tag to runner out. See '**Tag**.'

Outfield, The - The area of the field between the base paths and the perimeter wall or fence.

Outfielder - There are three men who patrol the outfield, spread out clockwise from left field through center field to right field. Their job is to catch fly balls (balls batted into the air) and to field groundballs that pierce the infield. This is the place for the athletes on the roster, who are not just rapid across the grass but who are goalkeeper-agile, prepared to fling themselves with outstretched mitt to make a catch or a stop. This is hugely important in the context of a game: the margin between a made catch and a double, triple or even home run is minimal. A ball high enough to creep over the center field wall for a homer is legally takeable if he can reach over the wall far enough. That's the text book version. The Red Sox play Manny in left field. Sometimes you can hide a guy who's none to athletic at first base, but not always.

Out In Front - A batter gets out in front of a change up, and misses, when he swings too early at the ball not arriving as quickly as expected. His bat is out in front of his body.

Out Of A Jam – Pitching term. If a 'jam' is a tight spot or difficult situation, you get 'out of one' with some good pitches if the count is 0 and 2 or similar, and when there are men on base but you don't let any of them score. If the bases are loaded, conceding one run may still be getting out of a jam.

Out Of here! - A sufficiently enthused sportscaster may well announce the fact of a home run by using this phrase, 'out of here' meaning that the ball has been hit clean out of the playing area. See *'That ball is gone!'*

"Out" Pitch – Most, if not all pitchers have a favourite pitch. They often like to throw it to get the third strike on a hitter. It's likely to be a fastball, a slider or a splitter.

Outrighted –In short, if you're outrighted, you're thrown off the roster at the end of the season down to the minor leagues to clear space for new trades.

Outside - Term used to describe a pitch that is too far away from the batter to land in the strike zone. *"That's outside for a ball."* A ball in this area is also '**off the outside**,' or *'off the outside corner.'*

Outside corner - The strike zone being fridge-shape, its outside corner is the whole of the left hand edge as you look at it from behind the pitcher. This is a great place for a pitcher to land the ball on a regular basis as it's just about the worst place from the hitter's point of view: he'll be looking to leave these expecting or hoping them to be called a 'ball' by the umpire. This is often a more lethal pitch than one on the inside corner, being further away from the batter's pulling swing.

Overhand (curve balls) - Type of curve ball thrown 'over arm,' rather than the more old-fashioned 'roundhouse curve' which is thrown with a round arm action. Overhand or overarm has the throwing arm coming through high past the pitcher's ear; roundarm means the arm will pass the body below shoulder height.

Overgripping - A problem for pitchers sometimes. Gripping the ball too hard, probably through fear of failure or wanting to succeed too hard, losing movement, accuracy or both.

Overpowering Fastball - What every pitcher wants: to be able to blow away the batters with a lightning quick fastball. It's not a case of the fastball having some movement on it, it's just the sheer speed that makes it overpowering.

Overswinging – A batter swinging too hard at the ball. Usually results in the eye being taken off the ball, which causes the miss and the strike or the mis-time and the pop-up or groundout.

Overthrowing - When a pitcher is trying to throw the ball too hard and is likely to lose accuracy and further, hurt his arm.

Over The Bag - is fair – A batted ball that passes over any part of the bag (the base) at first and third is deemed to be in fair territory.

Over The Plate - The plate in this case is the same as the strike zone, so over the plate is where not to put the ball if you're a pitcher. It's really saying that it's a bad pitch, landing more or less over the middle of the strike zone.

P

Paced – Peculiar verb often used in journalism to describe usually a hitter leading the team to a win. *'Green paced the Dodgers to a three run win in the sixth.'*

Painting (The Outside Corner) - Term descriptive of the pitcher's trade. Here it's suggested clearly that it's an art. Painting the outside corner means putting it continually in that spot. That placement is a notoriously difficult one for the batter. For example, just this morning I watched Manny Ramirez, the Red Sox slugger on his way to the Hall of Fame if current trends continue (see Bill James' *The Politics of Glory*, chapter 14, *Hall of Fame Standards*), strike out on three pitches on the outside corner looking. The last pitch was probably a ball, but still: point made, I think.

Palmball - This is a type of change up where the ball is gripped with much of one side in the palm (pitches are usually delivered with the fingers plus some wrist action).

Passed Ball - A ball which goes past the catcher (so shouldn't it be called a "past ball?") *which he is expected to catch,* allowing the runners to advance or the batter to go to first base if it's a third strike. This error, charged to the catcher has the same name.

Payroll – Hugely important factor in baseball success, the club's wage bill, as baseball is a sport, which does not have transfer fees, normally. The culture is one of trading players, not cash. The owners with or prepared to spend, very considerable sums of money on wages to secure the superstars tend to have the best ball clubs. However, this "fact" is contradicted by "*Moneyball.*"

Peg - A phrase for throw, now a little outdated.

Pelted – Describes a pitcher getting taken for a lot of hits and runs.

Pennant - A pennant is a metaphorical trophy for the winning of a division. There used to be two: the American League pennant and that for the National League when each only had one division. Now that there are six, there are six pennant races. Ball clubs winning their league would usually take advantage of the right to display their achievement on a flag atop a flagpole at the ballpark. Most all clubs still do put these achievements on display, but not necessarily in the form of a flag.

Pennant Race - Following on from above, a pennant race is what a team is in or involved in if it has a chance of winning a division. If a division is dominated by one team then it's a pennant race of one or there isn't one that year, depending on your viewpoint. A pennant race doesn't genuinely begin until August, at the earliest.

Pepper/Pepper Game – A pre-game and spring training warm up exercise, much played since way back in time, where a batter knocks a baseball at a circle of fielders, one of whom catches and throws back as fast as he can and so on and so on.

Perfect Game - Exceedingly rare, this is when a starting pitcher goes the nine inning distance without giving up a single hit, walk or hitting a batsman. The fielding side must prevent the making of an error that allows a batter to get safely to first. Only fifteen perfect games have been pitched in 103 seasons of major league play. The most recent was in 1999, pitched by David Cone of the Yankees until Randy Johnson pitched one last season for the Diamondbacks, the 17th in major league baseball history.

Perfect Inning – Where a pitcher gets three outs with no batter getting on base: so no hits, no errors, no walks and no hit batters.

Phantom Tag – When a fielder tries to con the umpire that he's made a tag on a base runner: he swings his arm in a tagging motion knowing he can't quite reach the runner.

Phantom Throw – These are more common, where the fielder tries to con the base runner into thinking he has the ball in his hand when he hasn't. It's done to make the runner pause on his way to the next base and so giving the defense a better opportunity of making an out.

Pheenom (pronounced '*Feee-nom)* - A brilliant new young player is a 'pheenom.' A diminutive of the word 'phenom-enon,' you'll be shocked to know.

Pick - Good defensive play by an infielder.

Picking Your Spots - This phrase describes a pitcher aiming for certain parts of the strike zone (or just outside): pitching for or with placement and accuracy.

Pickoff (throw) - The base runner looking to steal a base has the danger of being 'picked off' to contend with. If the base stealer takes off before the pitcher is in the stretch position: is about to make his pitch, the pitcher can pull out of the pitch and throw to first base. If the base runner can't get back and touch the base (or 'bag') before the pick off throw hits the glove of the fielder at first base, he's out. This out possibility leads to a lot of (sometimes) tedious throwing from pitcher to the first baseman to deter the runner from stealing a base.

Pilot – Alternative and at present, unfashionable term for manager.

Pinch Hitter - A manager can substitute one hitter for another at any time, traditionally only late in the game. The substitute is always called a 'pinch' hitter. The pinch hitter goes into the batting line up in the same place in the order as the player he has replaced. The fielding capability may be weakened as a result in the AL. In the NL, the potential for bringing in pinch hitters opens up a channel for all sorts of strategic changes. If at the end of the sixth inning in a game with home field advantage, you want to take out your starter, you can bring in a pinch hitter for him at the bottom of that inning, thus strengthening your offense. At this stage, a National League manager may like to use a different relief pitcher for the seventh, eighth and ninth for just this reason.

Pinch Runner - Just as you can replace a batter at any time, so you can a runner. A pinch runner comes in when a team really needs a run. So an improved runner may not only get round the bases quicker on someone's hit, but he may be much more likely to steal a base to get something going too. The runner bats in the line up now, thus the batting strength may be weakened for the rest of the game, unless he is then replaced by a pinch hitter. Pinch running is exceptionally important, as I am only just learning and can win ball games in late innings. An oddity it may be in a country where we expect all professional sportsmen to be exceptionally fit where any running is involved, but major league baseball has a number of right lardos and slackers who go round the bases like hippos after a large meal. Hence the regular need for pinch runners. To be fairer, in the AL, the designated hitter position has allowed old guys with dodgy knees to prolong a career. They can often still hit great, but can't run.

Pine Tar – A substance batters rub on the handle of the bats for a nice firm dry grip. This would appear to be dark viscous stuff originally distilled from pinewood and used for donkey's years by the pros. The Franklin company does a stick of it that you can get for $6.99 from your local sports store (if you happen to live in America). But it's white, so where the tar action's happening in it, you'll have to guess.

Pitch - The term for the delivery of the baseball to the catcher where the pitcher tries to get the batter out and the batter tries to hit the ball. See below for details and 'sequence pitching.' The centre of the action and the mystery of baseball.

Pitch Around Him - This is what the defensive team may do when they have a highly toxic hitter at the plate such as Bonds or ARod. The idea is to tempt him with wider, higher, lower pitches out of the strike zone to try to induce a mistake, but more so to avoid throwing something to him he can actually hit. Thus pitching around is more than half way to the intentional walk.

Pitcher - The player who throws the ball at the catcher, aiming to get the batter, who stands in between, to either miss the ball, hit it along the ground to a fielder or in the air to a fielder. The pitcher is the only man who is not a "position player."

Pitcher's Count – A count with more strikes than balls. See **"The Count (Pitch)."**

Pitcher's Mound - see **'The Mound.'**

Pitcher's Ballpark – The opposite of a **'Hitter's Ballpark,'** one where the outfield is large and the fences a long way distant from home plate, so the number of homers hit there is below the average. Indoor parks (those in Toronto, Minnesota, Montreal and Seattle, Houston, Phoenix and Tampa Bay when the retractable roofs aren't retracted) tend to have 'dead' air that causes the fly ball to flop somewhere over the warning track, and are never subject to a wind blowing out toward center field, so tend to favour pitchers. For most of the twentieth century parks helped the pitcher because they were so big. The 'cookie cutter' parks of the Sixties and Seventies didn't help the hitters either. The shrinking strike zone of the 1990s saw a boost in hitting and there is no sign that anyone in the game (apart from pitchers of course) wants a return to the attritional baseball of the Dead Ball Era and the mid-to-later sixties where guys could pitch a two-hitter and lose 0-1. So expect all future new parks to be 400' away in center and about 320-330 distant at the foul poles, making for fields that are fair game for the slugger.

Pitcher's Team - A team considered to be particularly strong in pitching. They will have excellent starters and depth in high quality relief pitching.

Pitch Him Away - This means a pitcher is aiming his pitches as far away from the batter's body as he can. He is trying to hit the outside corner of the plate while the batter has to reach for the pitch somewhat. Some batters like the ball here while some prefer it rather more in on the body ('inside'). They all like it down the middle.

Pitching Change - These can be made at any time during a game and their number is only limited by the number of pitchers available on the roster. It is not unusual for a manager to use seven or eight pitchers if he thinks he needs to or has to, if they're all getting beat up by the hitters.

Pitching Coach - The pitching coach always sits in the dug out with the manager and is the coach of first resort if a pitcher is getting into trouble. See **'Coaches.'**

Pitching Duel - A low scoring game where pitchers of both teams are giving up few hits and fewer runs, often none. So-called connoisseurs of baseball, or rather, traditionalists, love the pitching duel. It's the "pitching as high art" theme for the intellectual lover of the game. You, on the other hand, may find it boring.

Pitching Duet – This term describes a game which is/was a battle between two pitchers who were allowing the other team very few runs or none.

Pitching Gem - Frequently used term to describe an exceptional performance by a pitcher (naturally). This will often mean that he pitched a complete game: went the whole nine innings.

Pitching Match Up - The two starting pitchers facing each other on the given day, e.g., Beckett v Schmidt.

Pitching Rubber – In 1893 a new rule was brought in, moving the distance from home plate to pitcher's box to 60 feet, 6 inches (it had been 45 feet in the first year of the majors in 1876, then 50 feet in 1881), where it has been ever since. The distance from the centre of home plate (this accounts for the 6 inches) to the pitching place was marked at the pitcher's end by a piece of rubber, twelve inches long and four inches wide. At the point of delivery, one foot must be in contact with the rubber. In 1895 it was increased in size to 24 by 6 inches, where it has remained.

Pitching Screen – In daily batting practice, practice pitchers do a lot of throwing below the speed of match pitchers; batters want to get the feel of the ball coming off the bat a long way for the sake of their confidence. This threatens the integrity of the bodily health of the practice pitcher who will now be in the way of a lot of batted balls; thus the need for a protective screen. This comes up to waist level and stops bruised shins and knee injuries.

Pitching Staff - Collective term for the entire group of pitchers a ball club has on its roster. Most clubs will keep a pitching staff of close to fifty per cent of their 25 and 40 man rosters.

Pitch Out - This is used to signify the procedure for an intentional walk. The catcher moves to the first base side of home plate a few feet where the pitcher lobs four consecutive 'pitches' well out of reach of the frustrated batter. Where you might expect the batter to stand with his hands by his side waiting for his trip to first base, he always shapes to hit, as if the pitcher and catcher will suddenly revert to real pitching. They never do, though. There's something slightly demeaning in seeing Barry Bonds still forlornly waggling his bat as the four balls go sailing by two metres away when you know he'd love to be swishing his bat at real pitching.

Pitch Selection - The phrase 'pitch selection' tells you something immediately about pitching: it's a matter not of brute force but of intelligence. Strategy plays a highly important role in the struggle between pitcher and batter. The one struggles to gain the upper hand against the other. The advantage is with the one who statistically succeeds more often: the pitcher. He is able to hurl this small projectile from a distance of only sixty feet, six inches at an absurdly high pace. Furthermore, only he knows what he's going to throw next from what is potentially a very considerable storehouse of weaponry. To win the duel he will very often select each pitch in the at bat from this store in order to defeat the batter with three strikes or a false stroke: sliders, two-seam and four-seam fastballs, sinkers, change ups, curves, splitters in or away, frighteningly high or deceptively how. All the batter has is his eyesight, his trained instincts, experience and a swing of the bat when his eye is in harmony with his brain. See *'Sequence pitching.'*

Pitch To Contact – Type of pitching where his aim is to make the batter hit the ball. If this sounds odd, the idea is that pitching close to or in the difficult parts of the strike zone will constantly produce groundball outs. Or if there is good movement on the pitches, it should produce swinging and some   called, strikes. In theory, giving up walks shouldn't happen.

Place Hitting - This is the tactic or skill of hitting a pitch into the outfield or outfield spaces either through or over the infield for bases as opposed to trying to hit the long ball out of the park for a home run. Not your slugging approach to the game, which has been the fashion for the overwhelming majority of hitters for a number of years now.

Plate, The - Frequently used shorthand for home plate.

Plate – (v) If you see something like, "Ordonez' single plated the eighth run," it means that the Maglio Ordonez hit a single which brought a base runner across home plate for the team's eighth run of the game.

Plate Coverage – The extent to which a batter is able to master the plate geographically with the bat. This is a defensive issue primarily: he's covering the plate so he can fend off a pitch on the outside corner. This threatens the batter because he likes to leave a pitch outside the strike zone for a ball so he can "get ahead" of the pitcher (more balls than strikes in the count always pressurizes the pitcher to throw over the plate, an easier pitch for the batter to hit).

Plated, Run – If a run is plated, it's scored.

Plate Discipline – This describes the hitter's ability to limit his swings during an at bat to pitches that can reasonably said to be hittable. Pitchers, usually when ahead in the count, will seek to tempt batters to swing at pitches out of the strike zone and so get easier strikes or outs. The big hitters, the sluggers, always looking to hit home runs can be said to have at best indifferent plate discipline (Vladimir Guerrero and Jim Thome come obviously to mind here) while lead off men often have great discipline, knowing that to get on base, anyhow, any way, is the key.

Platooning - This is a term one frequently comes across in reading books about the past. It refers to the practice of not having a first choice catcher or first baseman or shortstop (etc), but alternating between two players. It used to be used where a player was ageing and couldn't play every day, or where a team didn't have an outstanding player in that position. Many teams platoon their catchers, where the strain of all that bending is too much for one man to go 162 games. The Boston Red Sox platoon two catchers because their knuckleballer Tim Wakefield and their sinkerball pitcher Derek Lowe like being caught by a particular pitcher, the number two Doug Mirabelli.

Play – (n) This is *such* a useful term for broadcasters: we should use it in our own sports in the UK I think. In the US a 'play' is a potential act a fielder should or is about to make. When he acts: tries to pick up a grounder and throw to first base successfully for a put out, there is immediately a play to be made. In the language, he is trying to 'make the play.' In baseball, a play 'exists' then, when there is the potential for a fielder to field the ball, catch the ball or throw the ball. There might be two plays as a result of one batted ball: the ball has to be gathered in by the fielder and then there may well be an opportunity to throw the hitter out. However, it is not quite all encompassing. A pitch is not a play and neither is what the batter does with it. But as soon as the batter makes contact with the ball there is bound to be at least one a play to make, unless the pitch goes for a home run, which comfortably clears the fence. If it's creeping over, technically there's a possibility that an outfielder may be able to jump up over the height of the wall and make the catch. Make the play, in fact.

Play Every Day – Euphemism for playing in every game and for being in a club's first choice nine for each game. If you play 'ever day' you're a regular.

Play Offs – In baseball today, at the end of a 162 game *regular season*, eight teams, four from each league, play off for the honour of making the World Series, a sort of Cup Final and League Championship hybrid. Each group of four comprises the winners of each of the three divisions, East, Central and West, plus the team with the best win-loss record of the remaining teams across the three divisions. This place is called *the wild card*.

The four are paired and play a best of five game series. These are called Division Series (NLDS/ALDS). The two winners then play off against each other for the right to play their mirror image in the other league in a best of seven series. These are called Championship Series (NLCS/ALCS). The winning teams from each league then play *The World Series*, again in a best of seven *set*.

Plunk - Slang term for a hitter being hit by a pitch.

Pop - A pitch with 'pop' on it is one with really good or extra speed.

Pop Fly – A pop fly is a mis-hit that goes high into the air for what should be an easy out in the infield, unless it loops over into the crowd to become a foul ball.

Pop-Up - A ball hit into the air in baseball is described in two ways. If it's hit over the infield - in which case the batter's got a decent bit of bat on the ball, probably - it's a fly ball; if it simply loops up into the air from a miss-hit inside the infield, it's a 'pop up.' If it goes up a long way it's a 'pop fly,' but if it doesn't, it's just a pop-up. It should end with an easy catch unless it arcs over into the crowd in which case it's a foul ball.

Porch – Now that ballpark design has returned to the double-decker grandstands of the past, we have the return of the "porch" (see Camden Yards and The Ballpark In Arlington). The term refers to 'stands with upper decks that sit invitingly close to home plate for the slugger. The "short porch" describes one particularly close to the batter's box.

Position Player - All members of the fielding side apart from the pitcher can and often are referred to as 'position players.'

Post-Season - When the teams have played 162 games, the first part of the season is over, the regular season, and we now have the play offs (four Division Series then two Championship series), then the World Series. All games after the regular season constitute the 'Post-Season.'

Pound (the fastball) – Phrase for what sluggers do when they hit a lot of fastballs to the deep outfield for extra base hits or right out of the park.

Pound The Strike Zone – A pitching strategy where he throws most of your pitches at the strike zone, keeping walks to a minimum and hoping for a lot of groundball outs. If a pitcher cannot reliably keep the ball down, this is not a good idea.

Powdered It – Ball hit very hard, usually for a home run

Power Hitter - A batter who specializes in power: hits for home runs and a lot of doubles.

Power Alleys, The - The gaps in left-center and right-center field, where the sluggers are wont to hit the ball, for doubles and triples.

Power Pitcher - One who relies on the fastball (speed) for success rather than finesse and subtlety.

Production – Slightly abbreviated form of "run production." A hitter's production is his ability to produce runs on the basis (mostly) of hits and home runs.

Productive Out – An out which is of some use to the side, like a sacrifice bunt or a sacrifice fly, because it advances one (or more) of the baserunners.

Prospect - A term for a young, talented player with a lot of potential. They are often trade-fodder.

Protecting The Plate – This means getting the bat on a difficult pitch to stop yourself being struck out when there are two strikes on you. It may also mean the batter positioning himself closer to the plate than he'd normally like so as to cover the pitch on the outside corner. Against the power pitcher this will increase his chances of being struck by the ball pitched inside, so caution is required. This is an essentially defensive position, one not taken normally by the very best hitters in the game unless they're facing the very best of pitchers. The term can also be used in terms of the pitcher's response to a batter crowding the plate. He makes a pitch or two inside, towards the batter's body to get him to back off the plate and give him the chance to see the 'imaginary' strike zone and his catcher clearly.

Protection - Batters wear all manner of protection: batting gloves, helmets, lower leg and wrist and lower arm guards and groin protectors. Though ex-pitcher and broadcaster Eric Baat has written almost sneeringly about the batters, cosseted by all this equipment, they're a very brave bunch of sportsmen if you ask me with a swerving solid ball hurled at them from 60 feet at up to 100 mph.

Some First Uses: Catcher's mask: James Tying of Harvard 1877. Chest Protectors for catchers: 1887. Catcher's gloves: 1890s. Charles Bennett; Shin Guards: 1906 Red Dooin, inside the socks; Roger Bresnahan 1907, outside the socks. Helmets: since around 1905 by individual players, by teams since the 1941 Brooklyn Dodgers, then adopted piecemeal. In 1971, wearing a helmet became mandatory.

Pull - This is what batters usually do when they make contact with the baseball. It means a right-handed batter hitting the ball into left field. This tends to occur most often because a horizontal swing of any bat-shaped object will cause the object to describe a right to left arc. The pulling of the ball thus occurs 'naturally;' this is true for both left and right-handed hitters. A player who only pulls the ball is thus more limited than one who is able to hit the ball **'the other way.'**

Pulling The String - A phrase used to describe a pitcher who has really good control of his pitches: change ups; curves; sliders and the like, to constantly defeat the attempts of the batters on the opposing side to make a hit. It's as though they have the hitter on a string.

Punch Out – Strike out.

Put Down A Bunt - Same as 'laying down' a bunt: it means putting a bunt into operation, or trying to.

Put Guys/Him In Motion – Base runners are not supposed to steal bases without the permission of the managers at the time they are on base. If the manager allows it, the runner will get a coded sign from the manager or from a base coach to whom the skipper has sent a sign. Allowing base runners to steal is often known as "putting guys in motion": allowing them, getting them to steal some bases to try to *get something going*," to score some runs.

Put Him Away – Strike a batter out.

Put Him On – This is code for the **intentional walk**. If a manager decides to have the pitcher walk a hitter, the decision has been made to 'put him on:' put him on base.

Put Out – When a batter is caught out or when the batter puts the ball in play only to be thrown out at first base it can be called a 'put out.' Not to be confused with a 'force out' which is only applied to a base runner being thrown out running to the next base.

R

Racism - 28 year old Frank Robinson was taken on by the Brooklyn Dodgers organization in 1946, thus breaking down the rusty, fetid wall of racism separating black Americans from their birthright: to be major league baseball players of the USA if that's what they wanted to be: if they were good enough. And of course, they were more than good enough. It came as a pleasant surprise recently to find the Hall Of Fame website for the first time and realise that pre-1947 brilliant Afro-Americans, who'd played in the Negro Leagues, had been admitted. Robinson played under immense pressure as the first non-white major leaguer, and many, many others now faced the opprobrium of racism from inside the game. It doesn't take a genius to notice what baseball had been missing all those years: think what we all would be missing right now without Barry Bonds, Alex Rodriguez, Sammy Sosa, Bartolo Colon, Manny Ramirez and Carlos Delgado, and what relative poverty the game would have suffered without Hank Aaron, Willie Mays, Jackie Robinson, Bob Gibson et al. With the gene pool being expanded by the inclusion of players from Central America, Puerto Rico and Mexico, it's safe to say that the average major league player is significantly better than his counterparts when the game was exclusively white. That's a controversial view, and it's not original, but it seems obvious to me.

Radar Gun - Pitches are measured for speed at every ballpark and displayed on some sort of video screen after a pitch for attendees to take notice of if they want.

Rain Check – For over 120 years some clubs have taken to the practice of giving out ticket portions to fans who have paid their entrance to a game only to see it rained out. The rain check allows them to use it as entrance to another game later in the season or the same game the next day.

Rain Delay – An officially stated delay to a ballgame due to rain. American summers are hot so the occasional heavy summer storm is to be expected. On the east coast the season begins in a precarious spring where English style frontal rain can ruin the day until April is out.

Rain Out – Universal term for "match abandoned" due to rain.

Rally – I always thought this meant coming from behind to level a score or take the lead, but in the States it means in baseball to put a bunch of hits and runs together.

Range - This is a term that relates to a fielder's ability to make successful plays. It's also turned into a statistic used to compare players in the same position across different teams: 9 x Plays Made per innings played. There is a further stat here, 'range factor,' calculated by adding putouts to assists x 9 divided by innings played.

RBI (Run Batted In) - The number of runs a hitter has 'batted in,' base runners brought across home plate for a run on his hits (or from being hit or being walked with the bases loaded) is one of the prime valuation mechanisms of a batter. The best hitters will be looking to cross the one hundred for the season mark around early to mid August. The RBI leader every year brings in between 140 and 160, and this is true for both leagues, give or take the odd blip in the National League. In 2001 Sammy Sosa broke the NL record with 160 and Manny Ramirez, then at Cleveland batted in 165 runs, the most since 1930 in that league. Last season, incidentally, Miguel Tejada of Baltimore led both leagues with 150.

A hitter bats a run in when a runner crosses the plate on one of his hits. If two men come in on a hit (usually a double) he gets two: if he hits a home run then he picks up an RBI for himself and one for every base runner. A grand slam then nets four RBIs to the hitter. If a batter hits the ball in play but is thrown out, he still gets the RBI if a man on third crosses the plate. Same with a sacrifice bunt or hit. However, if, with no outs, he hits into a double play with a man on third who comes home for a run, he does not get the RBI. Did you know that - which is code for 'I just found out by pure luck'- that if a runner on third comes in for a run on a wild pitch, the hitter at bat gets credited with the RBI?

RBI Double - This describes a batter hitting a double that also brings a runner home. A 'two RBI double' tells you that two runs have been batted in on the hit.

RBI Single - As above, with the batter bringing a runner home with a single.

RBI Triple - Ditto, on an outfield hit which sees the hitter get around to third.

Reaches - If a batter "reaches" he gets on base.

Reaches Back - Applies to a pitcher really digging back.

Receiver - Alternative usage for catcher.

Red Ass - A 'red ass' is a player, usually an infielder, who plays with real fire and intensity. He gets his red ass from diving in the dirt on the base paths.

Regular Season - The baseball season is divided into two phases: the regular season of 162 games (yes, new fans, check it out: 162! it's not a misprint) and the post-season, containing two sets of play off games before the baseball equivalent of the finals: the World Series which determines the champion baseball team of the season.

Relay Throw - Same as a cut off throw where an outfielder throw from deep is intercepted by an infielder so the ball can be moved as rapidly as possible to one of the bases for a force out attempt.

Relief - Where a fresh pitcher is brought to the mound after the starting pitcher has completed the number of innings required of them by the manager.

Relief Pitcher - The timing of the appearance of a reliever depends upon the manager and his reading of the game. Normally there are two catalysts: the pitcher getting spanked by the opposing batters and giving up a mounting number of runs and the successful starter beginning to tire. In the case of the former, bringing in a new pitcher (never a 'replacement' or 'substitute,' always a reliever) may well be an easy decision to make and the latter somewhat harder. The shrewd manager may pull the starter *before* he starts getting hit, rather than keeping him in until fatal damage is done in a couple of swift, devastating blows. The 2003 American League Championship Series, a titanic seven game struggle between ancient rivals the Boston Red Sox and the New York Yankees, was decided by the fateful decision regarding relief pitching. 5-2 ahead after seven innings, Sox pitching star Pedro Martinez was fatefully left in the game when almost the entire on-looking baseball world expected, and in the case of Sox fans begged, manager Grady Little to bring in his hitherto exceptionally successful team of relief pitchers. In the eighth inning, a burst of hitting from a flagging superstar saw the Red Sox lead vanish. They lost in the tenth. Little lost his job. 'Deservedly so,' said almost everyone.

Reliever - Short hand for a relief pitcher.

Reserve Clause - The dreaded reserve clause was in operation in major league baseball from its inception in 1879 until December 1975 when the power of the players finally broke it. Under the clause, a player could be held under contract by a club indefinitely: had the power to "reserve" his services from one year at a time. This was one of the worst examples of twentieth century American hypocrisy: this was the land of the free and above all, free trade, and yet when legally challenged, for example by Curt Flood in 1973, the Supreme Court refused to declare that an

American ballplayer was free to play   where he was most wanted or for the club who bid highest for his services. Instead they ruled that baseball was an anomalous business: that what was a restriction of freedom in all other circumstances in American society was not to be recognized as such in baseball because, when it came down to it, they accepted the owners' argument that the end of the reserve clause would take salaries through the roof, destroying baseball in the process.   They were able to act illogically and in terms of natural law, 'illegally' because of baseball's unique place in American society and history.

This all came to an end with the victory of free agency in '75 when at last, Andy Messersmith of the Dodgers and Andy McNally of the Expos successfully challenged the law. The owners agreed to put the clause to a three-man arbitration panel and lost the vote 1-2. Baseball survived. What a surprise. See also, *'Ten Day Rule'*.

Resin Bag - If you see something that looks like a pair of rolled up white socks with a bobble on the end on the back slope of the pitching mound, it's the resin bag. Pitchers grab this so that some white powdered resin puffs out on to their hands to keep them dry so they can grip the baseball with absolute assurance.

Rest - The time between pitchers' outings is called 'rest.' This is a vital issue for all the starters; the toll on their arms of throwing a hundred-plus pitches is often considerable. See '*Short Rest.*'

Retired - A batsmen who is 'out' is 'retired' by the fielding side. Both an individual batter and a team are talked of as being 'retired,' as in '*Buerle retired the side in order in the fifth.*' See '**In Order.**'

Retired Numbers - There is a strong tradition at each of the baseball clubs in the country to honour a great player on that team by retiring his number, to take it out of commission so no one else can use it. The latest to receive the accolade was Tony Gwynn of the San Diego Padres in June 2004.

Rhubarb – Old-fashioned term for baseball fight or heated argument.

Ribbie – (n) Short for RBI, occasionally used.

Ridiculous – A voguish high compliment for a great pitcher or hitter, as in "ridiculously good."

Riding - Historical term for players slagging each other off to put them off during play, an enormous amount of which used continually to go on until recent times. Cricket's 'sledging.' You might also read about a hitter 'riding' a home run, however, meaning he hit the ball real good out of the park.

Right - 'Right' is used a shorthand for 'right field.' A batter may be heard to have 'lined out to right,' meaning that he hit a line drive that was caught on the full by the right fielder. '*He hits that to right,*' means that the batter has hit the ball into right field over the infield.

Right-Center - Geographical term, describing the direction the batter has hit the ball, e.g., 'Ichiro *flies out to right-center.*'

Right-Center Gap – A pitch here, the space between the center and the right fielders should be good for a double: a triple if hit hard enough and if it rolls awkwardly enough.

Right Field - The outfield is split into three equal but imaginary geographical areas: left field, center field and right field. The right-hand third of that area is always called 'right field.'

Right Field Corner - Where right field meets the right field line extending all the way back to home plate is this area of difficulty for the right fielder. In some ballparks the corner is oddly shaped making it difficult for the right fielder to collect the ball quickly and cleanly.

Right Fielder - The outfielder who patrols right field.

Right Field Line - Line of white 'paint' which extends at ninety degrees to the third base line towards the perimeter fence dividing fair territory from foul.

Right Field Umpire - In the World Series only, there is a right field umpire who is responsible for that sector of the outfield. Because there is no extra center field umpire, this umpire has to take the whole right sector of the outfield, but he may be overruled on calls by the home plate umpire, who is effectively the chief of umpires.

Right-Hander – Not a term for a batter: it's for a pitcher who throws, well, right-handed.

Ring, World Series - The players on the roster of the World Series winning team are each awarded an inscribed ring (as opposed to medals awarded in football). The players prize them hugely. They name the player, the teams, the score and the year.

Rips – (n) 'Last Rips' might be heard to describe a team's batters going out for the ninth inning. 'Rips' are swings of the bat.

Rip(s) – (v) When a hitter "*rips it right over the wall in center field*" he hits a ball very hard. Same as *"drills it."*

Road Trip - When a team goes to play a series of games against another 'away from home,' they go on a road trip, even if they fly everywhere these days. These can be as long as a week and a half.

Role Player – Player who doesn't play in the line up every day, but who has a useful specialty, such as fast speed on the bases (so is used as a pinch runner) or excellent defensive skill (so is brought into the infield in the late innings to protect a lead or stop the bleeding). He'll *sit* most of the time.

Roller - Whilst a grounder is a legitimate way to try to get a hit, a roller just rolls fairly meekly off the bat for a probable out.

Rookie - A rookie is a term used in all major American sports and means a player in their first year in the big leagues, so long as he has had 130 at bats, pitched 50 innings or spent 45 days on the 25-man roster.

Rookie Season/Rookie Year - A rookie season is a player's first season where he plays a significant number of games. If in 2004 a player makes four appearances then in 2005 he makes 120, 2005 is his rookie year.

Round Tripper - Euphemism for home run.

Rope 1- (n) Is a hard hit line drive.

Rope 2 – (v) If a pitcher is described as getting 'roped' it means he went for a lot of hits.

Roster – Unlike all British sports, baseball teams have an official, limited number of players in their "first team squad" each season, a "roster" or list. Players can be moved on and off this roster at will throughout the season. The 25-man roster is used throughout the season up to the 1st of September, when the club can expand to a 40-man roster for the rest of the regular season. The eight play off teams have to switch back to a 25-man roster for the duration. At the end of the regular 162-game season, managers pick their 25-man roster for each series. They are not committed to the same 25 for all play off games. See '*Sent Down*' and '*Called Up.*'

Round Tripper - Another term for a home run.

Rubber Arm – If a pitcher has one of these, then he's got an arm that never gets damaged and never wears out. Roger Clemens would seem to be the best example of this phenomenon at the moment. He's 41 at 7-0 for Houston on the 2004 season as I write. The opposite of the rubber arm is the glass arm, the fragile one belonging to the pitcher who breaks down a lot.

Rubber, The - The rubber is the honour of winning a series of games, classically an odd number so that one team has to be victor. A rubber over four games or two can be won 3-1 or 2-0. 4-0 and it's a *sweep.*

Rubber Game - The rubber game is the deciding one in a series with an odd number of games, i.e. the third in a three game series, the fifth in a five game series and so on.

Rule 5 Draft – A rule to stop rich teams stockpiling young talent in their farm systems. If a player is not on the team's 40-man roster at the Nov 20th deadline and he has been with the club for 3 years (or 4 if signed before the age of 17), he can be drafted by another club. If acquired in this way, the drafting club has to keep the player on the 40-man roster for one whole season or it has to offer the player back for half the original $50 000 draft fee. Because of this, Rule V drafts number around a dozen per year. As with organised drafts of high school and college players each June, the team with the worst record the previous season has first pick, and so on.

Run Batted In (RBI) - See '*RBI.*'

Rundown – This describes a situation where a man on base is committed to running to the next base and is caught between two fielders, one of the bases behind and one on the base in front, one of who has the ball. Escape is almost impossible for the baserunner as he has to run to a base without skirting off into the outfield: he has to stay on the base path. He is almost always tagged out by an infielder, though a real speedster has been known to unnerve infielders sufficiently to cause wild throws. An inept fielder may let the runner dive under the tag occasionally. These days, a rundown means an inevitable out in 99% + cases.

Runner – Short for 'base runner.' As soon as he gets on base, the batter is now a 'runner' and his job is to get round the bases to score a run.

(The) Runner Advances - See '*Advance The Runner.*'

(The) Runner Goes! – The base runner on first (say) has the choice of whether to try to steal a base or not. When he decides to make the attempt, "the runner goes!" Note that the decision is normally made from the bench by the manager rather than by the runner.

The Runner Holds – If he stays, he holds. The runner may be 'held' by a pitcher who is aware of the imminent steal and is ready to throw to the base rather than pitch. Some pitchers are much easier to steal on than others. Left-handers are harder to steal on at first base because their head is angled to face the first base line.

Runners On The Corners - Lovely expression, which means that there's a base runner at, bases one and three: spells severe danger for the fielding side.

Running Game – A style of baseball, this is the opposite of the team that gets most of its runs by making big hits. So, the running game is about running the bases hard and with speed, running aggressively trying to stretch singles into doubles, doubles into triples, stealing bases as often as you can and bunting often. The 2003 Florida Marlins won a World Series with this tactical approach.

Run Out – A batter is required to 'run out' a ball that's batted straight to a fielder: run as hard and as fast as you can. Some hitters are keener than others to make the 100% level of effort expected by the team.

Run Producer – A 'run producer' is a hitter who makes a lot of hits and bats guys in with singles and doubles and homers. A good run producer will be a guy who makes around 150 hits a year (or more) and gets 100+ RBIs.

Runs - There is no alternative usage to the name for what is scored in baseball. It's 'runs.' A run is only scored when a base runner crosses home plate successfully.

Runs (vb) – A pitcher who has movement on his pitches to the side (as opposed to the curve which loops) "runs" the ball away or into the batter. He makes it move one way or the other.

Run Scored - When a base runner crosses home plate he scores a run and this is immediately chalked on to his statistics. The number of runs a player scores in a season has been used a lot traditionally as a measure of his prowess, but his RBI total is more significant. Sure, to score a run you have to get on base, which usually means he's made a hit, but he might have got there through a walk because of bad pitching.

Note that once the third out is made to end the inning, a runner who has crossed the plate from third base before the out is made *does not score*. Normally for example, if the batter flies out in the outfield the runner can tag up to score - he can leave third base the moment the catch is made. When the third out is made with the catch, the inning is immediately over and no runs can be scored. Normally, i.e. with none or one out, a player can score from third if he crosses home plate before the batter is thrown out at first base or before a force out is made on a runner leaving first or second base. In the case of the third out being made however, the run is crossed off. There is one exception: when the third out is NOT made on a force play, for example one caused by a runner trying to make it back to one of the bases (a rundown). If the runner at third crosses home plate before the runner is thrown out trying to make it back to second (or first in the case of the hitter flying out for the *second* out – the man caught returning to the base makes the third out), the run counts, because it is not a force play.

'Run Scoring Double' - This denotes a batter having hit a double and got at least one man who was on base at the time of the hit, home. Hence 'run scoring single' and 'run scoring triple.'

Run Support - What a pitcher needs to get the win: the batters on his team scoring some runs. You'll hear something like, '*the Expos pitchers just aren't getting enough run support this year*' in context.

S

Sabermetrics – Derives from the Society For the Advancement Of Baseball Research (SABR), a body of individuals who are dedicated to the study of baseball, both to uncover the sport's history and to develop a better understanding of the game through statistics and the careful scrutiny thereof.

Sacrifice Fly/Sac Fly - To advance a runner (to move a runner around the bases nearer home and the precious run), a hitter may well be expected to sacrifice himself. Here he hits the ball deep – a fly ball - into the outfield giving the runner(s) sufficient time to move to the next base (see '**tagging up**'). 'Sac' fly is often heard shorthand for 'sacrifice.' The sac fly is a tactic to be used when there are no outs or one. If there are two outs, the sac fly is useless, as the caught ball will immediately end the inning. Even if while the ball is in the air a runner has made it home, the 'run' doesn't count.

Sack – Another term for the physical base out there on the diamond, so called because the bases used to be small stuffed canvas sacks or bags. This is to prevent runners being injured when sliding into the bases. Today they're made of softish rubber. attached to the ground by a metal spike.

Sacks Full – Same as 'bases loaded:' there's a man on each base.

Sacrifice Bunt (Sac Bunt) - A bunt may also advance the runner(s). Although a bunt might be so well executed as to enable the batter to reach first in time, it very often results in the batter being thrown out at first. Thus the concept of sacrifice. Again, this is not to be attempted with two outs!

Safe – Is when a runner makes it to base safely: he's not 'in,' he's 'safe.'

Safe At Home - When a runner makes it home on a close play to score a run.

Safely - To 'hit safely in nine straight games' is to make one hit (at least) in each game.

Safety - n A hit. The term directly reflects the essential fact about baseball, proved over and over from the start of the organized game that the competitive advantage is essentially with the pitcher. The notion of the batter getting on base representing 'safety' expresses the insecurity of his job.

Safety Squeeze - A *squeeze play* where the runner only leaves third for home if the bunt looks good enough for him to make it home; a low risk squeeze play, in other words.

Sail - If a fastball has "sail" on it, it has sideways movement on it. Bob Feller comments on this aspect of pitching in his chapter from Donald Honig's *They Used To Play On Grass*.

Salaries - See **'Payroll.'**

Sandlot - If and when you start reading about old baseball players and old baseball, you'll come across the term "sandlot," as in 'Yeah, I used to play a lot of sandlot ball when I was a kid." It's origin is in a roughly diamond shape patch of sand on a park where kids could play baseball, but it's become a generic term for baseball played in a non-organized way on any old spare patch of ground or in a park.

Save, The - When a team is leading in the eighth or ninth inning, a specialist pitcher will probably be brought in to hopefully preserve the lead successfully - close the game out. If he does so, he gets the save. This is no mere conceptual matter: if the gap between the teams at the end of the eighth inning is more than three runs, it is not a save situation: there is nothing to 'save' quite, because normally a team will not be able to pull back three runs in one inning. It happens rarely these days because of specialist closers who throw hard, are fresh and who specialize in this job.

The closer's record is kept close eye on throughout his season: number of saves achieved against saves blown. The team doesn't have to go on to lose for the closer to blow the save. If he comes in at 5-4 and gives up a tying run before being taken out of the game ('pulled' or 'yanked'), the save is blown. His job is to keep the team ahead and that's it. Usually the closer comes in for only one inning, the ninth; only occasionally does he arrive on the scene earlier. Seeing a team lose a lead in the eighth makes one think, 'why didn't he bring in Gagne?'(or Rivera - name your favourite closer). After all, one inning is nothing. The apparent madness is only explained by the fact the team plays on around 27 days a month and the closer may be needed for many of these games. Therefore, you don't want to wear him out, thereby generally blunting his effectiveness. The all-time save record is Eric Gagne of the Dodgers' 118 game streak between 2002 and 2004.

Scattering Four Hits Over Five Innings - An odd verb, 'scattering,' is used in baseball to describe the number of hits a pitcher gives up during his time on the mound, but used it is with great frequency in press reports of games.

Scorer - Each game has an official scorer. His job is crucial. He is the one who decides between an error and a hit.

Scores (a Run) - When a base runner touches home plate before he can be tagged out by the catcher or a.n. other fielder, a run is scored. This run is both credited to the team and to the runner's record.

Scoring - Just as cricket matches are scored carefully on an official scorecard and many amateur ones, so are baseball games. They need to be so that absolutely precise records of players' performances can be logged for statistical history. There is very much a standard method. Space prevents a full explanation of it here, but there is an excellent website devoted to the art: www.baseballscorecard.com.

Scoring Position - When a batter, now a runner, arrives at second base he is now in scoring position, very much a positive for the offensive team and a cause for concern for the fielding side. This is because he is now within one hit of getting home to score a run. A grounder or line drive through or over the infield will often be enough to allow a man in scoring position to sprint around the last two bases, what with the runner allowed to move off - *take a lead off* - second base towards third before the pitcher pitches.

Screen - The screen is a huge sheet of clear Plexiglass protecting the spectators immediately behind home plate from foul balls being sliced into their faces and cold drinks.

Screwball - Once called the Fadeaway Pitch, invented by Walter Johnson of the Washington Senators, this one is murder on the arm. The name comes from the twist the pitching arm has to make, putting tremendous strain on the upper arm, to get the ball to spin in the correct fashion to make it swerve into the right handed batter. If the natural twist of the arm and wrist is anti-clockwise, the action of the normal lateral curve ball, the unnatural twist is the other way, it turning over and around in a screwing motion. This then, is a pitch dangerous to the health of the pitcher and out of the question for a youngster. It is now rare in the game. **Scroogie** is an alternative term for the screwball.

Scrub - A squad player who rarely gets picked.

Second - Short for 'second base.'

Secondary Average - In his essential book, *The Baseball Abstract*, where Bill James assesses and gives a 1-100 rating in baseball history for each of the positions on the field (top 100 catchers, first basemen, etc), he uses the term '*secondary average*' to get a deeper and wider picture of a hitter's worth beyond his batting average, the stat considered by most everyone in the game to be definitive. Secondary average is worked out by dividing the hitter's total bases (Hits + Walks + Stolen bases) divided by At Bats (over a given period). It's slugging average plus stolen bases and walks. This is not widely used, however. Whether this stat gains ground in the game in future is moot. It probably will.

Second Base – 90 feet from first and third, and 127 feet, 3 3/8 inches from home plate in a dead straight line is second base, with the pitching rubber directly in between. With TV flattening out angles so much, it's sometimes hard to remember that second base is the apex of the diamond, a fully 20 yards "north" of first base.

Second Baseman – This position is no longer one where the man stands on the second base bag: he plays near second base. The orthodox position for him is to play in the gap between the bag and first base for the right-handed hitter. The distance between the second baseman and the bag and the shortstop and the bag should be the same. The pitcher theoretically plugs the route to second base, though batted balls usually whiz past him at tremendous speed. The second baseman will be near enough to the bag at second to be there in less than three seconds so he is available to make the double play and to tag out a runner coming from first. So, because this fielding position is of critical importance, second basemen are agile guys who have quick hands and feet and who can throw hard and accurately.

Second Base Umpire – Stands adjacent to the bag at second to make in/out calls at that base.

Second Division – See '*first division.*'

Second Guessing – Not a phrase we use here: to second-guess is to bleat and moan about what the manager *should* have done in a given situation. "He should have pulled Clemens after he gave up that hit in the seventh." "No he shouldn't, what he should have done was pull Berkman in the eighth because he'd obviously been shaken up by that flying hot dog thrown from the crowd. He should have sent in a pinch hitter." Etc, etc.

Seeing Eye Single - Batter who gets to first base on a grounder that threads its way through the pitcher and fielders up the middle.

Sends The Runner - When there is a stolen base attempt, and when there is a hit and run, it's the manager who makes the call and 'sends the runner.'

Sent Down - Quite frequently a player on the roster of a major league team gets moved down to the club's minor league teams in Triple A, Double A and so on. When this demotion happens they are 'sent down' to the minors. Sometimes pitchers and batters are not quite demoted but sent to regain lost confidence. They might also be sent down whilst in recovery from a long-term injury to get some competitive practice.

Sequence Pitching - For those annoying people you know around you who still call baseball "glorified rounders," you can begin their journey out of ignorance by talking to them about pitching strategy, one of the arts of the pitcher. Pitcher's are always trying to outthink the hitter. Until the 50s, the fastball pitcher still tried to prosper through sheer speed, with maybe a curve and a change up thrown in. These days, the whole process is usually an elaborate one. A top class pitcher can select from a number of pitches and a number of locations and a number of speeds and he sequences them according to his needs, his guesses and his mental acuity. Most obviously, a couple of pitches to the inside corner will be followed by a pitch away. Or he throws one in on the hands after a two sliders away. And so on. However, on a 3-2 count, most will bottle out of an off-speed pitch or a curve and throw the fastball. "With the bases loaded and a 3-2 count, almost everybody in the stadium knew I was probably going to throw a fastball," a dejected pitcher by the name of Thomson said after a loss in 2004. In which case, you should have thrown your change up, son. See '*Setting Up The Hitter*.'

Series - Games of baseball are always in sequences of two or more. The group of games is almost always called a 'series.' Very occasionally it's a '*set*.'

Series 2 - Shorthand term for a World Series.

Set (position) – Position held by pitcher immediately prior to releasing the ball, where he is facing the batter, has placed his back foot on the rubber and has both hands in front of his body and comes to a complete stop. What the material difference is between this and the windup position in the official rules I don't know. The pitcher can either pitch from the windup position or set position: the definitions are almost exactly the same. Anyhow, the point is this: the pitcher must not try to surprise the batter with a quick pitch or pitch with elaborate sideways movement with his legs or take a run at the batter and pitch: he must come to a point of stillness on the mound where the batter knows that from here he is going to throw the ball, with a preliminary stretch or not (with men on base he throws without a leg kick to reduce the base runner's chance to steal a base). If the pitcher does not do this with a runner on base a balk is called and everyone advances one base. So, what we see on the mound prior to each and every pitch is carefully (I wouldn't say precisely) defined in the rules.

Set Down (The First Four Batters) - To 'set down' means to 'get out' or more properly, 'retire' a batter.

Sets Up Outside, The Catcher – Where the catcher 'sets up' is where he positions himself to receive the pitch. This is done partly to help the pitcher, giving him a target to aim at. There is a strong school of thought that says that the hurler's job is to throw at the catcher's glove. Here, if he 'sets up outside,' he moves from his normal center of the plate position to his right to the outside corner of the plate. He places his mitt emphatically where he wants the pitch to arrive. See also '**Framing the ball.**'

Setting The Table – The job of numbers 1 and 2 in the hitting line up is to get on base so that numbers 3 and 4, the positions of the best sluggers on the team, can 'drive them home,' make some hits so they can advance around the bases to score some runs. This is called '**Setting the table.**'

Setting Up The Hitter – One of the most important aspects of pitching strategy where the pitcher tries to fool the hitter into thinking he's going to get one type of pitch only to throw another. This is normally done on two strikes so that the pitcher can get the strikeout. Typically, on an 0 and 1 pitch he might throw inside for a strike. If it works and he gets strike two, he might throw another inside. Even if it's a ball for 1 and 2, the hitter has to be wary of the next pitch arriving this time on the corner for strike three if he doesn't make contact with it. In which case he's set up for a pitch on the outside corner, a contrasting pitch that the pitcher hopes the hitter won't be expecting. Contrast is the key.

Set Up Man - The set up man is a relief pitcher who usually comes in during or for the seventh or eighth inning, theoretically to keep hold of a lead before the closer comes in to finish the job off.

Seventh Inning Stretch - Though six out of nine is not even close to halfway (last time I looked), after seven innings the crowd gets to its feet for a stretch after sitting for so long watching the game. Only there's a lot of crowd movement for refreshment and bladder relief and there's nothing to stop you getting to your feet between earlier innings, so it's scarcely required. Anyway, in this pause, ballparks have played the anthem '*God Bless America*' since 9/11, which is respected by all and sung by at least some. At Wrigley Field, home of the Cubs as you may well now know, it having been mentioned here for about the fourth time even if you're a new fan, there is a seventh inning stretch tradition of singing '*Take Me Out To The Ball Game*,' led by a local (actors Bill Murray or John Cusack, for example) or indeed national celebrity (Ozzie Osbourne did the honours on one occasion in 2003). This tradition was established by local sportscaster Harry Caray who wore vast spectacles and whose caricature is drawn on a section of perimeter wall. Actually the song is sung during the SIS at many ballparks. In April 2004 at Fenway Park when I was there, we had both. The custom of the seventh inning stretch, by the way, has been in operation since 1869 at least.

Shagging balls - Have a cheap laugh with your friends with this one. Shagging balls is what fielders do in outfield practice: chasing down and/or catching hit balls.

Shagging flies - Have another one! This means specifically practicing the catching of balls batted high into the air.

Shakes Him Off – A pitcher's choice of pitch is made by the catcher, who shows the pitcher a sign before he goes into his set position. If a pitcher doesn't agree, he shakes his head almost imperceptibly at his battery mate. This is 'shaking him off.' The catcher will then probably make another suggestion via a finger sign if the pitcher gives him a chance, which he can either shake off again or nod his head slightly to let the catcher know that he agrees. One of the issues here is that the catcher should know what type of pitch is coming in as this gives him a much better chance of catching it.

Shallow – A term to describe the area of the outfield between the infield and the immediate geographical domain of the outfielder who normally positions himself approximately 25 to 30 metres from the fence. Thus, when a broadcaster says a batter pops up into 'shallow right,' you can picture with accuracy where the ball has gone. A 'shallow fly' is quite common also.

Shelled – A team heavily defeated, like the New York Giants in their last ever game at the Polo Grounds before moving west on 29th September 1957. Pitchers can get shelled also.

Shine Ball – A ball with some shine on it, from sweat or Vaseline is another of those doctored pitches outlawed in 1920. The shine makes the ball deviate hugely on its way to the plate.

Short - A truncated version of 'shortstop.' A 'hopper to short' means a hit ball that bounces several times on its way to the shortstop area of the infield.

Short Hop - While we 'take the ball on the bounce' or on the 'half-volley,' in the States they take it on the 'short hop.'

Short Reliever - Code for a closer or any pitcher pitching for around an inning or less. He may be said to pitch "in short relief." See "**Long Reliever.**"

Short Rest - If a starting pitcher starts a game with less than the established four-day gap he is supposed to need for his arm to recover he is said to be 'pitching on short rest.' This tends to happen a lot in the post-season when situations go critical and games become 'must win.'

Shortstop - The glamour position in the infield. He is the lynch pin of the four, often making crucial plays in an area to where the pitch is often pulled by the hitter. The best fielder in the team, one with great hands and a bullet throw fields there. Miguel Tejada of the Orioles, Edgar Renteria of the Cardinals and Derek Jeter of the Yankees are all notable short stops.

Shot - A solo, two run or three run 'shot' is a home run with the run-value added. A three run shot is one where there were two men on base when the hitter hit the homer.

Show Bunt - When a batter gets into that crouch and slides one hand down the barrel of the bat immediately prior to the pitcher releasing a pitch that he intends to bunt, he 'shows' bunt. (See '**bunt**' immediately if this explanation is nonsensical to you).

Shut 'em down – If a pitcher did this, he didn't allow the opposing hitters a run, over however many innings he went (pitched for).

Shutout/Shut Out - When a pitcher prevents the offensive opponents over a number of innings. The complete game shutout is normally nine of course, but it can be said that 'Willis shut out the Orioles in the first seven innings.'

Side-arm pitcher - Also called a 'sidewinder,' this is a pitcher who seems to throw almost underarm, as the release point is down around his knees, but is called a 'side-arm' pitcher because the arm is approximately horizontal on release of the baseball. Poor Byung Yung Kim is perhaps the best known of these at the moment, though the Oakland A's have a great exemplar called Chad Bradford who is well worth observing. Unfortunately he is only a reliever. Generally this style is way out of fashion.

Side Goes Down In Order - Means no one getting on base in the inning: three batters were removed in strict order in the line up. The 'side' only refers to the three batters, not the whole team. '*Side Retired In Order*' has the same meaning.

Signs - Signs are hugely important. These are made by from two directions for two purposes: to give advice or instructions to the pitcher in terms of where to direct the pitch and which type of pitch to select next and to give instructions to the batter or the base runner in terms of how to proceed. 'Signs' is to be taken literally, not metaphorically: a system of coded signals are devised and revised continually by all baseball teams, both amateur and professional, to make sure that players know what to do in a given situation but the opponents don't. The most obvious signing you'll see in a telecast is the pitcher signaling with his fingers on the inside of his thighs to the pitcher, to tell him what pitch to throw. But also, the manager sends signs throughout a game to batters to tell them to hit and run or bunt or to swing at the next pitch, and to baserunners too, telling them to steal or that the hit and run is on. Or not in all cases, where appropriate. See '**Stealing Signs.**'

Silent Bats - This is what a team has when they can't get a hit.

Single - A single is a hit that takes the hitter to first place. This can seem small beer compared with the mighty home run, but it is vital that a team gets men on base as frequently as possible in the course of a game so it must not be underestimated. The hitter who just mis-timed a pitch through the infield to get on, could easily be stealing a base within about sixty seconds and be in scoring position.

Single 'A' - Lowest rung of the echelon of baseball just below the major leagues or if you like, the third highest of the minor leagues.

Sinker (Ball) - A sinker is a pitch which has a deadly trajectory which sees it dropping alarmingly as it reaches the batter. It is very hard for a batter to hit a ball with such a flight path. This pitch is said to 'fall off the table.' Specialist sinkerball pitchers are fairly rare in the game. Derek Lowe of the Red Sox is an example.

Sit – Short for sitting on the bench, i.e, not playing in the starting nine.

Sit Back On (A Fastball) – Means "waiting for" the fastball or whatever pitch the batter is waiting for. If he's waiting for a certain type of pitch, he's also "looking" for it.

Sitting On (The Fastball) – Also means 'waiting for the fastball.'

Situational Hitting – Sounds complicated, but isn't: S.H. is matching what you do as a hitter at the plate to the needs of the team. For example, if the team has a man on third base with none or one out, a batter might (or arguably "should") look for a pitch he can lift deep to the outfielder (to make a **sac fly**), putting enough distance between the fielder when he catches it and home plate thus enabling the man on third to come in to score (after ***tagging up***). A slugger who looks for a safe single instead of swinging for the fences in the same situation in order to bring a man home is another example.

6-4-3 Double Play - The most common double play: the shortstop fields the grounder, throws to second base for the first out who then throws to first for the second (out). The five-four-three 'round the horn' is also common: third baseman to the second to the first. See '***Fielding Positions.***'

Skid – If a player is in a skid, he's having a very bad run or "trot" as cricket's Richie Benaud might say, as in "Pujols is currently in a 1 for19 skid." As if.

Slap Hitter – A slap hitter doesn't hit powerfully, but, with a larger margin for error than the slugger, makes regular contact to all fields, getting a lot of singles and some doubles. He might hit a home run occasionally. Juan Pierre of the Marlins is a slap hitter.

Slide – In baseball, the base runner's face-first or feet-first slide is to get to the base faster than he would on his feet, to avoid being forced or tagged out. It also makes it harder for the fielder on base to tag the runner: his target is smaller and now traveling a mite faster through the air. The target may also be more elusive: the runner may slide wide of the base and the fielder but touch the bag with his hand or his foot as he goes past. To old timers, sliding these days is a lost art; few players make a specialism of the practice and simply slide in a straight line at the bag. One of the spectacular sights in baseball is to see a batter (technically now a 'runner') sliding into one of the bases bringing up a spray of gravel and effecting a collision with an infielder for good measure. This is also immediately followed by an umpire making a characteristically extravagant signal to indicate the runner's status, in or out, spreading the arms wide and ram rod straight to denote 'in' or punching the air manically in a state of apparent furious anger. Wonderful. Master of the art, Ty Cobb had at least four types of slide.

Slider - A very common and dangerous pitch. It has almost the same speed as the fastball but breaks away from the batter - e.g. right-hander to right-hander - as it crosses the plate. It was described by one pitcher in the 30s, just after its discovery, as being like a car swerving off the road. Its widespread arrival did not occur until the 1950s (some would say '60s) and helped to bring about the decline in hitter numbers which eventually led to the major changes of 1969 when the mound was lowered to ten inches (from fifteen). Its late break away, at fastball speed, confounded batters, and well directed with heat, still does. Joe Morgan, in the latter part of 2004 began to use the term "*slide piece,*" which he probably picked up off some clubhouse floor somewhere.

Slug Bunt - See 'fake bunt.' But what a phrase this is. You've got to love a sport that has a piece of slang like this.

Slugfest - A game with a high number of long hits, particularly home runs. The score will be high, probably for both teams. 9-8 will do, though these days there will almost always one team per night that goes into double figures.

Slugger - A slugger is a batter whose specialty is the long hit, the towering home run. It's suggestive of brute force rather than style or finesse; however, a stylish big hitter can still be referred to as a "slugger." Note that the slugger will tend to strike out a lot more: the price paid for the much smaller margin for error in the big swing.

Slugging Average - See '***Slugging Percentage.***'

Slugging Percentage – An important batting statistic that measures run producing effectiveness. It is calculated by taking his total number of bases gained from hitting successfully – singles + doubles + home runs – and dividing it by his number of at bats. Slugging averages for a season of over .500 are pretty good. The top class hitter goes into the .600s. Bonds after 2000 hit .688, 2001 .863 (when he broke the home run record), in 2002 .799, in 2003 .749 and last season .807. He has been first in the field since 2001. In 2004 he averaged .812, the second highest of his career.

Slump - If a hitter (though it's a phrase that can also be applied to a pitchers) is out of form he is said to be in a slump. This phrase is appropriate to the game because statistics, a player's 'numbers,' are universally used to measure a player's performance and ability. The depth and length of the slump will be thus measured. For example, a hitter batting two-for-twenty four in his last five games is in a bad slump. A player in a slump can be said to be '*slumping.*'

Slurve - Slang for the cut fastball, that mongrel pitch of a curve and a slider.

Small Ball - Hitting strategy is not simply hoping that all nine hitters are going to smash home runs every inning; far from it. A subtler but essential stratagem is to get as many batters as possible to first base, then moving them around the bases, eventually getting them home. This is the style of baseball that Babe Ruth to a large extent put to the sword. Before he came along at the end of the 1910s, hitting a home run was considered vulgar by the baseball writing and thinking fraternity. 'Small ball,' as it was known, was the done thing, the proper way of playing the game.

Smoked it! - Hit a pitch with considerable velocity, probably for a home run.

Snag - A snag is a catch, especially when it isn't a straightforward one: where a little effort or skill is required to secure it in the glove.

Snapped An 0-13 Streak - A bad slump might see you in a negative streak like this: when you (eventually) come out of it, you don't 'break' it you 'snap' it.

Snapped off a curveball - Alternative term for 'throwing' the curveball. The snap comes from the sound the fingers make as the pitcher imparts spin on the ball at the point of delivery.

'Something On It' - No, nothing to do with ballpark refreshment (ha, ha) but if a fastball has something on it, it's particularly quick.

Southpaw - As in boxing, a term for a left-hander. Used for pitchers through its apparent origin: when a left-handed pitcher pitched in the Cubs' old West Side Park ground, their arm was to the south.

Sparkplug - A player whose personal performance and attitude influences positively the rest of the team, especially in terms of a team's run production. Often a lead off hitter.

Spit Ball - Now outlawed, the spitball used to be an every day phenomenon. It would be called ball tampering in cricket. Many pitchers used to put spit on the ball or any other unnatural substance that worked, to give their pitches alarming movement. Often referred to as the 'spitter,' it was outlawed in time for the 1920 season, because of the terms of the game having turned so dramatically into the favour of the pitchers since the turn of the twentieth century. In the wake of the Black Sox Scandal the powers that be needed to boost the image of the game. In addition to making the ball harder - from this date we have the 'Lively Ball Era,' ball tampering was made illegal, frankly, to give the batter a chance; the spitball was devastating and expertly delivered, was deemed almost impossible to hit.

When the spitter was outlawed in 1920, confusingly, seventeen practitioners of the art were allowed to be the last guys to use it until they each retired. The most famous of these was Burleigh Grimes. In the Seventies, fellow Hall of Famer Catfish Hunter was strongly suspected of using the pitch, and a number of others surreptitiously tried to use moisture and substances various. The close up TV camera has done away with this traditional way of cheating.

Spit - The capacity of baseball men to empty their mouths of all traces of saliva, players, coaches and managers all, is nothing short of astonishing. Note that they do this (and have always done, this is no modern phenomenon) mostly at their feet in the dug out. All these multi-millionaires and superstars treading in each other's warm, wet, slimy gob: I'm no prude, but it's not exactly the most pleasant aspect of watching the game.

Spitter - See **"Spitball."**

Split Fingered Fast Ball - This pitch, the "splitter" revolutionized pitching in the mid-1980s. It was invented in the late 70s by one Bruce Sutter, a Cubs reliever, who won a Cy Young award on the back of it, in '79. Five years later Roger Craig in, pitching coach to the Detroit Tigers, started to teach his version of it to his men (why Sutter's pitch wasn't copied by others I have yet to discover). The pitch is so called because of the way the ball is gripped (you can follow this by going to get a tennis ball, which has seams in exactly the same places as a baseball). Pick up a ball and you'll hold it most probably with your first and second fingers pointing away from you (you're not picking up a handful of sand on a beach to chuck at your little brother, but gripping a computer mouse). This looks like a 'V' right in front of you. If you now push the two fingers wider apart, still along the seams, you almost have the grip for the splitter: you've split your two fingers wide. Finally, because the pitch is thrown hard, like a fastball, you need to hold the ball towards the end of your fingers. This differentiates it from the forkball – the two fingers make a fork shape (as in fork in the road) – which is thrown as a **change up** pitch and held in the palm of the hand to assist the slower release of the ball.

The damage done by the splitter is that the laws of physics caused it to drop like a bomb around about the exact moment it arrived at the plate, which made it practically un-hittable. Pilgrims made their way to Craig's house from across the States, pitching coaches mostly, to learn its secret. Roger Angell, again in "*Once More Around The*

Park," chapter entitled "*The Arms Talks*," is talking from the year 1987 there, and posits the notion that the splitter is in the midst of destroying batters' numbers. This realignment of the pitcher-hitter relationship didn't quite happen (judging by last night's results where every score seemed to be about 8-7, Angell was worrying about nothing). Batters either got used to it, or spotted its imminent arrival through pitchers being unable to disguise the fingers-wide-apart grip and used a universal latent ability to accommodate the new challenge.

'Spot A 3-run rally in the seventh' - *Spot* is the key word here, used as a verb. Spotting three runs means putting three together on the board. It's also used as a noun, as in 'four run spot in the ninth.'

Spotting (The Inside Corner) - This is putting the pitch on the batter nearside of the plate. Similar to 'painting' the inside corner.

Spring Training - Baseball's 'pre-season,' it begins in February and runs to late March. The whole squad goes to a southern state, usually Florida or Arizona, where the climate is warm enough for them to prepare for the new season. There is almost a mystical reverence for spring training; some fans take a vacation to watch the team play numerous practice games against minor league teams and other major leaguers.

Squeaker – Game where one team wins narrowly, squeaking through by one run.

Squeeze Play – Term that describes the attempt to bunt a man home from third. There are two types: the normal squeeze play where the man on third breaks for the plate only when the hitter has made contact with the ball and the *suicide squeeze* where the man on third runs on the pitch. It's suicidal because if the hitter fails to make contact (to 'lay down the bunt'), the catcher needs only to make a simple tag for the out and should have plenty of time to do it. He should also make it comfortably if decent contact is made on the bunt, as by the time the ball strikes the bat, he'll be half way home. Typically a National League ploy. See also '**Safety Squeeze**.'

Squibber – Same as a roller, a poorly hit groundball.

Staff – Short for 'pitching staff,' the club's pitchers on its 25-man roster.

"Staked Sabathia To An Early Lead" - An odd verb, "stake," as it refers to a team's batters putting runs on the board early for the pitcher. This is formed from the concept of the hitter's job being to help the pitcher, to give him "run support."

Standings - Baseball's equivalent of league tables.

Stand Up Double - The 'stand up' part means that the hitter was able to make it to second base without having to slide, i.e., easily. Also '**Stand Up Triple**.'

Starter - Shorthand for starting pitcher.

Starting Pitcher - One thing that the new baseball fan has to get to grips with as soon as possible is the pattern of a team's pitching, the fact that it's organized. Over the course of each game the coach deploys a *team* of pitchers, not just one. Well okay, occasionally he uses only one, but today this is rare. If this is surprising, it's simply because if a pitcher goes the distance of nine innings or more, he's going to throw something between 120 and 160 pitches and his arm is going to be very sore. The stress of throwing a ninety mph pitch on the arm and shoulder is huge. The conventional wisdom now is that you let your starter throw around a hundred pitches. You must not wear out his arm but you want your opening pitcher, your starter, to do a lot of damage to the other team: to shut them down for as long as possible. A club's pitching is focused around a group of *starting pitchers*, five in number, who are supposed to be the best in the organization. A ball club is arguably only as good as its starting pitching. Few have five who have tremendous talent at this level, who have the quality of endurance as well as those of speed, variation, guile and aggression. Most will be lucky to have two, men who they can describe as 'aces.' Here's where money counts: a lot of payroll can buy a lot of great pitching. Conversely there's the Billy Beane method in Oakland, which has it that there is a mass of great pitching talent out there in America: the trick is knowing how to spot it. Anyhow, the starter's job is to pitch as many innings of shut out ball or as near to that as he can get, as possible, before handing over to the relievers, to the bullpen.

Starting Rotation - One major job of the coach now is to manage the starters effectively. This means rotating them so that they face hitters most suited to their strengths, or pitch in certain types of ballpark rather than others and keeping them from getting tired. The rotation of five is larger than at any other time in the game's history. At the climax of the season, the World Series, coaches rotate their starters with more desperation than care. In a do or die set of between four and seven games, the five man rotation is often thrown out the window so that Johnny Ace and his colleague Joe can pitch the manager and the club to glory. Classic example: 2001: the Arizona Diamondbacks' pilot Bob Brenly in the seven games made sure not only that aces Randy Johnson and Curt Schilling went twice, but that both aces were used as relievers. In the all-important Game 7, Johnson started and Schilling finished the Yankees off. No regular relievers were used in the 2-1 ninth inning victory.

Station – Base.

Statistics - 'Aaron Boone became the first third baseman to make three errors in a World Series Since 1948.'

Statistics 2 – Baseball would not be baseball without the constant logging of statistics and the poring over them by fans. If there is great depth to the following of baseball as a fan, they add either one very thick layer to the activity or several thinner but still substantial ones. Every activity on the field of play is counted and measured. The relative prowess of players is huge to fans and followers, supported by the existence of awards and the Hall of Fame, and this minute statistical measurement allows for constant, relentless study, contemplation and argument. Following baseball is about following a team, but in doing so, absorbing the culture of the game even from the United Kingdom is as much a necessity as something that happens anyway. The culture contains stats at its very heart. Or do I mean head? We know Barry Bonds is great because of his monumental slugging average, from his vast total of career home runs and from his high batting averages over the past few seasons. We know Ruth is King because after all this time he is still No. 1 in so many statistical tables. We will always know that Walter Johnson is great not only because his contemporaries have left records behind telling us how hard he threw and how hard he was to hit, but because his win-loss ratio was so good and his ERA so low, and even more so because that indefatigable statistician-writer Bill James has proved it with numbers beyond dispute. It's hard to resist the temptation to say that if as a new fan you're not interested in numbers, you're missing about half of what baseball is all about.

Statistics 3 – It's a peculiarity of baseball culture that only regular season statistics "count." A player's lifetime and seasonal stats are *not* his regular season and play off stats combined, just his regular season ones.

Stays Alive - Describes a batter with two strikes against him hanging on for dear life in the batter's box: he's probably just **fouled out off.**

Stays On It - If the batter doesn't try to pull it you may hear the broadcaster tell you that the batter 'stays on it,' goes rather more with the direction of the ball thrown toward him. It's less likely for a hitter to a homer going the other way but it does happen, especially to very powerful hitters.

Stealing A Base – An essential element in the game, particularly in the 1880-1960 period. For a team looking at an alternative stratagem to scoring runs by hitting homers, getting a base runner from first to second is important. The way to achieve this is to get him to steal a base: in other words, to run to the next pitch while the pitcher is in the act of delivery. As the pitcher goes into his wind up, that body curling prelude to the baseball actually leaving the hand, the runner at first can afford to be as much as six to eight feet toward second base: it called 'taking a lead.' At some risk admittedly, the runner is gambling that even if the hitter doesn't hit the next pitch, he can get to second base before the catcher can throw it to second base. If he does he's 'stolen second.' The steal from first to second is by far the most common, but stealing third from second is definitely a do-able proposition, especially a left-handed pitcher who is looking at first base as he winds up and then delivers.

Stealing a base is a risky move often taken by really fast running hitters. Slower, older, bulkier hitters don't bother to make the manoevre usually. Note that a runner can still steal a base after an out is made: this is not illegal. The ball is still 'live' until the next pitch is thrown. Last season, Reggie Sanders of the Cardinals stole second base after a batter fouled out in front of the first baseline dug out. The infielders turned to go back to their positions, leaving no one guarding first and second so Sanders took off and stole the base.

Stealing Home – Up until the 1960s runners used to steal home base: in other words, as the pitcher pitches, leave third to try to score a run. If you think about this, it should be impossible unless the batter makes good contact - in which case technically, it's a **squeeze play** - the catcher should easily tag out the runner. However, it used to be the case that the runner could knock the catcher out of his path to home. If in the process the ball broke free, then the run was scored. It is also marginally possible for the runner to slide under or around an anxious, incompetent or less than agile catcher. The arch home plate stealer of all time was Ty Cobb (retired 1928), who stole home a record 37 times, and in the 40s and 50s Jackie Robinson resurrected it to some extent. In this modern age of cleaner play (thanks to TV) the move is considered totally suicidal.

Stealing Second - This is the same as a stolen base. Most times second base is stolen, the runner taking off from first.

Stealing Signs – This is one of the arts of the game. While signs are pieces of coded information - catcher to pitcher, manager to batter – to hide the intentions of the players to their own advantage, stealing or working out your opponents' signs will nullify their gain and help you to win. The most important signs to steal are those of the pitcher-catcher relationship: if a batter can know what pitch he's about to get, he's much, much more likely to hit it. Sign stealing is not something that appears to be happening in the game now, but it is much written and talked about in oral histories from the early 20th century. See '*tipping pitches.*'

Stolen Base - See '**Stealing A Base.**'

Stole The Bag – Stole a base.

Stopper 1 - An alternative term for a closer; you want your relief pitcher here to keep the lead, stop the opposition from scoring.

Stopper 2 - An alternative term for a catcher.

Straight Down Broadway – Another brilliantly colourful euphemism for a pitcher throwing one straight down the middle of the plate, representing a juicy opportunity for the batter.

Stranded Runners - Men left on base at the end of an inning.

Streak- The most common streak in the game - a streak is an achievement (or negative one) recorded in a consecutive number of games – is that where the batter makes at least one hit in the game. The record is held by Joe DiMaggio who went on a 56 game streak in 1941.

Streaky – Not lucky as in the British parlance, but tending towards slumps – runs of losses or games going hitless - and highs: weeks or months of hitting .400, as opposed to more consistent achievement (or lack of it). A streaky hitter is inconsistent, has good runs and bad ones.

Stretch, The 1 – After studying this in a number of books and listening to a lot of commentary, I'm not sure that a lot of people in the game are totally sure what the stretch is in pitching, particularly the difference between the set and the stretch. Here's my attempt. A pitcher pitches from the stretch when there is a base runner, which is to say that he pitches from a still position without a big windup, having clearly having collected a sign from the catcher and having stood still in the set position. The set, remember, is that still point where it is clear that the pitcher is about to go into his wind up and deliver the ball. The point is, he doesn't go into a windup, which would make it easy for a baserunner to steal a base. That said, Dickson has a meaning of the stretch as the pitcher bringing both hands behind his head ready to pitch "to loosen up the muscles" which only confuses matters and clearly isn't what the ESPN commentators mean these days by the stretch. If there is any actual stretching going on, it's when the pitcher reaches back, as he has to do, to get some forward momentum going into his pitching stride. The point of the windup after all is to make it easier to throw the ball with great velocity. This is incredibly hard to do unless your body is moving forward towards the target. Set? Stretch? It's all fairly confusing because the official rules are so hard to follow. Check 'em out and throw cabbages at me if you think I'm wrong.

Stretch, The 2 - The stretch is the last part of the season. "*The Dodgers will have to do a lot better down the stretch to have a chance of making the play offs.*"

Strike - A strike is a ball that crosses the plate within the **strike zone**, the area above the 17-inch wide home plate deemed fair for a pitcher to throw the ball. There needs to be an agreed fair place to put the ball, otherwise the pitchers would be forever throwing the baseball four feet wide. The batter has to have a reasonable chance of making contact with the pitch. Strikes are what the pitcher wants to throw and what the batter does not want called against him. Three of them before four balls and he's out.

Strike Called - See '*Called Strike.*' No, this is not a joke.

Strike On The Inside Corner - This tells you which part of the zone the ball has passed through for a strike. The inside corner is bottom right of the rectangle or top right, inside being the part of the zone nearest the batter. The geography is commented on as precisely as this when the umpire calls a strike.

Strikeout – If, with two strikes on or against the batter, the pitcher throws a pitch past the swing of the batter, strike three is called and the batter is out. This particular type of batter retirement is called a 'strikeout' and it doesn't matter if the pitch was missing the strike zone: if the batter swings and misses, it's a strike. The number of strikeouts a pitcher throws is a measure of how dominant he is. A real ace who pitches mostly fastballs is likely to be known for his ability to blow the batters away. **Abb. SO** & **K.**

Strikeout Pitch – A lot of pitchers have a pitch that they habitually use when they have two strikes on a batter, to try to finish off the hitter. This is his "strikeout pitch." Commonly, it's the fastball, but not always. It could be a slider or a sinker, but not the curve. The curve is still regarded as a risky pitch and not one used in this way. I may well be wrong but I don't think there's a single pitcher in the majors whose strikeout pitch is the curve ball.

Strike Zone - This is the invisible rectangle of space a pitcher has to throw through to gain a strike on a batter. It is fifteen inches wide and as high as the distance between a batter's chest ("the midpoint between the top of the shoulders and the top of the uniform pants," to quote the most recent official rule book) and "the hollow below the knee." Because in play it is only defined by the eye of the home plate umpire and therefore cannot be absolutely precise, there is often controversy and argument when a player is struck out by a pitch that passes close by home plate.

The strike zone has varied in dimension through baseball history. In 1969 it was reduced in height to between armpits and knees because at the time pitchers were so dominant, hardly any runs were being scored. The present official definition means it's smaller still, which goes a long way to explain why so many hits, homers and runs are registered now.

Strikes The Side Out - When a pitcher removes the three batters in the inning with strikeouts. It's a fairly rare event now and one only likely to be achieved by a fastball pitcher and a brilliant one at that. Most pitchers do not average more than one 'K' per inning over a season.

Strikes The Side Out In Order - When the above is achieved by a pitcher striking out three batters straight - no one got on base during the inning. This is even rarer. The record number of strikeouts in a game is 20 (held by Kerry Wood and Roger Clemens who's done it twice). The maximum possible is (obviously) 27 in the normal course of events (beyond normal is extra innings).

Struck Out - If you're struck out it means you weren't thrown out or caught out but that three strikes were called against you.

Struck Out Looking - If a batsman has two strikes against him at an at bat, and is the victim of the third without swinging the bat, he is 'struck out looking,' i.e., watching the pitch cross the plate and not trying to hit it. Always makes the batter look somewhat foolish; however, there is such a thing as a bad call by the umpire and the fact that pitchers are looking to hit the corners of the strike zone with the pitch. By and large though, the umpires are very accurate indeed with their calls.

Stud – Alternative for a pitching ace, a real star.

Stuff - Stuff is what a pitcher has: it's his range of pitches, his speed, the intelligent way he uses his armoury. "He's got great stuff" is what you might often hear in these terms.

Submarine Pitch(er) – About the same thing as a side-armed pitcher, one who doesn't throw the ball 'normally,' 'over-hand' as it's called in baseball, but who delivers the ball with an arm down by their knees. In the mid-19th century, all pitchers threw this way. Gradually, as the game moved towards 1900, more and more pitchers threw overhand because it was easier to generate power that way.

Subway Series - Any series of games between the New York Mets and the New York Yankees, because, if the label has a literal origin, fans can shuttle between stadiums via subway

Suicide Squeeze – See *Squeeze Play*.

Suit – Old fashioned term for a baseball uniform. Hence, to 'Suit Up' is to put on your uniform.

Sweet Spot - "I believe in the sweet spot," says Crash Davis (Kevin Costner) early on in *Bull Durham*. This is the apparent fact that there is a 'central' spot on the barrel of the bat which, when contact is made, sends the ball further: the timing seems perfect and no vibration can be felt through the hands. Same thing with a good cricket bat. It's about five inches up from the end of the bat, dead centre.

Swept - This is a universal phrase used to describe what we'd call a 'whitewash,' a series where all the games are won by one of the teams. As in, 'I see the Red Sox swept the Yankees four to nothing pigs must be flying across the moon as I speak.'(originally written prior to G7).

Sweeper - You might here a broadcaster talk about a "sweeping breaking ball." The sweeping describes lateral or downwards movement on the pitch. The pitch is sometimes called a "sweeper." Great curveball practitioners are often described as having a "sweeping curve." It's one with a whole lot of movement on it.

Swings From The Heels – When a batter takes a *big* swing at a pitch.

Swinging Strike – Strike where the batter swings and misses.

Swipe Tag – Tag made by fielder when having to reach out with the glove to touch the runner, not being as close to him as he (the fielder) would like.

Switch Hitter – In baseball a common phenomenon is the switch hitter who bats both ways, left or tight handed, or more accurately, from both sides of the plate. Many are players of the highest class: Bernie Williams of the Yankees and Bill Mueller of the Red Sox, to name but two. Mickey Mantle was perhaps the greatest. The advantage of the switch hitter is mainly in being able to switch from left-handed to right-handed to face a leftie pitcher. Traditionally and statistically, left-handed batters do not fare well against left-handed pitchers.

T

Table Setter - A table setter is a batter whose job in the line up is to get on base rather than make the big hits that score the runs in spectacular fashion. He 'sets the table' for the big hitters to come in and 'clean up'. He is normally the lead off man, though a number two may have the primary function to do the same job. See *'Clean Up Hitter.'*

Tag - A tag is an active move made by a fielder to put a runner out when he's trying to advance around the bases. If you've ever played 'Tag,' 'Tig' It' then you'll know exactly what fielders have to do to tag out a runner: touch any part of his body or uniform before he touches the base (or 'bag') with any part of his. Fielders must have the ball in their hand to successfully 'apply the tag.'

Tagged out (the runner) – A player is 'tagged' or 'tagged out.'

Tags Up - This gives a different meaning to the term 'tag.' Here tagging up is what a runner does to advance to the next base when a hitter is caught (and put out) in the deep. The distance between the fielder making the catch and the intended base in this case is far enough for a runner to move say from second to third base in the time it takes for the fielder to throw the ball to the man on the bag at third, usually diving frantically to make it. It follows then, that 'tagging up' can also bring in a run: a runner at third base is allowed to advance to home plate if he can get there before the throw. **Note:** Look out for a batter talking about "tagging one" which means hitting the ball hard and deep.

Tail – A pitch which moves in or away or down on the batter in the last few feet of its journey to the plate is said to have a tail: it describes the late movement on the pitch.

Take A Strike – Batters have to decide at the plate whether to swing at a pitch or not; it takes three strikes to get them out, remember. If a batter decides not to swing at a pitch he 'takes a strike.' On a count of 2 and 0 (2 balls, no strikes) or 3 and 0 he may decide to leave the next pitch deliberately, come what may, in the hope of a fourth ball and a free pass to first base. This will depend on the hitter and whether the manager gives him the **green light** to swing. Just "take" is often heard, as in "Rolen takes for strike one."

Take Me Out To The Ball Game - Famous old song about the game that is sung in almost every ballpark during the seventh inning stretch, or was until 9/11 since when *God Bless America* has somewhat taken over. Jack Noworth wrote the words in 1908 on a train ride in Manhattan. Albert Von Tilzer added music and it became a big hit the following year. It's the chorus that's sung at the ballpark: *'Take me out to the ball game/ Take me out with the crowd/Buy me some peanuts and crackerjacks/ I don't care if I never get back/ Let me root, root, root for the home team/ If they don't win it's a shame/ For it's one, two, three strikes you're out/ At the old ball game."* It's an American baseball cliché really.

Takes Outside - If a batter 'takes outside' he decides not to swing at a pitch on the outside half of the plate that crosses for a strike or a ball. *Takes inside* also. *"Hafner takes inside for a strike."*

Take The Loss - The pitcher 'takes' this. Losing and winning is the most common way of measuring the effectiveness of pitchers. So if the starter leaves the game at 0-5, no matter what the inning, it is he who no, not 'loses:' takes the loss. However, if the starter is taken out of the game (see *'Yanked'*) with a score in his team's favour of 2-1, but the team goes on to lose 2-5 it is the pitcher who concedes the third run who takes the loss. This business can get more complicated. Try this scenario: the starter is taken out of the game at 2-1. The first reliever comes in and quickly gives up hits that put two men on second and third base. He is then removed and replaced by a second reliever. His first pitch is hit into the outfield for a triple from which both base runners score. The batting side goes on to score two more runs against a fourth pitcher in the ninth to lose 2-5. Who takes the loss? You got it? Not the second reliever giving up the triple but the first reliever. What do you think now about these people around you who call baseball 'glorified rounders?' See also **'The Decision.'**

Taken Out Of The Game - Means the same as being substituted in football.

Takes Him Deep – When a pitcher is 'taken deep' he's been hit for a home run.

Tally – Run scored, as in "Penny gave up a tally in the third."

Tape Measure Blast/Shot – Literally, a hit so huge that it requires a tape measurement to see if it's some sort of record, either for the player, the club or baseball itself. This is a long-held tradition so that the comment is not used metaphorically all the time, just most of the time. Thus we know back to the Ruth era how big a lot of home runs were. Indeed, it was the new phenomenon of huge hitting that Ruth brought to the game in the late 1910s that began home run measurement.

Tapper – A ball mis-hit by the batter softly along the ground, often bobbling, to an infielder who almost invariably makes the easy out.

'Tater - Home run.

Tattooed It! - Mashed it, smoked it, hit it out of the park.

Tear – If a player or team 'goes on a tear' (pronunciation as in ripped clothing) they win a lot of games or make a lot of hits.

Ten Day Rule – An old repressive rule for all ball players until free agency was established that enabled a club to cancel a player's contract without compensation at ten days' notice: like when a player received a career threatening or ending injury. Nice.

That Ball Is Gone! - A phrase interchangeable with 'out of here;' in other words, this effervescent ejaculation may be made by the sportscaster to announce to the world that someone has hit another homer.

Third - Simply shorthand for third base.

Third Base - The third of the bases the runner has to reach or touch on his way home. Indeed, a competent team or perhaps effective manager is expected to get you home from here by one means or another. Time for a sac fly if there are less than two outs.

Third Base Coach – See 'Coaches.'

Third Base Line - The painted white line, dividing fair from foul territory that extends from home plate to the perimeter fence at a ninety-degree angle to the first base line. This is a great place for a batter to hit the ball. As the third baseman usually plays a little towards the infield of the bag, the ball often scoots low into the outfield corner; the outfielder in left field has to run back and across to fetch the ball, often waiting for it to bounce off at least one part of the wall, followed by a slow dribble, by which time the hitter may be on second and anyone in scoring position, home.

Third Baseman – The third baseman is very much a specialist position and requires several skills at a high operating level. He must have a great eye, great hands, a missile of a throw (to cross the 127 foot distance in an instant to first base to make putouts) and much agility to stop low pulled balls by right-handed hitters. Its nickname is "**Hot Corner**".

Third Base Umpire – Makes calls on whether batted balls are fair or foul and adjudicates out-calls at third base.

Thirty Game Season – Pitchers winning 30 games in a single season. They are extinct now, because starting pitchers rarely go beyond seven innings and now that pitchers pitch on a five-man rotation. In the first seventy years of major league baseball pitcher started forty-plus games, so the list of those with two thirty game seasons, thirty wins that is, contains no present day pitchers. The last pitcher to achieve this feat was Danny Maclain of the Detroit Tigers in 1968 in the AL. This was a blip. His most immediate predecessor was Lefty Grove of the Philadelphia As in 1931. You have to go back seventy years this year to find the last achiever in the NL: Dizzy Dean of the St Louis Cardinals. Then you have to go to 1917 and Grover Alexander of the Phillies for the next. Only two pitchers have reached 25 in the last three decades so it is highly probable we'll see Winston Churchill again before we see a thirty game winner. See '**Twenty Game Winner.**'

Thirty Steals (per season) - An established benchmark for base stealers. Get to this figure and you're an expert.

Thirty Steals, Thirty Home Runs - This is an achievement combo that has reasonably wide recognition, though it's not a *huge* deal. This is perhaps surprising when one considers its rarity. In the AL it's only been done eleven times, all bar one since 1922. In the National League with its stronger tradition of **small ball** the number is thirty-two. Willy Mays of the Giants was the league's first 30-30 guy in 1956, showing clearly that in modern times ball players are fitter and faster, especially with the addition of black players when the race barrier finally cracked in 1947. See '**Forty Steals and Forty Home Runs.**'

Three Hundred (.300) - See '*Two Hundred.*'

Three Hundred Wins (in a career) – This is the benchmark of a truly great pitcher, a major and rare achievement. It proves not only tremendous pitching skill and know-how but stamina, strength and survival temperament. Even most great pitchers fall by the way side through worn out arms and nearby body parts before they can get to 300 wins. So, there was much hoo-haa about Roger Clemens' arrival into this room in the hall of pitching greats in 2003. He became only the 21st man ever to reach this number. Last season Greg Maddux of the Cubs became number 22. (See '**Four Hundred Wins**')

3000 Hits - Only 25 hitters in the history of baseball have made this many career hits. The statistic is pretty telling as sheer longevity cannot take a player this far. You have to be brilliant and have a body made out of second hand trucks to do it. A word for no. 25, Roberto Clemente: he manage to join the club before dying in a plane loaded up with relief supplies for Nicaraguan earthquake victims in 1972 at the age of 38.

3-2 Pitch, 2 Outs – On a count of 3-and-2 with 2 out, if there are any base runners on, they should "go" on the pitch: run like shit to the next base as the pitcher lets the ball go. Why? Because there is nothing to be lost. If the pitcher throws a ball, they can't be out; if he throws a strike, the inning is over. If the ball is hit into play, it's to your advantage to be as far away from your base as you can be. So in this situation, listen out for "the runners go."

3-4 – An excellent night's work. Now we're looking for how many bases and homers.

Three Up, Three Down - This is the same as the side being retired in order and is very frequently used at the end of an inning that was over in a flash.

Throw out - A 'throw out' occurs when a batter is out by being unable to make the next base as a result of a throw. I bet that surprised you. See '**Relay Throw.**'

Throw Strikes – This is what the pitcher is often exhorted to do when his location is not good. It means to throw accurately and get the ball over the plate. The phrase is also used to describe a pitcher performing well (he's 'throwing strikes'). The more obvious meaning is used also: to throw the ball over the plate *and* defeat the batter. The context will tell you which meaning is being used.

Thrown Out Of The Game - The equivalent to being sent off in football. It's always for dissent though it could also be for cheating. There is no problem about a substitute however, unlike soccer: another player will be brought into your role at no extra cost. A huge number of players were ejected from the early days of organized ball through to the period after the Second World War. Television seems to have had the effect of reducing the frequency: players were less inclined to display their pettiness (arguably) and lack of discipline in front of a sizeable chunk of the population; or in front of family and friends. Radio may have reduced it also before the arrival of TV in the late 40s. I noted with interest recently (Sept '04) a pitcher get immediately and unceremoniously jerked by an ump for disputing a call with one simple body gesture. Football could do with some of that, if you ask me.

Tied At 6 – Means the score is "6-6" between whatever teams are playing. If a hit **unties the score** it puts one team ahead of the other.

Tight Spin - It's a compliment to the pitcher if he throws his curveball with tight spin: the "tighter" the spin, the faster the ball is revolving through 360 degrees as it travels to the plate. This results in the ball dipping further, making it harder for the batter.

Tipping The Batter – To tip your pitches to the batter means not to conceal them properly. Often the way the pitcher grips the ball will reveal what type of pitch is coming next; thus you'll see him setting himself for his wind up with the ball behind the glove. Only at the last second or so will the batter then get a chance to see his grip which may let on to what's coming.

Tommy John Surgery – Tommy John was a pitcher who in 1974 tore an ulna collateral ligament in his pitching arm. Told by the Dodger to "make up something," meaning an ointment or salve to try to deal with the problem (this was the traditional way), one Dr Jobe decided to embark on experimental surgery. He transplanted a tendon, surplus to the requirements of his other arm, to the injured one, both above and below the elbow. To do this he had to drill through the bone. Not only did it work, it actually strengthened John's arm to the extent that he went on to win more games per season than before. He won 170 games in total post-recovery. He, John, not Jobe (who has since performed more than 250 operations) gave his name to the breakthrough procedure.

Too Low For A Ball - Simply used on commentary to tell you that the pitch was below the required height for a strike. It must be at least level with the 'hollow below the knee.'

Tools – These are a player's skills, the things he is good at, the tools of his trade. In classic definition, the tools of a ballplayer are his ability to run, throw, field, hit and hit with power. However this isn't a hard and fast definition. The pitcher can have his own tools and the batter his. These days the hitter's tools will include his ability to hit for average, to bring a runner home, to bunt, to run, to steal bases, to hit to the opposite field. The pitcher will be expected to have at the very least, a hot fastball, a curve, a changeup, a slider and excellent location.

Tools of Ignorance – These are the skills of the catcher and originate from a self-deprecating catcher by the name of Muddy Gruel in the 30s. The notion of the catcher being historically a bunch of numskulls doesn't really wash, however, especially when you see these guys catching 95 mph fastballs and throwing bullets to second base to prevent a stolen base. The term though is ironic and a little like the goalkeeper in football: he's supposed to be mad to do his job, throwing himself at the feet of onrushing strikers in the same way as a catcher is stupid as in mad to spend half the day wrecking his knees and having to catch or block ninety mile an hour missiles.

Top Of The Order - The top of the order consists of numbers one, two and three batters in the official batting line up.

Top of the first - An inning has two halves: the first is always the 'top.' The phrase is in universal usage and has been for many, many years. So "top of the first," "top of the second" and so on.

Toss - Nothing to do with coins or tennis, this is an alternative to a throw.

Tossed – Short for "tossed out of the game, the punishment for exuberant dissent.

Touch Up - If a pitcher gets "touched up" it means he got hit, usually for home runs. A pitcher can also be "touched" for runs too, e.g.: "Garciappara, who touched Roa for the fifth grand slam of his career."

"Touches All Four" – See immediately below.

Touches 'Em All - Yet another piece of code for the home run.

Towering Pop Up - Often used to describe a mis-hit that goes way up in the air within the infield. If it goes out beyond the infielders it's a towering 'fly.'

Trade - Where we have "transfer" in football we have "trade" in baseball. Always. Trades are made throughout the season until the July 31st deadline as the "pennant race" time of the season nears. They are made by the front office, usually the General Manager, not by the field manager who may or may not be even consulted on the needs of the team/ball club. The trade system reveals a part of the culture of the game where players are often dealt with as expendable items. Unless a free agent, players do not refuse to be traded. If their contract is traded, they have to go and play for the new team. Players, even Garciaparra when traded to the Cubs in 2004, are apt to be told without warning that they've been traded. Trades are often complicated. Club A may acquire a star from Club B in return for as many as three or four players. The GM of A may have no intention of using one or more of these, but acquire them to immediately trade to Club C for a player he wants from them. For a superlative exposition of the trading system, read chapter six, *The Trading Desk* particularly, but really, read the whole thing.

Trapped – When a fielder traps the ball he stops it with his glove as opposed to catching it.

Trick Pitch – In the early day of baseball, the fastball was the norm. Pitches which beat the batter or induced him to make a mistake through movement from side to side or by arriving more slowly than expected – the change up – were known as 'trick pitches,' as if the pitcher wasn't playing fair by not throwing straight so the batter could easily see what was going on.

Triple - This is a hit that gets the batter round and into third base. The record number of triples per season and in a career (the latter record is held by Sam Crawford with 312) is not going to be beaten unless ballparks become huge again, which is desperately unlikely unless humans are replaced by robots or something. Hits that went for triples in the 20s and 30s now would either be doubles or home runs.

Triple 'A' - (AAA) The level of baseball just below the majors is '*Triple A.*' This is a level then which contains a lot of players who either have or will play a lot of major league ball, and yet the games here are played to small audiences.

Triple Crown - This term signifies the batting achievement of being the highest home run hitter, being top of the batting averages and top of the RBI list in the same season. The honour is accorded per league. This is such a rare event it hasn't been done in either league since Boston's Carl Yastrzemski did it in the AL in 1967 and hasn't been done in the National League since *1937*.

Triple Play - A rare event in baseball, this is when three men are put out on one pitch. It might occur like this: the hitter hits a line drive straight to the short stop or second baseman (Out No. 1) who then steps on the bag at second base to put out a runner who is off the bag at second rather than well on the way to third (2), before throwing to the catcher to trap a man leaving third for home (3). It needs to begin with a caught ball because there usually isn't time to throw and tag out three runners. See *Unassisted triple play.*

Trot In Double - Runner makes it to second base comfortably, very similar to stand up double (or triple).

Turn It Over 1 – This describes the turning over of the wrist in the opposite way in the making of the pitch. In effect this is a screwball motion. The natural movement of the wrist and hand is to come down the right hand side of the ball, both turning clockwise. This normally causes the ball to swerve away from the right-handed hitter. If a pitcher can turn his fastball over he should be able to make it swerve in to the batter. See **"screwball."**

Turn It Over 2 – A double play is sometimes described as being 'turned over.'

"Turns On That One" – When a batter pulls the ball and his body turns with the swing of the bat in the direction of the departed ball. Not your classic stepping into the ball with an elegant swing.

Turn Two – Means to make two outs on one play; bring off a double play in other words.

12-6 Curveball – Describes the curve ball that starts way high - 12 o'clock - and drops like a bomb into the strike zone over the plate – to 6 o'clock; an almost impossible pitch to hit.

Twenty Game Winner (in a season) - This is the present gold standard for pitchers: twenty wins in a season. Over and over again in baseball books and articles you will find 20 wins in a season as being the mark of the truly successful pitcher. It's a slightly flawed measurement system in two ways: firstly, you might win games because you have brilliant hitting to back you up and secondly, in the last twenty years, the rarity of pitchers going the full nine innings (now they're thoroughly doing their job if they complete seven) means that really good pitchers can leave a game leading 3-1 only for their bullpen to blow the advantage. Therefore it has become increasingly hard for top class pitchers to go far enough in games to win twenty in a season. In earlier times, pitchers *normally* went the distance, so their performance could be more directly gauged.

Two Bagger – A double. So a 'three bagger' is a triple.

2-4 – Better. Did he hit a double? Home run? That's .500. Good night.

Twin Bill – Code for a doubleheader (two games played between the same teams on the same day).

Two Hundred (.200) - If you're 'batting two hundred' you're on the Mendoza Line and you ain't good enough for the majors or, you're a good player going through a bad slump. The hundreds are the standard measurements of batting success. Three hundred and you're having a fine season. Bat four hundred for the season and you'll suddenly become the most famous sportsman in America because no one has batted .400 since Ted Williams in 1941. Back at .200, you might see someone hitting this at the start of a season, but over 100 + games, quality always has out. No really good player slumps so badly they dip down this low or anything like. .200 for a whole month, never mind season is plain bad. See '**Batting Average**'

Two Hundred Hits (per season) - One of the benchmarks for the quality hitter; one of the numbers to aim for each summer: 200 hits is a great season.

Two Hundred Wins - A really good career record for a pitcher is two hundred or more wins. Most pitchers with 200 wins are in the Hall of Fame.

Two Out Double - It's thought noteworthy to attach 'two out' to a hit by the commentators to emphasize the importance of that hit - the inning is on the verge of being over - and when a batter makes a hit in a clutch situation it's considered automatically to be a feather in his cap. It's thought that the better the player the more likely he is to produce when the chips are down. Inferior hitters are deemed likely to fold in this situation. This is a somewhat traditional view and one refuted by some statisticians. Hence also 'two out single,' 'two out triple,' etc.

Two Out Rally – The rally with two outs turns up in reports because the inning's almost over and hey, isn't it remarkable that the player/team started putting some hits together just one out away from the end of the inning. There are so many two out homers and rallies that it really shouldn't be a big deal. There's a natural element of drama in there, I suppose, that can't quite be gainsaid.

Two-Seam Fastball - This fastball will move in the air in or away from the hitter or can be a sinking fastball, depending upon where and how the fingers grip the ball. This differs from the basic four-seam fastball in that it moves significantly more in the air. Unlike the four, the first two fingers are held along the seam (not across). For more detail see Joe Morgan's excellent *Baseball For Dummies*, where he tells us that a variation of the two-seamer is to grip the ball across the seam but at the narrowest part so it is two seams going across rather than two seams underneath the fingers. This is supposed to produce more sideways movement. See also **Four-Seam Fastball**.

Two Strike Count - A 'pitcher's count.' Two strikes have been called against the batter at this point in the at bat: one more and the batter is out. You don't get 'one strike count.' When there are two strikes, the batter could be out in the next few seconds so you better sit up and take notice!

2000 Hits (in a career) - You have to have been a great player to make this many hits in a career. Only 78 hitters have made over 2,500 in history. Many fantastic players never made it to 3000, including Babe Ruth, Ernie Banks, Reggie Jackson and Lou Gehrig. The further back you go in time the shorter players' careers were, or to put it rather better, the further forward you come, the better the medical health and fitness of players, the longer the careers and the more total hits the greats can make.

Tying Run (is at the plate) - Nice concept and often heard: "the tying run comes to the plate," says the sportscaster with the Royals 4-2 behind the Astros. This means that there is a man on base somewhere and that it'll be 4-4 if the hitter decides it might be a great time to ding one into the stands. It's more to signify the fact that a tied score is theoretically one hit away, as if you weren't aware. The tying run is sometimes referred to as the 'tying man.'

U

Umpires - Baseballs have umpires not referees. They are four in number in each game apart from the World Series when suddenly this isn't enough and an extra two are required, one on each of the baselines in the outfield. That said there was a very sticky moment in the AL Championship series in 2003 when a hit by the Red Sox bounced off the right field pole. According to the rules this is a home run but it was not spotted by the nearest umpire at first base. He signalled a foul ball but was overruled by the home plate umpire, the senior official in each game, who presumably had better eyesight or who was actually watching. See **Home Plate Umpire**, **First Base Umpire**, **Second Base** & **Third Base Umpire**.

Umpiring Signals – The established call for 'out' in a close call is for the ump is to punch an imaginary gut in front of him in somewhat energetic fashion. The closer the call, the more violent the punch. 'In' is denoted by the arms being spread wide. At home, the signal for a 'strike' is either to clench the fist and hold it up with a vertical arm more or less in front of the face, or to turn sideways and point a cocked first finger at an imaginary caught-red-handed rule breaker three yards away. You have to shout '*Straa-eeee!!*' or something similar loudly enough for them to hear in the bleachers. The strikeout signal is something else. For most, this requires an excited turning to the side and pretending to rip a telephone book in half when the third strike comes at a crucial time. Each umpire has his own signature, however. It's one of the best things about baseball, I think, the strikeout signal. I like the one they make when they throw a player or manager out of the game, as they try to throw their arm out of its socket as they point to the direction of the locker room; as if they actually wanted to bodily throw the guy out of there.

Unassisted Double Play - This is where an infielder produces both outs in a double play on his own without another fielder touching the ball. Ways of doing this: first out by an infielder catching a hit ball (a 'line drive') then putting out a runner between bases. If a man is in the process of leaving second base as the ball is hit, the fielder just needs to step on second base. Alternatively, after catching the line drive to put out the hitter, he might tag a runner who has "taken a big jump" off first base: meaning that he is quite a distance from first as the ball is hit. See also '**Rundown.**'

Unassisted Triple Play: This is such a rare event it's only happened 12 times in modern major league history: eleven times in regular play and once in the 1920 World Series. It's worth mentioning the latter just so as to tell you about the guy's name who executed it: Bill Wambsganss (that is not a misprint either). Following on from the paragraph above on the unassisted double play, the extra out may be achieved by being able to put all three of the outs together mentioned above: catch, treading on the bag and tagging out a runner. The last **Unassisted Triple Play took place on** August 10, 2003 when **the** Atlanta Braves shortstop Rafael Furcal at St. Louis, in the fifth inning, caught a line drive from the bat of pitcher Woody Williams, stepped on second to retire catcher Mike Matheny (at second base on the pitch), then tagged Orlando Palmeiro (on first) returning to first base for the third out. The one previous to that one was in 2000. A chapter of *The Glory Of Their Times* by Lawrence Ritter is devoted to Bill W.'s own thoughts on his career, including a full account of his big moment in baseball history.

Uncle Charlie – "Any time [as a pitcher] you get in front of a hitter like that, you're more than likely to get one or two heaters. Just don't miss them, because Uncle Charlie is next." Ellis Burks, April 2004. "Uncle Charlie" is the dreaded curve ball.

Under Protest - A game of baseball can be played 'under protest' to register a club's dissent at the result of a previous game, a loss being incurred through some sort of foul play or in the case of the Chicago Cubs in the 2003 post-season, bad luck. I'm talking about the infamous interference by a fan along the third base line when he caught a ball that supposedly was about to plop into the glove of a left fielder for a crucial out. As David Lengel commented at the time on the programme, there was little effective that the Cubs could have done after the match. There is no precedent for the game to be replayed through fan interference. They could only play the next game 'under pro-test,' which would have been nothing more than symbolical, showing their displeasure and total belief in the fact that a monstrous baseball crime has been committed against them. In the event they made no formal protest, no doubt because it would not have done much to focus the team for the next game.

Unearned Run - This is about pitchers. At some point in baseball history it was decided that if a run was scored as a result of a fielding error it shouldn't count against the statistical record of that pitcher. Thus was born the unearned run. If a runner crosses home plate through a fielding error or who got on base in the first place because of one, this run does not count against the pitcher. It's considered that without the fumble, the batter would be thrown out at first or the man at third thrown out at the plate, thus the occurrence is not the pitcher's fault. If a pitcher is taken out of the game with, say, two men on base, and they go on to score as a result of a pitch thrown by the reliever, the runs count against the yanked pitcher who put them there in the first place. To work out a pitcher's unearned runs from a box score line, you take the number under '**R**,' runs scored (while this guy was pitching) and subtract the number under '**ER**,' his earned runs. For example,

Boston	*IP*	*H*	*R*	*ER*	*BB*	*SO*	*HR*	*ERA*
Schilling (W, 1-0)	6.0	4	1	0	1	4	0	0.00

Kurt Schilling here in Game 2 of last year's World Series gave up a run in his six inning, but as you can see, it was unearned. Notice too that his ERA is 0.00, emphasizing that no runs were debited to his account.

Uniforms – Not "kit" then, but "uniform." The uniform, to my surprise and in my ignorance, has always been a serious subject for baseball fans, and there is great enthusiasm for their history, which has been interesting and varied. We are now in an era of retro-tradition with uniforms. After the comically ghastly experiments with gaudy stripes in psychedelic acid trip combinations of bright colour in the 70s and 80s, the thirty clubs all play in traditional white at home, and in grey away, just as recommended in the laws of the game. Designs are plain, clean and classic, with minimal embellishments. Alternative jerseys tend to be the same: as classy as hell. Due to authentic replica jerseys costing around $149.99, I cannot confirm for you that those the players wear are made of superior, softer material, compared to those you see in stores in the States that cost a good bit less but come in a shiny material somewhere out of 1987.

Untied It – Phrase to describe (usually) a hitter putting his team ahead with a hit. "Giles untied in the bottom of the ninth with a two-out double to right."

Up - 'Up' is where the pitcher should not 'leave' the ball: put it. 'Up' is around the level of the waist. Here the batter may well dump you out of the field or hit a long ball for a double or triple. *"If Contreras keeps leaving the ball up, he's going to get hit."*

Up The Ladder – A pitcher goes up the ladder when he throws the ball at the top of the strike zone or higher, especially after a couple of knee high pitches. Done deliberately, this change of geography is often enough to surprise the batter into swinging too late – if he chooses to swing.

Uppercut – This describes the swing of the home run hitter. This was Babe Ruth's swing that hit 714 dingers. To hit the ball high and out of the ballpark, it's necessary (as you can readily imagine, I expect) to strike the baseball from "underneath," from bottom to above: a level swing won't do it. Well, not as many as 714 times in a career anyway.

Upstairs - ...describes a pitch high in the strike zone or just too high for a strike. If a pitcher "goes upstairs" he throws there. He'll often do that after setting up the hitter with a pitch at the bottom of the zone, especially with a sinking fastball if he has it in his armoury. A lot of sluggers find the hard one upstairs hard to resist.

Up The Middle - This is going to be a hit: a well struck ball struck by the batter through the pitcher at the mound, who isn't in much shape for fielding at the end of his delivery, or to the side of him, is likely to pierce the infield defense. Seeing as second base is immediately behind the pitcher, you might expect the second baseman to cut off balls hit straight, but they stand on the first base side of the bag.

V

Velocity - Unlike cricket's fast bowlers, the speed of a pitcher's delivery is referred to as his or its 'velocity.' 'Speed' is usually used in the context of a hitter's 'bat speed' or a runner's 'speed around the bases.'

Victory - Same as a 'win,' used in the context of the pitcher's running record for the season and for a career. Pitchers not only 'get the win' but, you'll hear, 'get the victory.'

W

Waivers - When a play is *put on* waivers, his club is announcing to the other 29 clubs that he's available for a trade. In other words, put up for transfer whilst still under contract. If a club takes the player, they "claim" him. There was an interesting example of this in Boston last winter when Manny Ramirez was put on waivers. The only way they could finance a trade with the Texas Rangers for Alex Rodriguez (it's killing me not to say "wanted to *buy* ARod") was by off-loading Manny: putting him "on waivers." On a vast salary at Fenway of $20 per annum, a tab that his new ball club would have had to pick up, there were no takers.

Walk - If a pitcher throws four pitches which are left alone by the batter and fall out of the strike zone before he can throw three strikes, the batter gets a free pass to first base: a 'walk' in fact. This is also known as a 'base on balls' (as in the pitcher getting to first base on four balls thrown by the pitcher). Most batters trot there; Pete Rose used to full there at full pelt, but he was a one-off. See **'Intentional Walk.'** Tactically, walks are disastrous concessions of a base to the offensive team. The worst time to give up a walk, by common consent, is to the lead off hitter in the ninth inning when the closer is trying preserve a lead.

Walk In A Run – Phrase used when the bases are loaded and a pitcher throws four balls before three strikes. The bases are now over-loaded so the man on third has to get out of the way, crossing home plate for a run. The batter who 'draws' the walk gets the **RBI.**

Walk off home run - The game is tied at 1-1 in the bottom of the ninth (and last inning - last before extra innings are played anyway). You come up to bat. You get a pitch straight down the middle. You swing, you make great contact, you smoke it to left field and it flies out of the park, it's gone. You've hit the winning run; the game is over. There is no need for the inning to be completed so it isn't. Everyone can now walk off the field and get showered and changed. You've just hit a 'walk off home run.' It's the most dramatic event a game of baseball can produce. Only *you* don't walk off; you trot round the bases to be met at home plate by most of the organization's roster to be banged on the helmet in celebration. It's the miserable fielding side that does most of the walking off.

Wall (Outfield wall) - This is the construction that separates the playing field from the crowd. It varies slightly, occasionally significantly from ballpark to ballpark. The measure of the home run varies too. In some, only over the wall is a homer. In others you'll see a horizontal line painted on it in center field to show you that a hit below it and you keep running, on it or above it you can trot around the bases at your own speed. Some walls are famous like the green monster in left field Fenway Park, Boston, others have people painted on them, famous players and their achievements: 500 home runs, team achievements: 'World Series Champions 1986,' a much-loved broadcaster at Wrigley Field. There are scoreboards on many. Some are a broad, boring expanse of nothing, which is more than a shame. These days they are all padded to prevent outfielders from having to be scraped off the *warning track* when they go for a deep fly ball.

Warm Up Pitches - The pitchers are allowed five of these when they come out to the mound, so that there is a pause in the action every time there is a pitching change. They are also allowed (and take) five warm up pitchers before the start of each half of an inning.

Warning Track - In front of the outfield wall in every ballpark there is a wide orange gravel border. This might be to enable grass-cutting equipment to move easily to all parts of the field without ruining the precious grass, you might think (if you're me). It's called the 'warning track' and is literally to warn outfielders of the nearness of the outfield fence or solid wall so they don't crack their skulls into pieces, or didn't long ago when the term was coined and the padding wasn't there.

Waste Pitch – Pitch thrown by a pitcher with at least one strike, usually two, which is aimed to tempt the batter into swinging at a pitch out of the strike zone. If the batter swings and misses, he gets the strikeout (or another strike); if the batter leaves the pitch, it's only one ball.

Weaver Watch - Controversy at Baseball On 5! During season 2003 the Yankee pitcher Jeff Weaver came in for a lot of stick from viewers and David Lengel alike for having a number of terrible games. DL went as far as to call him 'a clown.' In the televised Red Sox game in late July that year he sunk his own reputation down further by openly showing dissent in the dug out when reliever Hammond blew his 3-0 lead and win. David, out of intense guilt calmed things down somewhat after this, which was a shame because for a lot of viewers, *Weaver Watch* was great fun, especially for those who don't like the Yankees. So, when Weaver came in as a late-inning reliever for Game 4 of the World Series and gave up the walk off homer that brought the Marlins level with the Bombers 2-2, some of us thought it was funny. I also found out at this time that Steinbrenner paid him a salary of $4.1 million in 2003, something that got me through many a traffic queue when I was so bored I thought I would turn into a vase. But he was subsequently traded to the Los Angeles Dodgers and had a good 2004, at which point *Weaver Watch* died.

And with Derek proving to be such a nice guy when the show's producer Erik Jansen interviewed him in Montreal last September, good thing too.

Went Down On Strikes – Means the batter got struck out.

Wheelhouse - A phrase meaning right down the middle, usually the batter's favourite place to get a pitch.

Whif/Whiffed - Struck out. "*Then Greene whiffed to end the inning.*"

Wickets - The ball sometimes goes 'between the wickets' of a fielder, meaning between their legs. I like the reference to the very early days of organized cricket when the wickets consisted of two stumps linked by a single stick on top.

Wild Card - This is huge. There are six divisions in the two leagues. The winners of each go straight into the post-season play-offs and have an equal chance of winning the World Series, give or take a little home field (dis)advantage. To make up an eight team, four pairing "quarter-final" (the phrase 'quarter final' is never used however, nor is 'semi final'), two teams are added, one from each league. The club with the best second place winning percentage in each league goes to post-season play and this is known as winning the wild card.

This system, in place since 1994 and the creation of two extra divisions, is still controversial. Purists like the old system when simply the winners of each ten-team league played off against each other in the World Series. Much as with the play off system in UK football, however, the play offs have stimulated the game for spectators and keep the season alive for more teams for longer: there are now many more meaningful games.

So, if your team is miles behind an excellent one; they're twelve games out and it's already June, don't despair: there is still the wild card place to play for and teams have won the World Series from the wild card position: Anaheim in 2002 and the Marlins in 2003.

Wild Pitch - A wild pitch is one that gets past the catcher, not because the catcher goofs (this would be a 'passed ball') but because the direction of the pitch is wayward. Importantly, a runner may move around the bases on a wild pitch and thus a poorly directed pitch, usually one which first bounces into the dirt and skids on under the catcher, can cost the team a run if there's a man on third right there, or put a man in scoring position where just now he was only on first base and no obvious threat. A batter cannot run on a wild pitch unless there are two strikes against him. Note that a batter can be technically struck out, but if the pitch he swings and misses becomes wild, he can run to first base.

Williams Shift - See '**Infield Shift.**'

Win, The – "The decision" is a very big deal indeed in baseball. The guy pitching when the team is ahead, or pitching when his offence gets to "go ahead" run will get the win on his record. Pitchers are rated and therefore rate themselves by two key stats: their ERA (runs conceded without being caused by errors) and their won-loss record. The greats are measured primarily by their win-loss record: winning 20 games in a season is considered the benchmark of the 'great' or highly successful pitcher. Win 20 games for 3 seasons in a row and you're well on your way to the Hall Of Fame, which is where every player wants to be. See also '**Decision**' and '**No Decision**' and '**The Loss.**'

Windup - If there's one single thing that Brits know about baseball it's that the guy who sends the ball up to the batter goes through a grotesque series body contortions to do it. This is called the windup. It is a coiling up of the body into a ball of latent energy, like winding up a child's toy before it explodes in a blur of motion across a room.

Windups now are very conservative. Some old photos of pitchers show a front leg lifted *waayy* into the air and the pitching arm almost touching the ground behind his back, his whole body shape making a tilted 'H.' It's hard to believe this type of motion didn't cause every pitch to hit the crowd thirty feet high and rising.

Windup Position – A technical term in the official rules of the game for pitchers. When they take their position on the mound with one (back) foot on the pitching rubber and the other in front towards the batters box, and place both hands in front of their body, they are said to be in the "windup position." From here he can either pitch to the batter, send a pickoff throw to a base or "disengage" by dropping his hands to his sides, at which point he goes out of the windup position. From here he can rock back and go into his leg kick, "preliminary" movements to releasing the ball. See "**Set Position.**"

Winningest - The flip side of the losingest coin. You want to describe the manager or the team with the best winning-losing ratio? Use this.

Winning Percentage - The ongoing record of a team during a season is not expressed by the number of points they have as in British sport because teams are not awarded points for wins. Simply, the team with the best winning percentage, expressed as a decimal fraction, sits at the top of the division table. A team that wins 12 of its first 20 games will have a score of .600 (expressed verbally as 'six hundred') and this will put them at the top of the table. Even the best teams in baseball will have to expect to get beat two games out of five, usually more. (See, **'Five Hundred'**)

World Series – An Abb. For 'World Championship Series,' the final series of the season, played off between the winners of each of the major leagues since 1903. The first winners were the Boston Americans, as the Boston Red Sox were then named, beating the Pittsburgh Pirates 5-3. The World Series has been played every year since bar two: 1904, when John McGraw, manager of the New York Giants, refused to meet the winners of the American League, probably because he didn't want to lose (to Boston: he let his pennant winning team take on the Philadelphia A's in 1905 however, and won) and 1994 when it was wiped by a player strike.

World Series Champions - Established title of the winners of the World Series

World Series Ring – See, **'Ring, World Series'**. This isn't a joke either.

Wrong Field - Another term for the 'opposite' field, the right half of the outfield for a right handed hitter. By now you'll know that the word 'wrong' is used because the natural thing for a hitter to do is pull the ball to left field.

Y

Yanked - A player pulled out of a game by the coach, be he pitcher or hitter is said to have been 'yanked.'

Yakker – A big curve or other breaking ball.

Yard – Common expression for the inside and perimeter of the ballpark. See (**'Goes Yard'**)

Z

Zone, The - Shorthand for strike zone, as opposed to being 'in the zone,' that state of blissful inner harmony containing the perfect focus of concentration that golfers and tennis players are often described as being in.

APPENDIX: FOLLOWING THE GAME

For anyone out there who is new to following baseball and who wants some advice on where to go to keep abreast of what's happening between shots of *Baseball on 5*, here goes.

Internet

This is your main supplier of information and there is a wealth of fantastic websites. Start with the institution that effectively owns the whole game, Major League Baseball and their **MLB.com.** Their main page will tell you what the up-to-the-minute news is in the game headline wise, but it's very much in the corporate vein: you won't find criticism or controversy here, really. But click on the "Stats" tab on the horizontal menu and you'll get access to a vast amount of statistical information, both past and present. Their historical stats section is excellent. With a bit of probing you can find historical leaders in almost every category you can think of. Indeed, every player's record in the history of the game is in there too. To get your team's stats, go to the "Teams" section (either top left or bottom left of main page) and scroll down to whichever it is. You'll immediately be connected to the organisation's official website. Again, the stats section is great and pretty easy to negotiate. The history sections are brief and bland but the stadium sections are useful if you're planning a visit. Further, the site gives you fabulous pitch-by-pitch coverage via its "Gameday" service. Whoever you follow, you can watch each pitch on your monitor screen, with moment-by-moment changes in hitter stats. It has everything but actual pictures and it's free. If you want video coverage, you can get that from MLB but you have to pay.

The ESPN website is also excellent **(ESPN.com).** The baseball section is easy to find and contains a voluminous amount of info: the stats section gives you a game by game account of not only the current season but the three below that also, with good details of pitchers. There's also good stuff on stadiums and individual players, including salaries. For history of individual players I use **BaseballLibrary,com** for great stories and anecdotes, especially those from the past. It's completely comprehensive. Baseball Almanac is also terrific for lists. If you want to know who Cy Young's team mates were at the Red Sox in 1905, for example, this will give it to you, or indeed the whole St Louis Browns roster for 1939, and it's a very easy site to use. It has superbly complete awards lists and achievements of clubs and players, including Hall of Famers (as you'd expect). It has loads of other stuff too, easily accessed on its left hand menu I also like Baseball-Reference.com for quick access to player stats, manager stats and park stats and use it a lot.

A great way of plugging into your favourite team is to find a local newspaper which has good and detailed coverage of your team (there'll be one) and click on its sports section. You may have to pay a fee (eg, New York Times) but it isn't much. I use the Globe for following Boston, it's free and it's excellent. Tons of articles, a good blog, load of photos, etc, etc. For me this is an essential source.

TV

If you're relatively minted and have a vast fat of time to burn, you can subscribe to NASN (North American Sports Network) for about twenty quid a month and watch live games every day and the news back-up stuff too.

Annuals

The Sporting News does 'em all and they're the best around. Don't take my word for it, take Erik Janssen's. I can tell you about three, because I have copies. Firstly, we have *The Sporting News Complete Record Book 2003 Edition* (556 pp): worth having for club records season by season and leaders in hitting, pitching and fielding, individual and team and for billions of records. Secondly, there's *Baseball Guide – The Ultimate 2004 Baseball Guide* (632 pp): this has some overlaps with the latter but covers an actual baseball season (in this case 2003) club-by-club. Thirdly, here comes *The Official Major League Baseball Fact Book – 2004 Edition* (423 pp): this is bigger, has pictures and has club game-by-game accounts of the season as well as quite detailed statistical coverage of every season in baseball dating back to 1876, Still not finished. Fourthly *Baseball Register 2004* (688 pp) which deals mostly in players, present and past, with their career numbers in detail and though I don't have one, looks worth having from the descriptions of it I've read. Finally, *Scouting Notebook 2004* (713 pp) also deals mostly in players but is more technical, as you can see from the title. So between them, *TSN* gives you over 2000 pages of baseball guide each spring. Sound great? Possibly. In reality, what they should do is collapse 5 into 3: one covering the previous season and clubs; two detailing the players past and present, and three, a record book, because there are loads of overlaps representing padding to sell more copies (or TSN are full of stupid people) with the present format. My second criticism is huge: like this page, the size of the type in the first three above is tiny and therefore desperately reader-unfriendly. The layout is poor and amateurish, often crushing information together with no regard for the reader. For good measure, the photos in the fact book are faint and small and therefore completely pointless. Next year I'm buying the Guide and the Register unless I can find better. And if I'm putting you off, Erik buys 'em every year and so does most everyone else, apparently.

For depth of statistical and theoretical analysis, you'll need to join **SABR and/or SABR UK** if you're particularly interested in the British game and its history. Has excellent links to a large number of US sites and can be found at **SABRUK.ORG.**